THIRD
EDITION

CONSUMER
Behavior
An Applied Approach

Nessim **Hanna** | Richard **Wozniak** | Margaret **Hanna** |

D1569779

Kendall Hunt
publishing company
4050 Westmark Drive • P O Box 1840 • Dubuque IA 52004-1840

Book Team

Chairman and Chief Executive Officer   Mark C. Falb
President and Chief Operating Office   Chad M. Chandlee
Vice President, Higher Education   David L. Tart
Director of National Book Program   Paul B. Carty
Editorial Development Manager   Georgia Botsford
Developmental Editor   Denise M. LaBudda
Assistant Vice President, Production Services   Christine E. O'Brien
Senior Production Editor   Mary Melloy
Senior Permissions Editor   Colleen Zelinsky
Cover Designer   Jancll Edwards

Front cover images:
(ties) Image © stephen rudolph, 2009. Under license from Shutterstock, Inc.
(shoes) Image © Thor Jorgen Udvang, 2009. Under license from Shutterstock, Inc.
Back cover images:
(ties) Images © Elnur, 2009. Under license from Shutterstock, Inc.

All Shutterstock images used under license from Shutterstock, Inc.

BRIEF CONTENTS

CONTENTS

PART 2   INDIVIDUAL INFLUENCES ON BEHAVIOR   109

CHAPTER 4 Consumer Perception   111

CHAPTER 5   Consumer Learning and Memory   149

CHAPTER 6   Consumer Attitudes   191

CHAPTER 7 Motivation and Emotion   231

CHAPTER 11 Group Influence 391

CHAPTER 12 The Family and Generational Cohorts 429

CHAPTER 15 Culture and Microcultures   541

FOREWORD

The conceptual foundation of consumer behavior relies heavily on theories, concepts, and models developed in the behavioral sciences with proper orientation toward business, particularly marketing, situations. The analysis and understanding of human behavior are usually based on the S-O-R model generally followed by the authors of *Consumer Behavior: An Applied Approach,* third edition, as suggested by the framework outlined in the preface of the book. Accordingly, behavior is said to be determined by forces within the individual as well as in the situation.

The authors cover the five psychological processes of perception, learning, attitudes, motivation, and personality. The manifestations of these processes obviously differ from one person to another. This is why people vary in their responses even to the same business events and marketing situations. Yet a marketer usually looks for common forces among people toward which he or she directs the marketing policies and promotional programs. Some of these forces can be found in the social environment and cultural spheres that bond people together. Since these forces differ from one society to another, it is expected that consumer behavior would vary across nations. A careful consideration should be given, therefore, to the unique forces that characterize the social and cultural milieu of each country.

The second half of the twentieth century has witnessed the prevalence of the *system's approach* in the management and organizational literature. The approach emphasizes, among other things, the *interdependencies* among various parts of the organizational system. This approach has found its way to the general orientation of the book through the cross-functional approach, so cleverly articulated by the authors, and as highlighted by the chapter-opening vignettes, end-of-chapter cross-functional debates, and points of view. This orientation has been further strengthened in the current third edition and is an important distinguishing feature of the book.

The authors have also adopted active individual, group, and self-learning approaches, with extensive use of the most up-to-date tools of information technology. Real-life applications are emphasized through the real-world opening vignettes, global, ethical, and in-practice application boxes, and cases about known companies in the United States and oversees, thus enriching and broadening the scope of knowledge of the students about American business experiences and what is happening worldwide. This will enhance the marketability of the book in other countries, and will enhance the globalized trend of educational programs everywhere.

This is a wonderful book that I have very much enjoyed reading. I strongly recommend it to colleagues in universities here in the United States and overseas.

Ahmed A. Abdel-Halim, Ph.D., Professor Emeritus, Alexandria University, Egypt, Former Dean, College of Business & Economics, United Arab Emirates University, UAE Former Management & Marketing Department Chair, Illinois State University at Normal–Bloomington, Illinois

PREFACE

The recent unprecedented economic challenges that confronted our economy since the year 2008 continue to impact every aspect of our lives. The burst of the housing bubble, the downturn of the stock market, the escalating credit crunch, the rising prices of food and energy, the loss of jobs, and the overwhelming national debt, as well as the cost of two wars, have all contributed to a domestic stagnation that engulfed not only our society but extended to the entire global economy.

From large corporations and small businesses, to individual consumers and families, the shocks emanating from Wall Street and the host of economic ills that accompanied the market collapse have shattered confidence in both business and government, and necessitate the recasting of business plans and government regulations. They also altered the manner in which consumers are learning to cope with these new realities of the marketplace. For example, American shoppers today are abandoning more expensive alternatives and trading down to store brands, smaller cars, and discount stores. Bargain hunting and coupon clipping have become routine for many consumers. Pricey retailers, vacation resort operators, as well as bars and restaurants, are but a few of the businesses that have witnessed the major effect of the economic downturn.

The problem that America is facing today is not simply a domestic one. It is a worldwide phenomenon encompassing both developed and underdeveloped nations. This global inclusion is an expression of the interdependency that has developed between nations today. The recent trend toward increased global cooperation among blocks of countries was envisioned with the objective of obtaining high standards of living for all participants. Thus, the traditional perspective of isolation as the principle of choice among countries is no longer useful nor practical in organizing and enhancing economic activities. This same principle of interdependency that works well in the global arena also holds great merit when applied to conventional marketing practices on the micro level.

Within the confines of the interdependency concept and its proven positive effect on business operations, firms today should no longer be viewed as collections of separate and independent units or departments, where each specializes in a singular activity such as engineering, purchasing, finance, accounting, selling, or human resources. Rather, today's successful business operations are based on sophisticated organizational arrangements that apply the team approach to managing operations—where representatives from various disciplines within the organization interact and equally cooperate in bringing new products and services into the marketplace. This cross-functional view of contemporary business operations had been the core of success for countless foreign firms, especially in Europe and Japan.

We feel so strongly about the cross-functional approach that we have brought it into *Consumer Behavior* in two major ways. First, every chapter ends with a cross-functional debate exercise tied to the chapter's opening vignette. These are intended to help students apply the chapter's principles to other business-related disciplines such as accountancy, management, finance, production, and law. For example, the opening vignette in Chapter 6, "Consumer Attitudes," concerning Tiger Woods as a product endorser, is extended to the financial ramifications for Nike.

This is not all. The cross-functional approach is brought in a second way. Each chapter contains three cross-functional points of view in the end-of-chapter material. These segments expose students to related disciplines and show them the interrelationship of marketing and consumer behavior to other functional areas of business. For example, in Chapter 6, the three cross-functional points of view focus on:

- *Finance and Economics*—how consumers' attitudes toward the health of the economy affect its actual performance
- *Politics*—smear campaigns that political candidates often use to win votes, and
- *Ethics*—the fashion industry's tendency to create different fashions every year in an effort to generate sales.

A cross-functional approach is only one of many things we have done in *Consumer Behavior*. All of these things have a common goal: to get the students involved. This is why we wrote the book. Thomas Jefferson once wrote, "Tell me and I'll forget, teach me and I may remember, involve me and I'll learn." We wanted to bring this principle to life in the consumer behavior field.

Special Features

Numerous features will keep students interested in the subject and will help them visualize applications of consumer behavior principles. Specifically:

- An **opening vignette** and **Internet exercise** at the beginning of each chapter ease readers into the topic. The Internet exercise directs students to one or more Web sites to help answer questions. For example, students are directed to visit Weight Watchers' Web site to explain the strategies that the company uses to encourage the one-third of the U.S. population who are overweight to change their eating habits and lifestyles.
- Each chapter contains three entertaining and informative **applications boxes** that tie in with chapter material. Each box is linked to the Internet and contains thought-provoking questions about specific Web sites. For instance, in Chapter 6, these boxes are:
- **"Consumer Behavior in Practice":** A box on the sentiment-expression business of greeting cards. Students are directed to Hallmark's Web site and are asked what attitudinal factors explain the practice of sending greeting cards.

- **"Global Opportunity":** A box on women's cosmetics in Europe directs students to the Web site of Eurochic Cosmetics. Questions elicit different preferences for cosmetics in the U.S. versus Europe.

- **"Ethical Dilemma":** A box on the Body Shop and its founder's alleged fabrication and exaggeration of the natural derivation of the company's products send students to the company's Web site to help them make up their own minds.

- Each chapter has a two-page original **case** covering an issue or a problem facing a real-world company. These cases include ones such as "Warner Bros. Eyes China," "A Japanese *Good-Housekeeping* Magazine," "Planning for the New Volkswagen Beetle," "America's Love for the Emerald Bottle," and "Club Med Woos Families." These cases are followed by questions designed to get students to seek additional information about the company—usually from the Internet.

- Each chapter ends with a **summary** and two types of questions, five **review questions** and three **discussion questions**. The discussion questions are specifically designed to test students' ability to apply the concepts learned in the chapter to other issues in the business world.

Discussion Questions

1. Procter & Gamble offers a large number of brands within a given product category. For example, in the area of laundry detergents alone, the company produces over a dozen different brands (among them Tide, Biz, Cheer, Dash, Bold, Gain, Era, Solo, Dreft, Ivory Snow, Oxydol). This practice, known wide dissimilarities in the needs of persons who travel for business versus those who travel for leisure. Based on these differences, prices quoted to business travelers are considerably higher than those charged for leisure travel. Speculate on the differences between the needs of these

---

Review Questions

1. A number of variables have been used to segment consumer markets such as demographic, psychographic, and geodemographic variables among others. Discuss what is meant by psychographic segmentation and the role of AIO inventories in categorizing consumers into various segments.

4. Marketing managers evaluate each market segment against a number of criteria to determine whether or not it should be pursued by the firm. Explain what these criteria are.
5. Briefly explain the interrelationship between the three steps of segmentation, tar-

---

Summary

This chapter addresses the topics of segmentation, targeting, and positioning. These are necessary and inseparable components of any marketing strategy. Segmentation entails dissecting the heterogeneous overall market for a product or service into a number of more homogeneous submarkets or niches. Targeting means reviewing and selecting ment strategy, (3) concentration strategy, and (4) customization strategy. The attractiveness of various market segments is typically evaluated with regard to seven factors: (1) size, (2) potential, (3) measurability, (4) accessibility, (5) compatibility, (6) stability, and (7) defendability. When a company has decided on the segment(s) it elects to

---

- A **running glossary** of terms is provided in the page margins to highlight key terms and help students review chapters at a glance.

These features, and the accompanying ancillary package, will reduce time-consuming preparations. They provide creative, hands-on projects and application-oriented assignments designed to actively involve your students in the learning process.

How Is *Consumer Behavior: An Applied Approach* Organized?

The text starts with the individual influences on behavior and then broadens the perspective to include relevant social/cultural forces. The text can be broken into three major sections:

Part 1 sets the groundwork of the text.

- **Chapter 1**, "Introduction to Consumer Behavior," examines the key approaches to the discipline of consumer behavior and the forces that drive human action. Unique to this chapter is the coverage of customer touchpoint management, as well as ten emerging trends in contemporary society that are expected to have a significant bearing on our lifestyles and consumption patterns. Ramifications of these current trends are examined both from marketing strategy and consumer behavior perspectives.

- **Chapter 2**, "Consumer Research," emphasizes the need to learn as much as possible about the consumer. It lists the sources of primary and secondary data from which such knowledge can be obtained. Unique to this chapter is its emphasis on the role of the Internet as an indispensable source of data acquisition. Through the Internet, researchers can track search engine Web site visitors, conduct online surveys, access data, and receive advice. The chapter also touches on the practices of database marketing and data mining. It then proceeds to look at the ethical issues involved in conducting consumer research.

- **Chapter 3**, "Segmentation, Targeting, and Positioning," identifies the segments to which consumers belong. The chapter examines the five approaches of market segmentation: geographic, demographic, geodemographic, psychographic, and behavioral. The discussion then progresses to cover targeting strategies, such as the undifferentiated, multisegment, concentration, and customization approaches. The chapter concludes by explaining tactics that can be used to position a product or a business in the marketplace. Unique to this chapter is the treatment of segmentation, targeting, and positioning as inseparable, interlocking activities. Also, there is expanded coverage of positioning tactics.

Part 2 deals with individual influences on behavior.

- **Chapter 4**, "Consumer Perception," examines the topics of exposure, attention, sensation, and interpretation of sensory input. The chapter covers stimulus, individual, and situational factors that influence perception. Other topics covered include Gestalt psychology, perceptual categorization, and inference. Unique to this chapter is its extensive coverage of imagery.

- **Chapter 5**, "Consumer Learning and Memory," examines learning theories including classical conditioning, operant conditioning, and cognitive learning, as well as how marketers apply these concepts. The chapter covers hemispheric specialization of the brain, vicarious learning, learning curves, habit, and brand loyalty. It concludes by examining the memory processes of information retrieval and loss. Unique to this chapter is the reshaping of the concept of classical conditioning into a fully cognitive theory, as well as extended coverage of the processes of memory, retention, and retrieval.

- **Chapter 6**, "Consumer Attitudes," examines the way attitudes develop, function, and the extent to which they determine our behavior. The chapter delves into a number of attitude models, including the traditional model and the multi-attribute model. It goes on to explain the theories of reasoned action, goal pursuit and trying, and attribution theory. The topic of attitude change is then treated from the perspectives of cognitive consistency and information processing. Unique to this chapter is its coverage of the recent theories of goal pursuit and trying, as well as online applications of the ELM.

- **Chapter 7,** "Motivation and Emotion," examines the types and elements of motivation and briefly highlights the major schools of thought concerning the origins of human motivation. The chapter investigates motivational conflict. It concludes with a discussion of emotions versus moods and shows how marketers may apply emotion in their promotional strategies. Unique to this chapter is its extensive coverage of the topics of consumer emotions and moods.

- **Chapter 8,** "Personality, Lifestyle, and Self-Concept," examines the nature of personality and briefly explains a number of personality theories such as the Freudian Psychoanalytic Theory, Neo-Freudian Theories, and the Trait Theory. The chapter progresses with a discussion of psychographics and VALS™ and its implications to marketers. Unique to this chapter is its expanded coverage of the self and the ramifications of this concept to marketers.

- **Chapter 9,** "Consumer Decision Making," examines the consumer decision process and the extent to which it takes on a rational and/or emotional tone. The chapter goes on to cover programmed versus nonprogrammed decisions and progresses through the stages of the consumer decision-making process. These entail problem recognition, search activity, identifying and evaluating alternatives, purchase, and postpurchase considerations—including customer satisfaction and complaints. Unique to this chapter is its clear and practical treatment of Prospect theory, and extended coverage of customer satisfaction.

Part 3 addresses social and cultural influences on our consumption behavior. However, to prepare students for this shift in emphasis, Chapters 10 and 11 cover communication and diffusion of innovations.

- **Chapter 10,** "Diffusion of Innovation," investigates the four elements of the diffusion process including innovation, the channel of communication, the social system, and time. The chapter progresses by covering the stages of the adoption process. It concludes with a discussion of the barriers to new product adoption in the form of value, usage, risk, tradition, and image obstacles. Unique to this chapter is its presentation of Rogers's revised innovation decision process rather than his traditional, more-familiar stages of the adoption process.

- **Chapter 11,** "Group Influence," investigates the meaning and importance of groups. The chapter delves into the types of social groups, including virtual communities, and the roles and statuses of group members. It then proceeds with a discussion of the types of social power including reward, coercive, legitimate, referent, and expert. The major thrust of the chapter deals with reference groups and their types and degrees of influence. The chapter concludes by addressing implications of reference group influence to the fields of marketing and consumer behavior. Unique to this chapter is its practical rather than theoretical slant.

- **Chapter 12**, "The Family and Generational Cohorts," examines the meaning of family and the process of consumer socialization, with special emphasis placed on the nature of family decision roles. The chapter moves on to discuss the family decision-making process and alludes specifically to children's influence on family decisions. The chapter also covers the family life cycle. Unique to this chapter is its extended coverage of nontraditional living arrangement patterns prevalent in contemporary society and generational cohorts and their implications for marketing strategists.

- **Chapter 13**, "Personal Influence and Word of Mouth," investigates the process of personal influence, opinion leadership, and word of mouth, as well as e-fluentials and viral communication. The chapter covers models of the influence process and delineates the various methods used to identify opinion leaders. The chapter concludes by citing strategic applications of personal influence and word of mouth to the field of marketing. Unique to this chapter is the industry-driven rather than theoretical focus of presentation, as well as the expanded coverage of methods to harness positive word of mouth and combat negative word of mouth.

- **Chapter 14**, "Social Class," investigates the concept of social stratification and the evolving social class structure in the United States versus that found in other cultures. The chapter progresses with a discussion of the methods used to measure social class and examines the impact of social class on consumption patterns. The implications of social class standing for purposes of market segmentation, targeting, and positioning are also highlighted. Unique to this chapter is its coverage of the ever-evolving class structure in the United States and how it affects the practice of marketing.

- **Chapter 15**, "Culture and Microcultures," investigates the meaning of culture. Unique to this chapter is its creative organization around Hofstede's as well as Harris' and Moran's sociocultural dimensions. The chapter focuses on microcultures, with special emphasis given to African-, Hispanic-, and Asian-American consumers, as well as microcultures of consumption. It concludes by citing implications of culture and microcultures to the field of consumer behavior and marketing strategy.

Organizational Framework of This Text

The diagram in Exhibit P.1 is a simplified representation of the treatment given to the subject of consumer behavior throughout this text.

The framework commences with a depiction of the consumer research process, whose objective is partially to provide information about consumers' needs, characteristics, and preferences for various brand alternatives. This first step is followed by the segmentation process, with involves dissecting the potential market for a product or service into a number of subgroups, each with its own unique but identifiable needs and preferences. Marketing managers can then decide which segment or segments to pursue.

Individual Influences
on Behavior

Communication

Social and Cultural
Influences on Behavior

Perception

Learning
and
Memory

Beliefs
and
Attitudes

Consumer
Research

Market
Segmentation

Motivation
and
Emotion

Consumer
Decision
Making

Group
Influences

Family
Influences

Personal
Influences

Social
Class

Personality
Self-concept,
and Lifestyle

Adoption

Culture and
Microculture

Diffusion

Feedback

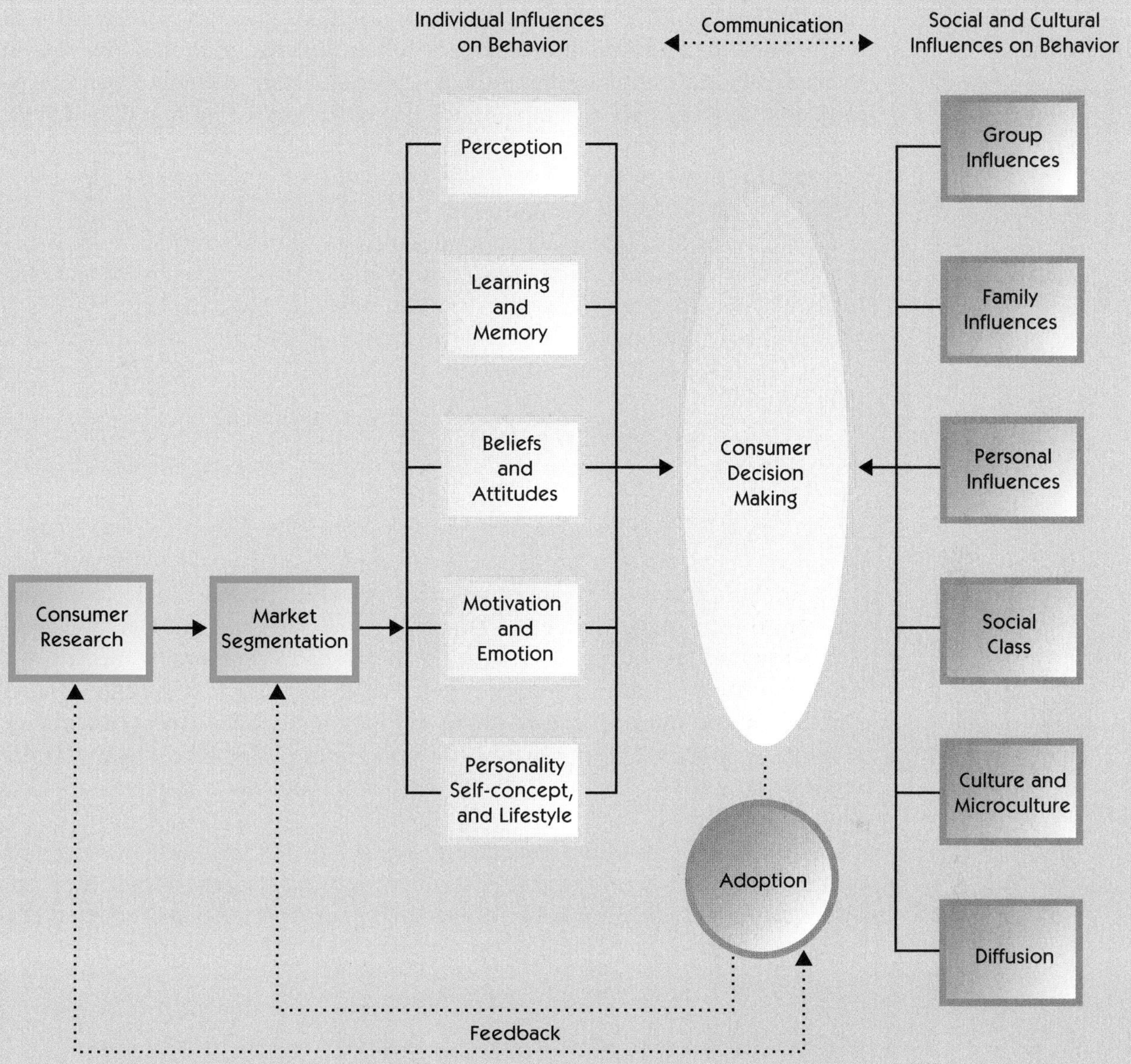

The framework then proceeds to consider the two broad sets of factors that largely influence consumer choice making; namely, individual influences and social and cultural influences. The first group, labeled *individual influences*, includes personal factors such as perception, learning, attitudes, motivation, and personality. Marketers attempt to influence consumers' perception, learning, and attitudes through product offerings, advertising, or salespeople, and other individual factors such as personality are taken as givens.

The second major group of influencing factors on decision making is brought about by the environment of which the consumer is part. This group of factors is labeled *social and cultural influences*. Components of this set include group, family, and personal influences. In addition, this set encompasses the ramifications of social class and culture on consumption patterns, as well as the effect of diffusion efforts brought about by change agents. The reason for including diffusion as part of the social and cultural influences on behavior is that other people's acceptance and use of products and services have a bearing on our own decision to accept and use these same products and services. For instance, person-to-person communication through the electronic media is not a one-sided phenomenon.

The framework addresses the communication flows between the environment and the consumer. Such communication, either interpersonal or mass, determines the probability and direction of consumer choices. This process is shown as a two-sided flow between the individual and the social and cultural forces. Each set of factors influences the other while being influenced by the other.

In light of the interaction of these two broad sets of forces, consumer decisions are made. In response to influence from an ad, a recommendation from a friend, or a temporary price reduction, consumers may decide to purchase or adopt a product. The framework thus shows adoption as an outcome of decision making.

Although adoption seemingly represents the last link in the decision-making process, most marketers consider it the start of a relationship with the consumer. Postpurchase evaluations occur as consumers begin to use a product. Product performance is evaluated against consumer expectations and sacrifice of resources. The result of this evaluation directly influences whether or not the consumer repurchases the same brand. This relationship in the framework is shown as a dotted-line feedback loop that connects adoption with the consumer.

The role of consumer research reappears at this juncture. Through research, marketers can determine consumer reactions and attitudes toward the brand as well as explain and predict future purchase intentions. A dotted line between feedback and consumer research reflects this interaction.

How Does *Consumer Behavior: An Applied Approach*'s Ancillary Package Uniquely Aid Professors in Their Teaching?

No consumer behavior textbook would be complete without a solid, up-to-date, ancillary package. Whereas a consumer behavior text should provide both theory and case examples that clarify and help students understand major concepts, the ancillary package should integrate theory with real-world practice by offering support materials that both instructors and students find useful.

A password-protected Web site includes:

- **An instructor's manual** that includes: chapter outlines/lecture notes; answers to review questions; answers to discussion questions; and solutions to case questions.
- **A test bank** that includes over 1,100 questions—a combination of multiple-choice and true-false items—prepared in part by Martin Meyers of the University of Wisconsin—Stevens Point. This test bank has been carefully edited and expanded by the authors to include many of their own exam questions.
- **A PowerPoint presentation** of lecture outlines and schematic diagrams found in the textbook.

ACKNOWLEDGMENTS

We are fortunate to have worked with some wonderful people who generously donated their time and effort to make this textbook and its ancillary package a reality. We are particularly indebted to Ms. Denise LeBudda, Editor; Ms. Mary Melloy, Senior Production Editor; Ms. Colleen Zelinsky, Senior Permissions Editor; as well as Ms. Tina Bower, Editor of the second edition, and all the kind folks at Kendall Hunt who made the publication of this third edition a reality.

Reviewers

We gratefully acknowledge the constructive comments of the colleagues who provided reviews for this text:

Carol Arnone
Frostburg State University

Stephen Baglione
Saint Leo University

Darren Boas
Hood College

Richard (Mike) Dailey
UT Arlington

Mary Edrington
Drake University

Susan Emens
Kent State University—Trumbull

Kimberly Folkers
Wartburg College

John Frasco
*Central Connecticut
State University*

Richard Heiens
*University of South Carolina
Aiken*

James Hess
Ivy Tech Community College

Eva Hyatt
Appalachian State University

William Lundstrom
Cleveland State University

Janet Lyons
Utah State University

Lawrence Marks
Kent State Univeristy

Michael J. Messina
Gannon University

Linda Mullen
Georgia Southern University

Chandran Mylvaganam
Northwood University, Michigan

Robert Owen
*Texas A&M University—
Texarkana*

Karen Palumbo
University of St. Francis

Janis Petronis
Tarleton State University

Carmen Reagan
Austin Peay State University

Scott Roberts
Roger Williams University

Annette Ryerson
Black Hills State University

Tom Schmidt
Simpson College

Ken shaw
SUNY Oswego

Harry Shrank
Temple University

Ross Steinman
Temple University

Karen Stone
Southern New Hampshire
University

Leona Tam
Old Dominion University

Keith Wade
Webber International University

Scott Weiland
Penn State Worthington Scranton

Gerald Weisenfeld
Troy University Montgomery

Jingyun Zhang
Bowling Green State University

We sincerely hope that every professor or student who uses this textbook finds it to be as interesting and enjoyable an experience as we have encountered in the process of writing it.

Nessim Hanna
Richard Wozniak
Margaret Hanna

ABOUT THE AUTHORS

The lead author, **Dr. Nessim Hanna** received his Ph.D. in Marketing from the University of Illinois at Urbana. He is Professor Emeritus of Marketing, Northern Illinois University, DeKalb, IL, and is presently the Vice President and Chief Marketing Officer of Efficient BioSystems, Inc., located in Darien, Illinois. His areas of expertise in the fields of consumer behavior, pricing, international marketing, as well as cross-functional business disciplines prompted many domestic and international universities to invite him as Visiting Professor to teach and to help in establishing their curricula. Included in this group are schools such as American Graduate School of International Management (Thunderbird, AZ); Norwegian School of Management (Oslo, Norway); and Hong Kong Baptist University (Hong Kong, China); the University of Petroleum and Minerals (Saudi Arabia); and the University of Cairo (Egypt).

Dr. Hanna has published intensively in the fields of consumer behavior, marketing management, pricing, and international marketing. He has over thirty-five articles published in refereed journals, such as *Journal of Marketing, Psychology and Marketing,* and *Journal of Academy of Marketing Science.* In addition, he has published over forty refereed conference papers. He is also the author of a number of textbooks on pricing and principles of marketing, as well as global business operations and institutions. His *Pricing Policies and Procedures* has been translated into the Czech, Polish, and Russian languages.

Dr. Hanna is on the editorial board of a number of domestic and international professional business journals. He has done consulting for and has conducted executive seminars on behalf of many companies and organizations, such as General Motors, Motorola, Honeywell, ServiceMaster, ARAMCO, Petromin, and Saudi Airline Top Management Group, as well as most recently for the Middle East Securities Executive Training Center. He has served as a keynote speaker for many organizations, including SAMMY, The National Association of Purchasing Managers, The American Management Association, and The American Marketing Association.

Dr. Hanna was appointed by The American Marketing Association Global Division as Coordinator of the International Activity Group (IAG) for the entire Middle East. He also established a number of faculty-student exchange programs between U.S. universities and other overseas institutions, such as the Norwegian School of Management and the Hong Kong Baptist University, among others.

In addition to his responsibilities at Efficient BioSystems, Inc., Dr. Hanna's activities include writing a number of executive training manuals, as well as conducting a number of executive overseas training programs for Middle Eastern and Asian business and financial executives.

Supporting author, **Mr. Richard Wozniak** received his B.S. in Marketing, B.A. in Spanish, and M.S. in Marketing from Northern Illinois University. He is a faculty member in the Department of Marketing, College of Business, at Northern Illinois University, in DeKalb, IL. He has taught under-graduate and graduate marketing and business-related courses for the past 30 years. In addition to his teaching, Mr. Wozniak has extensive business experience in the fields of retailing and wholesaling, working with companies such as Masterpiece Studios, Marshall Fields (now Macy's), A. Marcus, and Rockford Tool. Mr. Wozniak also does consulting for various not-for-profit organizations, including the Roman Catholic Archdiocese of Chicago. Mr. Wozniak has presented a number of papers on the topics of teaching statistics and research methods at regional conferences. Mr. Wozniak's invaluable contributions to this book include library and online research, as well as word processing of the entire manuscript and its supplements. In addition, he managed databases and classroom tested text-related materials.

Supporting author, **Ms. Margaret Hanna, APN, WHNP-BC, CCHP**, is presently a healthcare provider at San Quentin Correctional Facility in San Quentin, CA, a position she has held since 2006 after leaving her previous post as President of DermaCare Plus, Inc. in Elmhust, IL. Ms. Hanna brings a fresh perspective to this project as she synthesizes her expertise in medicine with her skills in the business field. In addition to her demanding career, she has authored and published many articles on various business issues related to the field of healthcare marketing. She has also presented papers on healthcare issues at business and medical conferences, both domestically and abroad. Ms. Hanna conducted seminars for healthcare administrators and served as a consultant for a number of medical groups and U.S. hospitals. Her business practice provided tremendous insights for the applied approach followed in this textbook, and her editorial capabilities added depth and clarity to the coverage.

GROUNDWORK OF THE TEXT

Introduction to Consumer Behavior

LEARNING OBJECTIVES

- To comprehend the dynamics of the Consumer Behavior discipline.
- To recognize the multi-disciplinary nature of this subset of human behavior.
- To gain insight into factors that influence purchasing decisions.
- To develop a basic understanding of the marketing concept.
- To explore the dynamic trends that shape our society.
- To grasp implications of the macro and micro trends on behavior.

KEY TERMS

consumer behavior
marketing concept
agents of change
telecommuting
ethical absolutism

ethical relativism
craft ethics
green marketing
global village

People in the United States are probably the most diet-conscious consumers in the world. In 2007, statistics from the Calorie Control Council, a trade association for diet-food makers, reveal that more than 95 million U.S. adults are now dieting and routinely consume foods with labels such as *diet, light, reduced calorie, low cholesterol,* and *low fat.* Store shelves are loaded with low-calorie food products ranging from Diet Coke to Slim-Fast. According to DataMonitor, the diet business in the United States and Europe combined mushroomed into an estimated $100 billion industry in the year 2008. Significant demand for weight-loss and diet products has helped to diversify this market and partition it into a number of distinct market segments that include diet foods and beverages, artificial sweeteners, diet pills and plans, medically supervised programs (e.g., weight-loss surgery), as well as health clubs, just to name a few.

Yet a study by the American Obesity Association reports that in 2007, approximately 127 million adults in the United States were overweight, 60 million were obese, and 9 million were overly obese.[1] Moreover, the study revealed that obesity among children is increasing at an even more alarming rate. Figures from 2007 show that 25 million children in the United States between the ages of 6 and 19 are overweight or obese. Americans may be consuming diet products and attempting to fight this weight epidemic; but at the same time, they appear to be gaining weight and inches around the waistline.

Whatever the reason, marketers are quick to capitalize on this and other consumer behaviors in the marketplace. Producers and marketers alike have adjusted their product offerings and strategies to accommodate consumers' desires to feel good about themselves. For example, clothing manufacturers who used to produce most garments in slender cuts have faced dwindling sales as consumers can no longer fit themselves into their usual clothing sizes. In response to consumer weight gain coupled with the corresponding phenomenon of weight-gain denial, clothing manufacturers embarked on a tactic known as vanity sizing. *Vanity sizing* is the practice of enlarging the actual size of garments but keeping the same smaller-size designation on the label. For example, a garment currently labeled size 8 may actually be a formerly size 10 item. Consumers psychologically feel better about a brand that allows them to fit into small sizes, suggesting they still have the figure and physique of yesteryear.

Airlines and theaters are working to eliminate complaints from dissatisfied customers who feel that seat dimensions are unsuitable to their body frames. Automakers are designing larger and wider models that are capable of accommodating the obese. Similarly, furniture makers are producing larger, sturdier chairs, couches, and bed frames that can withstand excessive body weight. One industry in particular now faces an intriguing question. In the field of promotion, advertisers are wondering whether the slim, trim, or even waiflike look of yesteryear's models remains relevant, or whether the era of full-bodied models has arrived.[2]

> *Issues related to diet and weight have created abundant opportunities for marketers in the areas of food and beverages, clothing, and exercise. Think of some such products that you purchase. Are they priced, promoted, or distributed differently from regular products?*

Why or why not? Check out a company involved in the diet-weight business by visiting Weight Watchers at www.weight-watchers.com. Also visit a plus-size and super-size ladies' fashion company at www.mylesahead.com. What motives do these companies stress to get consumers to buy their products or services?

What Is Consumer Behavior?

Welcome to the field of consumer behavior. As an interdisciplinary field of inquiry, **consumer behavior** focuses on the consumption-related activities of individuals. It investigates the reasons behind and the forces influencing the selection, purchase, use, and disposal of goods and services in order to satisfy personal needs and wants.

consumer behavior
the study of how consumers select, purchase, use, and dispose of goods and services to satisfy personal needs and wants

The field of study known as consumer behavior is a fairly young discipline. In fact, the first textbooks that specifically addressed the topic were written only as recently as the 1960s. Among the pioneers in the discipline of consumer behavior were James F. Engel, David T. Kollat, and Roger D. Blackwell, as well as John A. Howard and Harold F. Kassarjian, whom many have come to regard as the fathers of consumer behavior.

Consumer behavior is a subset of a larger set of activities consisting of all human behavior. It includes everything that occurs as prospective customers for products and services become actual customers. Interestingly enough, much of consumer behavior does not necessarily involve purchasing per se. It also encompasses such activities as browsing, influencing others, being influenced by others, and complaining about and returning products, as well as exposure to the media.

More specifically, the study of consumer behavior investigates the way individuals choose, purchase, use, and dispose of goods and services in order to satisfy personal or household needs. Savvy marketers today think of consumers in terms of their product and service needs throughout their lives. This view, which is known as the *customer lifecycle*, focuses upon the creation and delivery of lifetime value to the consumer during every interaction in a consumer's relationship with a firm. This relationship extends throughout the various stages of the purchase process, starting from one's interest and search for a product, to purchasing it, to using it, to replenishing or replacing it, to finally retiring or recycling it. In each one of these customer lifecycle stages, marketers attempt to improve their customer centricity through a better understanding of customer interactions or consumers' *touchpoints* with the firm. The goal of Customer Touchpoint Management (CTM) is to enrich customers' experiences with the firm during all interactions, both personal and mechanical, that they would normally experience during their relationship lifecycle with the firm.

Some of the influences that shape consumer choices and tendencies are internal processes, such as our own thinking, feeling, and desiring. Other influences spring from environmental factors, such as social forces (whether group or interpersonal) and economic, situational, retail, and promotional considerations. Somehow, all these forces combine and dynamically interact to produce shopping behavior, the objective of which is to satisfy human needs and wants.

Many forces combine to produce shopping behaviors; the objective of which is to satisfy human needs and wants.

The term *consumer behavior* differs from a similar term, *buyer behavior*, in that buyer behavior is an umbrella term often understood to encompass business-to-business purchasing as well as personal consumption. Business-to-business buying entails the procurement processes and activities of producers and intermediaries in the marketing channels, as well as the acquisition procedures of other organizations and institutions. Business-to-business buying is beyond the scope of this text, which primarily focuses on consumer behavior.

Human behavior is an extremely complicated subject, and consumer behavior is no less complex. Analysis of consumer behavior in the field entails surveying numerous theories and published research studies that offer insight into purchasing tendencies. The ultimate goal is to help marketers better understand the processes and activities of consumer behavior, and thus to anticipate how marketing strategies and tactics will influence consumers and affect the products and services various types of consumers will buy. In other words, as marketers come to understand consumer behavior, they are better able to predict how consumers will respond to various environmental and informational cues. For example, the September 11, 2001 attacks on the United States and the heightened level of apprehension and anxiety that followed caused many Americans to reexamine what really matters in their lives. Many are focusing more on keeping their homes and families secure, purchasing products that promise safety, and seeking better understanding of foreign cultures. Marketers can then configure and fine-tune their strategies and tactics accordingly. Additionally, in today's highly competitive marketplace, a sound understanding of consumer behavior helps marketers gain a competitive advantage and establish positive and lasting customer relationships.

Approaches to the Discipline of Consumer Behavior

In today's world, goods are produced and services are planned in anticipation of future demand. Meanwhile, consumer preferences and tastes constantly change. Styles quickly become fashionable and then go out of vogue. It becomes increasingly important that marketers know what consumers need and want, how they spend their resources, and how they decide where to shop, when to buy, and what to purchase. In short, timely knowledge of consumer behavior is a prerequisite for marketing success. For instance, companies that were able to anticipate the surge in consumers' need to feel secure developed numerous successful products and services ranging from home security systems to "smart" credit cards that defy fraudulent use.

The discipline of consumer behavior can be approached in a number of ways. At the individual level, we can examine intrapersonal influences on consumption such as perceptions, learning, attitudes, motivations, and personality. We can then broaden our view to examine group, interpersonal, cultural, and cross-cultural influences. Conversely, we can also begin by examining cultural and social forces that influence consumption and then narrow down the focus to personal factors. In this text, we begin our investigation of consumer behavior at the level of individual influences and then broaden our focus to consider social and cultural influences.

Throughout the stages of its development, the study of consumer behavior borrowed heavily from other fields of knowledge to enhance our understanding of human consumptive activities. In this sense, the investigation of consumer behavior can be viewed as interdisciplinary, spanning the spectrum of the behavioral sciences. Among the disciplines that contribute most to the understanding of consumer behavior are psychology, sociology, social psychology, cultural anthropology, and economics.

Psychology investigates the mental processes and behavior of individuals as they react to stimuli in their environment. Researchers of consumer behavior and marketing practitioners make extensive use of psychological concepts, including perception, learning, memory, motivation, emotion, personality, and self-image.

Unlike psychologists, sociologists generally focus on groups and social institutions as primary units of analysis. *Sociology* canvasses the collective behavior of individuals as groups, organizations, institutions, and entire societies. Researchers of consumer behavior and marketing practitioners alike are interested in status and role structures within various groups, as well as group norms and values.

Social psychology probes the way individuals relate to other individuals and function together within groups. The purchase of many products is socially motivated, and many products and services are used in group settings. In this regard, researchers of consumer behavior and marketers are interested in reference groups and opinion leaders that consumers look to when they make purchasing decisions.

Anthropology delves into people in relation to their culture. In addition to examining the influence of society on individuals, anthropologists explore artifacts and behavior patterns from the past. They also conduct comparative studies that cross cultural boundaries. Studies of cross-cultural consumer behavior are particularly valuable for marketers involved in global business.

Economics examines people's production and the exchange of resources for goods and services. In economic terms, the study of consumer behavior emphasizes *demand* more than *supply*, assuming that offering a supply of goods and services that truly matches market demand is preferable to undertaking the task of creating demand for what sellers happen to supply.

No single discipline adequately explains all aspects of consumption. For example, pure economic theory could lead one to assume that consumers always behave rationally, act on complete market information, and maximize the satisfaction they obtain from every dollar they spend. Traditional economics cannot account for the influence of internal forces, such as human needs and wants, attitudes, emotions, personality, and risk perception. Nor does it take into consideration the impact of external factors, such as culture, social class, the situational context, reference groups, opinion leaders, word of mouth, and marketing communications.

Psychology, sociology, social psychology, anthropology, and economics as well as other fields offer diverse perspectives from which marketers hope to gain meaningful insights about the factors that influence consumption patterns.

What Do Buying Decisions Involve?

To see what consumer behavior entails, consider the hypothetical case of Mr. and Mrs. Donato and their two young children, John and Kathy, as together they contemplated the acquisition of a family pet. After weeks of deliberating, the Donatos had decided to get a puppy. Nearly all the households in the neighborhood had dogs, and John and Kathy had repeatedly asked their parents for one. The parents believed it would teach the kids a great deal about responsibility and caring for others. The tasks of feeding the dog, walking it, grooming it, training it, and cleaning up after it were therefore delegated to the children.

The family borrowed several books about dogs from the local library and surfed the Internet to learn exactly what they were getting themselves into. Professional breeders were one source; others included pet shops, animal shelters, and individuals who ran classified ads in the local newspaper offering puppies for sale. After considering these sources, Mr. and Mrs. Donato decided to take John and Kathy to visit the local pet shop.

The parents had no strong preference for any particular breed or gender, and several large and small breeds, as well as mixed breeds, were available. The prices varied markedly, ranging from $800 for a purebred, show-quality malamute to $150 for a six-month-old mixed breed. Although Mr. and Mrs. Donato had originally agreed to spend no more than $400 on the purchase, John and Kathy instantly fell in love with a frisky gray-and-white husky that carried a price tag of $500.

Mr. and Mrs. Donato had a number of questions to ask the salesclerk. In just a few moments, they needed to learn as much as possible about caring for the new addition to their household. The clerk informed the Donatos that the city required dog owners to buy a license and that periodic shots were needed. The family bought a brush, a collar and leash, a feeding bowl, some toys, and a large basket where the dog could sleep.

A professional breeder happened to be waiting in the store's checkout line. She advised the Donatos that huskies need plenty of exercise and a large, fenced-in yard. She reminded them that responsible owners have their animal spayed or neutered in order to help control the pet population. She also recommended obedience school in order to train the pet properly.

The Donatos asked the breeder about the type and amount of food that would be best for the dog. Choices emerged again regarding which brand to purchase and the quantity to buy, as well as where to buy it. Better-quality foods were often available for cheaper prices at pet superstores. This fact, however, did not preclude the possibility of buying dog food from the pet store where the family bought the puppy. The only problems with buying the food there were limited choices and higher prices.

Selecting a veterinarian was not an easy task either; a dozen were listed in the Yellow Pages. The parents sought the advice of other pet-owning friends. Fortunately, a colleague at work recommended a competent veterinarian who charged reasonable prices for the required services. The Donatos called her for an appointment.

The decision to purchase a puppy involves a considerable amount of prepurchase deliberation.

Consumer Behavior: The Forces Behind Human Actions

This brief scenario illustrates a number of important concepts drawn from the field of consumer behavior. The decision occurred within a *family* setting where the parents *rationally* sorted out and weighed the pros and cons. Afterward, different family members played different *roles* in the *decision process*. The children were the *initiators* of the process. The parents were *motivated* to make the purchase by a desire to teach their kids a sense of responsibility, which they deemed an important *cultural value*. Mr. and Mrs. Donato must have *perceived* that buying a pet was a worthwhile investment. A particularly favorable *attitude* toward dogs, as compared to cats or other animals, was instrumental in the decision to acquire the puppy.

The decision to purchase the puppy was a *high-involvement* process, because adopting a dog is significant and relevant to the way a household functions. Consequently, a considerable amount of *pre-purchase deliberation* might be expected. Interestingly, the final selection may have been somewhat *impulsive*, because the narrative offers no evidence that the members of the family had read up on the traits of the chosen breed. Experience alone will tell whether the characteristics of the husky will match and complement the *personalities* and *lifestyle* of the owners.

The influence of *reference groups* came into play when the parents considered the fact that most families in their *middle-class* neighborhood owned dogs. In addition, Mr. and Mrs. Donato relied on the professional breeder as an *opinion leader* when they sought advice about food for the pet. *Word-of-mouth communications* helped them select a qualified veterinarian.

Purchase of the puppy brought about the *need* for additional expenditures on various products and services. Pet food and various accessories need to be purchased when the puppy is brought home. A trip to the vet is required for shots, and the puppy may be sent to obedience school for training. After the dog has become fully integrated into the household, many *low-involvement* purchases may also be made, such as toys, biscuits, and doggie treats.

Consumer Behavior in Practice

Is a Chicken Really a Chicken?

Before Frank Perdue, chickens had been thought of as much a commodity as beef or fish. For a newcomer to the broiler business, it would not be a smart idea to use advertising to gain market access, because such commodity advertising benefits all the players in the market, not just the newcomer. To enter the market against fierce competition, Frank Perdue, president of Perdue Farms, sought to communicate a strong differentiation for his brand of commodity chickens by marketing a brand-name chicken—something unknown in the broiler industry at that time. To make his chickens brand-identifiable would allow him to command premium prices for them and avoid the price competition that is characteristic of many commodity markets.

But what would differentiate his chickens from others so they would be identifiable to consumers? Perdue decided to add marigold petals to the chickens' high-nutrition diet. This gave the broilers a golden-yellow appearance instead of the usual pale-flesh color, a change that consumers interpreted as a sign of freshness and quality. He also planned to sell his broilers fresh rather than frozen, because consumers perceive fresh birds to be more flavorful.

With this plan of action, the only thing left for Perdue was to communicate the new image to the public, which he did through heavy spending on advertising. Perdue appeared personally in his company's television commercials, and his face appeared in full-page newspaper and magazine ads and on subway posters. He bragged in these ads about the soft life his tender chickens led, the quality food they consumed, the pure water they drank, and the tender loving care they received.

The results were astounding. Thousands of consumers called Perdue's headquarters daily asking where they could buy his chickens. Sales figures grew rapidly into the hundreds of millions, and the company attained unheard-of success within a few years. Even though Perdue's chickens commanded a premium price, consumers were willing to pay it because they believed in the quality of the chicken. Satisfaction was guaranteed; refunds were given to any dissatisfied customer. Today, the company is one of the largest and most profitable broiler producers in the United States, with annual sales in 2007 in excess of $3.4 billion. The company is ranked as the third largest poultry firm in the United States and presently provides food as well as agricultural products and services to customers in more than 50 countries.[3]

Frank Perdue originated the concept of branding chickens. Prior to Perdue's innovative approach, chickens were generally regarded as commodity products. How does branding affect consumers? Why do consumers usually seek branded products even though they are more expensive than their nonbranded counterparts? Are consumers wrong in doing so? Visit Perdue's home page at www.perdue.com and observe the strategies the company uses to promote its products and educate the public concerning them. How are these strategies different from those of other poultry producers?

The Role of the Marketing Concept in Exchange Processes

The activities of buying, selling, and marketing are certainly not new to the world. On the contrary, these tasks in some form or another are as old as the existence of humans on the planet. Cultural anthropologists have discovered murals on the walls of Egypt's more than 5,000-year-old Pharaonic temples that depict ships bringing ostrich feathers, ivory, rare woods, and monkeys into the country. These items were traded by merchants from Lebanon, Assyria, and Ethiopia in exchange for Egyptian chariots, wheat, and horses. It is only in recent times, however, that business practitioners have come to appreciate the vital role of the consumer as the core of all marketing activities. Firms today increasingly subscribe to an operating philosophy known as the **marketing concept**, in which the consumer is the focal point of company activities—production, new-product research and development, pricing, distribution, and promotion. The marketing concept embodies "the view that an industry is a customer-satisfying process, not a goods-producing process. An industry begins with the customer and his/her needs, not with a patent, a raw material, or a selling skill."[4] In this regard, the task of marketing is frequently described in terms of generating, expediting, and consummating exchanges between buyers and sellers in order to satisfy consumer needs and wants.

Inherent in any discussion of consumer behavior is the notion of exchange. Exchange occurs when resources of any variety are transferred between the parties to a transaction. In other words, exchange means relinquishing something of perceived value (cash, credit, labor, goods) in return for acquiring something else of perceived value (products, services, ideas). For successful exchanges to occur, there must be at least two parties—each of which possesses something desired by the other. Each party must be able to communicate with the other and to deliver on any commitments that are made. In addition, each party must believe that it is desirable—or at least acceptable—to deal with the other, and both parties must be free to accept or reject any offer from the other party.[5] Exchanges occur between individuals and other individuals, between individuals and organizations, and between organizations and other organizations.

The material possessions we own, the services we use, and the activities we engage in are largely by-products of marketing actions that somehow have influenced our purchasing behavior. We all witnessed the Beanie Baby craze in the 1990s, which prompted many consumers to collect them and even use them as investment tools. In a similar way, the make, model, and year of the car you drive, the services of the bank you frequent, and the sports outing you may have planned are some of the components of daily life that are influenced by marketers and their role as **agents of change**.

Some writers even go to the extent of stating that marketing is "the creation and delivery of a standard of living."[6] That is to say, in our society, marketers as agents of change have brought about the high standard of living to which we have grown accustomed. The claim is that our lives have become happier, more varied, and interesting due to their efforts.

In this view, what we purchase is based on what we see and learn. Much of what we see and learn results from marketing tactics, such as glamorous advertising, clever promotions, creative store displays, and the availability of a multitude of convenient and helpful customer services. For example, many of us would have been unable to purchase our homes or most of the durable goods we own if it were not for the creative financing and credit policies that marketers provide.

Although many of these marketing efforts help us to experience a more enjoyable lifestyle, at the same time we are victims of some such efforts. Consider, for example, the automakers' policy of introducing new auto models

marketing concept
an operating philosophy in which the consumer is the focus of all company activities

agents of change
entities that actively strive to reshape consumers' beliefs and behaviors

annually. This action makes the previous year's model, at least psychologically, seem old. This strategy prompts many car owners to upgrade to the new model. Similarly, think of the fashion industry's seasonal changes in clothing styles. When the new styles appear, most fashion-conscious consumers feel obligated to replace their suddenly outdated wardrobe. Contemplate further the decision of an electric power company to construct a nuclear energy–generating facility, whose cost and potential hazard to the society and environment are significantly high.

In such cases, do marketers have *the right* to act as agents of change for the public? Many societies attempt to find ways to cushion the effect of some of these changes through social action groups and governmental regulatory agencies. In addressing these changes, however, the challenge often lies in the difficulty of determining whether the change in the long run is beneficial to the entire society.

The Influence of Macro Forces on Consumer Behavior

Children born in recent years take for granted a world their grandparents could not have envisioned. During the twentieth century, humans have witnessed unprecedented technological progress. Never before has the pace of change been so brisk. The first half of the 20th century brought about the invention of automobiles, airplanes, radio, television, and telephones as well as many household appliances such as refrigerators, washing machines, and clothes driers. During the second half of that century, computers, satellites, and interactive media have altered the way we communicate. Supersonic jets and feature-loaded automobiles have changed the way we travel. Ingenious financial networks and investment programs have reshaped the way we plan for retirement. High-tech medical equipment and miracle drugs extend our lives. Eclectic forms of marketing have refashioned the way we shop.

As a result of a virtual information explosion, consumers now constitute the most knowledgeable generation in the history of humankind. Computer makers and software companies have made it easier than ever for consumers to get whatever they need—products, services, or information—wherever and whenever they want it via the Internet. It is possible to order groceries electronically and arrange a convenient delivery time. In the area of financial management, online payment of bills and investment in the stock market have become realities. In the workplace, innovative arrangements such as job sharing, flextime, and telecommuting offer viable alternatives to the traditional 9-to-5 positions at an employer's location. In the field of entertainment, over 1,000 cable and satellite stations have come into being. A telecommunications network supported by orbiting satellites makes it possible for consumers to reach anyone in the world and to witness global events as they occur.

As advances in technology have changed consumer lifestyles, marketing practices, in turn, have had to respond. Strategies ranging from precision targeting to customization of products have emerged. Creative selling tactics, advanced networks of distribution channels, and novel ways to motivate consumers to buy, as well as means to finance purchases, have also come about.

Such progress, however, does not come without costs. As consumers become increasingly overwhelmed by the deluge of new product offerings and glut of information, decision processes become more complicated. When sorting through and processing this information about products and services become monumental tasks, many consumers simplify their purchasing decisions by buying on impulse or relying on brand loyalties.

In the wake of this profusion of information, some unscrupulous marketers have seized the opportunity to employ puffery, deception, and manipulation to sell their products and services. Concern over unethical practices has motivated many private as well as public bodies to take steps to protect the public from misrepresentation and fraud. Many companies have adopted a philosophy of relationship marketing, in which firms develop a loyal clientele by forming and solidifying long-term customer alliances that are based on trust. Many industries have adopted codes of ethics to which member firms are expected to adhere. When self-regulation has proven to be inadequate, government bodies have had to step in to protect consumer rights.

Today's marketplace is a very different place from what it used to be. Consumers in highly developed nations have come to demand convenience and the immediate satisfaction of their needs and wants. They expect product-related facts to be instantaneously accessible but seldom use all the available information. These and a host of other trends create opportunities for innovative marketers who are open to change and willing to adapt to a dynamic marketplace. These same trends, however, pose serious threats to marketers who resist change or cannot adjust to it.

Emerging Trends in Contemporary Society

In the twenty-first century, a number of trends seem to be emerging. The following sections detail ten trends that will undoubtedly influence consumer behavior and consequently the way marketers conduct business. The trends are

1. Growth of the information superhighway
2. Focus on health, fitness, and beauty
3. Shifting roles of men and women
4. Telecommuting and the office of the future
5. Personalized economy
6. Concern about personal safety
7. Diversity in the workplace and marketplace
8. Focus on ethics
9. Ecological consciousness
10. Rise of the global village

GROWTH OF THE INFORMATION SUPERHIGHWAY

Communication in cyberspace is where the future for marketers lies. Technologies brought about by the electronic revolution and facilitated by orbiting satellites and fiber optics have made it possible to be in touch with anyone anywhere. The 2009 International CES ad in Figure 1.1 reflects the wide-sweeping diffusion of the information super-highway throughout contemporary society.

Figure 1.1

American consumers have more electronic gadgets and communicate more through these digital devices than consumers in perhaps any other society.

In the near future, machines will emerge as true collaborators. They will have sufficient understanding of human language and culture to monitor trends on their own. It has been estimated that by 2030, the available computer hardware will exceed the memory and processing capacity of the human brain by a factor of thousands, freeing the human brain from the time-wasting activities in the human diary.[7]

Since the 1990s, electronic telecommunication has arisen as the newest and most powerful means for marketers to reach consumers. Computers, databases, multi-media devices and phones, e-mail, fax, voice mail, interactive audiotext and videotext, and caller-number identification have brought about new and powerful marketing tools that allow marketers to satisfy consumers' desire to save time and still acquire products or services specifically geared for their needs. New techniques allow companies to segment the market down to just a few people. In promoting their products or services, marketers have learned how to make details about their products, often in the form of transmittable information, accessible on demand at places and times convenient for consumers.[8]

In addition to wireline e-commerce, today the evolution of the handheld devices incorporating WAP and GPRS technologies has accelerated the convenience of digital commerce. Mobile commerce, which facilitates business transactions through wireless devices, enables users to access the Internet anywhere they happen to be. Smart phones now offer fax, e-mail, Internet access, and phone capabilities all in one. In the next few years, m-commerce is expected to surpass wireline e-commerce as the method of choice for digital commerce transactions.[9] M-commerce will certainly affect many industries, including financial services (encompassing mobile banking), telecommunications (encompassing bill payments), services and retail structure (encompassing placement and payment for customer orders), and information services (encompassing financial, sports, and world news).[10]

However, many individuals and groups remain excluded from taking advantage of these growing technologies. For example, many poor, less-educated, or elderly persons lack relevant skills or access to computers, cell phones, and PDAs. Similarly, some developing and Third World nations lack the same technology. Thus, the world can be divided into two groups: Internet *haves* and *have-nots*. The benefits of the electronic age can accrue only to the privileged haves, at the unfortunate exclusion of the have-nots. However, Asian markets, which are growing at a staggering pace, accounted for 50 percent of the total worldwide Internet subscriber base in 2008.

From a consumer behavior perspective, the growth of the information superhighway has expedited access to any desired facts or news. It enhances the quantity and variety of sources. It allows for timely and up-to-date data to reach consumers wherever they may be. It facilitates communicating with others and performing transactions from convenient locations. It inspires unlimited entertainment choices made possible through the merging of various media. Moreover, advances in technology have made electronics smaller, versatile, faster, and cheaper. All of this increases the power of individual consumers.

FOCUS ON HEALTH, FITNESS, AND BEAUTY

While consumers enjoy the convenience of on-line shopping, Webcasting permits marketers to push information out across the internet.

The fitness craze of the 1980s, which was primarily fueled by a desire to look good, is being supplemented today by one that emphasizes longevity and good health. Today, a growing segment of the public is focusing on nutrition and exercise as means for health maintenance, cutting down on fat, cholesterol, and calories. Such inclinations have created golden opportunities for marketers of a vast array of products and services ranging from fat-free, low-calorie foods and drinks to vitamins, diet centers, and medical corrective procedures. The Sports Club/LA ad in Figure 1.2 reflects the widespread interest of many consumers in joining health clubs and in adopting a regimen of diet and exercise.

In addition, vanity seems to have become the order of the day. This trend can be attributed in part to the aging of the baby boomers. Billions of dollars are spent every year on hair implants, facelifts, plastic surgery, body-part enhancements, liposuction, tanning, and other weapons against what is considered unattractiveness. Men as well as women are becoming avid users of these services. For example, according to the American Society of Plastic Surgeons, in 2007, over 11 million surgical and nonsurgical procedures were performed. Among the surgical procedures, there were 329,000 breast augmentations, 307,000 nose reshapings, 302,000 liposuctions, 233,000 eyelid surgeries, and 146,000 tummy tucks. In the nonsurgical area, there were 3.8 million Botox injections, 965,000 chemical peels, 714,000 laser hair removals, 634,000 microderm abrasions, and 778,000 hyaluronic (e.g., Restylane) injections. Demand for nutritional supplements, such as vitamins and minerals, is also rising. Americans spend more than $35 billion on nutritional supplements per year. And if we add in expenditures in the weight-loss supplements market totaling $46 billion, the figure climbs to $81 billion annually.[11]

Figure 1.2
This ad from the Sports Club/LA reflects an increasing health awareness trend among many consumers who now realize that fitness can only be attained through exercise and diet.

From a consumer behavior point of view, the emphasis of contemporary society on fitness and beauty has caused some consumers to become virtually addicted to health foods, vitamins, and exercise. Others have quit smoking or chosen a vegetarian lifestyle. Still others spend lavishly on beauty aids and treatments. Many have come to think that being beautiful or handsome is a near requirement for success in business.

SHIFTING ROLES OF MEN AND WOMEN

The traditional roles of men and women in our society are being completely redefined. The gap between new and traditional gender roles at home, at work, and in the marketplace is a direct result of the advances made by women in terms of education, career choices, stature, and earning power. Add to this the fact that 48.5 percent of all U.S. households are headed by unmarried adults, and more single-person households—nearly 29 million of them—now exist in the United States.[12] Products that have been traditionally targeted to men, such as automobiles and computers, are now increasingly being targeted to women as well. Other products and services traditionally targeted to women—such as foods, household cleaners, children's products, and cosmetics—are increasingly being targeted to men. Today, for example, many men find themselves having to adjust to the task of raising a child. A number of Web sites now offer advice and support for child-rearing dads. These sites are designed with user-friendly headings such as "colic—how to deal with this dreadful crying" and "diaper rash—preventing it and dealing with it."

For marketers, these changes translate into a need for new targeting and positioning tactics. Companies face the task of continually reassessing and redefining the sales and advertising strategies they need to aim at different markets. For example, women today bring in half or more of the income in 55 percent of U.S. households. Single women are also the sole wage earners in 27 percent of U.S. households, and 30 percent of working wives out-earn their husbands. Women are also the driving force in the growth of Internet commerce. Forty-one percent of today's 55 million Internet shoppers are women. They represent 45 percent of the 9.2 million online book buyers, 38 percent of the 7.2 million CD/video buyers, 24 percent of the 5.4 million buyers of computer hardware, and 53 percent of the 4.5 million online buyers of clothing.[13] Women also spend more than $300 billion annually on vehicle purchases, maintenance, and repair, and they buy more than half of all the new vehicles. As a consequence, automakers, insurance companies, and marketers of financial services are now vigorously pursuing the female market. Others, such as marketers of sporting equipment, tools, and hardware, are recognizing for the first time the power of female buyers.

Subaru of America, for example, embraced the notion of marketing to women. The company launched an ad campaign in 2000 called "What Do I Know?" in which female athletes were showcased. Subaru's executives feel that women are an essential component of the automotive market, and that they possess significant buying power that cannot be ignored. Similarly, at

General Motors, both the interior and exterior design engineers for the 2008 Chevy Malibu were women. Carmakers are increasingly turning to women to determine the design and comfort of vehicles. Volvo Car Corporation, for example, in an effort to appeal to the female market, recruited a panel of women to build a car specifically designed for that market. The panel's efforts resulted in the creation of the Volvo YCC, which stands for "Your Concept Car." The YCC was debuted at the Geneva International Motor Show in March 2004. In addition, the panel's ideas resulted in the new Volvo C70 car, which was introduced in Australia in September 2006. Computer companies are following similar strategies. Compaq, for example, is reaching out directly to women through an advertising campaign that reflects the importance of computers in a woman's life. According to Woman Trend, a Washington, D.C.–based market research firm, women decide what to buy in 80 percent of families. In the case of travel expenditures, women are the deciders in 80 percent of families. They are also the deciders in 70 percent of families for medical expenses, and in 55 percent of families for both automobile and insurance purchases. In addition to their role as deciders, women are the primary shoppers in nearly two-thirds of households.[14] On the other hand, men in families are tackling more child-rearing responsibilities. They are going to the grocery store, transporting kids to and from piano lessons, and showing up for parent–teacher conferences.

From the perspective of consumer behavior, role redefinitions have influenced who shops, who cares for children, and who makes buying decisions in the household. Moreover, they have necessitated the redesign of many products and forced stores to adjust their operating hours and product mixes. Given these gender trends in audience composition, marketers must be alert to these changes in order to properly cater to the behavioral and attitudinal factors influencing their ever-changing market.

TELECOMMUTING AND THE OFFICE OF THE FUTURE

Beyond a doubt, companies in the new millennium will increasingly play a larger role in family life. Flextime, job sharing, and telecommuting will move off the pages of human resource journals onto boardroom agendas. One example of this trend is the shift in the perks companies now offer. Businesses have shifted from providing designated benefits, such as sick and vacation leaves, to more flexible offerings. One prevalent trend is the dependent flexible spending account, which provides dependents with their own flex spending options. Another is flextime, which gives the employees options beyond the standard 9-to-5 office hours. In addition, many companies provide paid family leaves beyond the Family and Medical Leave Act (FMLA) minimum requirements. Some offer child-oriented benefits, such as child-care referral services, allowing parents to bring children to work in emergency situations, as well as offer emergency/sick child care services. Still others provide other services such as adoption assistance, or help with education by offering college/school selection and referral services and by granting scholarships for family members of employees. Moreover, in the sphere of aging parents, some companies help employees in their responsibilities for them by providing eldercare referral service benefits, or offer company-supported eldercare centers.[15] While the offering of these perks has been curtailed to some extent due to the present adverse business conditions, firms are more likely to reinstitute them once the economy recovers.

One example of flextime is telecommuting. More people are working at home in *virtual offices*, thanks to advances in telecommunication and satellite facilities. The revolution in communications technology over the past two decades has made information not only inexpensive but also readily available to those with the skill to use it. Whether they are called telecommuters, business owners, virtual staffers, or moonlighters, an increasing number of U.S. workers are escaping the confines of their offices and conducting business operations from their homes. No longer are they stuck in rush-hour traffic, worried about arriving late for their jobs or for dinner. They simply work at home, where technology has transformed their residences into telecommunication centers. Telecommuting, as this remote work style is known, is predicted to become the office environment of the future.[16] A recent report has revealed that people are starting home businesses at a rate of 2 million per year.[17]

Some companies find that permitting employees to work from home enhances their productivity, reduces the company's operating costs, and allows employees the flexibility and comfort of working from the environment of their choice.

Telecommuting is what happens when employees or contractors work at home full- or part-time using PCs, modems, faxes, cellular phones, remote LAN access, and other communications equipment.[18] Over the next few years, as technology continues to spread through the society, the work-at-home labor force—which totaled 45.1 million in 2005—is expected to swell to record numbers.[19]

Among the reasons propelling the use of remote work styles are skyrocketing real estate costs and traffic problems, security concerns after 9/11, as well as improved worker productivity and employees' needs for flexible work schedules. Moreover, passage of the Americans with Disabilities Act mandated handicapped-accessible workplaces. The ability to be mainstreamed with access to data via computers and phone lines in one's home eliminates disparities between disabled and nondisabled workers.[20]

Companies using this work arrangement report hundreds of thousands of dollars of annual savings in the cost of leased office space. They also are able to attract and retain highly skilled workers and managers who would be discouraged from joining or remaining in the firm if they had to be physically present at the workplace. Merrill Lynch and AT&T are among the companies that sanction formal telecommuting programs. Today, half of AT&T's 50,000 managers worldwide telecommute.[21]

From a consumer behavior perspective, telecommuting necessitates maintaining a home office equipped with state-of-the-art telecommunications devices. Further, because workers are homebound, the need for transportation is reduced. This fact has ramifications on the demand for a number of products

telecommuting
an arrangement whereby employees work at home using PCs, modems, faxes, and other communications equipment

and services such as gasoline, automobiles, public transportation, auto insurance, and car repair services. Also affected is demand for child-care facilities and baby-sitting services. In fact, in 2006, home workers' shift in consumption patterns caused a fall of around $360 million in spending on such services.[22] From another point of view, the need for an efficient package-delivery system becomes increasingly apparent.

PERSONALIZED ECONOMY

Successful businesses today are those that intimately know their customers and design strategies that cater to the very specific needs of their clientele—even down to the individual level. It has been suggested that three properties characterize today's personalized economy.[23] The first of these is *custom design* of products or services that are marketed to ever-smaller consumer segments. In addition to tailors, shoemakers, fashion designers, painters, lawyers, physicians, plumbers, repair workers, and decorators who have always individualized their services, producers of products that are mass-produced—such as automobiles, motorcycles, and electronics—have also hopped aboard the personalization bandwagon. In the age of the TiVo, the iPhone, and iPod, consumers increasingly expect to custom-tailor their products. Dell Computer has done this successfully for years, so has Levi's with its customized jeans, and Land's End with its custom-fit service on the firm's Web site. Customers measure themselves, detail their style preferences, and answer questions about their figure. A customized garment arrives on their doorstep three weeks later. Other customized products include shoes, travel, food, financial services, cosmetics, bicycles, dolls, and even automobiles. In the field of entertainment, cable and satellite customers can view almost any movie or show on demand.[24]

Immediacy in providing products and services to customers is a second trait of the personalized economy. Convenience for customers is replacing convenience for sellers. Shoppers have come to demand the amenities of around-the-clock shopping services. They have learned to rely on electronic and mobile commerce, along with their facilitating financial instruments, such as credit and debit cards. Through these conveniences, consumers are able to place orders or secure cash wherever and whenever they want.[25]

The third feature of the personalized economy is *value*. Value is provided when sellers gear product features and service benefits to the specific needs of particular customers, or when they create innovative products for which certain buyers willingly pay premium prices. Products and services ranging from tailored clothing and customized furniture to corrective and cosmetic surgeries represent instances where superior value to consumers results from the personalization process.[26]

From a consumer behavior perspective, a rise in the standard of living has caused many consumers to crave products that reflect their individuality. Even though these products often carry a lofty price tag, consumers willingly pay the premium price to acquire the distinction and self-expression that personalized products offer. The SITEL Corporation ad in Figure 1.3 highlights the trend toward customization.

Figure 1.3

Customization is increasingly becoming a successful strategy for many businesses that produce consumer as well as business products. This ad from SITEL Corporation emphasizes products and services with no forced fit and suggests customization as the appropriate course of action.

CONCERN ABOUT PERSONAL SAFETY

Despite recent declines in official crime statistics, violence continues to devastate the present generation just as surely as plagues wiped out people in the Middle Ages. Violence has come to be regarded by many as a primary problem of contemporary U.S. society. Gangs, juvenile criminals, and drug traffickers are among those responsible for the high crime rate. Fueled by neglect, abuse, violence at home, glamorization of violence on TV, and weapons that fall into the wrong hands, crime seemingly has reached epidemic proportions. Among members of street gangs, crime has become the norm, not the exception. Gang members freely set aside the traditional norms and values of the culture to adopt a microculture complete with its own rules, codes, language, and criminal patterns.

For example, the Bureau of Justice Statistics estimated that there were 1.4 million reported violent crimes in 2006. This figure decreased by .5 percent since the year 2000.[27] According to the Justice Department, in 2006 there were over 17,000 murders, 92,000 cases of rape, 447,000 robberies, 2 million burglaries, and 1.2 million motor vehicle thefts.[28] Gang violence ranging from random drive-by shootings and drug trafficking to rape and murder has become common news items in the media today.

In the past few years, one of the major "anti-victimization fears" that consumers started to feel is identity theft. A recent survey conducted by the Federal Trade Commission (FTC) estimated that over 10 million American consumers, or about 4 percent of the adult population, became victims of identity theft in 2007.[29] In such cases, however, the financial losses are usually suffered by credit issuers and banks. Victims are seldom held responsible for fraudulent debts incurred in their name. Identity theft can take a number of forms, but almost always involves the misappropriation of names, Social Security numbers, credit card numbers, or other pieces of personal information for fraudulent purposes. Many victims do not even realize that their identities have been stolen until they see mysterious charges on their credit card statements or get turned down for credit. The FTC survey estimated that victimized consumers spent over 250 million hours in 2007 attempting to recover from identity theft.

In an attempt to address these types of consumer fears, legal action in Congress and the courts has been initiated. A number of bills pending on the Hill address a host of privacy matters, including allocating authority to the FTC for privacy protection, increasing penalties for identity theft and computer crimes, and tightening amendments to the Electronic Communications Privacy Act of 1986. Of particular importance is a bill that would set a national standard for mandatory disclosure when consumer records are compromised. This is due to widespread break-ins and mishaps with massive databases of confidential consumer information that many companies have been unable to protect in the past few years.

Crimes, on the other hand, left consumers searching for means by which they can protect themselves. Many consumers have resorted to arming themselves with personal-protection devices ranging from mace and pepper sprays to concealed handguns. Some are having sophisticated alarm systems installed in their homes and cars. Moreover, an increasing number of financially capable families (the "haves") are moving into restricted-access communities to escape fear of becoming crime victims. Today, gated communities, such as *Hidden Hills* in California and *Tuxedo* in New York, are estimated to exceed 40,000 residents each in population. Some, such as Nevada's *Green Lake,* are larger still and house over 60,000 residents.[30] The Loop-Loc Pool Covers ad in Figure 1.4 on page 23 addresses the safety concerns of homeowners relative to toddler's access to swimming pools.

DIVERSITY IN THE WORKPLACE AND MARKETPLACE

Diversity in the workplace is here to stay. Recent reports indicate that 52.3 percent of today's workforce is made up of women, people of color, and immigrants. By 2025, Whites will hold a mere 60.1 percent of the population, Blacks 13 percent, Asians and Pacific Islanders 6.7 percent, Native Americans 0.8 percent, and Hispanics 19.4 percent.[31] This expansion in racial, ethnic, and cul-

Figure 1.4

"Is your pool cover safe?" is a catchphrase used in this ad from Loop-Loc Pool Covers to raise concerns about pool safety and accidental drowning incidents. The illustration suggests using tough Loop-Loc pool covers to prevent such occurences.

tural diversity carries significant implications for management of the workforce as well as for marketers of products and services. The ad in Figure 1.5 on page 25 affirms that diversity and inclusion constitute the foundation of Bank of America's corporate culture.

Historically, immigrants were attracted to this country by the prospects for personal freedom, greater prosperity, and a brighter future—a promise known as the *American dream*. As years passed, ethnic minorities became increasingly assimilated into the mainstream and made impressive strides in the workplace. In the 1990s, the continued influx of immigrants as well as minorities and women into the labor market has resulted in a multicultural workforce composed of a rich mixture of demographic and lifestyle groups. Whereas observers used to assume that the United States was a melting pot of different races, nationalities, and religions, more current evidence suggests that the nation more closely resembles a salad bowl, in which diverse groups maintain many identifiable elements of their heritage and tradition.

Diversity has proven to be a great asset, offering divergent perspectives and enhancing creativity and innovation within the workplace. Enrichment in work quality due to the inclusion of employees with diverse experiences and backgrounds is one often-mentioned benefit. Social and political pressure also motivate many firms to actively seek diversity in their workforces.

In 2004, *Fortune* magazine undertook a study of *Fortune 1000* companies and the 200 largest privately held U.S. companies to determine the 50 best firms for minority employment. The results revealed the positive impact of diversity on these organizations' bottom line and identified diversity training as an inseparable component of the diversity initiative.[32] The study indicated that positive outcomes resulting from diversity included improved corporate culture, recruitment, client relations, and higher employee retention.

From a consumer behavior perspective, product adaptation has become increasingly necessary to suit the tastes and behavior patterns of distinct ethnic groups. Products such as hair-care items, cosmetics, and foods, among others, have been adjusted to suit the unique needs and preferences of diverse groups. Similarly, in response to diversity, various broadcast stations and print media that target their content to distinct publics have mushroomed. In the realm of response to promotion, Mexican Americans, prevalent in the West and Southwest, have been known to react differently to certain sales promotions and advertising messages than Cuban Americans in the Southeast and Puerto Ricans in the Northeast.[33] So what marketers may regard as a seemingly homogeneous group may in fact consist of different communities, each with unique preferences and patterns of responding to promotions.

FOCUS ON ETHICS

The majority of polls conducted on business ethics in the United States reveal an alarming state of affairs: The public believes the level of business ethics has declined during the past decade. For most people, hardly a day passes without a media report about unethical or illegal business practices ranging from corporate malfeasance such as Bear Stearns, AIG, CitiGroup, Fannie Mae, and Freddie Mac, to price-fixing, kickbacks, and fraudulent advertising claims. This situation has created skepticism and cynicism toward business and has yielded outcries from the public to place professionals and business organizations under closer scrutiny.

For example, the Index of Investor Optimism, created by UBS and Gallup, reports that investor optimism in February 2008 reached a low of 45—a figure

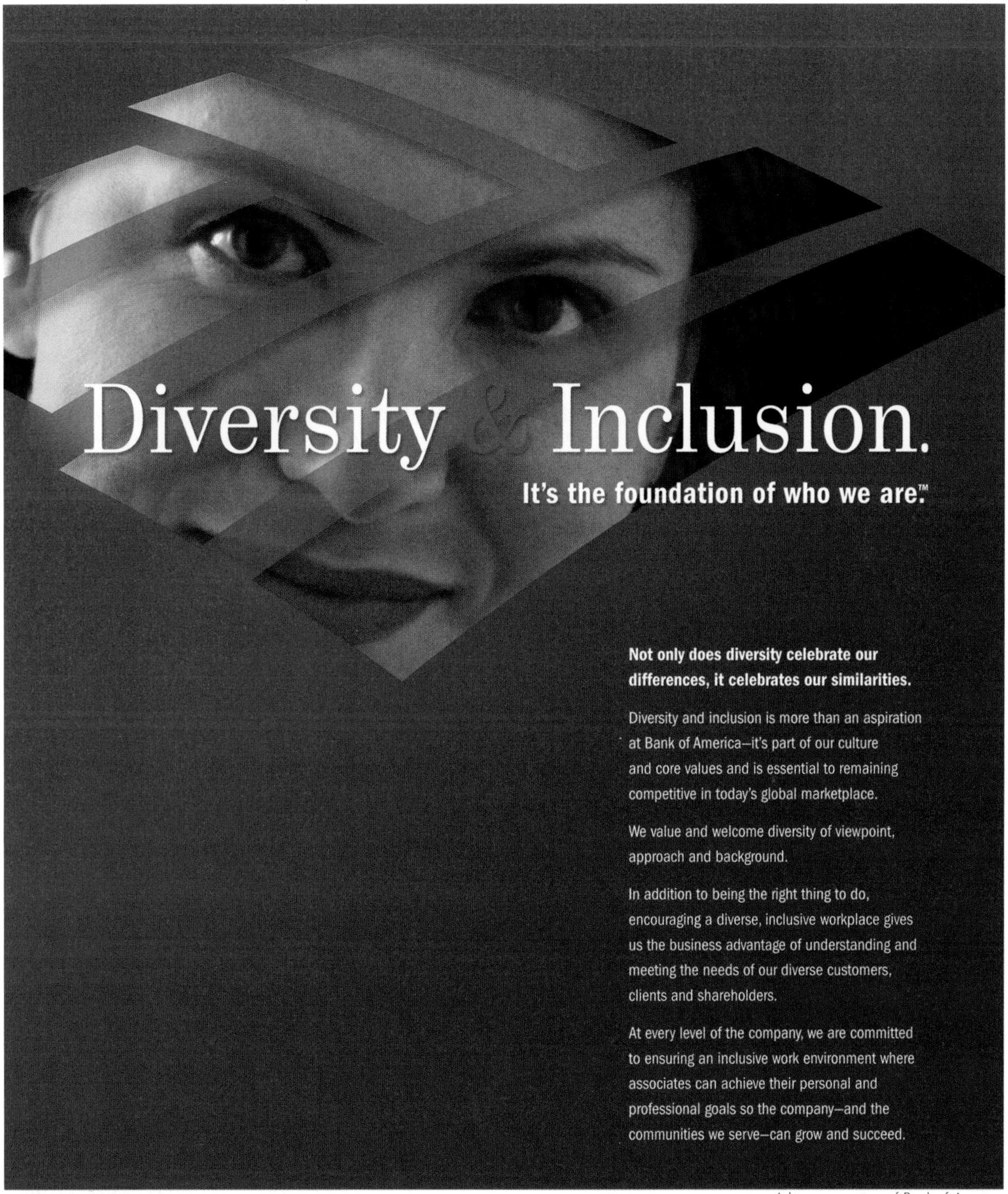
Diversity & Inclusion.
It's the foundation of who we are.™
Not only does diversity celebrate our differences, it celebrates our similarities.
Diversity and inclusion is more than an aspiration at Bank of America—it's part of our culture and core values and is essential to remaining competitive in today's global marketplace.
We value and welcome diversity of viewpoint, approach and background.
In addition to being the right thing to do, encouraging a diverse, inclusive workplace gives us the business advantage of understanding and meeting the needs of our diverse customers, clients and shareholders.
At every level of the company, we are committed to ensuring an inclusive work environment where associates can achieve their personal and professional goals so the company—and the communities we serve—can grow and succeed.

Ad image courtesy of Bank of America

Figure 1.5

This ad from Bank of America asserts that to remain competitive in today's global marketplace, diversity has to be an integral element in the culture and core values of any business.

below its post–September 11 slump of 50—due to perceptions that the economy is heading for a recession.

The drive for ethical behavior comes from individuals' desire to live in a just and fair society. Any society in which individuals lack a sense of ethics is likely to falter. This is particularly true in countries such as the United States and most developed Western nations, where people place a high value on the principles of private enterprise, free markets, open competition, and profit motive. When business managers operate in accord with accepted principles of right and wrong, however, the decisions they make are apt to be ethical. The difficulty lies in defining what is right and what is wrong.

Ethical absolutism, the assumption that there is one true ethical or moral code, may prove to be unworkable because of the varied values held by different individuals. **Ethical relativism**, on the other hand, may prove to be more practical in bringing about ethical decisions.[34] This principle recognizes the diversity of value systems and suggests we analyze the moral consequences of our acts.

Today, a form of morality dominant among business managers is called **craft ethics**.[35] This is a kind of ethical relativism whereby managers learn what their profession mandates in particular situations and then follow that mandate. Craft ethics is not based on what a manager personally believes would be moral. Rather, it entails an outward look at what others in one's profession would regard to be right or wrong.

Firms as well as trade associations have been taking a number of steps to improve the ethical climate of their businesses and industries. For example, a majority of large corporations, such as IBM, Sears, Ford, and Motorola, as well as the American Marketing Association (AMA), have adopted codes of ethics that reflect these organizations' commitment to proper operating standards. These codes provide managers with useful operational guidelines for ethical decision making. In addition, many firms have established audit committees on social responsibility, whose charge is to oversee the ethical marketing climate in the organization. Many companies also hold periodic management seminars that deal with questions of ethics. Goals of these activities include sensitizing managers to ethical problems specific to the firm's operations and providing answers to unique ethical questions that managers may face. A few firms have also established positions for resident ethicists on their staff to provide guidance and direction for ethical matters within their organizations.

Consumer concern for ethical business behavior has given rise to advocate groups that act as watchdogs for fraudulent and deceptive business practices. These groups expose companies that are deemed to engage in wrongdoing. Their actions range from filing lawsuits to organizing boycotts against offending firms. The government, in response to consumer pressure, has enacted a number of laws such as those mandating truth in lending, advertising, packaging, and labeling. These actions have sensitized many companies and institutions to ethical issues and prompted them to enact ethical codes as well as to train their employees to avoid actions that may be construed as ethically questionable.

ethical absolutism
an ethical framework that assumes there is one true ethical or moral code

ethical relativism
an ethical framework that recognizes the diversity of value systems and the moral consequences of an act

craft ethics
ethical relativism whereby managers learn what their profession mandates in a situation and follow that mandate

Ethical Dilemma

If We Err—It's Yours, Free!

Many consumers experience the frustration of reaching a store's checkout counter only to discover that they are being charged prices for products that are higher than those posted on shelf labels. Such overcharges represent a multimillion-dollar fraud that, it is alleged, some retailers intentionally engage in solely to pad their profit margins. Such practices impair consumer satisfaction and store loyalty. Retailers claim that prices programmed into computer systems are nearly 100 percent accurate and that problems arise in the logistics of getting corresponding prices on shelf labels to match those entered into the computer. With a range of 30,000 to 50,000 separate items in the average grocery store, retailers argue, sporadic mistakes are likely to occur. In addition, competition has prompted stores to make price changes—typically hundreds per week—increasing the opportunities for human error.

Scanners were introduced in supermarkets in 1974. Computerized scanning developed to simplify pricing, control inventory, and help retailers keep accurate records. Since manufacturers began bar coding packages and retailers shifted from manual to computerized operations, automated pricing procedures have accelerated customer checkout procedures and spared retailers the labor-intensive practice of price marking individual items. Retailers in most states are no longer required to stamp prices on merchandise.

Consumer activists, law enforcement agencies, journalists, consultants, academicians, and retailers themselves have inquired into the frequency with which scanning errors occur. Estimates range from a low of 2 percent of all items scanned in some studies to a whopping 10 percent in other investigations.

The cumulative impact of scanning errors on consumer satisfaction and loyalty is significant. Grocery store exit interviews reveal that 1 to 3 percent of shoppers switch stores if they feel that price discrepancies are commonplace. To minimize the negative effects of scanning errors on customer satisfaction and loyalty, most retailers today offer guarantees that allow consumers to receive items free of charge or at a discount if they scan inaccurately. Although this policy may confirm to customers that errors are unintentional, it also insulates retailers to some extent from potentially substantial legal liabilities. In such cases, claims of *intent* to deceive or defraud customers are more difficult to substantiate.[36]

The widespread use of scanning technology in retail stores is no surprise, considering the myriad benefits it offers to both retailers and consumers. What specific benefits does this technology offer each group? Visit the price check report of the Federal Trade Commission at www.ftc.gov/reports/scanner2/scanner2.htm, and ascertain whether or not it is realistic to believe that scanning errors can be eliminated entirely. If so, how? Also suggest ways that data collected by scanners can be used for purposes of researching consumer behavior.

ECOLOGICAL CONSCIOUSNESS

As concern for the environment becomes increasingly universal, a positive shift in public attitudes toward firms and products that protect the environment seems to be taking place. A recent Roper Starch Worldwide study, for example, segmented the green consumer market into five shades of green. They range from a 15 percent core of educated, upscale individuals who are willing to pay a premium or forego certain conveniences to ensure a cleaner environment to 37 percent of the public, who are nonenvironmentalist. These green consumers, according to J. Ottman Consulting, can further be classified by the type of environmental issue that concerns them. Three distinct groups can be

As concern for the environment becomes increasingly universal, there has been a positive shift in public attitude toward products that protect the environment.

observed. The first is *Planet Passionists*, whose aim is to protect wildlife and keep the environment clean for recreational purposes; a *Health Fanatics* group, which focuses on the health consequences of environmental problems arising from such things as radiation, toxic waste, pesticides, and exposure to the sun; and a third group of *Animal Lovers* whose goal is to protect animal rights and prevent cruelty against them.[37]

It is clear that environmentalism has become a major force worldwide in the twenty-first century. In the United States, for example, recent Gallup polling data show that the number of Americans who say they worry about the environment "a great deal" or "a fair amount" increased from 62 to 77 percent between 2004 and 2006. The main concern is related to the issue of what to do about conserving our planet's precious remaining resources, protecting Earth's fragile ecosystems, and providing a sustained quality of life for humans in the coming decades. Terms that have become a standard part of day-to-day conversations among Americans are *clean energy, renewable energy, greenhouse gasses, global warming, climate protection, sustainability, energy efficiency, ecosystem, hybrid technology,* and *green products*.

Today, many environmental actions are being mandated by federal, state, and local governments. For example, in 2007, President Bush in his State of the Union address called for a nearly fivefold increase in the nation's alternative fuel consumption by the year 2017. In addition, the refocusing of environmental concern from issues such as drinking water, which were local and concrete, to climate change, which is global and abstract, brought about a post-Katrina movement under the banner of "sustainability."[38] Architects vie to create the most sustainable and energy-efficient commercial and residential structures; energy companies race to produce alternative fuels and search for sources of renewable energy; and automobile companies strive to release the most efficient hybrid vehicles. The result for our economy is product innovation that addresses the need for sustainable solutions to contemporary ecological issues.

In the United States, a shift in consumer behavior toward supporting green marketing has become evident. **Green marketing** refers to the practice by manufacturers of wrapping their products in the glow of environmental good deeds. Some manufacturers push the environmental soundness of their products. Others extol their packaging, whereas still others simply create a link between their brands and some environmental cause.

green marketing
advocating the environmental soundness of products and packaging

Recent evidence of consumers' support for green marketing can be observed among both the affluent and the budget-conscious. An example of one affluent new customer category is the so-called LOHS, which stands for Lifestyles of Health and Sustainability. Its market, for everything from organic cosmetics to eco-resort vacations, is estimated to surpass $200 billion. Green products have also made broad inroads among the budget-conscious masses. Wal-Mart has been a leader among large retailers in this new trend. Its actions, such as producing garments from organic cotton or using polymer derived from corn instead of oil in wrapping products, have resulted in increased sales as well as an enhanced corporate image. For example, at Sam's Club outlets, consumers snapped up 190,000 organic-cotton yoga outfits in ten weeks.[39]

Consumers and producers alike must fully understand what it means to *go green*. For example, consumers need to be able to distinguish between honest and deceptive environmental claims concerning products and packaging materials. Consequently, it is imperative that producers differentiate between product and container when claiming environmental benefits in advertising.

The FTC has recently published *Guidelines for the Use of Environmental Marketing Claims*, a document using real-world examples to interpret the laws that pertain to labeling and packaging. All labeling, advertising, and promotional claims, explicit or implicit, and whether advanced via words, symbols, emblems, logos, depictions, or brand names, are regulated. This includes any claims of environmental attributes in connection with the sale or marketing of a product or package, whether it is sold for personal, commercial, institutional, or industrial use.[40]

From a consumer behavior perspective, increasing environmental awareness has resulted in a surge of environmentally friendly products, a greater acceptance of recycled products and containers, and a wave of legislation addressing environmental issues. In addition, ecological issues are increasingly becoming integrated into the educational curriculum and political systems.

RISE OF THE GLOBAL VILLAGE

Business activities are no longer confined to the domestic market. U.S. and foreign businesses compete in an increasingly interdependent global economic environment. A growing number of U.S. firms export, import, or manufacture products abroad. Similarly, many foreign-based companies now operate in the United States. Whether or not any given business organization is directly involved in exports and imports, it cannot avoid being affected by competition from abroad and by major global events such as the collapse of communism in Russia, the emergence of the European Union (EU), the Gulf Wars, the September 11th attacks on the United States, the Afghan and Iraq wars, or the crisis in Iran. In this sense, borders between countries are disintegrating, creating what has become known as the **global village**.

Among the trends leading toward a globalized economy is the rise of economies such as China and India, and the acceptance of the free-market system in Eastern Europe and many developing countries in Asia and Latin America. For example, in Eastern Europe and the Baltic States, once satellite nations of the former USSR, the shift from a restrictive Marxist system to a relatively free marketplace has created bountiful opportunities for marketers. Similar open-market systems are evolving at an amazing pace in once-poor and closed societies, such as China and India. The Chinese economy, for instance, has grown at an average of 9.6 percent a year since it began to embrace a market economy in 1978. The economy of China is expected to overtake that of the United States by the year 2030. Similarly, the Indian economy has grown at an

global village
the increasingly interdependent global economic environment

GLOBAL OPPORTUNITY

India's New Challenge to the Automotive Industry

In 2007, Mr. Ratan Tata, Tata Motors' CEO, announced to shareholders that the company planned to launch a new ultra-inexpensive vehicle into the Indian market in early 2008. The planned vehicle is temporarily called the "One-Lackh Car" in reference to its price of a lackh, or 100,000 rupes, which at current exchange rates equals about $2,500. Presently, the car has been given the name Nana.

The car, which is a four-door sedan with a rear 33 horsepower engine, will be able to seat four to five passengers. Tata's initial production capacity is planned to be 100,000 units per year. However, the company is about three years from completing a factory capable of producing 250,000 cars per annum. With this affordable vehicle, the company expects to trigger a revolution in car ownership, not only in India but also throughout the developing world.

With a very low rate of car ownership among Indians and the escalating per-capita income there, Tata is betting on overwhelming success for its new vehicle. In fact, only 8 Indians out of every thousand currently own a car, compared with about 750 per thousand in the United States.

As India's booming economy pulls millions of people into the middle class, those consumers who previously purchased motorbikes and scooters would be able to trade up to a low-priced vehicle. If Tata lures away a mere 10 percent of the 6.5 million Indians who presently buy motorbikes every year, the company would not only attain its highest sales expectations, but would also have expanded India's car market by more than half.

Building such an ultra-cheap car in that part of the world is possible due to low manufacturing costs that prevail in almost all developing countries. Tata's officials estimate that their engineering costs alone are about one-half of what they would be in Europe or in the United States. Moreover, labor cost is a fraction of that paid by European or U.S. carmakers. Tata is also able to cut costs by buying auto parts through Internet auctions.

Regarding the car's design, Tata tapped the skills of Italy's Fiat, with which it has a joint venture in India. The company also used the expertise of British engine designers from the West Midlands region in Britain, some of whom had lost their jobs due to closures of some automakers in Britain over the past few years.

Tata Motors is not only counting on high sales volume in India, but plans to export its car to Southeast Asia and Africa, as well as other developing nations. Tata Group believes the company can eventually sell over 1,000,000 vehicles per year worldwide. Affordability and fuel efficiency are the two major driving forces underlying the forecasted overwhelming demand.

Other competing carmakers are not standing still against this new threat. Fiat, General Motors, Renault-Nissan, Honda, Hyundai, Suzuki, Toyota, and Volkswagen are all busily working on producing low-cost vehicles. Renault-Nissan has recently announced that the company was looking at building a similarly inexpensive car in India. However, it is doubtful that any of these competing companies would be able to match the cheap price of the "One-Lackh Car."[41]

The success of Tata Motors in the production of an inexpensive vehicle has many implications, not only for the Indian economy, but also for the auto industry in the United States and in the world as a whole. In your view, what is the likelihood of success of this new car in India? What is its likelihood of success in other developing countries, such as those in Southeast Asia and Africa? If this car were to be introduced in the United States, would it likely meet with success? Explain. What would be the effect (if any) of this new car's introduction on other auto manufacturers in developed nations? Learn more about Tata Motors by visiting www.msnbc.msn.com/id/20394364/; www.seekingalpha.com/article/12684-tata-motors-corporate-background-for-the-attractive-indian-automaker; and www.treehugger.com/files/2007/07/3000_dollar_car.php

average annual rate of over 8 percent since it began its economic reform in 1991. India has been labeled as the "back office to the world." Of the world's 500 largest companies, 400 of them outsource to India.[42] Most of these countries are privatizing their previously state-owned enterprises, establishing market-driven pricing systems, and relaxing their import controls. It is expected that in the early twenty-first century, many of these nations will rank among the most important emerging markets for U.S. businesses.

Another trend reflecting the globalization of markets is the rapid growth of regional free trade areas, such as the North American Free Trade Area (NAFTA), the Asian Free Trade Area (AFTA), and the European Union (EU). NAFTA partners, for example, had agreed in 1991 to eliminate all tariffs between the United States, Canada, and Mexico in staggered intervals over a 15-year period—i.e., 2006. Nontariff barriers along with a variety of foreign investment restrictions were also targeted for elimination.

From a consumer behavior point of view, one distinguishing trait of today's global scene is the commonality of needs among consumers in different countries. Whether in Tokyo, Moscow, Berlin, London, Hong Kong, or Bangkok, consumers—particularly those in the middle class—have begun to seek the new products and services they have learned about in the media. Walking through the streets of any of these cities, we are likely to observe people wearing Levi's jeans or Nike shoes and using iPods and iPhones.

Ramifications of Current Trends for Consumers and Marketers

Trends such as those cited in this chapter constitute significant forces that have influenced where people live, how they live, what they value, how they earn their living, the roles they play, how they relax, how they communicate, where and how they shop, and the products they use. Today's consumers have found new ways to become more informed, are savvier, and have become more powerful in the process. Moreover, they have developed a sense of entitlement. That is to say whether the issue involves health, recreation, ethical matters, or environmental concerns, consumers have high expectations from the businesses that serve them. Adept marketers realize that they must adjust to the opportunities and challenges presented by these and other trends in the marketplace. It remains to be seen which companies will successfully adapt to these trends, precisely how firms will respond, and how consumers and government bodies will react to the actions of business. A thorough understanding of the market environment, consumers in it, and prevailing competitive forces, as well as current product and service offerings is vital for marketing management, which must draw up a mission statement and set workable strategies for the firm. Marketing research provides the necessary insights. Through research, marketers identify the best prospects for their product or service, the needs and preferences of these prospects, and how best to approach them. Hence, the topic of consumer research merits discussion at this point and is covered in chapter 2.

A Cross-Functional Point of View

These Cross-Functional Point of View segments are intended to help students visualize the connection between consumer behavior and other disciplines—particularly business fields. This type of material can also be used to check students' understanding and reactions to issues raised in these exercises as they relate to the field of consumer behavior.

Consumer behavior is a broad topic that borrows from other business and nonbusiness disciplines and at the same time has ramifications for them. Some of the implications of consumer behavior on other fields include the following:

- **Production/Inventory:** One of the major challenges that marketers of consumer goods face is the speculative nature of consumer demand. Consumer goods must be produced in advance of actual demand in anticipation of purchase action. This phenomenon is known as "speculative production." For example, manufacturers of women's fashions have to plan garments' materials, designs, styles, and colors eight months ahead of the season, produce them four months in advance, and distribute them two to three months before the season begins. This aspect of marketing consumer goods adds an element of risk to suppliers of such items because it requires them to predict future consumer purchase preferences and trends precisely. However, anticipating consumer tastes and purchase actions is not easy or foolproof. Manufacturers and distributors alike often find themselves stuck with huge inventories of unsalable products that nobody wants.

- **Management/Strategy:** When it comes to executing a management strategy such as customization, Andersen Windows seems to have found the right formula. Originally, the company mass-produced its windows. As recently as 1980, the company manufactured a range of standard windows in large batches. When the company found out that the market was asking for more unique windows, it rolled out a broad variety that exceeded 86,000 styles. When contractors visited a retailer, however, a mind-boggling array of choices confused them and made it difficult to figure out what they wanted. The net effect of this complexity threatened the mere existence of the company. In the early 1990s, the company responded by developing a new interactive, computerized version of its catalog whereby a salesperson can help customers add, change, and strip away features until they have designed a window that pleases them. Now a customer can get anything from a 20-foot-high gothic window to a 20-inch screen.

- **Promotion/Ethics:** In the past, patients who thought they might have a medical problem went to their doctor, discussed their symptoms, and took the medicine the doctor prescribed. Today, many patients walk into doctors' offices asking for specific drugs they heard about on TV or read about in a magazine. Many pharmaceutical companies today are bypassing physicians and going directly to consumers with their prescription drug ads. In 2007, the *New England Journal of Medicine* reported that expenditures by pharmaceutical companies on direct-to-consumer prescription drug ads in 2005 reached $29.9 billion. As direct-to-consumer ads continue to claim a greater share of pharmaceutical companies' marketing budgets, some questions arise concerning the morality of this type of promotion as well as how physicians will react to such manipulative efforts.

These issues, and a host of others like them, serve to show that consumer behavior transcends the field of marketing to other business disciplines.

Summary

For purposes of this text, *consumer behavior* refers to the field of study that addresses how people buy and why they act as they do. More specifically, the study of consumer behavior investigates how individuals plan, purchase, use, and dispose of goods and services that satisfy personal or household needs. Some of the influences that shape consumer choices and tendencies entail internal processes, such as thinking, feeling, and wanting. Other influences involve environmental factors, such as social, economic, situational, and promotional considerations. Somehow, all these forces combine and dynamically interact to produce shopping behavior, the objective of which is to satisfy personal needs and wants. The analysis of consumer behavior entails surveying various theories and research studies that offer insight about purchasing tendencies. Marketers need to understand what consumers need and want, how they spend their resources, and how they decide where to shop, when to buy, and what to purchase. In short, knowledge of consumer behavior is an essential prerequisite for marketing success. The ultimate goal of this field of endeavor is to help marketers *predict* consumer behavior.

As we enter the twenty-first century, a number of trends will undoubtedly affect consumer behavior and, consequently, how marketers conduct business. This chapter briefly examines a number of these trends. The specific trends covered include (1) growth of the information superhighway; (2) focus on health, fitness, and beauty; (3) shifting roles of men and women; (4) telecommuting and the office of the future; (5) personalized economy; (6) concern about personal safety; (7) diversity in the workplace and marketplace; (8) focus on ethics; (9) ecological consciousness; (10) rise of the global village.

In our society, marketers—as agents of change—are largely responsible for bringing about the high standard of living to which we have grown accustomed. Although many of these marketing efforts help us to experience a more enjoyable lifestyle, we are at the same time victims of some such efforts.

Review Questions

1. Comment on the statement "consumer behavior is a field of study that borrows heavily from other disciplines," and explain why such borrowing is necessary to fully understand consumption-related behaviors.
2. An obvious trend in contemporary society is the shifting roles of men and women. What are some of the ramifications of this trend to decision-making and purchasing behavior in the household?
3. Personal safety and security have become major concerns for many people. These concerns have affected two consumer-related behaviors—products that consumers buy to enhance their sense of safety *and* changes in the ways people shop for products and services. Detail what is meant by each of these changes in consumer behavior.
4. There appears to be a discrepancy between some people's claims about their

concern for the environment and the products they actually purchase—many of which lack environmental sensitivity. How do you account for the discrepancy between what people say and what they do? Do marketers share the blame for this phenomenon?

5. A recent trend in corporate America is the practice of accommodating the family life of its employees. Systems such as telecommuting, flextime, and job sharing are being offered to allow employees to work at home, have flexible hours, or care for children. What will this trend mean for marketers? What types of products or services will most likely be affected by this trend?

Discussion Questions

1. A commercial from Volvo, which aired a few years ago, depicted a Volvo Turbo Sportswagon accelerating faster than a BMW in a 0 to 60 mph performance test. Suspecting that the ad was based on questionable testing procedures, BMW accused Volvo of deceptive advertising. In fact, Volvo admitted to authorities that it had hired a freelance auto journalist to conduct the acclaimed test instead of employing an independent research laboratory. In your opinion, with whom does the responsibility for monitoring the integrity of such business practices rest? Should it be the corporations themselves, competitors in the industry, the government, or consumer groups?

2. Some companies are attempting to capitalize on the racial, ethnic, and cultural diversity that exists within contemporary society. Increasingly, marketers are coming to view minority groups as offering potentially lucrative markets for products and services. For example, Mary Kay and L'Oreal are among the companies that design cosmetics, beauty aids, and hair-care products that suit the skin tones and hair features of minority consumers. What other producers or service providers have found opportunities in targeting minority consumers? In your opinion, what other manufacturers or service providers are likely to find such opportunities?

3. Many companies today use telecommuting work styles to improve productivity, reduce operating expenses, and save employees' traveling time and cost. Georgia Power, for example, implemented a telecommuting project in 1992 with 14 employees working from home. The firm has now expanded the project, having realized savings of $100,000 in leased office space alone. In your opinion, what products or services are likely to experience increased demand as a consequence of this growing trend? What products and services are likely to experience a decline in demand as a result of this trend?

To use the Cross-Functional Debate, the class can be divided into teams. The first team takes one point of view concerning the issue presented; the second the opposing viewpoint. The teams then debate and bring up issues related to other disciplines addressed in the exercise. Others in the class serve as judges and can pose their own questions or comments to the debating teams.

In reference to the chapter's opening vignette, assume that a company manufactures a line of fashions for full-figured individuals and distributes them through its own king- and queen-size retail outlets. The types of costs incurred to manufacture and distribute these garments are more numerous and higher than for standard fashions. Having divided the class into two teams—a cost-accounting team and a marketing management team:

1. Assume the role of cost accountants. List the cost-related categories associated with this type of specialty operation, and defend the idea of following a cost-based pricing strategy.
2. Assume the role of marketing managers. Respond to the claims made by the first team, and advocate instead a psychological rather than a cost-based pricing strategy.

CASE

What's in Your Burger?

Recent media reports revealing that Americans get over one-third of their daily calories from restaurant foods have raised major health concerns among many consumers. This concern has resulted in a new drive to require food establishments to provide critical calorie information on their various menu items. Disclosing to consumers how these menu items would affect their waistline is seen by many as desirable and necessary information to help customers make healthy menu choices.

The practice of listing vital information including ingredients and calorie content of foods is mandated by the Food and Drug Administration (FDA) in the United States for all processed foods. All grocery items we purchase in the supermarket carry labels that provide such detailed information. Studies show that 75 percent of supermarket customers check label information, and half of those who do report that they have changed their brand choices based on that knowledge. However, surprisingly, when it comes to meals purchased by consumers in restaurants or fast-food establishments, this practice is overlooked.

This situation has caused many consumers to question this inconsistency in government food information mandates. A recent Keystone Center report revealed that national polls indicate 60 percent of restaurant patrons felt caloric content should be listed on menus. However, the Center, in the meantime, found that only one-half of the 300 large restaurant chains surveyed provided some nutritional information on meals served. Some major restaurants, such as Ruby Tuesday, Subway, McDonald's, and TGI Fridays, among a few others, have voluntarily begun to provide more caloric information about menu choices, but the majority of others have failed to follow suit.

The latter restaurants argue against such a move by citing costs associated with providing calorie information. Laboratory work required to calculate calorie content of one menu item can exceed $100; thus an entire menu can cost between $12,000 to $50,000. Other restaurant operators also question whether the public *truly* wants such information to be provided. Such knowledge, they argue, may enhance patrons' guilt feelings as they consume their choice of menu items.

The FDA and members of Congress have been considering measures that would require restaurants to provide such information. For example, Sen. Tom Harkin (D-Iowa) and Rep. Rosa DeLaura (D-Conn.) introduced bills in 2004 that would require fast-food chains to list calorie counts on menu boards, as well as on printed menus. However, such legislation was defeated in Congress, as it faced strong opposition from the National Restaurant Association. As a result, the FDA does not have the legal authority to mandate that restaurants take such action. The final responsibility for making the right menu choices, therefore, rests mostly with individual consumers. To help consumers dine healthfully, nutrition experts suggest a few strategies that include ordering an appetizer instead of an entree, sharing an entree with a friend, or asking for a take-out box at the beginning of the meal so as to avoid overeating. As always, the true secret in staying healthy, they claim, is moderation in our food consumption.

Questions

1. While food processors in the United States are required by law to list calories and vital nutritional information on food labels sold in grocery stores, restaurants in many states are not required to disclose the same. How do you explain such contradictions? Do you favor passing laws that would require restaurants to list calorie content on menu items? Why or why not?

2. Some restaurants do not provide calorie counts on their menus or menu boards, but provide that information online or in separate booklets placed on dining tables. For example, the chain Ruby Tuesday provides that information in a booklet called "Smart Eating Guide" placed on every table during meals. Others, like McDonald's, print the information on their paper placemats. Do you believe these are sincere efforts to provide such information? Do you consider these methods effective in helping consumers to choose wisely? Why do restaurants resort to these questionable methods of disclosure and avoid making such information more readily available?

3. Since consumers are left with the major responsibility for making the right food choices in restaurants, what would you suggest as strategies that consumers may follow or knowledge they may need in order to maintain a healthy lifestyle? Do you expect that everyone would be equally interested in getting this type of information or following food consumption guidelines? Why or why not?

Notes

1. "Obesity Rate in the United States Still Climbing," *Forbes* (August 27, 2007) p. 1.

2. "Land of the Fat," *Scanorama* (December 1994-January 1995), p. 69; Jerry Knight, "America Getting Thinner? Fat Chance," *Chicago Sun-Times* (September 4, 1994), p. 4; Bill Ingram, "Fed Up with False Hope," *Chicago Sun-Times* (September 4, 1994), p. 4.

3. Purdue Chicken, "Purdue Farms Is One of the Nation's Leading Poultry Companies," www.purdue.com/company/about/index.html, 2007.

4. Theodore Levitt, "Marketing Myopia" *Harvard Business Review* 53, no. 5 (September–October 1975), pp. 26–44 and 173–81.

5. Franklin S. Houston and Jule B. Gassenheimer, "Marketing and Exchange," *Journal of Marketing* (October 1987), pp. 3–18.

6. E. Jerome McCarthy and William D. Perreault Jr., *Basic Marketing*, 10th ed. (Homewood, IL: Irwin, 1990), p. 8; Malcolm P. McNair, "Marketing and the Social Challenge of Our Times," in Keith Cox and Ben M. Enis (eds.), *A New Measure of Responsibility for Marketing* (Chicago: American Marketing Associations, 1968).

7. James Burke, "Inventors Inventions," *Time* (December 4, 2000), pp. 65–74.

8. George Spitzer, "The Electronic Consumer," *World Monitor* 4 (April 1991), p. 64.

9. K. Andrew Burger, "Greasing the Wheels of M-Commerce, Parts 1 and 2," *E-Commerce Times* (June 12, 2007).

10. William O'Neal, "Go Gadgets Go," *Spirit* (July 2007) p. 111–116.

11. "The U.S. Weight Loss and Diet Control Market," Market Data Enterprises, www.marketresearch.com/product/displayasp?productid=1075148&xs=r; Miranda Hitti, "Breast Implantation Tops List for Women, Nose Jobs for Men," *Web MD Medical News* (March 23, 2007).

12. U.S. Census Bureau, Current Population Survey, 2004.

13. Marti Barletta, *Prime Time Women,* www.trendsight.com/index.php?option=tom_content&task=view&id=95&Itemid=, 2007.

14. "Market Research and the Women's Automobile and Travel Markets," *Road & Travel,* www.roadandtravel.com/company/marketing/marketresearch.htm, 2007.

15. Pamala Paul, "Flexing Our Options," *American Demographics* (July 2001), pp. 10–12.

16. Merlisa L. Corbett, "Telecommuting: The New Workplace Trend," *Black Enterprise* (June 1996), pp. 256–60.

17. Carol Leonetti Dannhauser, "Who's in the Home Office," *American Demographics* (June 1999), pp. 50–56.

18. "Telecommuting Trends Surface in New Report," *Telecommunications* (July 1992), pp. 9, 12.

19. Thomas W. Gainey, "Flextime and Telecommuting: Examining Individual Perceptions," *Southern Business Review* (Fall 2006).

20. For an opposing point of view concerning this trend, see Arlie R. Hochschild, "There's No Place Like Work," *New York Times Magazine* (April 20, 1997), pp. 50–55.

21. Dannhauser, "Who's in the Home Office."

22. Thomas W. Gainey, "Flextime and Telecommuting: Examining Individual Perceptions," *Southern Business Review* (Fall 2006).

23. Cheryl Russell, "The Master Trend," *American Demographics* (October 1993), pp. 28–37, Lisa T. Cullen, "Have It Your Way," *Time* (December 23, 2002), pp. 42–43; and Rebecca Gardyn, "Swap Meet," *American Demographics* (July 2001), pp. 51–55.

24. Amanda Gore, "StyleShake Brings Bespoke Fashion Online," *Personal Edition* (October 23, 2007), www.psfk.com/category/trends/all_about_me/customization.

25. Cover story, "The Vanishing Mass Market," *Business Week* (July 12, 2004); Jack Aaronson, "Mass Customization with a Personalized Experience," *ClickZ* (July 22, 2004).

26. Verne Kopytoff, "'Your Name Here' Goes Global," *Chronicle* (July 19, 2005), www.sfgate.com/cgi_bin/article.cgi?file=/c/a/2005/07/19.

27. U.S. Dept. of Justice, FBI Crime Justice Information Services Division, 2006.

28. Ibid.

29. Federal Bureau of Investigation, *2007 Financial Crime Report*, www.fbi.gov/publications/financial/fcs_report2007/financial_crime_2007.htm, 2007.

30. Steve Macek, "Gated Communities," *St. James Encyclopedia of Pop Culture*, www.findarticles.com/p/articles/mi_G1epc/is_tov/ai_2419100492.

31. Alison S. Wellner, "The Next 25 Years," *Am. Demo.*, (April 2003), pp. 24–27.

32. Cora Daniels, et. al., "50 Best Companies for Minorities in an Ideal World," *Fortune* (June 28, 2004).

33. Raymond Kotcher, "Diversity in Today's Workplace and Marketplace," *Public Relations Quarterly* 40 (Spring 1995), pp. 6–9.

34. Donald P. Robin, "Value Issues in Marketing," in Charles W. Lamb Jr. and Patrick M. Dunne (eds.), *Theoretical Developments in Marketing*, (Chicago: American Marketing Association Proceedings, 1980), p. 142.

35. Nancy Kubasek et al., "The Seductive Danger of Craft Ethics for Business Organizations," *Review of Business* 17, no. 2 (Winter 1996), pp. 23–29.

36. Tim Triplett, "Scanning Errors Likely to Take Toll on Customer Satisfaction," Marketing News 28, no. 16 (August 1, 1994), pp. 1, 6; "Store Scanners Err on Buyer's Side," *Chicago Sun-Times* (October 23, 1996), p. 61; Stephen Benjamin, "Six Stores Pay Fines for Price-Scanning Errors," *North Carolina Dept. of Agriculture and Consumer Services* (September 13, 2007).

37. "Green Marketing and Eco-Innovation," *J. Ottman Consulting Inc.* 10, no. 3 (2004), pp. 2–3; and Rebecca Gardyn, "Being Green," *Am. Dem.*, (September 2002), pp. 10–11.

38. Jerry Adler, "Going Green," *Newsweek* (July 17, 2006), pp. 43–52.

39. Ibid.

40. J. Stephen Shi and Jane M. Kane, "Green Issues," *Business Horizons* (January–February 1996), pp. 65–70.

41. Simon Robinson, "Utopian Vision," *Time* (October 8, 2007), pp. 1–5; Z. O. Greenburg, "India Automaker Banks on World's Cheapest Car," *Forbes* (August 23, 2007); www.msnbc.msn.com/id/20394364/; www.seekingalpha.com/article/12684-tata-motors-corporate-background-for-the-attractive-indian-automaker; and www.treehugger.com/files/2007/07/3000_dollar_car.php.

42. Robyn Meredith, *The Elephant and the Dragon* (Norton, 2007).

Consumer Research

CHAPTER 2

LEARNING OBJECTIVES

- To become familiar with the discipline of consumer research.
- To understand the need for gathering information about consumers.
- To probe sources of consumer information as well as their types and features.
- To gain insight into the advantages and limitations of observation versus self-report data collection methods.
- To recognize the ethical ramifications inherent in conducting consumer research.
- To explore the role of motivation research.
- To comprehend the nature of database marketing and data mining.

KEY TERMS

consumer research
secondary data
primary data
focus groups
experiments
test markets
consumer panels
database marketing
data mining
motivation research
projective techniques

Thematic Apperception Test (TAT)
cartoon
verbal projective
free word associations
controlled word associations
chain word associations
sentence completions
picture-sorting techniques
shopping list technique
Zaltman Metaphor Elicitation Technique (ZMET)

In 2007, Caterpillar, which is known for its earth-moving equipment, undertook a database marketing project to enhance its truck-engine market share. Caterpillar builds and sells to truck manufacturers $2 billion worth of large-truck engines per year. These manufacturers, who are basically assemblers, purchase their truck engines from various truck-engine makers such as Caterpillar.

The objective that Caterpillar had hoped to accomplish with this project was to determine its potential universe for truck-engine sales. Such information can help the company properly direct sales efforts, allocate promotional outlays, and strategically plan its future production operations.

From the company's internal databases, along with external motor-carrier and trade data, Caterpillar was able to construct a file of 110,000 customers, consisting of 8,000 mid-range fleets and 34,000 heavy-duty fleets. By injecting into this information other data Caterpillar assembled on NAICS code, truck-owner locations, engine models, number of trucks, and trucking category, the company was able to predict which non-customers were most likely to buy. As a result, customers and prospects were grouped into 83 Heavy-Duty Groups and 34 Mid-Range Groups; each group was then assigned a score representing its importance.

This analysis allowed Caterpillar to determine which were the high-value customers and prospects. It thus became possible to determine which groups of customers or prospects should be targeted by the sales force. It also allowed the company to develop sets of different promotional messages specifically designed to appeal to the needs of each market segment.[1]

As marketers become better at individualizing their relationships with customers, they may be re-creating the personal touch of yesteryear when shopkeepers knew the clients well and paid utmost attention to their specific needs.

> *Many companies today have come to realize that mass-marketing is no longer a viable strategy. As a consequence, firms increasingly develop a profile of consumers who constitute the best prospects for specific goods and services. Learn more about database marketing by visiting* www.dbmarketing.com/articles/Art164.htm. *Also visit a company involved in data mining at* www.kdnuggets.com/companies/products.html. *Are the benefits of having this information worth the cost and effort required to obtain it? Why or why not? How do you feel about the privacy issues associated with database marketing?*

Database marketing allows marketers to accomplish precision targeting—a necessity for success in today's highly segmented marketplace. In an increasingly competitive environment, consumer research—when properly conceived, conducted, and interpreted—is a very valuable input for designing, executing, and overseeing a firm's marketing plan.

This chapter touches on a number of issues that attempt to clarify who the consumer is, what needs and wants he or she may have, and why consumers purchase products and services. Today's marketing managers cannot function without information. Managerial decisions on issues ranging from product design to advertising appeals depend on the availability and quality of information about the single most important player in the marketplace—the consumer.

What Is Consumer Research?

Consumer research consists of the diverse and systematic methods that marketers employ to investigate the internal, environmental, and social factors that affect consumer decisions and exchange processes. Important areas of consumer research include perception, learning, memory, attitudes, motivations, lifestyles, and influence patterns as well as frequency of product use, where products are purchased, and consumers' media habits.

consumer research systematic methods used by marketers to study consumer decisions and exchange processes

The goal of consumer research is to understand the processes of selecting, purchasing, using, and disposing of goods and services. Studies about the ways consumers satisfy their needs and wants and the role models on which they pattern their behavior can enrich marketers' understanding of how shoppers arrive at purchase choices and why they make the selections they do. With these insights, marketers find themselves in a better position to predict consumers' reactions to product attributes and brand images, selling prices and price incentives, methods of distribution, and promotional efforts.

The list of potential applications for consumer research is endless. One objective is to segment the market for products and services and to profile those consumers who constitute the target market. A second objective is to identify consumers' beliefs, attitudes, intentions, and behavior with respect to a brand. A third goal of consumer research is to ascertain what adds perceived value to goods as well as to discern what builds brand loyalty among consumers. In brief, through consumer research, marketers attempt to design products with desirable features, position them properly in the marketplace, price them sensibly, distribute them effectively, and promote them to those most likely to buy. The ad in Figure 2.1 from Hoovers highlights the advanced research services the firm provides to its clients, which include conducting competitive analyses, building targeted customer lists, as well as performing risk assessments.

Information about the Consumer

In today's competitive environment, some of the most important questions that marketers must answer are who are their company's customers; what are their characteristics; how geographically dispersed are they; and why, where, and when they purchase the firm's products. Such knowledge is essential before any marketing activities can be undertaken. In this section, we cover several types of consumer information that can be beneficial to marketers.

THE PURCHASE SITUATION

Among the things marketers need to understand about consumers is where they purchase a product, how often they buy it, how they pay for it, and the way they choose between alternative brands.

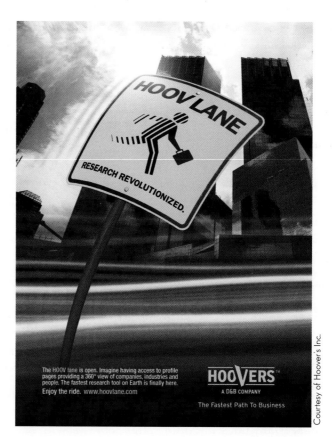

Figure 2.1

This Hoovers ad promotes the company's advanced research services, capable of providing savvy research profiles on companies, industries, and people that Hoovers offers to enterprises, small-business subscribers and executive accounts.

Regarding the issue of store choice, conventional wisdom has it that perception of a product's image is closely related to that of the store from which it is purchased. Designer brands of clothing and high-quality perfumes are usually sold in prestigious retail outlets for this reason. Similarly, the issue of how often consumers purchase a product has ramifications for manufacturers' production scheduling, inventory systems, and distribution policies. Likewise, the way consumers pay for a product is important in determining whether financing arrangements and credit policies are needed to facilitate purchase. Monitoring customers' brand choices enables a marketer to calculate the firm's market share and identify possible brand strengths that can be used to enhance the brand's market position.

BUYERS

Information about buyers' characteristics and background is also valuable. As marketers, we need to learn about buyers' *demographic characteristics*—age, income, gender, marital status, family size, and education—all of which can help us determine what to market, to whom, where, and at what price.

Another important type of useful information is the *psychographic profile* of consumers, which relates to their activities, interests, and opinions and reflects their lifestyle in general. For example, knowing consumers' media habits helps marketers decide where to reach them through advertising.

PRODUCT USE

Knowing how buyers use a product is also beneficial to a company and provides a basis for making decisions such as how to improve product design and which appeals should be stressed in advertising. For example, when Campbell Soup Company learned that most often consumers use its mushroom soup as an ingredient in casseroles, the firm switched its promotional strategy for this product from ads that suggested soup for lunch to publishing casserole recipes.

CUSTOMER LOYALTY

Brand loyalty, or the extent to which a consumer purchases the same brand instead of other brands in the same product category, is an important tendency to monitor. This importance stems from the impact of brand loyalty on the firm's promotional strategies. In cases of companies that have high brand loyalty, special deals or promotions by other competing brands will not succeed in luring away a brand's present customers. Conversely, brands with low levels of consumer loyalty can be vulnerable as promotions from competing firms can easily tempt these individuals.

MARKET SEGMENTS

No single product can appeal equally well to every consumer in the marketplace. Marketers recognize the heterogeneity of markets and, for this reason, divide the total market for a product or service into smaller, more homogenous segments. Each segment consists of a subgroup of buyers based on certain characteristics or behaviors that are relevant to the product or service offered. Marketers then design their product, pricing, distribution, and promotional strategies to cater to the needs and wants of each segment they target. This practice, known as *market segmentation*, cannot be accomplished without information on the diversity of the marketplace and on the various subgroups it encompasses.

CUSTOMER SATISFACTION

Intense competition in today's marketplace has prompted many companies to adopt innovative practices such as total quality management (TQM) and customer satisfaction assessment techniques to gain a competitive edge. TQM involves adjusting the firm's products to ensure customer satisfaction. Both Rolls-Royce and General Motors try to establish what quality level their target market expects and then attempt to market cars that continually surpass expectations. Customer satisfaction surveys attempt to measure how satisfied or dissatisfied customers are with a company's product, service, or image. The firm then uses the satisfaction data to improve, adapt, or create a new product or service or adjust an existing one.

The six categories of informational needs cited earlier exemplify the various types of data that marketers need in order to make sound business decisions. Other types of helpful information relate to consumers' attitudes, opinions, awareness, knowledge, intentions, and motivations.

Needless to say, consumer researchers have to tap a variety of sources to collect such information. In the next sections, we briefly cover secondary and primary sources of information and demonstrate how these sources can help marketers in their pursuit of effective means to promote their goods and services.

Sources of Information

SECONDARY DATA

secondary data
information or statistics not gathered for the immediate study at hand

Secondary data are information or statistics not gathered for the immediate study at hand, but gathered previously by someone else for some other purpose. For example, company records, books, government documents, periodicals, and computerized databases are some forms of secondary data. The most significant advantages of secondary data are the time and expense they save researchers. A researcher investigating a consumption pattern such as the extent of credit card use should focus first on secondary data before embarking on conducting a consumer survey. The sought information may be available from commercial sources, saving the researcher considerable effort. Not only are secondary data useful as a means of conducting a preliminary assessment of the issue under study, but also they are sometimes the only way to get data where the company lacks the resources necessary to conduct a field survey.

Secondary data can be obtained from three types of sources: libraries, nonlibrary sources, and the Internet. The first source—which includes books, periodicals, government documents, and computerized databases—can be accessed in different ways. Books are located through the library's electronic card catalog. Periodicals are accessed through various online indices and abstracting services. Government documents are accessed through specialized indices. Computerized databases and other sources of information such as annual reports can be found in business libraries and by browsing the Internet.[2]

Nonlibrary sources, such as company files, trade associations, government sources, media, and local establishments like chambers of commerce and better business bureaus, can also provide a wealth of information on a multitude of topics.

Today, the Internet has become a valuable tool for acquiring secondary data. It provides instant access to information and statistics about industries and companies. In addition, it connects researchers to newsgroups, where they can post queries and receive answers.

Despite the advantages of secondary data, two main limitations—fit and accuracy—face the researcher who attempts to use this type of data. Concerning fit, because the data were originally collected for purposes other than the project at hand, rarely do the data precisely suit the specific problem the researcher has defined. The difficulty may lie in the currency of the secondary data or in the units of measurement the researcher employed to report the data. Accuracy, on the other hand, depends on the expertise of the supplying organization in collecting the data or its motives for doing so. Some research, for example, is conducted to support a debatable view or to carry on some sort of propaganda campaign for an entity or cause. In addition to these two limitations, users of secondary data should also be concerned with the completeness and timeliness of the secondary sources they use.

PRIMARY DATA

Primary data are originated by the researcher for the purpose of the investigation at hand. For example, if a hospital were to contact a sample of recent patients and ask their opinion about the quality of care they received, this would entail collecting primary data. Unlike secondary data, where the needed information may require a few hours to gather, data for a survey may take months to acquire and cost tens of thousands of dollars to obtain. This process may require the researcher to design a data-collection instrument, devise a sampling plan, hire and train a field staff to gather the data, and process and analyze the data.

There are two main methods by which primary data can be collected. The first is observation of events or occurrences. Information gathered through this procedure is called *observational data*. The second method involves asking people questions. Information acquired through this method is called *self-report data*. This section covers six methods of gathering primary data: observation of consumers, consumer surveys, focus groups, experiments, test markets, and consumer panels.

Observation of Consumers

Data can be gathered by observing people, objects, or events. Observation can be made by human observers, where one or more individuals are trained to observe a phenomenon and record what they see. For example, Mattel Toy Company often invites children to play in a room containing various toys, and observers record which toys children play with most. Similarly, observers sometimes pose as shoppers and visit stores, car dealerships, or restaurants and record data about the service they receive. Observation also can be made by mechanical methods. For example, Kmart has installed a radarlike system that tracks customer traffic in its stores to identify crowded departments. Customer service can then be improved by directing more sales help to these departments as well as opening more checkout lanes.[3] Similarly, A.C. Nielsen Company connects "People Meters" to the television sets in participating households. The people meter's function is to provide information on what TV shows are being watched, the number of households viewing, and which family members are watching.

Observations can be made in a number of ways. They can be disguised or undisguised. In the first case, subjects do not know they are being observed. For example, Motel 6 uses its own representatives, who pose as soap sales-people

Information about food brand purchases can be obtained in a natural setting with a supermarket's "preferred-customer card."

staying in the motel, to ask guests what they think of the facilities.[4] In undisguised observation, the subjects know they are being watched. In the case of A.C. Nielsen's TV show ratings, for example, participants are aware that their viewing habits are being monitored. As a result, they may behave differently—a tendency that may produce less-accurate measurements of the phenomenon under study.

Observations can be obtained in either natural or contrived settings. Information about food-brand purchases, for example, can be obtained in a natural setting such as a supermarket that uses a system of "preferred-customer cards." When customer ID cards and the items shoppers purchase are scanned at the checkout counter, the products and brands purchased are linked to the buyer's household and electronically recorded.[5] In contrived settings, on the other hand, consumers may be brought into a controlled environment to test a specific variable. In advertising research, for example, people are brought to a lab and shown different ads projected at different speeds or lighting conditions. Researchers then monitor the respondents' physiological response to the ads by measuring such things as their eye pupil dilation or galvanic skin response (perspiration in the palm of the hand).

Observation is useful to learn about overt consumer actions; however, it does not permit researchers to obtain other relevant information about consumers such as their emotions, mental processes, and background data. This is where the need arises for consumer surveys.

Consumer Surveys

Whereas observation is often best suited for exploratory research, surveys are best suited for descriptive research. Surveys are particularly useful for consumer research because they permit gathering plentiful data by means of a questionnaire. A structured questionnaire with prespecified questions allows researchers to decide on the type of information to seek, how it should be gathered, and from whom. Use of questionnaires also means that respondents are asked the same question in the same way and in the same sequence, which facilitates tabulating and analyzing the data collected.

Through surveys, broad coverage of the population is possible. The relatively low cost of surveys allows researchers to acquire data from many respondents. Cooperation is also enhanced when researchers place minimal demands on respondents who participate in the survey.[6]

Surveys typically take one of five forms: personal surveys, intercept surveys, telephone surveys, mail surveys, and online surveys. In personal surveys, face-to-face interviews are conducted at respondents' homes or offices. This method allows control over who actually answers the questions and gives the interviewer a chance to explain questions or probe respondents' answers more deeply. However, because interviewers must travel to respondents' locations, this method is relatively costly.

Intercept surveys are also face-to-face interviews. However, they are conducted with people intercepted at some public location, such as a shopping mall. Intercept surveys are less costly than personal surveys because travel costs are virtually eliminated. Malls provide easy access to a general population that is appropriate for many types of consumer research.

Telephone surveys involve calling respondents and briefly interviewing them over the phone. This method is widely used in consumer research. It offers much wider population coverage than intercept interviews. Phone surveys can be conducted quickly and inexpensively.

In mail surveys, respondents complete and return self-administered questionnaires that have been sent to them. Compared to the other data-gathering methods (except maybe online surveys), mail surveys are the least expensive type because they require no interviewing staff. However, mail surveys carry the limitations of lacking control over who responds, time delays in getting replies back, and a low response rate.

Online surveys are conducted with visitors to an Internet site. Sometimes, these surveys are part of the registration process to gain access to the site. Online surveys use questionnaires similar to those employed for intercept surveys. They are usually brief and simple to respond to. A frequently encountered problem, however, is a low response rate, which reduces their usefulness, because respondents represent only a small share of the population.

Focus Groups

A **focus group** usually consists of 8 to 12 people drawn from the population relevant to the issue under investigation. Unlike surveys, focus groups do not use structured questionnaires. The moderator of a focus group starts only with an explanation of the topic to be covered and merely facilitates the respondents' flow of thought regarding the topic. Sessions usually last somewhere between 90 minutes to 2 hours.

focus groups
sessions where 8 to 12 people—led by a moderator—freely discuss a topic

The strength of the focus group method lies in its ability to acquire numerous and diverse views from respondents. It allows for spontaneity, and ideas may simply drop out of the blue during a focus group session. Furthermore, the group setting allows for idea generation and snowballing. A comment from one participant can trigger a chain of responses from the other members present.[8]

Focus groups are currently one of the most frequently used techniques in consumer research. They can be used to learn how consumers use a product or what a product means to them. Focus groups conducted by Nabisco, for example, revealed that many adults view Oreos as a cherished memory of childhood and perceive the cookie to be almost magical in its ability to make them feel good. This revelation led Nabisco to design its successful "unlocking the magic of Oreo" advertising campaign.

Similarly, focus groups can be used to find out consumer views about a product or brand as well as consumers' expectations of that product or brand. Ray-O-Vac found through a series of focus groups that consumers wanted brighter, more modern, and more dependable flashlights, and that they were willing to pay for the added durability. These insights led the company to develop its line of Workhorse flashlights, which regenerated a mature market.[9]

Grab Those Vodka Bottles Before They're Gone

People in different nations vary in their reaction to consumer research, particularly when they are approached by an outsider whom they do not know. International researchers must contend with a wide range of cultural diversity, which can be observed in the marked differences in language, religion, culture, values, and traditions.

Differences between countries can influence the type of research design that is deemed appropriate for the foreign market. For example, in vast countries like China and India, the distances between markets render a large-scale study difficult and costly. Methods of collecting data must also be adjusted to suit the infrastructure of the specific nation. In many developing countries, telephone ownership rates are low, requiring interviewers to travel long distances to contact respondents. Mail surveys in such countries may also be hindered by unreliable postal delivery. Customs and traditions also play an important role in the acquisition of the needed data. In Asian and Latin American countries, due to the traditions of courtesy and respect, respondents are likely to give high approval ratings for products or services being tested, even though their evaluations do not realistically reflect their true feelings. In Russia, responses to a survey can be colored by product shortages sometimes experienced by consumers in the marketplace. In one study, when a Russian respondent was asked to state her choice of which of several brands of vodka she would select, her answer was that she would buy all of them, because they will not be in the stores the next day.

Language and translation can also play a significant role in wording the research instrument. Accurate translation equivalence of expressions, slogans, and brand names is important, first, to ensure that the respondents understand the questions, and second to ascertain that the researcher understands the responses.[7]

Culture permeates every aspect of buying and product consumption, as well as people's reactions to selling techniques, promotions, and research. Learn more about a specific culture, such as Japan. Visit www.jinjapan.org/today/culture.html. Assume that you were asked to conduct a product feasibility study there. What might you try to avoid in your communication or research techniques applied there?

Recently, in order to offer clients a less expensive and quicker way to do consumer research, some consumer research firms have begun to conduct focus groups over the Internet.[10] Although capable of providing a speedy and low-cost means of acquiring data online, this technique is not without flaws. Critics of the approach contend that online chat sessions lack several critical components of genuine focus group research, such as authentic group dynamics and the inability to observe nonverbal or facial input of participants.[11]

Experiments

experiments
investigations that manipulate one or more casual variables to measure the effect on one or more dependent variables

Experiments are research investigations where researchers actively manipulate one or more experimental or causal variables, then measure the effect of this manipulation on one or more dependent variables.[12] For example, Smucker's created several jelly formulations by varying the levels of sweetness, consistency, and fruit-flavor intensity. Smucker's then recruited homemakers to serve the jelly to their families for a couple weeks. Reaction of the homemakers and members of their households were obtained on dimensions such as appearance, spreadability, and how well their kids liked the product. In this case, the researchers actively manipulated the experimental variables of sweetness, consistency, and fruit-flavor intensity of the jelly and then measured the effect of these manipulations on the dependent variables—homemakers' and kids' reactions to the jelly formulations.

Experiments are often used when researchers desire to control the effects of extraneous variables and, in so doing, to isolate the effect of manipulated variables. In this manner, researchers can verify whether or not these variables do in reality affect the dependent variable.

Variables such as appearance, sweetness, consistency, and flavor intensity were manipulated to research consumer preference of Smucker's jelly.

Two types of experiments are used in consumer research—the laboratory experiment and the field experiment. In a lab experiment, researchers observe respondents' reactions to manipulated product variable(s) in a laboratory-like setting. For example, a company wanted to know whether consumers would purchase shopping goods (such as gift items, clothing, or accessories) from a vending machine. Such machines, the firm thought, would be desirable in airports and bus or train stations. In a lab experiment, the company placed a variety of shopping goods in vending machines at a research facility, gave 30 subjects $100 each, and asked them to spend it on goods from the machines. The goal was to determine which items would pique interest and thus qualify for inclusion in the final list of product offerings. If the same research were to be conducted in the field, however, the researchers would have had to place the vending machines in airports and bus or train stations to produce consumer responses that are more authentic than those generated in the lab.

Test Markets

In an effort to predict the sales or profit consequences of a new or improved product, a company may actually market it in a small number of carefully selected medium-size cities so its actual market performance can be gauged. **Test markets** provide an acid test of the level of customer acceptance a product will achieve before the firm invests in a full-scale market introduction.

Test marketing is not restricted to predicting the sales potential of new or improved products. It provides an effective method of evaluating practically all aspects of a company's marketing program. Companies use it to test such things as the impact of change in retail price on a product's market share; the effect of different promotions (such as ad campaign themes or coupons) on sales; and the desirability or undesirability of a package design. For example, before Wendy's introduced its "Big Classic" hamburger, it reportedly spent $1 million testing the sandwich and its package among 5,200 people in 6 cities. The final product was a quarter-pound square beef patty in a sandwich that came in an almond-colored styrofoam box with a dome sculpted to resemble the bun's top.

test markets
evaluating a product or strategy in limited geographic areas

Although the test market is considered the final gauge of consumers' acceptance of a product, package, or ad copy, test marketing has some major drawbacks. Test markets are expensive—often costing hundreds of thousands of dollars. Moreover, they may delay a product's launch. Another problem with test markets is lack of control the testing organization has over competitive reactions, which can range from copying the new product to sabotaging the test. Competitors often jam tests of a competing brand by cutting prices of their own brands or by using heavy couponing to disrupt the test. For example, when Scope test-marketed a new flavored antiseptic mouthwash in Kansas City, Listerine responded with heavy local couponing and introduced a new low-priced product to distort the test market results for Scope.

To get the benefits of test marketing without the cost and other problems, companies today test products in "virtual markets, where shopper participants belonging to a select panel of consumers are chosen to participate in these tests." A "shopper" sitting behind a computer monitor travels through a "virtual store" and does his or her normal shopping. The shopper picks a package from the shelf by touching its image on the screen, examines it, then either purchases it by putting it into his or her "cart" or returns it to the shelf. This system can substitute for a real test market at a fraction of the cost.[13]

Consumer Panels

consumer panels
groups of research
participants who
provide purchase
and consumption
data over time

Consumer panels are groups of research participants who agree to provide information over time. This information may be obtained through observation, as in the case of Nielsen's TV audience panel, or may be provided by self-reports, such as when household panelists record their purchases in a diary or complete periodic questionnaires.

Because panels allow tracking a specific household's purchasing behavior over time, they are useful in studies dealing with brand switching and other changes in buying behavior due to promotions. For example, if Procter & Gamble distributed a 75-cents-off coupon for Crest toothpaste, the company can use grocery panel data to determine the percentage of people who used the coupon or switched from another brand because of it.

There are two types of panels: true panels and omnibus panels. True panels are used to provide repeated measurements of the same variables. For example, for its SCANTRACK service, the A.C. Nielsen Company maintains a panel of 40,000 households nationwide who are given handheld scanners with which they record every item they purchase. Similarly, National Purchase Diary (NPD) maintains a large consumer panel of families who record their purchases in a paper diary after every shopping trip.

The omnibus panel, on the other hand, is not used to provide a "moving picture" of the same variable. Rather, panel members may be asked to evaluate advertising copy at one time, whereas at another time they may be asked to provide their views about a new product. In such cases, separate subsamples selected from the larger panel may be chosen for each study. This choice is usually based on desired characteristics of the subsample members. For example, if the Parker Pen Company wanted to evaluate a new writing instrument, a subsample of individuals who expressed interest in writing instruments may be selected from the larger pool.

Current Issues in Consumer Research

Present-day technology has had an impact on consumer research. Improved methods brought about by recent technological breakthroughs have made it possible for researchers to acquire sophisticated data about consumers more quickly and easily. In this section, we cover three topics: using the Internet as a tool in consumer research, the proliferation of database marketing, and the up-and-coming data mining technique.

USING THE INTERNET AS A TOOL

One tool in consumer research is the Internet. It has at least four applications: tracking visitors to an Internet site that contains information or advertising, posting a questionnaire on the Internet to collect data, locating secondary data on a variety of topics, and posting questions to a newsgroup asking for advice.

Tracking Internet Visitors

In the realm of tracking visitors, companies can count the number of *hits* on various parts of a Web site (i.e., the number of times a visitor goes to a home page). Companies are also interested in the number of downloads for specific material. For example, when Volkswagen ran a promotional campaign for the new Beetle, it counted the number of hits on its Web page to determine the extent to which the campaign sparked interest in the car. In another use, hits can measure advertising effectiveness. A company like Motorola, for example, pays for Web *banner* ads only if viewers of these ads use the link to hit the advertiser's home page. Similarly, of special interest to companies is *page view*, the number of times a page is actually accessed by each visitor, as well as *stickness* of a Web site i.e., a site's ability to hold viewers measured in terms of time spent at a site per visit.

Many companies perform the services of tracking visitors to a Web site. In addition, various software types allow for tracking Web site visitors. Among the first type are companies such as VisitorTrack, VisiStat, and Boldchat, which provide realtime visitor tracking services and proactively engage online visitors. Software types, on the other hand, include Track4Win, SpectorPro, and WhosOn. In addition, keeping track of traffic going through your blogs and your RSS subscriber can be accomplished through services such as Google's FeedBurner and other sites such as AlexaStat, Technorati, PageRank, Digg, and Slashdot. This acquired information can then be used to target special messages of interest to a Web site's visitors. For example, an advertising service called *DoubleClick* can identify the type of site that users come from when they visit a new site and then choose advertising messages that match the visitor's likely interests.

Researchers use the Internet to deliver online questionnaires.

Online Surveys

Regarding online surveys, many companies such as Domino's Pizza and Qantas Airlines ask visitors to their Web sites to answer questions on a variety of topics, such as product performance, usage, and buyer demographics. These surveys provide an inexpensive and quick method of data collection.

Many companies handle the task of online surveys. Survey Lot.com is a hosting site that offers a number of participating online survey firms that pay participants to complete a questionnaire. These surveys usually focus on subjects such as customer satisfaction, market research, testing new products/services, and opinion surveys. Amounts paid to participants range from $25 to $125.

Despite the growth potential expected for online surveys in the near future, they are not without faults. Limitations relate to the representativeness of the responding sample that provides the data. Consumers using the Internet are not necessarily typical of the population at large. Surveys have shown that Internet users tend to be younger, better educated, and more technologically adept. As such, other consumer subgroups in the population might not be proportionally represented among respondents. Moreover, because questionnaires are sometimes posted at company Web sites, respondents who see and respond to them are limited to those who have some interest in the firm. It is also questionable whether respondents who are paid for taking the online survey truly reveal their genuine feelings. Based on these and other limitations, online surveys are often supplemented with other methods of data collection, such as phone, mail, or intercept surveys.

Data Acquisition

The Internet is an excellent source of data on many consumer-related issues. Some of this information is free, but some is only available at a charge. Information found on the Internet is current and easy to access. Because all surveys begin with an exhaustive search for available secondary data, the Internet is a useful source for relevant information—both domestic and global.

Sites such as Google, Yahoo, Ask, LiveSearch, and Dogpile have become popular among computer users looking for information on the Web. These services offer *search engines* that sift through the Web looking for sites that contain the needed information. All of them allow the user to enter one or more keywords and search the databases of Web sites for all occurrences of those words. They then return listings of sites that the user can go to by simply clicking on the name.

In addition to search engines, the researcher can use subject directories on the Web to explore a topic. Two types of directories exist. The first is the *academic and professional directories* which are created by librarians or subject experts, mostly in academic institutions. INFOMINE, from the University of California, is an example of an academic directory. The second type of directories is the *commercial portals*, such as Craigslist which provides links to a wide range of topics such as entertainment, commerce, hobbies, sports, travel, and other topics not necessarily covered by academic directories.

For information about a specific company, the company's home page is the first place to look. Internet addresses for most companies are simple to figure out intuitively by simply employing the company's name or initials as part of the address. For example, Sony's home page can be found at www.sony.com.

For a wide variety of industry and demographic statistics, the U.S. Census Bureau's home page, www.census.gov, provides researchers with a wealth of data through links such as *County and City Data Book* as well as the *Statistical Abstract of the United States.* International information regarding various countries can be obtained at the Central Intelligence Agency's Web site, www.cia.gov and then click "library."

For financial information on industries and companies, a variety of sources such as the *Wall Street Research Net* at www.wsrn.com, CompanyLink at www.hoovers.com, Bloomberg at www.blomberg.com, and My Money at mymoney.gov can be valuable.

For demographic information, business news, and industry information, a source such as newarkwww.rutgers.edu/guides/business/mkt-sources.htm can provide the researcher with a variety of current consumer data.

General Information

In some instances, a researcher may lack expertise about some research procedure, locating specific data, or some consumption-related topic, such as purchasing, using, or fixing a product. In such cases, it is possible to post such questions to a newsgroup or listserv and await a reply from someone who may have the answer. *Newsgroups* are electronic bulletin boards where such messages can be placed. These messages can then be accessed by anyone who visits the site. Similarly, *listservs* are electronic mailing lists that automatically send messages to list subscribers. There are hundreds of newsgroups and listservs on the Internet that can accommodate any type of question or message that users may have. Newsgroups can be accessed by using an Internet browser such as *Microsoft Internet Explorer* and a newsgroup-searching device such as groups.google.com/. Similarly, a list of consumer-related listservs can be found at MouseTracks, whose Web address is nsns.com/MouseTracks.

DATABASE MARKETING

Another growing area of consumer research brought about by advances in computer technology is **database marketing.** An increasing number of marketers, including those involved with catalog sales, record clubs, and credit card companies, invest heavily to build databases that enable them to figure out, among other things, who their customers are, which of these customers are likely prospects for specific product or service offerings, and which customers are more profitable. This process has become possible via a new generation of faster and more powerful computers that have enabled marketers to zero in on ever smaller and more precise niches of the population and probe specific customer profiles. For example, at FedEx, the company's database has

database marketing
the gathering, analyzing, and finding of specific information about propects

been instrumental in separating between the *good*, the *bad*, and the *ugly* customers.[14] The *good* customers spend a lot and require little service and marketing investment. The *bad* ones spend just as much but cost more to keep. The *ugly* spend little and show few signs of spending more in the future. Armed with this knowledge, FedEx was able to turn the *bad* customers into profitable ones by charging them higher shipping rates. For the *ugly*, the company stopped marketing to them altogether. By so doing, the firm was able to bring its costs down. Similarly, Capital One, a credit card issuer, became one of the world's largest and most profitable companies through the use of what it calls its Information-Based Strategy (IBS), which helped the company distinguish between profitable and nonprofitable clients to permit getting rid of the latter.

To build their databases, companies collect mountains of data about their customers. Every time customers send in a coupon, fill out warranty cards, or enter a sweepstakes, they volunteer information about themselves that gets fed into a computer somewhere. To that information, marketers add data from other sources, perhaps purchased from companies such as Donnelley, Metromail, or R.L. Polk. These firms collect vast amounts of data from public records such as drivers' licenses, auto registrations, and mortgage/tax roles and sell them to other users.

Once data about consumers have been collected, the computer—with help of sophisticated statistical techniques—merges the different sets of data into a single coherent database.

Among the more challenging tasks in database marketing is how to build the required database and what types of data to include in customers' files. The goal, of course, is to include data that help identify consumer characteristics relevant to the company's operations. For instance, would home ownership information be valuable to a company in the video-rental business? Or would magazine-subscription information be valuable to a company that sells toys for children? The job of continuously updating the database poses yet another challenge. In the consumer goods field, updated information may come from a variety of sources, including the company's records of consumers' product and service purchases, consumer purchases from other companies including online orders, retail checkout scanner data, purchased lists from outside vendors, sweepstakes entries, consumer inquiries and calls to 800 numbers, as well as other consumer databases.

DATA MINING

data mining
the computer software that sifts through mounds of data to find meaningful relationships

A new class of software technology known broadly as **data mining** has revolutionized analysis of companies' databases. Data mining tools can sift through mounds of data on customers and identify relationships that are worth noting. It can *see* patterns that might otherwise take tens of human years to find.[15]

Data mining has helped many companies to zero in on the individual customer in a kind of cybernetic intimacy.[16] For example, when MCI wanted to learn more about its customers and classify them into a number of meaningful profiles, it combed marketing data on 140 million households. Each household was evaluated on as many as 10,000 attributes including factors such as income, lifestyle, and past calling habits.[17] Through data mining, MCI was able to compile a set of 22 detailed—and highly secret—statistical profiles of its customers. Similarly, Fleet Bank analyzed information concerning more than 100,000 customer loans in order to predict such things as which customers might prepay and which ones might become delinquent. The data analyzed ranged from the age and zip code of customers to the source of their loan and whether or not it had been converted from a previous one. Data mining allowed the bank to set rules for identifying loans likely to yield the highest profits. Based on this information, the bank was able to adjust its rates and fees accordingly.[18]

Today, many companies are taking great interest in data mining procedures due to its numerous advantages. Data mining, for example, can identify which customers are profitable so that price incentives or promotional expenditures can be matched to the profitability of each. It is also used to model interpurchase times (length of time between purchases) to allow a company to know when to call on customers or when to drop a customer from the active customer database. It sifts through records of various products or services that consumers have purchased so the firm can cross-sell other items to them. Of course the number of applications to which data mining can be put is as diverse as the information contained in the database itself.

Motivation Research

Marketers and advertising agencies have become increasingly interested in why consumers behave as they do and why they select one product or brand instead of another. **Motivation research** explores the *why* aspects of human behavior with qualitative rather than quantitative research approaches.[19] This research is designed to delve below a subject's level of conscious awareness and uncover hidden motivations. Although such influences are difficult to determine, they may be central to understanding certain purchasing behaviors.

motivation research
the study of the *why* aspects of consumer behavior

Motivation research employs a set of techniques, such as projective tests and depth interviews, that were originally developed for use in clinical psychology and have been adapted for consumer research purposes.[20]

One of the reasons behind the need for motivation research is variation in consumers' willingness and ability to provide the information that marketers require. Individuals may or may not know their motives, or they may be unwilling to reveal what they do know because they feel it is personal or fear that it is socially unacceptable. In other instances, consumers do not express their motives simply because they are unaware of the forces that underlie their behavior.

Consumers who are able and willing to discuss their buying motives when directly questioned represent the easiest situation for marketers to handle. Their motives often relate to aspects of products such as brand attributes, benefits, and image. Such motives are conscious, and subjects do not attempt to hide them.

In some instances, consumers may not reveal their true buying motives either because they are personal or because they are unaware of them.

However, even when consumers are aware of their basic motivations, they are often reluctant to admit or reveal information that is personal or unpleasant or shows them in an unfavorable light. Direct question-and-answer approaches are ineffective under such circumstances. To overcome consumer reluctance to cooperate, marketers rely on projective techniques, which are based on the idea of relieving subjects of direct responsibility for the feelings they express. These methods have subjects assume the role of someone else and speak on their behalf. In doing so, respondents reveal their own motives.

Consumers who are unaware of their motives and cannot directly report them present a challenge for researchers. In this case, projective techniques as well as association tests can be helpful.

PROJECTIVE TECHNIQUES

projective techniques
the psychological techniques that reveal the *real* reasons behind consumption behaviors

Projective techniques are a set of specialized research tools that may be employed within the context of an in-depth interview to delve into a respondent's psyche and unravel the *real* reasons behind his or her consumption patterns.[22] Projective techniques take a variety of forms. For example, subjects may be shown ambiguous pictures or told about situations on which they are then asked to comment, thereby projecting themselves into the scene or predicament. Among the most popular projective tests employed for purposes of consumer research are the Thematic Apperception Test, cartoons, and verbal projectives.

Thematic Apperception Test

Thematic Apperception Test (TAT)
a test where respondents interpret an ambiguous situation

Some projective techniques are labeled *storytelling techniques* because they rely on pictorial stimuli such as photos, drawings, or cartoons that subjects are asked to explain. One such test is the **Thematic Apperception Test (TAT)**. In marketing applications, researchers design ambiguous illustrations or photographs depicting some phenomenon of interest such as shopping and purchasing circumstances, product use, or social situations. Some pictures are clear representations; others are more obscure. The respondent is asked to explain what is going on and what the outcome might be or to tell a story about each picture. Because few clues are available in the picture, subjects draw from their own personality traits, experiences, motivations, feelings, and imagination and, by doing so, reveal something about themselves. Their responses are used to assess motives, beliefs, and feelings about the phenomenon under investigation.

The government is cracking down on the cigarette industry.

Exhibit 2.1

A Marketing Application of the Cartoon Technique

After a researcher shows a respondent this cartoon, the researcher asks the respondent, "What comment does the wife make in response to her husband's statement?"

Cartoons

In the **cartoon** variation of the TAT, empty *balloons* appear near the mouths or heads of characters in an illustration. Sometimes, one character is shown posing a question or statement to another. The respondent replies by providing the missing portion of the dialogue and in so doing, projects his or her own beliefs, feelings, or motives onto the characters in the picture. An example appears in Exhibit 2.1.

cartoon
a test where respondents provide missing dialogue in a situational drawing

Verbal Projectives

In **verbal projectives**, words rather than pictures set up a situation or a problem. The respondent is asked to complete a story by surmising what the character might think or do in the suggested circumstances (or with the product) and what kind of person might be involved in that situation. In a classic example, an auto manufacturer asked people what *they* wanted in a car. Most wanted a safe, functional, conservative vehicle. When the same manufacturer asked respondents what their *neighbor* wanted in a car, the reply was very different. Subjects said their neighbors wanted a flashy vehicle with lots of horsepower and style; very few subjects mentioned safety.

verbal projective
a test where respondents complete an incomplete story

ASSOCIATION TESTS

Association tests are based on immediacy of subjects' responses to a stimulus word or phrase that the interviewer poses. The immediate response is assumed to curtail self-censorship. That is to say, an individual lacks time to come up with logical or socially acceptable answers to the words or phrases provided. Responses, thus, are presumed to be a respondent's *gut* reactions to a stimulus. Commonly used association tests include free word associations, controlled and chain word associations, and sentence completions.

Consumer Behavior in Practice

Torture Those Creepy Males

A few years ago, McCann-Erickson, a large advertising agency, was approached by its client to determine why low-income women in the South, a key market segment, were not purchasing Combat, a new brand of roach killer in a plastic tray. Widespread household-infestation trouble indicated that tremendous sales potential existed among this group. However, women remained loyal to the traditional bug sprays they had used for years.

The agency knew that earlier advertising had been successful. Women knew about Combat and believed it killed roaches effectively, neatly, and inconspicuously. Nonetheless, they still weren't buying it.

Agency psychologists determined that conducting motivation research would help in this case, because they suspected that hidden motives were behind women's reluctance to accept Combat. As a result, they conducted in-depth interviews and asked women to sketch the roaches and compose brief stories to explain their drawings. It amazed researchers to discover that all the roaches drawn were males!

Women perceived roaches as sneaky male scavengers. They associated roaches with men who had abandoned them, left them feeling poor and powerless, or mistreated them in the past. The agency concluded that women prefer spray roach killers over products that do not permit users to see roaches suffer and perish.

According to Paula Drillman, the research director and agency's director of strategic planning, killing roaches with conventional bug sprays and watching them squirm and die allow women to express their hostility toward men and gain greater control over the roaches.[21]

Marketers sometimes attempt to discover hidden forces behind consumer acceptance or rejection of products. In the case of Combat, the roach killer, what hidden motives caused rejection of the product? To see an example of a site designed to promote understanding between the sexes, visit Balance Magazine at www.balancemagazine.com. Can such sexist feelings be soothed?

Free Word Associations

In **free word associations**, a researcher dispenses a list of words one at a time to a respondent. Subjects are asked to respond immediately with the very first word that comes to mind for each. For example, in a study of cooking oil, key words in the list given to respondents might include *cholesterol, fat, health, heart, margarine, butter*, and *cost*. Responses are analyzed according to the frequency with which they are given as a reply, the average amount of time that elapses before a response is given, and the number of subjects who do not respond at all to a test word after a reasonable time. Free word associations have been used to test brand names for recognition, awareness, and recall as well as for possible negative connotations. They can also be used to uncover feelings about new products, and to identify key words for advertising and promotion.

Controlled and Chain Word Associations

Controlled and chain word associations are variations on free word association. In **controlled word associations**, subjects are instructed to respond with a certain type of response, such as recalling brand names. For example, in a study of consumer brand recognition, respondents may be asked to respond with the first brand name that comes to mind after hearing a product class, such as paint, detergent, toothpaste, or any other type of product. In **chain word associations**, subjects must respond with a series of words to reach deeper feelings. For example, respondents are asked to list the first four or five words that come to mind for each stimulus word. In response to the stimulus word *doughnut*, a subject may reply with a sequence of words such as *chocolate, sugar, breakfast, calories*, and *fat*. Knowledge of such psychological associations can be helpful to marketers in the areas of product design or formulation, labeling, and promotion.

chain word associations
association tests in which subjects respond with a series of four or five words

Sentence Completions

Another popular variation of free word association is **sentence completion**. Sentence completions give subjects a more directed stimulus than simple word associations. Respondents are asked to complete each thought with the first phrase that comes to mind. The following phrases illustrate sentence completions.

sentence completions
association tests where respondents complete sentences with the first phrase that comes to mind

> The average person considers rock-and-roll music . . .
> *When you first get a new car . . .*
> *Housecleaning would be so much easier if . . .*
> *People who smoke cigarettes . . .*

OTHER MOTIVATION RESEARCH TECHNIQUES

A number of other techniques are also employed for purposes of motivation research. They include various types of picture sorting, the shopping list technique, and the Zaltman Metaphor Elicitation Technique.

In **picture-sorting techniques**, subjects are given stacks of photos with people's faces (where each face represents a particular emotional reaction) or stereotyped figure sketches that typify various ethnic, lifestyle, age, occupation, and income groups. Subjects are asked to sort out those representing typical users of various products, brands, or patrons of particular stores. BBDO Worldwide Advertising Agency uses a method called *photosort* in which subjects view a photo deck depicting diverse types of people and indicate which brands of product they feel those portrayed would use. The types of people that subjects associate with different brands offer insight into the way these consumers perceive the brands themselves.[23]

picture-sorting techniques
tests where respondents sort a stack of pictures to reveal stereotypes

Shopping List Techniques

In the **shopping list technique**, a researcher reads or shows a shopping list to a respondent and asks what kind of consumer wrote it. Respondents express their own motives and attitudes as they infer those of someone else. For example, in a classic study conducted a number of years ago, direct-questioning interviews identified poor flavor as the reason consumers disliked instant coffee. Blind taste tests, however, strongly suggested that poor flavor was merely a rationalization. To identify the real cause, marketers showed respondents one of two shopping lists. Both lists included bread, ground meat, carrots, baking powder, peaches, potatoes, and coffee. One list, however, contained "Maxwell House (drip ground) Coffee" and the other, "Nescafe Instant Coffee."

shopping list technique
a test where respondents surmise the type of person who buys items on a list

With respect to instant coffee, research using the *shopping list technique* revealed that respondents were not dissatisfied with instant coffee's taste, but rather, with the idea of using it.

Zaltman Metaphor Elicitation Technique (ZMET)

a test where respondents provide images that represent their feelings about a topic

Subjects were asked to characterize the woman who purchased the groceries. Descriptions indicated that compared to the drip-ground buyer who was perceived as a good wife and thrifty, the instant coffee purchaser was thought to be lazy and a poor planner. Results indicated that respondents were not really dissatisfied with instant coffee's taste, but rather that the idea of using it was unacceptable. Thus, respondents had projected their own feelings about instant coffee onto the description of the hypothetical woman who purchased it.[24] A follow-up study a number of years later found no significant differences between subjects' descriptions of hypothetical regular and instant coffee shoppers.[25] By then, convenience foods had become staples of the U.S. diet.

Zaltman Metaphor Elicitation Technique (ZMET)

The **Zaltman Metaphor Elicitation Technique (ZMET)** is designed to elicit metaphors that can help researchers explore ideas that are deeply held by consumers regarding a variety of issues, such as brands, companies, purchase situations, product-usage patterns, or product concepts. In the ZMET, each participant is asked to collect a minimum of 12 images representing his or her thoughts or feelings about the research topic gathered from any source such as family albums, catalogs, or magazines. For example, in a study of women's thoughts and feelings about buying and wearing panty hose, twenty women were "Z-Metted." Each collected a dozen pictures from magazines, catalogs, and family photo albums. A review of these photos showed two types of images. The first consisted of pictures of steel bands strangling trees, twisted telephone cords, and fence posts encased in a tight plastic wrap. The second group of pictures were of flowers resting peacefully in a vase, a luxury car, and an ice cream sundae spilled on the ground.

The meaning of the first group of pictures is not hard to figure out. Many women view panty hose as hot, uncomfortable, and confining. However, the second group of pictures revealed a "like–hate" type of relationship. The flower vase picture indicated that wearing panty hose makes women feel thin and tall. The expensive car picture expressed a feeling of luxury felt when women wore panty hose. The spilled ice cream sundae represented embarrassment caused by stocking runs.[26] Such insights are important from a marketing standpoint because they provide a basis for understanding consumers and guide the manner in which marketers appeal to their diverse needs.[27] Findings from the panty hose study, for example, led hosiery manufacturers to alter their advertising appeals to include images reflecting luxury and allure.

However, it is important to recognize that because motivation research is exploratory in nature, it only offers insight and suggests hypotheses for more structured, quantitatively oriented investigations to be conducted with larger, more representative samples.

Ethical Issues in Consumer Research

A number of ethical issues need to be addressed when conducting consumer research. In some instances, researchers deliberately mislead or withhold information from respondents. At other times, researchers promise to hold all replies in strict confidence and then fail to do so. In still other cases, survey results are exaggerated, falsified, or misrepresented. These and other ethical violations arise in consumer research as they do in all other aspects of life. In some cases, the ethical lapses are deliberate; in other instances, they occur because researchers are unaware of their ethical responsibilities and the consequences of their actions.

Consider, for instance, the following scenarios:

A number of ethical issues need to be addressed when conducting consumer research.

- The manufacturer of a brand of toothpaste conducted a national survey among dentists to investigate which brand of toothpaste they recommend to their patients. The survey asked 500 dentists to pick the one brand they would most likely recommend to their patients from a list that included a choice between only three alternatives: the company's "brand A," a competitor's "brand B," or "none of the above." Four hundred out of the 500 dentists selected the "none of the above" choice. Seventy-five of them marked "A," and 25 marked "B." The manufacturer of A used the results of the survey as the basis for a national ad campaign claiming that "dentists choose brand A 3-to-1 over brand B as the toothpaste they would most likely recommend to their patients."

- A poll sponsored by the disposable diaper industry solicited respondents' views regarding the controversial issue of disposable diapers and their potentially harmful effects on the environment. The survey began with the statement, "It is estimated that disposable diapers account for less than 2 percent of the trash in landfills. In contrast, beverage containers, third-class mail, and yard waste are estimated to account for 21 percent of the trash in landfills. Given this, in your opinion, would it be fair to ban disposable diapers?"

- While conducting a telephone survey, an automobile manufacturer told respondents that the purpose of the study was to determine consumers' attitudes toward the company's cars and to assess their future buying intentions. In reality, the objective had nothing to do with consumer research. The acquired information was simply handed over to local dealers, who made sales calls to likely buyers.

- The manager of a Wal-Mart store caught a person writing down the prices of merchandise on the store shelves. When confronted, the individual claimed to be a university student doing a class project on competitive pricing. In reality, he was an employee from a large national chain of discount stores and was gathering pricing data so his firm could match or undercut Wal-Mart's prices.

Ethical issues such as these often arise in the realm of consumer research. In the first case of the toothpaste manufacturer, obvious and deliberate misinterpretation and misrepresentation of the data occurred. In the second case, the disposable diaper industry provided a statement that would certainly bias the responses received. In the auto manufacturer's case, the action simply amounted to selling under the guise of consumer research. In the last case of copying prices, the employee lied to conceal the identity of the sponsoring party and the purpose for which data were collected.

One useful way of determining whether or not a researcher's actions are ethical is to be cognizant of ethical standards in at least four areas related to a researcher's obligations toward research participants. These include protecting participants from harm; safeguarding participants from being deceived; ensuring that participants are informed about the study and are willing to participate; and guaranteeing that acquired data will be held in strict confidence.[28]

PROTECTING PARTICIPANTS

A primary obligation of a researcher is to protect participants from any physical or psychological harm that the research procedures may inflict. For example, physical harm may arise in a taste test where some participants have allergies to particular ingredients in the foods being tested. It may also arise in an olfactory test, where respondents are allergic to certain scents. In addition, physical harm may result from certain laboratory equipment such as a pupil-dilation apparatus used to test respondents' reactions to different advertising messages.

Psychological harm can result when respondents are pressured, embarrassed, made to feel guilty, or generally subjected to mental stress. For example, some survey respondents might feel embarrassed by the fact that they have not yet tried a certain product or that they cannot afford it. On other occasions, respondents feel pressured to provide personal and often intimate information they don't feel comfortable sharing. Such circumstances should be minimized when conducting consumer research projects. Although it is true that nothing in life is risk free, the risks posed by consumer research should not exceed those posed by everyday life.

AVOIDING DECEPTION

Another obligation of the researcher is to safeguard participants against deception. Consumers are often victims of deceit practiced by some unscrupulous marketers and fund-raisers who, under the guise of conducting research, attempt to sell them something or solicit donations to some cause.

Because many people like to express their opinions about products and issues, phony consumer researchers sometimes pretend to be interested in obtaining respondents' views about some issue, topic, or product. For example, an unethical fund-raiser might ask respondents four or five questions as a ploy. As the respondent gets involved in supplying the supposedly solicited views, the interviewer concludes with a request for a contribution. Many respondents find it difficult at that point in the interview to turn down the request. Of course, the interviewer had no intention of using the data obtained. This technique is often practiced by political parties and some nonprofit groups. In other instances, respondents may be asked to provide information detrimental to their self-interest. Consider the case of a consumer researcher who asks respondents to indicate how acceptable different prices are for a certain product. The purpose of the research is to determine consumers' price sensitivity with the ultimate goal of raising the current price to the highest possible level without risking a negative effect on sales. It is obvious that such practices are deceptive and cross the lines of ethical behavior when conducting consumer research.

INFORMING PARTICIPANTS

A third obligation of the researcher is to ensure that research participants are well informed about the purpose and procedures of their research. Such knowledge allows respondents to determine whether or not they should participate.

In some cases, the researcher deliberately falsifies the purpose of the study. For example, in the case of measuring consumers' price sensitivity mentioned earlier, the researcher never divulges the *real* reason behind the survey and claims that the objective of the study is to reduce rather than to raise prices. Similarly, in cases of fund-raising and selling under the guise of research, respondents may never be told what the true objective is.

Deception also occurs when researchers camouflage the identity of the organization sponsoring the research. A company may hire interviewers to acquire information about a competitive firm by instructing interviewers to claim they are working for the competitor. Moreover, interviewers may lie about the length of the survey. An interviewer, for example, may tell respondents that a 20-minute interview will take only a few moments of their time. Such actions are obviously unethical, because they fail to disclose information necessary for respondents to decide whether or not to participate.

HONORING PROMISES OF CONFIDENTIALITY

A final researcher obligation is to hold data that participants provide in strict confidence. Preservation of participants' anonymity is an important step, because the information acquired about consumers' opinions, behavior, or demographics can be valuable to other agents. Purchase-related data, for example, can be of great use to product–service sellers. Consumer demographics as well as lifestyle data can be of great interest to database markets. Customer financial data can be valuable to investment and insurance companies.[30]

Researchers should routinely remove any details that can identify specific respondents from the research report. This is particularly important for sensitive types of research when respondents provide potentially damaging views such as in the case of political and religious opinions on controversial issues. In such cases, anonymity for the purpose of protecting the respondent from reprisals or litigation is essential.

Through consumer research, companies gain valuable knowledge about consumers such as their purchasing habits, their product use, and their demographics. Through this process, marketers come to recognize that people possess different needs and wants and that they often satisfy their desires dissimilarly. The varied needs and wants of consumers must be taken into account

Ethical Dilemma

Do You Know Where Your Health Profile Is?

Drug companies are very interested in knowing what doctors prescribe for their patients when they visit their offices. These companies are paying huge sums of money to acquire such private and personal patient information. The beneficiary of such transactions happens to be the prestigious American Medical Association (AMA), which continues to sell such detailed physician data to the pharmaceutical industry. In fact, in 2005, the AMA made more than $44 million from the sale of database products to pharmaceutical companies, which represented 16 percent of the AMA's budget.

Such information is collected through drug reps' handheld computers that they carry when they visit doctors' offices. While they are at these offices, they obtain a detailed profile of the doctor's prescribing history for his or her various patients. The AMA combines this information collected by the reps in a physician's "Masterfile," and then sells the document to health information organizations.

These health information companies then pair the identifying information with prescribing records from pharmacies, a practice commonly known as *prescription data mining*. The package is now ready for sale to the eager pharmaceutical companies.

Armed with this knowledge of each doctor's individual prescribing habits, pharmaceutical companies use the data to tailor their sales pitches specifically to each physician. This step includes providing each physician with various types of drug ads, pens, pads, stethoscopes, booklets, calendars, and a multitude of other free benefits and giveaways designed to encourage these doctors

to prescribe more brand-name, higher-priced drugs marketed by the brand-name companies.

While the original intention of collecting such data from physicians was for the purpose of public health research, the realities of the situation point to the fact that this objective has been replaced by one of merely allowing pharmaceutical companies to enhance their bottom line.

Many observers criticized this practice and questioned its ethical ramifications. A number of policymakers, physician groups, and medical societies have come out against this practice. Their outcry has prompted a number of states, such as Maine, Vermont, and New Hampshire, to pass legislation banning the sale of information detailing what drugs doctors are prescribing to their patients. However, these efforts have been challenged by both the AMA and the data mining companies, based on their claim of "First Amendment rights."[29]

Most patients are unaware of the fact that their private health and prescription information is being sold, not just by the AMA, but by pharmacies as well. To learn more about this questionable practice, visit the Web site of PAL at www.prescriptionaccess.org/blog/?p=59 and NLARX at http://nlarx.com/membernews/nh.html. In your opinion, how can such practices harm patients and society as a whole? How would you respond to the argument of companies that collect, analyze, and sell medical data that such restrictions violate their free-speech rights?

when companies design their product and service offerings. This realization is the foundation for what is known as market segmentation. **Market segmentation allows marketers to see clearly the diversity within their markets and uncover possible opportunities** that may exist or to identify niches whose needs have been poorly met by other product and service offerings. Market segmentation together with the closely related concepts of targeting and positioning are the topics that constitute the next chapter.

A Cross-Functional Point of View

The topic of consumer research has a number of implications for business disciplines other than marketing. Relevant issues might include

- **Privacy/Cost:** Drug company reps who visit doctors' offices carry with them handheld computers that record which physicians prescribe which drugs and how often. For many years, the AMA recognized the important role such private information can play for pharmaceutical marketing purposes. It embarked on selling such information from its "Masterfile" to companies that purchase it in order to promote their drug brands to physicians who underprescribe their branded medications. In addition to this ethically questionable practice by the AMA, buying and selling of this sensitive information is a major factor in inflating the price paid by patients for drugs.

- **Legal:** A reporter from a popular magazine was known for his reports on controversial issues and his exceptional ability to acquire information from difficult and secretive sources. In a report he wrote on the Ku Klux Klan, he alluded to interviews he had conducted with various leaders of the group and facts he had acquired about them. When the article was published, an irate group took the matter to court and demanded that the reporter release the names, locations, and other data he had obtained about the KKK. Consultation with a legal adviser informed the reporter that when private information is subpoenaed, there are only limited legal safeguards to protect the identity of those individuals if the detailed information about them still existed in the reporter's file. The only protection for their identity is when their identifying information has already been removed. Information cannot be destroyed *after* being requested by a court.

- **Ethics:** Recently, a regional fruit juice company developed a lemonade that came in a variety of flavors. Although company executives believed that the product had great promise, they felt that it would be necessary to obtain positive test market results for the lemonade in order to convince the trade of the product's sales potential and to get wholesalers and retailers to handle it. With this objective in mind, the executives set out to test-market the lemonade in three towns where the company had a strong reputation and a solid distribution network. For purposes of the test, the executives contracted specific stores in these three towns where the company's other product sales were excellent. These were the only stores chosen to carry the tested lemonade. Three months later, the positive test market results materialized, and the executives felt confident to approach the trade with these excellent findings.

These issues, and a host of others like them, serve to show that the topic of consumer research transcends the field of marketing to other business disciplines.

Summary

Consumer research consists of the diverse and systematic methods that marketers employ to investigate the internal, environmental, and social factors that affect consumer decisions and exchange processes. The goal of consumer research is to understand the processes of selecting, purchasing, using, and disposing of goods and services. Marketers conduct consumer research to segment markets and profile those consumers who constitute the target market; to identify consumers' beliefs, attitudes, intentions, and behavior with respect to a brand; and to ascertain what adds perceived value to goods and discern what builds brand loyalty among consumers. Through consumer research, marketers attempt to design products with desirable features, position them properly in the marketplace, price them sensibly, distribute them effectively, and promote them to those most likely to buy.

Marketers are interested in information about purchase situations, buyers, product use, customer loyalty, market segments, and customer satisfaction. Some of this information is acquired via secondary data, which are information and statistics that were not gathered for the immediate study at hand. Secondary data include information found in libraries, company files, government documents, periodicals, computerized databases, and the Internet. For many studies, however, primary data acquired through original research becomes necessary. Primary data can be obtained via observation of consumers, consumer surveys, focus groups, experiments, test markets, and consumer panels.

Present-day technology has had an impact on consumer research. Increasingly, marketers turn to the Internet, build sophisticated databases, or employ data mining to gain a better understanding of consumers.

Motivation research, one type of consumer research, explores the *why* aspects of human behavior. Consumers may be aware of the reasons behind their behavior and willing to discuss them, be aware of their motives but unwilling to discuss them, or be unaware of the internal forces that impact their behavior. A number of projective techniques such as the TAT, cartoons, and verbal projectives along with associative techniques as well as other miscellaneous procedures such as picture sorting, the shopping list test, and the ZMET can be employed to reveal hidden or otherwise unspoken consumer motives.

A number of ethical issues need to be addressed when marketers conduct consumer research. These include protecting participants from physical or psychological harm, avoiding deception, adequately informing research participants, and honoring promises of confidentiality.

Review Questions

1. Cite some forms of consumer research and show how marketers can use the information acquired to understand consumers better.
2. Identify some uses of the Internet for purposes of conducting consumer research.
3. Progressive marketers find databases to be useful in a number of ways. Explain how.
4. Identify and discuss an important ethical issue that marketers should address when conducting consumer research.
5. What causes reluctance on the part of consumers to discuss the reasons for their consumption behaviors? How can researchers overcome this tendency?

Discussion Questions

1. In the 1980s, PepsiCo conducted blind taste tests between Pepsi and Coca-Cola drinks. Respondents were given two anonymous samples to taste and were asked to select the one they preferred. Pepsi was the brand chosen most often. Assuming that sweetness had something to do with the results, Coca-Cola executives embarked on developing a sweeter-tasting cola. Thousands of respondents participated in lab and field tests of the new cola. In practically every case, subjects preferred the taste of the new, sweeter cola. Encouraged by the test results, the Coca-Cola Company introduced New Coke to replace the original formula. Coca-Cola executives were shocked, however, at the negative and even hostile reception that New Coke encountered in the marketplace. In your opinion, did research respondents provide false information when they gave their positive product evaluations? In retrospect, how should researchers have interpreted respondents' replies?

2. Today, many retail stores rely heavily on scanning technology to monitor consumer buying habits. One method of using this technology entails *preferred-customer cards* presented at checkout counters to track consumer purchases via Universal Product Codes. A more sophisticated system, known as *The Incredible Universe*, is a bar-coded plastic identification card used by customers while visiting a store. It tracks how many times each customer comes into the store, how long he or she stays, and where in the store he or she has been. In what ways could this information be useful to retailers? Do you think the benefits of these systems justify their cost? Do you think monitoring devices such as these invade shoppers' privacy? Why or why not?

3. Marketers who need international demographic data must deal with the frustrating issue of data recency. The United States takes a census every 10 years, which is the typical frequency. Japan conducts its censuses every 5 years. France takes a census irregularly; since the 1960s, the interval has been about 7 years. In what used to be West Germany, the most recent census is dated 1987. Some northern and western European nations are abandoning censuses altogether and are relying on population registers to account for births, deaths, and changes in marital status or place of residence. Considering these variations, what advice can you give marketers to help them obtain a more precise profile of a foreign country's population?

In reference to the chapter opening vignette's examples regarding the increasing dependence of businesses on databases, assume that a group of entrepreneurs is studying the feasibility of opening a doll manufacturing plant. Unlike the cost-efficient method of mass-producing dolls in a standardized format, these entrepreneurs hope to offer ethnic-featured, anatomically correct, customized dolls that bear the face of a specific child. Toward this end, the following steps must be undertaken:

1. Databases of households that buy dolls from toy chains, specialty doll stores, and mail-order houses, as well as from other sources, must be purchased.
2. Analysts must sift through these databases to determine the ethnicity and other relevant characteristics of each doll-buying household.
3. A promotional packet must be developed to inform prospects that dolls could be specifically customized with each child's likeness and other personal attributes.

4. These promotional packets must then be mailed to every identified household.

A cost accountant reviewing the projected figures realizes the following:

1. The cost of doll production would double as a result of customization.
2. Purchasing the databases would cost tens of thousands of dollars.
3. Sifting through the mounds of data to determine household attributes would require hundreds of labor hours.
4. Costs would also be incurred to prepare and mail the promotional packet.

The end result would triple the selling price per doll. From the perspective of economic theory, would the high selling price seriously impair demand for the doll? For a product of this type, would the notion of a downsloping demand curve apply?

CASE

Tiger Toy Company of Hong Kong

As Susan Klein sat at a corner table in the Tiger Toy Company's cafeteria, overlooking Victoria Bay in Hong Kong, she could see the magnificent skyline of the city and watch the hustle and bustle of the many commercial and leisure boats crossing the harbor. Ms. Klein, the international director of sales for the Tiger Toy Company in Hong Kong, was waiting for her boss, Mr. W. L. Chung, president of the company, to discuss with him a second report she had prepared about U.S. companies' efforts to reach kids.

Mr. Chung is a modest, white-haired man in his late fifties who has successfully headed the company over the past 12 years. He transformed the company from a small Chinese manufacturer of a single line of dolls to a giant company that manufactures hundreds of lines of toys ranging from stuffed animals and key-wound toys to high-tech electronic gadgets.

Although the company sold its products worldwide, the United States was its major market, accounting for over 60 percent of its sales. A few months ago, Mr. Chung realized that despite the importance of the United States as a major market for toys, the company really didn't know much about the size of the kids' market there or that market's purchasing power. At that time, he asked Ms. Klein to find out these facts for him. Ms. Klein then prepared her original report informing him that in the United States in 2006, there were 50 million kids between the ages of 4 and 14, who reportedly spent an estimated $75 billion on various products and influenced the spending of another $500 billion by their families.

Impressed with these figures, Mr. Chung decided to pursue the U.S. kid market more vigorously and asked Ms. Klein to prepare another report on strategies companies selling to U.S.

kids employ in order to learn about their likes and dislikes.

As Ms. Klein poured herself a second cup of green tea, Mr. Chung finally walked into the cafeteria and sat down across from her. Ms. Klein handed him the new report she had prepared. Mr. Chung leaned back in his chair, sipped the green tea she poured him, and started to read the report. The document revealed some of the innovative strategies marketers in the United States employ to get closer to kids as a way of gaining knowledge about their lives and thoughts. The report highlighted a number of these strategies as follows:

- Levi Strauss supplies kids with video and disposable cameras and asks them to record diaries about how they and their friends spend their time. The objective is to reveal what goes on in a kid's world.
- Delta Airlines promotes its Fantastic Flyer program for kids aged 7 to 14 that rewards them with *Fantastic Flyer* magazines, birthday greetings, special foods and gifts during flights, and bargain fares for their parents. The goal is to generate future customers for Delta.
- Mattel brings a number of children into a test facility, provides them with a large selection of toys, and observes which toys children are most attracted to.
- Pepsi's ad agency, BBDO, arranges for groups of high school kids to spend entire weekends at posh hotels to get their reaction to Pepsi ads.
- Nickelodeon has online chats with 150 kids aged 7 to 11 every Wednesday to get their feelings about diverse topics, such as favorite movies and music.
- BKG America, a New York–based research firm that specializes in researching children, wires up 5,000 to 10,000 children and adults on computer networks to be used as focus groups in cyberspace. The company provides free America Online software to reward them for participating.
- Sega of America conducts dialogues online with kids, capturing thousands of names every day, which the company adds to its database as future prospects.
- Kid2Kid research firm hires kids as young as age 14 to moderate focus groups of peers. These kids are used to test new products, packages, or ads planned for the children's market.
- Levi Strauss hands kids $50 to $100 cash and asks them to record how they spend every penny of it.

As Mr. Chung read the report, he began to realize that the job of finding out how U.S. kids feel about his company's toys or which lines they like best would be a challenging task. Not only would he have to decide which strategy to follow to get the desired information, he would also have to select the research firm that could do the job in the most efficient and cost-effective way.

Questions

1. Which research strategy from among those cited would you recommend that Mr. Chung consider for purposes of learning about kids in the United States? Justify your recommendation. Would that research strategy apply equally well to other countries where the toy company sells its products?

2. Although Levi Strauss's main business involves apparel and accessories, why does the company resort to strategies such as having kids record diaries or tracing their money-expenditure patterns? Is such practice ethical?

3. In addition to the information Ms. Klein provided in her two reports, what other types of data does the Tiger Toy Company need to get a clear picture of the children's toy market in the United States?

Notes

1. Arther Middleton Hughes, "Database Marketing Has Arrived," Database Marketing Institute (November 27, 2007), www.dbmarketing.com/articles/Art215.htm; Arthur Middleton Hughes and Ian Gilyeat, "Database Marketing Drives New Corporate Strategy," Database Marketing Institute (November 27, 2007); www.dbmarketing.com/articles/Art178.htm; Arther Middleton Hughes, "Building Caterpillar Market Share with a Database," Database Marketing Institute (November 27, 2007), www.dbmarketing.com/articles/Art215.htm.

2. Diane Crispell, "How to Hunt for the Best Source," *American Demographics* 11 (September 1989), p. 46; Jack Edmondston, "Syndicated Research Is Wonderful, Right?" *Business Marketing* 79 (August 1994), p. 12; Martha Farnsworth Riche, "Look Before Leaping," *American Demographics* 12 (February 1990), p.18; F. Patrick Butler, *Business Research Sources: A Reference Navigator* (Boston: Irwin/McGraw-Hill, 1999).

3. Francine Schwadel, "Kmart Testing 'Radar' to Track Shopper Traffic," *Wall Street Journal* (September 24, 1991), pp. B1, B7.

4. Carol Hall, "King of the Road," *Marketing & Media Decisions* 24 (March 1989), p. 86.

5. For more detail on observation studies, see Paco Underhill, *Why We Buy* (Upper Saddle River, NJ: Simon & Schuster), 1999.

6. Gerald Meyers, "Interviewing Trade Execs Is Not Like Interviewing Consumers," Marketing News (June 7, 1993), pp. H20–H21; Ronald Czaja and Johnny Blair, *Designing Surveys* (Newbury Park, CA: Sage, 1996).

7. Tim R. V. Davis and Robert B. Young, "International Marketing Research: A Management Briefing," *Business Horizons* (March/ April 2002), pp. 31–38; and Nessim Hanna, "In the Middle East, Think Twice Before You Conduct a Survey," AMA *International Conference,* Delhi, India (January 1987); Nessim Hanna, "In the Middle East, Think Twice Before You Conduct a Survey," a paper presented at the American Marketing Association 1987 International Conference, "International Marketing Strategies: West Asia," Delhi, India, January 4-7, 1987.

8. Thomas L. Greenbaum, *The Practical Handbook and Guide to Focus Group Research* (New York: Lexington, 1993); Jane Farley Templeton, *The Focus Group: A Strategic Guide to Organizing, Conducting, and Analyzing the Focus Group Interview* (Chicago: Probus, 1994); Jack Edmondston, "Handle Focus Group Research with Care," *Business Marketing* 79 (June 1994), p. 38; Thomas L. Greenbaum, "Who's Leading Your Focus Group?" *Bank Marketing* 25 (March 1993), p. 31; John Hoeffel, "The Secret Life of Focus Groups," *American Demographics* 16

(December 1994), pp. 17–19; and Arch G. Woodside and Elizabeth J. Wilson, "Applying the Long Interview in Direct Marketing Research," *Journal of Direct Marketing Research* 9 (Winter 1995), pp. 37–55.

9. Jennifer Riddle, "Complaining Customers Get Firms' Attention," *Wisconsin State Journal* (June 22, 1986), p. 2.

10. Thomas L. Greenbaum, "Internet Focus Groups: An Oxymoron," *Marketing News* (March 3, 1997), pp. 35–36.

11. Kim Komando, "3 Reasons to Use Online Customer Surveys," Microsoft Small Business Center (2007), www.microsoft.com/business/resources/marketing/small-business-market-research.aspx.

12. David R. Boniface, *Experimental Design and Statistical Methods for Behavioural and Social Research* (London: Chapman and Hall, 1995); D. R. Cox, *Planning of Experiments* (New York: John Wiley, 1991); Roger E. Kirk, *Experimental Design: Procedures for Behavioral Sciences* (Monterey, CA: Brooks-Cole, 1995); Paul R. Rosenbaum, *Observational Studies* (New York: Springer, 1995); B. J. Winer, *Statistical Principles in Experimental Design* (New York: McGraw-Hill, 1991); Warren F. Kuhfeld, Randall D. Tobias, and Mark Garratt, "Efficient Experimental Design with Marketing Research Applications," *Journal of Marketing Research* 31 (1994), pp. 545-57; Terance A. Shimp, Eva M. Hyatt, and David J. Snyder, "A Critical Appraisal of Demand Artifacts in Consumer Research," *Journal of Consumer Research* 18 (December 1991), pp. 273-83.

13. Raymond Burke, "Virtual Shopping," *ORIMS Today* (August 1995), p. 28.

14. Paul C. Judge, "What've You Done for Us Lately?" *Business Week* no. 3595 (September 14, 1998), pp. 140-45.

15. John W. Verity, "Coaxing Meaning Out of Raw Data," *Business Week* (February 3, 1997), pp. 134-38; see also Rod Newing, "Data Mining: Data Mining Has Become One of the Latest Trends in Using Data," *Management Accounting (British)* 74 (October 1, 1996), pp. 5-6; Martin Marshall, "Data Mining: Rich Vein for Marketers, *Communications Week* (January 13, 1997), p. 1; Robert D. Small, "Debunking Data-Mining Myths—Don't Let Contradictory Claims about Data Mining Keep You from Improving Your Business," *Information Week* (January 20, 1997), p. 55; Emil T. Cipolla, "Data Mining: Techniques to Gain Insight into Your Data (Technology Information)," *Enterprise Systems Journal* 10 (December 1, 1995), pp.18-22; Michael Schrage, "Data Mining in a Vicious Circle," *Computerworld* (June 30, 1997); Anthony Agresta, "At the Leading Edge of Data Mining," *Marketing Forum* (September 1, 1997).

16. "A Potent New Tool for Selling: Database Marketing," *Business Week* (September 5, 1994).

17. Verity, "Coaxing Meaning Out of Raw Data."

18. Judge, "What've You Done for Us Lately?"

19. "Qualitative Research—A Summary of the Concepts Involved," *Journal of the Market Research Society* 21 (April 1979), pp. 107–24.

20. Dennis Rook, "Researching Consumer Fantasy," in Elizabeth C. Hirschman (ed.), *Research in Consumer Behavior* 3 (Greenwich, CT: JAI Press, 1990), pp. 247–70; David Mick, M. De Moss, and Ronald Faber, "A Projective Study of Motivations and Meanings of Self-Gifts: Implications for Retail Management," *Journal of Retailing* (Summer 1992), pp. 122–44; Mary Ann McGrath, John F. Sherry, and Sidney J. Levy, "Giving Voice to the Gift: The Use of Projective Techniques to Recover Lost Meanings," *Journal of Consumer Psychology* 2 (1993), pp. 171–91; see also Barbara Stern's analysis of Dichter's Handbook—"Literary Criticism and the History of Marketing Thought: A New Perspective on 'Reading' Marketing Theory," *Journal of the Academy of Marketing Science* 18 (Winter 1990), pp. 329–36.

21. Ronald Alsop, "Advertisers Put Consumers on the Couch," *Wall Street Journal* (May 13, 1998), p. 17.

22. Dennis W. Rook, "The Ritual Dimension of Consumer Behavior," *Journal of Consumer Research* 12 (December 1985), pp. 251–64.

23. Alsop, "Advertisers Put Consumers on the Couch."

24. Mason Haire, "Projective Techniques in Marketing Research," *Journal of Marketing* 14 (April 1950), pp. 649–56.

25. Frederick E. Webster and Frederick von Pechmann, "A Replication of the 'Shopping List' Study," *Journal of Marketing* 34 (April 1970), pp. 61–63.

26. Daniel H. Pink, "Metaphor Marketing," *Fast Company* (April–May 1998), pp. 214–29.

27. Gerald Zaltman, "Metaphorically Speaking," *Marketing Research: A Magazine of Management and Applications* 8, no. 2 (Summer 1996), pp. 13–20; Gerald Zaltman and Robin Higie Coulter, "Seeing the Voice of the Customer: Metaphor-Based Advertising Research," *Journal of Advertising Research* 35, no. 4 (July–August 1995), pp. 35–51.

28. Ishmael P. Akaah, "Attitudes of Marketing Professionals Toward Ethics in Marketing Research: A Cross-National Comparison," *Journal of Business Ethics* 9 (January 1990), pp. 45–53; Ishmael P. Akaah and Edward A. Riordan, "Judgments of Marketing Professionals about Ethical Issues in Marketing Research: A Replication and Extension," *Journal of Marketing Research* 26 (February 1989), pp. 112–20; Joel N. Axelrod, "Observations: Politics and Poker: Deception and Self-Deception in Marketing Research," *Journal of Advertising Research* 32 (November–December 1992), pp. 79–82; Stephen B. Castleberry, Warren French, and Barbara A. Carlin, "The Ethical Framework of Advertising and Marketing Research Practitioner: A Moral Development Perspective," *Journal of Advertising* 22 (June 1993), pp. 39–46; Thomas Exter, "What's a Researcher to Do?" *American Demographics* 11 (February 1989), p. 8; Susan S. Jarvis, "Potential Malpractice Lawsuits: New Impetus for the Marketing Professional to Adopt Research Standards?" *Journal of Business & Industrial Marketing* 8 (1993), pp. 13–16; S. W. Kelley, O. C. Ferrell, and S. J. Skinner, "Ethical Behavior among Marketing Researchers: An Assessment of Selected Demographic Characteristics," *Journal of Business Ethics* (August 1990), pp. 681–88; Christine Moorman, Rohit Deshpandi, and Gerald Zaltman, "Factors Affecting Trust in Market Research Relationships," *Journal of Marketing* 57 (1993), pp. 81–101; Edward J. O'Boyle and Lyndon E. Dawson Jr., "The American Marketing Association Code of Ethics: Instructions for Marketers," *Journal of Business Ethics* 11 (December 1992), pp. 921–32.

29. Robert Restuccia and Linda Vaias, "Prescription Mining Raises Millions for Doctors' Group," *San Francisco Chronicle* (July 25, 2007), p. B9

30. Archie B. Carroll, "Ethical Challenges for Business in the New Millennium: Corporate Social Responsibility and Models of Management Morality," *Business Ethics Quarterly* (January 2000), pp. 33–42.

Segmentation, Targeting, and Positioning

LEARNING OBJECTIVES

- To grasp the limitations of adopting a mass-marketing strategy.
- To comprehend the concepts of segmentation, targeting, and positioning.
- To identify the major segmentation variables for dissecting markets.
- To explore the various market-targeting strategies.
- To determine criteria for an effective positioning strategy.
- To examine the tactic of repositioning.

KEY TERMS

mass-market strategy
market segmentation
market targeting
positioning
geographic segmentation
demographic segmentation
geodemographic segmentation
psychographic segmentation
AIO inventories
behavioral segmentation

market profile
undifferentiated strategy
multisegment strategy
concentration strategy
customization strategy
mass customization
personalization
perceptual map
repositioning

Marketers realize that in order to succeed in today's increasingly fragmented marketplace, they have to isolate key market segments and reach these segments with the maximum possible impact. Innovative programs such as the following attract customers, enhance customer retention levels, and increase business:

- In 2007, the Kimberly-Clark Corporation launched a Web site labeled *parentstages.com*, the first online network designed to enable parents to quickly access the best parenting information available on the Web. This site is designed to help moms and dads through the various stages of parenthood. The *parentstages.com* network is comprised of a number of leading online partners, including *ivillage.com*, *urbanbaby.com*, and *totalwoman.com*, among others.

  The site is a virtual compass that helps busy parents quickly navigate their way through the wealth of parenting information available on the Web. This service marks the first time a wide range of parenting information from independent unbiased sources has been gathered into a single site.

- One way that large-scale marketers like Kraft are going after consumers is through targeted messages via e-mail, Internet, or custom-publishing projects. Kraft, for example, publishes seven different custom magazines for seven different customer profiles, from empty-nesters to large families. The editorial content and recipes are tailored to those profiles, and the mailings are personalized so the recipient's name appears throughout.

Targeting strategies such as these have become common in today's marketplace. For Kimberly-Clark, the high cost of developing the database was offset by the benefits of identifying an important market segment—expectant mothers—to whom the company's products are promoted. In this manner, the image of Kimberly-Clark becomes firmly established in the minds of the soon-to-be mothers as an empathetic, competent provider of baby products and related services. In the case of Kraft, through the successful packaging and entertainment perspective, Kraft's *Food & Quality* magazine has become the number one return on investment (ROI) of any of the company's marketing initiatives.[1]

Today, more than ever, marketers recognize the importance of precision targeting. Many have established innovative programs designed to initiate relationships with prospective customers and lure them to the company's brand. Cite one such program you have participated in. How does this program work? Learn more about Kimberly-Clark's new initiative by visiting its Web site at www.parentstages.com. What types of information does the company provide to help parenting, even though many visitors to the site may not be customers of the company? Do you think its strategy is effective? Why or why not?

Marketers for Kimberly-Clark have established innovative programs designed to initiate relationships with prospective customers.

© 2009, Monkey Business Images, Shutterstock, Inc.

This chapter addresses the strategies of market segmentation, targeting, and positioning. It also delineates tactics that marketers employ to achieve their sales, market-share, and profit goals. The reality is that people possess different needs and wants and often perceive and act on their desires differently. Rarely do firms today claim that everyone is a prospect for their products or services.

Mass Marketing

In 1908, Henry Ford introduced the new Model-T automobile to the market. His concept was simple—use economies of scale to produce a standardized, low-priced automobile that could be purchased in any color the customer desired—as long at it was black. Demand for the Model-T was so great that consumers flocked to purchase the car.

As time passed, the Model-T suffered the consequences of inflexibility because Ford overemphasized standardization and uniformity. Ford's basic premise that customers have homogeneous preferences proved to be incorrect. Consumers' needs for automobiles began to shift toward heavier, closed-body cars that were more comfortable and more colorful. Ford's highly standardized operations, as well as its specialized workforce and facilities, made it difficult to respond to changing customer needs. However, its chief rival, General Motors, had the flexibility to respond quickly to evolving consumer needs by introducing new automobile designs, such as the 1923 Chevrolet, which embodied the innovative features consumers had come to desire. These designs helped General Motors enhance its market position against Ford's Model-T. As a consequence, in 1927 Ford closed down operations for an entire year, at enormous cost, in order to retool and introduce the revised Model-A.

It is clear that Ford, in his Model-T introduction, employed a **mass-market strategy**, a philosophy based on the assumption of a single, large, homogeneous marketplace with common needs. Focusing on these common needs, Ford introduced only one product to appeal to everyone in the market. Other companies that followed this same strategy have ranged from the early Coca-Cola Company, which originally sold Coke in its familiar 8-ounce green-glass bottle and in only one flavor, to the Bell System, which introduced the early rotary-dial black telephones.

mass-market strategy
a philosophy that presumes consumers are uniform and that broad-appeal products and marketing programs suffice

Today, however, traditional mass-market approaches aimed at building huge customer or client bases are frequently ineffective. Large groups of consumers are, in reality, heterogeneous, consisting of smaller, more homogenous subgroups with common demographic or lifestyle characteristics. Consequently, mass-marketing approaches have largely been replaced by strategies to match the product to the market.

SEGMENTING CONSUMER MARKETS

Three major steps are necessary and inseparable components of any successful product–market matching strategy. The first step is market segmentation. **Market segmentation** is the act of dissecting the overall marketplace into a

market segmentation
the act of dissecting the marketplace into submarkets that require different marketing mixes

EXHIBIT 3.1   **Components of a Market Matching Strategy**

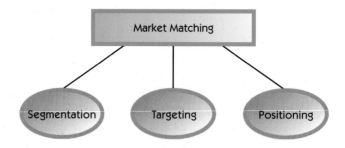

market targeting
the process of reviewing market segments and deciding which one(s) to pursue

positioning
establishing a differentiating image for a product or service in relation to that of the competition

number of submarkets that may require different products or services and thus can be approached with different marketing mixes. The second step is **market targeting**, which is the process of reviewing the segments that result from implementing the first step and deciding which one or ones the company can feasibly pursue. The selection of which market(s) to pursue is usually determined on the basis of a feasibility study, considering such things as a company's strengths and weakness, the opportunities and threats it faces, as well as a parallel analysis of the competition and overall industry trends. The third step is positioning. **Positioning** establishes an intended and differentiating image for a company's brand, product, or service. This image should communicate to the target segment(s) the uniqueness of the brand. These three steps are depicted in Exhibit 3.1.

Market Segmentation

By segmenting the market into a number of submarkets or *niches*, in which customers have distinct and somewhat similar needs, a marketer can determine which one or ones to target and accordingly design an appropriate marketing mix for serving and reaching each. For example, commercial airlines divide travelers into two major segments: business and leisure travelers. The first segment is characterized by interest in on-time departure and arrival, frequent daily flights, good service, and comfortable seats. Business travelers are less concerned about ticket prices and seldom purchase tickets in advance or remain at their destination over a weekend. Leisure travelers, on the other hand, are more interested in low-priced tickets than in precise departure or arrival times. This group usually purchases tickets in advance and remains at a destination over a weekend. Based on these differences, airlines have designed separate pricing structures for the two segments—a high price for the business traveler and a low price for the leisure traveler. Airlines promote these services differently to each segment, emphasizing those aspects that are important to each.

Market segmentation allows marketers to see clearly the diversity within their markets and uncover opportunities that may exist or segments whose needs have been poorly met by other offerings. For example, in the area of purchasing technology products, the technology consultant firm Forrester Research, Inc. has been surveying consumers annually since the late 1990s regarding their motivation, buying habits, and financial ability to purchase technology products.[2] Forrester's scheme separates people into ten categories that range from career-minded "Fast Forwards," who own an average of 20 technology products, to their less-affluent counterparts, the Techno-Strivers, who are at ease with technology, and use it at home, in the office, or for play. Other categories include "New Age Nurturers," who spend big sums on technology for home use and the "Hand-Shakers", the older and wealthy consumers who let younger assistants handle computers and other technology in the office. Such annual study has been of interest to many major companies such as Sprint, Visa, Ford, and Bank of America that started to use results of the study to identify products and services that these categories of consumers may be drawn to.[3]

In order for separate market segments to exist, there should be differences in the responses of the subgroups to product design, price, distribution, or promotion. If each subgroup were to respond in the same manner (for example, by purchasing products in the same amount or with the same frequency), then they would *not* be real market segments. Consumer research can determine likely sources of variation in consumer responses, and it is identifying the *response* that matters: Simply finding differences in consumers' characteristics is not enough.[4]

Marketers may opt to use one **segmentation variable** or several, whether geographic (location, climate), demographic (age, family life cycle, gender, race and ethnicity, occupation), geodemographic (consumer clusters and zip codes), psychographic (lifestyle, personality), or behavioral (usage rate, end benefits sought, brand and store loyalty). For example, a fashion firm may use differing climatic conditions between *geographic regions* as the sole segmentation variable. This clothing firm may offer a heavier and warmer garment line for consumers located in colder climate regions of the country and a lighter line for consumers in warmer regions. Alternatively, the firm may elect to employ additional segmentation variables such as *demographics* (offer separate fashion lines for men and for women), geodemographics (offer an expensive line of clothing directed to clusters of consumers residing in certain zip codes based on a scale of affluence), *psychographics* (offer sports lines for joggers, tennis players, and golfers), or *product-relevant behavior* (offer lines of formal and casual wear). Exhibit 3.2 depicts these five classes of segmentation variables, and the next sections cover each one in detail.

Segmenting Consumer Markets   EXHIBIT 3.2

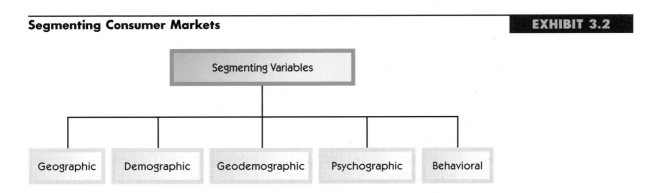

geographic segmentation

a partitioning of the market based on climate, location, surroundings, and terrain

When products are bought, used, or sold differently in various areas of the marketplace, it makes sense to use geography as a basis for market segmentation. Markets then are divided into subcategories such as regions, counties, cities, and towns that typically reflect varied consumer wants and product usage patterns.

Geographic dissimilarities between regions include climatic conditions, location, surroundings, distance, and terrain. These geographic differences precipitate the formation of different tastes, preferences, and activities among consumers residing in various parts of the marketplace. Marketers, in response, may need to develop separate marketing mixes to target consumers in diverse geographic sites. Many companies now *regionalize* their marketing programs and *localize* their products, as well as their advertising and selling efforts, in order to better suit the needs and preferences of individual regions, cities, and even neighborhoods. For example, S. C. Johnson & Son, maker of the Raid line of bug killers, has recently started using a geographic segmentation approach to market its line. The company promotes cockroach zappers in areas of heavy roach infestation such as Houston and New York, and flea sprays in flea-bitten cities such as Tampa and Birmingham.[5] This new segmentation strategy has led to an increase in Raid's market share in 16 out of 18 regions. It has also led to an increase of more than 5 percent in the company's market share in the $1 billion-per-year U.S. insecticide market.

When it comes to driving and preferences for vehicles, a greater percentage of consumers in the Southwest drive pickup trucks. More Northeasterners prefer vans, whereas Californians love high-priced imported cars such as BMWs and Mercedes-Benzes. Geography also appears to affect size preferences among car consumers. Whereas Texans like big cars, New Yorkers prefer more compact vehicles.

Advertisers on network television often run regional ad campaigns directed to consumers in different areas with their own unique tastes and preferences. Likewise, magazine and newspaper publishers often print different editions to accommodate the needs and interests of readers in diverse geographic areas. Many newspapers, for example, come in urban and suburban editions in order to carry news stories, editorials, and ads relevant to those readers who reside within a specific trading area. The ad in Figure 3.1 illustrates how *Parade*, a magazine inserted into hundreds of newspapers, enables advertisers to cover the national market or selected areas of the country.

DEMOGRAPHIC SEGMENTATION

demographic segmentation

a partitioning of the market based on factors such as age, gender, income, occupation, education, and ethnicity

Demographics are the most common basis for segmenting consumer markets. Marketers' preference for using demographic data to segment markets rests on the relative ease of measuring them as well as their close link to demand for many products and services. Demographic variables such as age, stage in the family life cycle, gender, income, occupation, education, religion, nationality, and race are commonly used by marketers because they usually correlate with

With Parade, you can cover the entire United States or just some of it.

As a marketer, Parade offers you the ability to custom-make your market. Whether it's metro areas, rural areas, the Corn Belt, Snow Belt or growth areas, Parade gives you a choice of any, or all, of over 300 markets. So no matter who you're trying to reach, you can dress your media plan accordingly.

PARADE
81 million readers in just 48 hours.

Figure 3.1

Today many newspaper and magazine publishers realize the importance of covering news and events relevant to local publics. In this ad, Parade magazine emphasizes its custom design, enabling it to serve the needs of both national and local advertisers.
(Created by Warwick Baker O'Neill for PARADE Magazine. Reprinted with permission of Parade Publications.)

consumer preferences, needs, and usage rates. For example, gender is an important segmentation variable in the case of clothing, cosmetics, skin-care products, and hair-coloring products. Similarly, stage in the family life cycle is important in determining the need for housing, furniture, appliances, children's products and services, and electronic gadgets.

Another reason for the value of demographic variables as a basis for market segmentation is the wealth of demographic data available from numerous sources, including the U.S. Census Bureau and various commercial and noncommercial entities such as Simmons Market Research and Donnelley Demographics. Demographic data are easily acquired and quite simple to use.

Age

Because consumer capabilities and wants change with age, age can be a significant segmentation tool for many firms. Crayola Company, which typically caters crayons toward 4- to 8-year-old children, has recently discovered a significant potential market consisting of girls between the ages of 8 and 12.[6] The company introduced a line of six do-it-yourself boutique-style jewelry kits called *Jazzy Jewelry*. Crayola executives felt that this product line extension was needed because jewelry has become a booming field, with girls becoming sophisticated at a younger age. Kellogg is another company that targets children. Cereals such as Fruit Loops, Apple Jacks, Honey Smacks, Fruity Marshmallow Krispies, Coco Krispies, and Cinnamon Mini-Buns are targeted for children.

In This Fight, Barbie Isn't the Winner

In marketing its toys internationally, Mattel appears to have misread the cultural values and traditions of Middle Eastern families. In her almost 50 years of existence, Barbie, Mattel's busty plastic doll with its outfit for every mood, has seen great success in most countries of the world. But one thing the blonde beauty was unable to do was to be considerate of the Muslim values and traditions that prevail in many parts of the Middle East and Asia.

Into her place now has stepped Fulla, a doll basically built on the same chassis as Barbie. Fulla has black hair, auburn-colored eyes, and a wide selection of head scarves. She even comes with her own prayer rug.

The doll has become a marketing phenomenon from Morocco to Iraq to Saudi Arabia. Since its launch in 2003, it has taken over the display shelves in toy stores in the Middle East and replaced, to a great extent, its American rival.

Fulla was the brainchild of a Syrian entrepreneur, who, like Mattel, is having the doll mass produced in China. The two dolls are made from the same materials, and are the same height, 11.5 inches. The only change that differentiated the two dolls was to flatten out Barbie's chest. Unlike Barbie's fashionable flair, Fulla is dressed in a full head-to-toe *abaya*. However, she—like Barbie—has a range of outfits and fashion accessories at her disposal. There are no bare arms, legs, or cleavage—nothing except the black *abaya* and another outfit featuring a white head scarf. Fulla has no male friends, but her creators added a protective brother doll in 2006.

Toy store operators in the Middle East say that Fulla is so popular among families there that they cannot keep up with the demand. It is outselling her rival Barbie by a 40-to-1 margin. The success of Fulla is merely a reflection of the fact that the values that Barbie conveys are not the ones that Muslim parents want to instill in their kids. All of this represents quite a lesson to be learned by producers who want to globally market their products.[7]

Although many U.S. Products find their way to foreign markets, manufacturers need to be cognizant of cultural differences not only in environmental, physical, and legal standards, but also of differing values and traditions that prevail in these foreign countries. Learn more about Mattel American Toy Company by visiting the Web site www.encyclocentral.com/12538Mattel_American_Toy_Company.html. Also learn about foreign cultures by visiting the University of Virginia Faculty Experts Guide at www.virginia.edu/facultyexperts/?root_id=1173 In your opinion, why should designers of toys or other products adjust their specifications to each country's standards? Would the costs of such adjustments justify the objective of enhancing product exports?

However, the company also produces other cereals for adults, such as All-Bran, Special K, Fiberwise, and Product 19 as well as smart start.

Harley-Davidson also recognizes that age plays an important role in identifying its market. The median age of a Harley customer is 47 years. Seven years ago, it was 43. Ever more accountants, physicians, and engineers are now entering the ranks of the Harley Owner Group (HOG) in larger numbers.[8] Similarly, when General Nutrition Company discovered that 30 percent of U.S. consumers age 35 and over take vitamins regularly, it opened a chain of natural food and vitamin stores to capitalize on this market segment. Coca-Cola's Sprite team created the The Sprite Yard—a mobile social network primarily directed to teenage and young adult audiences that allows them to share content, pictures, messages, and calendars with their friends as well as immediately redeem codes found on bottle caps for content on their phones.[9]

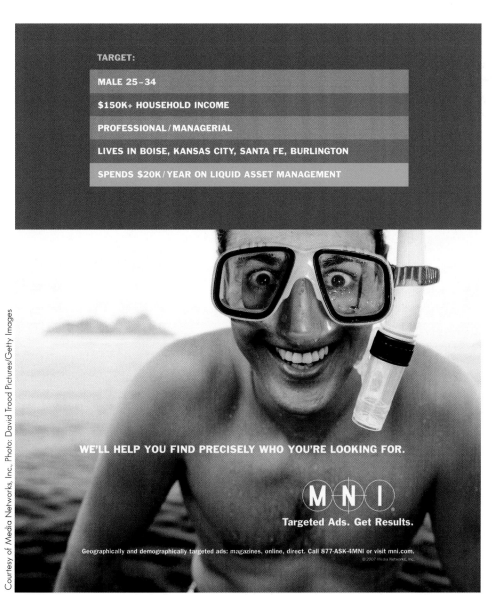

Courtesy of Media Networks, Inc., Photo: David Trood Pictures/Getty Images

Figure 3.2
Today, many advertisers realize the importance of specifically reaching their target market rather than wasting advertising dollars on non-prospects. In this ad, MNI emphasizes its services that enable advertisers to reach precisely whom they are looking for

In recent years, more and more companies have been targeting the baby boomers (born between 1946 and 1965). Since January 1, 1996, members of this group have been turning 50 years of age at the rate of 10,000 a day. Companies that offer financial services, leisure goods, pharmaceuticals, and preventative health care products and services are finding lucrative opportunities in this segment. The ad in Figure 3.2 informs prospective clients how MNI, a targeted-advertising agency, enables advertisers to reach precisely the type of consumer they are looking for.

Family Life Cycle

Stages of the family life cycle (a series of life phases that most families go through starting with young single individuals and ending with sole surviving spouses) present another demographic segmentation variable. Each stage of the cycle brings changes that, in turn, affect the family's needs, resources, and expenditure patterns. Many hotel chains, such as Hilton, Hyatt, Marriott, and Westin, have had to rethink their pitch to customers based on this segmentation variable. Many two-career couples, with or without children, are unable to take long trips because of their jobs or their children's schooling. In order to capitalize on their needs, business hotels in downtown areas designed brief weekend escapes for families where Internet access, pay-per-view movies, fitness centers, and diverse dining options are available. These hotels have started offering discounted weekend rates and allow children to stay in their parents' room free of charge. Packages are supplemented with amenities and services including special children's menus, cribs, bed rails, video games, and even flame-proof bathrobes for kids.[10]

The singles market is another significant life cycle segment. Defined as over 25 years old and divorced, widowed, or never married, this group represents a major market for many products and services. Great Expectations, the largest video dating service in the United States, successfully tapped this market and built a $80 million business with over 100,000 members. This segment is also of prime importance for such diverse products and services as fast foods, apartments and condominiums, entertainment, bars, and liquor.

Changes in the composition of families in the United States and the emergence of nontraditional families such as single-parent households have created new market segments. These segments have become an important targeting focus for support groups such as Parents Without Partners and child-care firms such as Kinder-Care Learning Centers.

A more complete discussion of the family life cycle, as well as various age groupings that are meaningful to marketers, is presented in Chapter 12. The ad in Figure 3.3 illustrates how G + J offers magazines for women of all ages—teens, expectant and new moms, home enthusiasts, and household decision makers.

Gender

Gender is also used as a basis for segmentation for a variety of products and services ranging from cigarettes to cosmetics. For example, a number of cigarette companies target women through brands that include Virginia Slims, More, Dawn, Capri, Superslims, Chelsa, and Eve Ultra Light 120s. In the diet field, companies such as Weight Watchers' Healthy Choice, Stouffers' Lean Cuisine, and Kraft emerged with a broad line of low-calorie foods that to a large degree are targeted to women. Diet centers, such as Jenny Craig and NutriSystem, also benefit by appealing directly to women.[11] Cosmetic companies have also been in the forefront of gender-based segmentation, offering preparations specifically formulated for men and for women.

Likewise, some pharmaceutical companies have found gender segmentation valuable in creating new market opportunities. A number of years ago, Pfizer Pharmaceuticals introduced Viagra to treat impotence, a sexual dysfunc-

Figure 3.3
Because needs, resources, and consumption patterns change as people pass through successive stages of the family life cycle, marketers can successfully use this concept to market products and services designed specifically for consumers at particular stages. In this ad, G + J offers a magazine for every stage of a woman's life.

tion that affects millions of men. Also, a large number of pharmaceutical companies produce and sell over 40 brands of oral contraceptives as well as infertility drugs to women.

Race and Ethnicity

The sheer size and purchasing power of the growing base of Hispanic-American, African-American, and Asian-American minorities make these groups rich frontiers for U.S. marketers who use race and ethnicity to segment markets. Minorities tend to favor products and media vehicles that are geared toward them. Merely translating the English copy of an advertising campaign into another language or replacing the image of a white model with an ethnic stand-in has insufficient appeal.

Products and services targeted on ethnic bases range from clothing and cosmetics to foods. JCPenney, for example, caters directly to African Americans by carrying merchandise such as African-styled clothing. Most telephone companies, banks, and large retailers, as well as many government offices today cater to various ethnic groups by employing operators who speak the same languages as callers. Magazine and newspaper publishers cater directly to ethnic groups through newspapers and magazines that reflect their experience and speak to them in a relevant way. Cosmetic companies produce beauty aids and hair-care products that fit the skin tones and hair features of each market segment. Supermarket chains adjust the product mix that each of their stores carry, based on the ethnic makeup of the trading area in which the store operates.

Occupation

Education, occupation, and income tend to be closely related, so much so that they are frequently used together as a composite index of an individual's or household's social class. Despite the high correlation of these three, some companies segment their market based on occupation alone in the belief that it is a more important determinant of consumer behavior than income. Occupational breakdowns include a large number of categories, ranging from professional and technical workers to homemakers.

InterPage, a U.S. fax company offering e-mail, fax, voice, and paper messaging on the Internet, has seized a large chunk of the enhanced messaging system from its major competitors by employing an occupational profile of paging systems users.[12] Among the primary user groups are hospitals and clinics (doctors, nurses, patients), nursing homes, hotels, government offices, military installations, restaurants, multi-departmented corporations, small-business owners, salespeople, and other professionals such as lawyers, who needed to be in contact with their home offices. InterPage proceeded to target each user group separately with models of wireless messaging solutions that each specific customer segment would likely prefer. In so doing, the company gained a competitive edge and succeeded in capturing a larger market share from its competitors.[13]

GEODEMOGRAPHIC SEGMENTATION

geodemographic segmentation
a partitioning of the market by considering data on neighborhoods, zip codes, or census tracts

Blending geography and demographics has led to the formation of a new technique known as **geodemographic segmentation**.[14] This technique is designed to explain and predict behavior by using typologies;—that is, by placing consumers into categories whose members are assumed to behave similarly. Geodemographic cluster systems sort U.S. neighborhoods on the basis of their income, educational attainment, occupation, home ownership rate, family type, age grouping, and other characteristics. These systems have proven successful in store-location analyses, directing advertising media buys, locating pockets of prospects for a product or service, and providing direct marketers with a highly effective tool for precision targeting.

The 1980s and early 1990s saw the proliferation of large, data-rich household databases developed by the direct-marketing industry. The U.S. Census also provides data on census tracts or block groups. Research firms such as Nielsen Claritas blend the two to create a cluster system in which consumer categories could be assigned to small units of geography, such as Zip code, Zip + 4, or census tract and block group. The assumption is that "birds of a feather flock together." In other words, people who live within the same neighborhood tend to be much alike and buy the same types of products and services. Based on this assumption, a Zip code can classify individuals according to their tastes. Exhibit 3.3 shows a map that uses geodemographics for segmentation purposes.

PRIZM

One of the earliest efforts in geodemographics is PRIZM (Potential Rating Index by ZIP Market), originally developed in 1974 by Claritas Inc., now Nielsen Claritas. This geodemographic taxonomy of U.S. consumers has become one of marketers' favorite tools for locating prospects.[15]

To develop its PRIZM system, Nielsen Claritas used a combination of census data and information generated by everything from car warranties to

EXHIBIT 3.3

Zip PRIZM Cluster Assignments—Louisville, KY.

This map from Nielsen Claritas depicts the categories of people who occupy various census tracts and block groups in a large metropolitan area. Courtesy of Nielsen Claritas.

Louisville, KY: S. Hancock St. & E Market St.
5 and 10 Mile Radii Showing Dominant PRIZM Cluster by ZIP Code

Dominant PRIZMne Cluster by ZIP Code

- 03 - Movers & Shakers
- 05 - Country Squires
- 09 - Big Fish, Small Pond
- 10 - Second City Elite
- 11 - God's Country
- 15 - Pools & Patios
- 19 - Home Sweet Home
- 20 - Fast-Track Families
- 23 - Greenbelt Sports
- 25 - Country Casuals
- 27 - Middleburg Managers
- 30 - Suburban Sprawl
- 33 - Big Sky Families
- 36 - Blue-Chip Blues
- 37 - Mayberry-ville
- 39 - Domestic Duos
- 46 - New Beginnings
- 49 - American Classics
- 51 - Shotguns & Pickups
- 52 - Suburban Pioneers
- 53 - Mobility Blues
- 54 - Multi-Culti Mosaic
- 59 - Urban Elders
- 61 - City Roots
- 65 - Big City Blues

grocery-store reward cards. The company characterized 66 distinct types of U.S. households. These household types are assigned colorful and distinctive labels, such as "Young Digerati," another called "Up-and-Comers," as well as "Country Comfort" and "Shotguns and Pickups." For example, ZIP codes classified as "Young Digerati" are the dual-income couples who live in chic condos in the most-fashionable urban areas, whereas "Up-and-Comers" are the recent college graduates hoping to jump-start their careers while still enjoying their free time.

These segments include not only basic demographics as age and household income, but also capture everything from where people buy their clothes to which magazines they read. Through this system, both marketers and consumers can learn just about everything they need to know about a city or a neighborhood. Home buyers, for example, can find helpful information ranging from house values to school ratings. Marketers, on the other hand, can construct a precise profile of consumers in a category. The category "Country Comfort," for instance, is characterized by consumers who prefer trucks, SUVs, and minivans to cars, and are active in home-based activities such as gardening, woodworking, and crafts. Members of the "Shotguns and Pickups" cluster, meanwhile, drive pick-up trucks and often own hunting rifles. Nearly one-third of these individuals live in mobile homes.[16]

A number of other companies in addition to Nielsen Claritas provide similar segmentation and targeting tools. Among them are **CACI** and **ACORN** systems, and ESRI Business Information Solution's **Community Tapestry**. This latter system, for example, provides detailed descriptions of American neighborhoods and divides U.S. residential areas into 65 segments based on demographic variables such as age, income, home value, occupation, household type, education, and other consumer behavior characteristics. The tapestry segments are organized into 12 **LifeMode** Summary Groups that are characterized with similar demographics and consumption patterns, as well as into 11 **Urbanization** Summary Groups with similar levels of density. Neighborhoods with the most similar characteristics are grouped together, while neighborhoods showing divergent characteristics are separated.

The PRIZM system assigns colorful labels to describe household types. "Up-and-comers" are recent college graduates hoping to jump-start their careers while still enjoying their free time.

© 2009, Emiliano Rodriguez, Shutterstock, Inc.

Another tool in the segmentation and targeting arena is the **PersonicX** household-level segmentation system, developed by **Acxiom**. It provides marketers and advertiser with a detailed profile of prospects at the household level. The system groups consumers into 70 clusters and 21 life-stage groups based on several factors, such as media preferences, shopping patterns, and financial standing. Titles assigned to such groups include "*Trucks & Trailers*," "*Country Ways*," "*Humble Homes*," and "*Apple Pie Families*." Such names profile each segment's lifestyle characteristics. The *Trucks & Trailers* segment, for example, represents people between the ages of 30 and 45, either married or single with no children, who own or rent, have annual household income of less than

$100,000, and live in rural areas. In its updated form, PersonicX now enables marketers to reach targeted segments both on and offline, thereby helping to hone their value strategies and promotional tactics.[17]

Examples of How One System (PRIZM) Has Been Used

By matching up its PRIZM clusters with information from other databases, Nielsen Claritas can tell its clients where their customers reside. For example, for a dog food company, Nielsen Claritas was able to determine that dog ownership was highest among *Kids and Cul-de-Sacs* and *God's Country* clusters, and to show the client which ZIP codes, census tracts, or blocks in the entire nation were characterized by these lifestyles.

In addition to the clustering system, PRIZM also provides consumption indices for a variety of product categories. The higher an area's consumption index number, the greater is its market potential for a specific type of product. For example, PRIZM publishes a market potential index for luxury cars.[18] Compared to the national average (for which the index equals 100), different areas of the country are categorized into five classes according to their sales potential. Areas with *high* sales potential are those with an index of 201 or more. Areas with *above-average* potential have a minimum index of 169. Areas with an index of at least 103 are designated as offering *average* potential. Areas with an index of 94 or less are considered *below average* and those with an index of 45 or less are regarded as offering *poor* potential.

A broad range of companies use PRIZM. Some merge it with their own internal databases or research to understand their markets better. BMW of North America has used Nielsen Claritas' marketing data for the purposes of site locations, market analysis, and sales performance analysis of the dealerships in its retail network. Similarly, AOL utilized PRIZM demographic segmentation as a core baseline for analyzing broad-based audience behaviors. By segmenting the audience in this manner, AOL was able to identify which segments used newer, emerging technologies with greater frequency. As a result, the company was able to apply the "emerging behaviors" as a filter to further identify its most valuable market segments.[19]

The number of companies keeping databases of individual consumers has exploded. Today, sophisticated computer programs used by marketers can combine information from several databases and put together a detailed picture of specific households or individuals. Similarly, supermarket checkout scanners enable many marketers to track the success of their products in the marketplace. Some experts believe that the future lies with technologies that count real people and actual purchases.[20]

PSYCHOGRAPHIC SEGMENTATION

Although age, family life cycle, gender, occupation, and other demographic variables are usually helpful in developing segmentation strategies, they often fail to paint a precise picture of different market segments. For example, there is little correlation between demographics and such things as consumer desire to travel, propensity for moviegoing, preferences for music, enthusiasm for sports, choice of investment opportunities, and affinity for smoking and drinking. These tendencies can, however, be explained through **psychographic segmentation**, which is the partitioning of the market based on consumers' lifestyle and personality characteristics.[22]

Psychographic profiles, descriptive sketches of individuals' lifestyles, are commonly obtained by having people respond to a battery of statements designed to reveal their Activities, Interests, and Opinions, hence the name **AIO inventories**. For example, an AIO inventory may include statements such as "I'd rather spend a quiet evening at home than go out to a party" and "I'd feel lost if I were alone in a foreign country." Respondents indicate how strongly they agree or disagree with each statement, usually on a six-point scale. Responses are then cluster analyzed, and results are cross-tabulated with a particular purchasing behavior of interest to the researcher. For example, a psychographic study may correlate ownership of foreign automobiles or interest in certain magazines to specific personality traits.

Today, a number of companies are using a new technique in this field known as *attitudinal data framing*. For example, CUNA Mutual Group, a financial services firm, uses this technique by mining its computer database to search for the motivations that triggered the purchase of financial products made by the company's investors. In other words, the company attempts to discover how and why its customers arrived at their purchase decisions.[23]

Several years ago, Gaines, formerly a pet foods division of General Foods, conducted a psychographic study of dog owners to classify households according to how they felt about their pets and to tie these feelings to the type of food a household's pets were fed most often.[24] In this investigation, five psychographic types of dog owners were identified. *Functionalist* owners, who kept a dog as a means of self or property protection, accounted for approximately 40 percent of the dog owners. These individuals showed little attachment to their dogs. *Family Mutt* owners, whose dogs served as pets for their children, represented about 25 percent and showed just somewhat more interest in their dogs. *Baby Substitute* owners, for whom a dog took the place of a child or a spouse, accounted for about 10 percent. They showed above-average attachment to their dog. *Nutritionalist* owners, such as breeders and consumers who were themselves diet conscious, accounted for about 13 percent and were very personally attached to their dogs. Finally, *Middle of the Road* owners, about 12 percent of dog owners, showed no distinctive characteristics.

Gaines found strong correlations between these psychographic categories and use of commercial dog food products. Members of the Baby Substitute and Nutritionalist categories bought the least amount of commercial dog food, whereas members of the Functionalist group bought the most. Because of their high degree of attachment to their dogs, Baby Substitutes and Nutritionalists were heavily involved in the choice of dog food, were least concerned about its cost, and displayed high interest in the quality and taste of the dog food. Gaines was able to introduce a line of premium priced and high-quality dog foods to suit the idiosyncrasies and preferences of the Baby Substitute and Nutritionalist segments.

Consumer Behavior in Practice

"Go On, Cut. You'll Be Brilliant"

Armstrong World Industries is a leader in the floor covering market and has successfully positioned its sheet-vinyl floor covering in the do-it-yourself (DIY) market. Originally, the company had observed that shoppers, after examining Armstrong's in-store displays, walked away without purchasing the product. Research revealed that although women generally drive the purchase decision in the DIY market, men are usually the ones left with the actual chore of installation. Armstrong also learned that fear of making the first cut is the major stumbling block against a purchase. Nearly 60 percent of the do-it-yourselfers cited fear of botching the job when they attempted to install the sheet-vinyl floor the first time.

Armstrong set out to combat this problem with a campaign that made a fail-safe promise to beginners: Make a mistake, and the company replaces the floor covering at no cost. Thus, the "Go on, cut. You'll be brilliant" campaign was born. Along with it, the company provided a *Trim and Fit* kit to help beginners do the job right the first time. The campaign was supplemented with point-of-purchase materials, permanent and temporary displays, and a toll-free number to provide beginners with installation tips.

The campaign was overwhelmingly successful. The biggest barrier to the purchase of the product had been substantially removed. Beginners were assured that even if they were to make a mistake, they would not have to pay for it. There was simply nothing to lose, so why not go ahead and do it?

Armstrong achieved a strong position in the DIY market because the company understood and empathized with the segment it targeted and spoke the language its prospects understood.[21]

The do-it-yourself market has grown substantially in the United States during the past two decades. To what underlying causes do you attribute this growth? Visit the Web site of Armstrong World Industries, Inc. at www.armstrong.com. What tactics does this company use to attract do-it-yourselfers? Also visit www.doityourself.com. Determine what types of projects are most likely to be popular among do-it-yourselfers. In your opinion, do any specific demographic or lifestyle traits characterize do-it-yourselfers or differentiate them from those who prefer to purchase already-complete, ready-to-use items?

One of the best-known and most widely used psychographic segmentation systems is VALS, developed by California-based SRI International. The VALS program is based on the assumption that people buy products and services and seek experience that can fulfill their preferences and give shape, substance, and satisfaction to their lives.[25] The current VALS program devises a system for placing consumers into one of eight clusters based on primary motivation and resources/innovation. It is presented in detail in Chapter 8, which deals with personality, lifestyle, and self-concept.

BEHAVIORAL SEGMENTATION

A final method used to segment the marketplace for products and services is **behavioral segmentation**. According to this method, buyers are divided into subgroups based on their attitude toward, usage of, commitment to, or reaction to a product. Identifying market segments based on actual product-related buyer behaviors, such as usage rate, benefits sought, brand and store loyalty, and

behavioral segmentation
a partitioning of the market based on attitudes toward or reaction to a product

marketing tactic sensitivity, is a suitable starting point for delineating market segments.

Usage Rate

Usage rate refers to the frequency or quantity in which consumers buy or use a particular product or service. For many products and services, a mere 20 percent of users account for approximately 80 percent of total product or service sales. This phenomenon is so common that it has become known as the *80–20 principle*.

Every product or service category has its users and nonusers. For marketers, it is critical to identify those within the total marketplace who belong to each group. Ameritech segments its service customers in order to pinpoint those who contribute most to the firm's profitability. By profiling heavy and light users, Ameritech is able to focus primarily on the first group through various price promotions and special service deals. Similarly, airlines, car rental companies, and hotels attempt to lure frequent business travelers, who constitute the heavy users of their services, via upgrades, discounts, and frequent-flier programs.

To attract nonusers, firms often rely on sales promotion in various forms such as product samples, coupons, rebates, bonus-size packages, premiums, and outright price reductions. Weight Watchers, for example, created a program called *Winners* through which new members can accumulate points redeemable for products such as sweatshirts, mugs, beach towels, coolers, and director's chairs. The more Weight Watchers' products and services purchased, the more points participants earn.[26]

Benefits Sought

Because different people seek different benefits from the same product or service, it is possible for marketers to use the benefits sought variable as a basis for segmenting the marketplace.[27]

Pharmaceutical companies often segment consumers on the basis of the benefits sought from medicine. Aspirin users take this medication to treat a wide range of ailments including headaches, muscular aches and pains, colds and flu, fevers, heart conditions, and menstrual syndromes. Other persons whose digestive systems are sensitive to aspirin turn to Tylenol (which contains acetaminophen, an aspirin substitute) in order to achieve pain relief without stomach irritation.

The success of online shopping versus shopping at traditional brick-and-mortar stores is largely based on the benefit of convenience to consumers. Toothpaste users seek to fight cavities, to whiten and brighten teeth, to freshen their breath, or even to prevent gum disease. Thus, the benefits that people seek when consuming a given product become the primary basis for segmenting the market.

Brand and Store Loyalty

Brand and store loyalty can also be means to segment the market. Brand loyalty is the tendency of some consumers to repeatedly select the same brand within a given product category. Store loyalty is a parallel tendency of some consumers to repeatedly patronize a particular retail establishment. To promote this tendency, many stores either offer preferred-customer cards or store credit cards to encourage customers to frequent the store. Brand loyalty may also lead to store loyalty, because consumers may prefer to patronize retail outlets that carry a particular brand of product. For example, consumers who like *Craftsman* tools must buy them at Sears, because the retailer's private brand of tools is not sold elsewhere.

Consumers can be classified as loyal or nonloyal, and even among loyal customers, the degree of loyalty varies. Consumers who are brand or store loyal in one product or service category might not be in another category, and their usual loyalties may lessen when competitors offer attractive incentives and inducements to switch brands via sales promotion. For marketers, recognizing such variations is helpful in adopting strategies to enhance loyalty. For example, to build loyalty, marketers have initiated frequent-shopper programs that entice and reward customers with financial contributions to retirement accounts, credits toward college tuition, and free travel.[28]

Marketing Tactic Sensitivity

Just as some consumers are more or less loyal to particular product brands, others are more responsive to certain marketing tactics. Some consumers, for example, are very price conscious, whereas others react primarily to perceived product quality. Still others respond to coupons, customer service, salespersons, advertising appeals, or word of mouth from their peers.

Many major retailers such as Sears sponsor store brands (like Kenmore or Craftsman) that offer value comparable to manufacturers' brands but sell for less in order to attract price-sensitive customers. Marketers of many food, beverage, and personal products offer sales promotion inducements such as coupons, rebates, bonus-size containers, "price-off promotions" and similar methods to lure value-conscious shoppers. Full-service department stores, such as Nordstrom and Macy's, employ salespersons on the selling floor who personally wait on customers. Such retailers also offer a wide spectrum of customer services such as personal shoppers, special orders, liberal exchange policies, delivery, gift wrapping, and nicely decorated waiting areas, in order to attract and keep those customers who are sensitive to in-store experiences.

Advertisers attempt to appeal to relevant buying motives in ads and commercials. Promoters of items such as baby products and life insurance, for example, frequently appeal to consumers' emotional buying motives through themes that emphasize the need to care for loved ones. Auto manufacturers such as Toyota and Honda target customers with appeals that express concern for the environment. Other car companies such as Mercedes-Benz, Jaguar, and Cadillac use status-related motives as the main focus for status seekers. Still others such as Volvo have employed feature-quality themes to appeal to drivers' safety concerns. The Bentley Continental GT automobile, depicted in Figure 3.4, emphasizes elegance and distinction, together with speed and security.

Market Targeting

So far, we have focused on the market segmentation process. Once this first analytical stage is complete, a portrait of the marketplace emerges. Called a **market profile**, this portrait includes the number of segments that exist within the larger market and outlines the characteristics and motivations of people or organizations within it, as well as competitors' positions relative to the specific product of interest.

Once the firm has profiled its market-segment opportunities, marketing managers have to evaluate the various segments and decide how many and which ones to target. Because companies vary in their size, financial resources, technical know-how, and marketing capability, they seek the best possible match between their characteristics and the desires and preferences of particular market segments. Whereas some firms with vast production facilities and capital strength, such as auto companies, can pursue a number of market segments at the same time, others that lack financing or other resources prefer to focus on a single segment.

There are four basic types of market-targeting strategies: (1) the undifferentiated strategy, (2) the multisegment strategy, (3) the concentration strategy, and (4) the customization strategy.

UNDIFFERENTIATED STRATEGY

A firm following an **undifferentiated strategy** essentially views the market as a single large domain with no individual segments. An undifferentiated approach is a *postage-stamp* strategy, meaning that the product is identical for

market profile
a portrait of the various market segments and competitors' positions in them relative to a specific product

undifferentiated strategy
a view that the market is a single large domain and that one marketing mix suffices

everyone far and near. Companies that follow this strategy assume that individual consumers have similar needs that can be met with a single marketing mix. An undifferentiated approach is feasible in the case of homogeneous product commodities, such as sugar, salt, rice, wheat, corn, and some categories of farm produce. Argo cornstarch, for example, uses an undifferentiated strategy and directs its product to the total market.

As we saw earlier in this chapter, companies employ this strategy when the product is relatively new to the marketplace and competition is minimal. The Hershey Company's first chocolate bar or the pioneering companies that produced the original white facial and bathroom tissues are but some examples of firms that have employed undifferentiated targeting. Advantages of this strategy mainly relate to savings in production and marketing costs due to standardization. An undifferentiated approach often makes good economic sense.

Ethical Dilemma

St. Ides . . . May Not Be Holy After All

Many corporations find it lucrative to target minorities such as African Americans and Latinos for a variety of products such as hard liquor, beer, and cigarettes. African Americans constitute a powerful consumer force that spends more than $960 billion a year on goods and services. Consequently, some companies within the alcohol industry pursue this segment with vigor. Marketing strategies have included endorsements by popular entertainment artists (Billy Dee Williams, Ice Cube), co-optation of popular culture music genres (rap music), donations to visible groups (African American Congressional Caucus), ads in African-American magazines (*Essence, Ebony, Jet*), and sponsorship of cultural events (Juneteenth celebration).

Millions of alcohol industry dollars are allotted annually to the goal of permeating the African-American market segment through products designed specifically for it. Recently, a controversial product, St. Ides, was targeted to African Americans. St. Ides is a malt liquor with the highest alcohol content of any mass-produced beer (8 percent of volume). Gangsta rap performers such as RUN-DMC and NWA have made the image of the 40-ounce St. Ides malt liquor bottle a popular symbol of masculinity. Other recording artists such as Ice Cube and King Tee promote St. Ides by proposing the 40-ounce container as a *single serving*. Posters depicting the artists

displaying a hand gesture with street-gang symbolism are also used in the St. Ides campaign.

Unfortunately, these tactics, which have proven successful, take full advantage of vulnerabilities within the African-American community. Department of Health and Human Services figures show a consistent year-to-year decrease in the life expectancy for African Americans. For example, African-American males have a higher incidence than whites of cirrhosis of the liver and cancer of the esophagus, both linked to alcohol consumption.[29]

Many marketers design and promote brands of products and services specifically for the increasing minority population. Critics of this practice argue that because minorities are part of the larger marketplace, their product and service needs are no different from those of other consumers. Thus, there is no need for differentiation. Such tactics, they claim, are merely a marketing ploy. With which opinion do you agree? Why? Visit the Web site of St. Ides at www.hiphop-elements.com/pv/2196/. What appeals does the company currently use in its commercials to promote its products? Do these appeals appear to target a specific market segment(s)? Are there any ethical ramifications of these efforts?

The combined impact of economies of scale and the benefits of workers' accumulated experience can produce significant reductions in unit costs.

In many instances, however, undifferentiated targeting emerges by default rather than by design. Companies continue to follow this strategy even after the market expands and competition intensifies. The result is often a stagnant and impotent product offering that commands little appeal. The firm then becomes vulnerable to competitive inroads and can easily lose its dominant market position. For example, Pepsi-Cola was able to capture a large market share from Coca-Cola when it offered different sizes of containers to the market in the late 1950s. Coca-Cola, realizing its failure to recognize the need for a multisegment strategy, followed Pepsi's lead and introduced different sizes and flavors. In so doing, Coca-Cola not only matched but surpassed Pepsi in introducing new flavors and sizes—a strategy that allowed Coca-Cola to regain its leadership position in the industry. The Coca-Cola ad in Figure 3.5 uses the brand's universal reputation to appeal to all types of soft drink consumers.

Figure 3.5

The Coca-Cola Company used an undifferentiated strategy when the product first appeared on the market. To some extent, the symbols employed in this current ad reiterate the original undifferentiated strategy.

MULTISEGMENT STRATEGY

A **multisegment strategy** entails serving two or more segments and developing marketing mixes to suit the needs of each. For instance, each of General Motors' brands, such as Chevrolet, Pontiac, Buick, Oldsmobile, and Cadillac, is designed to be targeted specifically to a particular market segment. In this case, all marketing mix elements—including the product, distribution, price, and promotion—are adjusted to match the characteristics of each targeted segment. Whereas the Chevrolet is designed to appeal to the budget-minded automobile buyer, GM's Cadillac line is targeted to upscale customers. Apple also employs a multisegment strategy for many of its new technologies such as *i*Phones and *i*Pods. The company analyzes ownership and market potential for all its electronic products among adults and teens. The survey measures household penetration of these technologies among these two groups, and goes further to quantify the purchasing intentions of each.[30]

Firms that follow a multisegment strategy serve a number of different market segments and offer a diversified product line. Market risk is low, because sales declines or losses in some segments are usually cushioned by profits realized in others. However, although a multisegment strategy can generate high sales and reduce market risk, it is accompanied by significant increases in the cost of doing business. To meet the requirements of dissimilar market segments, products have to be modified, which results in higher research and development, engineering, and tooling costs. Smaller production runs of each separate model mean higher costs per unit of output. Administrative costs of managing a diversified line escalate, and promotional expenses incurred to reach diverse market segments mount up.

On the other hand, the unique product features designed specifically to appeal to the peculiarities of each market segment allow the firm to charge higher selling prices. For example, when Apple recently introduced the *i*Phone, the company decided to charge a premium price.[31] Similarly, General Motors charges a higher price for a Cadillac than for a Chevy.

> **multisegment strategy**
> a view that the market consists of multiple segments, and each requires its own marketing mix

CONCENTRATION STRATEGY

A **concentration strategy** focuses marketing effort on one segment of a larger market and develops products and marketing programs tailored specifically to the needs and preferences of that segment. . . . For example, the King Size Company, a leading online retailer of big and tall fashions for men, caters specifically to the larger male.[32] The company realizes that millions of men in the United States weigh significantly more than their ideal body weight, enough potential customers to warrant a concentration strategy. To reach them, the firm mails out millions of clothing catalogs each year as well as sends out an e-mail newsletter to its customers and others who visit the company's Web site. This newsletter addresses matters concerning King Size weight issues and other topics of interest to this group. Other firms that use a concentration strategy range from distinctive automakers like Ferrari to food companies like Gerber (baby foods).

> **concentration strategy**
> a marketing effort that focuses on a single market segment

Advantages of the concentration strategy are many. The firm can achieve a prominent position in the market due to its precise knowledge of the specific preferences of its target market segment. It can enjoy operating economies in design, manufacturing, distribution, advertising, and promotion due to its focused view of the market. Firms using the concentration strategy often build a reputation for leadership in their field by serving the very specific needs of their clients.

Against these advantages, the concentration strategy may prove to be risky. A decrease in the size of the selected market segment, a decline in the segment's purchasing power, a change in customers' tastes, or the entry of a strong rival can spell disaster for a firm that keeps all its eggs in one basket.

CUSTOMIZATION STRATEGY

customization strategy
a personalized marketing effort to suit individual customer's needs

Many years ago, it was a normal practice for sellers to follow a **customization strategy** and individualize their goods to meet each customer's requirements. Tailors, shoemakers, clock makers, furniture artisans, and home builders, among others, customized their goods. However, as the marketplace grew in size and diversity, customization lessened, and products had to be produced in advance in anticipation of demand and stored until needed.

Customization, however, has not vanished. In small neighborhood stores, many proprietors know every customer by name and continue to offer personalized service. On a larger scale, some marketers—ranging from magazine publishers and greeting card companies all the way to sellers of personal computer systems—employ this strategy as a viable targeting option. For example, with the aid of computerized databases that contain geodemographic, lifestyle, and purchasing information about individual consumers, customized magazine issues now are published that contain ads matching specific subscriber profiles.[33]

mass customization
combining technology and customer information to tailor products and services to the specific needs of each customer.

The term **mass customization** has been coined to refer to efforts undertaken by manufacturers and marketers to combine the use of technology along with customer information to tailor products and services to the specific needs of each customer. Examples abound in the marketplace of companies that provide such customized products. In the watch industry, for example, Factory 121, a Swiss watch company, recently launched the Metropolitan Collection of customized watches, supported by a unique advertising campaign entitled "create your own time." The company, in the meantime, established a Web site where customers can create and design their own individually made Swiss timepieces in a fun and playful manner. Customers still get these watches at a factory-direct price.[34]

Similarly, mass customization has been accomplished in the dental industry. Today, new production methods can take dental impressions that are scanned in a 3-D computer tomography system, which subsequently produces the orthodontic device needed for straightening a specific adult's teeth. The process and materials used in manufacturing these devices are based on mass-manufacturing technologies, yet each patient's specifications are individually accommodated.[35] Other firms following a mass-customization strategy include Dell's "Build-to-order" computers and the tourism industry by offering package-holiday alternatives.

Mass customization, as a viable targeting strategy, is dependent on the likelihood that management can balance out the extra cost of giving each customer an individualized product or service against the profit potential that would be derived from increased sales and from willingness of customers to pay a premium for those customized products.

Personalization, which is a related concept to customization, has also been widely used as a targeting strategy. Personalizing standard items such as apparel, business supplies, calenders, baseball caps, mugs, pens, golf items, and even greeting cards has become a major selling strategy. American Greetings, Inc. initiated the personalization of greeting cards in 1992 by introducing *CreateaCard* kiosks and placing them in card shops throughout the country. Hallmark Corporation followed this action with its *Touch Screen Greeting* machines in 1993.[36]

One Japanese bicycle manufacturer uses a personalized process in fitting bikes to the needs of individual buyers.[37] Customers visit their local bicycle shop, where they are measured on a special frame. These measurements are then faxed to the factory where they are punched into a computer, which creates a blueprint of the desired bike in less than three minutes. The computer guides robots and workers through the production process, which yields a one-of-a-kind personalized bike within two weeks. The factory is prepared to produce any model from over 11 million variations in 199 color patterns.[38]

Personalization is also prevalent in the service industry. In fact, personalization has always characterized the marketing efforts of such service providers as physicians, lawyers, tax consultants, hairstylists, and interior decorators. The cost and commitment of resources necessary to implement a personalization strategy far exceed those required for producing standardized products or rendering standardized services. However, the higher level of customer satisfaction that results when consumers acquire precisely what they had in mind empowers companies employing this strategy to charge higher selling prices. The MetLife ad depicted in Figure 3.6 applies a customization strategy by offering pension plans to retirees that are specifically designed for each individual's needs.

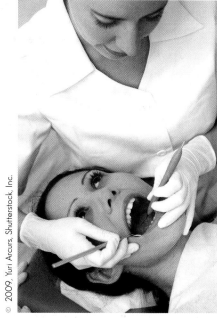
© 2009, Yuri Arcurs, Shutterstock, Inc.

The dental industry combines use of technology with customer information to tailor products and services to each customer.

personalization
making a product personal to the consumer. This concept is related to customization.

TARGETING CONSIDERATIONS

In selecting which market segment(s) to serve, a firm examines a number of criteria or features such as size, current sales potential, projected rate of sales growth, ease or reach, and expected profit margin. Not every segment presents a viable target market. Marketing managers evaluate each segment against a number of criteria to determine whether or not it should be pursued. These criteria include

- *Size:* The segment has to be large enough to warrant the resources and efforts necessary for a targeted marketing effort.

Figure 3.6

This ad from MetLife targets consumers concerned with retirement by offering them a customized pension plan. The company, like many others in today's marketplace, uses a service-customization strategy to address the unique needs of different consumer segments.

- *Potential*: A sufficient number of consumers in any targeted segment must possess a genuine need for the product or service offered, as well as the resources, willingness, and authority to buy.
- *Measurability*: The firm must assess whether or not research data are available in order to compare the segments' purchasing power, sales potential, costs, and potential profitability.
- *Accessibility*: The firm must be able to reach the consumers in each segment effectively and economically by means of its sales force, dealers and distributors, and available advertising media, as well as online.

- *Compatibility*: The product(s) and marketing mix necessary for the various segments under consideration must be consistent with company objectives, resources, know-how, and operations.
- *Stability*: The segment should be growing, or at least it should be relatively enduring. It must not be merely a temporary or fading one.
- *Defendability*: The firm must have the ability to defend its position against aggressive competitors.

Although some companies target the largest market segment or the segment with the greatest growth potential, the biggest or fastest-growing segment is not always the *right* segment for every firm. Small-size firms frequently lack the financial resources or competence to serve the largest market segments adequately. Often, the competition in the biggest and fastest- growing segments is too intense for smaller, weaker firms to break through and survive. Such firms may find it more advantageous to target a smaller segment and gain a large share, rather than target a huge segment and attract only a small share. In the toy industry, for instance, Ty Inc., which produces the authentic Beanie Babies, was able to make wide inroads in the toy market against giants such as Mattel and Fisher-Price.

Positioning

Once marketers have segmented the market and selected the target, their product or service offering needs to be properly positioned. Positioning strategy follows logically from targeting and has no significance apart from it. A product's *position* refers to the manner in which it is perceived by consumers, as compared to competitors' products and other products marketed by the same firm. This mental image that consumers hold of a particular product, service, brand, or store constitutes a significant factor in determining how it will fare in the marketplace. Ponder, for a moment, the images that are conjured up at the mention of brands such as Rolls-Royce and Kodak, or stores such as Saks Fifth Avenue and Super Kmart.

The decisions of marketing managers about what products to offer, prices to charge, promotional activities to undertake, and distribution channels to employ all affect the positioning of a brand in the marketplace. Fortunately, to a large extent, marketers can influence the formation of desirable mental images by planning and implementing a suitable positioning strategy. This process requires careful consideration of all product features as well as determination of the ways in which product characteristics, distribution, price, and promotion differentiate the brand from its competition.

In an effort to create this differentiating image, marketing managers attempt to ascertain how consumers perceive competing brands in the marketplace. One useful technique often employed to accomplish this objective is known as perceptual mapping.[39] **Perceptual maps** are *n*-dimensional comparisons that allow researchers to construct visual profiles for a number of related brands. For example, in comparing a number of competing brands of pain relievers along the *two* dimensions of *effectiveness in alleviating pain* (the horizontal axis), and *gentleness to the stomach* (the vertical axis), respondents

perceptual map
n-dimensional depiction that provides a visual profile of a number of brands for comparison purposes

would be requested to evaluate each brand on each of the two dimensions. The means of all respondents' evaluations for each attribute of every brand being compared are then calculated and plotted on a crosslike coordinate axis. A twodimensional perceptual map appears in Exhibit 3.4. As can be observed in this depiction, some pain relievers seem to have distinct images as indicated by the fact that they appear far apart from one another. Other pain relievers are perceived very similarly, as they appear to cluster together in a quadrant. The distance between any two brands in the map can be viewed as an operational measure of the disparity between their images.

Product positioning, therefore, is a strategic effort aimed at creating and maintaining in consumers' minds an image that will both distinguish a product from competitive offerings and give it an advantage in selected target markets. However, because not all brand differences are meaningful to consumers, a company should select a differentiating feature that is worthy of being established as a basis for positioning. Any selected feature should satisfy one or more of the criteria for positioning such as:

- *Desirability*, which implies a benefit highly valued by a large number of consumers
- *Uniqueness*, which denotes originality and exclusivity of the feature
- *Visibility*, which suggests a noticeable departure from features of competing brands
- *Affordability*, which suggests that the price is reasonable and fair

---

EXHIBIT 3.4   **Images of Pain Relievers: A Two-Dimensional Perceptual Map**

Consumer perceptions of some popular brands of pain relievers are charted in this map based on the two dimensions of effectiveness versus gentleness.

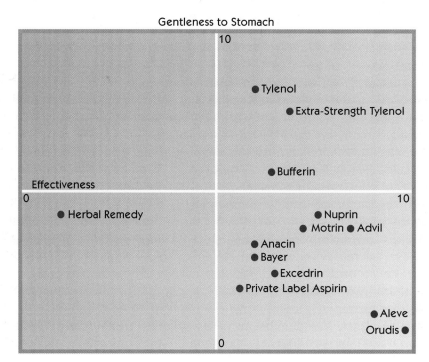

Examples abound in business literature of companies that were less successful in their positioning effort due to selecting marginal or irrelevant features. For example, when a Nexxus shampoo ad positioned the shampoo as capable of "bringing out the best in silver, gray, and white hair," few consumers were likely to admit that they were old and that their advanced age warranted using a shampoo specially formulated for the elderly. As a result, the expected sales did not materialize. Age denial worked as a deterrent to brand acceptance. Similarly, the American Association of Retired Persons, AARP, automatically mails to anyone who reaches 55 years of age invitations to join the association. Many of those are still active in the workforce; as such, they perceive retirement as a dormant, "not for me" lifestyle—a fact that causes most of these invitations to be ignored.

IRRELEVANT ATTRIBUTES AND POSITIONING

A number of researchers have suggested that it is possible to differentiate products by selecting attributes that *appear* to create a meaningful difference, when in fact, these features are irrelevant or nonbeneficial to consumers.[40] For example, many outdoor insect killers are differentiated on the basis of adding a pleasant scent to the spray, a characteristic that often reduces their effectiveness as bug killers. Similarly, mouthwashes are differentiated according to taste and color—features that have nothing to do with their potency.

It has been shown that these irrelevant features may work well in the short run. However, in the long run, competitors often recognize the vulnerability of irrelevant features leading to the introduction of new brands that grant consumers authentic benefits.

SELECTING A UNIQUE SELLING PROPOSITION

A positioning strategy that has worked well for a number of companies rested on the selection of a single benefit on which to differentiate a product. One researcher suggests selecting a *unique selling proposition* (USP) for each brand and focusing mainly on that proposition in all of the company's promotional efforts.[41] Volvo, for example, has used the superior safety record for its vehicle as its USP (selected as top safety pick for the year 2008). The continuous emphasis on this unique feature enables the company to achieve distinctiveness in a society where consumers suffer from an information overload. So Volvo may become perceived as "number one" in safety. According to Ries and Trout, occupying this premier stance is the ultimate goal of positioning.[42] This proposition is based on the belief that consumers arrange the brands they know in the form of a mental *product ladder*. For example, in the automobile safety arena, the ladder may be arranged as Volvo–BMW–Infiniti. The firm in the top rung tends to be remembered best.

According to another point of view, the late David Ogilvy, former creative head of Ogilvy & Mather International advertising agency, suggests that creating a product *personality* is the primary basis for a positioning strategy. After having created the desired product personality, marketers and advertisers then proceed to make a *large promise* of benefits for the consumer. They, of course, must make sure that the product *delivers* the promised benefits.[43]

Repositioning

Sometimes marketers decide to alter the way a product or service is perceived by consumers. The need for such a change may come about in response to a dynamic marketing environment, such as intensified competition, changing consumer tastes or lifestyles, and/or technological advances. Repositioning entails modifying an existing brand, targeting it to a new market segment, emphasizing new product uses and benefits, or altering a brand's image. Modifications in a brand's design, formulation, benefits, or name are likely accompanied by adjustments in its promotion, distribution, and pricing strategies. For instance, a reformulated soft drink in which NutraSweet replaces sugar as an ingredient offers a new benefit—calorie control. Marketers of this beverage may redirect product advertising in order to target consumers who are weight conscious or must restrict their sugar intake. Advertising appeals would likely tout the benefits of the sugar-free product.

Examples of companies that attempt to reposition their brands abound. For example, many high-tech businesses today have been repositioning themselves as e-business operations. United Airlines has recently attempted to reposition itself via an ad campaign called "Rising," which emphasized the company as the most passenger-centric airline, with a clear understanding of customer problems and the solutions required to fix them. Sears, in 2002, repositioned its operations under its then CEO—Alan Lacy by moving away from the perception of a traditional department store or discount operation to a broad-line retailer with service capabilities. This was accomplished by bringing in "better" products in the "good, better, best" continuum, updating the stores for a more inviting shopping experience, and offering advanced financial and credit services.

Cadbury confectionary company likewise followed a repositioning strategy to attract young adult consumers. All packaging, marketing communications, and point-of-sale (POS) displays were updated.

It should be noted, however, that marketing communications play a key role in the process of repositioning, as this is the main ingredient where images and perceptions are formed in the consumer's mind.

Repositioning usually entails a considerable investment of time and expense on the part of the company, because changing consumer attitudes is a difficult and slow process. Detailed coverage of attitude change appears in Chapter 6.

The first three chapters of this text attempt to sensitize you to the dynamics of the marketplace. Awareness of the emerging trends in the domestic and global market, coupled with a recognition of the diversity of consumers' needs and wants, will help you appreciate the complexity of factors that shape consumer behavior. More effort is thus needed to fathom the myriad personal and sociocultural factors that impact buying behavior. The remaining chapters of this book are devoted to exploring individual influences on consumer behavior such as perception, attitudes, and motivations as well as sociocultural influences such as reference groups, opinion leaders, and social class.

repositioning
modifying a brand, redirecting it, or stressing different features to boost sales

A Cross-Functional Point of View

The topics of segmentation, targeting, and positioning have a number of implications for business disciplines other than marketing. Relevant issues might include

- **Production/Global Business:** Because of different consumer preferences in foreign markets, product design or ingredients often have to be adjusted to suit the requirements of taste and use by foreign consumers. In addition, many nations have mandatory requirements and standards for imported products. For example, appliances may have to accommodate 220-volt, 50-cycle power standard prevalent elsewhere in the world. Automobiles may be required to have their steering wheels placed on the right side, and food items may have to be modified to suit local tastes. These product adjustments obviously entail additional cost. Before a company commits to doing business globally, a decision has to be made regarding the desirability of such adaptations and the ensuing ramifications of such actions from the perspectives of cost and brand image.

- **Human Resources/Costs:** Retail store operators know they cannot appeal equally to all consumers in the marketplace. They must decide what type of customers they will appeal to. Some retailers design their stores to appeal to affluent consumers, whereas others choose to pursue the working class. The first group usually adopts a full-service policy, which involves maintaining a large number of well-trained, well-groomed sales staff to serve its high-profile clientele. The second group usually adopts a self-service policy and limits its sales staff to a few, generally young and untrained individuals who can be hired at low cost. Costs of conducting business, and consequent selling prices, can therefore vary significantly between these types of stores. Retail store managers face the question of whether a policy of maintaining a high-caliber sales force at a high cost or limiting customer services but offering lower prices is a better alternative.

- **Ethics:** In some cases, selection of a targeting strategy is motivated by a company's realization that one segment is more vulnerable than the others. For example, a firm may target minorities, younger or older consumers, or the infirm with products or services that often carry a premium price tag. Although competition is often capable of removing such inequities in an economy like ours, it may take some time to eliminate some competitive advantages due to patent laws. The issue is whether or not consumer interests could or should be protected against such conspicuous practices.

These issues, and a host of others like them, serve to show that the topic of perception transcends the field of marketing to other business disciplines.

Summary

This chapter addresses the topics of segmentation, targeting, and positioning. These are necessary and inseparable components of any marketing strategy. Segmentation entails dissecting the heterogeneous overall market for a product or service into a number of more homogeneous submarkets or niches. Targeting means reviewing and selecting one or more market segments to pursue. Positioning establishes an intended and differentiating image for a product or service.

A mass-marketing approach, in which a standardized product is marketed to the entire marketplace, sometimes makes good economic sense for homogeneous commodity products. In a mass-marketing approach, economies of scale and accumulated experience work together to lower unit costs. Mass-marketing approaches have largely been replaced by market segmentation, which divides a body of consumers into smaller groups with common demographic or lifestyle characteristics. Marketers target specific segments, offer differentiated products, and design programs specifically suited to the needs and preferences of each segment selected.

Segmentation of consumer markets can be accomplished by using a number of variables. Segmentation can be based on geographic, demographic, geo-demographic, psychographic, and behavioral variables. Marketers can opt for single-variable or multivariate segmentation.

A market profile or portrait of the segmented marketplace emerges. Based on this profile, marketers decide which submarket(s) they should pursue or target. Four basic targeting strategies are (1) undifferentiated strategy, (2) multiseg- ment strategy, (3) concentration strategy, and (4) customization strategy. The attractiveness of various market segments is typically evaluated with regard to seven factors: (1) size, (2) potential, (3) measurability, (4) accessibility, (5) compatibility, (6) stability, and (7) defendability. When a company has decided on the segment(s) it elects to target, it develops a product mix and marketing mix appropriate for each segment.

Once marketers have segmented the market and selected their target market(s), their product or service offering(s) need to be properly positioned. Positioning strategy flows logically from the targeting strategy and has no significance apart from it. A product's position is the manner in which it is perceived by consumers in relation to competitors' products and other products marketed by the same firm. Because not all brand differences are meaningful to consumers, a company should select a differentiating feature that is worthy of being established as a basis for positioning. Any selected feature should satisfy one or more of the criteria for positioning that include (1) desirability, (2) uniqueness, (3) visibility, and (4) affordability.

Changes in the marketing environment sometimes cause marketers to reposition their products, changing the way a product or service is perceived by consumers by modifying an existing brand, targeting it to a new market segment, emphasizing new product uses and benefits, or altering a brand's image. Modifications in a brand's design, formulation, benefits, or name are likely accompanied by adjustments in its pricing, distribution, and promotion strategy.

Review Questions

1. A number of variables have been used to segment consumer markets such as demographic, psychographic, and geodemographic variables among others. Discuss what is meant by psychographic segmentation and the role of AIO inventories in categorizing consumers into various segments.

2. PRIZM is a geodemographic clustering system developed by the Nielsen Claritas Corporation. How is this system structured? For what purposes can this system be applied?

3. There are four basic types of market-targeting strategies. Compare and contrast what they mean to marketers.

4. Marketing managers evaluate each market segment against a number of criteria to determine whether or not it should be pursued by the firm. Explain what these criteria are.

5. Briefly explain the interrelationship between the three steps of segmentation, targeting, and positioning. Emphasize the logic behind the sequential ordering of these three steps.

Discussion Questions

1. Procter & Gamble offers a large number of brands within a given product category. For example, in the area of laundry detergents alone, the company produces over a dozen different brands (among them Tide, Biz, Cheer, Dash, Bold, Gain, Era, Solo, Dreft, Ivory Snow, Oxydol). This practice, known as a multibrand strategy, is applied by Procter & Gamble in other product categories, including toothpastes (Crest, Gleem, Denquel), bar soaps (Ivory, Camay, Lava, Zest, Safeguard, Coast), shampoos (Head & Shoulders, Prell, Pert Plus), and deodorants (Sure, Secret). Of course, each brand requires its own advertising budget, sales promotions, packaging, and so on. In your opinion, what is the logic behind incurring the added costs associated with a multibrand strategy?

2. The airline industry uses a differentiated pricing strategy when marketing travel services. Airlines have come to recognize wide dissimilarities in the needs of persons who travel for business versus those who travel for leisure. Based on these differences, prices quoted to business travelers are considerably higher than those charged for leisure travel. Speculate on the differences between the needs of these two groups that permit a two-tiered pricing program to work.

3. In recent years, products such as Uptown cigarettes as well as King Cobra, Old English 800, and Colt 45 malt liquors have been marketed to African Americans. Similarly, Capri, Misty, and Eve cigarettes are marketed to young females. In many economically depressed communities, state lotteries are heavily advertised on outdoor billboards. Discuss the ramifications of such actions in view of segmenting, targeting, and positioning strategies. Do you regard such actions to be socially responsible?

Cross-Functional Debate

Refer to the chapter opening vignette, regarding the innovative programs used by companies in order to attract customers. Assume that you are the marketing manager of Kimberly-Clark's Huggies Diapers Division, which the company considers to be a seperate strategic business unit (SBU) target. The financial manager of this corporation questions whether or not the proceeds from this segmentation-targeting effort would offset the following costs:

1. The cost of establishing a very specific database containing the names of expectant mothers, as well as the cost of establishing and maintaining a Web site specifically designed for that segment of women.
2. The loss of revenue due to online coupons, which ultimately result in lower prices for Kimberly-Clark's products.

3. The costs to produce the diaper samples to be mailed to new mothers and to develop instructional and promotional materials (creating, printing) to accompany these samples.
4. The costs of mailing these items to expectant and new mothers as well as coupon redemption costs.

Having divided the class into two teams, a marketing management team and a team of financial managers:

a. Assume the role of the marketing managers and defend your segmentation- targeting strategy.
b. Assume the role of the financial analysts and pose cost-related objections to the proposed segmentation-targeting strategy.

CASE

Warner Bros. Eyes China

Mr. George Jones, the president of Worldwide Licensing at Warner Bros. Consumer Products Division, is exploring the Chinese market as a possible new segment to add to the company's expanding movie licensing business.

Mr. Jones has observed the enviable success of packaged-goods and fast-food companies such as Procter & Gamble, PepsiCo, and McDonald's in capturing the wallets of this 1.2-billion consumer market. What makes China an attractive possibility is not just the mere size of the country, but rather its emerging middle class, which seems to be interested in anything that is Western. This group snaps up everything from Quarter Pounders and Coke to Pert shampoo and Crest toothpaste and seems to be brand conscious and receptive to advertising.

Along with this vast potential, however, lies the lumbering bureaucracy and strict controls the Chinese government places on foreign business. In the movie industry, just as with any other product, the problem is finding a way to get the film to the consumer. The China Film Ministry, which decides how many foreign films may be shown, favors homemade movies. It

stocks China's theaters with 200 homemade films a year and allows only 60 imported films. Moreover, regardless of the popularity of a foreign movie and its large audience draw, a film can be taken out of theaters in a few days and replaced with a Chinese film.

In addition, action films with special effects and high gadgetry, a popular type with Chinese moviegoers, face tough scrutiny from state censors, who often ask that cuts be made. This requirement mandates that films be adjusted to suit the needs of this foreign market.

Other additional features of the Chinese entertainment industry include its feeble infrastructure. Many theaters are not technologically advanced enough to handle present technically sophisticated films. In addition, the cut of the box-office receipts deducted by the government in the form of taxes is taken in ever-increasing amounts.

As Mr. Jones pondered these potential problems, he was wondering if it would be better to make films on location specifically for the Chinese market (as a means of ensuring a long-term presence in the country) or whether to pursue the market with his company's existing films.

Questions

1. In view of the opportunities and problems that Warner Bros. would likely face in China, do you recommend that Mr. Jones pursue the Chinese market at this time? Why or why not?

2. Assume that Mr. Jones has committed to serving the Chinese market. Considering potential costs and benefits, which strategy do you believe Warner Bros. should pursue: (a) Use present American films that may face discriminatory treatment and may require modification by Chinese censors, or (b) produce new films on location specifically for the Chinese market? Justify your decision.

3. In your opinion, does it make good business sense for American companies to pursue those often different and frustrating *foreign* markets? Wouldn't it be more advantageous to settle for the domestic market at the company's doorstep? Why?

Notes

1. "Kimberly-Clark Partners with Leading Online Parenting Content Providers to Launch Parentstages .com," www.prnewswire.com/cgibin/stories.pl?ACCT =104&STORY=/www/story104-17-20.

2. "Are Tech Buyers Different?" *Business Week* (January 26, 1998), pp. 64–65, 68.

3. *Ibid*.

4. David W. Cravens, *Stategic Marketing*, 5th ed. (Chicago: Irwin, 1997), p. 133.

5. Thomas Moore, "Different Folks, Different Strokes," *Fortune* (September 16, 1985), pp. 65, 68.

6. Judith D. Schwartz, "Back to School with Binney & Smith's Crayola," *Brandweek* (September 13, 1993), pp. 26–28.

7. Mark Mackinon, "Bye-Bye Barbie: Muslim Families Pick Modest Fulla Doll," *Chicago Sun-Times* (October 30, 2005), p. 44A.

8. Harley-Davidson Web site, http://investor.harley -davidson.com/demographics.cfm?bmlocale=en_us.

9. Vidya Lakshmipathy, et. al, "Sprite Invites Teens to Its Mobile Social Yard," *Forester.com Research* (December 31, 2007).

10. James S. Hirsch, "Vacationing Families Head Downtown to Welcoming Arms of Business Hotels," *Wall Street Journal* (June 13, 1994), p. B1.

11. Mollie Neal, "Weight Watchers' Winning Marketing Strategy," *Direct Marketing* (August 1993), pp. 24–26, 46.

12. "Business on Call," *Inc.com* (December 1996), www.Inc.com/magazine/19961215/2035 _pagen_2.html.

13. "US FAX Acquires InterPage—Strengthens Position and Extends Internet Offerings," *Business Wire* (December 1995), http://findarticle.com/p/articles/ mi_mOEIN/is_1995_Dec_19/ai_17899870.

14. Donald Cooke, "Understanding Geodemographics," *Business Geography* (January 1997), pp. 32–35.

15. Matt Rosenberg, "You Are Where You Live: Claritas PRIZM NE System Sorts Zip Codes into 66 Clusters," *About.com Geography* (January 17, 2006), http://geography.about.com/od/obtainpop-ulationdata/a/claritas.htm.

16. Sarah Max, "My Kind of Town," *Spirit* (September 2007), pp. 110–116; "66 PRIZM Marketing Segments," Nielsen Claritas PRIZM, www.claritas.com/ claritas/Default.jsp?ci=4&pn=prizmne_segments#24.

17. "Community Tapestry: The Fabric of America's Neighborhoods," ESRI www.esri.com/data/esri_data/ tapestry.html; "Acxiom Launches Online Segmentation Solution; New Tool Improves Speed, Ease-of-Use, and Accuracy in Household-Level Segmentation Analysis," Internet Retailer, (Press Release dated June 29, 2005); "ComScore Adds Acxiom PersonicX Segments to ComScore Segment Matrix Service," comScore, (June 10, 2008), www.comscore.com/press/ release. asp?press=2264; and www.acxiom.com/ personicx.

18. "Internet Solution Gives BMW Competitive Edge;" "AOL: PRIZM NE Makes a Difference in Determining Online Behaviors," www.claritas.com/claritas/ Default.jsp?ci=2&pn=cs_bmwusa.

19. "Claritas' Case Studies," www.Claritas.com/claritas/ Default.jsp?ci=2&pm=cs.

20. "They Know Where You Live—and How You Buy," *Business Week*, (February 7, 1994), p. 89.

21. Edward DiMingo, "The Fine Art of Positioning," *Journal of Business Strategy* (March–April 1988), pp. 33–38.

22. Joanna L. Krotz, "Divide and Conquer Your Customers with Psychographics," *Marketing Intelligence* (March 2004), p. 1

23. Ethan Boldt, "CUNA Mutual Group's Dave Griffith on Attitudinal Data Framing," *Target Marketing* (November 27, 2007), www.targetmarketingmag.com/story/print.bsp?sid=71956&var=story.

24. Scott Ward, "General Foods: Opportunities in the Dog Food Market," *Harvard Business School Case* no. 578162 (Cambridge, MA: Harvard Business School Publishing, 1978), pp. 1–37.

25. SRI Consulting Business Intelligence, "The VALS Types," 2003.

26. Neal, "Weight Watchers' Winning Marketing Strategy," pp. 24, 46–47.

27. Russell Haley, "Benefit Segmentation: A Decision-Oriented Research Tool," *Marketing Manaagement* 4, no. 1 (Summer 1995), pp. 59–63.

28. Shari Caudron, "Brand Loyalty: Can It Be Revived?" *Industry Week* (April 5, 1993), pp. 11–12, 14.

29. Maria L. Alaniz and Chris Wilkes, "Pro-Drinking Messages and Message Environment for Young Adults: The Case of Alcohol Industry Advertising in African-American, Mexican-American, and Native-American Communities," *Prevention Research Center* (Berkeley, CA: October 1, 1996).

30. "8th Annual Household and Teen CE Ownership Study," *Market Research.com*, www.marketresearch.com/product/display.asp?productid=1327723&xs=r.

31. Katie Hafner, "*i*Phone Owners Crying Foul over Price Cut," *New York Times* (December 7, 2007).

32. Vincent Alonzo, "The Bigger They Are . . . The Harder Some Marketers Try to Reach the Larger-Sized, Big-Spending Customers," *Incentive* (June 1995), pp. 57–60.

33. Stan Rapp and Tom Collins, *The Great Marketing Turnaround* (Upper Saddle River, NJ: Prentice Hall, 1990), pp. 97–98.

34. Frank T. Pillar (ed.), *Newsletter* TUM Research Center on Mass Customization and Customer Integration, 7, no. 1 (February, 2004).

35. *Ibid.*

36. M. R. Kropko, "Card Makers Struggling with Computer Kiosks," *Marketing News* 30, no. 12 (June 3, 1996), p. 6.

37. Susan Moffat, "Japan's New Personalized Production," *Fortune* (October 22, 1990), pp. 132–55.

38. *Ibid*

39. Jack Trout, Steve Rivkin, and Al Ries, *The New Positioning* (Boston, MA: McGraw-Hill, 1995).

40. Gregory S. Carpenter, Rashi Glazer, and Kent Nakamoto, "Meaningful Brands from Meaningless Differentiation: The Dependence on Irrelevant Attributes," *Journal of Marketing Research* (August 1994), pp. 339–50.

41. Rosser Reeves, *Reality in Advertising* (New York: Alfred Knopf, 1960).

42. Al Ries and Jack Trout, *Positioning: The Battle for Your Mind* (New York: Warner Brothers, 1982).

43. David Ogilvy, *Ogilvy on Advertising* (New York: Vintage Books, 1985); David Ogilvy, *Confessions of an Advertising Man* (New York: Atheneum, 1971); Ogilvy & Mather, *How to Create Advertising That Sells*, agency publication (May 1986).

INDIVIDUAL INFLUENCES ON BEHAVIOR

Consumer Perception

CHAPTER 4

LEARNING OBJECTIVES

- To define and comprehend elements of the perception process.
- To explore components of the human sensory system.
- To gain insight into the process of perceptual selectivity.
- To recognize the impact of stimulus, individual, and situational variables on perception.
- To become familiar with the Gestalt view of perception
- To understand the process of perceptual categorization and inference.
- To grasp the relationship between imagery and consumer perception.

KEY TERMS

perception
exposure
attention
sensation
synethesia
perceptual overloading
perceptual vigilance
selective exposure
selective attention
perceptual defense
selective sensitization
selective interpretation
adaptation
stimulus factors
individual factors
chunk
absolute (lower) threshold
terminal (upper) threshold
differential threshold or just noticeable
   difference (JND)

situational self-image
situational variables
gestalt
closure
grouping
proximity
context
figure and ground
perceptual categorization
surrogate indicators
prototype matching
perceptual inferences
schema
script
image
imagery
brand equity

One of the biggest issues companies have to face head-on is the quality of the image their products project to the public. Perhaps this concern is nowhere more evident than in the automobile industry, where image perception is the major factor determining what make of car consumers select.

With the sale of hybrid cars rising over 35 percent in 2007, the race among auto companies for the green market is definitely intense. By 2011, according to J. D. Power, car buyers could have over 75 hybrids to choose from, up from 14 in 2007. With a promising market of this magnitude, competition among the major save-the-planet cars is fiercely increasing.

The two major makers of hybrid cars are Toyota and Honda, which together control 90 percent of the U.S. hybrid car market. However, the success of each in luring customers to purchase their green cars is quite different.

Initially, Honda was out front with its hybrid cars, such as the 70-mpg Insight, introduced in 1999—a two-seat transporter that did not meet with much success. Later in 2005, Honda introduced the Honda Civic, which again faced a lukewarm reception. Consumers felt that the car looked just like the regular Honda, only with a hybrid badge on the trunk that was hard for anybody to notice. Consumers admitted that one major reason behind their purchasing a hybrid is the fact that they want other people to notice that their car is a hybrid and that they are doing something to help save the world's scarce resources. In this respect, they felt the Honda Civic is all but invisible.

What truly captured hybrid car buyers' interest is the Toyota Prius, a car with space-age styling and miserly mileage. With the overwhelming success of the Prius, Honda's Civic ranked second to Toyota despite the fact that Honda was the first to introduce hybrids to the United States. Toyota Prius has thus become the unchallenged leader in the hybrid car field and is outselling Honda's entire line of gas-electric Civics and Accords by five to one.

Actions Honda is taking to face this domination by Toyota include pulling the plug on its hybrid Accord due to its failure to attract buyers with its confusing formula of high horsepower and high price. The company is also working on a new high-profile hybrid—a Prius fighter, planned for 2009, code named "the global small hybrid," that is expected to have the highest mileage on the road. The car is designed to seat five passengers and carry a price tag of under $22,000.

Toyota, however, is not standing still against Honda's competitive efforts. The company intends to create an entire Prius car line, with different models all carrying the Prius badge. The three Prius models planned include a small car, a family car, and a crossover utility vehicle that would begin rolling out in 2009.

Toyota's executives have complete confidence that its Prius will continue to be a most successful hybrid. One Toyota executive commented on that success by saying that when people look back at the era of hybrids, the Prius will certainly be seen as the Model T of modern times.[1]

Honda Civic sales have significantly dragged behind those of Toyota's Prius, in spite of the fact that Honda was the first company to introduce hybrids to the United States. According to the Univer-

sity of Michigan's American Customer Satisfaction Index, which rates automakers based on owners' satisfaction, Toyota received a score of 87 out of a possible 100, while Honda's score was very close at 86. If these scores for the two companies are virtually identical, how do you explain the significant difference in sales figures? What factors influence hybrid car buyers in their selection of a car? Learn more about hybrid cars by visiting Hybrid Cars Reviews at www.consumersearch.com/www/automotive/hybrid-cars/index.html. In your opinion, will hybrid cars eventually replace all other car types?

This chapter begins by examining the stages of the perception process—exposure, attention, sensation, and interpretation—as well as its subjective and selective nature. We also continue to address stimulus, individual, and situational influences on perception. After discussing the gestalt view of perception, perceptual categorization, and perceptual inferences, the chapter covers the topic of brand imagery, brand equity, and risk perception.

What Is Perception?

Perception is the process of selecting, organizing, and interpreting sensations into a meaningful whole. In the past, methods of studying stimuli and measuring responses to them were restricted to examining the five senses. Today, however, the view that perception uses merely sight, hearing, smell, taste, and touch to comprehend the environment is inadequate. Although the senses do play a major role in our comprehension of an event, our interpretation of a sensation may lead to a false perception. Perception is highly subjective and therefore easily distorted.

perception
the process of selecting, organizing, and interpreting sensations into a meaningful whole

An individual's frame of reference affects the way he or she interprets sensations. For example, two friends may go to see the same movie but leave with different interpretations of the film. Their frames of reference, experience, and expectations are among the factors that influence their evaluations. Not only may different people perceive the same stimulus differently, but the same person may also perceive a given item differently at various times or under different circumstances.

Consumer perceptions are vital to marketers and often underlie the success or failure of products in the marketplace. For example, until recently, the Big Three U.S. automakers suffered from a poor-quality image. Consumers perceived cars produced overseas, particularly in Japan, to be of higher quality. Such perceptions caused many U.S. auto buyers to choose foreign-made cars, hurting the sales of U.S. automakers. In the past few years, however, U.S. automakers have worked diligently to improve the quality of their cars and have initiated promotional campaigns designed to enhance customer satisfaction with their cars. In 2005, for example, General Motors, Ford, and Daimler-Chrysler's Group have offered employee prices for all customers on most 2005 vehicles. And according to Autodata Corp., the big three U.S. automakers spent

Figure 4.1

This ad from Ford Motor Company announces the superior test results of the Camry, Accord, and Fusion models over imports.

an average of $4,239 per vehicle on incentives, compared with $2,372 for European brands and $1,619 for Asian brands. The ad from Ford in Figure 4.1 reveals to consumers the test results of *Road & Track* magazine's car enthusiasts. By putting Camry, Accord, and Fusion to the test, drivers rated the models—based on styling, handling, and performance—to be better than imports.

Three concepts are intimately related to perception: exposure, attention, and sensation. Acquisition of sensory information is possible only when consumers attend to stimuli they are exposed to. For example, commercials that escape viewers' attention produce no sensation and, thus, have no effect on behavior.

Exposure, Attention, and Sensation

exposure
the act of deliberately or accidentally coming into contact with environmental stimuli

The process of perception begins with exposure to a stimulus. **Exposure** occurs when individuals come into contact with environmental stimuli either accidentally or through their own deliberate, goal-directed behavior. Not all stimuli to which we are exposed, however, get noticed.

Attention refers to the allocation of mental capacity to a stimulus or task.[2] After choosing whether or not to expose themselves to a message, consumers may momentarily pay attention to a specific aspect of the stimulus that is within their range of exposure. Attention can be planned, involuntary, or spontaneous. Planned attention is goal directed; individuals use their attention—such as watching a TV commercial or reading an ad in a magazine—to help them perform a specific activity such as shopping. When external stimuli force their way into our awareness, attention is involuntary. Imagine, for instance, that a fire alarm were to sound as you read this. Your automatic reaction would be immediate involuntary attention to the alarm. Spontaneous attention, on the other hand, may be exemplified by shoppers looking for birthday gifts. They do not concentrate too narrowly on any particular product class; thus they may remain open to other stimuli. A perfume bottle noticed by accident while shopping at a department store is an example of a product that receives spontaneous attention.

attention
the allocation of an individual's mental capacity to a stimulus or task

Sensation refers to the responses of our sensory receptors (eyes, ears, mouth, nose, touch) to environmental stimuli, and the transmission of this information to the brain via the nervous system. This process represents the acquisition of raw sensory information received through the sense organs—a preliminary step in the processing of information.

sensation
the responses of a person's sensory receptors to environmental stimuli and transmission of this information to the brain via the nervous system

Sensory Systems

Environmental stimuli or sensory inputs are received through our five senses. Visualize for a moment a young woman shopping in an open fruit market on a sunny summer day. She *sees* the splendid colors of the different varieties of fruit, *smells* the sweet aromas of mangoes and strawberries, *tastes* a sample of a ripe pineapple, *hears* the calls of vendors promoting their fruits, and *feels* the weight and consistency of a melon as she examines it before purchase. The input picked up by her senses as she walks among the fruit stands is the raw data—ingredients in the initial step of information processing. Exhibit 4.1 depicts an overview of the perceptual process.

Just as the bright colors of the fresh fruits, their sweet scent, and their arrangement at the various stands aroused the shopper's desire to buy, so do the sensory qualities of nearly all products. These sensory qualities play an important role in enabling manufacturers to differentiate their products from those of competitors. For example, a number of years ago, Kimberly-Clark achieved a considerable gain in its sales picture by introducing colored and scented paper napkins and bathroom tissue. Many consumers preferred the innovative products over traditional all-white brands.

VISION

Researchers estimate that as much as 80 percent of what we receive from our environment is gained from vision. We tend to rely more on the other senses mostly when vision is unavailable (for example, in the dark).

EXHIBIT 4.1

An Overview of the Perceptual Process

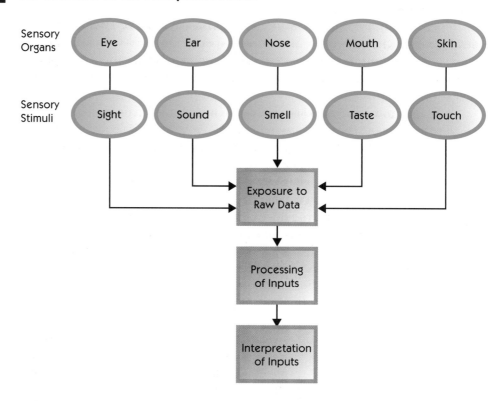

The first impression that a product, ad, or store makes on us depends largely on its physical attractiveness; this fact explains why marketers rely heavily on visual appeals in product design, packaging, ad layout, and store decor.

Visual perception is a multidimensional phenomenon involving seeing a number of elements of the product, such as its color, size, shape, and movement. One of the most obvious visual qualities we experience in a product is its color. Not only does color help attract our attention, it also influences our emotions and affects our moods. An examination of the colors in a Crayola crayons box reveals that while the original crayons had only six colors (black, blue, brown, yellow, orange, and red), today Crayola offers 120 crayon colors, including such ones as purple heart, razzmatazz, tropical rain forest, and fuzzy wuzzy brown. These varied colors and names have been proliferating and are now appearing in all types of product categories, such as ice cream, juice drinks, and nail polish. Consider for a moment, how colors are also used in the decor of various commercial establishments. Nightclubs use red light to create an aura of arousal and romance. Hospitals use pale greens and blues to create a

Sensory inputs are received through our five senses and play an important role in product differentation.

© 2009, dundanim, Shutterstock, Inc.

peaceful and relaxing environment. Mass-merchandisers use bright colors to attract shoppers' attention.

Similarly, color expresses emotions. Red roses symbolize love and yellow ones represent friendship. In many cases, specific cultural values are associated with color. In the United States, white connotes happiness and purity, whereas black is linked with death and mourning. In some Asian countries, however, the opposite is true.

Research shows that package color is an important factor in grabbing consumer attention amid the clutter of competing products. For shoppers who are not loyal to a particular brand, a change in package color can win their attention and enhance their consideration of a brand.[3]

Creative use of color by manufacturers is important, particularly in the area of product design and packaging. Clothing and cosmetics exemplify product categories in which color plays a major role in determining consumers' acceptance or rejection. A few years ago, for example, Wet and Wild nail polish, which came in a wide range of unusual colors, was an immediate hit among many young women.

SMELL

Scents play an important role in our lives. Odors can stir emotions, elicit memories, produce hunger, induce relaxation, or even repel us. The smell of chocolate as we enter a confectionery or the scent of perfume as we pass through the cosmetics section of a department store entices many shoppers to stop and purchase. Humans, like all animals, quickly learn to assign values to different scents. They come to recognize that the unpleasant smell of spoiled food means harm, and thus the food should be avoided. On the other hand, they are attracted to the smell of a freshly baked cake due to the perceived promise of tasty ingredients such as butter, eggs, vanilla, and sugar.

The same effect of olfactory cues holds true in the case of human relationships. Both sexes are programmed to search for certain types of mates. One of the most primal determinants in this process is the sense of smell; that is, a desirable partner must smell right. Moreover, scientists have cited various cases of the invisible influence of scent in our daily lives. One of the best-known examples of this phenomenon is the way the menstrual cycles of women who live together tend to synchronize.[4]

Responses to scents are culturally based. They result from prior associations between the scent and occasions or emotions that surrounded the presence of the scent. In the food category, for example, most people find the smell of fresh popcorn to be irresistible when they enter a movie theater. Garlic is viewed as delectable in Italy. Curry odors produce hunger sensations in India. Similarly, perfumes and colognes are capable of stirring up various feelings, emotions, or memories. The smell of someone's perfume or cologne, for example, is often a powerful enticement in a relationship—a theme that promoters of these products often utilize.

Realizing the positive effect of scent on consumption, some advertisers began using scented ads. In one type, a scented strip on the ad page releases

Figure 4.2

This ad for Giorgio of Beverly Hills contains a scent strip that allows consumers to sample the fragrance as an enticement to purchase the product.

a fragrance when the reader unfolds a crease. In another type, a scented spot produces a fragrance when the reader scratches it. Advertisers of a variety of products including perfumes, cosmetics, chocolates, and other foods and liquor have found that combining the scent with other elements of the printed ad tends to increase the effectiveness of their message. The perfume ad from Giorgio of Beverly Hills depicted in Figure 4.2 contains a scent strip that releases a fragrance when unfolded.

TASTE

Most scientists consider the sense of taste to be inseparable from the sense of smell. Receptors (taste buds) that reside on the tongue and palate combine with smell to produce familiar taste sensations such as saltiness, sweetness, bitterness, and sourness.

Taste has a significant effect on how foods and beverages fare in the marketplace—a fact that causes food and beverage processors to spare no cost or effort in ensuring that the taste of their products pleases consumer palates. Manufacturers of products ranging from cookies and snack foods to soft drinks, wines, and beers conduct taste tests either in an internal facility or through

Consumer Behavior in Practice

No Plastic Surgeon Is Needed for This Nose

New electronic noses are now available. With these devices, researchers can perform a variety of functions that range from measuring and quantifying smell to designing a desirable aroma that can be added to a product. At General Motors, for example, researchers have used the electronic nose to pinpoint and simulate the *new car* smell that is so inviting to new car buyers. Similarly, Volkswagen engineers believe that they have isolated a *quality* smell that can be incorporated into new vehicles. Unilever uses the mechanical nose for sniffing people's armpits to design effective and pleasantly aromatic deodorant-antiperspirant products. Perfume makers use the new noses to defend their brands against counterfeit fragrances. Food and beverage producers find them valuable in choosing the perfect aroma to add to their products.

The new nose technology came about as a by-product of research on the stealth aircraft program conducted for the U.S. military. During that project, researchers were enamored of certain polymers, or chains of molecules, that had the characteristics of conducting electricity and producing definite reactions to smell. Even though polymers were never used in building stealth aircraft, the published research was enough to encourage scientists to use them in developing the electronic nose. At Warwick University in Britain, scientists used the technology to produce the first electronic nose prototype in the mid-1980s.

The principle on which these mechanical noses operate is the ability of polymers to absorb scent vapors and match them with models retained in computer programs. Thus, an electric nose can sniff a particular wine of a certain vintage, determine if it smells identical to another batch, and identify any existing differences.

Applications for this high-tech nose are virtually limitless. One application can be found in the food industry. The machine can verify or discredit superiority claims made by marketers on behalf of their products. For example, freshness claims for foods or beverages can now be verified. The U.S. Food and Drug Administration's fish inspectors currently utilize electronic sniffers to grade fish at dockside inspections. Using the new nose eliminates disagreements between fishers and inspectors regarding the grades assigned to commercial fish.[5]

Scent and taste are integral factors when marketing foods, beverages, cosmetics, and a host of other products. Visit Huber the Nose at www.thenose.ch. Enumerate some specific products in which scents play an important role. What other products might be created or improved by adding scents to them? Do scents of places (e.g., stores) or objects (e.g., new cars) influence your shopping and buying behavior? Why or why not?

testing agencies such as Taste Test and St. Croix Sensory, Inc., which utilize professional sensory panelists who are trained to detect minute taste differences. Even schools such as Sensory Spectrum offer courses and seminars in taste perceptions.

An innovation in the sense of taste is the new electronic tongue, which was introduced in 1995 as a result of a joint Russian–Italian project. The electronic tongue, like its natural counterpart, can distinguish among a vast array of subtle flavors using a combination of the four elements of taste: sweet, sour, salty, and bitter. The electronic tongue is a silicone chip with small spherical beads a little wider in diameter than a hair. These beads act like test tubes, holding and analyzing liquid that is poured on them. The food and beverage industry uses the electronic tongue to monitor the flavors of existing products, and some have used the tongue to develop a digital library of tastes proven to be popular with consumers.

Acceptance of and preferences for new, unfamiliar taste sensations can be learned through familiarity. Many of us have developed an appreciation for foods that once were nontraditional to the American palate. Ethnic dishes, hot foods, and exotic spices are but a few examples of this phenomenon.

SOUND

Speech and music are two important weapons in the marketer's arsenal. Most marketing communications, including commercials, sales presentations, and stores' sound systems, employ speech or music. That is not to mention the extent of music as an industry in itself, with annual sales of music or music-related items amounting to hundreds of billions of dollars.

Making sense of speech is a cognitive process that involves our knowledge of meaning of words, how we string words together, our frame of reference, and the situation in which the speech is being presented. Music, on the other hand, has the ability to evoke feelings. In commercials, the choice of background music is a sensitive issue, because music can be used to set a desired mood, stir relevant emotions, or influence liking for the message. For example, research on the use of popular songs and song parodies in TV commercials for products including tennis shoes, soft drinks, and cookies revealed a positive effect of such music on consumers' recall of the ads.[6] Such recall is enhanced due to the emotional connections that many consumers have with a particular song or performer.[7] Likewise, advertisers have embarked on the music video approach popularized by MTV and VH1 and have used this format to build commercials and even entire campaigns.[8]

Research shows a positive correlation between music in retail settings and store sales. Research sponsored by MUZAK Corporation conducted in two grocery stores reported higher sales per customer when MUZAK music was played compared with radio music, contemporary environmental music, or no music at all.[9] Shoppers' pace of movement in a store was also influenced by music. Shoppers reportedly spent 17 percent more time traveling between two points in a store when slow versus fast music was played.[10] Perception of time spent in a store was also a function of the type of background music played. When shoppers were exposed to music they normally listened to, they reported spending less time in the store than they had in reality spent. In another study conducted in 2006, researchers investigated the effect of incorporating music into a Web site, which is the new major shopping environment for millions of consumers. The findings from the study also reveal that embedding background music in the homepage generated positive attitudes towards the Web sites.[11]

Noise, on the other hand, is negatively correlated with retail sales. Levels of anxiety and stress increase with the amount of noise in the shopping environment. Thus, a noisy buying experience may adversely affect consumers' evaluations of stores and products.

TOUCH

Have you noticed how children show affection toward animals by touching and petting them or how mothers demonstrate love by caressing and hugging an infant? Touch, in this sense, communicates feelings.

Writers suggest there are two types of touch: active touch and passive touch.[12] In the first case, an individual touches to express a feeling or to initiate a reaction. In the second case, the receiver feels the experience of being touched, such as how we feel when we receive a massage.

Touch is a component in many consumer behavior situations. It is part of the exploratory nature of human beings. In shopping, people often squeeze a melon, feel the texture of a fabric, or run their fingers through a fur coat. Physical contact with products provides consumers with vital information that, in many cases, is a main ingredient in their choice among competing brands.

Some observers believe that one of the drawbacks of electronic or catalog shopping compared with traditional shopping is the fact that it neglects the importance of product exploration and active touching that many consumer feel is a necessary component in their shopping experience. Researchers have found that products with primarily material properties, such as clothing or carpeting, are more likely to be preferred in shopping environments that allow physical inspection and touching than products with geometric properties such as packaged goods for which marketing online or through direct mail would be appropriate strategies.[13]

Although the five human senses are presented here separately, in reality, they are much more interrelated than we might suspect. Just as our sense of taste is highly dependent on the sense of smell, our human senses often work together in combination with one another. Many musicians and concert goers, for instance, report that they not only hear the music, they can actually *feel* it. For some people, the senses somehow fuse together and form a sort of sixth sense. This phenomenon is known as **synesthesia**. According to a recent report on CBS, some individuals report the ability to *taste* sounds or to *experience* colors.

synethesia
fusing together of the human senses

Input Variation and Its Effect on Sensation

Sensation depends on input variation. A more variable environment produces greater sensation than a constant environment, regardless of the strength of sensory input. Humans accommodate themselves to varying levels of environmental sensory input. When deprived of sensory stimulation for a time, we exhibit greater sensitivity to its return; hence the expression "It's so quiet, you can hear a pin drop." As sensory input decreases, our ability to detect change increases. We attain maximum sensitivity under conditions of minimal stimulation.

This fact has a number of important applications in marketing, particularly in the field of advertising. For example, consumers easily ignore ads when bombarded with a large daily dose of promotional messages. This tendency is a result of **perceptual overloading**, our inability to perceive all the stimuli that compete for our attention at any given moment. Humans also seem to have the

perceptual overloading
the inability to perceive all the stimuli that compete for an individual's attention at a given moment

perceptual vigilance
an individual's ability to disregard much of the stimulation one receives through the senses

ability to discard much of what they receive through their senses. This capability is referred to as **perceptual vigilance**. Perceptual vigilance has its roots in our tendency to be selective in what we perceive. Clearly, our senses are limited in their capacity to process all the stimuli in our surroundings. Hence, we attend to stimuli selectively.

Perceptual Selectivity

Each day, we are confronted with thousands of stimuli in the environment including ads in the media, products in stores, people, events, and situations. According to the president of Perception Research Services, an eye-tracking facility, the average supermarket shopper is exposed to 17,000 products in a shopping visit that lasts less than 30 minutes.[14] Because it is beyond a person's capability and interest to see everything there is to see, we screen out certain stimuli. This selectivity is of great concern to marketers, who attempt to communicate with their target audiences and surmount such blocking of information.

selective exposure
a tendency of people to ignore media and ads that address topics that are unimportant to them

SELECTIVE EXPOSURE AND ATTENTION

The selectivity process is like a series of filters or sieves that allows or disallows environmental stimuli to reach our consciousness. The first of these filters is called selective exposure. We exhibit **selective exposure** when we ignore media that address unimportant topics. Nobody pays attention to *every* ad, nor can anyone notice *all* the products in a supermarket. **Selective attention** refers to our tendency to heed information that interests us while at the same time we avoid information that is irrelevant, threatening, or contrary to our beliefs. Heavy smokers, for example, are unlikely to read reports from the Surgeon General that link cigarettes to lung cancer and heart disease. Exhibit 4.2 depicts the process of perceptual selectivity, indicating that perception occurs after environmental stimuli have been filtered through the processes of selective exposure and selective attention. Furthermore, the tendency of individuals to block threatening or contradictory stimuli from their conscious processing is known as **perceptual defense**. It serves as a defense mechanism to protect an individual's self-image and ego. We also perceive more readily information that is consistent with our own needs, beliefs, values, or attitudes. This tendency is known as **selective sensitization**. Sports fans, for example, are prone to keep up with their favorite teams and ignore others.

selective attention
a tendency of individuals to heed information that interests them and to avoid information that is irrelevant

perceptual defense
a tendency to block threatening or contradictory stimuli from extensive conscious processing

selective sensitization
a tendency to perceive more readily information that is consistent with one's needs and beliefs

selective interpretation
the act of combining relevant knowledge structures with expectations and intentions to derive meaning from a stimulus

SELECTIVE INTERPRETATION

Once an external stimulus attracts our attention, our perceptual system begins to consciously process it by means of **selective interpretation**. In interpreting a stimulus, we scan our memory for cues or relevant knowledge from prior

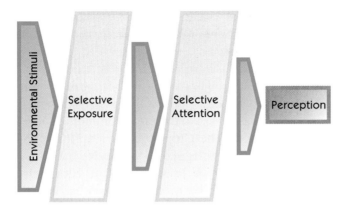

learning and experience. We combine these cues with our expectations and intentions in order to interpret the stimulus and derive its meaning, which may or may not coincide with the intended meaning.

Marketers know that it is not what they say that matters, but rather what customers hear or want to hear that counts. Recently, G. Heileman Brewing Company, makers of Old Style Beer, ran a billboard ad in Chicago featuring infamous gangster Al Capone with the caption "Al persuaded all his friends to try Old Style." Although Heileman said the ad was one of a series designed to show how long Old Style had been available in Chicago, many viewers believed it perpetuated ethnic stereotypes. Heileman realized that viewer perceptions had distorted the intended meaning and promptly withdrew the ad in response to public outcry.[15] In another recent example, Nike recalled 38,000 pairs of shoes bearing a logo that turned out to be inadvertently offensive to the Muslim community. The logo in question resembled the word *Allah*, which translates as "God" in Arabic. The notion that Nike would place the name of the deity on footwear was regarded by some to be a sacrilege. In response, Nike communicated sincere apologies for any unintentional offence. In addition to the recall, 30,000 pairs of shoes with the controversial logo were diverted from marketplaces such as Saudi Arabia, Kuwait, Indonesia, and Turkey to other markets.[16]

ATTENTION STIMULATION

The phenomenon of perceptual selection provides a major challenge to marketers today. They must contend with TV viewers who *zap* (switch channels) programming and *zip* (fast forward on VCRs) commercials. This is particularly true today due to the availability of products such as TiVo, which consumers can use to skip commercials altogether when viewing a program. Marketers must also deal with speed readers who seldom pay attention to print ads. In short, they must present messages to an audience that may not be interested in attending to them. On the other hand, many readers of special-interest

T.V. advertisers employ a tactic known as *roadblocking,* so that a person switching channels will be exposed to the same commercial on whatever channel is being watched.

publications read them cover-to-cover, ads and all, and even save them for future reference.

To combat selective exposure, marketers plan the placement of ads so that target consumers are most likely to be exposed to them. For example, some TV advertisers employ a tactic known as *roadblocking.* They arrange to air the same commercial on all networks at approximately the same time or during the same period, so that a person switching channels will still be exposed to the same commercial on whatever channel is being watched. To overcome selective attention, advertising appeals are designed to coincide with target consumers' lifestyles and needs. Another method is to address consumer fears or solve some problem, such as bad breath, hair loss, or dandruff. Choice of an appropriate medium is also important. Ads for expensive cooking utensils, fine wines, gourmet chocolates, and exotic desserts are more appropriate in *Bon Appetit* magazine than in *Business Week.* Because children influence the product choices their parents make, commercials for a kid's breakfast cereal are more effective during Saturday morning cartoons than on late-night talk shows.

ADAPTATION LEVELS

Humans are able to adapt to a wide variety of physical, social, and psychological conditions and develop familiarity with stimuli, especially those they experience regularly, to the point where the presence of a stimulus fails to produce its characteristic sensation. While having lunch at the university cafeteria, you may be bombarded with sensory inputs such as noise generated by other students, background music, the smell of food, and the sight of people carrying trays. Yet you may still manage to read the assignment for an upcoming class without being bothered by the surrounding commotion.

One method some TV commercials use to deviate from the audience's prior **adaptation** level is to create the impression of loudness by filtering out any noises that may drown out the ad's primary message. By removing low-frequency sounds that can mask higher frequencies, advertisers can ensure that sound in commercials is perceived at or near optimal levels. Departing from prior adaptation levels does not necessarily mean making clever, brilliantly executed presentations of stimuli. In some cases, monotonous or dull presentations can also be noticed, so long as they are different or unfamiliar.

adaptation
an indifference to a stimulus to which an individual has become overly accustomed

Stimulus and Individual Factors of Perception

As we discussed in the section on sensory systems, marketers attempt to design the physical attributes of products, brands, packages, ads, and stores to attract or direct consumer attention and entice prospects with merchandise offerings. The physical characteristics of objects are referred to as **stimulus factors**. They produce the physiological impulses that in turn produce a sensation. These factors (such as size, color, shape, taste, or smell) are the primary elements of the object that interact with our sensory systems to produce a sensation.

Just as the properties of one stimulus differ from those of other stimuli, human beings also differ from one another. **Individual factors** of perception are qualities of people that influence their interpretation of an impulse. Examples of individual factors include consumers' needs, interests, beliefs, experiences, feelings, expectations, memories, personalities, self-perceptions, lifestyles, roles, risk tolerances, attention spans, and mental sets. Any of these may affect our perception of products, services, brands, stores, ads, or policies.

The needs of individuals, for instance, influence their perception. Those who shop for food while hungry find everything appetizing. Consequently, they are prone to spend more on groceries. An individual's interests can determine whether or not he or she subscribes to specific magazines or watches particular TV programs. A person's beliefs about various restaurants, prior experiences with them, and feelings toward them influence where he or she might take a friend for dinner. Our expectations about the future and tolerance for risk can influence our willingness to invest in the stock market. We tend to prefer products and brands that complement our personality, self-concept, and lifestyle. The type of car a person drives, for example, reflects his or her self-perception and communicates something about the person to others. The role we play at the moment also influences our perceptions. In the role of a busy student, we may eat fast-food lunches, but as a single parent, we may pack nutritious lunches for our school-age children.

Span of attention, another individual factor of perception, deals with limitations on a person's ability to process bits of information. Humans can attend to only a small number of items at any given time. This limit appears to range from five to seven chunks of information, where a **chunk** is an organized grouping of data inputs. Social security numbers, for instance, are partitioned into three chunks—a three-digit number, two-digit number, and four-digit number. The length of time that stimuli can hold a consumer's attention also appears to be brief, often only a few seconds. Children, in particular, have very short attention spans.[17] Consequently, advertisers continuously provide appropriate cues in ads and commercials to recapture the audience's attention. For example, TV commercials for toys use special photographic angles, fast action, appealing colors, upbeat music, and other happy children to capture and hold kids' attention. Similarly, print ads for fast foods often depict mouth-watering close-up photos of a product to appeal to hungry consumers' taste buds.

An individual's mental set or perceptual style describes our tendency to process information and react in a certain manner under given circumstances. For example, an individual may be predisposed to consistently react positively to innovative ideas or to resist new ways of performing familiar tasks. People inclined to behave in particular ways often find it difficult to change.

Although stimulus attributes and perceiver characteristics or conditions affect the way we perceive objects, the notion that perception can be

stimulus factors
the physical characteristics of an object that produce physiological impulses in an individual

individual factors
the qualities of people that influence their interpretation of an impulse

chunk
an organized grouping of data inputs

explained solely in terms of stimulus and individual factors is debated, especially by gestalt psychologists, whose views we discuss shortly.

Threshold Levels

Every human sensory process (sight, hearing, smell, taste, and touch) has an upper and lower limit of responsiveness. For example, humans cannot hear high-pitched whistles that dogs respond to easily. The study of the link between physical stimulation and resulting sensation is called *psychophysics*. It investigates the relationship between the psychological and the physical worlds.

There are three thresholds for each sense: an absolute threshold, a terminal threshold, and a differential threshold or just-noticeable difference (JND). The **absolute threshold** is the lowest level at which an individual can experience a sensation. It is the point below which the physical stimulus can no longer be detected. Absolute limits can theoretically be established for every type of sensation.

absolute (lower) threshold
the lowest intensity level at which an individual can detect a stimulus

The **terminal threshold** is the point beyond which further increments in the intensity of a stimulus produce no greater sensation. Would adding a third scoop of raisins to Kellogg's Raisin Bran add to the taste? Would adding more perfume to a bottle of Chanel's Egoiste aftershave improve its scent? Would mixing an added blend of coffee beans to Maxwell House Coffee improve the taste? Obviously, if such changes resulted in higher cost but had an undetected effect on quality or taste, they would be unwarranted.

terminal (upper) threshold
the point beyond which further increases in the intensity of a stimulus produce no greater sensation

The **differential threshold** or **just-noticeable-difference** (JND) is the smallest increment in the intensity of a stimulus that can be detected by an individual and still be perceived as an increase or decrease. In 1834 Ernst H. Weber, then a pioneer in the study of psychophysics, quantified the relationship between the intensity of a stimulus and the change in intensity that is required to produce a recognizable difference. According to Weber, the size of the least detectable change in the intensity of a stimulus, the JND, is a function of the initial intensity. For example, if the study lamp on your desk contains a 200-watt bulb, you are unlikely to notice an increase or decrease of a single watt in the intensity of light. However, if your room were illuminated by a single candle, you would immediately notice an additional candle's light. Similarly, a rebate of $200 for purchasing a $60,000 BMW would probably go unnoticed, but a $200 rebate offered by Sears toward the purchase of a $500 washing machine would immediately be detected by the marketplace.

differential threshold (JND)
the smallest increment in the intensity of a stimulus that a person can detect

WHAT THE JND MEANS TO MARKETERS

A number of potential applications for the JND exist in marketing. These relate to pricing, product sizing, and packaging strategies. Whether marketers desire a change (such as altered package size, higher or lower price, or adjusted product quality) to be discernable by consumers or not, they need to estimate the JND.

Clothing retailers, for example, find that markdowns of less than 20 percent from the original price of a garment have little effect on enhancing sales. For

Ethical Dilemma

Challenging Your Freedom of Choice

Back in 1957, a researcher by the name of James Vicary claimed that by flashing messages to audiences on a movie screen at a high speed, he could induce them to unconsciously follow the action proposed by the message. Vicary claimed he was able to influence audiences in a New Jersey movie theater by getting them to purchase more cola and popcorn by merely projecting phrases instructing patrons to consume these products.

This phenomenon became known as *subliminal persuasion*, an involuntary outcome that is based on the premise that our attitudes and behaviors may be changed by stimuli that we do not or cannot consciously perceive—that is, stimuli presented to people at an intensity below their absolute threshold. Vicary's claims were promoted in a book entitled *The Hidden Persuaders*, which resulted in a public outcry and suspicions of a government conspiracy.

In subliminal messages, only a couple of words or a single image can be perceived by the unconscious mind. Therefore, the simpler the image or word is, the more likely it would be subconsciously registered.

It was only natural that some advertisers and other promoters of public opinion quickly envisioned the presupposed benefit of this technique in enhancing their causes. In practice, these practitioners are alleged of using variations on this technique to accomplish their objectives by embedding subliminal messages into films, TV programs, ads and commercials, acoustical media, self-help CDs, and rock music.

Public concern about the issue was sufficient to cause the FCC to hold hearings in 1974, which resulted in an FCC policy statement indicating that subliminal advertising was "contrary to public interest" and "intended to be deceptive." Furthermore, a study by the United Nations concluded that "the cultural implications of subliminal indoctrination is a major threat to human rights throughout the world."

There is a great deal of debate regarding the effectiveness of subliminal persuasion. Psychologists insist that subliminal messages have an effect only when these messages are goal-relevant to a specific individual; that is, if the suggested action in the subliminal message is of no pertinence to the individual, the message would be ineffectual.[18]

To consumers in any free society such as ours, freedom of choice has been a prized value with regard to our behavior and consumption. Do you believe subliminal persuasion can hinder such free choice? How ethical do you believe this technique is? Since it is hard to know when and if you are being exposed to subliminal persuasion, what would you suggest to prevent abuse of manipulative tactics? Learn more about these issues and others by visiting www.csicop.org/si/9611/judas_priest.html

consumers to believe they are getting a bargain, the markdown must be 20 percent or more. On the other hand, if the intention is to raise prices, marketers may want the effect to go undetected by the public. This is particularly true of manufacturers faced with rising costs of product ingredients. They debate whether to raise prices, with a possible negative effect on the company's competitive position, or alter ingredients (thereby reducing the quantity or quality of the product). In either case, the move is usually designed to be below the JND to produce the least disruptive effect on the company's competitive position.

Many companies use a strategy of downsizing (decreasing package size while maintaining the price) to combat rising costs. Philip Morris cut the weight of its Brim coffee from 12 to 11$\frac{1}{2}$ ounces but left the can size and price the same. Similarly, Kimberly-Clark cut the number of diapers in a package from 88 to 80. These moves in effect raised unit prices while not informing consumers that they were paying more.[19]

The same philosophy guides manufacturers and retailers who practice price lining, a strategy of offering a class of products for sale at only a few price levels. A women's clothing shop, for example, may carry three lines of comparable dresses at a low, medium, and high price. With this practice, marketers create the impression of distinct and noticeable differences between the lines by widening the price gap between them. In doing so, they ensure that consumers are unlikely to perceive the lines as similar, even if in reality they are very comparable.

Some JND tactics that involve making undetectable reductions in package contents have been questioned from an ethical perspective. M&Ms brand candy, on the other hand, occasionally sponsors sales promotions in which bonus-size packages boast of 10 percent more candy at the regular selling price, a difference that the firm expects consumers to notice.

Situational Influences on Perception

As consumers we are usually affected by the situation in which we buy and use products; that is, the factors above and beyond our own characteristics and those of a product or ad. We may feel exuberant or despondent, leisurely at ease or pressed for time.[20] We often tailor our purchases according to how we feel at any given time and the specific circumstances in which we find ourselves. Such behavior reflects our **situational self-image**, the physical and mental state we are experiencing at a specific moment in time.[21] For example, a person facing a frustrating situation may tend to smoke, drink, or overeat.

Situational variables are environmental circumstances that constitute the context within which purchases, product usage, and product-related communications occur. There are five classes of situational variables: (1) physical surroundings, (2) social surroundings, (3) task definition, (4) time, and (5) antecedent states. Like stimulus and individual factors, they influence the way we perceive an object or event as well as how we respond to it.

PHYSICAL SURROUNDINGS

Physical surroundings at any given site include its readily apparent properties, which act on our five senses. For example, Macy's department store in midtown New York, with its elegant fixtures and impressive displays, exemplifies a certain type of physical surrounding. Physical surroundings also include store location, parking facilities, and product assortment. Retailers orchestrate layout (the visible arrangement of merchandise and promotional materials), atmospherics (decor, sounds or music, lighting, aromas, temperature, humidity), customer services, and a variety of other factors including employees' dress, presentation, and demeanor to generate the desired perception of their stores. Clutter in the aisles, on-sale promotions, stock outs, and return policies, as well

situational self-image
the physical and mental state a person is experiencing at a specific moment in time

situational variables
environmental circumstances that constitute the context within which transactions occur

as some elements beyond a retailer's control such as the weather, can likewise influence shoppers' perceptions.

While this variable is obviously applicable to physical retail stores, similar principles apply to virtual stores visited by consumers who shop online. A creative and compelling Web site with a distinctive logo, digital photography, print collateral, rich interactive media presentation, music, and Flash as well as clever graphic design is necessary to create the desired positive effect in an online environment.

SOCIAL SURROUNDINGS

Social surroundings are a second set of situational factors. These include other persons present in the shopping environment, such as family members, store personnel and clientele, and the degree of crowding. For example, in a supermarket, parents are often pestered by their young children to buy junk food. Similarly, salespeople's characteristics and manners, as well as interpersonal interactions occurring in the vicinity, are all elements of the social surroundings.

Situational variables influence the way we perceive an object or event as well as how we respond to it.

TASK DEFINITION

Task definition, a third situational factor, reflects an individual's defined role in the shopping process. For example, one parent may assume the role of purchasing clothing for a family's young children. Task definition may also be the shopper's reason for engaging in a particular behavior. When invited to a dinner party, we may purchase a bottle of wine as a gift for the hosts that is markedly different from one intended for our own consumption. Marketers can build on the concept of task definition to enhance sales. Department stores, for example, encourage engaged couples to sign up for bridal registries. This service facilitates for a couple's friends and relatives the task of purchasing wedding gifts.

TIME PERSPECTIVE

Time perspective is a fourth situational factor. Time can be regarded absolutely or relatively. In absolute terms, time dimensions are, for example, hour of the day, day of the week, or season of the year. In relative terms, time can be regarded in relationship to some past or future event (such as time since or until meals or a paycheck). Consumers differ in their perception and use of time, which they spend in ways that generally reflect their lifestyle. The appeal of many products rests on their ability to save time. Both the absolute and relative dimensions of time influence how consumers behave in the marketplace. For example, working consumers often shop evenings and weekends. People tend to spend more right after getting paid than later in the period between checks. Similarly, last-minute Christmas shoppers face a very different situation than individuals who complete their holiday shopping early.

Due to the immense growth in online buying, the element of shopping time has undergone drastic changes. Consumers can make purchase decisions more efficiently and conveniently on the Web, where a great variety of products is available along with information about where to get the best deal. Moreover, there is no need for the shopper to go through the time-consuming efforts of traveling, dealing with salespeople, and waiting in line at checkout counters, as is the case in conventional retail stores.

ANTECEDENT STATE

Antecedent state, a fifth situational factor, is the physical or psychological state of an individual immediately preceding his or her current state. Antecedent states are temporary. They can be classified as momentary conditions or momentary moods. Momentary conditions include such circumstances as having cash on hand or none at all. Momentary moods are states like being happy or sad, calm or angry, relaxed or excited. Momentary conditions and moods can influence whether or not consumers buy, what they buy, and how much they buy.

Situational factors, separately or in combination, can exert a direct impact on purchase choices. They can also combine with the characteristics of a product or a consumer to influence purchases. For example, an elated executive who has just been promoted may decide to buy her husband an expensive set of golf clubs rather than a simple shirt for their anniversary. For marketers, knowing how a person feels and anticipating what is going on in the environment where a product is being purchased or consumed can help to better predict consumers' product and brand choices.

Gestalt Psychology

Gestalt psychologists suggest a different way of looking at perception. Unlike the traditional view, this perspective emphasizes perceiving cohesive wholes, recognizing meaningful patterns, and formulating total impressions rather than noting discrete elements of a stimulus.

gestalt
a view that people perceive cohesive wholes and formulate total impressions

Gestalt is a German word, roughly meaning *whole or total impression*. We do not notice or perceive solitary stimuli; rather, we perceive them as part of an overall pattern or Gestalt. In fact we strive to perceive cohesive wholes and meaningful patterns that are simple and complete rather than discrete components.[22]

To marketers, too, the total configuration of the marketing mix is more important than either product design, price, distribution, or promotion separately. A brand, store, or company image is a total perception formed by processing information from many sources over time. Marketers also know that altering a seemingly minor element of a product, package, or ad sometimes alters its entire character. In a classic case that occurred in 1985, Coca-Cola attempted to change the formula of its flagship brand. In blind taste tests conducted on 190,000 consumers, subjects were asked their taste preferences for the traditional Coke formula, the new formula, and Pepsi. New formula Coke was found to be the consistent winner.[23] The public uproar that occurred when the traditional formula was withdrawn from the market forced the cola giant to bring back Coke Classic.

Consumers usually perceive environmental stimuli in a manner consistent with certain Gestalt principles—closure, grouping, proximity, context, and figure and ground. Let us see how these are relevant to marketing strategies and consumer perceptions.

Closure is our tendency to perceive a complete object even though some parts are missing. Upon experiencing an incomplete stimulus, we mentally bring it to completion. In so doing, our active involvement with this stimulus helps us remember it better. Closure, for example, explains the popularity of soap operas. Viewers become *hooked* on a show out of the need to complete the story line. Similarly, advertisers sometimes use incomplete illustrations, words, or jingles to attract attention and enhance recall.[24]

Several Gestalt principles relate to grouping. **Grouping** is the human tendency to perceive large data chunks rather than small units. We integrate bits of information into organized wholes, which enables us to evaluate brands over a variety of product attributes. When prospective students evaluate universities they might attend, their perceptions often involve grouping. The process of assessing these schools is often based largely on global evaluation and overall reputation rather than on specific characteristics of each school under consideration.

Proximity is a gestalt principle that suggests an object may become associated with another because of spatial and temporal nearness to that item. Objects close together seem to belong together or appear related in some way. Nuts, when sold in supermarkets, could be displayed with snack foods or cake mixes and other baking-related items, in which case we mentally group them with these foods and perceive them as fattening. When they are shelved with health foods, however, we may perceive nuts to be nutritious items that are high in protein. Similarly, proximity relates to product-positioning strategy. Advertisers associate their brands with positive symbols, images, or situations during which the product is used. They also attempt to build associations between product purchase or use and some desirable outcome.

Likewise, the **context** or surroundings, circumstances, or setting in which stimuli occur affects the way we perceive them. For example, an article that appears in the *Wall Street Journal* would be perceived quite differently than the same story in a supermarket tabloid. The ruggedness of a four-wheel-drive vehicle may be expressed by picturing the vehicle against a mountainous terrain. Similarly, a hybrid or a compact car is perceived as a desirable vehicle in an era of fuel shortages and skyrocketing gasoline prices.

Figure and ground suggests that objects or figures are perceived in relationship to their background or ground. Interaction between the object and its background is instrumental in creating a desired perception.[25] Gestalt psychologists note that in organizing stimuli into wholes, people tend to distinguish

closure
the tendency to perceive complete structures even though some parts are missing

grouping
the tendency to perceive data chunks rather than separate units

proximity
the tendency to assume relatedness due to spatial or temporal nearness

context
the setting in which a stimulus occurs affects how it is perceived

figure and ground
objects are perceived in relation to their background

Figure 4.3

In this ad from Gucci, the watch is the dominant Figure, causing our eyes to focus directly on it. The background, however, adds the ambience of a romantic fantasy.

perceptual categorization
the tendency to group somewhat similar objects together

stimuli that are prominent (the figure that is generally in the foreground) from stimuli that are less prominent (those in the background). Both print ads and broadcast commercials as well as Web sites are usually designed so that the figure dominates, while other elements recede into the background. If the figure is dominant, it is more likely that the eye will go directly to it, particularly if the background has a softer or fuzzier focus. The Gucci ad in Figure 4.3 illustrates the principle of figure and ground.

Up to this point we have discussed the physical and psychological processes that interact to produce a perception. Another area that merits exploration is broadly referred to as perceptual categorization—consumers' tendency to place products into logical categories or classes. In so doing, we simplify information processing and, consequently, the task of buying.

Perceptual Categorization

We tend to group objects together and respond to their class membership rather than to their unique attributes. This enables us to process quickly and simply the large volume of stimuli to which we are exposed. For example, a customer notices an unfamiliar item in a supermarket. Based on cues from its whereabouts in the store and its package design, the consumer identifies the item as a pasta product. This process is called **perceptual categorization**. To categorize objects, we weigh cues from the stimulus item to possible matches in our long-term memory. We are likely to react to the item as we would to other elements within the same category. If we believe that pasta is a healthy and tasty alternative to high-fat meals, we may try the item; if we dislike spaghetti, we may avoid it.

Individuals formulate both generic product classes (detergents, snacks, cereals) and subgroups within broader categories (dishwashing detergents and laundry detergents). The more specific subgroups are often based on such factors as quality, durability, prestige, economy, and usage occasion. For example, consumers categorize both filet mignon and ground beef as food items. Filet mignon, however, is expensive and reserved for special occasions; hamburgers are ordinary-meal items. Marketers attempt to facilitate proper categorization of their products. For example, when Toyota introduced the Lexus and Nissan introduced the Infiniti, they were intended to be grouped with and compared to other expensive cars. To accomplish this objective, both companies produced a number of print ads and commercials that pictured the new models along with expensive, prestigious cars such as BMWs and Mercedes-Benzes in various settings. Similarly, when Honda introduced its gas-electric Civic and Toyota its Prius, both were perceived as environmentally-friendly vehicles.

As we saw in the previous chapter on segmentation, most marketers today do not try to make products all things to all people. Although it is essential that consumers recognize a brand as part of its appropriate product class, marketers do not want their brands to be perceived as duplicates of other brands. Rather, positioning strategies attempt to establish both correct brand categorization and brand uniqueness. For example, producers of analgesic products want consumers to classify their brands correctly as pain relievers but not to think all pain medications are interchangeable.

Marketers attempt to understand how people make judgments about the properties they seek in products. They also try to provide clear, unambiguous cues that enable consumers to categorize products as intended. For example, the original Listerine's antiseptic color, medicinal taste, and tingling sensation suggest that the product kills germs. The swirl inside the top of a jar of peanut butter or tub of margarine suggests freshness. The sound of a new car door's slam suggests how well constructed it is.

SURROGATE INDICATORS

Today, complexity among many consumer products, particularly technology items, has never been greater. Some of these products, such as TiVos, Treos, BlackBerries, Wi-Fi, HDTV, plasma screens, picture phones, digital cameras, iPods, and iPhones, have tens or even hundreds of features or applications. Consumers, in many cases, struggle to appraise and evaluate the features of these gizmos and their uses. Keeping pace with such products' new attributes requires significant time and technical knowledge on the part of the consumer. However, since the majority of the consuming public often lacks both the technical expertise and the time required to understand, evaluate, and compare between these brands, consumers simplify their choice process by relying on substitute cues to categorize the brands or their features. For example, if a consumer is contemplating a purchase of a digital camera, the shopper may use cues such as price/brand as benchmarks to guide his or her choice. These cues—price and brand—are called **surrogate indicators**. We use surrogate indicators to place products into categories or discern uniqueness among brands within the same product class. For example, a recent study revealed that consumers rely on manufacturer reputation, the variety a brand offers, retailer reputation, and product warranty as useful surrogate indicators in selecting products. Other common surrogate indicators include brand name, price, and physical appearance.[26] Packaging and guarantee, when they serve as signals of product quality to consumers, are also surrogate indicators. Country of origin, in many cases, is also used by consumers as a substitute cue. Country of origin affects the perceived value of a product. A consumer's prior experience with a country's product, as well as his or her cognitions and feelings about that nation's image, has a major influence on that person's purchasing behavior. Just as Japanese autos, French perfumes, and Swiss watches are highly valued by many consumers, other countries' products, such as toys or seafood from China, may not fare so well.[25]

surrogate indicators
the cues that consumers rely on to place products into categories

© 2009, Kmitu, Shutterstock, Inc.

As suggested by the adage "You get what you pay for," consumers often use price as a surrogate indicator. We tend to rely on price as an indicator of product quality when we face risky situations, when we lack confidence in our ability to assess quality directly, and when we suspect significant quality or price variations exist among brands. For different types of merchandise, we as consumers formulate notions of *expected price* that serve as reference points in judging the prices we encounter in the marketplace. Over time, these expected prices remain flexible. As selling prices rise and fall, we adjust our price expectations according to market realities and personal experiences.

Price, however, is not always the most important influence on our perception of quality. Other factors such as brand names, store images, prior brand experiences, and specific product-quality attributes can temper the impact of a price–quality relationship we perceive and even overshadow it. Thus, our overall product perceptions blend information we derived from price, other external cues, and judgments of intrinsic product attributes.

Our overall product perceptions blend information from price, brand name, physical appearance, retailer reputation and other judgements.

PROTOTYPE MATCHING

rototype matching
the tendency to compare brands in a product category to the category's leading brand

A phenomenon closely related to perceptual categorization is known as **prototype matching**, our tendency to compare brands in a product category against the exemplar brand in that category. For example, various brands in the luggage category would likely be compared to a leading brand such as Samsonite. A given luggage piece, therefore, would be judged as acceptable or unacceptable according to how closely it matches the attributes of the category exemplar. Prototype matching explains the power of a brand leader to set the standards for the rest of the product category.[27]

Perceptual Inference

perceptual inferences
beliefs based on prior experience that a person assigns to products or stores

Individuals form associations between stimuli. They develop beliefs about products, brands, stores, and companies based on previously acquired information and their own experiences with the stimuli. **Perceptual inferences** are beliefs based on these forms of prior knowledge and experience that a person unconsciously or consciously comes to assign to products, brands, or stores.[28] For example, previous learning may cause consumers to associate high price with superior quality and, consequently, to anticipate a higher level of satisfaction when they select expensive brands and models.

To prompt inferences concerning product quality, marketers may incorporate appropriate sensory cues into their product design. For example, Pine-

Sol's strong antiseptic aroma implies that it disinfects as it cleans. Imperial Majesty perfume by Clive Christian of London comes in a Baccarat crystal bottle with an 18K gold bottle collar adorned with diamonds, giving the perfume the prestige it deserves when it is sold at Harrrod's in London and at B. Goodman in New York city for $2,150 an ounce.

There are three types of perceptual inferences. *Evaluation-based inferences* are judgments leading to a consistently positive or negative brand evaluation. Someone who has had a positive experience with a Magnavox TV may conclude that all Magnavox merchandise is good. This is called the *halo effect*. After a bad experience with the TV, the same person may conclude all Magnavox merchandise is inferior (a negative halo effect). Some inferences are *similarity based*. We may base our beliefs about a brand on its similarity to other products, simply linking unfamiliar products to familiar ones. For example, a shopper may associate with ketchup a new condiment packaged in a tall, slender bottle. Still other inferences are *correlational*, based on drawing conclusions from the general to the specific. For example, a consumer may believe that the higher the dosage of pain reliever in a headache remedy, the more quickly the brand works. Thus, the brand containing the highest dose of medicine has to relieve pain the fastest.

Schema and Scripts

Consumers store in their memory categorized information about objects. As they gain shopping experience, they recall information in an orderly manner that permits them to buy more efficiently. A **schema** is an organizing framework, a set of expectations that provide a structure for understanding and interpreting new information. A major food processor spent heavily to develop a tastier ketchup with a process that preserved the tomato's aromatic qualities and natural flavor. Upon introduction in supermarkets, however, the ketchup flopped. Why? The new process had eliminated the overcooked, scorched flavor that seeps into ketchup made by conventional processing. Unfortunately, it was precisely this flavor that most consumers identify as the taste of genuine ketchup. The firm adjusted its equipment to overcook and scorch and successfully reintroduced an *improved* ketchup. The original ketchup simply didn't fit into consumers' schema of what *real* ketchup should taste like.

schema
a structure for understanding and interpreting new information

Consumers have general schemas and subschemas. An individual may, for example, have general schemas about automobile makes and subschemas about specific car features, such as four-wheel drive, convertible top, stick shift, and automatic transmission. Similarly, a person may have general schemas about retailers and subschemas about various types of stores, such as department stores, discount stores, supermarkets, and convenience stores.

Scripts refer to our knowledge about the appropriate behaviors to perform in response to recurring events that we may encounter. For example, as we order a product online, return a purchased merchandise item to a store, or negotiate the purchase price of a new car, we act out a script, a behavior

script
the knowledge about procedures to follow in recurring situations

sequence appropriate for the situation. In buying a new automobile, for instance, we may (1) order the make, model, style, color, and various options; (2) agree on the delivery date; (3) negotiate a price; and (4) complete the details of a financing plan.

Scripts include our expectations about locations, situations, people, specific behaviors to perform, and outcomes of that behavior. They organize our knowledge about what to do in familiar situations and let us anticipate the outcome of our actions. Once activated, a script automatically guides most relevant behavior so that we don't have to make many deliberate, conscious decisions when faced with a similar situation. Scripts facilitate shopping. Rather than organizing information from scratch, we rely on experience to develop routines leading toward product purchase and use.

Perception and Images

Simply stated, image is a person's net impression of what a company, product, brand, or store is all about. Armani suits, for example, convey a different image from those purchased at Sears. Sources of images include sensory information from various sources such as advertising, personal experience, and symbols that people have come to recognize and respond to.

Martineau, based on the earlier work of Levy, characterized *image* as "the total set of attitudes, the halo of psychological meanings, the associations of feeling, the indelibly written aesthetic messages over and above bare physical qualities."[29] In other words, image invokes a functional and psychological portrait that a stimulus paints in consumers' minds.[30] It is the mental picture, personality, and feelings that an object conveys to consumers.

To attract customers, manufacturers and retailers must project an image that is acceptable to their target market. Consumers frequently form preferences for one brand or store over another because of its image. The way a brand or store is perceived and what it communicates about the consumer to others can be more important than how well a product works or how much a dealer charges. Thus, it is imperative that both manufacturers and retailers become cognizant of the many factors that contribute to brand and store images. The ad in Figure 4.4 depicts how Guess Jeans uses a sexy image to promote its products.

Image building presents a challenge for marketers because a mental image encompasses many facets, such as impressions of product attributes, types of people who use a brand, and situations surrounding brand use. Images can be built around notions of economy, safety, reliability, pleasure, status, distinctiveness, or other aspects of the product that may be of interest to the target market.

A product's image can differ greatly from its physical attributes. For example, it is often the image we hold of food or beverage items that determines our preferences for them. Consumers frequently find it difficult to believe that brands in certain product categories are virtually identical. They come to insist on a particular brand largely due to image-building factors

Reprinted with permission of Guess, Inc.

Figure 4.4

Wearers of Guess Jeans make a fashion statement.

Source: Photographer: Ellen von Unwerth, Art Director: Paul Marciano.

initiated by marketers such as branding, packaging, pricing, and promotion rather than due to physical product differences. The significance of brand image quickly becomes apparent in the case of a blind wine taste test performed at a winery in California. In that test, which took place in 2007, researchers gave respondents unidentified samples of red wines such as Merlot and Cabernet Sauvignon. Some of the samples were exclusive French brands; others were expensive competing California brands, as well as wines from Charles Schwab's own winery. To everyone's surprise, the inexpensive $1.99 bottle of Charles Schwab's wine was rated as high or even higher than equivalent competing wines for which consumers pay significantly higher prices. The point is that both the famous labels and higher prices elevated consumers' perception of the taste and quality of the designer-brand wines.[31]

Like products and brands, stores also have images. Establishments such as Bloomingdale's, Saks Fifth Avenue, Nieman Marcus, and Crate and Barrel project very different images than Target, Kmart, Wal-Mart, and Filene's Basement.

In selecting stores, consumers look for those that match their self-concept. Some stores intimidate a shopper, whereas others are comfortable to patronize. For some consumers, the same store is regarded as an acceptable source for some types of merchandise but not for others. A shopper may perceive Sears to be a good place to buy appliances and housewares, but not clothing. However, as part of its strategy to overcome this less-than-glamorous perception of its fashions, Sears recently acquired Lands' End and started offering that line of clothing in its stores.

Because stores cannot be all things to all people, retailers attempt to create images congruent with the self-image held by the market segment they target. Store images are shaped by retailers' merchandise assortment, level of customer services, pricing policies, promotional activities, reputation for integrity, degree of community involvement, and atmospherics. Atmospherics entail all the various physical elements in a store's design, both inside and out, that appeal to customers' emotions and stimulate buying. Interior atmospheric elements include sensory factors such as layout (arrangement of departments, width of aisles, grouping of products, location of checkout areas), store fixtures, merchandise displays, wall and floor coverings, lighting, colors, sounds, scent, neatness, degree of crowding, personnel, and clientele. Exterior atmospheric elements include location, appearance of the storefront, display windows, entrances, and degree of traffic congestion.[32]

Interestingly, consumers formulate images of stores regardless of whether or not retailers deliberately attempt to convey a specific image. Furthermore, Mazursky and Jacoby found that store attributes consumers employed while constructing images appeared to vary.[33] Although brand name appeared to be the most important cue when consumers formed impressions about the quality of merchandise, the number of salespersons per department seemed to influence most strongly customer images concerning quality of service.

IMAGERY AND PROMOTION

imagery
the way consumers visualize sensory information in working memory

Imagery is a process by which we visualize sensory information in our working memory. Working memory refers to our ability to hold and manipulate information in the mind over short periods of time. For example, when we give directions to an out-of-town friend, we use mental imagery to picture the roads, exits, traffic lights, and stop signs to verbally express our memory of the route. Imagery is helpful to consumers in at least two ways. It helps them to recall and express information they have stored in their memory. It also facilitates consumers' comprehension when products or situations are presented in a pictorial or graphic form.

Imagery is therefore important as a perceptual tool in promotion. In advertising, for example, imagery is created largely through illustrations. Pictures may be used to demonstrate how a product is used. Research shows that dually coded pictures (pictures that show the brand name along with the product) increase recall of the brand name.[35] This enhanced recall is thought to be the result of our seeing the information in two different forms—verbal and pictorial.

Global Opportunity

What Do James Dean, Cowboys, and Latin Americans Have in Common?

Levi Strauss Company markets products in 70 countries around the world. The company owns and operates plants in 25 countries and has licensees, distributors, and joint ventures in many others. One of the pressing decisions the company faces in creating a uniform image throughout the world is whether to apply a worldwide strategy to all advertising or settle on localized campaigns for each country in which Levi's products are sold. By allowing the localization of Levi's advertising, the company fears that it may appear as separate and distinct firms in different nations. The fact that local advertising agencies in some countries are quite sophisticated whereas ad agencies in other nations lack expertise in creating and casting commercials would nurture such an impression. On the other hand, a uniform worldwide advertising strategy would tend to ignore differences that characterize consumers in various countries.

In determining which strategy is best, the company reviewed its current ads in various countries. For example, in European television, Levi's commercials project a super-sexy appeal. In the minds of at least some company executives, this is an objectional personality for the brand. In Latin America, Levi's ads addressed a family oriented, largely Catholic market. There it was found that the quality of the creative work was substandard. In the United Kingdom, ads emphasized Levi's as an American brand starring a cowboy in a Wild West fantasy setting. In Japan, to overcome competition from other jeans brands, Levi's positioned itself as legendary American

jeans with commercials bearing the theme "Heroes Wear Levi's." Japanese Levi commercials featured clips of cult figures such as James Dean. In Brazil, where consumers are more strongly influenced by European fashion trends than by American trends, the French-filmed commercials featured cool young Parisians amidst a wild traffic scene. In Australia, creating brand awareness was the focus of Levi's advertising campaign. Commercials emphasized the brand name and Levi's quality image.

It appeared that while the advantages of employing a uniform advertising strategy in all markets were clear, the disadvantages are just as real. The unique needs of each market could not be met with a single worldwide advertising strategy. Moreover, implementation of a centralized advertising strategy would require an organizational structure that is considerably different from Levi's present one. Finally, local advertising agencies in different parts of the world often resist outside suggestions to change the way they conduct their business.[34]

Levi Strauss is a name known worldwide. The company's garments and jeans are popular in almost every country in the world. Learn about Levi's involvement in the international market by visiting its Web site at www.eu.levi.com. What benefits do foreign consumers perceive in purchasing Levi's, which they must often buy at exorbitant prices? Are these perceived benefits identical to those sought by U.S. consumers?

Together with the other ingredients of the marketing mix, promotion—and advertising in particular—plays an important role in establishing and enhancing favorable corporate, brand, and store images.[36] Because of advertising's ability to generate images, it has sometimes been referred to as the business of *image management*—creating and maintaining images and meanings in a consumer's mind.[37]

IMAGE CHANGE

The public's positive image of a firm is vital for its continued success. Images can range from clear to vague, from strongly positive to neutral or even negative. A favorable image virtually ensures continued attractiveness of the firm and becomes a valuable asset that is cherished and protected. A negative image, on the other hand, can seriously impair a firm's ability to do business and could even threaten its survival. As a result, image protection and restoration strategies may take the form of aggressive, reactive, or defensive moves.[38]

Management may take a firm's positive image for granted until something unfortunate occurs and executives are faced with a negative image to rectify. Because attitudes are slow to change, image correction is a time-consuming process. Examples abound in corporate history of companies that were faced with the challenge of changing negative images. Some of the most famous incidents in recent times include TJX Inc. (the corporate parent of T. J. Maxx and Marshalls), with its massive customer data security breach; Glaxo Smith Kline, with its *Avandia* diabetic medication linked to heart attacks; Merck with its *Vioxx* arthritis medication connected with cardiac events; oil companies' conspiracy to raise gasoline prices both after Iraq's invasion of Kuwait as well as during the war in Iraq; and the mortgage industry's deceptive subprime lending practices that led to the collapse of the U.S. housing market in 2007.

BRAND EQUITY

brand equity
the added value a brand name brings to a product beyond its functional worth

The most successful brands within their product category develop brand equity. **Brand equity** is the added value a brand brings to a product beyond the item's functional value. For example, when brands like Nike or Reebok add value to athletic shoes and exercise gear, these brands are said to possess brand equity. Companies develop equity for their brands by consistently delivering high quality, building strong associations between a brand and a set of benefits (such as Sony's association with innovation and high quality), and developing a consistent image through sponsorship of humanitarian and environmental causes, the use of logos, trademarks, trade characters, or spokespeople.[39]

Brand equity increases profits and market share. It also enhances both customer and distributor loyalty to a brand. When firms apply brands with strong equity to new products or new lines of products, consumers are more apt to try them. Firms with brand equity may also allow other companies to license their brand for use on noncompeting products (such as Chanel Sunglasses and Harley-Davidson beach towels).

So far we have seen that consumers do not purchase objectively defined products. Rather, consumers buy products as they perceive them to be. They attend to only particular product attributes and process only a fragment of the advertising messages directed to them. What consumers learn about products, services, brands, and stores is largely an outcome of their experiences. What may seem obvious and critical for marketers may prove to be too subtle or even trivial for consumers. It is for this reason the study of consumer perception alone is insufficient to explain their behavior in the marketplace. It is equally important to understand how consumers *learn* about products, services, brands, and stores, which is the topic of the next chapter, dealing with consumer learning and memory.

RISK PERCEPTION

Perception of risk is a fact of life. Any task we undertake in performing our day-to-day activities involves some sort of risk or uncertainty. Whether you are driving your car, purchasing stocks through a broker, or at a store or online buying a product, you are taking a certain degree of risk.

Risk perception is a subjective judgement that we make about the characteristics and severity of uncertainties we face. Individuals confronted with the same decision perceive different degrees of ensuing loss or harm. Variations in the perception of risk are due to a number of individual factors that include a person's prior knowledge and experience, one's emotional state, his or her choice of exposure to the source of risk, degree of expected loss, whether or not the risk is within one's control, the level of uncertainty associated with the outcome, and the risk/benefit ratio of the consequences of an action. For example, a high sensation-seeking individual (i.e., one who craves challenges and thrills), such as a skydiver or mountain climber, perceives the risk of these activities differently than an acrophobic person.

Perception of risk is inseparable from any investigation of consumer behavior. Consumers incur various degrees and varieties of risk in the execution of every marketplace transaction. There are generally five types of risk that consumers experience. The first of these is **functional risk**, that is, whether or not the purchased product or service will perform as expected. A second type of risk is **financial risk**, that is, whether the product or service is worth the investment required. A third type is **physical risk**, whicht questions the danger the product or service poses to the individual or the environment. The fourth type of risk is **social risk**, which seeks to ascertain how significant others will perceive the purchase choice. The fifth type of risk is **psychological risk**, that is, the chance that a faulty choice may bruise the buyer's self-image.

Both consumers and sellers attempt to reduce the degree of risk perception in business transactions. Sellers, for example, adopt various risk-reduction strategies to aid buyers, including offering 100% satisfaction guarantees, warrantees, refunds, samples, and free non-committing trial periods. They also enhance the benefits accrued from a purchase in order to equalize the relationship between risk/benefit paradigm. Consumers, on the other hand, attempt to reduce risk by comparing various competing offerings, acquiring product information from multiple sources, selecting reputable brands and vendors, and seeking endorsed brands, as well as relying upon other surrogate indicators like price.

Unfortunately, the concept of risk perception had become abused to some degree by less-than-scrupulous marketers. Some vendors have come to recognize the power of preying upon consumers' perceptions of risk and fears of uncertainty. Often, vulnerable consumers fall prey to tactics where marketers cite harm if purchase action is not taken. Examples abound in the fields of pharmaceuticals, insurance, health and beauty products, weight-loss clinics, and a host of home-security products and services.[40]

A Cross-Functional Point of View

The topic of perception has a number of implications for business disciplines other than marketing. Relevant issues might include

- **Legal Issues:** Torts arise from differing perceptions of what is right and wrong or where responsibility lies in cases of product liability. Ponder the cases of smokers who claim to have developed cancer as a result of smoking, patients who claim to have been harmed by taking the drug Vioxx, or men who have suffered heart attacks as a result of taking Viagra. From a perceptual point of view, with whom does responsibility lie? Have marketers *deliberately* promoted cigarettes as desirable and thus shaped faulty consumer perceptions of them? Were consumers deceived by these positive images? What are the potential ramifications of such actions?

- **Production Costs/Ethics:** Relying on a brand's reputation for high quality, managers of a well-known high-fashion clothing company decided to compromise on fabrics used for its garments by replacing them with cheaper imported substitutes without consumer knowledge. It also elected to manufacture its wares in a foreign country using cheap labor in order to reduce production costs. Unsuspecting consumers continue to patronize the brand, unaware of the cost-reduction measures implemented by the firm. Is it ethical for companies to rest on their laurels even if that means selling seemingly the same quality product?

- **Sales/Supply Chain:** Consumers often come to perceive a certain brand (such as Maytag appliances) as superior to its competition and highly desirable to own and use. Due to this perception on the part of consumers, sales reps of this brand's sponsoring firm in turn come to perceive their company to be important enough to qualify as the *channel captain*. That is to say, the company is entitled to occupy a position of authority and power in the distribution channel and should possess the right to dictate to dealers how to promote, price, and display the company's products. Dealers perceive that if they were to refuse to conform, they stand a chance of losing the franchise to sell the highly demanded brand. How can producers get better cooperation from channel members other than resorting to coercive tactics that may serve to damage relationships within the supply chain?

These issues, and a host of others like them, show that the topic of perception transcends the field of marketing to other business disciplines.

Summary

This chapter examines the physiological and psychological bases of perception and explains human perceptual processes. The process of perception begins with exposure to the abundant stimuli in the environment. Because perceptual processes are selective, some—but not all—stimuli may attract an individual's attention. Sensation occurs when an individual's sensory receptors transmit sensory data to the brain via the nervous system. Sensory systems include vision, smell, taste, sound, and touch. Perception occurs as individuals subjectively organize and interpret sensations.

A traditional notion views perception as the outcome of interaction between characteristics of stimuli, characteristics or conditions of perceivers, and situational factors. In this view, factors such as threshold levels (absolute, terminal, or differential) influence perceptual processes. The gestalt view, on the other hand, emphasizes perceiving cohesive wholes, recognizing meaningful patterns, and formulating total impressions rather than noting discrete elements. Consumers usually perceive stimuli in their environment in a manner consistent with gestalt principles, including closure, grouping, proximity, context, and figure and ground.

Individuals tend to group stimuli together into classes to facilitate dealing with them. This tendency is known as perceptual categorization. We consciously or unconsciously formulate beliefs about unfamiliar stimuli and assign meanings to objects based on other available information. This tendency is known as perceptual inference.

Schema are organizing frameworks that provide individuals with a structure for understanding new stimuli. Scripts suggest appropriate behavior sequences for particular environments and situations.

Image entails an individual's net impression of what a stimulus is all about. Product, service, and brand positionings must be appropriate for the particular market segment to which they are targeted. Firms may take proactive or reactive-defensive approaches to combat an unfavorable image. Among a firm's greatest assets is the ability of its brands to add value to products and services. This added value is known as brand equity.

Risk perception is a subjective judgment we make about uncertainties we face. Risk can take the forms of functional, physical, social, and psychological disposition.

Review Questions

1. Considering perceptual threshold levels, researchers agree that there are three threshold levels for each sense: an absolute threshold, a terminal threshold, and a differential threshold or JND. Explain what is meant by the JND and show how this concept can be of value to marketers.

2. As consumers, we are affected by the situations in which we buy or use products. These *situational variables* are environmental circumstances that surround product purchase, uses, or related information. Explain.

3. In contrast to the traditional view of perception, Gestalt psychologists suggest a different way of looking at perception. What does their view encompass? Briefly cite two Gestalt principles that you are familiar with and explain how they can be applied in marketing.

4. Image perception is an important topic for marketers. Image is a person's net impression of what a company, product, brand, or store is all about. Are images for a given product, brand, or store uniform among consumers? What factors affect image formation? How do marketers use *image* as a strategy for a brand or a store?

5. Many retailers use their pricing strategy to communicate desired images of product offerings to their customers. A high price can convey the impression of the superior quality and distinction of an item to consumers, while a lower price for the same product can cause it to be perceived as inferior or ordinary. Explain the psychological reasons behind this phenomenon, and indicate other surrogate indicators that can produce similar perceptual reactions in consumers.

Discussion Questions

1. Frank Perdue, of Perdue Farms, will go down in history as the man who transformed chickens from a commodity item to a brand-name product. Discuss what similar producers of commodity-type products have done and can do to create a recognized brand.

2. Community involvement is a popular strategy that many companies follow today to enhance consumers' perception of their corporate image. Many of these firms participate in sponsoring various humanitarian, charitable, and environmental causes, as well as athletic events. How effective do you believe this strategy is in enhancing or changing consumers' perception of the corporate image? Explain.

3. A few years ago, Dole Company, a producer of canned and fresh fruits and vegetables, developed a process that successfully maintained the fresh taste of pineapple juice when the product was packaged in cans. In taste tests, however, the juice did not appeal to subjects. Respondents indicated that they preferred the taste of juice canned by the traditional method. Discuss reasons why subjects in taste tests may have reacted in a manner that, in effect, rejects a superior product.

In reference to the chapter-opening vignette on the success of Toyota and Honda with their hybrid cars, it is surprising to observe that General Motors surrendered its title as the world's top-selling carmaker to Toyota, in part because GM underestimated drivers' appetite for leaner, greener cars—a desire fulfilled perfectly by Toyota's Prius. If you know that GM has always been a leader in pure research and development, spending $6.6 billion in 2006 on research, how can the research director of GM explain the skeptical view of stockholders that the company is a technological laggard when it came to hybrids and green technology? What can GM do to overcome this misperception?

CASE

A Japanese *Good Housekeeping* Magazine

Editors at Hearst, the giant publishing company, breathed a sigh of relief after the first issue of *Good Housekeeping* magazine hit the newsstands in Japan in early 1998. "It was a major challenge," commented one of the company's editors. The problem for Hearst was how to adapt the magazine's Middle American features and style to the Japanese taste. The challenge ranged all the way from choosing a name for the magazine to determining the usefulness of the Good Housekeeping seal of approval.

In selecting a name for the magazine, Hearst editors had to look for a Japanese equivalent, because most Japanese women had never heard of *Good Housekeeping*. If the company were to use an exact translation of the English title, the Japanese name would become *Kaji*. Literally, *kaji* means domestic duties and suggests images of servants' or maids' types of responsibilities. To prevent this negative connotation, the company kept the English name, but printed the word *Good* on the magazine's cover at triple the size of *Housekeeping*.

Editors at Hearst also realized that most of *Good Housekeeping's* U.S. articles would not suit the tastes of Japanese women. For example, articles dealing with womens' triumph over tragedy or their concern for domestic political or work-related issues are of no interest to Japanese women. These types of articles depress the women in Japan, who are accustomed to cheerful and amusing stories. Other features in the magazine such as "Best Loved Bible Quotes" would be out of place in a largely Buddhist nation. The seal of approval would also be confusing to Japanese consumers and would have to change. Instead, the company decided to use Japanese researchers called "GH Checkers" to test and rate various domestic Japanese products.

To best represent the Japanese views in the magazine, Hearst selected a Japanese editor for the job. She felt that some universal themes such as interior decoration, cooking, flower arrangement, and travel would be appropriate to include, but Japanese women are also interested in "aspirational" articles about an idealized America. For example, a feature that was received well in the first issue covered state-of-the-art New York kitchens as large as an entire apartment in Japan. Although such kitchens are a distant dream for most Japanese, it makes good sense to include such features because they kindle images of a fantasy world.

Questions

1. Hearst boasts that it distributed an ambitious 300,000 copies of *Good Housekeeping's* Japanese debut issue. From a perceptual standpoint, why would Japanese women be interested in an American-based magazine?

2. Think of some editorial features in the magazine publishing field that would seem universal—that are likely to be of interest to readers elsewhere. Alternatively, think of other features that would not lend themselves to transferability. Justify your views.

3. The executives at Hearst selected a Japanese woman as an editor to head the project. Why did the company take this action? What insights can such an editor bring to the Japanese edition?

Notes

1. Keith Naughton, "A Case of Prius Envy," *Newsweek*, (September 3, 2007), pp. 40-41.
2. Daniel Kahneman, *Attention and Effort* (Upper Saddle River, NJ: Prentice Hall, 1973).
3. "New Ideas MSI: Color Counts," *Marketing Management* 12, no. 4 (Aug. 2003), p. 2.
4. Maureen Morrin and S. Ratneshwar, "Does it Make Sense to Use Scents To Enhance Brand Memory?" *Journal of Marketing Research* 40, no. 1 (February 2003), pp. 10-16.
5. Kyle Pope, "Technology Improves on the Nose as Scientists Try to Mimic Smell," *Wall Street Journal* (March 1, 1995), pp. B1, B8.
6. Gail Tom, "Marketing with Music," *Journal of Consumer Marketing* 7 (Spring 1990), pp. 49-53.
7. James Vail, "Music as a Marketing Tool," *Advertising Age* (November 4, 1985), p. 24.
8. Ibid.
9. Jeff Ware and Gerald L. Patrick, "Gelson's Supermarkets: Effects of MUZAK Music on the Purchasing Behavior of Supermarket Shoppers," *MUZAK Research Report* (Seattle, WA: MUZAK, 1984).
10. Ronald E. Milliman, "Using Background Music to Affect the Behavior of Supermarket Shoppers," *Journal of Marketing* 46 (Summer 1982), pp. 86-91.
11. Jon Ma, "Emotional and Attitudinal Responses to Websites: The Impact of Background Music in Online Shopping," *AMA Proceedings* (Summer 2006), p. 219.
12. George Gordon, *Active Touch* (Oxford, England: Pergamon Press, 1980).
13. Deborah B. McCabe and Stephen M. Nowlis, "The Effect of Examining Actual Products or Product Descriptions on Consumer Preference," *Journal of Consumer Psychology* 13, no. 4 (2003), pp. 431-9.
14. Stephen MacDonald, "Form = Function," *Wall Street Journal* (January 22, 1988), p. 17.
15. Raymond R. Coffey, "Advertisers Should Bury Old Gangsters," *Chicago Sun-Times* (June 7, 1994), p. 3.
16. Donna Abu-Nasr, "Nike Bows to Muslims, Will Recall 'Air' Shoes," *Chicago Sun-Times* (June 25, 1997), p. 59.

17. Andrew A. Mitchell, "An Information Processing View of Consumer Behavior," in Subhash C. Jain (ed.), *Research Frontiers in Marketing, Dialogues and Directions* (Chicago, IL: American Marketing Association, 1978), pp. 189-90; Allan Greenberg and Charles Suttoni, "Television Commercial Wear-out," *Journal of Advertising Research* 13 (October 1973), pp. 47-54.
19. J. Karremans, "Beyond Vicary's Fantasies: The Impact of Subliminal Priming and Brand Choice," *Journal of Experimental Social Psychology*, vol. 42 (2006), pp. 792-798; Anthony R. Pratkanis, "The Cargo Cult Science of Subliminal Persuasion," *Skeptical Inquirer* (2006), pp. 8-11.
20. Pradeep Kakkar and Richard J. Lutz, "Situational Influence on Consumer Behavior: A Review," in Harold H. Kassarjian and Thomas S. Robertson (eds.), *Perspectives in Consumer Behavior*, 3rd ed. (Glenview, IL: Scott, Foresman, 1981), pp. 204-14.
21. Russell W. Belk, "An Exploratory Assessment of Situational Effects in Buyer Behavior," *Journal of Marketing Research* 11 (May 1974), pp. 156-63; U. N. Umesh and Joseph A. Cote, "Influence of Situational Variables on Brand-Choice Models," *Journal of Business Research* 16, no. 2 (1988), pp. 91-99; J. Wesley Hutchinson and Joseph W. Alba, "Ignoring Irrelevant Information: Situational Determinants of Consumer Learning," *Journal of Consumer Research* 18 (December 1991), pp. 325-45.
22. Harold H. Kassarjian, "Field Theory in Consumer Behavior," in Scott Ward and Thomas Robertson (eds.), *Consumer Behavior: Theoretical Sources* (Upper Saddle River, NJ: Prentice Hall, 1973); David Horton and Thomas Turnage, *Human Learning* (Upper Saddle River, NJ: Prentice Hall, 1976); Mary R. Zimmer and Linda L. Golden, "Impressions of Retail Stores: A Content Analysis of Consumer Images," *Journal of Retailing* 64 (Fall 1988), pp. 265-93; Gaetano Kanizsa, "Gestalt Theory Has Been Misinterpreted, but Has Also Had Some Real Conceptual Difficulties," *Philosophical Psychology* 7 (1994), pp. 149-62;

Michael Stadler and Peter Kruse, "Gestalt Theory and Synergetics: From Psychophysical Isomorphism to Holistic Emergentism," *Philosophical Psychology* 7 (1994), pp. 211-26; Julius Harburger, "Concept Closure," *Advertising Age* (January 12, 1987), p. 18.

23. "In This Taste Test, the Loser Is the Taste Test," *Wall Street Journal* (June 3, 1987), p. 33; Robert F. Hartley, *Marketing Mistakes*, 4th ed. (New York: Wiley, 1989), pp. 221-36.

24. James T. Heimbach and Jacob Jacoby, "The Zeigernik Effect in Advertising," in M. Venkatesan (ed.), *Proceedings of the Third Annual Conference* (Association for Consumer Research, 1972), pp. 746-58; Harburger, "Concept Closure."

25. Robin Pogrebin, "By Design or Not, an Ad Becomes a Fad," *New Yok Times* (December 24, 1995), p. E3.

26. Devavrat Purohit and Joydeep Srivastava, "Effect of Manufacturer Reputation, Retailer Reputation, and Product Warranty on Consumer Judgment of Product Quality," *Journal of Consumer Psychology* 10, no. 3 (2001), pp. 123-135. Niraj Dawar and Philip Parker, "Marketing Universals: Consumers' Use of Brand Name, Price, Physical Appearance, and Retailer Reputation as Signals of Product Quality," *Journal of Marketing* 58 (April 1994), pp. 81-95; William Dodds, Kent Monroe, and Dhruv Grewal, "Effects of Price, Brand, and Store Information on Buyers' Product Evaluations," *Journal of Marketing Research* 28 (August 1991), pp. 307-19; Kent Monroe, *Pricing: Making Profitable Decisions*, 2nd ed. (New York: McGraw-Hill, 1990); Tung-Zong Chang and Albert R. Wildt, "Price, Product Information, and Purchase Intention: An Empirical Study," *Journal of the Academy of Marketing Science* 22, no. 1 (1994), pp. 16-27; Donald R. Liechtenstein, Nancy M. Ridgway, and Richard G. Nitemeyer, "Price Perception and Consumer Shopping Behavior: A Field Study," *Journal of Marketing Research* 30 (May 1993), p. 242; Noel Mark Lavenka, "Measurement of Consumers' Perceptions of Product Quality, Brand Name, and Packaging: Candy Bar Comparisons by Magnitude Estimation," *Marketing Research* 3, no. 2 (June 1991), pp. 38-45; Rose L. Johnson and James L. Kellaries, "An Exploratory Study of Price/Perceived Quality Relationships Among Consumer Services," in Michael Housten (ed.), *Advances in Consumer Research* 15 (1988), pp. 316-22; Durairaj Mahaswaron, "Country of Origin as a Stereotype: Effects of Consumer Expertise and Attribute Strength on Product Evaluations," *Journal of Consumer Research* 21 (September 1994), pp. 354-65. Jonah Berger, et. al., "The Influence of Product Variety on Brand Perception and Choice" *Journal of Marketing Science*, vol. 26, no. 4 (July/August 2007), pp. 584-585; Peeter W. J. Verlegh, et. al., "Country of Origin Effects in Consumer Processing of Advertising Claims," *International Journal of Research in Marketing,* vol. 22, no. 2 (June 2005), pp. 127-139.

27. Mita Sujan, "Consumer Knowledge: Effects on Evaluation Strategies Mediating Consumer Judgments," *Journal of Consumer Research* 12 (June 1985), pp. 31-46; Eleanor Rosch, "Principles of Categorization," in E. Rosch and B. B. Lloyd (eds.), Recognition and Categorization (Hillsdale, NJ: Lawrence Erlbaum, 1978).

28. Joseph W. Alba and J. Wesley Hutchinson, "Dimensions of Consumer Expertise," *Journal of Consumer Research* 13 (1987), pp. 493-98.

29. Pierre Martineau, *Motivation in Advertising* (New York: McGraw-Hill, 1957), p. 146.

30. Pierre Martineau, "The Personality of the Retail Store," *Harvard Business Review* 36 (January-February, 1958), pp. 47-55.

31. Ron Kaspriske, "Uncorking a Few in the Wine Country," *Golf Digest* (September, 2007).

32. Lil Berry, "The Components of Department Store Image: A Theoretical and Empirical Analysis," *Journal of Retailing* 45, no. 1 (1998), pp. 3-20; and David Muzursky and Jacob Jacoby, "Exploring the Development of Store Images," *Journal of Retailing* 62 (Summer 1986), pp. 145-65.

33. Ibid.

34. "Exporting a Legend," *International Advertising* (November-December 1981), pp. 2-3; "Levi Zipping Up World Image," *Advertising Age* (September 14, 1981), pp. 35-36; and "For Levi's a Flattering Fit Overseas," *Business Week* (November 5, 1990), p. 76.

35. Ama Carmine, "The Effect of Perceived Advertising Costs on Brand Perceptions," *Journal of Consumer Research* 17 (September 1990), pp. 160-71.

36. Kenneth A. Hunt and Susan M. Keaveney, "A Process Model of the Effects of Price Promotions on Brand Image," *Psychology and Marketing* 11, no. 6, (November-December 1994), pp. 511-32; P. R. Dickson and A. G. Sawyer, "The Price Knowledge and Search of Supermarket Shoppers," *Journal of Marketing* 54 (July 1990), pp. 42-53; Joseph W. Alba, Susan M. Broniarczyk, Terence A. Shimp, and Joel E. Urbany, "The Influence of Prior Beliefs, Frequency Cues, and Magnitude Cues on Consumers' Perceptions of Comparative Price Data," *Journal of Consumer Research* 21 (September 1994), pp. 219-35.

37. C. Whan Park, Bernard Jaworski, and Deborah J. MacInnis, "Strategic Brand Concept Image Management," *Journal of Marketing* (October 1986), pp. 135-45; Thomas J. Reynolds and Jonathan Gutman, "Advertising Is Image Management," *Journal of Advertising Research* (February-March 1984), pp. 27-37.

38. Josee Bloemer and Ko Ruyter, "On the Relationship Between Store Image, Store Satisfaction, and Store Loyalty" *European Journal of Marketing* 32, no. 5/6 (1999), pp. 499-513.

39. Don E. Schultz, "Brand Equity Has Become Oh So Fashionable," *Marketing News* (March 31, 1997), p. 9; Kevin Lane Keller, "Conceptualizing, Measuring, and Managing Customer-Based Brand Equity," *Journal of Marketing* 57 (January 1993), pp. 1–22; H. Shanker Krishnan and Dipankar Chakravarti, "Varieties of Brand Memory Induced by Advertising: Determinants, Measures, and Relationships," in David A. Aaker and Alexander L. Biel (eds.), *Brand Equity and Advertising: Advertising's Role in Building Strong Brands* (Hillsdale, NJ: Lawrence Erlbaum, 1993), pp. 213–31; Peter H. Farquhar, "Brand Equity," *Marketing Insights* (Summer 1989), p. 59: Ama Carmine, "The Effect of Perceived Advertising Costs on Brand Perceptions," *Journal of Consumer Research* 17 (September 1990), pp. 160–71; Kenneth A. Hunt and Susan M. Keaveney, "A Process Model of the Effects of Price Promotions on Brand Image," *Psychology and Marketing* 11, no. 6 (November–December 1994), pp. 511–32.

40. Clinton M. Jenkin, "Risk perception and terrorism: applying the psychometric paradigm, *Journal of Naval Post Graduate School Center for Homeland and Security*, no. 2, (July, 2006); Jared Carbone, et al., "Can natural experiments measure behavioral responses to enviromental risks?," *Environmental and Resource Economics*, vol. 33 (2006), pp. 273–297.

Consumer Learning and Memory

LEARNING OBJECTIVES

- To grasp the meaning and range of the consumer learning process.
- To develop a basic understanding of selected learning theories.
- To explore the concept of Neo-Pavlovian conditioning.
- To become familiar with the notion of hemispheric specialization of the brain.
- To gain insight into the phenomenon of vicarious learning.
- To comprehend the nature of memory and its structure.

KEY TERMS

learning
low-involvement learning
high-involvement learning
classical conditioning
contiguity
contingency
congruity
operant (instrumental) conditioning
positive reinforcement
negative reinforcement
reinforcement schedule
continuous reinforcement
intermittent reinforcement
massed (concentrated) practice
spaced (distributed) practice
behavior shaping
ecological design
stimulus generalization
stimulus discrimination
cognitive learning

subjective experience
neo-Pavlovian conditioning
hemispheric specialization of the brain
left hemisphere
right hemisphere
vicarious learning
learning curve (experience effect)
brand loyalty
inertia
brand parity
mnemonic devices
sensory memory
short-term memory (STM)
encoding
long-term memory (LTM)
knowledge structures
information retrieval
retroactive interference
misinformation effect
proactive interference

One of today's persistent marketing problems is that consumers' purchasing habits are unpredictable. Consumers are too savvy to buy or stay with a brand on the strength of its name alone. They stray from their brands looking for alternatives that offer better price and value. The percentage of consumers who say they are loyal to well-known brand names has declined from a high of 82 percent in 1976 to around 50 percent today. This brand-switching trend is fueled by thousands of trading sites on the Internet, the availability of a gamut of private-label products, and the growing popularity of alternative retail outlets such as warehouse clubs and discount food and drugstores.

To businesses, brand loyalty translates into higher market share and profits. Programs have already been initiated by marketers to entice and reward loyal customers with bonuses such as frequent-flier schemes, financial contributions to retirement accounts, and even financial credits toward college tuition. Such rewards are instrumental in the consumer learning process of becoming store and brand loyal. These programs have come to be known as frequent-shopper programs. Other frequent-shopper programs initiated by grocery chains, such as Safeway, Jewel-Osco and Dominick's, offer immediate reinforcement with a discount off the purchase price when consumers use a preferred-customer card at the checkout counter. One of the hottest trends with credit cards these days is the varied rewards programs that companies offer to promote particular cards and to increase their usage. The different types of rewards customers can enjoy include lifestyle rewards, such as allowing cardholders to take vacations and go on other getaways, or to enjoy a "night out" once they have accumulated a certain number of points. Other rewards include cash-back offers, as well as air-travel miles, gift certificates, free merchandise, and member-only discounts.

In 2004, one interesting case of a reward program was put into place by the Hershey Chocolate Company, which rewarded candy lovers with free tickets to the movies. Hershey executives felt that candy and motion pictures go hand-in-hand and decided to reward their loyal customers with something that everyone enjoys doing—going to the movies. In this reward program, which was labeled "Hollywood Movie Magic," Hershey's chocolate lovers received movie tickets for the purchase of Milk Duds, Whoppers, and Hershey Bite brands.

Many companies today, such as phone companies, restaurants, car rental agencies, and hotels, realize the importance of such retention-intended frequent-shopper programs. Although such practices are expensive for participating companies, their cost is justified by the benefits of retained customers. They make good economic sense in light of the fact that the cost of retaining customers is minimal compared to the cost of acquiring new ones.[1]

Achieving customer loyalty is one of the foremost goals of marketing managers. Think of some programs that you personally have participated in (supermarket preferred-customer cards, frequent-flier miles) that are designed to enhance customer loyalty. Is the extent of your loyalty to a brand or store influenced by these programs? Visit Reward Credit Card at its Web site, www.rewardcreditcardsite.com *and determine if, besides economic benefits, there are any psychological forces behind choosing a particular credit card.*

All of the programs described above, whether they involve lifestyle rewards, receiving cash back, or granting air miles, have one thing in common—they reward customers for their patronage. Such reinforcements are major contributors to learning.

This chapter discusses learning as it applies to consumer behavior. We introduce three major learning theories: classical conditioning, operant conditioning, and cognitive learning. Although the bases for these theories are different, they are complementary—not contradictory. Each theory explains different types of learning from different perspectives. Other forms of learning, such as vicarious learning and habit formation, are relevant, and we explore them as well. Finally, we discuss memory and forgetting.

What Is Learning?

Learning infiltrates nearly all human behavior, and consumption of goods and services is no exception. Consumer behavior includes learning as both an adaptive and a problem-solving activity. Within economic, cultural, social, and psychological constraints, we exhibit behaviors that we anticipate will enable us to reach the various goals on which we focus. As we come to discover that certain behaviors produce results that are more satisfying than others, we reassess our decision processes and purchasing strategies accordingly.

DEFINITION OF LEARNING

Learning has been defined in a number of ways. In a broad sense, learning occurs when experience produces relatively lasting changes in a person's capabilities or behavior. More precisely, learning is any process by which changes occur in the content or organization of an individual's long-term memory.[2]

A few qualifications are in order. First, because learning frequently involves mental processes, it is not directly observable. Thus, we often measure it in terms of performance. Teachers measure student learning according to performance on exams; similarly, marketers may measure consumer learning as it is manifested in their shopping selections. Not all learning, however, produces immediate activity. Rather, it can offer information that may eventually lead to action. Whereas most retail newspaper ads and many Web sites seek prompt consumer responses, most manufacturer-sponsored TV and magazine ads are image builders that aren't expected to produce quick purchase reactions.

A second qualification governs the source of behavioral changes. Learning entails a change brought about by experience; our definition excludes behavior and ability changes that result from instinct and reflex, or growth and maturation of body tissues.

Third, the effects of learning are relatively long term. Learning is said to have occurred when a subject consistently responds in the desired manner. The definition excludes temporary changes precipitated by alcohol, drugs, or deprivation (hunger, thirst, fatigue).

learning
process by which changes occur in the content or organization of a person's long-term memory

Fourth, the term *behavior*, as employed in these definitions, covers both overt activities (such as shopping) and cognitive processes (such as problem solving and information processing). The ad from the Partnership for a Drug-Free America shown in Figure 5.1 alerts parents to the fact that a medicine cabinet in the home can pose as serious a problem for teens as having drug dealers in town.

RANGE OF LEARNING SITUATIONS

Humans, throughout their lives, acquire numerous skills that enable them to manage their daily lives. They learn language skills to interact and communicate with others. They learn to recognize and respond to symbols encountered in the environment such as packages and brand names. They learn how to process information to solve problems. They learn to think by mentally manipulating symbols representing reality to form combinations of meaning. This thinking leads to insight and an enhanced comprehension of relationships in a problem. Through a process known as consumer socialization, they acquire the knowledge and skills necessary to function in the marketplace. For example, they learn to read the small print in a contract or negotiate the price of a new car. Through familiarity with objects over time and the influence of others, consumers learn tastes for specific products, styles, and brands.[3]

low-involvement learning
a case where individuals are less motivated to attend to and process material to be learned

Applied specifically to the field of consumer behavior, learning occurs in situations ranging from low to high levels of consumer involvement. In **low-involvement learning** situations, consumers have little or no motivation to process the material to be learned. When consumers encounter ads in the media or on the Web for products they do not use or stores where they do not shop, they may lack the incentive to attend to and process these messages.

high-involvement learning
a case where individuals are motivated to process information to be learned

In **high-involvement learning** situations, on the other hand, individuals are motivated to process the information to be learned. A consumer who plans to buy a new automobile is likely to navigate the Internet searching for and checking out automotive Web sites and/or seek advice from others to learn as much as possible about the car's features, performance capabilities, and gas mileage. The degree of consumer involvement is a function of the interaction between an individual, a stimulus, and a situation.[4] For instance, consumers who lack interest in automobiles might merely glance at car ads. However, if an automobile ad features an admired superstar, many of these same individuals might attend to the ad and read it carefully to learn what the celebrity has to say. Similarly, consumers who generally ignore car ads would likely become more involved with automobile advertising when the need to buy a car arises.

Learning Theories

A review of the literature on learning reveals a number of different learning theories.[5] These can be divided among two schools of thought: behavioral-associationist theories and cognitive-organizational theories. Three learning

THERE'S A NEW DEALER IN TOWN.

These days, teens don't have to go out looking for drugs; they can just go to the medicine cabinet. Even as teen use of "street drugs" is on the decline, the abuse of prescription drugs is increasing. The perception is that they're safe even though abuse can lead to paranoia, addiction, seizures, and death. You can prevent abuse by safeguarding and monitoring your family's medications. Educate yourself. Find out more at theantidrug.com. You can stop the dealer.

Office of National Drug Control Policy / Partnership for a Drug-Free America

theantidrug.com **PARENTS.**
THE ANTI-DRUG.

Figure 5.1
The Partnership for a Drug-Free America warns parents of teens about the dangers of drugs currently sitting in the medicine cabinet of their own home.

theories apply particularly well to the attempts of marketers to stimulate or change consumer behavior and are covered in this chapter. These theories are (1) classical conditioning and (2) operant conditioning, which fall under the behavioral–associationist heading, and (3) cognitive learning, which addresses the mental processes by which people acquire knowledge and form concepts.

CLASSICAL CONDITIONING

classical conditioning
a view that learning involves linking a conditioned stimulus and an unconditioned stimulus

The term *classical conditioning* elicits thoughts of the well-known experiments by Pavlov with dogs.[6] The process of **classical conditioning** involves forming a connection between a conditioned stimulus (in Pavlov's case a bell) and an unconditioned stimulus (in Pavlov's case food) to teach a desired reaction (salivation at the tone of the bell). To form the link between the bell tone and food, Pavlov sounded a bell just before the dogs were exposed to food. The bell tone was the conditioned stimulus (CS) and food was the unconditioned stimulus (US). Eventually, after many repetitions, hearing the bell tone caused Pavlov's dogs to expect food and to salivate. The bell had come to produce the same response, salivation (UR), originally produced only by food. A connection had been formed, and a primitive variety of learning had taken place. A schematic conceptualization of this process appears in Exhibit 5.1.

Pavlov viewed conditioned responses as temporary and capable of being extinguished. The Russian word he used meant *conditional*, which suggests a temporary effect. Curiously, U.S. researchers assumed that Pavlov's interest was in the maintenance of responses and somehow translated his word as *conditioned*, which suggests the effects were permanent or final. Recognizing this departure from Pavlov's original intention, Krugman noted that long-term consumer likes and dislikes become part of an individual's personality in a way that briefly conditioned and easily extinguished conditioned responses do not.[7]

EXHIBIT 5.1   **Schematic Presentation of Classical Conditioning**

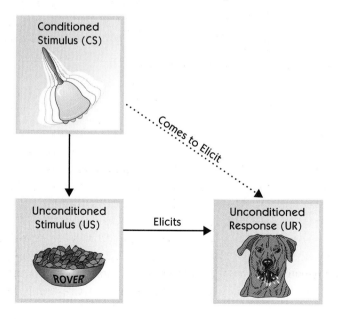

Ethical Dilemma

Cause Behind Cause Marketing

Astute marketers have cleverly used the concept of classical conditioning to get consumers to reach for their brands. The ploy involves forming a connection between their brand and a particular charitable cause. American Express first came up with the idea back in 1983. Each time the cardholder charged an item, the company donated a penny toward restoring the Statue of Liberty. The result was a few million dollars to refurbish the Lady, plus the heightened goodwill for AMEX. Known as *cause marketing*, the practice is one of the fastest-growing and increasingly-debated attempts by corporations to boost market share. Through the years, many examples of cause marketing were initiated, including Avon support of breast cancer research in the United States; Kimberly-Clark, Coca-Cola, and Nestle support of Children's Miracle Network; American Express donation of 2 cents per transaction to the Share Our Strength anti-hunger organization; and Midas support of Project Baby Safe. Other recent campaigns include Product Red, which is supported by many major corporations including Gap, Apple, and Motorola, to cure AIDS; Chilli's support for St. Jude's Children's Hospital; Lay's snacks for Make-A-Wish charity; and General Mills box tops for education.

The purpose of these affiliations between businesses and charities is obvious. Although conveying a positive message to the company's audiences is an important objective, causes are instrumental in moving cases of merchandise. Such relationships get consumers emotionally involved, which encourages them to switch brands and retailers. When consumers were asked their feelings regarding charitable tie-ins, 40 percent of women and 30 percent of men reported that they were more likely to buy a product or service if they knew that a certain amount of the purchase price was going to be donated to a cause or campaign.

Critics argue that many companies are insincere in their claims of support for charities. Sometimes companies donate just a minuscule fraction of the money they earn from the campaign to the chosen cause. Other times, companies' actions to support a cause wind up doing more harm than good. An example in point is BMWs Ultimate Drive Campaign in 1997, in which the firm donated a dollar toward fighting cancer for each mile potential customers test drove the company's vehicles. Yet the chemicals of car exhaust are established links to lung cancer. Similarly in 2007, Estee Lauder donated $500,000 from sales of its Pink Ribbon Collection of cosmetics to breast cancer research but refused to sign the Compact for Safe Cosmetics to ensure that its products do not contain chemicals that are suspected of contributing to the disease. Such instances of questionable cause-marketing practices are becoming commonplace and could pose a threat to legitimate companies that run cause-related marketing campaigns. As the public increasingly falls victim to cases of suspicious charitable solicitations, consumers could be turned off by cause-marketing campaigns.[11]

In your opinion, is cause marketing a desirable business practice? Discover why companies are interested in this endeavor by visiting www.tsaresearch.com/CRMFEATURE.html. For successful tie-ins between a brand and a charity, what prerequisites do you recommend? Is a natural fit between the product category and charity necessary? Why or why not?

Classical Conditioning and the Formation of Associations

The traditional interpretation of classical conditioning views learning as forming connections or associations between environmental events.[8] Some psychologists consider these associations to be nothing more than linkages between two concepts; other psychologists regard these associations as a fusing or blending so that two separate items are combined to form a larger unit that has no immediate resemblance to either item alone.[9] Associative learning via classical conditioning usually involves the organism's learning of an association between a conditioned (originally neutral) stimulus and an unconditioned stimulus, which could be biological (food, fragrance) or symbolic (the flag). In a consumer behavior context, conditioned stimuli include products, brands, and stores, whereas unconditioned stimuli might include celebrities, music, and humor. For example, studies have demonstrated that hearing music or humor we like or dislike while being exposed to products can directly affect our preferences for them.[10]

Research on the connection between music and sales involved the case of holiday music and holiday merchandise.[12] The study revealed that department stores that played Christmas music during the holiday season experienced on the average a 32.8 percent increase in sales volume of seasonal merchandise compared with stores that failed to play such music.[13] To summarize, through association, a product/brand (CS) can come to elicit liking/disliking (CR) analogous to the liking/disliking (UR) evoked by an ad's model, music, or humor (US).[14] According to one Coca-Cola executive, "Pavlov took a neutral object and by associating it with a meaningful object, made it a symbol of something else . . . that is precisely what we try to do in modern advertising."[15]

The traditional view of classical conditioning holds that conditioning represents the establishment of new reflexes (stimulus–response connections) that result from frequent pairings of a CS and US. In other words, classical conditioning is a low-level, mechanical process in which control over a response is passed from one stimulus to another.[16] From a consumer behavior perspective, this would suggest, for example, that if a particular piece of music emotionally excites the listener, then a brand paired with the same music should similarly stir the consumer.[17]

Learning Principles Under the Classical Conditioning Model

For connections to be formed under classical conditioning, four conditions must prevail—repetition, contiguity, contingency, and congruity. Repetition is the frequency of pairing a CS with an US. The more often the CS and US are coupled, the more quickly learning occurs.

Repetition is employed in scheduling media for a campaign. Advertisers reiterate their messages in many ads and commercials targeted to the same audience over a specified time period. Ad copy, especially in the broadcast media, repeatedly links the brand with its greatest benefit.[18] Figure 5.2 illustrates repetition by showing a series of photographs depicting various models of Mercedes-Benz automobiles.

Repeating advertising messages to an audience does, however, cause the impact of these messages to lessen. *Advertising wearout* is defined as diminished responsiveness of an audience to ads and commercials as a consequence of repeated exposure to them. Recently, new views regarding advertising wearout have appeared in the literature. For example, Hughes feels that wearout occurs when an ad no longer triggers recall of positive feelings from a viewer's long-term memory.[19] Wearout results, in part, from a viewer's adaptation to the ad as well as from lowered expectations of entertainment or new information from it.

Contiguity, a second principle, involves spacial and temporal nearness. Learning occurs more quickly when the CS is presented close to the US. In his

contiguity
the spacial or temporal nearness of objects

The most common photograph taken is with a loved one.

Unlike any other.   Mercedes-Benz

© Daimler-Chrysler AG.

Figure 5.2

In this ad from Mercedes Benz, repetition of the car's imagery over its lengthy history utilizes the concept of classical conditioning for the purpose of enhancing consumer learning.

experiment, Pavlov rang the bell (CS) at about the same moment he exposed the dog to food (US). If the bell were rung much earlier or later and in different surroundings, it would have been more difficult for the dogs to connect the bell tone with food. Marketers often try to associate products and product use with pleasant imagery through temporal or spatial proximity.[20] For example, sponsors advertise automobiles in luxurious surroundings, clothing and jewelry on attractive models, and beer and soft drinks in cheerful, party-like settings.

To expedite learning via classical conditioning, stimuli should be presented in the proper order. A third principle known as **contingency** states that the CS should precede the US.[21] Research suggests the CS has predictive or information value. It signals that the US is about to occur. Thus, the conditioned response (CR) is anticipatory.[22]

Finally, for associations to form between the CS and US, they must be related in some meaningful way. This principle is known as **congruity**, the consistency or relatedness of sequentially presented pairs of informational cues or concurrently encountered elements comprising a stimulus event.[23] Congruity

contingency
the notion that the conditioned stimulus should precede the unconditioned stimulus

congruity
the relatedness of sequentially presented informational cues

and incongruity influence our processing and memory for events. Incongruent information tends to be more difficult to encode and retrieve. Irrelevant information tends to produce lower recall.

OPERANT (INSTRUMENTAL) CONDITIONING

operant (instrumental) conditioning

a view that learning is driven by the positive or negative consequences of behavior

Operant or instrumental conditioning differs from classical conditioning in three significant aspects. First, unlike classical conditioning, which is driven by antecedent stimuli, operant conditioning is driven by the *consequences* of behavior as subjects discover that certain actions produce more desirable outcomes than others. Second, in operant conditioning, learning occurs not through repetitive responses to contiguous stimuli but through trial and error. When a behavior is followed by a reward, the subject is more likely to repeat that behavior. In other words, he or she forms a *habit* or response tendency. On the other hand, when a person's behavior is punished, the subject tests new responses and engages in alternate activities until his or her actions are suitably rewarded.

The third difference is that whereas classical conditioning involves stimulus substitution, operant conditioning involves response substitution.[24] In other words, fruitless behaviors tend to be replaced with ones that are reinforced. Consumers who are unsuccessful in obtaining a pleasing resolution to a buying situation are likely to modify their solution until a subsequent response is found to be more satisfactory.

Classical and operant conditioning are similar in one significant aspect. Both models of learning ignore mental processes such as perception, thinking, and reasoning. Subjects are passive and make no attempt to assess the nature of the situation. Nor do they actively examine alternate response modes. In conditioning models, learners do not think; they simply behave.

Like Pavlov, U.S. psychologist B. F. Skinner used animal experiments to develop his operant learning model. In Skinner's conditioning exercises, hungry pigeons and rats were placed in so-called Skinner boxes equipped with special mechanisms such as pecking keys and levers designed to dispense food when touched. Initially the pigeons and rats wandered restlessly in the boxes, until they accidentally hit the special mechanism and food pellets rewarded them. Soon the test animals came to manipulate the food-dispensing mechanism continuously, seeking food pellets. Once the mechanism had been disconnected, however, their rate of manipulation decreased and eventually stopped. At that point, extinction had occurred. That is, the behavior ceased because key pecking and lever pressing were no longer instrumental in producing rewards.[25] The process of operant conditioning is depicted in Exhibit 5.2.

How Operant Conditioning Works

Operant conditioning alters the likelihood that a behavior will occur by changing the consequences of that behavior. Unlike classical conditioning, operant conditioning proposes a sequence in which behavior occurs first, perhaps in reaction to a cue. The behavior is then reinforced (or punished),

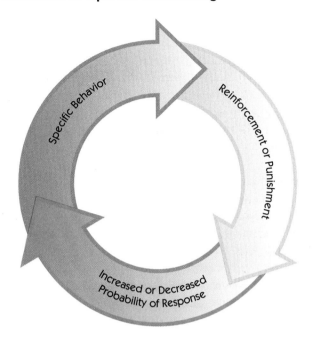

and the result is an increase (or decrease) in the probability that the response will occur again. Reinforcement and punishment are, therefore, *instrumental* in bringing about a behavioral change.

Reinforcement is a reward given to acknowledge a desired behavior and increase the probability that it will be repeated in the future. It can be positive or negative. **Positive reinforcement** encourages behavior with pleasant consequences such as fun, enjoyment, relaxation, or savings. Marketers offer attractive benefits and other rewards to establish and bolster desired consumer behaviors. As we saw at the start of the chapter, many firms, such as airlines and credit card organizations, reward customers with frequent-flier miles as a bonus when they use the companies' services. Cosmetics companies often give customers free gifts when they purchase a designated item or spend a specified amount.

Negative reinforcement, on the other hand, offers the relief or removal of some adverse situation to increase the frequency of a behavior or to boost sales. For example, Bayer Aspirin, Tylenol, and Advil promise pain relief. Other products such as antibacterial soaps, antiperspirants, mouthwashes, anti-aging creams and treatments, as well as teeth-whitening strips are all positioned to lessen various consumer fears and anxieties. The term *negative reinforcement* must not be confused with punishment.

Punishment is an aversive result that decreases the frequency of an undesirable response. Punishment can take two forms. Frequently it involves something that subjects perceive as painful or unpleasant. For example,

positive reinforcement
an inducement to repeat a behavior to receive a pleasant consequence

negative reinforcement
an inducement to repeat a behavior in order to remove an adverse situation

motorists who exceed the posted speed limit may, if stopped by the police, be required to pay a hefty fine. Punishment may also take the form of the removal of something desirable or pleasant. Reckless drivers with numerous traffic violations may, as part of their penalty, have their driving privileges suspended. Marketers do not have the power to punish consumers for not taking a suggested action in any direct form, although some observers regard certain marketing practices, such as fear and guilt advertising, as falling under this label.

REINFORCEMENT SCHEDULES

The pattern in which reinforcements are given is known as the schedule of reinforcement. Different reinforcement schedules lead to different patterns of learning. There are two main types of **reinforcement schedules**: continuous (total) and intermittent (partial) schedules. **Continuous reinforcement** schedules reward a desired behavior every time it occurs. Under conditions of continuous reinforcement, learning occurs more quickly, but the sought behavior ceases shortly after the rewards stop. **Intermittent reinforcement** schedules, on the other hand, reward a desired behavior only occasionally. Although learning does not occur as quickly as under continuous reinforcement, intermittent reinforcement slows down the process of forgetting. In other words, when learned under conditions of intermittent reinforcement, behavior becomes more persistent. Many gamblers persevere, even after repeated losses, precisely because they do not expect to win every time and thus never know when the next win might occur. The *next time* may provide the coveted payoff. Hence the residual effects of learning persist. The effects of continuous and intermittent reinforcement on forgetting and behavior maintenance over time are depicted in Exhibit 5.3.

EXHIBIT 5.3   **Rate of Forgetting**

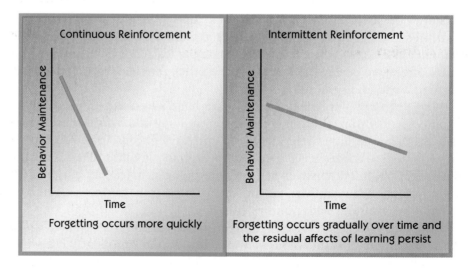

Continuous Reinforcement

Behavior Maintenance

Time

Forgetting occurs more quickly

Intermittent Reinforcement

Behavior Maintenance

Time

Forgetting occurs gradually over time and the residual affects of learning persist

PRACTICE SCHEDULES

Timing exerts important influences on learning. **Massed (concentrated) practice** condenses a learning schedule into a brief time span to accelerate learning. **Spaced (distributed) practice,** on the other hand, paces learning over a time interval to increase retention. Spaced practice typically involves several short learning sessions distributed over time with breaks or rest periods between them. Generally, massed schedules produce greater initial learning, but dispersed schedules produce learning that is more lasting. Traditional media schedules slot brief ads and commercials that recur over the duration of a campaign, approximating spaced learning. The recent *infomercial* phenomenon, on the other hand, might be compared to massed learning.

CHALLENGES IN APPLYING OPERANT CONDITIONING

One challenge that marketers face when applying operant conditioning concepts is that the desired behavior must occur first before it can be rewarded. For example, in the field of automobile sales, it is unlikely that prospects would be actively searching for a new car if their present vehicle were functioning well. Consequently, car dealerships need a strategy to entice prospects to visit their showrooms. Thus, where the probability that individuals will perform a desired behavior is small, marketers frequently rely on a process called behavior shaping. **Behavior shaping** is the process of breaking down a complex behavior into a sequence of simple component actions and then reinforcing the successive components to increase the probability that the final action will occur.

For example, an auto dealership can apply behavior shaping by mapping out a guided, step-by-step path that gradually steers prospects toward buying, rewarding them at each point along the way. First, the dealer may initiate a direct-mail campaign announcing the arrival of new models and offering visitors free refreshments, gifts, and opportunities to win prizes in hourly raffles. Second, the dealer may offer a $50 cash reward to test-drive a display vehicle. Finally, to encourage test-drivers to buy, a $1000 instant rebate may be extended to anyone who purchases a new car during the promotion period.

A second type of operant conditioning is known as ecological design. **Ecological design** is the calculated planning of physical space and other facets of the environment to modify human behavior or expedite a desired response. For example, auto sales personnel usually escort buyers into *closing rooms* to complete the details of a transaction. These environments are specially designed to relax buyers with soft colors, subdued background music, and customer service award plaques on the walls, as well as to minimize distractions and interruptions. This serene environment is instrumental in making customers feel more relaxed and in control of the situation—conditions that are favorable for conducting business.

Potential applications of ecological design are endless. Retailers seek convenient and accessible store locations with plenty of parking space to encourage shopping. They fashion selling-floor layouts and merchandise displays to expose

massed (concentrated) practice
lengthy learning sessions scheduled over a brief time period

spaced (distributed) practice
brief learning sessions intermingled with rest periods scheduled over a lengthy time period

behavior shaping
the process of breaking down a complex behavior into a series of simple stages and reinforcing the learner at each step

ecological design
the planning of physical space and other facets of the environment to modify human behavior

Figure 5.3

The concept of ecological design is illustrated in this ad from California Closets that depicts a functional yet attractive décor for contemporary homes.

See our new Lago™ finishes direct from Italy   **SPACE** TO BE

CALIFORNIA CLOSETS®

complimentary consultation | 800.274.6754 | californiaclosets.com
1000 Fourth Street , San Rafael

customers to a wide variety of merchandise and trigger impulse buying. In one case, a firm that operates several 7-Eleven stores addressed the problem of loitering in store parking lots by installing exterior speakers and playing Mozart, Mantovani, and 1960s folk tunes. Kids, who composed a large percentage of the loiterers, hated the music and searched for different sites to congregate.[26]

Other applications of ecological design relate to the fields of information technologies and Web design. Graphic artists employ animations, music, and color in order to reinforce the sponsor's image both online and offline and to make it easy to purchase the product with the click of a mouse. The California Closets ad in Figure 5.3 illustrates the desirable effect of an artistic environment that can enhance the aesthetics and value of a modern home.

APPLICATIONS OF CONDITIONING THEORIES: STIMULUS GENERALIZATION AND DISCRIMINATION

stimulus generalization
the tendency to assign commonality to similar stimuli

Among the tendencies that we learn through classical and operant conditioning are the abilities to generalize and discriminate. **Stimulus generalization** means that once learners acquire a response to a particular stimulus, this response may be elicited by stimuli similar to the original one. For example, a person who is positively impressed by the quality of one Japanese-made automobile may generalize this superior-quality perception to all Japanese-made cars. Similarly, a consumer's negative reaction to a product of a particular brand can extend to all other products bearing the same brand name. Whether positive or negative, this tendency for a widely known brand to influence consumers regarding products bearing the same name is called a *halo effect*.

Stimulus discrimination, in contrast, occurs when learners develop an ability to distinguish between, and respond differently to, similar—but nonidentical—stimuli. Even though research has shown that most consumers cannot distinguish between many brands of foods and beverages on the basis of taste alone, many people nonetheless develop a strong partiality for certain ones due to image-building marketing variables such as branding, packaging, pricing, and promotion. For instance, in a wine-tasting experiment reported on the ABC network in 2008, respondents were given two samples of wine representing the same brand. However, these subjects were told that the first wine sample came from a $5-per-bottle brand, while the second sample was taken form a $45-per-bottle brand. As expected, respondents rated the second wine sample significantly better in taste and higher in quality than the first. Some consumers develop keener discriminating capacities within a particular product category than others. Stimulus discrimination based on physical or psychological product attributes is the foundation of positioning strategy, which attempts to establish a competitive advantage or unique image for a brand in consumers' minds. A brand has a high chance of success if consumers can be led to discriminate between that brand and its competition—especially if the brand is noticeably better than other brands in some respect that is important to consumers. In some product categories, however, such as salt and sugar, brands are so similar that consumers usually do not care enough to discriminate between them. Such products are called *commodities*. Figure 5.4 depicts an ad from Lufthansa designed to gain a competitive advantage over other airlines by differentiating itself based on superior service offered to passengers.

stimulus discrimination
the tendency to distinguish between, and respond differently to, similar—but nonidentical—stimuli

COGNITIVE LEARNING

Human learning ranges from simple and mechanical habit formation to complex information processing. Although we engage in considerable trial-and-error behavior, we are not locked into a ceaselessly repetitive stimulus–response behavior mode. We can and do readily modify our response tendencies when insight and understanding direct us to a different view of a situation or when our goals or motivations change. We are information processors who continuously alter our response tendencies. For example, in studies involving children, researchers such as Peracchio demonstrated that the ability of children to make mature consumer decisions increases with age.[27] According to this view, kids can be segmented by age in terms of their stage of cognitive development or ability to comprehend concepts of increasing cognitive complexity.

Cognitive learning recognizes that we *think*, not just *do*. Cognitive learning pertains to changes in knowledge. It recognizes the active mental process through which people form meaningful associations among concepts, learn sequences of concepts, solve problems, and gain insights.[28] Cognitive learning

cognitive learning
a view that humans are goal-oriented, problem solvers and processors of information

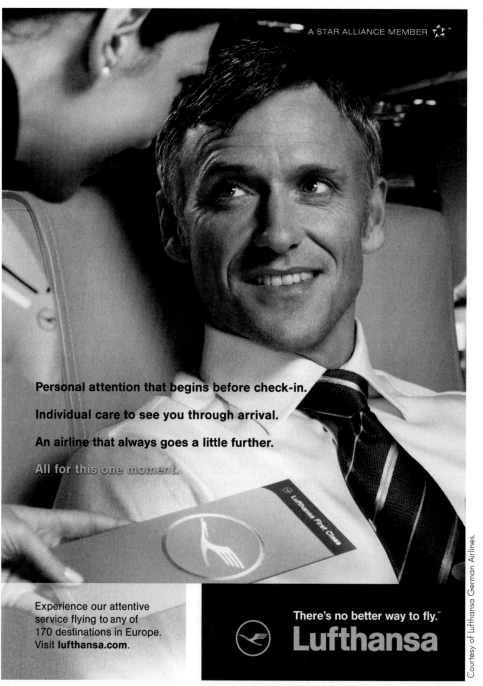

A STAR ALLIANCE MEMBER

Personal attention that begins before check-in.

Individual care to see you through arrival.

An airline that always goes a little further.

All for this one moment.

Experience our attentive
service flying to any of
170 destinations in Europe.
Visit **lufthansa.com**.

There's no better way to fly.™
Lufthansa

Courtesy of Lufthansa German Airlines.

Figure 5.4

By stressing the airline's motto of personal attention and individual care, Lufthansa
differentiates itself from others based on superiority of its in-flight services.

theory evolved from Kohler's experiments on apes.[29] In one experiment, a chimpanzee was placed in a cage. Bananas hung from the roof and boxes rested on the floor. The chimp tried but could not reach the bananas, until it solved the problem by moving a box beneath the bananas. Learning resulted from insight; it was not an outcome of a mere stimulus–response–reinforcement pattern.

Cognitive theory emphasizes our capacity for problem solving and understanding relationships. Learners recognize a goal, engage in purposeful behavior to achieve the goal, apply insight to devise a solution, and accomplish their goal. Cognitive theory acknowledges the role and importance of reinforcement. Unlike the case in operant conditioning, however, where rewards are not evident until after behavior has occurred, in cognitive learning subjects understand and anticipate their goal (reward) from the start.

Cognitive learning theory also recognizes the role of **subjective experience**—our beliefs, values, attitudes, expectations, insight, understanding, and meaning. We synthesize our personal beliefs, attitudes, and prior experiences to produce insight into new situations. The brain or central nervous system dominates as we approach problems sensibly, interpreting new information to develop fresh beliefs and meanings. With goal orientation and perceptive thinking, learners can apply insight and reasoning abilities and draw from prior knowledge to understand current problem situations, even though there may be no historical precedents in their experience.[30] The ad from Symantec in Figure 5.5 employs cognitive learning to convey to consumers specific information about the outstanding speed of Norton Internet Security™ 2008.

subjective experience
the notion that humans synthesize beliefs and experiences to gain insight into new situations

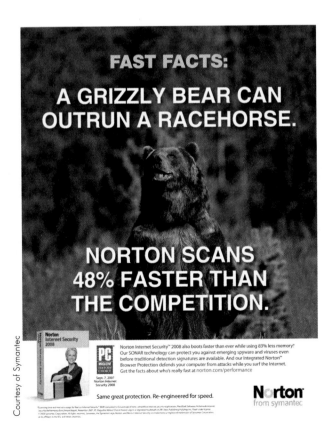

Courtesy of Symantec

Figure 5.5
This ad from Symantec provides documented facts regarding Norton's advanced scanning speed compared to the competition

Consumer Behavior in Practice

Channel Surfers Don't Seem to Zap this One

Based on the cognition view of learning, marketers have come to recognize the importance of providing detailed product information as a powerful promotional strategy. Major corporations, including Apple, Sega, McDonald's, State Farm, Fidelity Investments, and Toyota among others, have recently become users of infomercials. Through infomercials, advertisers can present a powerful demonstration of their product and cover in detail how it is used, how it works, its features, its benefits, and its maker. Time and space are the backbone of the technique. The expanded time frame enables advertisers to cover selling points completely and solicit viewers' requests for further information via visiting a Web site or dialing an 800 number. This is particularly important to first-time buyers and for complex purchase decisions. The supplementary facts and details can be vital toward building an ongoing relationship.

Infomercials are not just designed to accomplish direct sales. They can be effective in introducing new brands, building a database of inquiring prospects, driving or enhancing retail sales, routing customers to local dealerships, as well as sampling. One major advantage of infomercials to advertisers is the fact that results are immediate and traceable. If an infomercial does not work, advertisers would know within days or even hours. The success of infomercials is judged on the number of inquiries generated or product orders received.

Today, there are entire networks devoted just to airing infomercials all day and night. Infomercials have become a near staple on a number of TV channels, such as ION. Other channels that specialize in airing infomercials include Shop at Home, Shop NBC, HSN, QVC, Jewelry TV, America's Store, Gems TV, and Corner Store TV. A comparison of TV listings from 2007 with those of 1987 reveals that many broadcasters are now airing infomercials in lieu of movies or syndicated series runs. A newcomer to the field is TV4U.com, a Web site launched in 2007 that offers TV programming as well as infomercial videos on demand.[31]

The huge success that the infomercial format has achieved in recent years has changed the way many advertisers allocate their advertising budgets among different media types and various ad formats. Visit two infomercial Web sites at www.informercialindex.com and www.infomercialdrtv.com/ to learn how infomercials simplify life's choices by providing information. Do consumers equally rely on product information for all product choices? For what types of purchases are consumers most likely to seek product information? Is there a typical profile for the type of person who is likely to view infomercials?

Cognitive learning theory also recognizes the role of information processing in attitude formation and change by consumers—what we think, feel, and do. Examples abound in this area. In the political arena, the accessibility and wide appeal of television makes it an effective medium for providing prospective voters a convenient way to learn about political candidates and their stance on the key issues during an election year.[32] We can also envision how strategies such as persuasion can work effectively to promote various causes and issues, such as forwarding environmental concerns. Persuasion is a form of social influence that is accomplished more or less by guiding consumers toward accepting a new product, idea, attitude, or course of action by either rational or emotional means.[33] One recent application of an attitudinal model being applied in the field of education involved creating learning programs designed to reduce racial stereotyping and prejudice among children in the participating schools.[34]

NEO-PAVLOVIAN CONDITIONING

During the past two decades, some consumer researchers have begun to show renewed interest in classical conditioning. The traditional view of classical conditioning was of simple connections forming between stimuli and responses. The contemporary view, on the other hand, posits that learning is not simple, primitive, automatic, passive, or low involvement, but rather that it is a multifaceted process. Modern theorists no longer hold the notion that an organism's actions simply follow stimuli in a reflexive manner.[35]

The modern view of classical conditioning, sometimes called **neo-Pavlovian conditioning**, reshapes traditional classical conditioning into a fully cognitive theory.[36] It holds that learned associations are rich, often complex, and may involve relationships among multiple objects and events in the environment. In other words, neo-Pavlovian conditioning emphasizes cognitive associative learning, which is not mere acquisition of new reflexes but rather procurement of new knowledge about the environment, where one stimulus provides information about another. This view is based on an assumption of intelligence and information-processing capabilities of the organism. The Metra ad in Figure 5.6 attempts to form a mental association between taking the train and driving one's own car.

neo-Pavlovian conditioning
a view that reshapes traditional classical conditioning into a fully cognitive theory

Although the word *response* may suggest that what is conditioned in classical conditioning is overt behavior, a number of psychologists suggest that what is really conditioned is an *evaluative response* or attitude, and not overt behavior per se.[37] From marketers' point of view, attitudes that involve strong associations are highly functional. They free us from the effort required for deliberate reasoning and guide our behavior in a fairly automatic fashion. They serve to minimize information processing prior to initiating appropriate responses.[38] For example, consumers who associate the "Made in America" label with high quality and good workmanship tend to prefer to purchase products carrying this label over their imported counterparts.

Which Learning Theories Do Marketers Employ?

Marketers approach the topic of consumer learning from a number of angles, employing concepts borrowed from classical and operant conditioning as well as from cognitive learning. Sometimes the emphasis is on the way consumers form habits and become loyal to a particular brand. At other times, marketers are interested in how attitudes develop and change. In still other cases, marketers are concerned with the manner in which consumers process information and arrive at decisions.

A glance at the field of advertising reveals that advertisers use a variety of strategies to convey their messages. Many ads are founded on classical conditioning concepts. For example, Nike's campaign to promote the Air Jordan line of sneakers linked the athlete Michael Jordan to the benefits and style of the shoe. Other ads that emphasize product quality and positive product-use

Figure 5.6

This Metra ad, which draws a mental association between the train and a car, invites commuters to think of a train ride as a viable alternative to driving.

experiences draw from operant conditioning. Sony's ads, which emphasize the superior quality of its home electronics products, exemplify this approach. Still other ads present logical arguments supporting the choice of a specific brand or vendor. Every tax season, H&R Block runs ads that use this format, offering specific reasons why taxpayers should use the firm's services.

Thus, diverse perspectives such as habit formation *versus* problem solving and concept formation should not be considered contradictory but rather complementary to one another.[39] No single theory completely explains learning. Rather, each view helps explain those aspects of learning that the other views neglect or have difficulty addressing.[40] Conditioning theories offer insights into low-involvement buying (of products like detergents, paper towels, and toothpaste). Cognitive theories, on the other hand, relate to high-involvement purchasing (of cars, furniture, and clothing, for instance), where problem solving involves information search and brand evaluation.

Learning and Hemispheric Specialization of the Brain

During the past 35 years, researchers have become interested in the topic of **hemispheric specialization of the brain**. The basic premise of this concept is that the right and left hemispheres of the brain are not identical in their anatomy or function. They process, organize, and encode information differently, and each is capable of functioning in a manner different from that of the other.[41]

The **left hemisphere** is considered to be a rational-linear part of the brain that specializes in sequential processing, logical and analytical thinking, and verbalization. Expressions of language through speech are exclusively processed in the left hemisphere.[42] The acquisition of new habit patterns is also considered a function of the left hemisphere, which has the ability to analyze the common aspects of a task and formulate logical and meaningful relationships among them. Reading, for example, is considered to be primarily a left hemisphere function.[43] Mathematics, and in particular calculations and algebra, are also postulated to be left hemisphere operations.

The **right hemisphere**, on the other hand, is capable of multiple processing of incoming stimuli. The interpretation of complex visual patterns is predominantly a right hemisphere function. The right hemisphere is much more effective in the recognition of faces, whereas the left hemisphere remembers the names that go with the faces. The retention of visual patterns, such as geometric designs and graphs, falls in the domain of the right hemisphere.[44] It is also believed that iconic (graphic) memory is primarily a function of the right hemisphere.[45] As a result, iconic presentation of information, in the form of graphic displays, diagrams, and flowcharts, greatly facilitates both comprehension and retention of information.

However, research reveals that for many individuals, the brain's right and left hemispheres do not operate independently of each other, but rather work together to process information. This view of hemispheric specialization suggests

hemispheric specialization of the brain
a view that the left and right hemispheres of the brain process, organize, and encode information differently

left hemisphere
the area of the brain that specializes in analytical thinking, verbalization, and algebraic calculations

right hemisphere
the area of the brain that specializes in interpreting and recognizing visual patterns

that both modes of consciousness and cognitive style complement each other. Whereas the left hemisphere tends to be logical, the right hemisphere tends to be creative. Because information processing requires interhemispheric organization, marketers often attempt to stimulate both hemispheres for maximum effect.

One application of hemispheric specialization entails recognizing distinct styles of consumer learning. Because we perceive experience and information in different ways and process them differently, the combinations formed color our unique learning styles. According to the 4MAT® model, developed by Excel Inc., there are four major identifiable learning styles:[46]

- *Type One Learners* are primarily interested in personal meaning. For such individuals, marketers need to create a reason to know.
- *Type Two Learners* are primarily interested in the facts as they lead to conceptual understanding. Marketers need to give them facts that deepen their comprehension.
- *Type Three Learners* are primarily interested in how things work. Marketers need to let them try out a product or service.
- *Type Four Learners* are primarily interested in self-discovery. Marketers need to let them teach themselves and communicate the information they acquire to others.

Each of these four learning styles needs to be addressed using both the right and left hemispheres of the brain. Right- and left-brain dominant learners will be comfortable half of the time but will adapt their learning style the other half.

Another application of hemispheric specialization lies in the selection of promotional media used by marketers. Because the left hemisphere is involved primarily with language and logic, it is credited with processing the kind of information consumers receive from copy-heavy Internet sites and from the print media. The right hemisphere, which houses spatial perception, holistic understanding, perceptual insight, sensation, artistic talent, and recognition of faces, is credited with processing the kind of information we receive from TV commercials, as well as from highly visual Web sites.[47]

In the first case, arguments, logic, and cues presented trigger left-brain processing and generate cognitive activity that encourages consumers to evaluate the pros and cons of the product or message.[48] But in the second case of television or highly visual Internet sites, Hansen as well as Krugman suggest that the passive processing of images viewed on the screen falls in the domain of the right hemisphere, which deals with the visual and audible components of the commercial, including the creative use of symbols, music, and art.[49] Figure 5.7 from General Electric uses a cute analogy suggesting that the company merges high fashion (right brain) with high tech (left brain) to produce GE Profile appliances.

Learning in a Social Context: Vicarious Learning

Skinner, Tolman, Miller and Dollard, Bandura and Walters, and others have demonstrated that learning often occurs within a social context.[50] Consumer learning and behavior is largely social in nature and occurs within a social context.[51] The

High fashion marries high tech.

ERGY STAR® rated dishwasher and refrigerator • fast thaw • easy guide menu system • three direct feed wash arms • halogen

recise air convection system • sensor-controlled dishwashing • quick chill • electronic touch temperature controls • extra tall

True love is a GE Profile kitchen. Contemporary beauty is united with easy-to-use electronic controls and sensors. The result? The ability to make every meal amazing in a

room where everyone wants to hang out. Fashion and technology may seem an unlikely pair. But at GE Profile, they fall in love and make incredible kitchens together.

GE Profile™
GEAppliances.com

imagination at work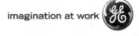

FIGURE 5.7

This ad from GE Profile addresses the roles of the right-brain (high fashion) and left-brain (high tech) in promoting its line of technically-advanced, fashionably-designed GE appliances.

cultural socialization process and influence of reference groups, opinion leaders, family ties, and significant others are but a few among the many social forces that sway and reinforce consumers' choices and shape their response tendencies.

People often alter their behavior after viewing the behavior of others. **Vicarious learning** is behavior change that occurs as a result of observing the activity of others, called models, and the consequences of their behavior. An individual who watches others receive rewards for engaging in a behavior learns to imitate their actions. Similarly, someone who sees others receive punishment for their deeds learns to avoid them. For example, highway drivers tend to slow down when they observe a police vehicle with lights flashing that pulls over a speeding auto.

vicarious learning
behavior change due to observing others and the consequences of their actions

Global Opportunity

No Images of an Ugly American Here

Western images and lifestyles have become highly desirable models emulated by millions of consumers worldwide. Vicarious learning has resulted in a world where similarities seem to exist in its four corners. Call it Planet Hollywood or Planet Reebok, our world today is characterized by a youth culture that has taken many of its cues from American pop culture. Kids in Hong Kong, Tokyo, Prague, and New Delhi are watching videos on YouTube, wriggling into Levi's jeans, and downloading the latest songs from iTunes. Fast-food restaurants such as McDonald's, KFC, and Pizza Hut have become favorite places where the young like to hang out. Colas and Baskin-Robbins ice cream have become staples in Cairo and Istanbul. American movies, TV soaps, and news programs such as CNN have captured the interest of consumers in hundreds of countries.

Beyond goods and artifacts, the largest influence of such a transnational trend lies in the domain of values. Through movies, TV programs, and other media forms, America is sending its values of upward mobility and individualism to Taipei, Saigon, and Bombay.

There are many benefits as well as problems associated with this trend. Among the benefits, a borderless economy promotes allegiances to products not to countries. More understanding and cooperation between countries emerge as a result of trade. When a New Yorker buys a Mustang from Ford Motor Company, 60 percent of his or her money goes to South Korea, Japan, Germany, Taiwan, Singapore, Britain, and Barbados, as these regions supply parts and components for the automobile. Trade thus replaces war, and goods replace bullets.

On the negative side, however, are countries that are likely to remain separated from this transnational trend. Countries such as Afghanistan, Ethiopia, Rwanda, and some other African countries are likely to remain isolated, further widening the gap between the haves and have-nots. Beyond these few nations, however, the rest of the world continues to offer endless opportunities for marketers of many U.S. products and services.[53]

The past few decades have witnessed unparalleled trade cooperation between countries of the world. Visit www.census.gov/foreign-trade/top/index.html to learn which nations are the top trading partners of the United States. How do you explain the fact that so many products today have become "world products," regardless of where they originate? Does this trend mean that in due time, homogeneity may characterize all world cultures?

Advertisers apply vicarious learning concepts in several ways.[52] To develop a desired behavior, ads depict models (similar to the target audience) who use a sponsor's brand with satisfactory results. This approach suggests that the same rewards—in the form of benefits or compliments from peers—are forthcoming if viewers use the advertised brand. For example, an ad for a diet pill may show before and after photos of a consumer to illustrate the brand's effectiveness. To alter a behavior, ads may depict the mishaps that result from not using the sponsor's brand and suggest that the dire consequences can be avoided with the right product choice. Insurance companies often use testimonials from victimized customers whose polices from these firms spared their families from enduring devastating consequences and losses. To build on responses already learned, ads depict models using familiar products in innovative ways or on occasions other than those with which the items are usually associated. A commercial shows a tennis player, fatigued after a tough game, taking aspirin to relieve aching muscles and finding relief. Although viewers already know that aspirin abates headaches, getting people to perceive aspirin as a muscle relaxer may create new sales opportunities.

Among the many ways that advertisers employ vicarious learning concepts is getting satisfied customers to offer testimony about the benefits or effectiveness of their brand.

Learning Curves

As we continue to learn, we gain experience in the task being performed. The effect of experience, primarily due to dexterity derived from repetition, is embodied in the adages "Practice makes perfect" and "Experience is the best teacher." A task becomes easier as the number of repetitions increases. This concept is known as the **learning curve** or **experience effect**. It has been of great interest to industrial and strategic market planners, who apply it as a cost-reduction measure. Applications extend beyond manufacturing to activities such as sales, marketing, and distribution. The cost (or effort) of performing these tasks also falls appreciably as a consequence of accrued experience.

The same phenomenon holds true for purchasing behavior. Consumers accumulate experience in performing shopping tasks and develop strategies to streamline the process. They develop shopping routines requiring minimal thought, effort, or search and draw from their experiences with various brands. Brand loyalty is partly a manifestation of the learning curve. As they experiment with available brands, consumers adopt effort-reduction strategies to simplify their shopping.

learning curve (experience effect)
the notion that tasks become easier as the number of repetitions increases

HABIT AND BRAND LOYALTY

As a result of learning, we develop consistent patterns of behavior that we engage in repeatedly and without conscious thought. This phenomenon is known as habit. Applied specifically to consumer behavior, habits result from strong drive–response chains, brand–product category associations, and behavior-reward experiences with particular brands within product classes.

Brand loyalty is a consumer's consistent preference for and purchase of a specific brand within a given product category over time. Without information seeking or brand evaluation, brand-loyal consumers *automatically* tend to repurchase the same brand. Their commitment to a brand serves two purposes. In the case of high-involvement purchases with a strong degree of personal importance and relevance such as a car, brand loyalty reduces risk and facilitates selection. On the other hand, in the case of low-involvement purchases with a minor degree of personal importance and relevance such as a candy bar, routine purchasing saves time and effort.

Marketers today attempt to develop brand loyalty through relationship marketing. *Relationship marketing* is a set of activities that marketers undertake to establish a positive tie with consumers. This bond encourages consumers to reduce their market choices voluntarily by engaging in an ongoing relationship with a marketer of a specific product, service, or brand or from a specific

brand loyalty
a consumer's consistent purchase of a specific brand within a product category

firm. Consumers may purposefully elect to reduce their choice options and maintain a continuing loyalty to a particular marketer.[54] Activities such as diligently attending to consumers' needs, providing high-quality customer services, seeking consumer input for purposes of product design, and maintaining open and effective communication with them are among the methods marketers employ to build and solidify lasting trust relationships.[55]

To assess the extent of consumer brand loyalty, researchers no longer rely solely on survey data. In-store scanners and customer ID cards (or *preferred-customer cards*) enable marketers to track customers' brand selections over time electronically. Assessing the extent of consumer brand loyalty also occurs for online purchases. Some research companies today specialize in tracking online purchases to learn the brands, quantities, and frequency of our purchases.

Brand loyalty is measured in terms of a subject's sequence or proportion of purchases within a product category. Some studies consider consumers to be *brand loyal* if they buy a given brand a specified number of times (typically three to five) in a row. In other studies, consumers are deemed *brand loyal* if a given brand constitutes a specified percentage of all purchases (typically 75 percent to 80 percent) in some product category within a stated period of time, such as three months.

Why Do Consumers Develop Brand Loyalties?

Some consumers repeatedly buy the same brand merely because it is familiar and doing so saves time and energy. They have no strong feelings about it one way or the other. This tendency is referred to as **inertia** and differs from genuine brand loyalty in that the former represents a case of low involvement. Such brand-purchase routines suggest arbitrary acceptance of a brand without any degree of commitment to it. Competitors who attempt to change consumer buying patterns based on inertia can often do so easily because they encounter little resistance to brand switching. In many but not all product categories, shoppers who find their usual brand to be temporarily out of stock or who come across price reductions, coupons, or point-of-purchase displays for competitive brands are apt to switch.

In the case of true brand loyalty, on the other hand, repeat purchasing of a brand reflects high involvement and a conscious decision on the part of consumers to continue buying the same brand.[56] The pattern of repetitive behavior results from underlying positive attitudes toward the brand that are due to brand attributes, experience with the brand, or emotional attachment (such as congruence with a consumer's self-perception or associations with prior events).[57] *True-blue* buyers are not open to change and may rebel when their preferred brands are altered, redesigned, or eliminated.[58]

Why Do Consumers Switch Brands?

In our society, where almost all products face stiff and relentless competition, every brand category becomes subject to commoditization. That is, the differentiating benefit of one brand over other competing brands tends to diminish or disappear. Some consumers have come to believe that no significant differences exist among brands. This notion, known as **brand parity**, is reflected in

inertia
a pattern of repeatedly buying a particular brand merely because it is familiar

brand parity
a situation where many consumers come to believe that no significant differences exist among brands

a survey showing that worldwide, consumers who use products such as beer, cigarettes, paper towels, soaps, and snack chips believe all brands are similar.[59] Interestingly, the same study found brand loyalty to be highest for cigarette purchases.

What happens after once-loyal consumers switch from their regular brands? Four purchasing-behavior patterns have been identified.[60] The first of these is *reversion*, in which consumers switch back to their original brand. A second possible pattern is *conversion*, wherein consumers remain loyal to the new brand. A third possibility is *vacillation* or random switching between the new and old brands. The fourth pattern is *experimentation*, in which consumers engage in further systematic trial of other brands. A study by Mazursky, LaBarbera, and Aiello measured consumer response to various incentives to switch brands.[61] There was a difference in behavior depending on whether brand switching was induced by extrinsic incentives (price, coupon) or intrinsic ones (desire to try a new brand). Unlike intrinsic motives, extrinsic incentives motivate consumers to switch despite a high level of satisfaction with the last-purchased brand. Such switching behavior results in weaker intentions to repurchase the new brand, however.

Memory and Retention

Maximizing consumer learning and minimizing forgetting are primary objectives of marketers. Information storage and retrieval processes are therefore of particular concern to advertisers, who hope the campaigns they design will make lasting impressions on their audience. Consider what happens when you look up a telephone number in a phone directory. Your eyes selectively focus on the required information among an array of published listings. An afterimage remains for a few moments—just long enough for you to dial the number. Unless you mentally rehearse the number or dial it frequently, however, you probably quickly forget it. In the process of seeking information, we all receive these kinds of stimuli and acquire much more than we need. Some of this data we remember, but the rest is forgotten.

In an effort to minimize forgetting, retention aids known as mnemonic devices have been developed to help people's retention processes. **Mnemonic devices**, which can be auditory or visual, promote retention of material by organizing it efficiently or identifying it with easily remembered symbols.[62] Advertisers frequently use music, rhyme, and rhythm to enhance memorability. Slogans and jingles such as Apple's "The power to be your best," Burger King's "Have it your way," and Ace Hardware's "Ace is the place with the helpful hardware man" are but a few of the more popular ones.

mnemonic devices auditory or visual aids that promote retention of material by identifying it with easily remembered symbols

Marketers frequently provide word associations for telephone numbers. For example, a carpet retailer may pay a premium rate for the number corresponding to C-A-R-P-E-T-S or 1-800-M-A-T-T-R-E-S. Other commercials cheerfully sing sponsors' phone numbers to make them memorable. Trademarks such as Nike's swoosh and McDonald's Golden Arches, as well as trade characters such as the Snuggles bear and the Michelin tire man use visible reflections of product attributes or benefits to enhance learning.

THE STRUCTURE OF MEMORY

Human memory is a complex mechanism. When information first enters our brain, it is directed through an area known as the hippocampus, which sorts it and directs it to other parts of the brain based on the information's importance or relevance. Memory consists of three storage systems: sensory memory, short-term memory, and long-term memory.[63] In **sensory memory**, incoming data undergo preliminary processing largely based on the physical qualities of a perceived object, such as its size, color, and volume. The instantaneous processing of visual and auditory data are referred to as iconic and echoic processing, respectively.[64]

After sensory processing, data input promptly passes into **short-term memory (STM)**, called the *workbench* for information-processing operations. In STM, we categorize, process, and hold information for a brief period. If the information is significant to us, it may undergo a process known as rehearsal. Rehearsal is silent, mental repetition of the data and linkage of it to other information. Rehearsed data become transferred to long-term memory within 2 to 10 seconds. Without rehearsal, we lose data inputs in 30 seconds or less.[65] STM's capacity to contain data is restricted to as few as 4 or 5 and perhaps up to 7 items at a time.[66] Sometimes too much data competes simultaneously for our attention. This situation, called *information overload*, can reduce STM's capacity to only 2 or 3 bits of data. Much information may be lost. Knowledgeable advertisers, as a result, attempt to keep their messages simple and uncluttered without too much information.

Rehearsal keeps information in STM long enough to be encoded. **Encoding** is a process through which we select words or visual images to represent a perceived object. Trade characters and suggestive brand names such as Mr. Clean, Green Giant, and Endust are symbols provided by marketers to facilitate the encoding processes.

Both visual and verbal data are important in forming an overall mental image to encode. It requires less time to learn visual than verbal information, as we saw in the section on hemispheric specialization of the brain. A print ad containing verbal information that is accompanied by an illustration is more likely to be encoded than verbal cues alone.

Long-term memory (LTM) is an information warehouse. Unlike STM, where information is held only momentarily, LTM retains information for a relatively longer span of time. Anderson, in what is known as the associative network model—a generally accepted representation of LTM—asserts that LTM can be represented as a network of nodes and connecting links, where nodes represent stored information or concepts, and links represent the strength of association between nodes.[67] For instance, consider the case of a consumer who ponders the purchase of a new iPhone, introduced in 2007. She already owns a cell phone and is familiar with most of its functions. She feels its performance is satisfactory for use at home, as well as on her job as a sales rep. Her liking of the new iPhone is strongly linked to its unique features, which make the functions of calling, text messaging, Web browsing, checking e-mail, contact management, playing music, taking photos, and watching videos so

---

sensory memory
a storage system in which incoming data undergo preliminary processing

short-term memory (STM)
a storage system in which an individual briefly holds a limited amount of information

encoding
the process of employing symbols such as words or images to store a perceived idea

long-term memory (LTM)
the information warehouse in which data are organized and extendedly stored

much easier. She strongly dislikes the fact that her present phone requires pressing many tiny buttons, navigating diverse interphases, and squinting at a tiny display screen. Unlike her present cell phone, she is thrilled that the new phone's interface is not fixed and rigid but fluid and molten. Her purchase would also be linked strongly to expectations of future upgrades from Apple, such as one that allows her to rent and upload movies. For her, purchasing the innovative iPhone is linked to a lesser extent to attracting the attention of her clients and others as she uses it.

© 2009, Andresr, Shutterstock, Inc.

Knowledge Structures include our personal experiences as well as information we acquire from the media, salespeople, colleagues, friends and family.

In LTM, information is organized and stored under cues or headings. If appropriate cues are present and if the setting and manner in which we process the information are suitable, then recall is simple.[68] If, however, appropriate or effective cues are absent, material cannot be recalled.[69] The more cues we use to store a piece of information in memory, the easier it is to retrieve it later on. For example, cues under which we may store aspirin in memory include usage occasions such as headaches and fever, brand names such as Bayer, and ad-photos of persons suffering from a cold or muscle pain.

Information stored in LTM is not passive. That is to say, we actively use **knowledge structures**, or arrangements of related bits of information, to store and organize information about products, brands, and retailers in memory. The way we interpret and respond to incoming messages depends on how the information fits into our knowledge structures. If new information coincides with stored information, the communication is more effective. On the other hand, if new information contradicts our stored information, we may become confused, and the incoming message will be less effective. Knowledge structures consist of more than just product types and brand names. They include our personal experiences as well as information we acquire from such sources as the media, salespeople, colleagues, friends, and family.

New information we gain also affects the structure of stored information. Information housed in LTM constantly goes through a process of reorganization, and new links between information chunks are always being formed. This process links fresh material to information already in storage in order to make new data inputs more meaningful.

knowledge structures
formations of related bits of information

Information Retrieval

When we sift through our LTM to find the specific information we need, we engage in information retrieval. **Information retrieval** is the process of activating previously stored information from LTM. A number of studies have addressed the topic of retrieval cues. This line of research was largely prompted

information retrieval
the process of sifting through memory to activate previously stored information

in the 1970s by Quaker Oats' famous "Mikey" commercial for Life cereal.[70] The classic Mikey commercial featured "Mikey," a difficult-to-please, four-year-old boy, who is offered a bowl of Life cereal—and starts eating it. The commercial featured the catch phrase "He likes it, Hey Mikey." The commercial was very popular and ran from 1972 to 1984, becoming one of the longest-running commercials of all time. Quaker added a still photo of Mikey to the lower right-hand corner on the front side of Life cereal boxes, hoping that consumers would link Life cereal with Mikey. Although a strategy like this should facilitate retrieval, mitigating factors may hinder it. When many brands advertise within a product category, for example, consumers find it more difficult to remember which ad is associated with which brand. Different consumers may also focus on different cues. Upon viewing the Life commercial, some consumers may not have noted the Life brand name but rather heard the taste and nutritional claims for the cereal. These individuals might fail to link the Mikey cue to the brand.[71]

Furthermore, researchers distinguish between information *availability* and *accessibility* in connection with information retrieval.[72] Even though information has been processed and stored in LTM, individuals are capable of retrieving only a small fraction of it.[73] Thus, availability of information in memory is a necessary but insufficient condition for its retrieval and subsequent use. Factors that influence information accessibility for retrieval purposes include (1) related learned information (in this case, that might be knowledge about Kellogg's and Post cereals), (2) self- or externally generated retrieval cues (such as thoughts of a healthy breakfast or the Mikey character), and (3) various encoding factors (humorous or serious appeal). When the retrieval procedure fails, it is an indication that extinction or forgetting has occurred.

Extinction and Forgetting

Extinction and forgetting are opposites of learning. Both involve loss of responses, skills, or cognitive material that once was learned and entered into memory. Better initial learning, of course, reduces subsequent loss. For this reason, marketers spend generously on intensive advertising campaigns over many media types during the introductory stage of the product life cycle. TV is a particularly effective medium for such undertakings because it accommodates visual and auditory images that correlate and reinforce one another.

As we saw in the section on conditioning, *extinction* is one type of learning loss. A break in the link between behavior and expected reward leads to a rapid decline in the probability that a response will be repeated. Once a brand no longer satisfies consumers, the likelihood that they will rebuy it decreases dramatically. Eventually, they may stop buying it altogether. In the absence of reinforcement, behavior ceases to recur, and extinction ensues.

Forgetting also involves learning loss. When we forget, material that was once part of our conscious mind recedes into the mind's unconscious recesses and is no longer available for voluntary recall. Forgetting occurs when a stimulus is no longer repeated or perceived. Cessation of brand use or discontinuation of brand promotion can cause forgetting. For example, Ingersoll which was once a popular brand of watches, is hardly remembered today. The ad from Pfizer in Figure 5.8 for Aricept, a medication for mild to moderate dementia of the Alzheimer's type, enumerates the benefits this drug offers to patients by assisting them to be more like themselves longer.

Confusion makes learning more difficult and increases the likelihood of forgetting. Ad clutter and competitive advertising often interfere with message reception and cause confusion in a consumer's mind. A consumer exposed to a multitude of TV commercials promoting different brands of detergents, each having numerous features, can easily become confused. This, in turn, weakens the stimulus–reward connection.

Advertisers combat forgetting with media schedules that maintain a target level of advertising repetitions. Some messages, called *reminder* ads, are specifically designed to echo and reinforce earlier promotional efforts.

Mere reiteration of the same messages, however, is likely to irritate an audience. One of the best methods to help people form a concept is to demonstrate it in myriad diverse specific circumstances. Advertisers, therefore, create campaigns consisting of several ads or commercials, each of which echoes the same theme but presents it in a different setting. For example, separate ads for an all-purpose household cleaner might depict diverse applications ranging from washing kitchen floors and family room walls to disinfecting bathroom bowls.

Forgetting occurs very rapidly in the period immediately after learning. It then slows down as time passes.[74] No evidence supports the notion that mere passage of time causes forgetting. Rather, forgetting results from the active process of acquiring new responses that replace and interfere with earlier remembered patterns. Two obstacles hinder retention processes, retroactive and proactive interference.

In **retroactive interference**, recent learning interferes with our recollection of previously learned material. For example, on viewing two ads in succession, both for competitive brands, we may find our memory of the second ad interferes with recall of the first. For example, in viewing two successive shoe ads from Adidas and Converse, the resulting interference caused by the second ad would most likely affect consumers' memory of the first ad. This tendency is due to the functional similarity of the advertised products and the likeness of the two messages.

One type of retroactive interference, known as the **misinformation effect**, occurs when misleading details are suggested to a person after witnessessing an event.[75] If an eyewitness to an incident is subsequently exposed to false details about it, the misinformation can impair the person's recollection of what really occurred and cause errors in his or her account of the event. The person may even come to believe the phony details if he or she has forgotten their source. This type of influence has often been applied by rival candidates during political campaigns. It usually takes the form of negative ads that provide false or misleading information about the other candidate's personality, views, or activities.

In **proactive interference**, prior learning interferes with recall of recently learned material. For example, familiarity with an established brand of film such as Kodak may overshadow a more recent brand such as Fuji. The processes of retroactive and proactive interference are illustrated in Exhibit 5.4 on page 181.

retroactive interference
a case where recent learning interferes with recall of previously learned material

misinformation effect
a case where false assertions taint a person's recall of what *really* occurred

proactive interference
a case where prior learning interferes with recall of recently learned material

"When Dad was first diagnosed with Alzheimer's,
I thought, what if I have to put him in a nursing home."

If caring for your loved one means everything to you, prescription Aricept can help.

- Aricept is a once-a-day treatment. It's for people with mild to moderate Alzheimer's disease.

- Studies showed it helped maintain overall function, which may include effects on memory and behavior.

- Aricept helps people be more like themselves longer.

Early treatment is key. Don't wait to ask your doctor about Aricept.

ONCE-A-DAY
ARICEPT®
(donepezil HCl)
5-MG AND 10-MG TABLETS

When Alzheimer's hits home
Aricept can help.

Important information:

Aricept is one treatment option you and your doctor can consider.

Aricept is indicated for mild to moderate Alzheimer's disease.

Aricept is well tolerated but may not be for everyone. Some people may have nausea, diarrhea, not sleep well, or vomit. Some people may have muscle cramps, feel very tired, or may not want to eat. In studies, these side effects were usually mild and went away over time. People at risk for stomach ulcers or who take certain other medicines should tell their doctors because serious stomach problems, such as bleeding, may get worse. Some people who take Aricept may experience fainting. Please see important Product Information on next page. For more information call 1-800-760-6029 ext. 68 or visit www.aricept.com

If you or someone you know needs help paying for medicine, call 1-888-4PPA-NOW (1-888-477-2669). Or go to www.pparx.org

 Partnership for Prescription Assistance

AR271436A

Figure 5.8

This ad from Pfizer suggests that Aricept, an Alzheimer's medication, can help patients' overall function, which may include effects on memory and behavior.

The Dynamics of Retroactive and Proactive Interference

EXHIBIT 5.4

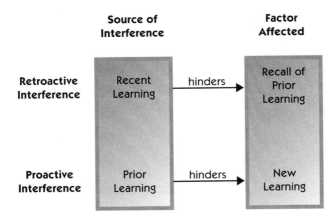

MESSAGE INTERFERENCE AND LIKELIHOOD OF RECALL

Forgetting that results from retroactive and proactive interference has important implications for marketers. Because we are exposed to such a large number of promotional messages daily, there exists significant potential for message interference. Confusion grows in proportion to the extent that competing ads push products from the same category or claim similar features and benefits.

Recent research findings indicate that interference effects occur only for unfamiliar brands.[76] Information about both familiar and unfamiliar competing brands was shown to have no effect on the recall of familiar brands.

Other recent research has found that a unique item in a series of relatively homogeneous items tends to be recalled easily, because the effects of retroactive and proactive interference are minimalized in this situation.[77] A case in point is Apple's iPod, which has dominated the digital music player scene since its launch in 2001. The famous commercials and print ads featured dark-silhouetted characters against bright-colored backgrounds. The silhouettes are usually dancing, and in TV commercials are backed by upbeat music while holding iPods and listening to them with Apple-supplied earphones. These distinctively appear in white so that they stand out against the colorful background and black silhouettes.[78]

Learning is a major determinant of human behavior. Consumers are not born with brand preferences; they learn them over time by being exposed to advertising, interacting with significant others, as well as their own experience with products. Learning is critical to marketers, who are charged with the challenging task of getting consumers to learn about their brands, often amidst clutter initiated by competitive messages. In this sense, the marketer is a teacher aiming to facilitate learning through advertising, personal selling, or even through instructional manuals that accompany products.

Our perceptual processes are integral companions to the learning process. That is to say, learning does not occur in a vacuum. New data—once perceived—are cast against knowledge and experiences already in memory, causing the individual to form feelings or attitudes toward the incoming information. The next chapter addresses the topic of attitudes—how they form, how they can be strengthened, and how they change.

A Cross-Functional Point of View

The topics of learning and memory have a number of implications for business disciplines other than marketing. Relevant issues might include

- **Human Resource Management:** Training and development are important issues that management must face because of their effect on employee productivity and operating costs. Training has a bearing on a number of issues such as ease and speed of employee learning, the frequency and cost of training programs, and the specific instructional methods to be employed. An alternative strategy that some companies have adopted is replacing part of the workforce with computers, robots, and other high-tech machinery. Labor unions, of course, fight such actions because of their negative cumulative effect on the workforce.

- **Pricing Strategy/Legal Considerations:** The concept of the *learning curve* or *experience effect* is important to industrial and strategic market planners who recognize that as workers accumulate more experience in performing a task, they become more efficient, and costs associated with performing the task decline. Based on this principle, some firms adopt a low-price strategy known as *predatory pricing*, which is designed to strip market share away from competitors. A company, for example, may calculate the low costs that hypothetically will prevail in, say, 2015 and

base on these costs a low price for the present time. As the firm realizes large sales volumes through the low price, the hypothesized low costs actually materialize, confirming what is known as a self-fulfilling prophecy. Costs decline due to the combined effects of enhanced economies of scale and the learning curve. From a legal perspective, are such pricing practices lawful? Does this strategy conform to standard and acceptable accounting practices?

- **Product Engineering:** As competition has forced manufacturers to keep adding advanced features to their products, many of these products—particularly home electronics—have become technically complicated and too sophisticated for average consumers to operate. Many consumers become confused and frustrated as they attempt to learn how to use the various features, often from cumbersome and unclear owners' manuals. Two managerial implications emerge from this situation. The first addresses whether or not all these high-tech features are really needed. The second implication addresses the clarity of owners' manuals that accompany a product. Might it be better if these products were simplified, lessening the required learning and lowering prices for consumers?

These issues, and a host of others like them, serve to show that the topics of learning and memory transcend the field of marketing to other business disciplines.

Summary

The three major schools of learning theories are (1) classical conditioning, (2) operant conditioning, and (3) cognitive learning. Under classical conditioning, it is assumed that learning occurs as the result of connections formed between a conditioned stimulus and an unconditioned stimulus. The major learning principles include repetition, contiguity, contingency, and congruity.

Operant conditioning theory posits that learning occurs via trial and error, as consumers discover that certain behaviors produce more desirable outcomes. Marketers face the challenge of getting a desired behavior to occur so it can be rewarded. In this regard, behavior shaping and ecological design can prove to be helpful.

Cognitive learning emphasizes goal-orientation, problem-solving, and information-processing capabilities of consumers, who continually alter their response tendencies to adjust to varying circumstances.

Renewed interest in classical conditioning, interpreted in a neo-Pavlovian sense, has reshaped traditional classical conditioning into a fully cognitive theory.

Whereas the left hemisphere of the brain is considered to be the rational-linear part, the right hemisphere specializes in iconic types of information, such as diagrams, graphs, faces, and names. Knowledge about the brain may be useful to marketers when determining which types of media are appropriate for their promotions.

Vicarious learning occurs as a result of observing the behavior of others and the consequences of their behavior.

When people repeatedly perform a task, it becomes easier as they accumulate experience. This principle is known as the learning curve or experience effect. The learning curve phenomenon is exhibited when individuals develop consistent patterns in which they engage repeatedly and without thought. Such patterns are called habits. Habit is manifested in consumer behavior as buyers develop shopping routines and brand loyalties.

Memory consists of three storage systems: sensory, short-term, and long-term memory. Retrieval is the process of activating previously stored information from LTM. Both information availability and accessibility have a bearing on a person's ability to retrieve stored information. When the retrieval process fails, it is an indication that extinction or forgetting has occurred. Retroactive interference (perhaps due to the misinformation effect) and proactive interference can hamper a person's recall of information.

Review Questions

1. Classical conditioning views learning as forming connections or associations between environmental events. How does learning occur under the classical conditioning model? What are the four prerequisites for this type of learning to occur?
2. How does operant conditioning as a learning theory differ from classical conditioning? Explain, and cite some of the challenges that marketers face in applying operant conditioning.
3. It has been claimed that the right and left hemispheres of the brain are not identical in their function—a tendency known as hemispheric specialization. Discuss what you know about this view, and explain how such distinction can be helpful to marketers in the selection of advertising media.
4. Explain what is meant by vicarious learning, and show how advertisers apply this concept to enhance the effectiveness of their messages.
5. The three components of memory are sensory, short-term, and long-term memory. What are the functions of these memory components? Is information passively or actively stored in long-term memory? Explain.

Discussion Questions

1. Many breakfast cereal producers make their box tops or UPC codes part of their promotional effort. Consumers are informed that if they mail in a specified number of box tops or UPCs, they will receive a premium free of charge or at a reduced price. What specific learning principles underlie this practice?
2. Although almost everybody is familiar with well-known cola beverages such as Coke, Pepsi, and RC, these companies nevertheless maintain large advertising budgets and continue to spend huge sums on ads and commercials that basically echo the same familiar themes. What is the purpose of advertising of this type? Is this type of advertising really necessary?
3. Motorola Corporation has initiated a policy of a virtually smoke-free workplace. Smoking is prohibited in company buildings, and employees who are spotted smoking inside their vehicles in the company parking lot are "punished" by the possibility of losing their jobs. How effective do you expect such coercive policies to be in modifying employees' habits? How might such strict policies influence employee morale?

In reference to the chapter opening vignette regarding programs undertaken by various companies to enhance customer loyalty, a familiar method is the practice of issuing *preferred-customer cards* that are scanned at the checkout counter, granting the customer various price discounts. Although economically beneficial to consumers, the private information about customer profiles along with a track record of their purchases is often released or sold to other institutions without consumers' permission or knowledge. From a legal point of view, are such retailers' actions defensible? Are consumers being injured? How? Who really *owns* this information? Is there any legal recourse consumers can take to protect themselves against this practice?

CASE

Travelodge Rewards Program

The executives at Travelodge Hotels recently met to discuss the Guest Rewards program called "Travelodge Miles" that the company has had in effect for a number of years. The program allowed guests to receive an eleventh night free after 10 qualified stays. This program made it easy for vacation travelers to earn a reward fairly quickly—a feature that helped somewhat to boost business.

A major issue on which the majority of the meetings centered was the recent shift in the travel market. There seemed to be a growing category of budget-conscious leisure travelers and corporate clientele brought about by concerns over the sluggish economy, shrinking financial resources, and worries about the future. As a result of these circumstances, Travelodge executives were concerned about what lies ahead for the hospitality business. The executives were closely examining a 2007 report known as the *National Leisure Travel Monitor*, published yearly by the Yankelovich partners. The report unveiled trends, facts, and predictions for travel in the year 2008, including: (1) short getaways of four nights or less, (2) fewer vacations taken by individuals and/or families, (3) word-of-mouth referrals as the most trusted source of travel information, (4) great interest in frequent-flier miles among leisure travelers, with almost half now participating in airline-sponsored programs, and (5) the majority of travelers who use airlines or hotel services book their vacations online.

In view of this report and other information drawn from comments generated through guest surveys and focus groups, the executives at Travelodge decided to launch a revitalized Guest Rewards program named TripRewards, designed to cope with the new trends the travel industry faces today. The program compensates frequent Travelodge and Thriftlodge guests for their patronage with rewards such as earning points for miles by staying at participating TripRewards hotels, which exceed 6,000 in the United States and Canada. These points are granted at the rate of 10 points per dollar spent on lodging, two air miles per dollar spent on lodging, or two rail points per dollar spent on lodging. Points can also be earned through purchases made at participating business partners such as florists, car rental firms, real estate companies, or when using the new TripRewards MasterCard credit card. These TripRewards points can be redeemed in various ways, according to customers' preferences. They can be used for free hotel stays, to receive gifts chosen from an attractive catalog, for meals in restaurants, or for other options such as movie passes or amusement park admissions.

To enhance the program's effectiveness, the executives at Travelodge had to make sure it is user-friendly for front-desk staff, management and corporate personnel, and, most important, the guests. By using a state-of-the-art swipe card technology, which automatically updates guests' points each time they stay at the chain, the program makes it easy and convenient for leisure as well as business travelers to use.

Questions

1. Travelodge claims that its revitalized Guest Rewards program, TripRewards, has been successful in attracting both leisure and corporate business travelers. From a learning point of view, what are the principles on which this program is based? How would you explain the success of this program?
2. Instead of the proposed TripRewards program, one Travelodge executive in the meeting suggested adopting the Travelodge rewards program presently being used in Canada. The Canadian program offers rewards based on the degree of guest loyalty and frequency of use of Travelodge. This program has three reward levels: blue, gold, and platinum. Blue members receive a permanent member card and 10 points for every lodging dollar spent. Gold members receive all blue member benefits plus early checkin and late checkout privileges. Platinum members receive all gold member benefits plus an extra two points for each lodging dollar spent, as well as complementary room upgrade and access to executive lounges. Do you think that differentiating the rewards based on guest loyalty is a good idea? Why or why not?
3. A participant in one of the focus groups the company conducted suggested that since many guests are unaware that these reward programs are available or seldom take advantage of them, it would be better for Travelodge to spend the program's costs in offering guests free gourmet breakfasts (not the usual donuts and coffee) and/or free high tea in the afternoon. Do you agree?

Notes

1. Ran Kivetz and Itamar Simonson, "The Idiosyncratic Fit Heuristic: Effort Advantage as a Determinant of Consumer Response to Loyalty Programs," *Journal of Marketing Research* 40, no. 4 (November 2003); Based on Shari Caudron, "Brand Loyalty: Can It Be Revived?" *Industry Week* (April 5, 1993), pp. 11–12, 14; "Credit Card Rewards Programs," *Creditor Web*, www.creditorweb.com/articles/credit-card-rewards-programs.html; Hershey's Foods Web site, www.thehersheycompany.com/news/release.asp?releaseID=398319.
2. A. A. Mitchell, "Cognitive Processes Initiated by Exposure to Advertising," in R. Harris (ed.), *Information Processing Research in Advertising* (New York: Lawrence Erlbaum, 1983), pp. 13–42; M. L. Rothschild and W. C. Gaidis, "Behavioral Learning Theory: Its Relevance to Marketing and Promotions," *Journal of Marketing* (Spring 1981), pp. 70–78; and J. P. Peter and W. R. Nord, "A Clarification and Extension of Operant Conditioning Principles in Marketing," *Journal of Marketing* (Summer 1982), pp. 102–7.
3. Morris B. Holbrook, "Nostalgia and Consumption Preferences: Some Emerging Patterns of Consumer Tastes," *Journal of Consumer Research* 20 (September 1993), pp. 245–56; Robert M. Schindler and Morris B. Holbrook, "Critical Periods in the Development of Men's and Women's Tastes in Personal Appearance," *Psychology & Marketing* 10, no. 6 (November–December 1993), pp. 549–64; Morris B. Holbrook and Robert M. Schindler, "Age, Sex, and Attitude Toward the Past as Predictors of Consumers' Aesthetic Tastes for Cultural Products," *Journal of Marketing Research* 31 (August 1994), pp. 412–22; Morris B. Holbrook and Robert M. Schindler, "Some Exploratory Findings on the Development of Musical Tastes," *Journal of Consumer Research* 16 (June 1989), pp. 119–24; Randall Rothenberg, "The Past Is Now the Latest Craze." *New York Times* (November 29, 1989), p. D1.
4. C. Huffman and M. J. Houston, "Goal-Oriented Experiences and the Development of Knowledge," *Journal of Consumer Research* (September 1993), pp. 190–207; S. A. Hawkins and S. J. Hoch, "Low-Involve-

ment Learning," *Journal of Consumer Research* (September 1992), pp. 212–25; N. M. Alperstein, "The Verbal Content of TV Advertising and Its Circulation in Everyday Life," *Journal of Advertising* 2 (1990), pp. 15–22; D. D. Muehling, R. N. Laczniak, and J. C. Andrews, "Defining, Operationalizing, and Using Involvement in Advertising Research," *Journal of Current Issues and Research in Advertising* (Spring 1993), pp. 22–57; T. B. C. Poiesz and C. J. P. M. deBont, "Do We Need Involvement to Understand Consumer Behavior?" in F. R. Kardes and M. Sujan (eds.), *Advances in Consumer Research* (Provo, UT: Association for Consumer Research, 1995), pp. 448–52.

5. Gordon H. Bower and Ernest R. Hilgard, *Theories of Learning* 5th ed. (Upper Saddle River, NJ: Prentice Hall, 1981).

6. Ivan P. Pavlov, *Conditioned Reflexes: An Investigation of the Physiological Activity of the Cerebral Cortex*, G. V. Anrep (trans., ed.) (London: Oxford University Press, 1927); Peter C. Holland, "Origins of Behavior in Pavlovian Conditioning," in G. H. Bower (ed.), *The Psychology of Learning and Motivation* 18 (Orlando, FL: Harcourt Brace Jovanovich, 1984), pp. 129–74; Kenneth Hugdahl, "Pavlovian Conditioning and Hemispheric Asymmetry: A Perspective," in G. Davey (ed.), *Cognitive Processes and Pavlovian Conditioning in Humans* (Chicester, England: John Wiley, 1987), pp. 147–82; Walter R. Nord and J. Paul Peter, "A Behavior Modification Perspective on Marketing," *Journal of Marketing* (Spring 1980), pp. 36–47; Terence A. Shimp, "The Role of Subject Awareness in Classical Conditioning: A Case of Opposing Ontologies and Conflicting Evidence," in Rebecca Holman and Michael Solomon (eds.), *Advances in Consumer Research*, 18 (Provo, UT: Association for Consumer Research, 1991), pp. 158–63; Elnora W. Stuart, Terence A. Shimp, and Randall W. Engle, "Classical Conditioning of Consumer Attitudes: Four Experiments in an Advertising Context," *Journal of Consumer Research* 14 (December 1987), pp. 334–49; Terence A. Shimp, Elnora W. Stuart, and Randall W. Engle, "A Program of Classical Conditioning Experiments Testing Variations in the Conditioned Stimulus and Context," *Journal of Consumer Research* 18, no. 1 (June 1991), pp. 1–12; Chris T. Allen and Thomas J. Madden, "A Closer Look at Classical Conditioning," *Journal of Consumer Research* 12, (December 1985), pp. 301–15; Lynn Kahle, Sharon Beatty, and Patricia Kennedy, "Comment on Classically Conditioning Human Consumers," in Melanie Wallendorf and Paul Anderson (eds.), *Advances in Consumer Research* 14 (Provo, UT: Association for Consumer Research, 1987), pp. 411–13; Francis K. McSweeney and Calvin Bierley, "Recent Developments in Classical Conditioning," *Journal of Consumer Research* 11 (September 1984), pp.

619–31; Calvin Bierley, Francis K. McSweeney, and Renee Vannieuwkerk, "Classical Conditioning of Preference for Stimuli," *Journal of Consumer Research* 12 (December 1985), pp. 316–23; Terence A. Shimp, "Neo-Pavlovian Conditioning and Its Implications for Consumer Theory and Research," in Thomas S. Robertson and Harold K. Kassarjian (eds.), *Handbook for Consumer Behavior* (Upper Saddle River, NJ: Prentice Hall, 1991), pp. 162–87; W. Jake Jacobs and James R. Blackburn, "A Model of Pavlovian conditioning: Variations in Representations of the Unconditioned Stimulus," *Integrated Physiological and Behavioral Science* 30 (January 1, 1995), pp. 12–33; Arjun Chaudhuri and Ross Buck, "Media Differences in Rational and Emotional Responses to Advertising," *Journal of Broadcasting & Electronic Media* 39 (January 1, 1995), pp. 109–25; B. F. Skinner, "Some Responses to the Stimulus 'Pavlov,' *Integrative Physiological & Behavioral Science* 31 (July 1, 1996), pp. 254–57.

7. Herbert E. Krugman, "Observations: Pavlov's Dog and the Future of Consumer Psychology," *Journal of Advertising Research* (November–December 1994), pp. 67–70.

8. Richard E. Petty and John T. Cacioppo, *Attitudes and Persuasion: Classic and Contemporary Approaches* (Dubuque, IA: Won. C. Brown, 1981).

9. Bennett B. Murdock Jr., "The Contributions of Hermann Ebbinhaus," *Journal of Experiential Psychology: Learning, Memory, and Cognition* 11, no. 3 (1985), pp. 469–71.

10. Gerald J. Gorn, "The Effects of Music in Advertising on Choice Behavior: A Classical Conditioning Approach," *Journal of Marketing* 46 (Winter 1982), pp. 94–101; Chris T. Allen and Thomas J. Madden, "A Closer Look at Classical Conditioning," *Journal of Consumer Research* 12 (December 1985), pp. 301–15.

11. Howard Schlossberg, "For a Good Cause," Promo 8, no. 3 (February 1994), pp. 38–50; John Graham, "Corporate Charity," *Incentive* (July 1994), pp. 51–52; and Geoffrey Smith and Ron Stodghill, "Are Good Causes Good Marketing," *Business Week* (March 21, 1994), p. 64; "Cause-Related Fraud on the Rise," *Incentive* (August 1994), p. 8; Udayan Gupta, "Cause-Driven Companies' New Cause: Profits," *Wall Street Journal* (November 8, 1994), p. B1; Mary Rowand, "Shoppers Turn to Web for Holiday Wish Lists," *AMA* (November 15, 2007); "Think Before You Pink," (November 2007), www.thinkbeforeyoupink. org/Pages/InfoMktgCampaigns.html; Cone Communications, "Cone Report Benchmark Survey," www. msen.mb.ca/crm.html.

12. "The Effect of Music in a Retail Setting," University of Washington, www.faculty.bschool.washington.edu/ ryolch/Research/atmosphe.htm.

13. "Music Motivates Impulse Buyers, Not Thoughtful Shoppers," *Monitor on Psychology*, vol. 36, no. 10 (November, 2005), www.apa.org/monitor/nov05/music.html.

14. Shimp, "Neo-Pavlovian Conditioning and Its Implications for Consumer Theory and Research."

15. Ibid.

16. Robert A. Rescorla, "Pavlovian Conditioning: It's Not What You Think It Is," *American Psychologist* 43 (March 1988), pp. 151-60.

17. Shimp, "Neo-Pavlovian Conditioning and Its Implications for Consumer Theory and Research."

18. Chris Janiszewski et. al., "A Meta-Analysis of Spacing Effect in Verbal Learning: Implications for Research on Advertising Repetition and Consumer Memory," *Journal of Consumer Research* 30, no. 1 (June 2003), pp. 138-150.

19. G. David Hughes, "Realtime Response Measures Redefine Advertising Wearout," *Journal of Advertising Research* (May/June 1992), pp. 61-77.

20. Rebecca Gardyn and John Fetto, "Where's the Lovin?" *American Demographics* 23, no. 2 (February 2001), pages 10-11.

21. John Kim, Chris T. Allen, and Frank R. Kardes, "An Investigation of the Mediational Mechanisms Underlying Attitudinal Conditioning," *Journal of Marketing Research* XXXIII (August 1996), pp. 318-28.

22. Robert A. Rescorla, "Pavlovian Conditioning and Its Proper Control Procedures," *Psychological Review* 74 (1967), pp. 70-71.

23. J. Meyers-Levy and A. M. Tybout, "Schema Congruity as a basis for Product Evaluation," *Journal of Consumer Research* 16 (1989), pp. 38-54; T. K. Srull, M. Lichenstein, and M. Rothbart, "Associative Storage and Retrieval Processes in Person Memory," *Journal of Experimental Psychology: Learning, Memory, and Cognition* 11 (1985), pp. 316-45; James J. Kellaris and Susan Powell Mantel, "Shaping Time Perceptions with Background Music: The Effect of Congruity and Arousal on Estimates of Ad Durations," *Psychology & Marketing* 13, no. 5 (August 1996), pp. 501-15.

24. J. Charles Jones, *Learning* (New York: Harcourt Brace Jovanovich, 1967), pp. 28-29.

25. B. F. Skinner, *The Behavior of Organisms: An Experimental Analysis* (New York: Apple-Century-Crofts, 1938); Gordon R. Foxall, "Behavior Analysis and Consumer Psychology," *Journal of Economic Psychology* 15 (March 1994), pp. 5-91; Blaise J. Biergiel and Christine Trosclair, "Instrumental Learning: Its Application to Customer Satisfaction," *Journal of Consumer Marketing* 2 (Fall 1985), pp. 23-28; Gordon R. Foxall, "The Behavioral Perspective Model of Purchase and Consumption: From Consumer Theory to Marketing Practice," *Journal of the Academy of Marketing Sciences* 20 (Spring 1992), pp. 189-98; Walter R. Nord and J. Paul Peter, "A Behavior Modification Perspective on Marketing," *Journal of Marketing* (Spring 1980), pp. 36-47; J. Paul Peter and Walter R. Nord, "A Clarification and Extension of Operant Conditioning Principles in Marketing," *Journal of Marketing* 46, (Summer 1982), pp. 102-7; Skinner, "Some Responses to the Stimulus 'Pavlov.'"

26. Dee Ann Glamser, "Mozart Plays to Empty Lot," *USA Today* (August 24, 1990), p. 3A.

27. Laura A. Peracchio, "How Do Young Children Learn to Be Consumers? A Script-Processing Approach," *Journal of Consumer Research* 18 (March 1992), pp. 425-40; Laura A. Peracchio, "Young Children's Processing of a Televised Narrative: Is a Picture Really Worth a Thousand Words?" *Journal of Consumer Research* 20 (September 1993), pp. 281-93; Carole Macklin, "The Effects of an Advertising Retrieval Cue on Young Children's Memory and Brand Evaluations," *Psychology & Marketing* 11, (May-June 1994), pp. 291-311; Jean Piaget, "The Child and Modern Physics," *Scientific American* 196 (1957), pp. 46-51.

28. Stephen J. Hoch and John Deighton, "Managing What Consumers Learn from Experience," *Journal of Marketing* 53 (April 1989), pp. 1-20.

29. Wolfgang Kohler, *The Mentality of Apes* (New York: Harcourt Brace & World, 1925).

30. Jennifer G. Paxton and Deborah R. John, "Consumer Learning by Analogy: A Model of Internal Knowledge Transfer," *Journal of Consumer Research* 24 (December 1997), pp. 266-284.

31. Chad Rubel, "Infomercials Evolve as Major Firms Join Successful Format," *Marketing News* 29, no. 1 (January 2, 1995), pp. 1, 36; and Chad Rubel, "Higher Costs Putting Infomercials to the Test," *Marketing News* 29, no. 1 (January 2, 1995), pp. 36-37; "TV4U.com Launches Infomercials and Channels on Their 21 Channel Broadband Network," *Newswire Today* (January 18, 2008), www.newswiretoday.com/news/13566/.

32. Mark Fitzgerald and Jennifer Saba, "Special Report: Outlook for Campaign Ad Revenue 2008," *Editor and Publisher* (December 18, 2007).

33. William D. Crano and Radmila Prislin, "Attitudes and Persuasion," *Annual Review of Psychology*, vol. 57 (January 2006), pp. 345-374.

34. Rebecca S. Bigler, "The Use of Multicultural Curricula and Materials to Counter Racism in Children," *Journal of Social Issues*, vol. 55, no. 4 (Winter 1999), pp. 687-705.

35. Geoffrey Cowley, "The Wisdom of Animals," *Newsweek* (May 23, 1988), pp. 52-59.

36. Shimp, "Neo-Pavlovian Conditioning and Its Implications for Consumer Theory and Research"; Shimp, "The Role of Subject Awareness in Classical Conditioning: A Case of Opposing Ontologies and Conflicting Evidence."

37. Shimp, "Neo-Pavlovian Conditioning and Its Implications for Consumer Theory and Research."

38. Ibid.

39. Rom J. Markin Jr., *Consumer Behavior, A Cognitive Orientation* (New York: Macmillan, 1974), p. 239.

40. E. R. Hilgard and R. C. Atkinson, *Introduction to Psychology* (New York: Harcourt Brace Jovanovich, 1967), p. 306.

41. I. L. Sonnier, *Hemisphericity as a Key to Understanding Individual Differences* (Springfield, IL: Thomas Publications, 1992), p. 7.

42. C. W. Burklund and A. Smith, "Language and Cerebral Hemispheres," *Neurology* 27 (1977), pp. 627–33; B. Samples, "Education for Both Sides of the Human Mind," *The Science Teacher* 42, no. 1 (1975), pp. 21–23.

43. M. Hunter, "Right-Brained Kids in Left-Brained Schools," *Today's Education* (November–December 1976), pp. 45–48.

44. D. Hines, "Independent Functioning of the Two Cerebral Hemispheres for Recognizing Bilaterally Presented Tachistoscopic Visual Half-Field Stimuli," *Cortex* 11 (1975), pp. 132–43.

45. C. W. Taylor, "Developing Effective Functioning People: The Accountable Goal of Multiple Talent Teaching," *Education* 94 (1973), pp. 99–110; E. P. Torrance, "Emergence of Identity Through Expressive Activities," *Elementary English* (1973), pp. 849–52.

46. Excel, Inc., "Major Premises of 4MAT®," www.excelcorp.com/4premis.html (1996) (accessed June 22, 1999).

47. S. Weinstein, V. Appel, and C. Weinstein, "Brain Activity Responses to Magazine and Television Advertising," *Journal of Advertising Research* 20, no. 3 (June 1980).

48. M. B. Holbrook and W. L. Moore, "Feature Actions in Consumer Judgments of Verbal vs. Pictorial Presentations," *Journal of Consumer Research* 8 (June 1981), pp. 103–13.

49. Flemming Hansen, "Hemispheral Lateralization: Implications for Understanding Consumer Behavior," *Journal of Consumer Research* 8 (June 1981), pp. 23–36; Herbert E. Krugman, "The Impact of Television Advertising: Learning without Involvement," *The Public Opinion Quarterly* 29 (1965), pp. 349–56; Herbert E. Krugman, "Memory without Recall, Exposure without Recognition," *Journal of Advertising Research* 17 (1977), pp. 7–12; Herbert E. Krugman, "Sustained Viewing of Television," paper presented at the Conference Board, Council on Marketing Research, New York (1980).

50. B. F. Skinner, *Science and Human Behavior* (New York: Macmillan, 1953); Edward Chance Tolman, *Purposive Behavior in Animals and Men* (New York: Appleton-Century-Crofts, 1932); N. E. Miller and J. Dollard, *Social Learning and Imitation* (New Haven, CT: Yale University Press, 1941); A. Bandura, "Social Learning Through Imitation," in M. R. Jones (ed.), *Nebraska Symposium on Motivation* (Lincoln, NE: University of Nebraska Press, 1962), pp. 211–69; and A. Bandura and R. H. Walters, *Social Learning and Personality Development* (New York: Holt, Rinehart and Winston, 1963).

51. Jagdish Sheth, "How Adults Learn Brand Preference," *Journal of Advertising Research* 8, no. 3 (September 1968), pp. 25–36.

52. Arjun Chaudhuri and Ross Buck, "Media Differences in Rational and Emotional Responses to Advertising," *Journal of Broadcasting & Electronic Media* 39 (January 1, 1995), pp. 109–25; Ross Buck, "Emotional Education and Mass Media," in R. P. Hawkins, J. M. Weimann, and S. Pingree (eds.), *Advancing Communication Science: Merging Mass and Interpersonal Perspectives* (Beverly Hills, CA: Sage, 1989), pp. 44–76; C. Pechmann and D. W. Stewart, "The Multidimensionality of Persuasive Communications: Theoretical and Empirical Foundations," in P. Cafferata and A. M. Tybout (eds.), *Cognitive and Affective Responses to Advertising* (Lexington, MA: Lexington Books, 1989), pp. 31–45.

53. "The Global Village Finally Arrives," *Time* 142, no. 21 (Fall 1993).

54. Jagdish N. Sheth and Atul Parvtiyar, "Relationship Marketing in Consumer Markets: Antecedents and Consequences," *Journal of the Academy of Marketing Science* 23, no. 4 (Fall 1995), pp. 255–71.

55. Regis McKenna, *Successful Strategies for the Age of the Customer* (Reading, MA: Addison-Wesley, 1991).

56. Jacob Jacoby and Robert Chestnut, *Brand Loyalty: Measurement and Management* (New York: John Wiley, 1978).

57. Anne B. Fisher, "Coke's Brand Loyalty Lesson," *Fortune* (August 5, 1985), p. 44.

58. Jacoby and Chestnut, *Brand Loyalty: Measurement and Management*.

59. Ronald Alsop, "Brand Loyalty Is Rarely Blind Loyalty," *Wall Street Journal* (October 19, 1989), p. B1. and Andrew Greenfield, "Brands That Get Noticed," *Marketing Research* 15, no. 2 (Summer 2003), pp. 228–32.

60. Raymond J. lawrence, "Patterns of Buyer Behavior: Time for a New Approach?" *Journal of Marketing Research* 6 (May 1969), pp. 137–44.

61. David Mazursky, Priscilla LaBarbera, and Al Aiello, "When Consumers Switch Brands," *Psychology & Marketing* 4, no. 1 (Spring 1987), pp. 17–30.

62. Naresh K. Malhotra, "Mnemonics in Marketing: A Pedagogical Tool," *Journal of the Academy of Marketing Science* 19 (Spring 1991), pp. 141–49.

63. Lyle E. Bourne, Roger L. Dominowski, and Elizabeth F. Loftus, *Cognitive Processes* (Upper Saddle River,

NJ: Prentice Hall, 1979); Donald A. Norman, *Memory and Attention* (New York: John Wiley, 1969); Peter H. Lindsay and Donald A. Norman, *Human Information Processing* (New York: Academic Press, 1972); A. Newell and H. A. Simon, *Human Problem Solving* (Upper Saddle River, NJ: Prentice Hall, 1972).

64. Bourne, Dominowski, and Loftus, *Cognitive Processes*; Ulrich Neisser, *Cognitive Psychology* (New York: Appleton, 1966); Robert G. Crowsers, *Principles of Learning in Memory* (Hillsdale, NJ: Lawrence Erlbaum, 1976); and Hershel W. Leibowitz and Lewis O. Harvey Jr., "Perception," *Annual Review of Psychology* 24 (1973), pp. 207-40.

65. Richard M. Shiffrin and R. C. Atkinson, "Storage and Retrieval Processes in Long-Term Memory," *Psychological Review* 76 (March 1969), pp. 179-93.

66. Herbert A. Simon "How Big Is a Chunk?" Science 183 (February 1974), pp. 482-88; George A. Miller, "The Magical Number Seven, Plus or Minus Two: Some Limits on Our Capacity for Processing Information," *Psychological Review* 63 (March 1956), pp. 81-97.

67. John R. Anderson, *The Architecture of Cognition* (Cambridge, Ma: Harvard University Press, 1983).

68. Gabriel Biehal and Dipankar Chakravarti, "Consumers' use of Memory and External Information in Choice: Macro and Micro Perspectives," *Journal of Consumer Research* 12; (March 1986), pp. 382-405.

69. Kevin Lane Keller, "Memory Factors in Advertising: The Effect of Advertising Retrieval Cues on Brand Evaluations," *Journal of Consumer Research* 14 (December 1987), pp. 316-33; Kevin Lane Keller, "Memory and Evaluation Effects in Competitive Advertising Environments," *Journal of Consumer Research* 17 (March 1991), pp. 463-76; Fergus I. M. Craik, "Encoding and Retrieval Effects in Human Memory: A Partial Review," in A. D. Baddeley and J. Long (eds.), *Attention and Performance* 9 (Hillsdale, NJ: Lawrence Erlbaum, 1981); Endel Tulving, "Relation Between Encoding Specificity and Levels of Processing," in L. S. Cermak and Fergus I. M. Craik (eds.), *Levels of Processing in Human Memory* (Hillsdale, NJ: Lawrence Erlbaum, 1979), pp. 401-28.

70. Keller, "Memory Factors in Advertising: The Effect of Advertising Retrieval Cues on Brand Evaluations";

Keller, "Memory and Evaluation Effects in Competitive Advertising Environments."

71. Ibid.

72. John G. Lynch and Thomas K. Srull, "Memory and Attentional Factors in Consumer Choice: Concepts and Research Methods," *Journal of Consumer Research* 9 (June 1982), pp. 18-36.

73. *Ibid.*

74. H. Ebbinghaus, *Memory*, H. A. Ruger and C. E. Bussenius (trans.) (New York: Teachers College, 1913); Hubert A. Zielske, "The Remembering and Forgetting of Advertising," *Journal of Marketing* 23, (January 1959), pp. 231-43.

75. Kenneth R. Weingardt, Elizabeth F. Loftus, and D. Stephen Lindsay, "Misinformation Revisited: New Evidence on the Suggestibility of Memory," *Memory & Cognition* 23, no. 1 (1995), pp. 72-82; D. S. Lindsay, "Misleading Suggestions Can Impair Eyewitnesses' Ability to Remember Event Details," *Journal of Experimental Psychology: Learning, Memory, and Cognition* 16 (1990), pp. 1077-83; Elizabeth F. Loftus, "Memory Malleability: Constructivist and Fuzzy-Trace Explanations," *Learning and Individual Differences* 7, no. 2 (1995), pp. 133-37; M. McCloskey and M. Zaragoza, "Misleading Postevent Information and Memory for Events: Arguments and Evidence Against Memory Impairment Hypotheses," *Journal of Experimental Psychology: General* 114 (1985), pp. 1-16; E. F. Loftus, H. G. Hoffman, and W. A. Wagenaar, "The Misinformation Effect," in M. L. Howe, C. J. Brainerd, and V. F. Reyna (eds.), *Development of Long-Term Retention* (New York: Springer-Verlag, 1992).

76. Robert Kent and Chris T. Allen, "Competitive Interference Effects in Consumer Memory for Advertising: The Role of Brand Familiarity," *Journal of Marketing* 58, (July 1994), pp. 97-105.

77. Robert Kent and Chris T. Allen, "Competitive Interference Effects in Consumer Memory for Advertising: The Role of Brand Familiarity," *Journal of Marketing* 58 (July 1994), pp. 97-105.

78. Chris Cadelago, "Forget MTV—Apple's iPod Ads Are the New Music Star Makers," *San Francisco Chronicle* (November 24, 2007).

Consumer Attitudes

LEARNING OBJECTIVES

- To define attitudes, ascertain their nature, and identify their sources.
- To recognize the ramifications of the four functions that attitudes serve.
- To become familiar with the tenets and applications of the traditional and multi-attribute attitude models.
- To develop a basic understanding of the theories of reasoned action as well as goal pursuit & trying.
- To learn about attribution theory as well as its behavioral implications.
- To investigate the roles of cognitive consistency and information processing theories in attitude change.
- To identify and comprehend the concept and application of the elaboration likelihood model.

KEY TERMS

attitudes
attitude object
valence
intensity
centrality
utilitarian function
ego-defensive function
value-expressive function
knowledge function
traditional model of attitudes
cognitive component
affective component
behavioral (conative) component
multi-attribute model
attitude toward-the-object

theory of reasoned action (TORA)
intention
attitude-toward-the-behavior
subjective norms
goals
attribution
attitude change
cognitive consistency
cognitive dissonance theory
postpurchase dissonance
information-processing approach
elaboration-likelihood model (ELM)
central route to persuasion
peripheral route to persuasion

Tiger Woods's coming out as a pro in August 1996 ignited a media frenzy. Although many people were skeptical about Tigermania, Eldrick (Tiger) Woods, who was then only 21 years old, quickly proved himself and continued his unprecedented career accomplishments. Now in his early 30s, Tiger Woods is master of all he pursues, having just been voted the PGA Tour Player of the Year by his peers for the ninth time in his 11-year career—a vote made easy by his seven victories in the 2007 season that included a 13th major and the PGA Championship at Southern Hills.

His charitable side is as impressive as his mastery of the game. He established the Tiger Woods Learning Center, a safe haven where kids can learn, explore, and know they will never be humiliated. Sixteen thousand middle-school and high-school children went through the learning center program, and an estimated 10 million children were helped in 10 years by this center, the Smart Something character development program, and the foundation's programmatic grants and Youth Clinics.

Not only has Tiger reshaped the game of golf with his championship performance, he has also captured the hearts of America with his enthusiasm and love for the game. The extensive media coverage of his participation in tournaments as well as his personal life and charitable undertakings have both directed attention to golf and generated enthusiasm and interest for the game among many young people of all races.

Seeing Tiger with the green Masters jacket around his shoulders, marketers were quick to envision his enormous potential as a pitchman. Companies such as Nike, American Express, Tag Heuer Watches, General Motors' Buick, Gillette, EA Sports, and Accenture recognize the value of engaging the golf world's most visible icon in promoting their products. Tiger's age also makes him a natural draw for young people. In 2007, Tiger Woods topped the marketability of any active athlete who ever existed.

Beyond Tiger's contributions as a product endorser, the very game of golf itself stands to benefit from increasing interest among young kids who hated golf, who found it boring, and who regarded it as for old fogies. Creating interest in the game among youth is not simply a matter of flooding the media with catchy ads and hoping that Tiger continues to dominate the sport. The real issue entails whether the golf industry will interest young people including minorities in the game or keep it an elitist sport. Tiger's recognition of this issue has prompted him to establish the Tiger Woods Foundation, the purpose of which is to bring golf to minority children across America.[1]

> *Interest in golf has escalated as a result of Tiger's widely publicized championships. What explains Tiger's influence? In our society, whose attitudes toward golf are most likely to be influenced by him? Visit the following Tiger sites:* www.tigerwoods.com *and* http://sportsbusinessdigest.com/?p=264. *Note the companies and products he promotes. When Tiger is used as a spokesman for products, does he influence attitudes toward golf or attitudes toward products? Please explain.*

This brief narrative about Tiger Woods and the golf industry serves to illustrate how attitudes toward a whole industry or a sport can be influenced by the accomplishments of just one person. Tiger's popularity is serving to change some previously held negative and indifferent attitudes toward the game. Among many young people including minorities, an apparently widely held belief exists that golf is a sport for elderly and affluent members of the white race. Consequently, few young people of all races participate in the sport. To what extent changing attitudes will alter the sport remains to be seen.

This chapter examines factors that influence the formation and change of beliefs and attitudes. An understanding of these factors is imperative for both makers of public policy and marketers alike in their effort to anticipate and influence human behavior. If companies are to successfully develop and market innovative products that are on the leading edge, it is essential for them to analyze consumer behavior to understand the attitudes that drive it.[2]

What Are Attitudes?

In 1935, Gordon Allport, an early researcher in the field of attitudes, suggested that the concept of attitude is probably the most distinctive, indispensable concept in social psychology. Current studies indicate that Allport's words are still true today. Some authors maintain that no other single influence is as important to the study of consumer behavior as the concept of attitude.

Attitudes are consistent inclinations—whether favorable or unfavorable—that people hold toward products, services, people, places, or events. They can be more formally defined as learned predispositions to respond in a consistent manner in respect to a given object.[3] Attitudes are thus *mental states* and part of our psychological makeup.

Let us look at the terms of our definition. Attitudes are *learned*. For example, media coverage or direct experience of the 9/11 attack on the United States resulted in overwhelmingly negative attitudes on the part of the public toward terrorists and terrorist groups such as *al Qaeda*. Similarly, from a marketing perspective, attitudes can be formed either as a direct result of experiences with a product or through information acquired from others, including the mass media. We are not born with attitudes; we develop them as we experience or learn about things surrounding us. Attitudes, however, are not synonymous with behavior. A person may hold a favorable attitude toward Porsche automobiles but may not purchase one due to the high cost.

Attitudes are characterized by *consistency*. This means that attitudes take time to develop and are stable and enduring. They are not cast in stone—they can be changed over a period of time, but this process is usually very slow. Consistency means that once negative consumer attitudes toward a product or corporation develop, marketers face difficulties in changing them.

Consumer attitudes are *responsive*. They form as we become able to judge a product or situation based on personal experience and acquired information or perhaps as we choose between a number of alternatives. For example, a positive experience with a Sony television may lead us to believe this brand is superior to other TV sets on the market. We may insist on purchasing a Sony, even if less-expensive alternatives are available. Our response does not have to be a purchase decision, however, and may simply entail recommending the brand to our friends.

attitudes
learned predispositions to respond in a consistent manner to a given object

attitude object
anything about which consumers can form an attitude

Anything about which we can hold an attitude is called an **attitude object**. People, products, services, brands, situations, companies, issues, and places are all examples. In the chapter opening vignette, the sport of golf is an attitude object. Many people have positive feelings toward the game, whereas others find it boring. Each group will react to golf in its own way. Those with positive attitudes may play golf on a somewhat regular basis or watch golf tournaments on TV. Those with negative attitudes will likely avoid golf altogether. Of course, there are those who are indifferent about the game and hold neither negative nor positive attitudes toward it. Such individuals may or may not play the game or watch a tournament, depending on the degree of their social involvement with peers or family members who enjoy the game.

Although attitudes are well entrenched in the theory and practice of marketing, a major problem is that they are not directly observable. Attitudes must be inferred from what consumers say or do, and even then they may remain ambiguous. An observer who sees an individual attending a religious retreat might infer that this person is in favor of religion. In reality, however, the person may be attending the retreat because of a need for social interaction, to meet friends, or to find a marriage partner. Despite these types of ambiguities, understanding attitudes is essential to marketers because attitudes serve as a link between consumers' perceptions and their actual behavior.

Valence, Intensity, and Centrality of Attitudes

valence
an attraction or repulsion felt toward an attitude object

Attitudes steer people in a particular direction with respect to an attitude object. This aspect of attitudes is called **valence**. Positive valence attracts individuals toward a stimulus object; negative valence repels them away from it. For example, Intel Corporation, maker of ultrafast computer chips, pays subsidies to computer advertisers who place "Intel Inside" slogans in their ads. This practice is an effective means of attaining positive valence for Intel.

intensity
the extent of how strongly an individual feels one way or the other about an attitude object

Humans, in general, hold many attitudes with varying degrees of fervor, called **intensity**. For example, many consumers feel strongly about the brand of beer or wine they drink. The more strongly they feel about the product, the less likely they will be to change to another brand. Conversely, if an attitude is weak, the behavior can be changed easily. The probability of attitude change varies inversely with the intensity of the attitude.

centrality
the extent of how closely an attitude reflects a person's core values and beliefs

Centrality of an attitude, on the other hand, refers to how closely an attitude reflects our core values and beliefs. Central values cover such things as patriotism, religion, ethics, political affiliation, and personal values and goals, all of which are resistant to change. A person who believes strongly in human rights will be critical of actions taken by countries that deny their citizens these rights. Consumers who are attracted to products such as Louis Vuitton purses or luggage, or Rolex watches and designer brands such as Yves Saint Laurent or Gucci exhibit a high level of attitude centrality because these items are psychologically important to them. Highly visible, expensive, and prestigious goods are often used as symbols to reflect one's self-concept and feelings of self-worth. People in many cases judge others' social worth based on their ownership of such possessions. However, fortunately, most shopping-related attitudes are *peripheral*. For instance, attitudes toward the cell phone service provider we choose or the Web site from which we purchase products or services are usually somewhat easy to change because they do not relate to our central values and beliefs. As such, peripheral attitudes are susceptible to change.

Sources of Attitudes

We learn, form, and acquire attitudes from many sources. The three major ones are personal experience with objects, social interaction, and exposure to mass media.

PERSONAL EXPERIENCE WITH OBJECTS

We constantly touch, taste, feel, try on, or examine objects we encounter. Based on this contact, we evaluate objects in our environment and form attitudes toward them. Marketers induce trials so that we can experience products and their benefits firsthand before purchasing them. For example, most major automobile companies fight to get rental companies to use their cars in order to expose the public to a particular model. When renters drive a model and are impressed by its look or performance, they develop positive attitudes that may lead to increased sales or positive word of mouth.

SOCIAL INTERACTION

People tend to acquire, through social interaction, the attitudes of family members, friends, neighbors, and colleagues and perhaps online communities. Social groups, peer groups, and work groups are also influential in molding a wide range of product- and service-related attitudes. Many young people today choose to get a tattoo or have their body pierced largely to fit into and gain acceptance by their peer group.

EXPOSURE TO MASS MEDIA

No one has ever been exposed to so much information as the present generation. The multitude of broadcast and cable networks, radio stations, computer networks, newspapers, magazines, telephones, faxes, and mail services have exposed us all to amounts of information no one ever thought possible. Events in other parts of the world are immediately communicated around the globe. With such an outpouring of information, the influence of mass media on attitude formation and change cannot be underestimated. Most products today have become equally universal; they are found in just about every country.

The Functions of Attitudes

Attitudes serve four functions: utilitarian, ego-defensive, value-expressive, and knowledge functions.[4]

UTILITARIAN FUNCTION

utilitarian function
the notion that some attitudes serve as a means to an end—gaining rewards or avoiding punishments

When products help us gain rewards or avoid punishments, they perform a **utilitarian function.** Cosmetics, antiperspirants, and mouthwashes help us to either look good or avoid smelling bad. If a product helps us achieve a desired goal, our resulting attitude toward it will be positive. Conversely, our attitude would be negative if the product did not contribute to reaching our goal. For example, economically minded travelers may form positive attitudes toward airlines with low ticket prices, such as SouthWest and JetBlue, because of the basic no-frills, low-cost transportation the firms provide. Fliers, on the other hand, may be negatively predisposed toward a particular airline that was responsible for lost baggage. To promote a product, marketers can emphasize a utilitarian purpose the item can serve. The ad in Figure 6.1 from firstSTREET presents agruments for and evidence of the comfort offered by the Sleep Better Memory Foam Ultra Mattress Topper, a high-tech sleep system that molds to consumers'

Figure 6.1
This ad from firstSTREET stresses the utilitarian advantage of getting a better night's sleep by using this memory Foam Ultra Mattress Topper.

body contours. By providing such facts, the ad highlights the utilitarian function of the brand and thus, elevates the resulting attitudes toward it.

EGO-DEFENSIVE FUNCTION

These attitudes serve the social-adjustment function, which translates into a tendency to conform to expectations of other to permit social interactions to run smoothly and more efficiently. For example, humans are known to protect their egos and disguise their inadequacies. Consumers therefore often prefer particular products because of their compensatory value, such as Viagra (for sexual potency) and Rogaine (for hair growth). Similarly, certain electronic keyboards compensate for players' lack of talent or training by automatically adding chords and rhythms that make inexperienced performers sound like professionals. Products such as these perform an important **ego-defensive function**. When the external environment presents threats to the ego, internal anxieties arise, and defensive behavior stems from attitudes that protect the ego's delicate sensitivities. Marketers recognize that some products are purchased to avoid anxiety-producing situations and offer reassurances of protection for consumers' ego states. Ads from Procter & Gamble for the company's Sure brand of antiperspirant illustrate these principles by depicting social situations where body odor could cause embarrassment. The ad copy challenges Sure users with the slogan, "Raise your hand if you're Sure!" Similarly, Kellogg's Special K breakfast cereal is promoted as a means of improving health and achieving weight control through its low-carb weight-loss plan. The ad in Figure 6.2 exemplifies an application of the ego-defensive function of attitudes by advocating the use of cosmetics to alleviate a woman's concern over her appearance.

ego-defensive function
the notion that some attitudes serve to protect an individual's ego or disguise a person's inadequacies

Figure 6.2
This Bed Head Cosmetics ad plays on women's sensitive ego-driven mechanism by suggesting that using the company's brand of cosmetics alleviates their concern about looking like one who just got out of bed.

VALUE-EXPRESSIVE FUNCTION

Attitudes serving the value-expressive function help consumers express their central values (such as patriotism) and idiosyncratic preferences (such as a preference for designer—label garments and expensive brands of home electronics), as well assist them in conveying their self-perception to others. Patriotic feelings, for example, which resulted from the 9/11 terrorist attack, generated significant changes in consumer attitudes and behavior toward a variety of domestic and foreign entities and issues. These attitudes had and will continue to have significant ramifications for our economy as a whole (such as the value of the dollar in foreign markets), and particularly for the dynamics of the marketplace. Affected sectors, for example, include financial services, travel, hospitality, housing, energy, and security.

By acquiring prestigious products, consumers attempt to convey to others their accomplishment and success.

© 2009, Pokrovskaya Elena, Shutterstock, Inc.

Another dimension of the value-expressive function of attitudes can be observed in our relentless effort to achieve self-enhancement, self-extension, and self-expression by communicating to others the values we revere, such as beauty, self-respect, freedom, pleasure, and accomplishment. Behavior stemming from such value-expressive attitudes demonstrates our core values. For example, some consumers prefer to purchase quality, expensive, prestigious, and distinctive products. Through such acquisitions, these consumers attempt to convey to others their accomplishments and success. Actions like this clearly demonstrate the potency of the **value-expressive function**. Capitalizing on these tendencies, marketers of consumer goods attempt to identify their brands with widely held or deeply seated values, portray their brands as means of expressing them, and surround their brands with symbols of them. Promotional strategies used by entities such as expensive automobile or motorcycle owners' groups, prestigious country clubs, and Ivy League colleges have been successful in attracting participants, members, or students by linking the advertiser to the values cherished most by these individuals. Luxurious automobiles are often promoted as self-expressive possessions due to their elegance and high price. The ad in Figure 6.3 from Mercedes-Benz communicates the value-expressive qualities of owning this new and prestigious 2009 SL automobile.

value-expressive function

the notion that some attitudes help consumers communicate the core values they revere to other people

KNOWLEDGE FUNCTION

Most of us seek simplicity, stability, and predictability in our interaction with our environment. Knowledge helps us simplify and give meaning to what otherwise would be a complex and chaotic universe. Attitudes that serve the knowledge function help consumes organize, structure, and summarize

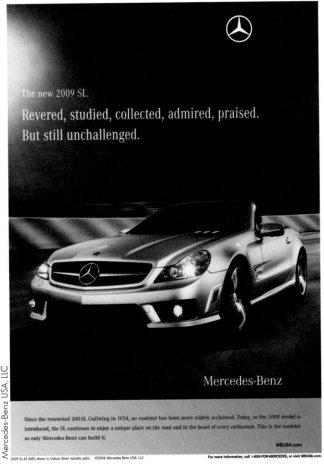

Figure 6.3

The caption "revered, studied, connected, admired, and praised" communicates the self-expressive value of acquiring this prestigous Mercedes-Benz automobile.

large amounts of complex information about attitude objects so that decisions concerning them can be made quickly and easily. The **knowledge function** of attitudes reflects cognitive theories of learning and information processing, which portray humans as information seekers. Our knowledge quest is prompted by curiosity and the desire to deal competently and effectively with life's varied predicaments. Based on this function, we form our particular attitudes, positive or negative regarding stimuli we encounter in our daily life.

The knowledge function offers insights for product-positioning strategies. Marketers must clearly and unambiguously position their brands and explain the benefits that differentiate a brand from its competition. One Heinz ad supplied information about the ingredients of its vinegar products. The ad indicated that whereas many white vinegars contain petroleum as a base, Heinz white vinegar is made from sun-ripened corn and that its cider vinegar is made from real apples. By providing facts about the firm's over

knowledge function
the notion that some attitudes provide people with a simple, predictable, and organized view of the environment

Consumer Behavior in Practice

What's Made Out of Rags, Pulp, and Ink and Is Value Expressive?

The greeting card industry is big business today, with annual sales exceeding $7 billion. Unlike selling tangible products, greeting card companies are in the *sentiment expression business*, where cards can produce sentiments of warmth, love, sympathy, humor, or even ease pain.

According to the Greeting Card Association, almost $7 billion worth of cards were sold in 2001. Two manufacturers dominate this business: American Greetings Corporation, the world's largest publicly owned greeting card manufacturer, and Hallmark Cards, Inc., the largest privately owned producer. Together, these two companies control about 80 percent of the present $7.5 billion U.S. greeting card market.

The history of mass-produced greeting cards can be traced back to nineteenth-century England and the United States. At that time, the advances of efficient, cost-effective color printing, coupled with low postage rates, brought about the birth of a new industry. By the late nineteenth century, a wide variety of mass-printed greeting cards were available for many occasions, such as Christmas, New Year's, Valentine's Day, and Easter. These could be found in neighborhood drugstores, general stores, and print shops.

As the public became accustomed to the idea of sending greeting cards for occasions other than the traditional ones, cards began to be offered for every event, holiday, and faith—covering themes as varied as life itself. Today, approximately 50 percent of the cards purchased annually are holiday related; the rest are *everyday types* of cards that are designed to express sentiments as diverse as human emotions. Approximately 90 percent of all cards are purchased by women. Thus, greeting cards are placed on highly visible permanent displays in outlets most often frequented by women.

Sales in this industry remained flat over the past ten years; American Greetings, Inc., and Hallmark are always on the lookout for new ways to boost their shares of the value-expressive market. Innovative ideas range from creating new occasions, such as Sweetest Day, when cards can be exchanged, to entering the high-tech arena. Electronic kiosks, originally placed in retail stores back in 1992, allow customers to personalize greeting cards. Through this customizing service called "Personalize It," customers can incorporate personal remarks into precomposed verses. However, while the idea of these kiosks was potentially profitable, a dispute over the ownership of the patent for the touch-screen technology emerged among Hallmark, American Greetings, and Custom Expressions, the company that had invented the technology behind the kiosks. Due to this dispute, Hallmark is expected to close many of these kiosks, since they failed to fulfill their early promise of profitability.

In 2007, an Internet card company called SendOut Cards.com was established. Through the services of this firm, customers can send either a conventional or customized card with their personalized message, and accomplish this task in less than 60 seconds—a convenience and speed that paints a rosy picture for the online service.[5]

Consumers in the United States, more so than those abroad, are likely to send greeting cards on various occasions to express diverse sentiments, such as affection, recognition, concern, remembrance, and sympathy. What factors explain this tendency among consumers in the United States? Visit the Hallmark Company and Send OutCards.com at www.hallmark.com and www. sendoutcards.com respectively. In your opinion, to what extent will customization capability enhance the market for greeting cards and the industry at large? How and why?

110-year-old, all-natural recipe for vinegar, Heinz used knowledge to positively influence consumers' attitudes toward the brand. Similarly, providing knowledge regarding the wireless capability of its printers is the basis of this ad from Hewlett-Packard in Figure 6.4.

Courtesy of Hewlett-Packard

Figure 6.4

This ad from Hewlett-Packard provides consumers with beneficial knowledge regarding its printers' capability of producing copies wirelessly from any room within a house.

The distinction we just drew between the various attitude functions (utilitarian, ego defensive, value expressive, and knowledge) helps marketers recognize that attitudes toward different product categories tend to be associated with different attitude functions.[6] For example, consumers tend to form utilitarian attitudes toward products such as kitchen disposal units or furnaces. Most people do not really care how a furnace looks verses how efficiently it operates. By contrast, attitudes toward perfumes, greeting cards, and clothing serve a value-expressive function. These products help us make favorable impressions on other people. Consequently, utilitarian ads are likely to be more effective in the case of the first type of products, whereas image-oriented ads are more suitable for the latter types.

Do Attitudes Determine Behavior?

Decades of research show that we *sometimes* act in accordance with our attitudes. At other times, however, we behave in a manner quite inconsistent with them. For example, an Insight Research Group in 2008 showed that 86 percent

CHAPTER 6 Consumer Attitudes 201

of Americans claimed to be environmentalists and say they are willing to make sacrifices for a better environment.[7] However, marketers have observed that when it comes to making concrete buying decisions, many are not the environmentalists they claim to be.

Researchers over the years have dealt with three fundamental issues: (1) *whether* a relationship between attitudes and behavior exists (that is, do attitudes influence behavior?), (2) *when* such a relationship is to be expected, and (3) *how* attitudes affect or guide behavior.

On the first point, *do attitudes relate to behavior*, researchers have found conflicting evidence. Corey, for example, examined the correlation between students' attitudes toward cheating and their actual cheating behavior and found it to equal zero.[8] Those who indicated negative attitudes toward cheating did cheat on a later test. Other evidence, however, shows a positive correlation between attitudes and behavior. For example, consumers who indicated having favorable attitudes toward coupons as a promotional practice tended to use them regularly when they shopped.[9]

Concerning the second point, *when a link between attitudes and behavior could be expected*, researchers have identified factors that are instrumental in determining whether the relationship between attitudes and behavior is strong or weak. Fazio and Ewoldsen cited a number of factors, called *moderating variables*, that govern this relationship.[10] These moderating variables include (a) qualities of the behavior (whether the behavior is general or specific), (b) qualities of the person (whether the person is inner or outer directed and whether or not the individual has a vested interest in the attitude issue), (c) qualities of the situation in which the behavior is exhibited (the physical and social surroundings, as well as the time context), and (d) qualities of the attitude itself (the apparent influence that the attitude exerts upon the individual).

To clarify, assume you enjoy sports and tennis in particular. Assume further that a friend were to call you on a sunny Saturday morning with an invitation to play tennis at an exclusive country club. Most likely you would accept the invitation unless you had an important prior commitment. In this example, the relation between the positive attitude toward tennis and acceptance of the invitation is strong. In terms of the four moderating variables, (a) the attitude object is specific—playing tennis on a nice morning, (b) the outing offers an opportunity to socialize, (c) the game will take place at a fancy country club, and (d) the exercise will do you good. These types of factors moderate the relationship between attitudes and resulting behavior.

The third point, *how attitudes guide behavior*, has been the subject of a great deal of research. Many analysts and users of attitude responses in marketing research feel that it is essential to understand the attitudes that drive consumer behavior. Consequently, they frequently overrate the importance of reported attitudes. Most survey questionnaires fail to follow up attitude questions with an action question, such as: "OK, if that's how you *feel* about it, then what are you going to *do* about it?" In short, reported attitudes do not always equal action.[11] However, because attitudes often seem to guide behavior, a clear understanding of the role of attitudes in purchase situations can provide marketers with the means of dealing with issues of attitude creation and change.

In the following sections, we present basic attitude perspectives, starting with the traditional model of attitudes, followed by the multi-attribute model, and then the theory of reasoned action.

The Traditional Model of Attitudes

In 1988, after many years of stable sales, the purchase rate of aspirin suddenly skyrocketed. The explosion in sales was due to a report in a medical journal stating that daily doses of aspirin can lower the risk of heart attacks in healthy adults.[12] This example represents one approach to examining attitudes as a means of guiding behavior. Consumers originally knew that aspirin is useful for relieving headaches, colds, and fever. The new information about its ability to lower the risk of heart attacks, however, created a new belief and a positive feeling toward aspirin as well as an enhanced tendency among many people to use it for that purpose. The result was a sudden increase in demand for the product. The **traditional model of attitudes**, called the tricomponent model, expresses this interrelationship and posits that attitudes consist of three components: *cognitive*, *affective*, and *behavioral* or *conative*.[13] A schematic diagram of the traditional model of attitudes appears in Exhibit 6.1. Each of these three components is described in the paragraphs that follow.

traditional model of attitudes
a view that attitudes consist of three components: cognitive, affective, and behavioral

COGNITIVE COMPONENT

The **cognitive component** is what we think we know about an attitude object. Our beliefs could be based on *knowledge* (one's experience documents that aspirin relieves pain and reduces the risk of heart attacks), *opinion*

cognitive component
what a person thinks he or she knows about an attitude object

Schematic Conception of Attitudes: The Traditional Model

EXHIBIT 6.1

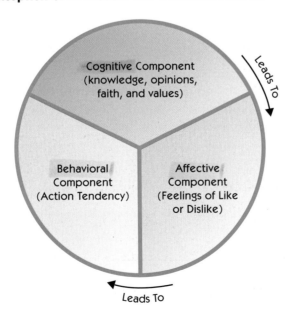

(inconclusive beliefs based on a medical journal's claims about aspirin's role in reducing the risk of heart attacks), *faith* (convictions about the integrity of the researchers and their methods), or *value systems* (people should heed medical advice to maintain good health).

AFFECTIVE COMPONENT

affective component
an individual's positive or negative reaction to an attitude object

The **affective component** of an attitude includes feelings of like or dislike, representing our reaction to the cognitive aspect of the attitude.[14] For example, after reading the medical journal's report about the way aspirin can effectively reduce heart attack risks, an individual begins to form positive feelings toward aspirin and commences to consider it as a viable treatment for maintaining good health.

BEHAVIORAL OR CONATIVE COMPONENT

behavioral (conative) component
a person's action tendency or intentions with respect to an attitude object

The **behavioral** or **conative component** of an attitude represents our tendency to respond in a certain way, as an expression of the favorable or unfavorable feelings formed earlier. The behavioral component may take the form of *overt behavior*. Consumers' rush to purchase and use aspirin after reading the medical report is a manifestation of the response to the positive feelings generated by the article. However, others react to this new information by doing nothing. Researchers attempt to assess the *intentions* of consumers in such cases by asking about their possible future actions relating to the product under investigation.

Attitude Components and Marketing Strategy

When marketers use the traditional model to create or change attitudes, they appeal to consumers at the *cognitive* level with informative messages, at the *affective* level with emotionally toned messages, and at the *behavioral* level with incentives such as samples, coupons, or rebates. For example, in 2007, Johnson & Johnson introduced a second-generation product, Listerine Whitening Quick Dissolving Strips, which dissolve in the mouth within 5 to 10 minutes. The main claim to fame of these strips is that with regular use, the strips will produce whiter teeth and freshen breath within two weeks. Johnson & Johnson is following the traditional attitude model in its new product launch. Working at the cognitive level, television spots were placed on broadcast and cable networks. These commercials opened with the words, "Tell Us Where You Whiten." The commercials used a slice-of-life format, showing consumers engaging and interacting. In addition to these ads, the firm sponsored ABC's "Good Morning America" program, on which the whitening strips were also mentioned. At the affective level, the company built on consumers' desire to look sexy and attractive, as well as emphasized the fact that the quick dissolving strips give users the freedom to go out in public. Johnson & Johnson's strategy also operated at the behavioral level by distributing as many as 17 million samples during the first year of the campaign, and attaching samples of the strips to other Listerine products. These strips were also given away at stores like Wal-Mart. The company dispatched teams of workers on motorcycles in 20 cities, giving away T-shirts that read "Do It Here. Do It There. Do It Anywhere." This refers to consumers' ability to use the whitening strips at any time and everywhere they go.[15]

In marketing a second generation teeth whitening product, Johnson and Johnson appealed to consumers at the *cognitive* level by stressing their desire to look sexy and attractive.

However, the traditional model of attitudes, despite its uses to explain attitude formation and change, tends to give the impression that overt behavior can be easily predicted from an individual's attitudes. In reality, as we've now seen, attitudes and accompanying behavior are often in obvious contradiction. This discrepancy renders false the notion that researchers can predict an individual's overt behavior through knowledge of that person's attitudes. Subsequent research efforts continued to address the issue of how attitudes guide behavior. One such effort by Martin Fishbein, a foremost researcher of attitudes, resulted in what is known as the multi-attribute model of attitudes. This model is briefly covered in the following section.

Fishbein's Multi-Attribute Model of Attitudes

The **multi-attribute model** differs from the traditional model of attitudes in a number of respects. It recognizes that the attitude object can have a number of attributes that differ in importance to the same individual. It is possible for a consumer concurrently to hold strongly positive feelings toward some features of a product and less positive or even negative feelings toward other attributes of the same item. Consumers concerned about their diet may select a fat-free brand of ice cream even though they find the taste to be less appealing than traditional ice cream.

Fishbein hypothesized that an **attitude-toward-the-object** is a function of (1) a person's beliefs about an object (the object's inclusion of a number of characteristic attributes) and (2) the person's evaluative aspects of those beliefs (that person's appraisal of the presence and desirability of each of these characteristic attributes in a brand). He proposed that through quantification of these two variables, it becomes possible to arrive at a numerical evaluation of attitudes toward a product. This, in turn, would allow marketers to use such knowledge in evaluating or comparing between a number of competing brands.[16]

To clarify, assume a study is conducted to compare three medium-priced brands of watches—Timex, Citizen, and Seiko. In this case, respondents are asked to identify the attributes they use to evaluate watches in actual purchase situations. Suppose the respondents identify four attributes: *attractiveness, brand reputation, price affordability*, and the watch's *special features*. Respondents are then asked to rate the importance of each of the four attributes by giving each a *numerical weight*. A six-point scale may be used for this purpose, where the higher number indicates greater attribute importance.

multi-attribute model
a view that attitude objects have a number of desirable or undesirable features that differ in importance to the same individual

attitude toward-the-object
an individual's overall appraisal (like or dislike) of an attitude object

EXHIBIT 6.2

A Respondent's Ratings of Three Brands of Watches Using Fishbein's Attitude-Toward-an-Object Model

Perceive Attribute	Weight Assigned to Each Attribute (Values range from 1–6)	Beliefs about Each Brand of Watch Numerical ratings (1–7) multiplied by weights (1–6)		
		Timex	Citizen	Seiko
Attractiveness	6	× 7 = 42	× 6 = 36	× 6 = 36
Brand reputation	5	× 4 = 20	× 7 = 35	× 5 = 25
Affordability	3	× 5 = 15	× 6 = 18	× 5 = 15
Special features	5	× 3 = 15	× 3 = 15	× 4 = 20
		92	104	96

Further, respondents in the study are asked to rate the extent to which each brand possesses these same attributes; that is to say, to give *numerical ratings* (say from 1 to 7) to each of these attributes as it exists in each brand. These numerical ratings reflect respondents' perceived presence or absence of each attribute in each brand. For example, if a respondent feels that the Citizen watch has a better reputation than the other two brands, the respondent may give it a high rating of 7. Exhibit 6.2 depicts the case of a respondent in the process of evaluating the three brands of watches mentioned.

Through this process the respondent's scores can be calculated for each brand by multiplying each *attribute's numerical rating* times its corresponding *weight*. In this case, the respondent rated the Citizen watch to be best among the three choices, giving it a composite score of 104 compared to 96 for Seiko and 92 for Timex. By summing the scores for each brand from all the respondents comprising the study's sample, an overall numerical score emerges for each brand. The watch with the highest overall score is judged to be the most preferred (has the strongest positive attitude) from the standpoint of the study's respondents.

Some researchers of consumer behavior believe that information obtained using Fishbein's multi-attribute model is relevant to marketers from a strategic point of view. The model enables marketers to ascertain brand strengths and deficiencies relative to the competition by determining how consumers evaluate brand alternatives on critical attributes. Revealing the brand's perceived strengths and weaknesses has implications for both brand design and promotion. For design, product weakness may signal the need to undertake corrective brand reformulation.

LIMITATIONS OF THE FISHBEIN MODEL

Some consumer researchers contend Fishbein's model tends to assume that when consumers hold positive feelings toward most or even some features of a product, the positive attitudes toward these features will translate into a purchase.

Limitations of this type have led psychologists such as Ajzen and Fishbein to abandon the study of attitudes-toward-objects and focus instead on attitudes-toward-actions.[17] This revised view looks not only at the features of the object but also at the consequences of the purchase. In other words, when considering the purchase of an Intel Centrino Pro Processor notebook, an individual may ponder such factors as mobility, increased productivity, information security, time saved, time required to learn, and many other aspects specifically relevant to that person. Therefore, from a consumer behavior point of view, it makes more sense to find out a prospective buyer's attitude toward the consequences of purchasing and owning the notebook rather than merely to identify his or her attitude toward its features. In this case, despite the positive feelings about the notebook's capability to secure information, the consumer may decide against its purchase due to perceived hindrances, such as the platform's requirement to have an enabled chipset with a connection to a power source and corporate network capabilities being limited to battery power.

Due to these concerns, Ajzen and Fishbein developed the theory of reasoned action to address the limitations of the previous view.

The Theory of Reasoned Action

According to the **theory of reasoned action (TORA)**, behavior is determined by a person's intention to behave.[18] **Intention**, in this sense, is a person's subjective resolution to behave in a certain way toward an attitude object. For example, women in Western societies buy cosmetic products with the intent of enhancing their natural beauty. Here, intention (looking attractive) determines the attitude toward the behavior (buying a brand of cosmetics). Such behavior is also influenced by the social norm governing the action to be taken (the society admires and rewards good looks). In contrast, in some traditional Islamic countries, women's use of cosmetics is frowned upon, and purchase of such items is often discouraged. According to this view, in taking action, a person considers, weighs, and combines the following two factors: (1) attitude-toward-the-behavior and (2) subjective norms regarding the behavior.

1. **Attitude-toward-the-behavior** is the belief that our behavior leads to specific outcomes (positive or negative) and our evaluation of these outcomes. For example, a couple contemplating adoption of a child would consider aspects of the adoption process such as going through a lengthy legal process, nurturing the child, forfeiting leisure time, incurring costs to raise the child, experiencing the pleasure of having the child, and anticipating love from the child, as well as their evaluation of these outcomes.

2. **Subjective norms** are our beliefs about what significant others think we should or should not do, as well as our inclination to comply with their specific desires. For a couple pondering adoption of a child, subjective

theory of reasoned action (TORA)
a view that attitude toward the behavior, intentions, and subjective norms determine behavior

intention
one's subjective resolution to behave in a certain way toward an attitude object

attitude-toward-the-behavior
one's overall appraisal of an act based on its consequences and one's evaluation of these outcomes

subjective norms
one's beliefs about what significant others think and inclinations to comply with their views

Global Opportunity

If It's Red, It Will Sell Better in Paris

The way people view products such as cosmetics and form attitudes toward them varies significantly from one culture to another. For example, in the case of women's cosmetics in Europe, color preferences vary dramatically by country as a function of the climate and quality of daylight in each nation. Whereas Italian women tend to buy shades of brown, French women prefer bold reds. Scandinavians, on the other hand, prefer dark shades of foundation because of their long winters and avid love of the sun. In Britain and Germany, pearly pinks are quite popular, although lilacs and some bolder colors sell well in this reunited market.

Concerning toiletries, the United Kingdom is a soap-and-talc-using nation. The rest of the European Union prefers shower gels, which Europeans redesigned with adult-oriented colors. Among European women, the French are best informed about issues of body care and cosmetics. Scandinavian women generally tend to be less sophisticated than most other Europeans about the nature, type, and effect of basic toiletry ingredients. Deodorants and antiperspirants remain very popular in Europe as the practice of taking baths or showers daily in many circles is more the exception than the rule.

Many of the gimmicks and novelties used in the United States to sell cosmetics and toiletries are largely unworkable in Europe. For American marketers, a more scientific, almost paramedical approach to promoting and selling their cosmetics in Europe would work much better. Europeans look for functionality and effectiveness, not narcissism. Vanity and superficial self-conceit are not highly admired values in most parts of Europe.[19]

Although use of cosmetics seems to be a universal phenomenon, their ingredients, shades, and application specifics vary from country to country. Visit L'ORÉAL at www.loreal.com and the government report Web site at www.cosmeticsdesign-europe.com. What factors might account for the differences in preferences and attitudes toward cosmetics in various countries? How would you explain negative attitudes toward cosmetics in some traditional Islamic countries?

norms would encompass their views regarding how their family and friends would perceive the action. Would these significant others be supportive, critical, or indifferent?

The more positively we view the outcome and the greater the approval from significant others we anticipate for the action, the more likely we are to arrive at the intention to undertake the action.

Although the views brought about by this theory may be plausible, the TORA fails to explain conditions where purchase situations are hindered by some adverse personal or environmental circumstances. The TORA presumes that if the consumer tries to act, no impediments are likely to stand in the way. That is to say, the formation of intentions in this case assumes the behavior is nonproblematic. In many instances, however, behavior can be impeded by real or imagined factors such as limits on consumers' ability, time constraints, and environmental contingencies. In the Intel Centrino notebook example cited earlier, either external (environmental) or internal (personal) impediments, such as insufficient resources to buy the notebook, unavailability of the desired model, or lack of self-confidence to understand the product's features, can thwart the action.

Theories of Goal Pursuit and Trying

According to these theories, pursuits where an individual thinks impediments stand in the way of attaining a desired objective are termed **goals**. In this view, virtually all pursuits are seen as goals.[20] That is why we often hear people say, "I have a goal of trying to lose twenty pounds in the next six months," or say, "I have a goal of trying to learn skydiving this summer." Because most actions are forestalled by some unforeseen event, and there is no certainty in goal achievement, behavior is reduced to merely *trying* to achieve the goal. That is to say, if consumers feel that a goal is too difficult to achieve, or a task is too complicated to handle, intentions to try subside. This phenomenon may explain why more people are not sky divers or Ph.D. candidates.

The theory of trying proposes that there are three attitudes toward goals: (1) attitudes toward the consequences of *succeeding* to achieve a goal, (2) attitudes toward the consequences of trying but *failing* to achieve a goal, and (3) attitudes toward the *process* of striving to achieve a goal.[21] In applying the theory to purchase situations, it becomes evident that consumer attitudes toward the consequences of success and failure to achieve a goal, as well as their attitudes toward trying, influence the adoption process for new products.[22] Consider, for instance, the case of novice skiers who are unlikely to take up the sport and buy the necessary gear unless they have both the desire to ski and the confidence in their ability to try and succeed in conquering challenging slopes.

Astute marketers recognize the importance of trials in getting consumers to buy their products. Because consumers, in this view, may perceive the purchase of a product as a goal, marketers can use strategies that enhance trial. They distribute free samples, allow product trials in the store, or send free trial issues to potential newspaper and magazine subscribers.[23]

An example of such marketing strategies is evident in the arena of selling time-share or retirement community properties. Retiring couples who live in cold climates often contemplate a move to a warmer location where they hope to spend the rest of their lives in comfort. Such a desirable goal, however, is often hindered by impediments such as lack of knowledge regarding which area is more suitable for living, what choices exist in the various locales, and what types of property can be acquired at what price. Further impediments may also include the necessity of selling the present residence, leaving friends and acquaintances behind, disposing of many accumulated possessions, as well as the difficulty and cost of the physical move itself. As a result, many such couples delay their plan to pursue such a goal for years or even suppress the need to move altogether.

Many property developers have recognized these tendencies and have designed strategies

goals
pursuits where an individual *thinks* impediments stand in they way of attaining a desired objective

All expense paid vacations to property destinations and valuable gift give-aways are successful sales tactics used to sell time-share and retirement properties.

© 2009. Christophe Testi, Shutterstock, Inc.

to reduce or remove the impact of the aforementioned impediments. Programs such as offering prospects an opportunity to see and experience the property have been implemented through deals such as brief all-expenses-paid vacations to the property destination that prospects *win*. Other deals may involve offering valuable gifts just for visiting the property site. Those who accept these offers sit through a sales presentation designed to accomplish two objectives: first, to reduce the psychological impediment of fear associated with approaching an unknown investment, and second, advance the desirability of the present choice through witnessing the impressive amenities of the property firsthand as well as taking advantage of the creative financial arrangements that facilitate immediate acquisition of the property. Such sales tactics have been highly successful in helping time-share and retirement property promoters to achieve admirable levels of sales.

Other applications of this theory include the case of car dealerships that recognize the goal of many consumers to acquire new automobiles. However, the financial impediment frequently hinders fulfillment of this goal. To overcome this barrier, dealers often offer new cars with no down payment required at the time of purchase. Moreover, these dealers arrange for convenient monthly payments that commence after a grace period. The same strategy has been used by dealerships of home furnishings, allowing consumers to acquire their needed furniture while removing the associated financial impediments. Marketers of major appliances and home electronics go even a step farther. Not only do they remove the financial barriers, they further eliminate the physical impediments of delivering such heavy items to consumers' homes and ridding them of the old units. It should also be obvious that the success of the credit card industry was largely based on the same premise—eliminating financial impediments that most of us face as we attempt to fulfill our goals of product or service acquisitions.

How Attitudes Are Formed

We form attitudes largely through association and learning, such as via classical and operant conditioning, as well as through cognitive learning.[24] (For a detailed discussion of these theories, see chapter 5 on learning.) In *classical conditioning*, a positive attitude (conditioned response) can be elicited by presenting along with the brand (conditioned stimulus) an attractive unconditioned stimulus. An advertising manager may therefore pair the brand with an emotionally appealing stimulus in order to generate a desired consumer response. Many U.S. producers of cosmetics and perfumes use French-sounding brand names for their products to create the impression that they are exotic and desirable French creations. Through such a link, a positive consumer response is produced toward the brand. Similarly, associating a shampoo with proteins known to provide shiny and silky hair, or a facial cream with Vitamin E known to restore health and radiance to the skin, brings about desirable linkages. In this manner, a positive attitude toward the shampoo or facial cream emerges. This strategy simply applies Pavlovian learning principles for purposes of attitude shaping.[25]

Similarly, the concept of family branding applies this classical conditioning viewpoint. Corporations such as Kodak, Sony, and General Electric use the same brand name on every product they produce. The positive connotations that the well-known brand carries transfers to any new item these companies introduce. Likewise, when Nike elected to use Tiger Woods as a celebrity endorser for its brand, the goal was to create a positive association between Tiger, who already enjoys a favorable attitude, and the Nike line of shoes and sports apparel.

Attitudes may also result from *operant conditioning*, in which learning occurs as a result of the consequences of the behavior itself. Rewards enhance attitudes toward a stimulus and increase the probability that a behavior will recur. During certain seasons of the year, such as the period before Christmas, many retailers open their doors early in the morning to accommodate shopping traffic. The first hundred or so customers, upon entering the store, may be given *early bird* gifts or discounts as rewards for shopping early. Such rewards are instrumental in developing positive attitudes toward the store as well as toward the shopping experience. Similarly, in view of the intense competition between cell phone companies such as Verizon, Cingular, T-Mobile, AT&T, Sprint, and others, these service providers attempt to enhance favorable attitudes toward their particular brand by offering various deals and specials ranging from free cell phones and accessories to extended free calling hours.

In the context of *cognitive learning*, consumers form attitudes about products based on both exposure to information about them provided by marketers as well as through consumers' own cognitions (knowledge, experience, and goals). A number of recently developed models known as *attitude-toward-the-ad* models attempt to explain the way we may form attitudes, feelings, and judgments about products as a result of our exposure to ads about them. These models, which apply under low-involvement conditions, suggest that where, when, and in what context an ad is seen are among the variables that may shape the attitudes we form toward the ad and, in turn, toward the product.[26] Examples abound in the advertising field of instances where liking of the commercial translated into positive attitudes toward the product. Among these examples are the caveman and gecko commercials of GEICO automobile insurance company for the firm's low-cost, minimum-coverage policies. In these cases, it is clear that liking toward the ad may transfer to the brand. Conversely, if consumers dislike the ad, negative feelings toward the brand may result. The Jose Cuervo ad in Figure 6.5 applies the attitude-toward-the-ad model by depicting a playful and intimate scene that catches the eye in the hope of creating a positive feeling toward the brand.

The role of cognition in attitude formation has stimulated research in yet another closely related area—our tendency to attribute causes to events we encounter. This tendency, known as attribution, has a bearing on the way we think of objects or situations around us and, in turn, how we coin our attitudes toward them.

Figure 6.5
In this ad from Jose Cuervo tequila, the playful situation depicted can affect consumer's attitudes toward the brand.

Attribution Theory

attribution
efforts to ascertain the causes of events in our lives

According to **attribution** theory, we attempt to ascertain the causes of events in our daily lives. We make hypotheses about why things happen and who or what is responsible for their occurrence. We also try to discern whether incidents are caused by something internal or external to us. If a homemaker buys a new brand of cake mix and bakes a delicious dessert, the homemaker can attribute the positive outcome either to one's own baking ability or to the qualities of the cake mix. This process through which we determine causality exerts an effect on the attitudes we form.[28]

We make attributions in part to determine how to respond to occurrences now and in the future. Homemakers who attribute their cake's success to their own ability would not necessarily form positive attitudes toward the new brand, because in their view any brand would do. If, however, they attribute the cake's success to the new brand, homemakers are more likely to develop positive attitudes toward it and select it again.[29]

Ethical Dilemma

Unconditional Love for Those Rain Forest Bath Beads

From a single, tiny hippy store in Brighton, United Kingdom, established by Anita Roddick several years ago, *The Body Shop* grew to one of the world's premier natural cosmetics companies, with more than 2,000 stores worldwide. What helped Roddick achieve this remarkable success is consumers' interpretation of her high-profile campaigns in support of politically correct causes. These campaigns centered around issues, such as using natural ingredients, ending animal testing, saving the whale, rescuing the rain forests, recycling, and AIDS awareness. By so doing, Roddick offered a *New Age* antibeauty message to a new generation of liberated women who resent companies' indifference toward the environment and was able to create strong and favorable attitudes toward her line. This strategy gave Roddick the explosive rise from obscurity to an environmental crusader and a feminist icon and helped her sell her bottles of Brazil nut hair conditioner, rain forest bath beads, and other products from the company's *Trade Not Aid line*. As such, Roddick became the heroine for many baby boomers and was dubbed "the Mother Teresa of Capitalism."

The end of the century, however, brought about a reversal in that rosy picture the company had enjoyed for years. An article in *Business Ethics* magazine questioned a number of the company's practices and claims. This article alleged that Body Shop's products were not so natural; its policies were not so environmentally conscious;

and its business practices were not so ethical. The article also revealed that the company did almost no trading with the Third World, had a poor record of charitable giving, and was under investigation by the Federal Trade Commission for franchise irregularities. Response to the article was overwhelming. An avalanche of mostly negative press coverage ensued, causing the company's stock to plunge by over 20 percent.

In March 2006, L'Oreal agreed to pay more than $1 billion to take over the Body Shop empire. However, controversy persisted surrounding claims that L'Oreal continues to test its products on animals, which contradicts the Body Shop's core value of "Against Animal Testing." As a result, there were many boycotts around the globe from consumers and other retailers, especially in the United Kingdom, where the company has its headquarters.[27]

The "idealism" strategy that Roddick used to sell her line of beauty products caused consumers to embrace the "natural" message enthusiastically. Roddick claimed that she did not just sell beauty and hope, but rather offered the promise of a better life. Visit the Web site of The Body Shop at www.the-body-shop.com. Do you think slogans and appeals such as these influence most people's attitudes and actions? Can misleading claims made by cosmetics companies hurt their cause? Why?

Attribution also provides insight for marketers in the area of promotional claims and how these claims affect the formation of consumers' attitudes. Prospects realize that some of the positive statements made by sellers about their offerings are ploys to generate purchases. Consumers in this case tend to discount such assertions as caused by the marketer's desire to promote their products—a feeling that reduces the effectiveness of the promotional effort. To avoid this possibility, researchers suggest the use of product disclaimers, or admission of some product limitations or disadvantages in comparison to the competition.[30] This strategy may enhance the credibility of the claims, creating a more favorable attitude toward a brand. Pharmaceutical companies' ads and commercials provide good examples of this strategy. The ads list the negative side effects associated with the medication being promoted and enumerate circumstances and patient conditions when the drug should not be taken.

How Attitudes Are Changed

As was pointed out earlier in this chapter under the heading "Valence, Intensity, and Centrality of Attitudes," the likelihood that an attitude can be changed depends on its centrality and intensity. Attitudes are difficult to change, and the likelihood of their change varies inversely with their centrality and intensity; that is, the more central or extreme the valence of an attitude, the more difficult it is to modify or restructure it.

For many marketers and advertisers, attitude change is a primary goal. **Attitude change** shifts a negative valence to a positive one or vice versa. It requires a change in the organization or structure of a belief, or a change in the content of a belief itself.

The real challenge to marketers arises when the goal is to create favorable attitudes toward a company or its products among consumers who do not regard them favorably. A number of theories govern the approaches that marketers use to achieve attitude change. The most frequently employed are cognitive consistency and information-processing theories.[31] Let us look first at how cognitive consistency theories can help in this regard.

THE ROLE OF COGNITIVE CONSISTENCY IN ATTITUDE CHANGE

The basic premise of **cognitive consistency** is that humans strive to maintain congruity between the three components of an attitude (cognitive, affective, and behavioral). Shoppers' purchasing behavior, for example, is expected to be consistent with their attitudes. The newly formed attitudes are also expected to be consistent with their values and personalities. Consistency theories actually encompass a large group of theories, including (1) cognitive dissonance theory, (2) balance theory, and (3) congruity theory.[32] These theories reiterate a recurring theme—a person's tendency to maintain harmonious relationships between the cognitive (belief), affective (emotional), and behavioral elements of an attitude. For the purposes of our present coverage, it suffices to view Festinger's cognitive dissonance theory to explain how creating a conflict (dissonance) can be instrumental in bringing about a desired attitude change.

COGNITIVE DISSONANCE THEORY

Cognitive dissonance theory assumes that we seek consistency among the three attitude components, as well as congruity between our values and the behavior we exhibit. Inconsistency among the components of an attitude produces psychological tension that motivates us to restore the balance. For example, individuals who go on a diet are much more likely to adopt foods that are made with various fat and sugar substitutes.[33] In so doing, such individuals maintain the psychological balance between beliefs (the need to loose weight) and actions (eating lower-calorie foods). If we experience dissonance between our beliefs and actions, we will either attempt to alter our behavior to be more consistent with our held beliefs or change our beliefs to become more consistent with our behavior.[34]

---

attitude change
a shift in the valence of an attitude from negative to positive or vice versa

cognitive consistency
a view that we strive to maintain congruity between beliefs, emotions, and behavior

cognitive dissonance theory
a view that inconsistency between a person's beliefs and behavior causes psychological tension

Festinger constructed cognitive dissonance theory within the confines of a free-will situation, where a person faces a free choice between a number of desirable alternatives. Dissonance occurs once the choice between alternatives has been made and, in this sense, is synonymous with postdecisional conflict. Suppose, for example, that an individual has to choose between two prestigious automobiles—a Mercedes-Benz and a BMW. In resolving this conflict, the individual selects and purchases the BMW. Once an alternative has been chosen, attractive features of the rejected alternative and unattractive features of the selected alternative start to become magnified in the consumer's mind. As a consequence, the consumer will experience **postpurchase dissonance**, a state of doubt regarding the wisdom of the purchasing decision. Because dissonance is felt as tension and psychological discomfort, the individual is motivated to resolve this condition by either revoking the decision (changing the behavior) or seeking out additional positive information to support it (reinforcing the original belief that led to the decision).

Marketers use dissonance to change attitudes. In creating a situation where information conflicts with beliefs, marketers hope that the resulting dissonant condition may lead to attitude or behavior modification. One popular strategy marketers use to conjure up dissonance is playing on consumers' fears. Insurance companies, pharmaceutical companies, medical centers, and investment consultants are among the many firms that use cognitive dissonance—precipitated by fear appeals—to change attitudes or improve feelings toward their products and services. For example, because many people do not like to think about death and the purchase of life (death) insurance, companies in this line of business attempt to overcome prospects' resistance by stirring their sympathy toward their family. Ads depict the bleak future that awaits a family's members if one were to die suddenly. Direct-to-consumer pharmaceutical ads are designed to raise consumers' fears regarding a variety of medical conditions. These commercials then encourage consumers to take the step of seeing their doctor and asking for the advertised drug. Similarly, American Express recognized the power of well-placed panic, fear, and anxiety in getting consumers to change their habit of carrying cash and instead using travelers' checks. Dramatic American Express TV commercials and print ads have portrayed desperate consumers stuck in dire situations in foreign countries without cash as a consequence of a stolen purse or lost wallet. Figure 6.6 displays a Liberty Mutual ad where arresting imagery crossed with reassuring copy is used to create dissonance.

Now let us turn our attention to the second approach to changing attitudes, known as information processing.

THE ROLE OF INFORMATION PROCESSING IN ATTITUDE CHANGE

Whereas the cognitive consistency approach emphasizes harmony among the components of an individual's attitudes, the **information-processing approach** emphasizes communicating relevant and appropriate facts to consumers. The underlying assumption is that consumers are rational and able to

postpurchase dissonance
a state of doubting the wisdom of one's choice after making a purchase

information-processing approach
an effort to provide facts to help consumers reach a logical conclusion

YOUR CAR BREAKS DOWN
IN THE MIDDLE OF NOWHERE.

WE'VE SEEN ENOUGH
HORROR MOVIES TO KNOW YOU
NEED A TOW TRUCK FAST.

You're out in the middle of nowhere. But with Liberty Mutual, you're not
out of luck. Our auto policies offer unlimited towing, with no mileage limit.
Taking responsibility. Getting you and your auto to safety. That's our policy.
For auto, home, or life insurance, call 1.800.4LIBERTY or visit libertymutual.com

Auto Home Life   Responsibility. What's your policy?

If you have purchased towing coverage, Liberty Mutual will pay for the cost of towing your car to the nearest repair
facility when you use a tow provider within our network. Not available in all states. © 2008 Liberty Mutual Group.

Liberty
Mutual.

Figure 6.6

This Liberty Mutual Insurance Group ad employs the concept of cognitive dissonance to
promote the company's services. The ad first creates a potentially traumatic situation, and
then resolves it by promising speedy rescues and unlimited towing services.

see the logic supporting an issue, causing them to adjust their behavior accordingly. This approach employs advertising and other forms of promotion specifically designed to produce the desired impact on the target audience.[35]

The information-processing model appears to be one of the most widely
used strategies in marketing, largely because it lends itself well to the mass
media. Its objective is to attain a change in the dynamics of an attitude through
a change in its cognitive component. Because consumers are logical creatures

McGuire's Information-Processing Model

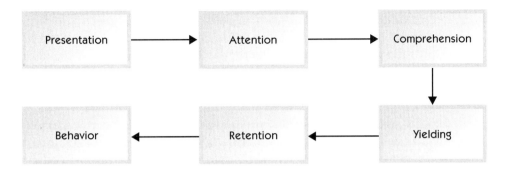

EXHIBIT 6.3

Source: William J. McGuire, "An Information-Processing Model of Advertising Effectiveness," a paper presented at the Symposium of Behavioral and Management Science in Marketing, Center for Continuing Education, University of Chicago, July 1969.

capable of comprehension, data analysis, and problem solving to arrive at a goal-directed behavior, it follows that presenting them with persuasive communication should make behavior change possible. After processing the new information, the consumer may decide to change behavior toward an attitude object. A number of years ago Burger King initiated an advertising campaign that explained to the public that Burger King's hamburgers are charbroiled, whereas McDonald's are fried. Individuals may conclude charbroiled is healthier than fried. If they do, their purchase behavior may undergo change.

If an individual is to be successfully persuaded, this person has to pass through a number of information-processing stages for maximum impact. McGuire, using an information-processing approach to explain attitude and behavior change, proposed a sequential series of six steps through which an individual passes in order to be effectively persuaded. Exhibit 6.3 illustrates them: presentation, attention, comprehension, yielding, retention, and behavior. Each of these steps can be assigned a certain probability of occurring, and the probability of an attitude change is the product of the probabilities of the individual steps.

As shown in Exhibit 6.3, a message intended to affect and persuade consumers must first reach them; it must also be presented in a way that wins their attention. Further, receivers must comprehend the arguments and conclusions contained in the message and note their relevance to them. Yielding to conclusions largely depends on the persuasiveness of the arguments and their relevance to receivers' needs. Finally, consumers must retain the conclusions until an opportunity arises to act on them.[36]

For marketers and advertisers, the result of persuasive communication depends on the degree of consumer involvement; that is, how important the attitude object is to the consumer. As we might expect, under conditions of *low involvement*, attitudes are less intense and are supported by less knowledge about the attributes of the stimulus. Such attitudes are more susceptible to change when individuals are exposed to persuasive arguments. For example, shoppers waiting in the checkout line at a grocery store may choose a brand of chewing gum that offers a two-for-the-price-of-one pack rather than their regular brand. For most consumers, chewing gum is a low-involvement product, and brand choice is not a significant issue. Promotional pricing strategies, thus, would likely affect brand selection.[37]

Under conditions of *high involvement*, on the other hand, consumers are motivated to think about the information presented. As a result, communication offering strong arguments and sound logic would likely be required to produce attitude change. For example, the Lunesta ad in Figure 6.7 makes a strong case for considering this medication to overcome insomnia. For high-involvement situations, the persuasiveness of a message in the form of convincing evidence is critical if attitude change is to be achieved.

Marketers use a number of strategies that stem from the information-processing model to change consumer attitudes. These include making direct comparisons against competitive brands, highlighting present brand attributes, adding new attributes, providing knowledge of alternatives or consequences, and changing the relative values of brand attributes. You are probably familiar with many of these.

MAKING COMPARISONS AGAINST COMPETITION

The comparison strategy attempts to change consumer beliefs about the company's products in relation to those of competitors by emphasizing its advantages against competing brands. Comparative advertising, used in many cases to accomplish this objective, presents the company's product along with another competing brand mentioned by name; the message explains how the company's product is better in some way than the other brand.

EMPHASIZING BRAND ATTRIBUTES

The second strategy for changing attitudes centers on enhancing consumer knowledge of certain attributes or features of the brand. This communication strategy highlights less-familiar attributes to create a positive disposition toward the brand.

ADDING NEW ATTRIBUTES

Another strategy for changing attitudes is to add one or more new attributes to the product in an attempt to increase its attractiveness. Car models may include a number of extra options as standard equipment. Breakfast cereal may be promoted as containing fiber, lowering cholesterol, and beneficial for the heart.

PROVIDING KNOWLEDGE OF ALTERNATIVES OR CONSEQUENCES

Providing consumers with evidence, facts, or figures that allow them to make an informed choice between existing alternatives is another strategy for changing attitudes. Through this exercise in logic, consumers can determine which alternative is best for them. Some Culligan ads, for example, explain

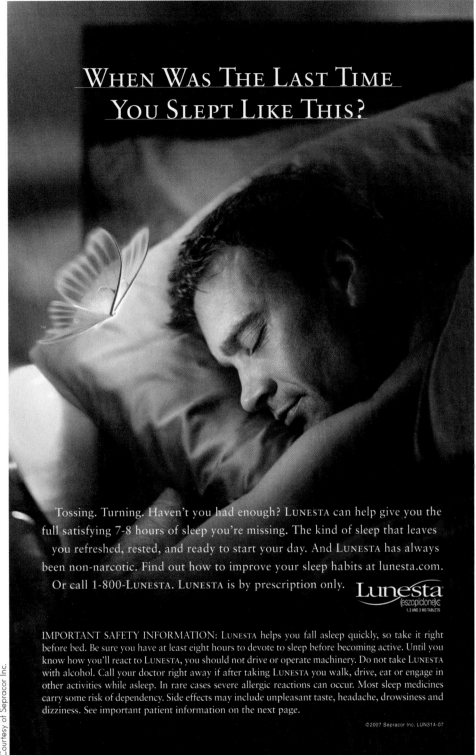

Figure 6.7

This Lunesta ad from Sepracor, Inc., makes a strong case for consumers to consider taking the drug in order to get a satisfying seven to eight hours of restful sleep every night.

to consumers the various impurities present in tap water and suggest a Culligan purification system as a solution to the problem. Competitors, such as Pùr, offer self-monitoring water filters that, ads claim, remove lead and other water contaminants, improve water taste, and tell owners when the filter needs replacement.

CHANGING THE RELATIVE VALUE OF ATTRIBUTES

Still another approach to changing attitudes toward a product attempts to shift the relative values of specific attributes the product possesses.[38] For instance, how desirable is the decay-prevention attribute in toothpaste? Could fresh breath and whiter teeth be as important, or more important? How important is style or design to automobile buyers? Could gas mileage or protecting the fragile environment be a more powerful attribute?

Many of the above strategies have been and continue to be successfully applied by marketers in their efforts to change consumer attitudes. Astute marketers have learned that attitude change is a slow, gradual, and difficult process, but in general it is more likely to occur (1) if consumers perceive greater benefit in a suggested course of action, (2) if consumers feel that their need has been satisfied more completely or easily by such an attitude realignment, (3) if a linkage has been formed between purchase of a brand and a specific consumer interest or cause, and/or (4) if incentives such as coupons, samples, rebates, sweepstakes, or give-aways have been made available by the seller.

CONSUMER REACTION TO MARKETERS' ATTITUDE-RELATED STRATEGIES

Up to this point, we have examined how marketers attempt to influence the formation or change of consumer attitudes as well as the strategies they use to accomplish these objectives. The other side of the coin, however, is the reaction of consumers as marketers seek to influence their attitudes. In other words, how do consumers react to these attempts, and how do they process the information marketers communicate to them? The elaboration-likelihood model addresses the ways consumers deal with these types of persuasive efforts.

The **elaboration-likelihood model (ELM)** proposes in general that an individual exposed to an ad will relate the information it contains to prior experiences, knowledge, and information to arrive at new ideas that were present neither in the ad nor in that person's previous knowledge set. This model also suggests that the degree to which a consumer *elaborates* on a message depends on its relevance to that person. The more relevant the message, the more elaboration occurs. The **central route to persuasion** requires greater elaboration; the **peripheral route to persuasion** requires less.[39] For example, a consumer who is experiencing hair loss would be more apt to elaborate on evidence provided in a message from Upjohn regarding its Rogaine hair treatment than another individual who is not losing hair. Similarly, research has shown that when evaluating products, some consumers are particularly concerned about how their use of that product will affect the image they project, which would lead to central processing. For others, however, image is unimportant, which would lead to peripheral processing.[40]

The central route to persuasion is presumed to prevail under conditions of high involvement. Here, the message recipient has both the ability and motivation to process the information. An individual is likely to think about the evidence and arguments presented in the message, determine whether they are compelling, and then develop his or her position on the matter. For example, a prospective buyer may be exposed to an ad containing arguments supporting the purchase of a hybrid automobile instead of a luxurious and expensive foreign car. The ad claims that by choosing the hybrid, the consumer would save money on gasoline and help protect the fragile environment. This prospect may find the evidence to be sufficiently compelling to select the hybrid instead of the foreign luxury car that was originally considered. Petty and Cacioppo suggest that the central route to persuasion can produce a lasting change in attitudes; however, they warn that this change may be difficult to accomplish. The ad in Figure 6.8 from Ford presents the claim of the "most fuel-efficient SUV on earth" to entice environmentalists as well as those concerned about fuel costs. By providing such facts about this green car, the ad employs the central route to persuasion.

The peripheral route to persuasion, on the other hand, is likely to prevail under conditions of low involvement. Here message recipients are unlikely to have strong feelings about the issue or possess a great deal of prior knowledge about it. Nor

THE MOST
FUEL-EFFICIENT
SUV ON EARTH.
THE 2008 ESCAPE HYBRID.

Courtesy Ford Motor Company

Figure 6.8
This ad from Ford provides solid reasons for preferring this new, environmentally-friendly SUV. Protection of the environment and saving fuel are but two of the features emphasized by this ad to entice prospective buyers.

would they devote a great deal of thought to the issues, evidence, or arguments presented in the message. The basis for this view lies in the observation that, in order to function in contemporary society, an individual must often act as a *lazy organism or cognitive miser*.[41] In many cases, people choose not to think a great deal about messages, issues, and arguments. Instead, they resort to some rudimentary means for deciding what is good or bad, desirable or undesirable. Individuals may simply respond to source cues (attractiveness, likability, credibility of a presenter) or apply uncomplicated rules of thumb (select the most advertised brand, choose the most expensive item, buy what happens to be on sale).

Recent research on the role of the elaboration-likelihood model in consumer processing of Internet advertising proposed a modified ELM that incorporates elements unique to the Internet environment.[42] Similar to the case of other media types, high involvement leads to click-through of banner ads via the central route. However, in low-involvement cases, factors such as larger-than-average ad size and dynamic animation tend to enhance click-through via the peripheral route. Other moderators of ad click-through were to be product-category relevance, attitude toward Web advertising, and consumers' experience with the Web.[43]

A Cross-Functional Point of View

The topic of consumer attitudes has a number of implications for business disciplines other than marketing. Relevant issues might include

- **Finance/Economics:** Consumer beliefs about the health of the economy have a lot to do with its actual performance. Some believe that low consumer confidence and fears of a recession can contribute to the economy's woes by inducing both consumers and businesses to cut spending. Less spending, in turn, can cause more trouble by forcing trapped employers to cut workers' hours or eliminate their jobs altogether. These actions would undermine consumer confidence even more. The effect can snowball as the economy declines and as pessimism increases. These fears about the economy can thus become self-fulfilling prophecies. Many observers, as a result, believe that we *can* scare ourselves into a recession.

- **Political:** In the political arena, recent election campaigns seem to have chosen a questionable route to persuade voters. Instead of debating issues of concern to the public, many candidates use smear campaigns that attribute lack of experience or a questionable voting record to their opponent. By creating negative attitudes toward the adversary, the candidate, in comparison, hopes to be viewed more positively. Significant expenditures are wasted every election year on such negative ads. In our society, one cannot help but wonder if such tactics—often involving exaggerations and half truths—are undermining our democratic system.

- **Strategy/Ethics:** In the clothing and fashion industry, new styles seem to be seasonally forced onto the marketplace. The new fashions are usually designed to be markedly different from those of the previous year and psychologically date last season's garments. The intent of the industry is simple—to get fashion-conscious consumers to feel negatively about their present wardrobe and prompt them to adopt the latest styles. In this manner, consumers' self-consciousness about their looks would generate the needed demand for the new fashion and in turn achieve the industry's sales goals. Whereas some observers condemn the practice as bordering on deception, others support it and argue that without it, the fashion industry would collapse and thousands of workers would be out of a job.

These issues, and a host of others like them, serve to show that the topic of consumer attitudes transcends the field of marketing to other business disciplines.

Because it would be impossible for most individuals to exert extensive mental effort to analyze all persuasive communications to which they are exposed, it may be sufficient in some cases for communicators to merely *expose* consumers to an issue or *remind* them of it, rather than present substantive arguments in order to achieve the desired attitude confirmation or change. By simply associating a product or issue with other positive information or desired goals the recipient may already hold, marketers could achieve their purpose of attitude change and behavior modification. The ad in Figure 6.9 from Light of Life Foundation applies the peripheral route to persuasion by the simplicity of its presentation.

At the heart of the study of consumer behavior is the notion that consumers attempt to accomplish some end result through the purchase and use of products or services. Through our discussion of the role of attitudes in shaping behavior, we have seen that the mechanisms by which attitudes influence actual behavior are quite varied. No simple relationship between attitudes and behavior applies to all products and situations. This realization brings to focus the need to understand other forces that impel our actions. The topic of motivation is presented in the next chapter to shed further light on the processes that underlie human behavior. In discussing motivation, the biological, social, and psychological bases for our actions will be examined along with an overview of the influence of emotions on our behavior.

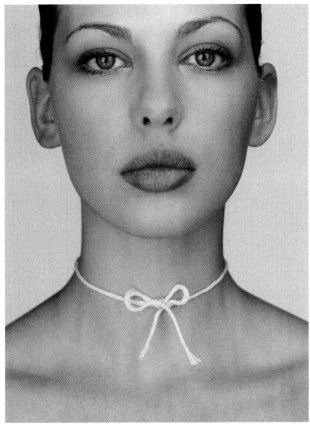

Remember to ask your doctor to check your neck for thyroid cancer. Light of Life Foundation checkyourneck.com

Figure 6.9

By minimizing verbal information about thyroid cancer, and utilizing a simple and attractive visual presentation, this Light of Life Foundation ad employs the peripheral route to persuasion.

Summary

This chapter addresses the properties of attitudes, the relationship between beliefs, attitudes, and behavior, and the factors that influence attitude formation and change. Attitudes develop largely as a result of personal experience with objects, social interaction, and exposure to mass media. Attitudes can serve utilitarian, ego-defensive, value-expressive, and knowledge functions for an individual.

Individuals *sometimes* act in accordance with their attitudes. At other times they behave in a manner quite inconsistent with their attitudes. A number of theories address the impact of attitudes on behavior. One such theory is the traditional model, which suggests that attitudes consist of cognitive, affective, and behavioral components. Another view posits a multi-attribute model in which individuals hold attitudes toward various facets of an attitude object. The theory of reasoned action distinguishes between attitude-toward-the-object and attitude-toward-the-behavior. It also recognizes the roles of intentions and subjective norms. The theories of goal pursuit and trying address individuals' attempts to reach a *goal* when real or perceived impediments stand in the way of attainment.

Attitudes are formed largely through association and learning, such as via classical and operant conditioning, as well as cognitive learning. Attribution is the process by which people hypothesize why things happen and who or what is responsible for various occurrences. Such attributions influence the way we perceive objects and, in turn, our attitudes toward them.

A cognitive consistency approach to attitude change posits that individuals strive for harmony between three components of an attitude (cognitive, affective, and behavioral). Cognitive dissonance theory assumes individuals seek consistency among the three attitude components, as well as congruity between their values and the behavior that stems from them. Inconsistency produces psychological tension that motivates a person to restore the balance.

An information-processing approach, on the other hand, emphasizes communicating factual, persuasive, and relevant messages to consumers in order to permit logical processing of ideas and, in turn, attitude or behavior change. This approach suggests five attitude change strategies for marketers: making comparisons against competition, emphasizing brand attributes, adding new attributes, providing knowledge of alternatives or consequences, and changing the relative value of attributes.

The issue of how consumers react to and process marketers' persuasive communications is addressed in the elaboration-likelihood model. In this view, the extent to which a consumer *elaborates* on a message depends on its relevance to that person. The more relevant the message, the more elaboration occurs. The central route to persuasion is presumed to prevail under conditions of high involvement. Under conditions of low involvement, the peripheral route to persuasion is likely to prevail.

Review Questions

1. It has been said that attitudes serve a number of functions for individuals. This distinction between attitude functions helps marketers recognize that attitudes toward different product categories tend to be associated with different attitude functions. Explain and give examples.

2. The traditional model of attitudes suggests that attitudes consist of three components. Cite and explain the operation of each. Can overt behavior be predicted easily through the knowledge of a person's attitudes? Why or why not?

3. The theory of reasoned action emphasizes intentions as a primary consideration in predicting behavior. Goal pursuit and trying theories, on the other hand, propose that attitudes toward the consequences of trying are the main predictors of behavior. Explain the difference between these two points of view.

4. For many marketers and advertisers, attitude change is a primary goal. In this endeavor, marketers use a number of strategies that stem from the information-processing model in order to change consumer attitudes. Explain these strategies. Is attitude change generally an attainable goal? Why or why not?

5. What are the tenets of the elaboration-likelihood model of attitude formation? What are the explanatory roles of the central and peripheral routes to persuasion presented in this model? Is such information useful for advertisers? How?

Discussion Questions

1. One phenomenon prevalent today is the practice of body piercing. Nose, lips, tongue, belly button, as well as other body parts are the subjects of such piercing. While from a medical perspective some regard the practice as risky and potentially infectious, body piercing continues to be popular. In terms of the theory of reasoned action, how would you explain the prevalence of this behavior? Whose subjective norms are at play in this case?

2. A TV commercial sponsored by an automobile battery company depicts a situation in which a frightened woman finds herself stranded with an unstartable car in a deserted street on a stormy night. An announcer's voice-over states that she would not have had to face this unnerving situation if her car had been equipped with the advertiser's brand of battery. How effective is this advertising format in changing attitudes? Do you think fear-raising approaches are appropriate appeals for marketers and advertisers to use? Why or why not? When might such appeals be more or less appropriate?

3. The advertising agency of a well-known Japanese automaker produces two distinct varieties of print ads for the car. The first type follows an *information-dominant* approach. In other words, ads provide a detailed description of the car's features and performance. The second type of ad follows a *visual-dominant* approach and includes a colorful picture of the car with an attractive model sitting behind the wheel, but no description of the car or factual arguments for owning it. Toward what end does the ad agency use each of these two disparate approaches?

In reference to the chapter-opening vignette, assume that you were the marketing or advertising manager at Nike who had originally in 1996 proposed signing a contract to use Tiger Woods, who was then 21 years of age and had just gone pro, as a spokesperson for the company. The manager suggested paying Tiger $40 million over five years for his services. Recall that this proposal was made *before* Tiger shattered records and won golf's most prestigious trophies, including the 2007 PGA Tour Player of the Year. Tiger's victories proved to be a windfall for Nike, but at that time this foresight did not exist. When the proposal was made by the marketing manager, how would you have defended it to the financial officers and shareholders of the company? Keep in mind that at this point, the company would be paying Tiger a huge sum, while his future as golf pro was unknown

CASE

Planning for the New Volkswagen Beetle

On a Monday morning, in mid-January 1994, Mr. Jens Neumann, the German board member in charge of VW North American operations, and Mr. Clive Warrilow, president of VW of America, received a memo from VW Chairman Ferdinand Piech requesting an urgent meeting on Wednesday of the same week.

As the three executives met in Mr. Piech's office, he explained the reason for the urgent meeting. "Gentlemen, for the last few weeks, I have been bothered with the thought of our declining market share in the U.S. auto market. I remember in 1970 when our Beetle was so popular in the United States and our market share was about 46 percent of all imports. That year, I recall, we sold over 569,000 vehicles. Now, however, we barely have 1 percent of that market. Where did we go wrong?"

"I know this is an unfortunate situation," responded Mr. Warrilow. "Since we stopped producing the Beetle back in 1978, most European automakers took over the U.S. market. The majority of the gain seems to be in the luxury car segment that includes Mercedes-Benz and BMW. These companies have been introducing new and exciting models," he added.

"This is precisely why we are meeting here today," said Mr. Piech. "I'd like to get your feelings about the possibility of introducing a new VW car to the U.S. market—not really new . . . what I mean, a makeover of our original bug."

"A makeover of the Beetle?" exclaimed Mr. Warrilow. "I thought when we dropped it back in 1978, it was because of the faltering demand for it."

"I know, I'm not really talking about producing the same car. I'm thinking of a new Beetle designed for an upmarket. I want to capitalize on the nostalgia as aging baby boomers in the United States who loved our car when they were young reach for symbols to prove they're still youthful," said Mr. Piech.

"How will this new Beetle differ from its predecessor?" asked Mr. Neumann.

"Well . . . I was thinking it would still have the distinctive half-moon shape, but it would be bigger and more powerful than the original Beetle, with standard features like air conditioning and a six-speaker stereo. Options could include antilock brakes and front-seat heaters," said Mr. Piech.

"Aren't these features going to raise the car's price dramatically?" commented Mr. Warrilow. "I thought one of the most attractive features of our original Beetle was its low price. Consumers in the United States loved the Beetle because the car was dependable and economical. They felt it was a pretty good bargain for the price. I recall the price was under $2,000 in the early 1970s. My question is—aren't we losing sight of what originally sold the car?" said Mr. Warrilow.

Seemingly ignoring Mr. Warrilow's last comment, Mr. Piech continued, "I was thinking a price of around $20,000 would be just about right. This price would give us a good profit margin, but more importantly it would fit the new lifestyle of the baby boomers. I want to give them a car that brings back good memories and is perceived as a fun car to have and drive around. Yet at the same time I want them to feel that the car is prestigious enough and would enhance their self-image when they buy one."

"I have a concern," Mr. Warrilow interrupted. "I recall that many Americans were leery about the safety of the original Beetle in case of an accident. How are we going to address this issue in the new car?" he asked.

"Well, we could place the engine under the hood instead of in the rear. In this case, the engine will act as a buffer between the driver and the other car in the case of an accident. This placement would also allow the engine to drive the front wheels . . . an added benefit in my opinion," explained Mr. Piech.

A minute of silence prevailed as the two men were thinking about what Mr. Piech suggested.

Finally, Mr. Warrilow broke the silence and asked, "Any idea of a timetable for introducing this car?"

"I was thinking of a launch in the spring of 1998," said Mr. Piech as he started to close an open file in front of him. "I'd like both of you to think about this idea and the possible reaction of the American consumer to this updated version of the Beetle. If it seems feasible, I'll get our engineers working on it right away."

Questions

1. By introducing the new Beetle, VW's hope was to capitalize on baby boomers' nostalgia. What attitudinal factors are at play in promotional appeals that build on nostalgia? How can such feelings be triggered?
2. How do you explain the success of the new Beetle knowing that vans, big sport-utility vehicles, and pickups are America's favorite cars and that the market for the two-door sports coupes in the United States is contracting rapidly?
3. Do you think that the introduction and popularity of hybrid automobiles and the continued consumer interest in these economical vehicles will negatively affect future demand for the Volkswagen? Why or why not?

Notes

1. "About Tiger," official Web site for Tiger Woods; http:www.tigerwoods.com/aboutme/default.sps?sid 5825&lid51 (accessed March 5, 2004); Jason Sherman, "For Sale: The Marketing of Professional Athletes," http://ct.cc.rochester.edu/issues/97spring/970424/sherman.html (posted April 24, 1997; accessed October 22, 1998); "All About Tiger, Biography," CBSSportsLine, http://cbs.sportsline.com/u/fans/celebrity/tiger/about/index.htm, and "1998 Tour Championship" (October 29–November 1, 1998, East Lakes Course, Atlanta, GA), http://tigersfans.com; Larry Dorman, "As Woods Enters Prime, Time Is on His Side," *The New York Times*, (December 13, 2007); Jon Show, "Tiger Woods Tops Marketability Survey of Sports Execs," *Sports Business Daily* (March 19, 2007).

2. Chet Kane, "Accessing Latest Trends? It's Attitude, Not Behavior," *Brandweek* (February 21, 1994), p. 15.

3. Martin Fishbein and Icek Ajzen, *Beliefs, Attitude, Intention, and Behavior: An Introduction to Theory and Research* (Reading, MA: Addison-Wesley, 1975), p. 6; Richard J. Lutz, "The Role of Attitude Theory in Marketing," in Harold Kassarjian and Thomas Robertson (eds.), *Perspectives in Consumer Behavior, 4th ed.* (Upper Saddle River, NJ: Prentice Hall, 1991), pp. 317–39.

4. Rajdeep Grewal, Raj Mehta, and Frank R. Kardes, "The Timing of Repeat purchase of Consumer Durable Goods: The Role of Functional Bases of Consumer Attitudes," *Journal of Marketing Research* 41, no. 1 (February 2004), pp. 101–115; Daniel Katz,

"The Functional Approach to the Study of Attitudes," *Public Opinion Quarterly* 24 (1960), p. 170; see also S. Shavitt, "The Role of Attitude Objects in Attitude Functions," *Journal of Experimental Social Psychology* 26 (1999), pp. 124–48.

5. Bristol Voss, "Selling with Sentiment," *Sales & Marketing Management* (March 1993), pp. 60–65; SIC 2771 Greeting Cards Forum, www.reference forbusiness.com/industries/Printing-Publishing-Allied/Greeting-Card.

6. Shavitt, "The Role of Attitude Objects in Attitude Functions."

7. "Survey Finds Majority of Americans Do More Than They Realize to Live 'Green', www.csrwire.com/news/10720.html.

8. S. M. Corey, "Professed Attitudes and Actual Behavior," *Journal of Educational Psychology* 28 (1937), pp. 271–80; see also C. Seligman et al., "Predicting Summer Energy Consumption from Home-owners' Attitudes," *Journal of Applied Social Psychology* 9 (1979), pp. 70–90.

9. Laurie Peterson, "Get Ready for Global Coupon War," *Adweek's Marketing Week* (1991), in William D. Perreault Jr. and E. Jerome McCarthy (eds.), *Applications in Basic Marketing*, 1993 ed. (Homewood, IL: Irwin, 1992), p. 151; Bill Wolfe, "Shoppers Save Coupons at a Healthy Clip," *Chicago Sun-Times* (October 18, 1998), p. 58A.

10. R. H. Fazio and D. R. Roskos-Ewoldsen, "Acting as We Feel," in S. Shavitt and T. C. Brock (eds.), *Persuasion: Psychological Insights and Perspectives* (Boston: Allyn and Bacon, 1994), pp. 71–93.

11. Thomas T. Semon, "Knowing Attitudes Is Nice, but Not Enough," *Marketing News* (October 21, 1996), p. 6; Kane, "Accessing Latest Trends? It's Attitude, Not Behavior."

12. Laurie Freeman, "Sales of Aspirin Soar After Study," *Advertising Age* (March 28, 1988), pp. 3, 74.

13. Milton J. Rosenberg, "An Analysis of Affective–Cognitive Consistency," in M. J. Rosenberg, Carl I. Hovland et al. (eds.), *Attitude Organization and Change* (New Haven: Yale University Press, 1960).

14. Joel B. Cohen and Charles S. Areni, "Affect and Consumer Behavior," in Thomas Robertson and Harold Kassarjian (eds.), *Handbook of Consumer Behavior* (Upper Saddle River, NJ: Prentice Hall), pp. 188–240.

15. Claire Atkinson, "Whiten Your Teeth Even While Walking the Dog," *The New York Times* (July 27, 2007).

16. Martin Fishbein, "An Investigation of the Relationship Between Beliefs About an Object and the Attitude Toward That Object," *Human Relations* 16 (1963), pp. 233–40; Fishbein and Ajzen, *Beliefs, Attitude, Intention, and Behavior: An Introduction to Theory and Research*; Icek Ajzen and Martin Fishbein, *Understanding Attitudes and Predicting Social Behavior* (Upper Saddle River, NJ: Prentice Hall, 1980); William L. Wilkie and Edgar A. Pessemier, "Issues in Marketing's Use of Multi-Attribute Models," *Journal of Marketing Research* 10 (November 1973), pp. 428–41; James R. Bettman, Noel Capon, and Richard J. Lutz, "Multi-attribute Measurement Models and Multi-attribute Theory: A Test of Construct Validity," *Journal of Consumer Research* 1 (March 1975), pp. 1–14; Michael B. Mazis, Olli T. Ahtola, and R. Eugene Klippel, "A Comparison of Four Multi-Attribute Models in the Prediction of Consumer Attitudes," *Journal of Consumer Research* 2 (June 1975), pp. 38–52; and David J. Curry, Michael B. Menasco, and James W. Van Ark, "Multi-attribute Dyadic Choice: Models and Tests," *Journal of Marketing Research* 28 (August 1991), pp. 259–67.

17. Fishbein and Ajzen, *"Beliefs, Attitude, Intention, and Behavior: An Introduction to Theory and Research."*

18. Ajzen and Fishbein, *Understanding Attitudes and Predicting Social Behavior*; see also Michael J. Ryan and E. H. Bonfield, "Fishbein's Intentions Model: A Test of External and Pragmatic Validity," *Journal of Marketing* 44 (Spring 1980), pp. 82–95; Terence Shimp and Alican Kavas, "The Theory of Reasoned Action Applied to Coupon Usage," *Journal of Consumer Research* 11 (December 1984), pp. 795–809; Richard L. Oliver and William O. Bearden, "Crossover Effects in the Theory of Reasoned Action: A Moderating Influence Attempt," *Journal of Consumer Research* 12 (December 1985), pp. 324–40; Blair H. Sheppard, Jon Hartwick, and Paul R. Warshaw, "The Theory of Reasoned Action: A Meta-Analysis of Past Research and Recommendations for Modifications and Future Research," *Journal of Consumer Research* 15 (September 1986), pp. 325–43; and Richard P. Bagozzi, Hans Baumgartner, and Youjae Yi, "State versus Action Orientation and the Theory of Reasoned Action: An Application to Coupon Usage," *Journal of Consumer Research* 18 (March 1992), pp. 505–18.

19. Allyson L. Stewart, "Toiletries, Cosmetics Marketing in Europe: Vive La Difference," *Marketing News* 28, no. 4 (February 14, 1994), p. 6.

20. I. Ajzen, "From Intentions to Actions: A Theory of Planned Behavior," in J. Kuhl and J. Beckmann (eds.), *Action-Control: From Cognition to Behavior* (New York: Springer, 1985), pp. 11–39.

21. Richard P. Bagozzi and Paul R. Warshaw, "Trying to Consume," *Journal of Consumer Research* 17 (September 1990), pp. 127–40; Richard P. Bagozzi, Fred D. Davis, and Paul R. Warshaw, "Development and Test of a Theory of Technological Learning and Usage," *Human Relations* 45, no. 7 (July 1992), pp.

659–86; Richard P. Bagozzi, "Attitudes, Intentions, and Behavior: A Test of Some Key Hypotheses," *Journal of Personality and Social Psychology* 41 (October 1981), pp. 607–27.

22. Bagozzi, Davis, and Warshaw, "Development and Test of a Theory of Technological Learning and Usage"; Bagozzi and Warshaw, "Trying to Consume."

23. Maureen Milford (Gannett News Service), "New Policy for Stores: Please Try It," *Chicago Sun-Times* (July 28, 1997), p. 48.

24. John Kim, Chris T. Allen, and Frank R. Kardes, "An Investigation of the Mediational Mechanisms Underlying Attitudinal Conditioning," *Journal of Marketing Research* 33, no. 3 (August 1996), pp. 318–28.

25. John Kim, Chris T. Allen, and Frank R. Kardes, "An Investigation of the Mediational Mechanisms Underlying Attitudinal Conditioning," *Journal of Marketing Research* XXXIII (August 1996), pp. 318–28.

26. Terence Shimp, "Attitude toward the Ad as a Mediator of Consumer Brand Choice," *Journal of Advertising* 10, no. 2 (1981), pp. 9–15; Pamela M. Homer, "The Mediating Effect of Attitude toward the Ad: Some Additional Evidence," *Journal of Marketing Research* 27 (February 1990), pp. 78–86; Thomas J. Olney, Morris B. Holbrook, and Rajeev Batra, "Consumer Responses to Advertising: The Effect of Ad Content, Emotions, and Attitude toward the Ad on Viewing Time," *Journal of Consumer Research* 17 (March 1991), pp. 440–53; Stephen P. Brown and Douglas M. Stayman, "Antecedents and Consequences of Attitude toward the Ad: A Meta-analysis," *Journal of Consumer Research* 19, (June 1992), pp. 34–51; Amitava Chattopadhyay and Prakash Negungadi, "Does Attitude toward the Ad Endure? The Moderating Effects of Attention and Delay," *Journal of Consumer Research* 19 (June 1992), pp. 26–33; Gabriel Biehal, Debra Stephens, and Eleonora Curlo, "Attitude toward the Ad and Brand Choice," *Journal of Advertising* 21 (September 1992), pp. 19–39.

27. Jon Entine, "The Body Shop: Truth and Consequences," *Drug & Cosmetic Industry* 15, no. 2 (February 1995), pp. 54–64: and R. Eisman, "Soul Searching at the Body Shop," *Incentive* (January 1995), p. 8; Harvey Mackay, "One Body Not Short of Soul," *Chicago Sun-Times* (October 21, 2007), p. A43; Liz Webber, "Business Work Mourns the Body Shop's Anita Roddick," *Inc.com* (September 11, 2007), www.inc.com/news/articles/200709/roddick.html.

28. Valerie S. Folkes, "Recent Attribution Research in Consumer Behavior: A Review and New Directions," *Journal of Consumer Research* 14 (March 1988), pp. 548–65; Robert Baer, "Overestimating Salesperson Truthfulness: The Fundamental Attribution Error," in Marvin Goldberg et al. (eds.), *Advances in Consumer Research* (Provo, UT: Association for Consumer Research, 1990), pp. 501–7; Valerie S. Folkes, "Consumer Reactions to Product Failure: An Attributional Approach," *Journal of Consumer Research* (March 1984), pp. 398–409; Richard W. Mizerski, Linda L. Golden, and Jerome B. Kernan, "The Attributional Process in Consumer Decision Making," *Journal of Consumer Research* (September 1979), pp. 123–40; Valerie S. Folkes, Susan Koletsky, and John L. Graham, "A Field Study of Casual Inferences and Consumer Reaction: The View from the Airport," *Journal of Consumer Research* (March 1987), pp. 534–39; Edward E. Jones et al., *Attribution: Perceiving the Causes of Behavior* (Morristown, NJ: General Learning Press, 1972); Jess Kellar Alberts, Yvonne Kellar-Guenther, and Steven R. Corman, "That's Not Funny: Understanding Recipients' Responses to Teasing," *Western Journal of Communication* 60 (September 1, 1996), p. 337; Steven G. Little, Robert C. Sterling, and Daniel H. Tingstrom, "The Influence of Geographic and Racial Cues on Evaluation of Blame," *The Journal of Social Psychology* 136 (June 1, 1996), pp. 373–79; Thomas Blass, "The Milgram Obedience Experiment: Support for a Cognitive View of Defensive Attribution," *The Journal of Social Psychology* 136 (June 1, 1996), pp. 407–10; John Maltby, "Attribution Style and Projection," *Journal of Genetic Psychology* 157 (December 1, 1996), pp. 505–6.

29. *Ibid.*

30. Robert B. Settle and L. L. Golden, "Attribution Theory and Advertising Credibility," *Journal of Marketing Research* 11 (May 1974), pp. 181–85.

31. Richard E. Petty, Rao H. Unnava, and Alan J. Strathman, "Theories of Attitude Change," in Thomas Robertson and Harold Kassarjian (eds.), *Handbook of Consumer Behavior* (Upper Saddle River, NJ: Prentice Hall, 1991), pp. 241–80; Paul W. Miniard, Sunil Bhatla, and Randall I. Rose, "On the Formation and Relationship of Ad and Brand Attitudes: An Experimental and Causal Approach," *Journal of Marketing Research* 27 (August 1990), pp. 290–303; Carolyn Tripp, Thomas D. Jensen, and Less Carlson, "The Effects of Multiple Product Endorsements by Celebrities on Consumers' Attitudes and Intentions," *Journal of Consumer Research* 20 (March 1994), pp. 535–47.

32. L. Festinger, *A Theory of Cognitive Dissonance* (Stanford, CA: Stanford University Press, 1957); Leon Festinger and Dana Bramel, "The Reactions of Human Cognitive Dissonance," in Arthur J. Bachrach (ed.), *Experimental Foundations of Clinical Psychology* (New York: Basic Books, 1962), p. 254; J. W. Brehm and A. R. Cohen, *Explorations in Cognitive Dissonance* (New York: John Wiley, 1962), Ch. 2; S. S.

Komarita and Ira Bernstein, "Attitude Intensity and Dissonant Cognitions," *Journal of Abnormal and Social Psychology* 69 (September 1964), pp. 323–29. F. Heider, "Attitudes and Cognitive Organization," *Journal of Psychology* 21 (1946), pp. 107–12; C. E. Osgood and P. H. Tannenbaum, "The Principle of Congruity in the Prediction of Attitude Change," *Psychological Review* 62 (1955), pp. 42–55; C. E. Osgood and P. H. Tannenbaum, "The Nature and Measurement of Meaning," *Psychological Bulletin* 49 (1952), pp. 197–237.

33. Food and Drug Administration, "Olestra and Other Fat Substitutes," *FDA Backgrounder* (November 28, 1995), www.fda.gov/opacom/backgrounders/olestra.html (accessed December 1, 1995).

34. Festinger, *A Theory of Cognitive Dissonance*; Festinger and Bramel, "The Reactions of Human Cognitive Dissonance"; Brehm and Cohen, *Explorations in Cognitive Dissonance*, Ch. 2; Komarita and Bernstein, "Attitude Intensity and Dissonant Cognitions"; Chester A. Insko and John Schopler, *Experimental Social Psychology* (New York: Academic Press, 1972), p. 109; William H. Cummings and M. Venkatesan, "Cognitive Dissonance and Consumer Behavior: A Review of the Evidence," *Journal of Marketing Research* XIII (August 1976), pp. 303–8; Dieter Frey and Marita Rosch, "Information Seeking after Decisions: The Roles of Novelty of Information and Decision Reversibility," *Personality and Social Psychology Bulletin* 10, no. 1 (March 1984), pp. 91–98; J. Cooper and R. H. Fazio, "A New Look at Dissonance Theory," in L. Berkowitz (ed.), *Advances in Experimental Social Psychology* (New York: Academic Press, 1984), pp. 229–66.

35. Durairaj Maheswaran and Brian Sternthal, "The Effect of Knowledge, Motivation, and Type of Message on Ad Processing and Product Judgments," *Journal of Consumer Research* (June 1990), pp. 66–73; Deborah J. MacInnis and C. Whan Park, "The Differential Role of Characteristics of Music on High and Low Involvement Consumers' Processing of Ads," *Journal of Consumer Research* (September 1991), pp. 161–73.

36. William J. McGuire, "An Information-Processing Model of Advertising Effectiveness," a paper presented at the Symposium of Behavioral and Management Science in Marketing, Center for Continuing Education, University of Chicago (July 1969); G. S. Day, "Theories of Attitude Structure and Change," in S. Ward and T. Robertson (eds.), *Consumer Behavior: Theoretical Sources* (Upper Saddle River, NJ: Prentice Hall, 1973), p. 326.

37. Michael L. Ray, "Marketing Communication and the Hierarchy of Effects," in Peter Clark (ed.), *New Models for Mass Communication Research* 2 (Beverly Hills: Sage, 1973).

38. Ashesh Mukherjee and Wayne D. Hoyer, "The Effect of Novel Attributes On Product Evaluation," *Journal of Consumer Research* 28, no. 3 (December 2001), pp. 462–472.

39. Richard E. Petty and John T. Cacioppo, *Attitudes and Persuasion: Classic and Contemporary Approaches* (Dubuque, IA: WM.C. Brown, 1981); John T. Cacioppo, Richard E. Petty, Chuan Feng Kao, and Regina Rodriguez, "Central and Peripheral Routes to Persuasion: An Individual Difference Perspective," *Journal of Personality and Social Psychology* 51, no. 5 (1986), pp. 1032–43; Scott B. MacKenzie and Richard A. Spreng, "How Does Motivation Moderate the Impact of Central and Peripheral Processing on Brand Attitudes and Intentions?" *Journal of Consumer Research* (March 1992), pp. 519–29; Ronald C. Goodstein, "Category-Based Applications and Extensions in Advertising: Motivating More Extensive Ad Processing," *Journal of Consumer Research* (June 1993), pp. 87–99.

40. M. Snyder and K. DeBono, "Understanding the Functions of Attitudes: Lessons from Personality and Social Behavior," in A. R. Pratakins et al. (eds.), *Attitude Structure and Function* (Hillsdale, NJ: Erlbaum, 1989), pp. 339–60.

41. R. E. Petty, "To Think or Not to Think, Exploring Two Routes of Persuasion," in S. Shavitt and T. C. Brick (eds.), *Persuasion: Psychological Insights and Perspectives* (Boston: Allyn and Bacon, 1994), pp. 113–47.

42. Sanjay Putrevu and Kenneth R. Lord, "Processing Internet Communications: A Motivation, Opportunity, and Ability Framework," *Journal of Current Issues and Research in Advertising* 25, no. 1 (Spring 2003), pp. 45–59.

43. Chang-Hoan Cho, "How Advertising Works on the WWW: Modified Elaboration Likelihood Model," *Journal of Current Issues and Research in Advertising* 21 (Spring 1999), pp. 33–50; and Gordon Bruner and Anand Kumar, "Web Commercials and Advertising Hierarchy-of-Effects," *Journal of Advertising Research* 40 (January/April 2000), pp. 35–42.

Motivation and Emotion

LEARNING OBJECTIVES

- To analyze and understand the concept of a motivated state as well as its arousal/direction prerequisites.
- To conceptualize five aspects of consumer motivation.
- To recognize the roles of needs, motives, goals, and desires in consumer motivation.
- To become familiar with the underlying assumptions of basic motivation theories.
- To comprehend the sources, types, and resolution of motivational conflict.
- To develop a basic understanding of the nature of human emotions and moods.
- To gain insight into how researchers measure human emotions.

KEY TERMS

motivation
arousal
direction
intrinsic motivation
extrinsic motivation
rational motives
emotional motives
needs
physiological needs
acquired needs
motive
goal
generic goals
brand specific goals
desires

instincts
homeostasis
high sensation seekers (HSS)
low sensation seekers (LSS)
optimal stimulation level (OSL)
general sensation-seeking scale (GSSS)
basic needs
instrumental motives
motivational conflict
approach-approach conflict
approach-avoidance conflict
avoidance-avoidance conflict
emotions
mood
bonding

Gambling, in one form or another, is presently within easy reach of nearly everyone. Lotteries, Native American and riverboat casinos, horse and greyhound racing, off-track betting, bingo parlors, and cruise ships are forms of gambling that have become so popular today among an estimated 80 million to 90 million people in the United States. Recent studies indicate that the take for commercial casinos alone reached $33 billion in the year 2006. The gambling trend is rapidly gaining momentum, with an estimated 5 percent annual increase in wagering since 2005. Leading these increases are casinos on riverboats and Indian reservations, video lotteries, as well as Internet and off-track betting. Today, there are casinos in 32 states; and every state except Hawaii and Utah offers some form of legal betting.

Two factors have underscored this growth in legal gambling: public demand for gambling-style entertainment and states' need for new sources of revenue. Public officials view consumers' desire and attraction toward gambling as an excellent opportunity to provide much-needed funding for education and other publicly supported activities. For example, in the case of state-sponsored lotteries, approximately one-third of the proceeds help fund education. The prize percentage may run from 50 to 65 percent, while the remainder goes toward administrative expenses, retailers' commissions, and advertising costs.

From a behavioral point of view, studies show that gamblers tend to continue to gamble whether they are losing or winning. When losing, gamblers continue to place bets in order to recover losses. When winning occurs, bets are made to win more. In either case, it is hard for gamblers to stop gambling. Psychiatrists report seeing more and more patients with gambling-related problems. Lawyers assert that gambling is to be blamed for an increasing number of bankruptcies and divorces. Law enforcement officials indicate that some problem gamblers are turning to crime to pay their gambling debts. However, despite these ills, growth of the gambling industry continues.

We may wonder what motivates people to gamble. Is it the excitement, thrill, and high they get when they gamble? Is it the fun and entertainment involved? Is it greed to acquire easy money or something one has not worked for? Is it the challenge gambling generates? Or is it, like drugs and alcohol, a compulsive escape from reality? Regardless of the underlying motive, the growing trend for embracing and enjoying gambling seems to be a sign of the times.[1]

> *What do you think about gambling in general? In your opinion, what internal and external forces motivate people to gamble? Learn more about various states' involvement in lotteries by visiting the Web site* www.mylottocorner.com. *Also visit, a site on federal gambling laws at* www.gambling-laws-us.com/Articles-Notes/. *What motivates the government of various states to sanction or sponsor gambling activities? Are such activities in the public's best interest?*

The forces that drive people to gamble are diverse and perplexing. An understanding of why people gamble can help either to cure a social problem or to capitalize on a business opportunity. Marketers of gambling operations can use this knowledge to find more effective ways to motivate consumers' participation in the activity. At the same time, this knowledge can assist promoters in their search for innovative gambling formats that would enhance an operator's market share.

This chapter emphasizes the importance of motivation and explains the various elements inherent in the motivational phenomenon. It then continues to briefly discuss theories of motivation and the role of emotions in determining behavior of consumers in the marketplace.

What Is Motivation?

It has been said that behind each human action lies a motive. If that motive could be understood, it would become possible to ascertain and even predict behavior. In solving criminal cases, detectives look for a motive to unravel the mystery. In industry, one of the major concerns is to motivate employees to work harder. In marketing, motivation is primarily an activity translated into the expenditure of billions of dollars spent annually on advertising and promotional campaigns designed to get consumers to buy.

Motivation underlies the reasons that impel people to undertake certain actions. It is a state in which our energy is mobilized and directed in a selective fashion toward states of affairs in the external environment, called goals.[2] This view of motivation reveals that two conditions must prevail for motivation to occur. The first is a state of **arousal** or tension; the second is an impetus or **direction** for the behavior. Arousal is a tension state resulting mainly from unsatisfied needs. Direction, on the other hand, is an end toward which behavior is prompted. The state of tension that exists as a need arises activates or moves the individual toward purposive behavior in the form of a goal. For example, dermatologists who use Allergan Company's Botox cosmetic injections typically promote this procedure by following this arousal-direction view of motivation. The theme of most of these ads depicts a "before" unflattering photo of women's faces ravaged with wrinkles, lines, and furrows around the forehead, eyes, lips, and neck—an image most consumers would find unsightly. The ads go on to show how this highly effective, non-surgical procedure can dramatically attain a desired facial rejuvenation and reduce the toughest wrinkles within days. The "after" effect of Botox is then expressed in the form of jubilant, delighted, enchanted, and gloating customers. This in-your-face approach, complete with unflattering images, is enough to create a tension level resulting in sales levels estimated to exceed 3.5 million injections in 2007.[3] The need-induced tension exerts a push on the individual to take the necessary action. This push gives both impetus and direction to the behavior. In this sense, tension is goal directing.

Various conditions can trigger arousal. *Physiological cues* such as stomach contractions, decreases in blood sugar levels, changes in body temperature, or secretion of sex hormones are a source of arousal. Arousal can also be generated by *emotional*

motivation
a state in which our energy is mobilized and directed in a selective fashion toward desirable goals

arousal
a tension state resulting mainly from unfilled needs

direction
an end toward which behavior is prompted

An understanding of why people gamble can help either to cure a social problem or to capitalize on a business opportunity.

© 2009, Yuri Arcurs, Shutterstock, Inc.

cues. Fantasizing may stimulate latent needs. People who are bored or frustrated when trying to accomplish their goals may daydream about more desirable alternatives. Individuals can also become aroused when something lessens their freedom of choice.[4] For example, television cable customers, frustrated with their providers' limited channel offerings, have taken their business to other companies such as Direct TV or satellite dish networks that offer extensive channels at reasonable cost. *Cognitive cues*, such as personal accomplishments or even random thoughts, can similarly trigger arousal. Conscientious college students, for instance, may start to think about studying abroad for a semester, doing an internship, or attending graduate school. Moreover, *environmental cues* such as aromas, ads, packaging, point-of-purchase displays, and price promotions may trigger arousal.

From a marketing and consumer behavior perspective, then, both arousal and direction are necessary prerequisites for a motivated state to exist. Promotions must both arouse prospects' desire for a product category and then clearly direct them to a specific brand. For example, a TV commercial by Pizza Hut shown during an evening talk show may depict a mouthwatering pizza being served at a social gathering. A couple watching the commercial suddenly develops hunger for a pizza. They respond to this hunger by picking up the phone and ordering a pizza from Pizzaria Uno, an Italian pizza parlor the couple prefers. In this case, it is easy to see that arousal succeeded, but direction failed. The couple's learned behavior (loyalty to Pizzaria Uno) altered the course of their direction. Pizza Hut created the motivation and paid for the commercial, but Pizzaria Uno reaped the benefits in the form of enhanced consumption of its pizzas.

Classifying Consumer Motivations

Researchers focus on understanding the motives that activate human behavior. Motives are psychological constructs hypothesized to explain behavior. They cannot be observed, but the behavior that results from them can usually be witnessed. Motives in this sense are abstractions postulated to explain observable behavior. They are frequently classified as conscious–unconscious, high–low urgency, positive–negative polarity, intrinsic–extrinsic, and rational–emotional. Let us briefly examine these classifications and ponder their significance to the study of consumer behavior.

CONSCIOUS VERSUS UNCONSCIOUS

Motives can be *conscious* (sometimes referred to as manifest) or *unconscious* (sometimes referred to as latent). In many cases, a consumer's motives are conscious, and the reasons for an individual's behavior are clear to him or her. Hence, because consumers are aware of their conscious motives, these motives do not have to be aroused.

Sometimes, however, an individual's motives are unconscious, and the person does not know why a particular behavior was undertaken. Some gamblers become hooked on gambling. They risk losing their wealth, jobs, or even families over it. In most cases, they have no explanations for their destructive habit. A variety of reasons can cause motivations to be unconscious. First, needs themselves remain unconscious as long as they are being satisfied.[5] Unless an individual's sinuses are congested, he or she rarely thinks of the body's need for oxygen. Second, certain needs have such low priority for individuals that they are unaware of them. Third, needs may be repressed. That is, some individuals may avoid admitting the existence of a need. For example, celibate priests or monks, in a search for higher principles, choose to deny the presence of sexual needs.

From a consumer behavior perspective, because unconscious motives are dormant and unrecognized, they must be drawn to the consumer's attention by the promotional efforts of marketers. Reaching awareness of motivations we did not previously recognize can trigger purchase action. As an example, most people tend to regard themselves as invincible and fail to recognize the need to arrange for their death. The funeral industry, in response to this tendency, has developed promotions and offers that make the emotion-laden purchase of a casket more like buying a piece of furniture.[6]

HIGH VERSUS LOW URGENCY

Motives can exert either immediate or delayed impact on behavior. *High-urgency* needs require immediate satisfaction. A consumer who needs to replace a furnace on a cold winter day or purchase a new suit for an upcoming job interview lacks the time needed to comparison shop and, consequently, may fail to get the best value. This urgency may in part explain why seasonal garments command their highest price at the start of the season. Consumers who need these seasonal products *now* are willing to pay whatever price it takes to acquire them.

The act of satisfying *low-urgency* needs, on the other hand, can be postponed. Consumers in this case have sufficient time to shop around and compare alternatives before buying. During periods of economic hardship or uncertainty, consumers tend to postpone the purchase of some durable goods (carpeting, furniture), because the purchase of these items is not urgent and can be delayed. Marketers, in this case, in order to stimulate purchase action and command better prices, attempt to create a sense of necessity and urgency for the products or services being promoted. The ad in Figure 7.1 from Delta Queen Steamboat Company offers a two-for-one fare incentive to get vacationers to book their trips early.

POSITIVE VERSUS NEGATIVE POLARITY

Motives, in addition, display polarity. That is to say, they positively or negatively influence people's behavior. *Positive influences* lead individuals toward desired goals. For example, many people take daily vitamin supplements to enhance the nutritional value of their diet. They also may use colognes or aftershave lotions in order to smell good. Conversely, *negative influences* steer people away from adverse consequences. For example, some consumers may

Figure 7.1
Delta Queen Steamboat Company creates a sense of urgency by encouraging vacationers to book their trips early in order to qualify for the 2-for-1 fares.

use gel toothpastes and mouthwashes to avoid bad breath, or they may use antibacterial soaps and antiperspirants to avoid body odor. Positively and negatively motivated groups of consumers may represent separate market segments. Although marketers usually employ positive brand benefits to entice consumers to follow a suggested course of action, they occasionally resort to negative motivating forces such as fear or guilt to bring about the desired change. Figure 7.2 from Trojan proposes a safe course of action that will protect sexual partners from regretful consequences.

Figure 7.2

This ad from Trojan uses the concept of negative polarity to promote the brand.

(Use of the TROJAN®, and the Warrior Head Logo®, and EVOLVE™ trademarks, and EVOLVE print ad for TROJAN® brand condoms is used with the express written permission of Church & Dwight Co., Inc., Princeton, New Jersey. TROJAN®, the Warrior Head Logo®, and EVOLVE™ are trademarks of Church & Dwight Virginia Co., Inc. © Church & Dwight Virginia Co., Inc. 2007.)

INTRINSIC VERSUS EXTRINSIC

intrinsic motivation
behavior undertaken for the inherent pleasure of the activity itself

extrinsic motivation
behavior undertaken in order to acquire rewards

Behavior can be intrinsically motivated or extrinsically motivated. In the case of **intrinsic motivation**, an individual engages in behavior for the inherent pleasure of the activity undertaken; behavior *is* the reward. An avid golfer, for example, may spend dearly on golfing because of sheer enjoyment and pleasure in the game itself. **Extrinsic motivation**, on the other hand, moves an individual to acquire rewards that are independent of the activity. Golf pros may participate in tournaments to win trophies and large monetary prizes. Playing the game, in such cases, is not motivated by the mere fun of the activity itself but rather by the prospect of making money.

© 2009, JupiterImages, Inc.

From a marketing perspective, behavior resulting from intrinsic motivation tends to be more enduring compared with that precipitated by extrinsic motivation. The pleasure of being involved in the activity itself ensures continued involvement and interest. Conversely, in the case of extrinsic motivation, once rewards cease, interest in the activity subsides. Marketers therefore try to create intrinsic motivation. Music and dance instructors, martial arts, yoga, pilates trainers; as well as coaches who give tennis and swimming lessons are but some examples of entities that attempt to help people derive enjoyment from the activity itself and keep them interested through intrinsic motivation.

Behavior resulting from intrinsic motivation tends to be more enduring than behavior precipitated by extrinsic motivation.

RATIONAL VERSUS EMOTIONAL

rational motives
those aroused through appeals to reason and logic

emotional motives
those aroused by stressing sentiments, fantasies, and feelings

Motives have also been classified as either rational or emotional. **Rational motives** are aroused through appeals to reason and logic. They stress objective, utilitarian goals such as economy, durability, quality, and dependability. Rationally oriented advertising offers a straightforward, no-nonsense, factual message. It attempts to build a persuasive and credible argument in support of a brand by presenting relevant information and without necessarily being artistic or clever.[7] Fast-food franchises, for example, have advertised that their hamburgers are 100 percent pure beef. Phone companies and Internet service providers promote their services by stressing rational appeals such as better value through lower rates, broader coverage, and faster connections. The ad in Figure 7.3 for Fellowes Shredders employs a rational appeal to promote the product.

Emotional motives, on the other hand, entail goal selection that relies on subjective criteria. Emotional motives have their origin in human feelings and impulsive or unreasoned promptings to action.[8] In other words, emotional purchases are often whimsical rather than based on information and prepurchase deliberation. According to Holbrook and Hirschman, emotional consumption can be characterized by "pursuit of fantasies, feelings, and fun."[9] These experiential aspects of consumption focus on the "symbolic, hedonic, and aesthetic"

Figure 7.3

This ad from Fellowes Shredders uses a rational approach to promote the brand. The tagline "the world's toughest shredder," combined with statistics on identity theft portray the brand as one that virtually eliminates the possibility of consumers becoming victims of this crime.

EXHIBIT 7.1 **A Partial Listing of Rational and Emotional Motives and the Appeals Used to Stimulate Them**

Rational Appeals	Emotional Appeals
Economy in purchase	Pride in personal appearance
Economy in use	Pride of ownership
Space saving	Ambition, competition, achievement,
Labor Saving	recognition
Time saving	Approval from others
Labor saving	Status, prestige, esteem
Increased performance	Individuality
More efficient performance	Play, sport, physical activity
Simplicity in operation	Rest, relaxation
Durability (long product life)	Appetite, taste
Availability	Curiosity
Low maintenance cost	Guilt
Quality materials	Fear
Quality workmanship	Patriotism
Convenience	Love of family
Safety and security	Loyalty

nature of consumption. Many emotional motives are linked to an individual's social and aesthetic requirements, as well as his or her self-concept. Such motives include status, belonging, beauty, pride, distinctiveness, and pleasure.

Until recently, emotions were regarded as enemies of pure reason. Modern discoveries, however, reveal startling new images from MRI and PET scans showing that emotion is at the physical center of our brains. Emotion is not nature's afterthought; it is one of the primary regulators of health, happiness, reasoning, and human actions. In other words, emotions can help people be more efficient with their reasoning abilities. Although feelings sometimes derail thought, more often they point it in the right direction.[10] In the field of children's apparel, Gymboree Company, which operates hundreds of mall-based stores, has cleverly used emotions to influence what otherwise might be a rational purchase decision. Its reputation for producing and selling colorful clothes, reinforced by its multihued logo "Quality clothes, colorful kids" tagline, has given the company its strong competitive edge and enabled it to carve for itself a substantial niche in the highly competitive market for children's clothing.[11]

Most promotional campaigns fall somewhere along a continuum between purely rational and purely emotional. That is, they combine both rational and emotional motivations but may lean in one direction or the other. Exhibit 7.1 contains a sample listing of rational and emotional consumer motivations to which advertisers commonly appeal. Note that some appeals could be placed under both headings.

Elements of Motivation

Four elements are inherent in motivation. They are needs, motives, goals, and desires. We discuss each briefly here in turn, but the separation is actually arbitrary because these concepts constantly overlap and interact. Motivation should be thought of as a dynamic process rather than as separate elements that make up the whole.[12]

NEEDS

Humans have diverse needs. Human requirements for food and drink, for safety, for social acceptance, and for achievement are but a few of the needs most of us are familiar with. **Needs** are internal forces that prompt behavior toward goal-oriented solutions. Unlike motives, needs do not necessarily trigger behavior. A person on a diet may, when feeling hungry, ignore the need for food. Similarly, a person who has recently quit smoking may suppress the desire for a cigarette.

Needs are usually treated under two broad categories, physiological needs and acquired needs.[13] **Physiological needs** are basic conditions that are required for the maintenance of life and the normal processes of health and growth. The human requirements for food, water, shelter, sex, and rest are examples. **Acquired needs**, on the other hand, are learned and conditioned by relationships with others in the environment and specific culture in which we are brought up. Consequently, these types of needs may vary cross-culturally. What may be deemed desirable according to one set of cultural values may be regarded as undesirable according to the values of a different culture. Attitudes concerning what is beautiful, modest, or fashionable differ from one society to another. Thus, needs for cosmetics, jewelry, or diet foods and beverages are not universal. These are sometimes referred to as secondary needs.

Even though we distinguish between physiological and acquired needs, much behavior reflects an interaction between the two types. For example, a warm piece of clothing may suffice for a wintry day to protect an individual from the cold, fulfilling an important primary need for bodily protection. However, the person may opt for purchasing a fur coat because of a strong desire for status and prestige. Both primary and secondary needs interact in this case to influence the purchasing decision.

needs
internal forces that prompt behavior toward goal-oriented solutions

physiological needs
basic bodily requirements essential to maintain life

acquired needs
drives that are conditioned by relationships with others in the environment

MOTIVES

Once a need has been activated, a state of tension exists that drives the individual to reduce or eliminate the need. In other words, the state of tension caused by an unfulfilled need creates a drive. A consumer who experiences such a state strives to reduce the tension by satisfying the need. For example, hunger is a basic need. When aroused in an individual, it becomes a **motive** for satisfying the need. The individual feeling the pangs of hunger may, for example, stop at Taco Bell to get a burrito. In this view, motives arise from states of imbalance or tension and carry out the function of energizing, activating, and directing the behavior toward desirable goals.

Motives, in the majority of cases, are directed toward reducing bodily deficiencies, whether biogenic or psychogenic. In addition, motives may direct behavior toward enhancing an individual's health, happiness, or well-being. They may also exist to push an individual away from dangerous places, situations, or harmful products. A motive, therefore, can direct us toward or away from some

motive
a state of tension that pushes an individual to act

object, place, or situation. Motives, moreover, may be activated toward behaviors that are legal, moral, and ethical; or conversely, they may be activated toward illegal, immoral, and unethical actions. Motives, as you can see, are capable of accommodating an endless diversity of human needs.

GOALS

goal
the sought-after objective of motivated behavior

Human behavior is not random or irrational but rather is goal directed. The sought-after result of motivation is some desirable **goal**.[14] The goal may be an object, an activity, or a situation toward which motivated behavior is directed. Goals *pull* individuals toward acquiring a reward. The challenge for marketers is to persuade consumers to perceive their product or service offerings as desirable goals that will satisfy their needs. Whereas needs and motives *push* the individual to correct a state of imbalance, goals *pull* the individual toward something perceived as desirable.

generic goals
nonspecific categories of products and services that can satisfy customer needs

Marketers differentiate between two types of goals, generic goals and product-specific goals. **Generic goals** refer to the general classes or categories of products and services that can satisfy certain consumer needs. For a commuter, automobiles (as opposed to using public transportation) may be considered one category among a number of alternative transportation means to fulfill daily travel needs. Automobiles, in this sense, comprise a generic class of products. Marketers are generally less concerned with stimulating primary demand for an entire product category, except perhaps in such cases as ads by the American Dairy Association, Florida Orange Growers Association, and California Raisin Growers' Association, as well as other industrywide trade organizations. The ad in Figure 7.4 highlights the benefits of milk and encourages drinking milk instead of sugary beverages in order to build a lean, healthy, and muscular body.

brand-specific goals
particular alternatives in a product category from which consumers can choose

Brand-specific goals, on the other hand, are the branded, identified, or labeled alternatives available in a category of products from which consumers select specific brands to satisfy their needs. In the commuter case mentioned earlier, the individual involved may decide to purchase an automobile and specifically choose a Ford Mustang to fulfill his or her travel needs. From a marketing point of view, the Ford Mustang is a brand-specific alternative. Mustang sales are most likely affected by the extent of promotional activities undertaken by Ford to stimulate demand for this model. So, unlike the case with generic goals for which needs may already exist, promotional programs are necessary to stimulate demand for product- and brand-specific alternatives. Every year, marketers allocate hefty sums of money to accomplish this objective. In 2008, NBC TV sold eighty-four 30-second ad spots during the Super Bowl at the incredible cost of $2.7 million per each 30 seconds of air time.[15] In 2008, the Super Bowl aired 50 minutes and 50 seconds of commercial time. Big advertisers such as Anheuser-Busch, Coca-Cola, PepsiCo Inc., Hyundai, Victoria Secret, General Motors, General Electric, and GoDaddy.com were among the takers.[16]

The selection of goals by an individual depends on a number of factors that characterize the person or the situation at the time the need emerges. Factors such as this person's physical, financial, and emotional conditions affect goal

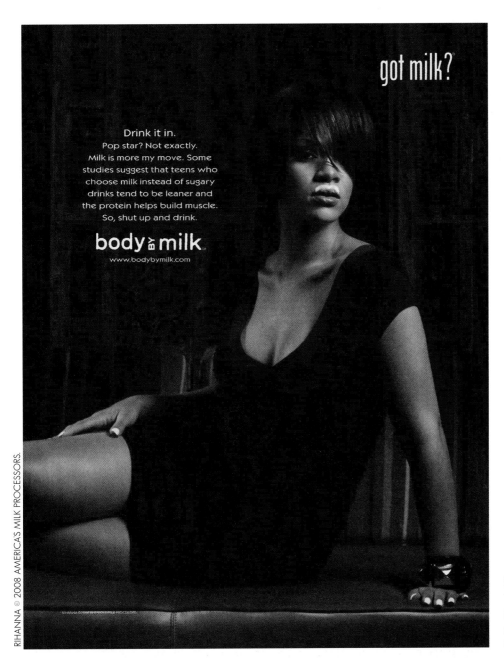

got milk?

Drink it in.
Pop star? Not exactly.
Milk is more my move. Some
studies suggest that teens who
choose milk instead of sugary
drinks tend to be leaner and
the protein helps build muscle.
So, shut up and drink.

body by milk
www.bodybymilk.com

RIHANNA © 2008 AMERICA'S MILK PROCESSORS.

Figure 7.4
This ad from Body by Milk promotes drinking milk without mentioning any specific brand.

selection. A graduating college student who is a first-time buyer of a new car may settle for a Hyundai rather than a BMW due to financial considerations. Cultural values and norms are another group of factors that influence goal selection. Whereas many people in the United States enjoy sunbathing, Middle Easterners avoid the sun due to a culturally based perception that dark skin is a sign of the working class and fair skin is a symbol of higher social stature.

In addition, products that consumers own or use such as the cars they drive, homes they buy, electronics they use, and clothes they wear convey something about themselves to people with whom they interact. The products consumers

BRUT

BRUT. THE ESSENCE OF MAN.™

Figure 7.5

Brut uses the likeness of a virile, muscular male model to suggest that users of Brut project an image that captures the essence of manhood

choose are, in reality, social symbols reflecting their self-image. They serve as a means of communication between an individual and his or her significant others. These symbols reflect images such as masculinity or femininity, ability, status, success, or any other desirable self-image feature an individual may desire to convey to others. Whereas many women in the United States aspire to lose weight, in some African countries, women prefer to gain weight, since a heavier body frame is deemed attractive. Figure 7.5 illustrates the use of reinforcing one's self-image as an appeal in advertising, prompting males to select Brut aftershave to express their manhood.

DESIRES

desires

passions that involve longing, yearning, and fervently wishing for something

Recently, some researchers of consumer behavior have directed attention to the concept of consumer desires. They define consumer **desires** as belief-based passions that involve longing, yearning, and fervently wishing for something.[17] This perspective attempts to acknowledge products' rich symbolic meanings and consumers' emotional involvement with coveted goods.

Desires involve an intensely passionate positive emotional attachment steeped in fantasies and dreams rather than based on reasoned judgments. Desires can be dangerous, because they often transgress the ordinary and border on being socially unacceptable. This transgressive character is part of their allure. Because of the dangers of losing control to a desire and the fear of appearing obsessed, consumers may try to tame and rationalize their desires so that they appear more socially acceptable. Ironically, however, doing so lessens the *mystical* power of current desires and leads toward developing new ones. Interestingly, once desired objects are ultimately obtained, consumers tend to become bored with them and desire new focal objects. The spectrum of human desires is endless. Desires vary by personality, gender, age, and culture. For example, when inquired about their desires, children in the United States tend to mention such things as toys, pets,

Ethical Dilemma

Challenging Children's Sensitivity to the Suffering of Others

Today, as many people seek to fill their leisure time with activities that involve adventure, promise fun, and provide a challenge, they find in electronic video games a practical venue to fulfill this need.

Video games in today's society have become extremely popular and are increasingly being allotted more time in the daily-life routine of many individuals. These games have been successfully marketed to and are easily obtained by both children and adults. It has been estimated that, on the average, boys spend 15 hours per week playing these games, versus 5 hours for girls.

Most of these games can be judged as having a positive influence on players, mostly through broadening their knowledge, improving their reaction time, and enhancing their creativity. As a learning tool for children in particular, these games may assist parents and educators in their mission to broaden a child's horizons and ensure the development of his or her ethical code, empathy, and concern for others. Through these games, children can also learn to take responsibility for their own actions.

One disturbing trend in this field, however, has been the proliferation of the violent variety of games. The content of this latter type has been claimed to encourage excessive aggression and cruelty among young people. Research has shown that such games may be more harmful than violent television shows and movies due to the fact that they are interactive, competitive, engrossing, and require the player to identify with the aggressor. As such, these games promote automatic aggression, and work to desensitize the players' reflective emotions, care for others, and responsibility for their behavior. The actions required from the players to successfully engage in the game involve a temporary yielding of the players' core values and moral judgement merely for the sake of winning.

The negative effect of these video games has raised major concerns of many groups, including parents, educators, law enforcement agencies, legislators, and mental health professionals. A Surgeon General's study along with a follow-up report by the National Institute of Mental Health identified three major effects of this type of violence on children's behavior. (1) Children may become less sensitive to the pain and suffering of others; (2) they may become fearful of the world around them; and (3) they become more likely to behave in aggressive and harmful ways toward others. In response to these concerns, some cities and states are now considering legislation designed to prevent the sale of mature-rated video games to children.[18]

The popularity of video games will continue to gain momentum as years go by. In your opinion, why are these games so popular among both the young and the old? How can society reduce the potential harm caused by certain types of these games? Do you think the benefits of the "good" games far exceed the social cost incurred because of the violent ones? For more information about the effect of violent games on children, visit www.psychologymatters.org/mediaviolence.html. Should legislation be enacted to restrict the sale and availability of such violent games? Defend your answer.

candy, ice cream, and trips to an amusement park. Women often cite shoes, designer-label clothing, jewelry, cosmetics, and expensive perfume. Men, on the other hand, often report a desire for fancy cars, electronic gadgets, and unique collectibles. Seniors frequently speak of travel and visiting exotic places. These emotional urges bring about a desired state of affairs that help us experience life at its fullest.

Now that we have examined the four elements of motivation, let us look at the numerous theoretical attempts to conceptualize human motivation and explain its underlying causes.

Theories of Motivation

A glance at the literature on motivation reveals an abundance of theories attempting to conceptualize human motivation. Although each has its own merit, the discussion of all of them is beyond the scope of this book. These various theories, however, can be grouped under four main categories: (1) instinct theories, (2) drive theories, (3) arousal theories, and (4) cognitive theories. Each category warrants some explanation.

INSTINCT THEORIES

Instinct theories of motivation suggest that behavior is innate. Humans, like all forms of animal life, are born equipped with **instincts**, the physical and behavioral characteristics of a species that enable it to survive. The origin of this approach to motivation dates back to the writings of the nineteenth-century naturalist Charles Darwin, who believed that instincts arise through a process of natural selection and are transmitted genetically to individual members of the species. Behavior and its underlying motivation reflect the process of adaptation of creatures to their environment.

Many theorists adopted this train of thought to explain various human tendencies. Freud's psychoanalytic theory viewed sexual instincts as a primary motivator of human behavior. Some of Freud's disciples, as well as others in disagreement with him, advocated that other human instincts supersede sexual impulses in directing behavior. Such impetuses include belonging, engaging in social interaction, maintaining meaningful affiliations with others, surmounting perceived inferiorities, striving for superiority, and overcoming childhood insecurities in relationships with parents. Still other theorists presented a variety of biogenic and psychogenic instincts ranging from curiosity to self-assertion.

Even though the value of instinctive theories in the motivation literature has been questioned, marketers still find instinct theories provide rich grounds for formulating advertising appeals. A quick glance at the field of advertising and promotion today reveals the diversity of appeals to various instincts, particularly those using sexual appeals. Typically, cologne, perfume, clothing, and alcohol ads appear to have the most sexual content in them. For example, one Guess Jeans ad shows a shirtless man lying near a woman wearing panties and an open blouse that barely covers her breasts. Another for Skyy Vodka shows a man from the waist down with legs apart, a bottle of vodka in his hand, and a woman wearing a skimpy bikini top lying underneath him. A third for Candies perfume shows a sexy, half-naked girl sitting on a sink straddling a handsome man who has his shirt off.[19] These erotic appeals seem to be popular among advertisers and range from subtle hints of sexuality to blatant displays of sexual encounters. Figure 7.6 depicts a sexy ad from Jockey For Her that is almost certain to attract readers' attention.

DRIVE THEORIES

A motive, as was discussed earlier, is an internal state resulting from either biological or psychological disequilibrium. When a person's physiological or psychological equilibrium is disrupted, motives drive this individual to restore

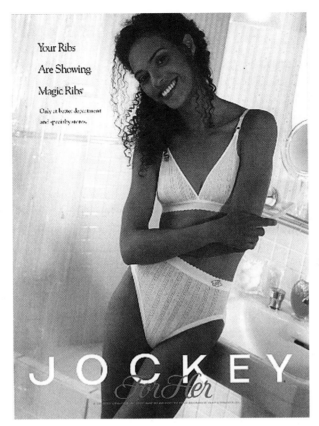

Figure 7.6
Ads like this one promoting Jockey For Her often use sexy models to create a desirable aura for their products.

prior equilibrium or balance. Back in 1939, one of the pioneer biologists named William B. Cannon coined the term **homeostasis** to explain the self-regulating mechanism of the body that is hypothesized to maintain harmony of all bodily systems. Body chemistry and the system's harmony are maintained in balance despite activities that may tend to change or alter their concentration or pattern. When this equilibrium is disturbed as a result of needs or external circumstances, the automatic homeostatic mechanism is no longer in harmony. This disequilibrium or imbalance causes the organism to be aroused to correct the deficit. Thus, tension reduction becomes the primary function of behavior. When homeostasis is restored, the internal stimulus subsides. In this event, motivation is seen as the driving force arising from homeostatic imbalance or tension.

In this view, the basic premise of drive theories is that individuals tend to shift from a negative state to a neutral state to maintain equilibrium. Applying this concept, some marketers resort to creating tension states for consumers and then offering their products, services, and brands as means of restoring balance. This tension-arousing format works best where consumers are already concerned about the issue raised in the ad and where the threat presented is not excessive. If the threat is too strong, it could cause consumers to block the

homeostasis
a self-regulating mechanism of the body that maintains harmony of all bodily systems

message. Use of this tactic is widespread in advertising and is reportedly found in over 15 percent of all television commercials.[20] Advertisers of insurance, for example, have used such tension-arousing appeals to spur interest in life, health, home, and auto insurance policies. The purchase of insurance coverage, in turn, relieves the aroused fears of consumers. Similar tension-arousing promotions sponsored by other firms or institutions have employed guilt appeals to make a case for not driving while intoxicated, for saying "No" to drugs, or for buying environmentally friendly products. Consumers who observe such recommendations need not feel guilty about their actions.[21] Advertisers of pharmaceuticals, security systems, and products designed to protect the elderly and children are among the many companies that use the tension-arousing format to promote their products and services. The ad from Clorox in Figure 7.7 highlights the potential danger presented by germs as children interact with other kids.

AROUSAL THEORIES

Activation or arousal theories suggest that people often seek stimulation instead of trying to avoid it. In this view, consumers move from a neutral state to a more desirable enhanced state. Examples of arousal-seeking behaviors include traveling to exciting places, experiencing thrilling rides in amusement parks, sampling exotic foods, and participating in or viewing high-risk sports.

High sensation seekers (HSS) are individuals who have a stronger-than-average need to seek and approach activities, situations, and ideas that are novel, changing, complex, surprising, and more intense. For HSS's, tour operators provide vacation packages that offer many exciting activities such as scuba diving, exploring ruins, deep sea fishing, and rock climbing. A recent report showed that 31 million Americans have taken what the Travel Industry of America (TIA) calls "hard adventure vacations" in the past five years.[22] These trips include such physically demanding feats as mountain climbing, skydiving, and cave exploring. Adventurous vacationers are more likely than the population as a whole to be male, young, and have high household incomes.

Some individuals, on the other hand, prefer to read a book, work on a computer, or watch TV in the comfort of their own home. Those persons who are less willing to seek and accept challenges are referred to as **low sensation seekers (LSS)**. The tendency of people either to seek or to avoid thrilling, challenging activities has been called their **optimal stimulation level (OSL)**.[23]

Researchers have attempted to develop various measures of the need for stimulation. For example, Zuckerman developed the **general sensation-seeking scale (GSSS)**, which is designed to measure individual differences in sensation seeking along four dimensions:

1. Thrill and adventure seeking
2. Experience seeking
3. Disinhibition, and
4. Susceptibility to boredom.[25]

high sensation seekers (HSS)
persons with stronger-than-average need to seek novel, surprising, and more intense activities

low sensation seekers (LSS)
persons who prefer less-thrilling activities

optimal stimulation level (OSL)
a measurement of people's tendency to seek or avoid thrilling, challenging activities

general sensation-seeking scale (GSSS)
a scale designed to measure individual differences in sensation-seeking tendencies

May they share secrets instead of germs.

Clorox® disinfecting products kill the germs that can make kids sick.

clorox.com

Use as directed on hard, non-porous surfaces

Figure 7.7

Building on parents' desire to protect their children from harm, this ad from Clorox highlights the danger of infections caused by transmitting germs, and suggests using Clorox as a means of eliminating this threat.

Consumer Behavior in Practice

Get 'Em While They're Still Young

Many marketers consider college students to be a fertile and desirable market to pursue. One reason is that they represent a good-sized market. In 2008, the number of students enrolled in institutions of higher education reached 18 million. A second reason for this market's attractiveness is that today's college students have more money than their predecessors, and they don't mind parting with it.

Companies that target the college student market use a variety of appeals. Realizing that this market is composed of a varied mix of high and low sensation seekers, these firms develop strategies to appeal to the whims of these various segments. There are companies such as tour operators and beer distributors that still cater to the spring break crowd and participate in rowdy contests, promotional beach games, and product giveaways during gatherings where surfing, romance, drinking, and wet T-shirt contests are the norm. Other companies, however, take a more responsible approach to reaching students. Ford Motor Company, for example, generates collegiate sales by offering students between $500 to $1,000 cash incentives to purchase a car. Verizon's tactics to lure college students include providing extra cell minutes, low rates, and prepaid plans. This is in addition to generous free night and weekend minutes. Verizon also provides a multicolored Web site (www.free2tlk.com) that offers students links to popular Web sites, information on popular phones and features, a text messaging directory, and a chance to sign up for service and win Sony wares.

In its effort to appeal to college students, Microsoft gives free access to some of its development, design, and gaming software to help spark students' creativity and enhance Microsoft's image. The free software, which is available through DreamSpark program to students, includes Microsoft Visual Studio 2008, Microsoft Expression Studio, and Microsoft Windows Server 2003.

Based on their realization that 76 percent of college students carry at least one credit card, these companies continue to vigorously pursue the collegiate market. Their arsenal includes T-shirts, iPods, and other gifts plus a host of benefits such as zero interest for a grace period as well as no annual fee. The goal behind all these efforts is obvious—by getting students to use their brands while in college, companies hope to create customers for life.[24]

Are the benefits to companies of using come-ons to attract college students worth the effort and cost invested? Visit www.free2tlk.com to learn how Verizon appeals to college students. Do you think that most college graduates maintain their college "product and brand relationships" in later years? In your opinion, what types of products can benefit most from this early familiarity?

This scale allows researchers to divide respondents into high and low sensation seekers based on the research evidence that the OSL is constant within an individual, but varies from one individual to another.

Arousal theories have affected marketing strategies in the areas of promotion and incentives. In such arenas, arousal is created through cues, symbols, and suggestions that stir all sorts of human emotions. For instance, in the area of promotion directed to high sensation seekers, marketers employ a number of arousal-generating tactics, such as depicting exotic adventures, unexpected riches, breathtaking activities, and romantic encounters to motivate a desired consumer response. One such tactic employed by Conejos Ranches in Colorado invites vacationers to experience a taste of the real West and participate in a working cowboy vacation. The experience includes taking part in a rodeo, working and moving cattle, sleeping in cowboy tepees, and eating chuck-wagon cooked meals.

Similarly, the U.S. Army in recognizing the difference between LSS and HSS employs two separate promotional strategies to attract recruits. Because the army needs LSS types for administrative jobs, one of the promotional strategies suggests to prospective enlistees the use of army training for career experience and college education. On the HSS side, especially for combat positions, the army uses more exciting promotional messages, such as those involving meeting challenges and facing risks.

Investment firms such as Dreyfus, Fidelity, and Smith Barney are also among those that serve both LSS (conservative) and HSS (speculative) investors as customers. By creating separate services—including newsletters, investment counseling programs, promotional packages, investment portfolios, and alternative levels of services—such firms are better positioned to address the goals and risk tolerance of different types of investors.

© 2009, Joe Gough, Shutterstock, Inc.

Demanding outdoor sports have always been a favorite of many high sensation seeking individuals.

COGNITIVE THEORIES

Cognitive theories presume that human beings are rational, intelligent organisms who use their physical and intellectual capacities to fulfill their conscious desires. In this view, humans are not mechanically driven by internal needs and motives and by external stimuli. Rather, they are viewed as information processors and problem solvers who have the ability to deal effectively with their environment. This view of human behavior recognizes the interdependence between the mental processes of learning, feeling, thinking, performing, perceiving, remembering, and forgetting. Behavior is seen as a continuous interaction between these mental processes and an active process rather than an act that emerges only when a need arises. Behavior is purposeful and a means that humans use for controlling life events that surround them as well as for controlling their own states. People select goals to accomplish objectives (to learn, to dominate, to master the environment, to control their behavior) and consciously monitor their behavior to ensure the accomplishment of set goals.

Marketers often apply cognitive theory when designing promotional appeals. Advertising copy that contains logical arguments enumerating a brand's features, advantages, or benefits can bring about a change in perceptions and incite motives for purchasing. Ads for hybrid automobiles, for example, often focus on objective reasons to choose this type of vehicle over others. Such ads usually emphasize the hybrid's benefits of saving money, and gas, as well as the environment. Similarly, ads from investment firms almost always provide facts about their financial accomplishments and earnings histories to convince consumers to choose their services over others'. Figure 7.8 depicts an ad for Morgan Stanley that employs a cognitive approach by providing information of interest to potential investors.

Figure 7.8

This ad from Morgan Stanley applies cognitive theory by informing consumers about two potentially beneficial investment opportunities in renewable energy and microloans.

In other applications, some marketers employ strategies designed to help consumers set goals and control their own state of affairs. Health clubs and diet centers often use appeals that encourage prospects to take control of their own predicament. Weight-loss or bodybuilding goals planned specifically for each individual are designed to promote a firm's services to customers who are eager to change their present states.

Whereas the motivation theories covered so far in this chapter emphasize the roles of forces such as instincts, drives, arousal, and cognition in instigating or guiding human behavior, other views on a universal *need hierarchy* and *social motives* have also been advocated as dominant influences on human behavior. Let us take a brief look at these views.

MASLOW'S HIERARCHY OF NEEDS

Abraham Maslow, a clinical psychologist, believed that human needs fall into a hierarchical pattern. The five **basic needs** that encompass most human goals are ranked in the hierarchy so that the higher-order needs arise only after the lower-order needs have largely been satisfied. If lower-order needs cease to be satisfied, an individual may regress backward in the hierarchy. Arranged from low order to higher order, these needs are physiological, safety, social, esteem, and self-actualization.[26]

basic needs
essential needs that include physiological, safety, social, esteem, and self-actualization needs

Maslow's hierarchy provides clues concerning which needs are driving behavior. He postulates that for higher needs in the hierarchy to emerge as motivating factors, those needs at lower tiers must first be largely satisfied. Stated differently, when needs at a particular level are frustrated or only partially satisfied, they persist as a dominating influence on behavior. One level of needs has to be sufficiently—but not completely—satisfied for the next level to emerge. Some overlap exists between each level, and no need is ever totally satisfied. Consequently, multiple levels of needs may affect individuals simultaneously.

Based on this view, in affluent societies such as the United States and Canada, because the lower-order (physiological) needs have largely been met, behavior *is* essentially motivated by higher-order needs such as belonging, esteem, and self-actualization. It would be only natural, then, to anticipate that advertising copy within affluent societies emphasizes success, esteem, prestige, distinction, and achievement as major motivators for stimulating buyer behavior.[27] The ad in Figure 7.9 suggests that by wearing Ocean Dream perfume, a woman can "leave an impression" on a man—a theme that implies distinction and esteem.

Maslow's hierarchy is often applied by marketers as a basis for market segmentation and product positioning, whereby specific promotional appeals are targeted to consumers at one or more need levels. For instance, four-star restaurants frequently sponsor ads that spotlight specific food and beverage items on their menu (a physiological appeal) and also stress their elegant dining atmosphere (a social appeal). Similarly, a beer ad that depicts a party atmosphere (a social appeal) may also speak of the brand's taste (a physiological appeal) and advise against drinking and driving (a safety appeal).

Figure 7.9
This ad from Giorgio Beverly Hills suggests elegance, distinction, and esteem by depicting an attractive woman leaving an impression on a man simply by wearing Ocean Dream perfume.

SOCIAL MOTIVATION THEORIES

Many theorists such as Murray and McClelland have assembled lists of *social needs* that, even though labeled as needs, are in reality motivational tendencies rather than needs.[28] We present them here to describe some of the motivational patterns of consumers. Murray's list of social motives, for example, includes 20 motives arranged in alphabetical order rather than in a hierarchy. According to Murray, any one of the 20 motives could be directing an individual's behavior, depending on that individual's environmental situation. Exhibit 7.2 lists Murray's social motives.[29]

Unlike Maslow's basic needs, Murray's social motives are instrumental. **Instrumental motives** describe learned patterns of behavior, such as harm avoidance, that are solicited in the service of a basic need. For example, a person who becomes hungry at midnight may temporarily bypass eating because the only restaurant open at this late hour is located in an unsafe part of town.

instrumental motives
learned, social patterns of behavior that are solicited in the service of a basic need

EXHIBIT 7.2	Murray's List of Social Motives			
abasement	autonomy	dominance	nurturance	sentience
achievement	counteraction	exhibition	order	sex
affiliation	defendence	harm avoidance	play	succorance
aggression	deference	inavoidance	rejection	understanding

From a marketing point of view, these *action-oriented* social motives are more effective as advertising themes than the basic needs suggested by Maslow. Whereas efforts to stimulate basic needs translate into the fulfillment of generic goals, social motive activation is more powerful in motivating product-specific and brand-specific choices. The ad in Figure 7.10 from the state of Ohio and directed to vacationers, employs the motives of play and nurturance as forms of social motivation to promote the state's various attractions.

Figure 7.10

The social motives of play and nurturance are being evoked in this ad from the State of Ohio. The ad highlights the excitement and surprise to be experienced when visiting the state's various attractions.

McClelland, on the other hand, conceived motives as the mainspring of action. The work of McClelland and his associates centered on a number of learned social motives such as uniqueness (assertion of individual identity). In particular, McClelland emphasized a trio of needs that appeared to play a significant role in interpersonal relationships. This trio consists of desires for power, affiliation, and achievement.

From a consumer behavior perspective, power, affiliation, and achievement motives are important because they underlie a great deal of consumption-related activity.[30] Products such as souped-up, high-performance sports cars and motorcycles would lend themselves well to promises of power for owners. Campaigns designed to recruit members for country clubs or fraternal organizations might employ themes of belonging, acceptance, and social approval. Campaigns for do-it-yourself products virtually guarantee successful achievement—even for novices, and investment organizations allude to substantial returns from investment opportunities. The ad from BMW Motorrad USA in Figure 7.11 employs the concept of power, suggested by McClelland, in order to promote the K1200R Sport motorcycle.

McClelland further suggested other characteristics and attitudes of achievement-motivated individuals. Among them is the fact that task achievement is more important to such persons than material or financial rewards.

Figure 7.11

This ad from BMW Motorrad USA applies the concept of power, suggested by McClelland's trio of needs, to promote the K 1200R sports motorcycle. The ad suggests that riders "unleash their edge" by experiencing the thrill of riding this powerful bike.

Task achievement also provides them with greater satisfaction than receiving recognition or praise. Such individuals exhibit a tendency to seek improvements and ways to do things better.[31]

Although Maslow, Murray, and McClelland presented needs and motives in different formats, their concepts are similar. Whereas Maslow's basic needs are common to all people, the environment is an important factor in social motives, which are learned. Human motivation is social in nature, and social motives play a major role in human interpersonal relations.

Now that we have examined various views concerning the origins and causes of motivation and considered the dominant forces that underlie a motivated state, let us move on to another motivational issue that addresses situations in which multiple needs arise simultaneously—a phenomenon known as motivational conflict.

Motivational Conflict

Four of the motivational theories examined earlier—instinct, drive, arousal, and cognitive—emphasize different forces as an explanation of motivated behavior. However, such distinctions between the theories are largely artificial. Human motivation is complex and reveals the influence of varied forces driven by multiple causes. For example, the motivation to reproduce can be explained equally well in terms of instinct, drive, or arousal theories. In this sense, these theories are complementary rather than contradictory. They shed light on the diverse sources of human motivation and suggest that motivation is a complex, multifaceted phenomenon.

Life would be simple if consumers could deal with their needs, motives, and goals one at a time. Unfortunately, seldom is this the case. More often, a combination of forces, which differ in direction and strength, operate on an individual concurrently. Sometimes consumer motivations are complementary; at other times they clash. Take the case of satisfying hunger and pursuing a healthy lifestyle. Unfortunately, when a hungry individual is about to indulge in a rich pizza, a conflict arises. Although pizza is one of this person's favorite foods, it is also high in fat, cholesterol, and salt. **Motivational conflict** occurs when multiple needs function simultaneously and fulfilling one goal causes another to remain unsatisfied. The end result of such situations is *frustration*—an emotional state that arises when barriers interfere with goal-directed behavior.

motivational conflict
situations in which multiple needs simultaneously act on an individual

A widely accepted treatment of motivational conflict by Lewin proposes that some forces precipitate movement toward a goal (approach), whereas other forces deter such action (avoidance).[32] Consumer purchasing usually involves some degree of conflict between an individual's desire to acquire product benefits and resistance against undesirable factors (spending money, investing time and effort, incurring risk). Knowledge of such consumer tendencies guides marketers in their quest for tactics designed to ease motivational conflicts in purchase situations. Tactics such as "buy now, pay later," "order through the Internet," and "return the product for a full refund" are but a few examples of tactics that marketers employ to reduce motivational conflicts for consumers.

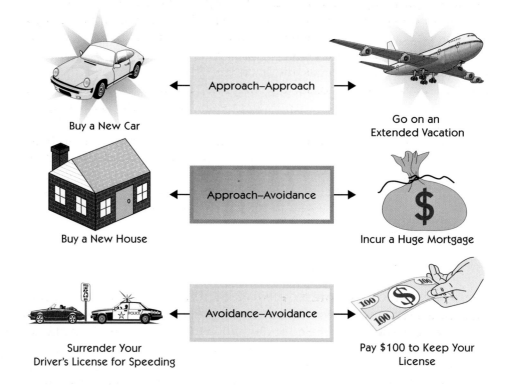

Buy a New Car — Approach–Approach — Go on an Extended Vacation

Buy a New House — Approach–Avoidance — Incur a Huge Mortgage

Surrender Your Driver's License for Speeding — Avoidance–Avoidance — Pay $100 to Keep Your License

Lewin identified three common types of motivational conflict. One type occurs when an individual must select between two attractive alternatives. A second type occurs when one's choice involves both positive and negative consequences. A third type occurs when a person must choose among two repulsive options. These are called approach–approach, approach–avoidance, and avoidance–avoidance situations, respectively. Exhibit 7.3 is a schematic diagram that summarizes these types of conflict.

APPROACH–APPROACH

approach–approach conflict

a situation in which a person faces a choice among two desirable alternatives

In **approach–approach conflicts**, consumers face a choice among desirable options. The more equal the attraction, the greater the conflict. For example, when browsing a restaurant's menu, we may find both steak and lobster appetizing. To help consumers resolve approach–approach conflicts, marketers may enable consumers to take advantage of multiple options simultaneously. Some restaurants, for example, offer surf-and-turf combination plates. Other businesses utilize strategically placed cues in the store to influence the brand selections of shoppers facing approach–approach conflicts. Such shoppers are quite susceptible to visual appeals, price offers, and other point-of-purchase enticements. Advertisers also often bundle multiple benefits in a single offer for the same reason. For instance, Verizon ads promise free cell phones, clearer sound quality, fewer dropped calls, better geographic coverage, and activation at no charge.

APPROACH–AVOIDANCE

The most typical buyer behavior situation is **approach–avoidance conflict** because, in every case, consumers must surrender money and time, forego other opportunities, expend energy and effort, and incur risks to procure product benefits. Consumers purchase products and services only when their anticipated satisfaction exceeds the sacrifice of resources required. Thus, marketers must convince consumers that product rewards exceed their cost. In the food and beverage industry, new product opportunities have evolved out of approach–avoidance conflicts. For example, diet beverages and low-calorie, reduced-fat meals now enable weight-conscious consumers to both enjoy these products and lessen their caloric intake. In other cases, marketers have developed alternative products for individuals who regret self-indulgent consumption. The popularity of imitation furs among some consumers is largely due to the ability of fake furs to eliminate guilt over slaughtering animals for the sake of fashion.

approach–avoidance conflict
a situation in which a person must surrender resources to gain a desirable outcome

AVOIDANCE–AVOIDANCE

Avoidance–avoidance conflicts require consumers to choose one of two unpleasant alternatives and are thus difficult to resolve. For example, automobile drivers eventually face the choice of paying a huge bill to repair an old car or coming up with the necessary financing to buy a new one. Similarly, college students want neither to be without a computer nor to spend hundreds of dollars to buy one. Under such circumstances, marketers may attempt to reduce the negative aspect of spending the money by extending payment plans, offering trade-in allowances, or donating some portion of a product's selling price to a charitable cause. Marketers can also increase the negativeness of avoiding the purchase of a product or service. For example, ads for Quick Lube oil-change service remind drivers that failure to change a car's oil and filter regularly can cause expensive auto repairs later. In an alternative strategy, marketers restructure a negative situation into a positive one to make it more attractive. For example, most heads of households want neither to risk financial ruin for their loved ones in the event of death nor to pay the high costs of life insurance. Recognizing this, many life insurance firms create combination insurance and investment programs to shift the focus from policy costs and death to retirement income and return-on-investment.

avoidance–avoidance conflict
a situation in which a person faces a choice between two undesirable alternatives

Now we shift our attention to a related and equally important topic in human motivation—that of emotions. We investigate the significant role they play in shaping our purchasing behavior as well as examine their influential place in the design of marketing strategy.

Emotions

Humans are emotional creatures.[33] Our behavior is influenced to a great extent by **emotions** such as love, fear, anger, envy, surprise, loneliness, sorrow, and happiness. Even the goals we select are chosen in the context of our emotional

emotion
a feeling state such as joy or sorrow

states. Everybody has experienced emotional motivation. Emotions are evolutionary adaptations, as they enhance our ability to experience and evaluate our environment. We sometimes visit malls, department stores, and shopping Web sites to alleviate boredom.[34] At other times, we contribute to charitable causes out of compassion for the less fortunate.

The significance of the topic of emotions to marketers stems from the realization that stirring consumers' emotions can be a powerful strategy in product and service promotions. American Greetings, Inc., and Hallmark, the greeting card giants, successfully use emotional themes to sell their cards. Similarly, ads from florists such as FTD and 800-FLOWERS suggest sending flowers as a delightful means of expressing emotions. Music recording companies use the emotion of nostalgia to sell golden oldies. The movie industry stresses emotions to bring back older movies such as *Gone with the Wind* and *The Wizard of Oz.* Television shows from the 1970s and 1980s return with cinematic makeovers. So far, consumers have seen shows such as *Scooby Do, Starsky and Hutch, Miami Vice, Lost in Space,* and *The Beverly Hillbillies.* Carmakers such as Volkswagen have reintroduced popular older models such as the VW Beetle to capitalize on nostalgic feelings toward the original Bug. Advertisers have been known to recycle ads from the past. Retro campaigns have been run for brands such as Energizer batteries, using the familiar Energizer Bunny who just keeps going and going and going, as well as for Oscar Meyer wieners, Aqua Velva (aftershave), and Reese's Peanut Butter Cup.[35] Other products or services for which emotions have successfully been tapped to enhance sales include Mickey Mouse pajamas, Buggs Bunny and Mr. Men T-shirts, Strawberry Shortcake cartoons, more superheros, "classic" cars, rock and pop music (on vinyl, CD, or live), furniture, and clothing.

For many consumers, a major part of the appeal in product acquisitions is the emotional value the product offers. In purchasing or receiving a gift, for example, it is often not the monetary worth of the gift that determines its value, but rather the emotions that the gift conveys. Many of us also attach varied emotions to our possessions. For example, we may have a favorite pen, book, CD, or may keep some memorabilia of our favorite athlete or movie star. When we travel, we often buy souvenirs from the places we visit and tend to stay in accommodations where we have had fond memories. In realizing these tendencies, marketers attempt to establish connections between their specific product or service and emotions—a strategy known as *bonding.*[36] Through this strategy, it becomes possible to stimulate the need for a specific product or brand simply by stirring the emotions that the marketer has successfully connected to it.

THE NATURE OF HUMAN EMOTIONS

For years, emotions were considered the base remnants of humans' animal selves imprisoned in primitive portions of the brain. Other thinkers have regarded emotions as ineffable ingredients of the human spirit, too elusive to capture. Recently, scientists have begun to capitalize on advances in brain

Global Opportunity

Honeydew Melon Wrapped in Black Velvet

Japanese consumers are much more attuned to emotional variables of products compared to their U.S. counterparts. The visual and graphic presentation of what they purchase is of vital importance to them. For example, one of the prime differences between Japanese and U.S. consumers is the way the former approach packaging. To them, design of the package is regarded as an essential motivational aspect of merchandising. Packaging is not considered a frivolous add-on to a product but rather an integral part of it. This view explains why a Japanese boutique would sell a single honeydew melon wrapped in black velvet or why a department store offers customers loose tea packed in crystal jars adorned with silk flowers. Everything in Japan is seen from the perspective of design. In a Japanese restaurant, for example, the entire atmosphere is designed to please the eye. The restaurant's menu, its interior decor, the food on the plate, and the uniform of waiters and waitresses all reflect meticulous attention to the emotional aspects of design.

One U.S. company selling rice crackers in Japan learned its lesson on emotions the hard way. Initially the firm packed its rice crackers in California-style bright-colored packs, with the word *California* printed on them. Japanese consumers liked the taste of the crackers, but the package flopped. When the package was changed to a Japanese-style design, complete with almond blossoms in pastel colors, the product flew off the shelf.[39]

Do emotional appeals affect consumers equally? What types of products lend themselves better to emotional appeals? Visit a Japanese Web site at www.jetro.go.jp. In your opinion, what other products or features of the Japanese society reflect that culture's appreciation for design and emotional presentation? Give specific examples.

scanning, pharmacology, and animal research to trace feelings along their journey through the corporeal landscape and the brain's complex circuitry. They are shaking up centuries-old notions of how humans feel, why they differ from each other emotionally, and what makes them feel the way they do.[37] Biology does not always support traditional notions regarding how feelings fit together. Happiness, for example, is not the opposite of sadness, and depression is not simply exaggerated sadness.

Some scientists believe that emotions are mainly a physical reaction to environmental events and situational stimuli. Emotions can be accompanied by physiological changes such as eye-pupil dilation, increased perspiration, more rapid breathing, increased heart rate and blood pressure, and elevated blood sugar levels. Physical symptoms of anger, for example, may include accelerated heartbeat, change in the rate of breathing, blushing of the face, and shaking. Emotions can trigger specific behaviors. Fear may cause one to flee; anger may trigger striking; grief may precipitate crying. Strong emotional responses, such as intense anger or fear, can prevent one from thinking clearly. Emotionally charged states (happiness, surprise, rage, distress) can amplify positive and negative experiences. Later, recollection of these events can affect individuals' subsequent behavior.[38] Memories of a pleasant dinner with a close friend at a nice restaurant may cause an individual to frequent that place and recommend it to others.

EMOTION VERSUS MOOD

mood
an individual's current
frame of mind

Whereas emotions entail an individual's response to particular stimuli in the environment, mood entails a temporary feeling state or frame of mind.[40] Moods are already present when consumers experience ads, retail stores, products, services, and brands.[41] For example, a person can be in a good mood due to receiving a promotion or in a bad mood due to problems experienced at one's place of work. These moods could have a bearing on whether or not consumers shop, when and where they shop, and whether they shop alone or with others.

Mood also influences the way we respond to shopping environments and cues, such as point-of-purchase displays and how long we remain in a store.[42] Retailers often try to *create* a mood for shoppers, even though customers enter the store with preexisting moods. For example, fragrance counters in some department stores are sprayed with perfume scents to create a mood. Likewise, in an online environment, the use of color, music, and animation all combine to put visitors in a positive and receptive frame of mind. When selling homes, realtors have been known to ask current occupants to bake a loaf of bread in the oven before agents show the home to prospective buyers. The smell of fresh-baked bread can create a positive mood due to associations with fond childhood memories. Consumers in a positive mood tend to recall more information about a specific brand than those in a negative mood. However, it is unlikely that attempts to induce a positive mood toward that brand at the point of purchase via background music or other means would exert a noticeable impact on its selection by consumers unless a previously stored evaluation of it already existed.[43]

Research suggests that being in a good mood can facilitate flexibility in a person's thinking, enhance the recall of stimuli, encourage someone to seek variety, and increase his or her willingness to try new things.[44]

When our mood is elevated, we tend to process information in detail, which leads to greater elaboration and recall.[45] Consumers engaged in the *internal search* stage of the decision process (sifting through memory for product knowledge) are likely to recall mood-compatible information, feelings, and experiences.[46] Consequently, marketers who put consumers in a good mood by using humor or pleasing visuals may enhance recall of positive product attributes. Isen and Means suggest that mood influences decision-making processes. They argue that when making purchase decisions, individuals who are in a positive mood tend to do so more efficiently.[47] For example, such persons are unlikely to waste time in reviewing information already examined.

From a consumer behavior perspective, some products seem to have mood-altering properties. Fragrances, alcohol, and tobacco are but some examples. It has also been observed that people sometimes use consumption to manage their moods. Cuba's Fidel Castro, the former president of Cuba, is reported to have said that he smoked a cigar under two circumstances: to celebrate when he was in a good mood and to console himself when he was in a bad mood. People in elevated moods also report a greater willingness to spend. On the other hand, people in bad moods tend to be more willing to spend on items with mood-elevating properties, such as chocolates and alcoholic beverages.

MARKETING AND PROMOTIONAL
APPLICATIONS OF EMOTION

According to McClelland, emotional arousal is the primary energizing force behind consumer behavior.[48] Emotionally toned ads that attempt to stimulate a positive affective response rather than provide information or logical arguments can therefore be effective motivators in this view. Consumers seek products whose primary or secondary benefits are emotional. Many products and services (movies, video games, many electronic gadgets and Web sites, and exotic travel destinations) offer emotion as a primary benefit. Other products offer emotion as a secondary benefit. Cars provide transportation and prestige; laptops offer productivity and convenience.[49] Acknowledging this fact, marketing communicators employ emotion within promotional campaigns in a variety of ways.

Ad campaigns frequently use emotions that directly relate to the product attributes and benefits. Many products offer emotional as well as utilitarian benefits. To illustrate, Cartier wristwatches, depicted in Figure 7.12, connote achievement, success, and distinction as well as denote time of day.

Other campaigns use emotions that do not directly relate to the product or its benefits. The goal of these remote emotional appeals is to increase the effectiveness of persuasive communications by increasing attention to the messages or making them more memorable. For example, humor has been used to sell

Courtesy of Cartier International

Figure 7.12

Ads like this one from Cartier, showing an impressive-looking watch, emphasize emotional buying motives such as beauty, distinctiveness, and prestige to raise consumer's interest in, and desire for, the brand.

products that aren't funny. Sex has been used to sell numerous products ranging from beverages and toothpastes to clothing and automobiles. Often, however, humor and sex have little or nothing to do with the goods being advertised.

HOW EMOTIONAL ADS WORK

Emotional ads trigger physiological and psychological reactions that can be both positive and negative. The goal of marketers, of course, is to get consumers to attribute an experienced pleasantness—benefits and satisfaction—to brand attributes. Some evidence suggests that when viewing ads, consumers can experience and respond to very low, but detectable, levels of certain emotions.[50] The perception of these emotions, even at these minimal levels, may affect cognition and behavior.[51]

It has been proposed that the goal of emotional advertising is bonding. As mentioned earlier, **bonding** involves connecting the consumer and the product through an emotional tie.[52] Through this link, it becomes possible to activate the need for the product simply by stirring the relevant emotion. Consider, for example, the well-established tie between individuals, red roses, and love. Consumers are likely to purchase red roses when love emotions are stirred in certain circumstances or on special occasions such as Valentine's Day or Sweetest Day. Emotional appeals also appear to hold the potential for enhancing the chance that a message will be perceived. Emotional ads can enhance attitude formation or change by increasing the marketer's ability to attract and hold attention. Viewers may be more apt to attend to ads that employ positive or even negative emotions than to neutral ads.

Similarly, emotional ads can amplify mental processing and increase consumer involvement with the product. For example, a Budweiser commercial shows two Dalmatian puppies exchanging envious glares as one gets to ride in a Budweiser beer wagon. Another commercial from Nike puts golfers in the shoes of skateboarders as they putt in fear of being chased off the greens by police. And an Australian public service announcement gets its message across as the drunk driving death of a father and his son is reenacted in shocking detail. By heightening a viewer's state of physiological and psychological arousal, emotional ads may receive more thorough processing and be remembered better than neutral ads.[53]

MEASURING EMOTION

Researchers have been employing a variety of verbal, visual, and psychological response tools to measure consumers' emotional responses to advertising. There are verbal measurement scales that involve extensive adjective checklists that consumers complete. These types, however, are often viewed as lengthy and time consuming for attaining the desired results. Visual measurement tools are also available and are done via handheld dial-turning instruments that consumers manipulate while watching the commercials being tested.

The PAD (Pleasure-Arousal-Dominance) Semantic Differential Scale devised by Mehrabian and Russell is currently the most widely used and validated instrument for measuring emotional response. The PAD Scale is based on sets of emotion-denoting adjective pairs that tap into the intended emotion. For

bonding

the connecting of a consumer and a product through an emotional tie

example, "Happy–Sad" is used to assess levels of *pleasure*. The Self-Assessment Manikin (SAM) represents another method of measuring emotional responses. SAM depicts each PAD dimension with a graphic character arranged along a continuous nine-point scale. For *pleasure*, SAM ranges from a smiling happy figure to a frowning unhappy figure. For *arousal*, SAM ranges from sleepy with eyes closed to excited with eyes wide open. The *dominance* scale shows SAM ranging from a tiny figure representing a feeling of being submissive to a large figure representing an in-control sort of feeling. The correlations between scores obtained through SAM and those obtained from the PAD Semantic Differential procedure were impressive for all the studies that have been undertaken.[54]

In addition, BBDO Advertising Agency developed another method of gauging emotions based on facial expressions. This technique, known as the Emotional Measurement System (EMS), can be employed to gauge the emotions that an ad triggers. To test an ad, subjects are instructed to sort swiftly through 53 pictures and set aside those that reflect how they feel when viewing an ad under study. The percent of subjects that selects particular pictures yields a profile of viewers' emotional response to the test ad.[55] Four samples of facial expression photos from BBDO's EMS appear in Figure 7.13.

Throughout this chapter, we have seen that motivating consumers is a fundamental purpose of the marketing effort. The challenge for marketers lies in activating human motives and in getting consumers to perceive products and services as goals. Not all motivational appeals are equally capable of generating consumer response. Although the motivations underlying some purchases are quite simple, other purchases are influenced by more complex motivations.

One of the major factors that influences our tendency to respond to different motivational appeals is our personality. All of us have our own ways of dealing with the environment. These behavior patterns are unique to ourselves. Whether or not motivational appeals such as fantasy, sex, wish fulfillment, escape, fun, fear, guilt, and so forth have an influence on us is governed to a large extent by our personality and how we give meaning to the world around us. The next chapter examines the way our personality develops and how personality, together with our lifestyle and self-concept, shapes our consumption patterns.

Figure 7.13

These four photos of facial expressions from BBDO's EMS depict the emotions of surprise, happiness-playfulness, disgust, and distraction. Respondents use these and other similar photos to express how they feel about an ad or a product.

A Cross-Functional Point of View

The topics of motivation and emotion have a number of implications for business disciplines other than marketing. Relevant issues might include

- **Law and Ethics:** For many years, spring break has been associated with trips to beach towns for sun, surf, parties, and flirting. Unfortunately, a number of tour operators are subtly promoting the idea that foreign cities provide a haven for underage American students to drink and even take drugs without running afoul of the law. One company selling tours to college students is touting trips to Mexico, where the drinking age is 18 and is "rarely" enforced. Another operator promotes its tours by offering "50 hours of free drinking" over 7 days. On the travel Web site StudentSpringBreak.com, students are encouraged to visit Amsterdam during spring break, which the site calls a "pot-smoker's paradise" due to its liberal drug laws.

- **Business Strategy:** Creativity and product innovations are the core of the strategy employed by 3M to remain a market leader. The company set a goal for each of its 40 divisions to generate at least 25 percent of its income from products introduced within the last 5 years. To accomplish this objective, 3M motivates every employee, not just the firm's engineers, to become a "product champion." The company allows employees to spend up to 15 percent of their time working on projects of personal interest. Once a new idea created by a product champion appears promising, the project is placed in the hands of a multidisciplinary venture team headed by the product champion. Moreover, the company hands out its Golden Step awards each year to the venture teams whose new products earn more than $2 million in U.S. sales within 3 years of their introduction. If this strategy is so successful for 3M, why don't more companies follow it?

- **Finance:** The intense competition between credit card companies has prompted all of them to look for creative means to get customers to favor one card over others. For example, many of them no longer charge an annual fee for the card. Some offer cash rebates based on charged purchases, whereas others offer an initial low annual percentage rate (APR) and encourage users to transfer high-rate credit card balances to the specific card being promoted. Some offer long-term low APRs calculated on the basis of the Prime plus a modest interest rate, whereas others motivate users by perks, such as travel rewards, accident and luggage insurance, and auto rental insurance when the card is used for paying the charges. Still others offer picture-personalized as well as affinity cards and supply 24-hour toll-free phone numbers for services such as security, road and travel, and merchandising. By making it so easy for most people to get credit, some wonder if this accessibility is desirable in our society.

These issues, and a host of others like them, serve to show that the topics of motivation and emotion transcend the field of marketing to other business disciplines.

Summary

Motivation is a state of the individual in which bodily energy is mobilized and directed in a selective fashion toward states of affairs in the external environment, called goals. Motives can be conscious or unconscious. They can be based on needs that have a biological or psychological origin. In addition, motives can be classified as high versus low urgency, positive versus negative polarity, intrinsic versus extrinsic, or rational versus emotional.

Needs or requirements can become motives, which, in turn, lead individuals toward action. For marketers, it is necessary to both arouse consumers and direct them toward specific products, services, or brands, which consumers are persuaded to perceive as goals. Desires are steeped in fantasies rather than reasoning and refer to belief-based passions that involve longing, yearning, and fervently wishing for something.

A number of theories attempt to explain human motivation. These include instinct, drive, arousal, and cognitive theories. Instinct theories suggest that the origins of human motivation are innate and reflect adaptation of species to the environment. Drive theories suggest that disturbances, disharmony, or imbalances of an individual's body systems tend to be reduced or eliminated by means of an automatic and internal homeostatic mechanism, which seeks to rectify the disequilibrium. Arousal theory suggests that individuals seek stimulation instead of trying to avoid it. It also suggests that there exists an optimal stimulation level that individuals seek to maintain. Cognitive theories view humans as rational, intelligent creatures who have the mental capability to pursue goals they set for themselves. Other views of motivation include Maslow's self-actualization theory, which rank-ordered five basic human needs, and social motives theories, which list a number of social needs as the basis of human motivation. As individuals attempt to satisfy their needs and attain their goals, motivational conflicts may arise.

Emotions are distinguishable, relatively strong, and largely involuntary feelings that arise in response to particular stimuli in the environment. Promotional strategies employ emotions in a number of ways. Although ads often use emotions that relate to product attributes and benefits, some ads attempt to increase the effectiveness of persuasive messages by using emotions that do not directly relate to the product, its features, or its benefits. Emotional ads not only try to trigger positive physiological and psychological consumer responses, they also attempt to achieve bonding; that is, to get consumers to somehow *connect* with the product or brand.

Emotions can be measured in a variety of ways. One method involves extensive adjective checklists that consumers complete. Another is accomplished by using visual measurement tools that allow consumers to manipulate a handheld dial to record their feelings while viewing ads or commercials. However, the PAD Semantic Differential Scale along with The Self Assessment Manikin (SAM) are currently the most widely used tools to measure emotions. Emotions can also be measured by decoding facial expressions via use of the EMS Facial Photo System developed by BBDO Advertsing Agency.

Review Questions

1. It has been proposed that four key elements of motivation are needs, motives, goals, and desires. Briefly explain each, and show how these four elements overlap or interact in producing a motivated state.

2. Two of the theories that attempt to conceptualize human motivation are instinct theory and cognitive theory. Briefly explain each, and compare and contrast their basic tenets.

3. One of the assumptions made by arousal theories of motivation is the tendency of consumers to seek stimulation. In this regard, these theories classify consumers into *high versus low* sensation seekers. Explain these typologies and show how marketers can benefit from knowledge of such consumer classifications.

4. In the sphere of motivational conflict, Lewin identified three common types of conflict. What are these three types of motivational conflict? How do these types of conflict relate to the field of consumer behavior? Explain through an example.

5. Distinguish and contrast between human emotions and moods. What causes each to come about? What implications do these two states hold for marketers?

Discussion Questions

1. Legal gambling has been an effective method for many states to raise revenue without raising income or property taxes. Several states have banded together to create superlotteries. What motivational influences can be used to entice prospective ticket buyers? Discuss the ethical aspects of encouraging people to gamble. How would you counter social critics who argue against government involvement in encouraging people to gamble?

2. The success of companies such as Hallmark cards, 1-800-SEND-FTD (flowers), and firms that bronze children's shoes can be traced to emotional responses on the part of consumers. Discuss.

3. Many manufacturers use cause marketing (a practice in which a company donates a portion of sales proceeds to support a cause in the public's interest) as a method to motivate consumers to purchase their brands of products and services. What is the basis behind the success of this strategy?

Cross-Functional Debate

In reference to the chapter opening vignette on gambling, assume that you are responsible for managing a state lottery. Unexpectedly, spokespeople from many special-interest groups begin to attack the lottery on the grounds that it siphons money from those who can least afford to play. In view of the crisis, the media pick up on the debate. As a state lottery manager, you are being interviewed by the media and are given an opportunity to defend the role of the lottery in raising funds needed by the state. What points would you make in defense of the lottery? How are critics of the lottery likely to counter your defense?

Frequency Program for a Car Rental Company

It was about 10:00 on a Wednesday morning in January when Deirdre Girard, principal of PreVision Marketing Inc., along with two of her staff consultants, was getting ready to head to the company's conference room to meet with two executives from a large national car rental company. PreVision Marketing Inc. is a consulting firm that has designed hundreds of customer retention programs for clients such as U.S. West, Toys "Я" Us, Safeway, and Nissan. Ms. DeMoranville, the promotion director of the car rental company, and Mr. Wagle, the company's national sales director, were paying a visit to PreVision to discuss the possibility of developing a frequency marketing program for their firm.

As the executives settled in their seats in the elegant conference room, Ms. Girard introduced the guests and welcomed them to the company's headquarters. Ms. DeMoranville began the conversation by explaining the purpose of their visit. "Thank you for giving us this opportunity to speak with you today regarding our need for a frequency marketing program. As you know, our company is in the car rental business...a competitive business to say the least. Until now, we haven't had a frequency program that we can call our own. A few years ago, we signed an agreement with a domestic airline to offer discounts to its customers when they rent our cars. Of course, the benefit from this program was mutual, but I wouldn't call the program a smashing success when it comes to retaining customers. That is why we hope that with your expertise and cooperation, we can develop an effective reward program that offers our customers benefits capable of creating repeat business."

Mr. Wagle, who up to this point was listening in while jotting down some notes on a scrap of paper, joined the conversation. "At the start, I would like to say that our company would be leery of programs that offer customers the moon without being able to deliver. I cringe every time I think of the Pepsi fiasco a few years ago with the Harrier jet. A business student bought enough Pepsi stuff with redemption points to qualify for the jet shown in TV commercials. Pepsi, of course, couldn't deliver because it is illegal for a civilian to own a national defense weapon. We would like a down-to-earth program...something that our customers would find exciting and rewarding, yet something we could also deliver without losing our shirt."

"Just to know where you're coming from," asked Ms. Girard, "how do you feel about programs like the ones used by credit card companies, such as Citi AAdvantage? These credit card companies offer free deals including air travel, entertainment, food, retail merchandise, and much more from a wide array of national corporate partners of the credit card companies."

"In my opinion," responded Ms. DeMoranville, "there are two problems with these programs. One problem I often read about is that if every customer used the free travel miles, the airline industry would go bankrupt. That is why these offers are now being adjusted to allow for the expiration of these air miles after a certain date, as well as to restrict their use to certain dates." She paused for a moment and then added, "The second problem I see is that many customers are not even aware of most of the deals extended to them by such companies. Moreover," she continued, "they seldom take advantage of these offers; nor do they even care to sign up to qualify for the rewards"...These two issues concern me, and we will have to consider them in any retention program we choose to adopt."

The discussion went on for another two hours and a number of relevant points were raised and discussed. Finally, as Ms. DeMoranville looked at her watch and realized it was time to break for lunch, she remarked, "We have a proposition for your company. We would like you to come up with a number of ideas for a retention program specifically designed for our car rental business. Perhaps then we can get together again and discuss which ideas seem to be most workable for our purposes. We have about six months to come up with a program before our fiscal year starts in July. We'll need to allocate funds in our budget for this program in the new fiscal year. Do you think this leaves you sufficient time to work on the project?"

As PreVision executives confirmed their intent to promptly and diligently take on the project, Ms. Girard knew in her heart that it would pose a challenge. Her expertise had taught her that merely copying another company's customer retention program never works and that unless the loyalty program was totally customized for the specific company, it would most likely be doomed to fail.

Questions

1. Do you agree with Ms. DeMoranville that some customer retention programs such as those used by credit card companies are too broad for both their sponsors and patrons?
2. In your opinion, what are the psychological/motivational forces that render many of the customer retention programs successful? What reasons underlie the failure of others?
3. What features would a retention program designed specifically for the car rental company include? Please cite features that you personally consider to be most enticing.

Notes

1. Sean Flynn, "Is Gambling Good for America?" *Parade* (May 20, 2007), www.parade.com/articles/editions/2007/edition_05-20-2007/gambling.
2. Theodore M. Newcomb, Ralph H. Turner, and Philip E. Converse, *Social Psychology* (New York: Holt, Rinehart and Winston, 1965), p. 22.
3. Christine Bittar, "Allergan Set to Make Juvederm a Name," *MediaPost Publications* (January 25, 2007).
4. Jack W. Brehm, "Psychological Reactance: Theory and Applications," in Thomas K. Skrull (ed.), *Advances in Consumer Research* 16 (Provo, UT: Association for Consumer Research, 1989), pp. 72–75.
5. Wroe Alderson, "Needs, Wants, and Creative Marketing," *Cost and Profit Outlook* 8 (September 1955), pp. 1–3.
6. Gordon Fairclough, "Casket Stores Offer Bargains to Die For," *Wall Street Journal* (February 19, 1997), pp. B1, B10.
7. Scott Rockwood, "For Better Ad Success, Try Getting Emotional," *Marketing News* (October 21, 1996), p. 4.
8. Melvin T. Copeland, *Principles of Merchandising* (New York: A. W. Shaw Company, 1924), pp. 155–67; see also Carol Morgan and Doron Levy, "Why We Kick the Tires," *Brandweek* 38, no. 36 (September 29, 1997), pp. 24–28; Bill Bachrach, "How to Influence Human Behavior," *Executive Excellence* 12, no. 1 (January 1995), pp. 12–13.
9. Morris B. Holbrook and Elizabeth C. Hirschman, "The Experiential Aspects of Consumption: Consumer Fantasies, Feelings, and Fun," *Journal of Consumer Research* 9 (September 1982), pp. 132–40.
10. Dr. Henry H. Lodge, "Why Emotions Keep You Well," *Parade* (June 17, 2007), p. 17.
11. Becky Ebenkamp, "Color Coordination," *Brandweek* (January 12, 1998).
12. William N. Dember, "The New Look in Motivation," *American Scientist* (December 1965), pp. 409–27.
13. Chester R. Wasson, Frederick D. Sturdivant, and David H. McConoughy, *Competition and Human Behavior* (New York: Appleton-Century-Crofts, 1968), pp. 27–28.
14. Alain Jolibert and Gary Baumgartner, "Values, Motivations, and Personal Goals: Revisted," *Psychology & Marketing* 14, no. 7 (October 1997), pp. 675–88.
15. "Nielsen Recap of 2008 Super Bowl Advertising (February 7, 2008), http://biz.yahoo.com/prnews/080207/nyth105b.html?.v=1.
16. PR Newswire, Nielsen's Recap of 2008 Super Bowl Advertising (February 7, 2008), www.sys-con.com/read/497950.html
17. Russell W. Belk, Güliz Ger, and Søren Askegaard, "Consumer Desire in Three Cultures: Results from Projective Research," *Advances in Consumer Research* 24 (1997), pp. 24–28; Russell W. Belk, Güliz Ger, and Søren Askegaard, "Metaphors of Consumer Desire," *Advances in Consumer Research* 23 (1996), pp. 368–73.
18. "Violent Video Games—Psychologists Help Protect Children from Harmful Effects," www

psychologymatters.org/videogames.html; "Violence in the Media—Psychologists Help Protect Children from Harmful Effects," www.psychologymatters.org/mediaviolence.html; Jeanne B. Funk, "Children and Violent Video Games: Are There 'High Risk' Players?" http://culturalpolicy.uchicago.edu/conf2001/papers/funk1.html.

19. T. Baranski and J. Batt, "Women and Advertising: A Little Too Sexy?" *Synergy*, www.bgsu.edu/departments/tcom/faculty/ha/sp2003/gp1/Article1.html (accessed February 20, 2008).

20. Lynette S. Unger and James M. Stearns, "The Use of Fear and Guilt Messages in Television Advertising: Issues and Evidence," in P. E. Murphy et al. (eds.), 1983 *AMA Educators' Proceedings* (Chicago: American Marketing Association, 1983).

21. Joseph D. Brown and Russell G. Wahlers, "The Environmentally Concerned Consumer: An Exploratory Study," Journal of Marketing Theory & Practice 6, no. 2 (Spring 1998), pp. 39–47; Laura M. Litvan, "Going 'Green' in the '90s," Nation's Business 83, no. 2 (February 1995), pp. 30–32; "Packaging Assumes a Key Role in Green Cosmetics Image," Drug & Cosmetic Industry 156, no. 2 (February 1995), pp. 34, 100; Maria K. Magnusson et al., "Choice of Organic Foods Is Related to Perceived Consequences for Human Health and to Environmentally Friendly Behavior," *ScienceDirect* (February 2003), pp. 109–117.

22. Matthew Klien, "Top Lines," American Demographics (October 1998), pp. 12–13; Tia Travel Statistics and Trends, www.tia.org/Travel/travel/traveltrends.asp-81k (accessed February 20, 2008).

23. George Kish and Gregory V. Donnenwerth, "Interests and Stimulation Seeking," *Journal of Counseling Psychology* 16 (1969), pp. 551–56; Nessim Hanna and John Wagle, "Who Is Your Satisfied Customer?" *The Journal of Consumer Marketing* 6 (Winter 1989), pp. 53–61; Richard Oliver, "Effect of Expectation and Disconfirmation on Post-Exposure Product Evaluations: An Alternative Interpretation," *Journal of Applied Psychology* 62, no. 4 (1977), pp. 480–86; Nessim Hanna, Rick Ridnour, and A. H. Kizilbash, "Optimum Stimulation Level: Evidence Relating to the Role of OSL in Predicting Sales Personnel Performance," *Journal of Professional Services Marketing* 10, no. 1 (1993), pp. 65–75; Jan Benedict, E. M. Steenkamp, and Hans Baumgartner, "The Role of Optimum Stimulation Level in Exploratory Consumer Behavior," *The Journal of Consumer Research* 19 (December 1992), pp. 434–48.

24. Peter Piazza, "Microsoft Will Lure Students with Free Software," *Data Storage Today* (February 18, 2008); Becca Madder, "Wireless Companies Boost Efforts to Lure Young Buyers," *Business Journal* (November 30, 2001); Jessica Silver-Greenberg, "College Students Majoring in Credit Card Debt," *Business Week* (September 5, 2007).

25. M. Zuckerman, "Development of a Sensation Seeking Scale," *Journal of Consulting Psychology* 28 (1964), pp. 477–82; "Form V Sensation Seeking Scale: SS" (Zuckerman, 1979), in William O. Bearden, Richard G. Netemeyer, and Mary F. Mobley, *Handbook of Marketing Scales* (Newbury Park, CA: Sage, 1993), pp. 172–76; "Measuring Sensation Seeking," NIDA Notes (July–August 1995), www.nida.nih.gov/NIDA_Notes/ NNVol10N4/MeasureSens.html (accessed January 8, 1998).

26. Abraham H. Maslow, "A Theory of Human Motivation," *Psychological Review* 50 (1943), pp. 370–96; Abraham H. Maslow, *Motivation and Personality* (New York: Harper & Row, 1954); Abraham H. Maslow, *Motivation and Personality*, 2nd ed. (New York: Harper & Row, 1970); Abraham H. Maslow, *Toward a Psychology of Being* (New York: Van Nostrand Reinhold, 1968), pp. 189–215; Rudy Schrocer, "Maslow's Hierarchy of Needs as a Framework for Identifying Emotional Triggers," *Marketing Review* 46, no. 5 (February 1991), pp. 26, 28.

27. David Glen Mick and Corinne Faure, "Consumer Self-gifts in Achievement Contexts: The Role of Outcomes, Attributions, Emotions, and Deservingness," *International Journal of Research in Marketing* 15, no. 4 (October 1998), pp. 293–307.

28. A. Henry Murray, *An Exploration in Personality: A Clinical Experimental Study of Fifty Men of College Age* (London: Oxford University Press, 1938), pp. 80–83; A. Henry Murray, *Explorations in Personality* (New York: Oxford University Press, 1938); Bernard Weiner, *Theories of Motivation* (Chicago: Markham, 1972), pp. 173–74; Stuart J. Agres and Morty Bernstein, "Cognitive and Emotional Elements of Persuasion," in David W. Stewart (ed.), *Proceedings of the Division of Consumer Psychology* (Nashville, TN: American Psychological Association, 1985), pp. 1–2; Karl W. Jackson and Dennis J. Shea, "Motivation Training in Perspective," in Walter Nord (ed.), *Concepts and Controversy in Organizational Behavior* (Pacific Palisades, CA: Goodyear Publishing, 1972), p. 106; David C. McClelland, *Studies in Motivation* (New York: Appleton-Century-Crofts, 1955); David C. McClelland, "Business Drive and National Achievement," *Harvard Business Review* (July–August 1962), p. 99; "Achievement Motivation Can Be Developed," *Harvard Business Review* 5, no. 24 (November–December 1965), p. 178; Abraham K. Korman, *The Psychology of Motivation* (Upper Saddle River, NJ: Prentice Hall, 1974), p. 190; David McClelland, J. W. Atkinson, R. A. Clark, and E. L. Lowell, *The Achievement Motive* (New York: Appleton-Century-Crofts, 1953); David C. McClelland,

Personality (New York: William Sloane, 1951); David C. McClelland, "Achievement and Entrepreneurship: A Longitudinal Study," *Journal of Personality and Social Psychology* (April 1965), pp. 1, 389–92; W. J. McGuire, "Psychological Motives and Communications Gratification," in J. G. Blumer and C. Katz (eds.), *The Uses of Mass Communications: Current Perspectives on Gratification Research* (Newbury Park, CA: Sage, 1974), pp. 167–96; and W. J. McGuire, "Some Internal Psychological Forces Influencing Consumer Choice," *Journal of Consumer Research* (March 1976), pp. 302–19.

29. Murray, *Explorations in Personality*; Murray, *An Exploration in Personality: A Clinical Experimental Study of Fifty Men of College Age*.

30. Mick and Faure, "Consumer Self-gifts in Achievement Contexts: The Role of Outcomes, Attributions, Emotions, and Deservingness."

31. "David McClelland's Motivational Needs Theory," *Business Balls*, www.businessballs.com/davidmcclelland.htm; "McClelland's Theory of Needs," *NetMBA*, www.netmba.com/mgmt/ob/motivation/mcclelland/.

32. Kurt Lewin, *A Dynamic Theory of Personality* (New York: McGraw-Hill, 1935).

33. Carroll Izard, *Human Emotion* (New York: Plenum Press, 1977); Marquis, "Our Emotions: Why We Feel the Way We Do; New Advances Are Opening Our Subjective Inner Worlds to Objective Study. Discoveries Are Upsetting Long-Held Notions."

34. R. A. Westbrook and W. C. Black, "A Motivation-Based Shopper Typology," *Journal of Retailing* (Spring 1985), pp. 78–103; T. C. O'Guinn and R. W. Belk, "Heaven on Earth," *Journal of Consumer Research* (September 1989), pp. 227–38; G. D. Mick, M. DeMoss, and R. J. Faber, "A Projective Study of Motivations and Meanings of Self-Gifts," *Journal of Retailing* (Summer 1992), pp. 122–44.

35. Karen Brooks, "Retro Hits and Myths," *Couriermail.com.au* (October 9, 2007); www.news.com.au/couriermail/story/0,23739,22557533-27197,00.html.

36. "Connecting Consumer and Product," *New York Times* (January 18, 1990), p. D19.

37. Marquis, "Our Emotions: Why We Feel the Way We Do; New Advances Are Opening our Subjective Inner Worlds to Objective Study. Discoveries Are Upsetting Long-Held Notions."

38. Joel B. Cohen and Charles S. Areni, "Affect and Consumer Behavior," in Harold H. Kassarjian and Thomas S. Robertson (eds.), *Perspectives in Consumer Behavior*, 4th ed., (Upper Saddle River, NJ: Prentice Hall, 1991), pp. 188–240; Madeline Johnson and George M. Zinkhan, "Emotional Responses to a Professional Service Encounter," *Journal of Service Marketing* 5 (Spring 1991), pp. 5–16.

39. Helen Chang, "New Packaging Boosts U. S. Food Sales in Asia," *Journal of Commerce* (May 31, 1989), p. A1; Alexander Besher, "Packaging, Design Aren't Frivolous in Japan," *Chronicle Features* (August 24, 1990), p. 26; Nessim Hanna and Tanuja Srivastava, "Cultural Aspects of Gift Giving: A Comparative Analysis of the Significance of Gift Giving in the U.S. and Japan," *World Marketing Congress Proceedings* VIII (1997), pp. 269–73.

40. Meryl Paula Gardner, "Mood States and Consumer Behavior: A Critical Review," *Journal of Consumer Research* 12 (December 1985), pp. 281–300; Robert A. Peterson and Matthew Sauber, "A Mood Scale for Survey Research," in Patrick E. Murphy et al. (eds.), 1983 *AMA Educators' Proceedings* (Chicago: American Marketing Association, 1983), pp. 409–14.

41. Barry J. Babin, William R. Darden, and Mitch Griffin, "Some Comments on the Role of Emotions in Consumer Behavior," in Robert P. Leone, V. Kumor, et al. (eds.), 1992 *AMA Educators' Proceedings* (Chicago: American Marketing Association, 1992), pp. 130–39; Patricia A. Knowles, Stephen J. Grove, and W. Jeffrey Burroughs, "An Experimental Examination of Mood Effects on Retrieval and Evaluation of Advertisement and Brand Information," *Journal of the Academy of Marketing Science* 21 (Spring 1993), pp. 135–42; Rajeev Batra and Douglas M. Stayman, " The Role of Mood in Advertising Effectiveness," *Journal of Consumer Research* (September 1990), pp. 203–14.

42. Gardner, "Mood States and Consumer Behavior: A Critical Review"; Ruth Belk Smith and Elaine Sherman, "Effects of Store Image and Mood on Consumer Behavior: A Theoretical and Empirical Analysis," in Leigh McAlister and Michael L. Rothschild (eds.), *Advances in Consumer Research* 20 (Provo, UT: Association for Consumer Research, 1993), p. 631.

43. Knowles, Grove, and Burroughs, "An Experimental Examination of Mood Effects on Retrieval and Evaluation of Advertisement and Brand Information."

44. Alice M. Isen, Paula M. Niedenthal, and Nancy Cantor, "An Influence of Positive Affect on Social Categorization," *Motivation and Emotion* 16, no. 1 (1992), pp. 65–78; Alice M. Isen, "Some Ways in Which Affect Influences Cognitive Processes: Implications for Advertising and Consumer Behavior," in Alice M. Tybout and P. Cafferata (eds.), *Advertising and Consumer Psychology* (Lexington, MA: Lexington Books, 1989), pp. 91–117; Barbara E. Kahn and Alice M. Isen, "The Influence of Positive Affect on Variety Seeking Among Safe, Enjoyable Products," *Journal of Consumer Research* 20, no. 2 (September 1993), pp. 257–70.

45. Isen, "Some Ways in Which Affect Influences Cognitive Processes: Implications for Advertising and Consumer Behavior," pp. 91–118.

46. Alice M. Isen, Thomas Shalker, Margaret Clark, and Lynn Karp, "Affect, Accessibility of Material in Memory and Behavior: A Cognitive Loop?" *Journal of Personality and Social Psychology* (January 1978), pp. 1–12; see also Edmund T. Rolls, "A Theory of Emotion and Its Application to Understanding the Neural Basis of Emotion," *Cognition & Emotion* 4, no. 3 (1990), pp. 182–84; Meryl Gardner, "Effects of Mood States on Consumer Information Processing," *Research in Consumer Behavior* 2 (1987), pp. 113–35; T. J. Olney, M. B. Holbrook, and R. Batra, "Consumer Responses to Advertising," *Journal of Consumer Research* (March 1991), pp. 440–53; S. P. Brown and D. M. Stayman, "Antecedents and Consequences of Attitude toward the Ad," *Journal of Consumer Research* (June 1992), pp. 34–51: G. Biehal, D. Stephens, and E. Curlo, "Attitude toward the Ad and Brand Choice," *Journal of Advertising* (September 1992), pp. 19–36; P. A. Stout and R. T. Rust, "Emotional Feelings and Evaluative Dimensions of Advertising," *Journal of Advertising* (March 1993), pp. 61–71; P. M. Homer, "The Mediating Role of Attitude toward the Ad," *Journal of Marketing Research* (February 1990), pp. 78–88; and B. Mittal, "The Relative Roles of Brand Beliefs and Attitude," *Journal of Marketing Research* (May 1990), pp. 209–19.

47. Alice M. Isen and Barbara Means, "The Influence of Positive Affect on Decision-Making Stategy," *Social Cognition* 2, no. 1 (1983), pp. 18–31; Carlos A. Estrada, Alice M. Isen, and Mark J. Young, "Positive Affect Improves Creative Problem Solving and Influences Reported Source of Practice Satisfaction in Physicians," *Motivation and Emotion* 18, no. 4 (1994), pp. 285–99.

48. Weiner, *Theories of Motivation*: Agres and Bernstein, "Cognitive and Emotional Elements of Persuasion"; Jackson and Shea, "Motivation Training in Perspective"; McClelland, *Studies in Motivation*; McClelland, "Business Drive and National Achievement"; "Achievement Motivation Can Be Developed"; Korman, *The Psychology of Motivation*; McClelland, Atkinson, Clark, and Lowell, *The Achievement Motive*; McClelland, *Personality*.

49. C. Campbell, The *Romantic Ethic and the Spirit of Modern Consumerism* (Oxford: Blackwell, 1987).

50. Julie Edell and Marian Burke, "The Power of Feelings in Understanding Advertising Effects," *Journal of Consumer Research* 14 (December 1987), pp. 421–33; Robert A. Westbrook, "Product/Consumption-Based Affective Responses and Postpurchase Processes," *Journal of Marketing Research* 24 (August 1987), pp. 258–70.

51. Chris Allen, Karen Machleit, and Susan Marine, "On Assessing the Emotionality of Advertising via Izard's Differential Emotions Scale," in Michael Houston (ed.), *Advances in Consumer Research* 15 (Provo, UT: Association for Consumer Research, 1988); Haim Mano, "Emotional States and Decision Making," in Marvin Goldberg et al. (eds.), *Advances in Consumer Research* 17 (Provo, UT: Association for Consumer Research, 1990), pp. 577–84.

52. "Connecting Consumer and Product," *New York Times* (January 18, 1990), p. D19.

53. M. Friestad and E. Thorson, "Emotion-Eliciting Advertising," in R. Lutz (ed.), *Advances in Consumer Research* 13 (Provo, UT: Association for Consumer Research, 1986), pp. 111–16.

54. John D. Morris, "Observation: SAM: The Self-Assessment Manikin," *Journal of Advertising Research* (November–December, 1995).

55. G. Levin, "Emotion Guides BBDO's Ad Tests," *Advertising Age* (January 29, 1990), p. 12.

Personality, Lifestyle, and Self-Concept

LEARNING OBJECTIVES

- To explore the various theoretical views of the meaning, nature, and development of personality.
- To grasp the basic tenets and marketing applications of a number of popular personality theories.
- To be able to compare and contrast selected basic personality theories.
- To recognize the role of lifestyle and psychographics in developing consumer typologies.
- To become familiar with the tools of AIO inventories as well as the VALS system for purposes of market segmentation.
- To analyze the importance of the self-concept and examine the way it influences consumer purchasing patterns.

KEY TERMS

personality
id
superego
ego
reality (objective) anxiety
neurotic anxiety
moral anxiety
defense mechanisms
fixation
neo-Freudian theory
compliance-aggressiveness-detachment
  (CAD) scale

trait theory
traits
personality tests
psychographics
AIO inventories
VALS
self-concept
extended-self
possible-self
self-product congruence
symbolic self-completion

From the dawn of history, physical beauty has been a valued goal. A variety of beauty practices have prevailed in various cultures over the ages, such as binding the feet; puncturing the ears, nose, and belly buttons; enlarging the lips; and tattooing the skin. Tombs in Egypt, for example, have revealed that women in the time of the Pharoahs used lip gloss, rouge, powder, eye shadow, nail polish, perfumes, and creams to enhance their natural beauty. Various cultures, as well as different periods of history, tend to subscribe to a desirable look or *ideal* of beauty. Present-day views regarding what is beautiful are very different from those of the past. In the United States, for example, the ideal figure of women has changed radically over the years. In contrast to the frail, underfed, and delicate look of women that prevailed in the nineteenth century, or the straightlaced look with corsets popular in the early twentieth century, today's beauty ideal is the healthy, vigorous, and relatively athletic look, but very thin and busty. By contrast, in the African country of Mauritania, being heavy is considered attractive. The heavier the woman is, the more desirable she is perceived by eligible men. Chances for marriage dramatically increase with gains in a woman's weight and size.

An individual's body image is an inseparable component of his or her concept of self. Body image is the subjective evaluation of one's physical appearance. In judging how attractive their physical self is, individuals compare how closely their look corresponds to the image that society values. Social comparison is a known human tendency. Consumers see idealized images in person, in advertising messages, in movies, and on television. Consciously or unconsciously, they compare themselves with these prototypes. The comparison often leads to dissatisfaction to the extent that self-perceptions do not match up with idealized images. Dissatisfaction has led, at least in our society, to the proliferation of products and services ranging from diet foods to exercise equipment, from cosmetics to plastic surgery, and from tanning salons to hairstylists. Many people willingly go to great lengths to change aspects of their physical selves. Recognizing this tendency, marketers frequently create insecurities in the minds of consumers regarding their appearance by emphasizing disparities between the real and ideal self. Consequently, consumers become vulnerable targets for purchasing the recommended product or service offerings.

Because advertising generates social comparisons, and advertisers tend to portray *better-off* others, such as happy, beautiful, or wealthy people, it has been censured by critics as a major cause of consumer dissatisfaction. Advertisers argue that temporary dissatisfaction is beneficial and constructive. It motivates consumers and stimulates them to buy products or use services that improve their appearance and eventually enhances their self-image and satisfaction with themselves.[1]

> *Do you agree with the assertion that advertisers' depictions of thin and attractive models in ads are ineffective and undesirable today because the practice causes unhappiness in many less-attractive women due to self-comparisons? Learn about models available for ads by visiting New Faces Models and Talent at the*

firm's Web site www.newfaces.com/ and Models.com at www.models.com In your opinion, would consumers respond more positively to ads that depict more "typical" and not-so-glamorous models? Would you expect men and women to respond similarly to such ads? Explain.

Although it seems natural today to think about consumers in terms of having self-concepts that they attempt to protect and enhance through the purchase of products and services, this concept is a relatively recent view of people. The significance of this view lies in the observation that consumers' feelings about themselves shape their consumption practices. Many products from clothes to cosmetics are bought because a person is attempting to manifest a positive attribute or hide a negative aspect of self.

In our social interaction with others, we tend to automatically assign them certain personality traits that we presume they possess.

Personality has been investigated from many different points of view. Freudian theory, for example, emphasizes a conflict system between competing forces within an individual's psyche. The trait approach, on the other hand, hypothesizes that sets of inner personal attributes distinguish one individual from another. Many other explanations of personality also prevail.

This chapter examines personality from a number of theoretical vantage points while underscoring their marketing implications. We also examine consumer lifestyles as a basis for segmenting markets, targeting prospects, and positioning products. We conclude by addressing the self-concept and its impact on consumer buying tendencies.

What Is Personality?

At one time or another, nearly everybody has gone on a blind date. Usually the first question posed to the matchmaker relates to what the prospective escort is like. "He [or she] has a great personality" is a frequent reply. After the date, however, one party may conclude that the companion had "no personality at all."

In casual conversations, the word *personality* often refers to whatever one individual observes in another person. In this sense, personality is the striking overall impression that a person leaves with others.[2]

The term *personality* is derived from *persona*, a Latin term for the masks worn by actors on stage in ancient Greek and Roman theater. In the absence of a standard definition, the following represents the authors' view of personality's structure and functioning:

Personality is the sum total of an individual's inner psychological attributes. It makes individuals what they are, distinguishes them from every other person, demonstrates their mode of adjustment to life's circumstances, and produces their unique, stable pattern of responding to environmental stimuli.

This definition highlights a number of properties that characterize personality. First, it is unique. Personality is one among many internal properties of individuals that, together with environmental factors, shape human behavior. Individuals appear to possess distinctive qualities or unique clusters of attributes that distinguish them from others. Personality is unique to each individual, and no two people are identical. Second, personality is consistent. The preceding definition acknowledges that considerable stability, consistency, and predictability permeate a person's personality. The attributes that distinguish an individual are reasonably consistent across diverse sets of circumstances. Personality is not, however, fixed or rigid. Third, personality is not static. It evolves as part of a gradual maturing process and may be further altered by abrupt or pivotal life events such as a career change, the conception or birth of a child, divorce, a serious accident, or the passing of a loved one.

Diversity of Personality Theories

Although personality theories offer fascinating insights into human nature, little agreement exists about how the topic of personality should be approached. The number of personality theories is as impressive as the variation among them. Acknowledging that psychologists offer many and diverse opinions concerning personality formation, Hall and Lindzey submit that "no substantive definition of personality can be applied with any generality" and that "personality is defined by the particular empirical concepts which are a part of the theory of personality employed by the observer."[3]

One view of personality assumes that humans possess traits that determine their personality. In other words, if an individual behaves in a sociable, adaptable, achievement-oriented, or independent manner, it is so because that person possesses the corresponding traits. A second view postulates that an individual's personality is the result of events experienced in the past, especially during childhood. Freud, for example, believed that parent–child relationships during the first five years of life largely determine adult personality. A third view proposes that personality reflects striving on the part of an individual to acquire rewards and avoid punishments in the here and now. Safe driving, for example, has its rewards. Drivers who prudently obey traffic regulations and hope to arrive at their destination safely without getting a traffic violation are viewed as possessing cautious personalities. A fourth view speculates that personality unfolds in the quest to achieve goals and someday realize one's inherent potential. Conscientious students, for example, may have ambitious career plans. In a fifth approach, some researchers attempt to link personality to birth order (firstborn child, middle child, last-born child, only child).[4] According to this view, individual personality differences arise from the family setting, as siblings compete for parental attention.[5]

In recent years, personality research has taken a new direction. Many psychologists have come to reject the notion that there are cross-situational consistencies in behavior. In other words, they no longer propose that there exist broad patterns of behavior that permeate *all* the circumstances we encounter. Rather, many researchers today propose that behavior is situational, determined by the circumstances that surround a specific event. Studies investigate specific issues (such as problem solving, information processing, impulse buying, and bargain hunting) in specific situations and study how various personalities interact with the unique set of circumstances in order to produce behavior. In this view, behavior is governed not by all-determining personality traits but rather by personality *styles* that tend to be exhibited in particular situations. For example, individuals are not equally susceptible to persuasion on *all* topics or from *all* information sources. Similarly, individuals who shop compulsively in one product category (such as buying antique furniture) or shopping environment (such as buying at flea markets) may or may not do so in other product categories or buying environments.

© 2009, JupiterImages, Inc.

Many individuals enjoy frequenting flea markets, where a large variety of products and antiques can be found at bargain prices.

Most psychologists do agree that personality is largely the social outgrowth of an individual's experiences with other people, events, and objects. These influences shape what and how people think, feel, act, communicate, desire, and dream. Marketers who understand the characteristics that consumers share in common and those that differentiate them may discover valuable insights for market segmentation, targeting, positioning, and design of promotional appeals. To investigate the relationship between personality and purchasing behavior, this chapter briefly explores Freudian, neo-Freudian, and trait personality theories.

Freudian Theory of Personality

From the dawn of history, humans have attempted to explain why behavior varies from one individual to another. Some researchers advocated that heredity underlies variations in human behavior, whereas others proposed physical features such as the size of a person's skull or skin color as the basis for these differences. Today, however, many believe that within the individual exists a segment of the mind, known as the *unconscious*, that has the power to affect their feelings and behaviors. This approach has its roots in the theories of Sigmund Freud.[6]

Ethical Dilemma

Cosmetic Psychopharmacology and Designer Personalities

Depression strikes an estimated 20 million adult Americans each year. Studies reveal that regardless of race, depression seems to affect about twice as many women as men. This can be caused by a number of factors, such as postpartum depression, which can strike women who otherwise would have not suffered a depression disorder.[10]

Many depressed individuals seek ways to reduce and manage stress. Although no drug can encapsulate happiness and provide solutions for all human problems, a number of by-prescription-only medications, such as Cymbalta, Zoloft, Lexapro, Paxil, Luvox, Remeron, and Effexor, as well as others, allow some persons to be the fully functioning individuals they could be if they were not troubled by depression, obsessive-compulsive disorders, or bulimia nervosa (an eating disorder).[11] In specific cases, some of these medications have also been used to treat phobias, mood swings, and premenstrual syndrome (PMS). These drugs relieve the symptoms of depression by increasing the availability of certain brain chemicals called neurotransmitters. It is believed that these brain chemicals can help improve patients' emotional state.[12]

Although the benefits of antidepressants are plausible, the media as well as pharmaceutical companies have heralded an era in which it would appear that altering a person's personality might be as easy as changing one's hair color. Sensational journalism and advertising have left many people with the false impression that so-called *personality pills* or *happy drugs* can provide a quick pick-me-up and create designer personalities. To some extent, drug companies themselves may have fostered this perception. For example, depressed Americans have been targeted with a number of direct-to-consumer (DTC) campaigns, the purpose of which is to offer help against depression. Commercials for Cymbalta tend to heighten awareness of depression by indicating a checklist of symptoms the company views as indicative of this condition. One such commercial enumerates where depression hurts, whom depression hurts, and how depression hurts. Another suggests physical or mental conditions that consumers should view as synonymous with depression. The commercial then directs consumers to ask their physicians about Cymbalta's role in overcoming these depressed feelings.[13] This elevated awareness has caused many to believe they suffer from depression, and has even reached preschoolers, who now constitute the fastest growing market for antidepressants.

Pharmaceutical companies have even gone a step further in promoting the use of antidepressants. There are now anti-depression medications for dogs and cats. Clomipramine, an anti-depression medication, has already gained FDA approval for both human and canine use. It is currently being used for canines suffering from "separation anxiety" when a dog finds the absence of its owner too much to bear.[14]

To learn more about depression, visit www.upliftprogram.com/depression_stats.html. *Some people believe that promotional campaigns to inform consumers about depression symptoms are merely self-fulfilling prophecies. By detailing the symptoms, many individuals come to identify with them and begin to feel they must be going through a state of depression. This belief then enhances sales of the drug. Do you agree or disagree. Why?*

Freudian psychoanalytic personality theory significantly influenced our awareness of self and the understanding of our human makeup. It has been said that Freud invented psychoanalysis and revolutionized twentieth-century notions about the life of the human mind. His wide-ranging collection of metaphors concerning the mental life of human beings has largely become common knowledge.[7] According to Freud, personality is a result of a dynamic struggle between inner psychological drives such as sex and aggression and social pressures such as moral and ethical codes. In addition, Freud believed that individuals are aware of only a limited number of the forces that truly drive their behavior.[8]

According to Freud, personality is a result of an interaction between the three components of personality: the id, the superego, and the ego. The **id** is an unconscious reservoir of human instincts that seeks pleasure and demands immediate satisfaction, and is not regulated by right or wrong. The **superego** is a largely unconscious repository of social, moral, and ethical codes that restricts how far a person can go to acquire goals and steers instinctive drives into acceptable avenues. The **ego** is the conscious control center that mediates the id's uninhibited impulses and the superego's constraints. Each person must achieve balance as the id's desires encounter the ego's logic and the superego's prohibitions. The ego pursues the goals of the id in a socially responsible manner. In the Freudian model, sexually related biological motivation and continual conflict between the id, superego, and ego permeate human personality. The way children manage conflict determines their adult personality, and unresolved childhood conflicts continue to affect adult behavior.

In Freud's view, anxiety alerts the ego to potential danger and in doing so plays a major role in personality development. He discerned three types of anxiety. **Reality (objective) anxiety** is fear of tangible danger in the real world, such as fear of snakes, wild animals, fire, or storms. **Neurotic anxiety** demonstrates conflict between the id and the ego in that we fear the real consequences or punishment of our instinctual gratification. Those who consider shoplifting, for example, may fear getting caught by store security personnel and being sent to jail. **Moral anxiety** reflects conflict between the id and the superego; it is fear of our own conscience. Potential shoplifters may fear shame and guilt feelings—punishment from within—for behavior that violates the moral code.

To varying degrees, individuals employ defense mechanisms to keep anxiety within tolerable limits. **Defense mechanisms** are psychological realignments by which people unconsciously deny and distort frustrating or anxiety-producing situations to protect their ego. A partial listing of defense mechanisms with examples appears in Exhibit 8.1.[9]

According to Freud, personality develops as individuals progress through a sequence of psychosexual stages during infancy and childhood. These stages are named after erogenous zones of the body around which attention focuses. They include the oral, anal, and phallic stages, which Freud believed occur between the ages of one to five. Personality, according to this view, is fully developed by age five, and there is little that can be done to change it thereafter. **Fixation** or permanent halting of personality development may occur if children experience excessive frustration, anxiety, or even satisfaction at a particular stage.

id
a personality component that demands pleasure and immediate gratification

superego
the social, moral, and ethical component of personality

ego
a personality component that balances the id's hedonistic impulses and the superego's constraints

reality (objective) anxiety
the fear of tangible danger in the real world

neurotic anxiety
the fear of the negative consequences of instinctual gratification

moral anxiety
the fear of feeling shame and guilt

defense mechanisms
the tendency to protect our ego by denying and distorting anxiety-producing situations

fixation
a halt in personality progress at a particular developmental stage

EXHIBIT 8.1   **A Partial List of Defense Mechanisms**

Repression	Denying and concealing impulses that cause one's feelings of conflict, discomfort, or guilt. Consumers who go on a diet may repress their need for food in favor of the higher-priority goal of looking more attractive.
Rationalization	Reinterpreting and justifying one's behavior to make it seem logical and acceptable. Shoplifters may convince themselves that retailers "rip off" customers. Consumers frequently rationalize purchases about which they feel anxious or guilty.
Regression	Retreating to a previous, secure period of life and exhibiting immature behavior. For some, cigar and cigarette smoking may be regressive. They may unconsciously link the oral stimulation to the security of nursing at a mother's breast.
Projection	Attributing one's own disturbing impulses or faults to another person. One may reshape "I hate myself" into "He hates me." Contempt for another's conspicuous consumption may hide one's own greed or materialism.
Aggression	Resorting to assertive behavior to protect one's ego or interests. Some angry consumers may organize a boycott against manufacturers who use sweatshop labor.
Withdrawal	Removing oneself from a frustrating situation. Consumers who object to violence or sex in motion pictures may stop going to the movies.

MARKETING APPLICATIONS OF FREUDIAN THEORY

Promotional appeals frequently address the id, ego, and superego components of personality. The BMW ad in Figure 8.1, addresses the measure principle of the id by suggesting to the consumer that owning a prestigious car is merely a reward to oneself.

Advertisements frequently emphasize the pleasure and self-indulgent aspects of products. Whether the product depicted is a perfume or satin sheets, ads often attempt to address the pleasure principle of the id. Other ads employ sexual themes, sensuous illustrations or stories, and suggestive double meanings to promote various products and services. In still other applications of the id, ads often depict aggressive scenes or violent acts to promote sporting events, auto races, movies, and TV shows. Campaigns employing dream-sequence, fantasy, and wish-fulfillment themes are also sympathetic with the id's passionate cravings.

Sales promotion methods that address the ego or reality principle are also prevalent. Credit policies are often designed to appeal to the ego by glossing over the reality of spending money. Firms in many cases extend payment plans, buying incentives, or free goods or services to facilitate consumer purchases by temporarily underwriting some of the cost. Similarly, advertising occasionally appeals to an overburdened ego by offering consumers a way to escape

Figure 8.1
This BMW ad appeals to the pleasure principle of the id. It states that you owe it to yourself to drive a prestigious car.

from their conflicts. Advertising appeals stress the desirability of fleeing from and eluding life's troubles, pressures, and worries. Promotion for vacation resorts, pleasure cruises, and gambling casinos frequently employ escape, leisure, freedom, and fantasy appeals, but shows them reasonably priced to pacify the ego. The Princess Cruises ad displayed in Figure 8.2 employs such themes.

Promotional appeals also address the superego with references to social amenities, moral and ethical protocol, and tradition. Promotions frequently advance both legitimate and spurious arguments designed to help consumers surmount guilt feelings and rationalize or justify their purchases. De Beers uses the slogan "a diamond is forever," and both Honda and Toyota proudly claim that they are the most environmentally conscious auto companies due to their introduction of hybrid vehicles.

Neo-Freudian Personality Theory

Four disciples of Freud developed their own psychoanalytic personality theories. Rather than focus on the significance and consequences of sexual conflicts, the ideas of neo-Freudians Adler, Horney, Fromm, and Sullivan suggest that social variables and not biological drives underlie personality formation—hence the development of **neo-Freudian theory**.

neo-Freudian theory
a view that social variables rather than biological instincts and sexual drives underlie personality formation

Inspiring views as far as the eye can see —
and not a worry in sight.

Figure 8.2

In order to promote the firm's tours, Princess Cruises employs the theme of escaping completely via an extended vacation.

Adler proposed that personality is the set of behaviors an individual employs in pursuit of superiority and perfection.[15] Humans are social beings motivated by urges to compensate for or overcome inferiority complexes. Feelings of inferiority often develop during childhood as a result of perceived physical, social, or psychological disabilities. These impediments may be real or imagined. By age four or five, and as a result of parent–child interactions, individuals choose and create their own unique style of life. This lifestyle is the basic character that defines and shapes their behavior and attitudes and that determines those aspects of the environment to which they will attend. According to Adler, individuals are conscious of the goals they strive to attain and the behavior they engage in to achieve their personal goals.

Horney suggested that personality develops as individuals attempt to deal with anxiety.[16] Humans are born helpless into a potentially hostile world; early anxieties stem from parent–child relationships. Horney hypothesized that people develop one of three behavior patterns to deal with their childhood insecurities and later anxieties. The *compliant personality* moves toward people when troubled. Compliant individuals seek affection, appreciation, acceptance, and approval from others. The *aggressive personality* moves against people when troubled. Aggressive individuals desire to stand out and excel; they seek admiration, power, and exploitation of others. The *detached personality* moves away from others when troubled. Detached individuals seek self-sufficiency, independence, and unassailablilty.

Fromm asserted that humans feel lonely and isolated because they have become separated from nature and other people.[17] Fromm emphasized humans' need for love, fellowship, and security in order to overcome feelings of loneliness, alienation, and insignificance.

Sullivan considered personality "a hypothetical entity that cannot be separated from interpersonal relations" and "the relatively enduring pattern of recurrent interpersonal situations which characterize a human life."[18] According to Sullivan, humans continually attempt to establish rewarding interpersonal relationships. Social associations, however, may threaten people's security and produce anxiety. Progression through a series of developmental stages leads individuals toward a mature repertory of interpersonal relations by adulthood (the early twenties).

MARKETING APPLICATIONS OF NEO-FREUDIAN THEORY

Neo-Freudian personality theory directs marketers' attention to the social character of consumption. Many promotional campaigns emphasize social relationships and human interaction. The L.L. Bean ad in Figure 8.3 promotes its clothing catalog by depicting warm interaction in a family setting. Similarly, purchase and use of personal-care products such as soaps, antiperspirants, and mouthwashes reflect consumers' concern for positive interpersonal relationships and anxieties over potentially offending others.

We guarantee everything but the weather.

For a wide variety of gear and clothing that looks good, feels great, and is always 100% guaranteed, there's only one place to turn. The new L.L. Bean Fall catalog.

Call for your FREE Fall catalog. 1-800-987-2326.

Or shop on-line at www.llbean.com

L.L.Bean
FREEPORT, MAINE

Figure 8.3
Ads that depict happy moments spent with family or friends exemplify the use of neo-Freudian themes.

Cohen developed a **compliance-aggressivenes-detachment (CAD) scale** paradigm.[19] It was designed to classify subjects as high or low on Horney's hypo-thesized behavioral tendencies. The inventory asks respondents to finish 35 incomplete statements about various situations. On a 6-point scale ranging from extremely undesirable to extremely desirable, subjects indicate their feelings about each situation. Specific statements measure compliance; others measure aggressiveness or detachment. Sample CAD statements appear in Exhibit 8.2.

Using a sample of undergraduate male university students, Cohen administered the CAD inventory and asked brand preferences in 15 product categories where Horney's social traits seem to operate. Finding that personality differences had a generally small—but significant—effect on purchase patterns in 7 of the 15 product categories, Cohen suggested the link between personality and consumer behavior merits further investigation. Social-approval appeals, social-conquest themes, and individualistic or nonsocial-context promotional approaches could prove useful in targeting compliant, aggressive, and detached personality types, respectively. Since Cohen's study, CAD scales have been further tested and applied by marketers in a variety of studies covering topics such as purchase involvement, product evaluation, and social influences on buying.[20]

Although Freudian and neo-Freudian theories were useful to gain insight about the motivations that direct consumers' behavior, many researchers were uncomfortable with them largely because they lacked a quantitative dimension. Their usefulness depended on the researcher's interpretative skill. For this reason, interest grew in using standardized personality tests that are reliable and valid psychological measurements designed to identify and quantify personality traits. The relationship of these traits to consumer preferences and purchases can then be further examined. In the following section, let us examine trait theory and identify the role personality traits play in shaping consumption behavior.

Trait Theory

The trait approach to personality study, known as **trait theory,** classifies people according to their dominant characteristics or identifiable traits, which are manifested in the form of consistent responses toward environmental stimuli. **Traits** are thus characteristics that distinguish individuals from one another

---

EXHIBIT 8.2   **Cohen's CAD Scale: Sample Statements**

	Extremely Undesirable					Extremely Desirable
Being free of emotional ties with others is:	___	___	___	___	___	___
Giving comfort to those in need of friends is:	___	___	___	___	___	___
To refuse to give in to others in an argument is:	___	___	___	___	___	___

and that translate into relatively permanent and consistent response patterns. The trait approach to personality attempts to identify, through factor analysis and other statistical techniques, the predominant characteristics of human personality. Through standard psychological inventories, personalities are described and classified in terms of such traits as dominance, sociability, self-acceptance, responsibility, and so forth.

From a marketing perspective, the value of trait theory stems from the fact that because traits are considered to be attributes of the person and not of the situation, similar environmental stimuli or situations generally elicit a consistent response pattern from a particular individual. For this reason and because of the ease with which the trait approach can be applied, trait theory has been extensively utilized in marketing. A number of traits have been used as correlates in consumer behavior studies. *Innovativeness*, for example, is the extent to which an individual enjoys trying new things.[21] *Materialism*, a second trait, refers to the degree of importance that a person attaches to procuring and owning products.[22] *Self-consciousness*, a third trait, entails the extent to which a person deliberately monitors and controls the image of the self that he or she projects to others. *Need for cognition* is the degree to which someone is inclined to think about things.[23] Additional traits that have been frequently used in consumer behavior studies include *tolerance for ambiguity*, *dogmatism*, *category width*, *social character*, *compulsiveness*, *variety seeking*, *tendency to conform*, and *the need for emotion*. These traits are discussed in Exhibit 8.3.

One well-known instrument for measuring a person's personality traits or psychological type is the Myers-Briggs Type Indicator.[27] The four scales that the instrument measures are (1) extroversion/ introversion, (2) sensate/intuitive, (3) thinking/feeling, and (4) judging/perceiving. The various combinations of these preferences result in 16 personality types that are denoted by four letters such as INTJ (which stand for introversion, intuition, with thinking and judging) to represent a person's tendencies on the four traits. This instrument has been widely used for purposes of recruitment, career counseling, occupational choices, market segmentation, and dating services.

Sometimes researchers attempt to find out whether consumers who buy a specific product, possess a distinctive personality trait profile.

Recent research has found a strong relationship between personality traits and the biology of the brain.[28] For example, if two people were to experience a similar crisis (such as divorce, loss of a job, death of a family member), one individual may appear to fall apart while the other glides through it, seemingly in control. Why might they react so dissimilarly? The biology of the brain appears to play an essential role, contributing to an understanding of the individual differences in personality traits. Compelling evidence suggests that 50 to 70 percent of individual variation in personality trait scores is related to genetic influence, but the remaining 30 to 50 percent can be attributed to environmental influences.[29]

© 2009, , iofoto, Shutterstock, Inc.

Tolerance for ambiguity is a personality trait that refers to how individuals tend to react in situations that are novel, complex, or insoluble. Those with high tolerance for ambiguity deal with inconsistency in a constructive way. Those with low tolerance for ambiguity view it as undesirable or threatening.

Dogmatism is a personality trait that measures how rigid or unrigid a person is toward unfamiliar objects, individuals, or situations. Highly dogmatic individuals are less likely to be accepting of other views that are contradictory to the ones they hold.

Category width is a trait that measures to what degree an individual is likely to tolerate risk. It addresses the extent to which an individual is willing to accept poor or negative consequences or outcomes of decisions one makes.

Social character is a trait that identifies where an individual belongs on the continuum that ranges from being inner directed to being other directed. *Inner-directed* consumers tend to be more independent in their thoughts and behavior. *Other-directed* individuals, on the other hand, tend to look to others for direction as to what course of action is appropriate.

Compulsiveness is a trait that amounts to a form of addiction to a particular behavior. Compulsiveness extends beyond mere fixations of stamp, coin, and record collectors to include consumers with uncontrollable urges to shop, gamble, smoke, drink, abuse drugs, or indulge in sex.[24]

Variety seeking is a trait that distinguishes between people in terms of the extent to which they seek challenge, excitement, and variety in their lives.[25] *Low sensation seekers* prefer a quiet, calm, undisturbed existence. *High sensation seekers*, on the other hand, become bored if their lifestyle is void of challenge, excitement, and action.

Tendency to conform is a trait that distinguishes people based on their proclivity to conform to social pressures when making purchases. Individuals with a *low tendency to conform* go ahead with their intended purchases whether they shop alone or with a group. Those who exhibit a *high tendency to conform* tend to make many more changes in purchase plans when shopping with a group than when shopping alone.[26]

Need for emotion is a trait that distinguishes between people in terms of their degree of emotionality. Highly emotional individuals react more sensitively to objects and situations, whereas those who rank low on this trait react in an indifferent manner more frequently and to a wider range of events.

Innovativeness is a trait that reveals the extent to which individuals sense excitement and stimulation upon experiencing new opportunities, objects, or situations. They savor the new, the offbeat, and the risky. An emphasis on this trait of innovation is demonstrated by the ad in Figure 8.4 from BT, which highlights the firm's strategy of viewing clients' problems as opportunities to be pursued by the BT innovative team.

Bringing it all together

For some people it's a problem. For our innovators it's an opportunity.

Innovators think differently. Where most of us see barriers they see opportunities. They are mavericks, the unruly individuals who won't accept the way things are. And search for the way things should be. Our research facilities are full of these innovators. We encourage them to explore the seemingly unprofitable and unusual. Because we know that many of their ideas, considered off-beat today, could become tomorrow's next big thing. From greener networking and health monitoring, to flexible working and wearable technology, BT is innovating for companies and people in the UK and around the world. Find out more about this bigger thinking at www.biggerthinking.com

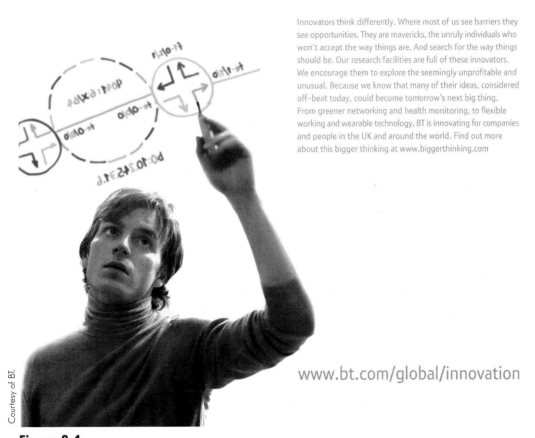

www.bt.com/global/innovation

Courtesy of BT.

Figure 8.4

Innovators tend to think differently and view barriers as opportunities. This ad from BT suggests to clients that the firm's team of innovators successfully explores the seemingly unprofitable and unusual.

Recently, a study addressed the issue of whether or not personality traits are genetically determined. The study provided the first confirmed association between a specific gene and a normal personality trait called *novelty seeking*.[30] Whereas previous studies have shown more generally that genes affect personality, as do an individual's life experiences, this discovery provided the first missing link between genes and personality by implicating a particular communication system within the brain. Such findings represent a possible step toward unraveling the genetics of personality. Perhaps with future advances in gene detection technology, it may become possible and useful for marketers of services such as insurance, investments, and travel to gauge the novelty-seeking tendencies of their clients in order to offer them programs specifically designed for their personality types.[31]

MEASURING TRAITS

Trait theory is built on a number of assumptions:

- Traits are identifiable, and a limited number of traits are common to most individuals.
- Traits are relatively stable and, regardless of specific environmental circumstances, exert fairly pervasive effects on behavior.
- Traits vary in intensity among different people, and the degree to which individuals possess various traits is measurable via questionnaires or other behavioral indicators.
- People who possess similar traits and trait intensities have similar goals and behaviors.

Advocates of trait theory speculate that if researchers can identify the particular combination of traits that an individual possesses and uncover the consistencies in his or her behavior, then it should be possible to make predictions concerning this person's behavior. Personality trait assessment relies on **personality tests**, paper-and-pencil questionnaires designed to measure one or more personality traits. To develop personality tests, researchers often start with subjects' replies to a number of questions that attempt to reveal their response tendencies (such as rigidity or openness). Respondents may be requested to agree or disagree with statements such as "There is usually only one best way to solve a problem" or "Most people don't know what's good for them." Likewise, respondents may be asked to respond to questions designed to express their likes or dislikes for particular situations or types of people.

Results of these tests produce trait profiles of participating individuals that are then correlated with data on their product purchases. The main purpose of this procedure is to identify behavioral patterns that can be generalized to an entire market segment. For example, researchers may seek answers to such questions as, "What is the trait profile of consumers who purchase convertible automobiles?" or "What traits identify those who purchase environmentally friendly products?"[32] As can be seen, the value of trait theory to marketing stems from the possibility of treating consumers who display similar personality traits as market segments and then developing appropriate appeals for such groups of consumers based on their distinguishing traits.

personality tests
paper-and-pencil questionnaires designed to measure personality traits

Consumer Behavior in Practice

A Cheerful and Good-Natured Stove

Is your refrigerator sensitive, gentle, and faithful? Is your microwave oven a male or female? Is your blender a teenager or a senior citizen? If these questions seem strange, they are considered very useful by many companies today that attempt to discover what human personality traits consumers assign to brands. In the minds of many consumers, products and brands take on personalities of their own. This *brand personality* is a valuable tool for both marketers and consumers alike. Marketers have long realized that consumers buy products and brands with personalities that match their own. Product personalities give consumers confidence in their purchase decisions, facilitate the choice process when selecting among competing brands, and enhance their loyalty to particular brands.

In a recent study by Whirlpool Corporation, researchers attempted to identify the personality traits that consumers assign to Whirlpool's brands. In one phase of the study, Whirlpool researchers asked respondents first to select adjectives from a list to describe familiar Whirlpool brands. Listed adjectives included such human personality traits as dependable, strong, independent, hardworking, trustworthy, and faithful. Second, respondents were instructed to indicate whether the brand is masculine or feminine.

The results were interesting. Whirlpool brands were viewed as gentle, sensitive, quiet, good natured, flexible, modern, cheerful, and creative. Personified, Whirlpool brand was perceived as a modern, family-oriented woman who lives the best of suburban life and is considered a good friend and neighbor.

KitchenAid was perceived as a modern professional woman who is competent, aggressive, and smart and who works hard to acquire the better things in life. She is sophisticated, glamorous, wealthy, elegant, fashionable, and innovative.

What is the value of all this? Companies say that this knowledge helps them to concisely establish the brand personality in all communications directed toward the market. Product personality also facilitates the creation of differences between brands for the purpose of attaining greater brand loyalty and gaining an advantage over the competition.[33]

The goal behind building a brand personality is to create a match between the personalities of customers and those of the brand. Visit the Web site of General Motors Corporation at www.gm.com. Consider several models of GM automobiles such as Chevrolet, Buick, Cadillac and Saturn. What type of brand personality does the company aspire to build for each model? What marketing strategies and tactics are employed in building unique personalities for each model?

In order to apply standardized personality tests in marketing investigations, marketers and researchers must first speculate which specific traits are likely to influence brand preference before choosing a particular personality test.[34] Merely borrowing standard personality inventories designed for clinical purposes and attempting to discover useful relationships between personality and shopping behaviors or brand preferences frequently produces poor results.[35] Clinical multitrait personality inventories were not designed to investigate consumer behavior.[36] Tailor-made personality inventories or modified personality tests that focus on specific constellations of traits that researchers suspect to be related to product use are more likely to be useful for purposes of consumer research than are standardized clinical tests.[37]

MARKETING APPLICATIONS OF TRAIT THEORY

Trait theory is one of the most often used methods for researching the link between personality and consumer behavior. As mentioned earlier, studies frequently search for correlations between a set of specific personality traits and consumer behaviors such as product purchases, brand choice, retail store selection, online shopping, media selection, and a variety of other factors. For example, one recent study found a measurable link between the personality traits of extroversion and neuroticism and postpurchase processes such as consumer satisfaction/dissatisfaction, loyalty, complaining, and word of mouth.[38]

Another study correlated the variety-seeking trait to consumption behavior and found interdependence between this trait and product choice, store choice, and susceptibility to advertising appeals.[39] The study reported that high sensation seekers, as a result of being intrigued with the prospect of *newness*, were more likely than low sensation seekers to be consumer innovators. As to store choice, the study reported that high sensation seekers tended to prefer shopping at downtown stores because they enjoy the noise and bustle of downtown. Low sensation seekers, on the other hand, were found to be typically mall and online shoppers who try to avoid the exciting but stressful downtown atmosphere. Reaction to advertising and susceptibility to different advertising appeals also varied between high and low sensation seekers. High sensation seekers were more likely to react favorably to informative advertising that appealed to their curiosity and tended to evaluate the merits of the advertised product on the basis of their own experiences. Low sensation seekers, on the other hand, were less apt to evaluate product merits on their own, except within the confines of reference group settings and the presence of a trusted celebrity or expert.

It has also been observed that consumers with opposite traits may still display the same purchase behavior. Two consumers on opposite ends of a personality-trait continuum, such as aggressiveness, may purchase the same sports car. The first may do so to express and match an outgoing self-image. The second may do so to offset or overcome feelings of insecurity.

Of course, marketers who plan to use personality traits as a basis for market segmentation have to make sure that groups of consumers possessing common personality traits are sufficiently large to offer genuine potential. They must further be demographically homogeneous or geographically clustered so that they can be economically reached through the mass media. Those traits that form the basis for segmentation should then serve as a guide in developing the appropriate marketing mix.[40]

Early researchers were able to devise instruments that combined the quantitative aspect of personality inventories with the qualitative information offered by psychoanalytic procedures. The result was an approach that was called psychographics—the science of measuring and categorizing consumer lifestyles. Psychographics offers insight into what goes on in the consumer's mind and seeks to identify individual consumption-related activities, interests, and opinions. The following section is devoted to a discussion of psychographics.

Psychographics

Psychographics, which investigates consumer lifestyles, differs from trait theory in that it explores the possibility of developing meaningful categories out of the infinite range of activities, interests, and opinions that characterize consumers. Psychographics is a research approach rather than a personality theory, whose aim is to assess consumers' lifestyles so that meaningful consumer typologies can be identified.

psychographics
a segmentation approach that classifies consumers based on their lifestyle

Marketers have long realized that, in many cases, demographic dimensions alone—such as age, education, income, occupation, sex, and marital status—fail to explain certain consumer behavior tendencies. For example, there is no relationship between demographics and smoking, drinking, preference for sports, going to movies, choosing music, and liking the outdoors. These tendencies reflect lifestyle preferences, which vary dramatically between people.

Psychographics uses statements designed to reveal the activities, interests, and opinions of consumers, commonly referred to as AIO. AIO inventories are constructed specifically for each study to assess the lifestyles of a target group in order to link AIO with a specific consumption behavior or preference, such as purchase and use of a certain product, service, or brand.

AIO inventories
questionnaires designed to reveal consumers' activities, interests, and opinions

AIO inventories typically contain a large number of statements. Respondents are instructed to express their degree of agreement or disagreement with each. *Activity* statements, for example, may include phrases describing what individuals do, what they buy, and how they spend their time. *Interest* statements may cover subjects' preferences, priorities, and concerns. *Opinion* statements may solicit respondents' views and perceptions on a variety of aspects related to their social, cultural, or economic surroundings as well as on the products or services that constitute the subject of the investigation. Exhibit 8.4 shows part of an AIO inventory designed to reveal store patronage patterns and preferences of a group of consumers.

Data obtained from AIO inventories are then analyzed using statistical techniques such as factor analysis, cluster analysis, and cross-tabulation. This analysis reveals meaningful groupings that seem to share a particular consumption tendency or that form a distinguishable profile. For example, data on attitudes of adults toward animal welfare, animal rights, animal experiments, animal testing, animal hunting, animals as pets, and animals as a source of food are usually obtained through AIO inventories. The Roper Center for Public Opinion Research and the National Opinion Research Center at the University of Michigan conduct such surveys and provide comprehensive data on distinguishable groupings within the public and their attitudes on these issues. Marketers then correlate these findings with consumer behavior and tendencies such as consumption of meat, purchase of cosmetics that have been tested on animals, acquiring pets and feeding them, as well as buying gear related to hunting for recreation and sport.

AIO inventories vary in the degree of their specificity. Researchers may aim at obtaining highly specific types of information that can be valuable in revealing consumption patterns for specific product categories such as pet food. On the other hand, AIO inventories may be designed to collect broad and

EXHIBIT 8.4   AIO Questionnaire: Sample Items

	Definately Disagree			**Definately Agree**		
I like to have a salesperson assist me in making a selection.	1	2	3	4	5	6
I like to stick to well-known brand names.	1	2	3	4	5	6
I shop a lot for specials.	1	2	3	4	5	6
I like to be considered a leader.	1	2	3	4	5	6
I like to feel attractive to the opposite sex.	1	2	3	4	5	6
I buy a lot of goods on impulse.	1	2	3	4	5	6
I like to go shopping with friends.	1	2	3	4	5	6
Good grooming is a sign of self-respect.	1	2	3	4	5	6
When buying clothing, I am more concerned with style than price.	1	2	3	4	5	6
Weekends are my favorite time to shop.	1	2	3	4	5	6
Store brands are just as good as nationally advertised brands.	1	2	3	4	5	6
I pay a lot more attention to prices now than I ever did before.	1	2	3	4	5	6

general types of information in order to identify meaningful consumer typologies or market segments. Typologies based on lifestyle can be useful in a variety of ways such as defining new-product targets, positioning products through advertising, designing campaign themes or appeals, and determining which media to use to reach various prospect groups.

A landmark effort in this area of psychographic/demographic segmentation is **VALS™**. The VALS™ system advocates that people buy products and services and seek experiences that fulfill their characteristic preferences and give shape, substance, and satisfaction to their lives. An individual's primary motivation determines what particular about the self or the world is the meaningful core that governs his or her activities. VALS™ isolates the patterns that reinforce and sustain a person's identity as the person expresses it in the marketplace.[41]

VALS™

a segmentation approach that classifies consumers according to primary motivations and resources/innovation

THE VALS™ SYSTEM

The VALS™ program proposes that consumer behavior is driven by three primary motivations: ideals, achievement, and self-expression. *Ideals-motivated consumers* are guided in their choices by abstract, idealized criteria, rather than by feelings, events, or a desire for the approval and opinion of others. *Achievement-motivated consumers* look for products and services that demonstrate success to their peers. *Self-expression-motivated consumers* are guided by a desire for social or physical activity, variety, and risk-taking.

In addition to segmenting by primary motivation, the VALS™ typology also segments by resources. The resources dimension, which is depicted as a continuum ranging from minimal to abundant, refers to the full range of psychological, physical, demographic, and material means and capacities that are available to consumers.[42]

The VALS™ system defines eight segments, roughly equal in size. Each segment has a unique combination of psychological attributes and demographics that underlie consumer decision making. As a result, each segment has a distinct consumer mind-set and exhibits distinct patterns of consumer behavior.

Exhibit 8.5 is a depiction of the eight VALS™ segments classified on the two dimensions of *primary motivation* (the horizontal dimension) and *resources* and *innovation* (the vertical dimension).

Exhibit 8.6 further clarifies the composition of each of the eight VALS™ segments and reveals particular and distinctive behavioral tendencies, attitudes, lifestyles, and decision-making patterns characteristic of individuals who fall into each segment.[43]

VAL™ Configuration of Consumer Categories **EXHIBIT 8.5**

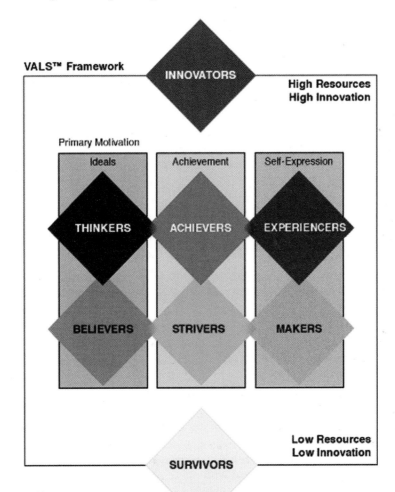

Innovators are successful, sophisticated, take-charge people with high self-esteem. Because they have such abundant resources, they exhibit all three primary motivations in varying degrees. They are change leaders and are the most receptive to new ideas and technologies. Innovators are very active consumers, and their purchases reflect cultivated tastes for upscale, niche products and services.

Thinkers are motivated by ideals. They are mature, satisfied, comfortable, and reflective people who value order, knowledge, and responsibility. They tend to be well educated and actively seek out information in the decision-making process. They are well informed about world and national events and are alert to opportunities to broaden their knowledge.

Achievers are motivated by the desire for achievement. They have goal-oriented lifestyles and a deep commitment to career and family. Their social lives reflect this focus and are structured around family, their place of worship, and work. Achievers live conventional lives, are politically conservative, and respect authority and the status quo. They value consensus, predictability, and stability over risk, intimacy, and self-discovery.

Experiencers are motivated by self-expression. As young, enthusiastic, and impulsive consumers, Experiencers quickly become enthusiastic about new possibilities but are equally quick to cool. They seek variety and excitement, savoring the new, the offbeat, and the risky. Their energy finds an outlet in exercise, sports, outdoor recreation, and social activities.

Believers, like Thinkers, are motivated by ideals. They are conservative, conventional people with concrete beliefs based on traditional, established codes: family, religion, community, and the nation. Many Believers express moral codes that are deeply rooted and literally interpreted. They follow established routines, organized in large part around home, family, community, and social or religious organizations to which they belong.

Strivers are trendy and fun loving. Because they are motivated by achievement, Strivers are concerned about the opinions and approval of others. Money defines success for Strivers, who don't have enough of it to meet their desires. They favor stylish products that emulate the purchase of people with greater material wealth. Many see themselves as having a job rather than a career, and a lack of skills and focus often prevents them from moving ahead.

Makers, like Experiencers, are motivated by self-expression. They express themselves and experience the world by working on it—building a house, raising children, fixing a car, or canning vegetables—and have enough skill and energy to carry out their projects successfully. Makers are practical people who have constructive skills and value self-sufficiency. They live within a traditional context of family, practical work, and physical recreation and have little interest in what lies outside that context.

Survivors live narrowly focused lives. With few resources with which to cope, they often believe that the world is changing too quickly. They are comfortable with the familiar and are primarily concerned with safety and security. Because they must focus on meeting needs rather than fulfilling desires, Survivors do not show a strong primary motivation.

Marketing Applications of Vals™

VALS™ has helped marketers select target markets, develop effective media plans, and create ads that match the attributes and images of products with the types of consumer who use these products. VALS™ appears to work best for product categories such as automobiles, homes, garments, jewelry, and furnishings, where emotional involvement impacts consumers' buying processes.[44]

Lack of consumer involvement or low involvement lessens the chance that marketers would create products or ad appeals for specific VALS™ groups. For example, it is unlikely that marketers of staple food products, such as milk and bread, would enhance their sales by targeting specific VALS™ segments. Believing that a single segmentation system cannot be applied cross-culturally, SRI Consulting Business Intelligence uses separate VALS™ systems for Japan and the United Kingdom.[45]

VALS™ has become a widely used tool for assessing and measuring cultural and lifestyle values and identifying consumer groups. Many firms and advertising agencies have jumped aboard the VALS™ bandwagon and subscribe to it annually. American Airlines, for example, employed VALS™ in order to identify its frequent-flyer customer group—business travelers—as the *Achievers*. Advertisers have come to realize that radio is a particularly good medium to reach some of the VALS™ groups. Because radio offers only a limited number of station formats, VALS's™ eight typologies seem to fit radio audiences fairly well. Conservative blue-collar workers with traditional values (i.e., the VALS™ *Believer* and *Maker* segments) often prefer country music stations. On the other hand, higher-income consumers over age 45 (i.e., the VALS™ *Innovator, Thinkers,* and *Achiever* segments) frequently tune to news and talk-radio stations.[46]

In a more recent application, VALS™ was used to identify likely adopters of innovative technologies. The ad from LG in Figure 8.5 depicts appropriate appeals for a specific VALS™ group where the matching of products and a particular consumer segment is the essence of the ad's appeal. Another company known as Intelligent Transportation Systems (ITS), which markets high-tech transportation systems (such as global positioning devices) was able to identify VALS™ *Innovators* as its best prospects because this category includes early adopters of new products.

The Self-Concept

Each of us has attitudes, feelings, perceptions, and evaluations of ourselves in terms of physical appearance, attractiveness, mental aptitude, capabilities, roles, and so on. Some of these attributes we like and others we deplore. The overall image that a person holds of him or herself is referred to as that individual's self-concept. The **self-concept** is the sum total of an individual's beliefs and feelings about him- or herself.

Although the self-concept is closely associated with personality, the concept of self is a narrower approach to the study of consumer behavior than the broader field of personality. It permits the specific focus on the individual and

self-concept
the overall image that a person holds of him or herself

7am-10am: Last minute client meeting in Beijing to discuss major structural change.

11am-4pm: Intense meeting with engineers to defy laws of physics.

7pm-11pm: Motivational meeting with contractors to pull off the impossible.

(11:10pm: Angry voicemessage from fiancée inLos Angeles complaining that you forgot to call.)

Life's

Good

(11:15pm: Call to fiancée to show her you never stopped thinking about her for a second.)

The LG 3G Phone enables you to see and talk to someone in real time.
When you need to most.

It's just one way LG makes life good. To see more ways, visit www.lge.com

Life's Good

LG

Figure 8.5

This ad from LG attempts to match the attributes and images of luxury brands with the type of consumer who is likely to purchase or use these products.

allows the measurement of conscious determinants that shape a person's behavior. The importance of the self-concept stems from the observation that consumers' feelings about themselves shape their consumption practices. Many products from clothes to cosmetics are bought because a person is attempting to manifest a positive attribute or hide a negative aspect of self.

The self-concept is a complex structure that can be described along many dimensions including both our self-assessment and the way others perceive us. We evaluate ourselves in relation to others as we go through life experiences. Starting with childhood, we begin to develop self-awareness, that is, awareness of the extent to which we are similar to or dissimilar from others. We learn our strengths and weaknesses and develop positive or negative feelings about what we are as a result.[48]

Self-concept also emerges from other people's opinions of us. We learn to perceive ourselves as others perceive us. Relationships with other people play a significant role in forming the self. We are constantly interpreting how others perceive the symbols we surround ourselves with. We adjust and pattern our behavior based on others' expectations, meeting some and failing others.

The self-concept is thus the outcome of a comparison between our actual standing on some attribute and an ideal. The ideal is our conception of how we would like to be. People often experience discrepancies between their actual and desired selves. For some individuals, this gap is wider than for others. Such individuals are particularly suitable targets for ad campaigns that use fantasy appeals as ways to cope with problems in the real world or to compensate for boredom.[49] Campaigns for Disney theme parks, films, videos, and related merchandise offer examples of ads that employ fantasy appeals.

VARIETY OF SELF-CONCEPTS

A variety of self-concepts have been identified in consumer behavior literature. Early work by Carl Rogers, a pioneer in the field of the self-concept, identified a number of components of the self such as the real-self (the individual as an objective entity), the ideal-self (what the individual would like to be), the self-image (how individuals see themselves), the apparent self (the self that others see), and the reference-group self (the self one imagines that others see).[50]

More recent research has added other concepts such as the extended-self and the possible-self. The **extended-self** is the self defined in terms of an individual's more important possessions.[51] The extended-self includes the home, clothing, car, and furnishings a person owns. Possessions, in this sense, are perceived as a confirmation or extension of the self-image. Such goods are said to possess *badge value* because they communicate something about their owners or users and how they feel about themselves. For instance, the J. Crew label on a pair of jeans suggests something different about the person wearing them than does Wrangler (the popular brand for rodeo riders and cowboys).

The **possible-self**, on the other hand, refers to an individual's perceptions concerning what he or she would like to become, what one could become, or what one fears becoming. The notion of possible-selves conveys a stronger future orientation than the other self-concept types.[52]

extended-self
the self defined in terms of an individual's possessions

possible-self
the self a person would like to or could become

Global Opportunity

For the Japanese: A Bowl of VALS™

SRI International, which created the VALS™ program for the U.S. market, undertook the task of conducting a similar analysis of the Japanese market. The study attempts to explain and model forces affecting social change in Japan. Japan VALS™ divides Japanese society into segments based on two key consumer attributes: *life orientation* and *attitudes toward social change.*

Concerning life orienteation—that is, what interests or animates a person the most, Japan VALS™ identified four life orientations, including traditional ways, occupations, innovation, and self-expression. Regarding attitudes toward social change, Japan VALS™ stratifies Japanese society into distinct layers that could be likened to an inverted bowl, where each layer of consumers is nested inside another. The change-leading segments of society are found in the outermost layers, whereas those who resist change are located in the center. In this depiction, change is diffused from one layer to the next though channels that are mainly influenced by different life orientations. Thus, Japan VALS™ clarifies the process of social change and innovation diffusion in the Japanese culture. Japan VALS™ stratifies the Japanese market into six layers, described as follows (with the first change-leading layer at the outermost rim of the bowl, and the sixth change-resistant layer at the center).

1. *Integrators* (4 percent of .the population) score high on innovation. They are active, inquisitive trendsetters who are affluent and informed.
2. *Self-Innovators and Self-Adapters* (7 and 11 percent of the population, respectively) score high on self-expression. They desire personal experience, fashionable display, and social activities.
3. *Ryoshiki Innovators and Adapters* (6 and 10 percent of the population, respectively) score highest on occupations. Education and career achievement are their personal focus.
4. *Tradition Innovators and Adapters* (6 and 10 percent of the population, respectively) score highest on traditional ways. They tend to adhere to traditional religions and customs.
5. *High Pragmatics and Low Pragmatics* (14 and 17 percent of the population, respectively) do not score high on any life-orientation dimension. They are inactive, are uniformed, and have few interests.
6. *Sustainers* (15 percent of the population) are people who score lowest on innovation and self-expression dimensions.

Benefits of studies like Japan VALS™ abound for internal marketers. Japan VALS™ facilitates achievement of objectives that relate to segmenting the Japanese marketplace, identifying unfulfilled consumer needs, generating new-product ideas, differentiating brands from the competition, forecasting change in the business environment, and communicating effectively with various target audiences.

Studies of consumer attitudes in various societies help marketers recognize differences between those prevailing in the United States and those of other countries. Learn more about Japan VALS™ and see the inverted-bowl depiction by visiting http://www.sricbi.com/VALS/JVALS.shtml and http://www.sricbi.com/VALS/JVALSbackground.shtml Based on this knowledge, what promotional themes should a clothing company such as Levi's use to sell its products in Japan? Should these themes be different from those used in the United States? Why or why not?

These different types of self-images manifest themselves in different buying situations. Because many consumption activities are related to self-evaluation, consumers reflect their values through the products they buy and activities they undertake. To be congruent with the reference-group self, for example, an individual may take up golf and buy all the necessary gear for the game to be accepted into a group. Deep inside, however, he or she may not really care for the game.

MEASURING THE SELF-CONCEPT

A popular method of measuring the self-concept involves use of the Q-sort technique. Q-sorting is a sophisticated form of rank-ordering. It involves giving the respondent a number of cards, usually somewhere between 60 and 120, where each card contains a statement or a situation for the respondent to evaluate. Each respondent is asked to sort these cards into a number of piles arranged by the researcher to reflect the degree of the respondent's personal assessment of each statement.

In using Q-sorts to measure the self-concept, a number of statements addressing various elements of the self are developed by the researcher. Each statement is then printed on a card. Respondents are given these cards and instructed to sort them into a predetermined number of piles (such as seven piles), based on how each respondent assesses these statements. The following is an example of a typical set of statements on a Q-sort designed to measure the self-concept:

Definitely me					**Definitely not me**	
1	2	3	4	5	6	7

I feel I am a bit of a swinger.
I feel more sophisticated than most people around.
I enjoy being alone.
I favor medical procedures to improve one's looks.
I always like to impress others.
I often fantasize about winning the lottery.
I usually take the initiative when meeting others.
I'm good at giving people advice.

The reason for having an odd number of piles in the Q-sort is to allow for a neutral position. Respondents are instructed to place into the neutral pile (pile 4 in the preceding example) those cards that are left over after other choices have been made. These are the statements toward which the respondent is indifferent. The number of cards to be placed in each pile is often designed to approximate the distribution of the normal curve. Data from the Q-sort are then analyzed through statistical techniques that may include factor analysis and cluster analysis.

Measurement of the self-concept via Q-sorting helps marketers identify clusters of individuals that exhibit similar concepts of self. The assumption is that people with similar self-concepts tend to exhibit similar consumption habits;

A person's role as teacher in a classroom can be completely different than his or her role in other aspects of life.

hence, such identification would help marketers decide on the appropriate strategies to target them.

SELF-CONCEPT AND SOCIAL ROLES

As consumers assume diverse social roles, they put on different selves like actors who perform in a theater. Each role requires its own script, props, and costumes.[53] A person learns what others expect from the role and develops the behaviors necessary to meet these expectations. Whether the role be that of husband, parent, boss, or student, different aspects of the self come into play and are manifested in a person's behavior. Some components of the self are more active in one role than in another. As a parent, the individual may be caring, affectionate, and giving—characteristics that may not be apparent in the same person's role as a boss. Some identities are more central to the self than others. An individual's identity as a parent can be more central than that as a tennis player. The degree of centrality of the identity (or lack thereof) is instrumental in determining the seriousness an individual places on performing what is expected from the role.

The importance of role recognition to marketers lies in the observation that people are often concerned about the impression they make on others. An elevated level of sensitivity about the image that a person communicates to those around him or her results in heightened concern about the appropriateness of one's consumption-related behaviors. Those who demonstrate greater public self-consciousness are sometimes referred to as *high self-monitors*. High self-monitors are intensely attuned to the way they present themselves within social environments. In contrast to *low self-monitors*, high self-monitors are more apt to select products based on their estimates of how these items will be perceived by others.[54] Such persons tend to be more interested in clothing and heavier users of cosmetics.[55] The degree to which a consumer is a high or low self-monitor can be gauged by the extent to which he or she agrees or disagrees with statements such as "I guess I put on a show to impress or entertain others" and "I would probably make a good actor."[56]

SELF-CONCEPT AND CONSUMPTION

Consumption of products and services contributes to the definition of the self. It has been said that you are what you consume. In other words, the products and services that people consume help them define their self-concept and social identity.[57] In addition, an individual's consumption of products and services affects other people's perceptions of him or her.[58]

People, more often than not, use another individual's possessions or consumption behavior to help them make judgments about who that person is. They often consider a person's clothes, make of automobile, dwelling, home decoration, and leisure activities to make inferences about that person's personality. Grubb and Grathwohl believe that one meaningful way of understanding the role of goods is to view them as symbols serving as a means of communication between individuals and their significant others.[59] In the same way that the use of certain products and services influences other's perceptions of who we are, these same products are instrumental in determining our own concept of self.

Many studies support the view that congruence exists between product usage and self-concept.[60] **Self-product congruence** refers to the tendency of individuals to select and use products that match some aspect of the self. Brands have personalities or images, and consumers seek those brands that match their self-image or the image they would like to project to others. These brand personalities can be more enduring and influential than the product's functional attributes. Differentiating brands can thus become possible through attaching emotional values into a brand to reflect a unique brand personality.[61] A recent study by Kressmann, et. al. tested the effect of self-image congruence on loyalty for car brands. Six hundred car owners were surveyed. The results documented the paramount importance of self-congruity in predicting brand loyalty.[62] Another study found that employed females were likely to shop for and wear those outfits that match their ideal career self-image. The more upward the career anchorage, the greater the preference among such employees for wearing businesslike outfits.[63]

Certain properties tend to characterize the products that consumers use as symbols. To qualify, the products must be visible in use; that is, conspicuous products that are readily apparent to others. Products such as automobiles, clothing, and furnishings are examples. The product class must also carry a distinctive brand name, steep price tag, or prestigious origin so as to allow formation of a stereotypical image of the user. One can easily see in Figure 8.6 how a familiar product such as a watch can become a symbol when it possesses a distinctive brand name.

self-product congruence
a tendency to select products that march some aspects of the self

STABILITY OF THE SELF-CONCEPT

Even though the self-concept is relatively stable, it is not static. Sometimes consumers change their self-concept as a result of encountering new experiences or as a consequence of a change they bring about in their own lives. For example, changing the appearance of the body through corrective and plastic surgeries or implants can bring about a change in the way people feel about themselves. Cosmetics, hair restyling or coloring, color contact lenses, dieting, as well as liposuction are other means people employ to improve their appearance. As a consequence, their initial self-concept goes through a corresponding change. Some people even hire professional image consultants to attain an appropriate and mutually agreed-upon self-image. Image consultants offer their clients advice on various personal attributes,

OYSTER PERPETUAL
COSMOGRAPH DAYTONA
IN 18 KT WHITE GOLD

WWW.ROLEX.COM **ROLEX**

NEW YORK   For an Official Rolex Jeweler call 1-800-367-6539. Rolex ⬥ Oyster Perpetual and Cosmograph Daytona are trademarks.

Courtesy of Rolex

Figure 8.6
Based on a global reputation for exceptional quality and high price, many affluent consumers seek a fine Rolex watch as a symbol of distinction.

such as clothing, color, presentation, appearance, posture, speaking, and media skills.[64]

A new experience in an individual's life can also precipitate change in his or her self-concept. For example, a U.S. executive who is assigned a new position in a foreign country, such as Japan, with unfamiliar customs and values may undergo some changes in self-concept. When consumers take on new, unfamiliar roles, they frequently rely on products as crutches to help them formulate a sense of identity.

A person with an incomplete definition of self tends to fill in the missing pieces of his or her identity by means of acquiring and displaying symbols that are associated with it.[65] This process of completing an otherwise deficient self is known as **symbolic self-completion**. Many recent college graduates, upon finding a job, buy a car, wardrobe, and other possessions appropriate for their new position. Once the self is complete, individuals may develop a sense of attachment to the objects they use to maintain their self-concept.[66] Such items—commonly referred to as security blankets—reinforce a person's sense of self, especially when he or she faces novel circumstances. For example, many newly hired employees place family photos on the desk in their office to make the environment seem more familiar and comfortable.

symbolic self-completion
a tendency to complement self by displaying symbols associated with one's identity

Although the self-concept is subject to change, this change process is usually gradual and slow. The self-concept held by an individual is a result of myriad experiences and influences that occur over the years. This characteristic gives the self-concept a persistent, durable structure. For example, it is unlikely that a single negative occurrence or even a few negative incidents would change a positive self-concept. The forementioned U.S. executive sent to Japan may experience recurrent work-related clashes with other Japanese executives, who strictly adhere to group consensus in decision making. These conflicts alone may not be sufficient to change the executive's personal values of individuality and autonomy.

So far we have seen how our personality traits, lifestyle, and self-concept influence what we purchase, use, and like. When we purchase an automobile, a garment, or even a bottle of cologne, we try to match the product's personality with our own. In addition, the products and services we buy and the material possessions we display convey meanings about ourselves to other people. We tend to surround ourselves with products and brands that reflect the images we would like others to hold of us.

The influence of personality, lifestyle, and self-concept is not only evident in the types of products and services we purchase to match our personality. This influence also extends to decisions concerning how we purchase them, where we shop for them, and the circumstances under which we acquire them. For instance, when we feel self-confident, we tend to buy things we might not ordinarily buy when we feel cautious. Confident investors, for example, are more likely than their more-cautious counterparts to consider risky, speculative ventures. Similarly, sociable shoppers may shop more often, spend more time doing so, and visit more stores than less-sociable ones do. Personality, then, has an important influence on the decision-making process—a topic that is covered in detail in the following chapter.

A Cross-Functional Point of View

The topics of personality, lifestyle, and self-concept have a number of implications for business disciplines other than marketing. Relevant issues might include

- **Management:** Leadership approaches vary within organizations. Leadership style in an organization appears to depend largely on the personality traits of specific managers. If the manager happens to have an aggressive and domineering type of personality, Theory X would likely prevail as a leadership style. The manager, in this case, would likely view subordinates as lazy, lacking ambition, and irresponsible. As such, autocratic managers are likely to resort to coercion, control, and threats of punishment to make employees more productive.

  On the other hand, if a manager happens to possess a humanistic and supportive personality, Theory Y would likely prevail as a leadership style. The nurturing manager, in this case, would tend to believe that subordinates not only will work hard but also will seek additional responsibility and challenge. In addition, if they are committed to the goals of the organization, they will exercise self-direction and self-control. In this view, the intellectual potential of average human beings is only being partially tapped.

  A glance at leadership styles in modern organizations reveals the presence of both management styles, but which style works best under what conditions is not always so clear.

- **Counseling/Ethics:** In contemporary society, personality-related disorders appear to be on the rise at an ever increasing rate. Depression, eating disorders, and phobias are but a few examples of such conditions. In view of the efforts that some desperate patients exert to seek help, an alarming phenomenon has surfaced. The media, a few years ago, raised allegations of a number of questionable treatment cases where some inexperienced therapists advise patients that their personality-related problems are the result of sexual abuse during childhood. In addi-

tion, these therapists used techniques such as visualization and hypnosis to convince patients that these alleged sexual experiences really *did* occur. Through the power of suggestion, patients eventually become convinced that the repressed memories of childhood caused them to *dissociate* and develop multiple personality disorders.

- **Human Resources/Cost:** In today's business world, hiring the right corporate leaders is of prime importance in a firm. The financial gains to be had in hiring the right executive are second only to technological advances. Among the tools developed recently for screening executives are the Myers-Briggs Type Indicator and its many variations, which sort out executives into 16 personality types. Associated with these types of tests is a technique known as the Assessment Center (which is not a place but a process) invented by the CIA's predecessor agency to identify potential spies. The approach was adapted by big corporations that needed to find steel-nerved types of executives to operate in hostile territory.

  Concerning the costs associated with finding the perfect executive, Assessment Centers tend to be more expensive than other kinds of evaluations. At $5,000 per head, some companies find the cost to be minor compared to the benefits gained. Not only does recruiting the right executive improve retention and reduce training costs, but such executives also tend to perform better and do so over a longer time period. Others, however, feel that for all its cost and complexity, the Assessment Center is not substantially more valid as a predictor of job performance than any other single--and usually cheaper--means of evaluation, such as more traditional personality profiles.

These issues, and a host of others like them, serve to show that the topics of personality, lifestyle, and self-concept transcend the field of marketing to other business disciplines.

Summary

For purposes of the study of consumer behavior, personality can be defined as the sum total of an individual's inner psychological attributes. Personality makes individuals what they are, distinguishes them from every other person, demonstrates their mode of adjustment to life's circumstances, and produces their unique, stable pattern of responding to environmental stimuli. Personality theories that are particularly relevant to the study of consumer behavior include Freudian, neo-Freudian, and trait theories.

Psychographics, which is employed to investigate consumer lifestyles, is related to trait theories. Psychographics is not a personality theory. Rather, it is a research approach whose aim is to assess consumers' lifestyles so that meaningful consumer typologies can be identified. Unlike trait theories, which classify people according to their dominant characteristics using personality tests, psychographic research employs AIO inventories. AIO inventories are constructed specifically for each study to assess the lifestyles of a target group. The objective is to link AIO with specific consumption behaviors or preferences, such as purchase or use of specific products, services, brands. The VALS program is a landmark effort in the field of psychographic research.

Consumers simultaneously hold a number of images of themselves. The self-concept is a complex structure that includes both an individual's self-assessment *and* the way one is perceived by others. A number of self-concepts are possible, including the real-self, the ideal-self, the self-image, the apparent self, and the reference-group image. The extended-self includes some of an individual's most important possessions, especially those with badge value. The possible-self includes an individual's perceptions concerning what he or she would like to become, could become, or fears becoming.

Product, brand, and service consumption contribute to an individual's definition of self. Consumers tend to choose products, brands, and stores that match some aspects of their self; to protect their self-images; and to buy products whose images correspond to, enhance, and communicate their self-concept, a notion known as self-product congruence. Goods often serve as social tools or symbols by which individuals disclose something about themselves to others.

Even though the self-concept is relatively stable, it is not static. Different factors related to the individual or ones' social environment can precipitate change in the self-concept. The term *symbolic self-completion* refers to ones' tendency to fill in the missing pieces of his or her identity by means of acquiring and displaying symbols that are associated with it.

Review Questions

1. Freudian psychoanalytic personality theory is based on a presumed interaction between three components of personality: the id, the ego, and the superego. Explain the basic tenets of this view, and show how advertisers use this knowledge to enhance the effectiveness of their promotional messages.

2. In contrast to Freudian psychoanalytic personality theory, trait theory classifies people according to their consistent responses to environmental stimuli. For purposes of making this theory operational, what are traits? How can these traits be measured? How do marketers correlate personality traits with their strategies? Give some examples.

3. Unlike personality theories, psychographics aims to assess consumers' lifestyles so that meaningful consumer typologies can be identified. What methods do researchers use to identify consumers' lifestyles? How is psychographics different from demographics?

4. A landmark effort in the areas of values and lifestyle research is the VALS™ program, developed by SRI International. What is VALS™? How can VALS™ help marketers segment the market more effectively? Give an example.

5. Whereas the self-concept is closely associated with personality, the *self* is a more narrowly defined notion. What is the self-concept? What are some of the forms the self-concept takes? Is the self-concept a factor in determining what a person consumes? Explain.

Discussion Questions

1. Recently there has been an obvious trend in TV programs and commercials to employ average-looking, plainly dressed, and sometimes overweight models and actors in contrast to the slim, trim, glamorous, and fashionably attired stars and models who dominated TV shows and commercials in the not-so-distant past. How do you account for this shift in strategy? Is the *waif* (ultraslim) look something of the past? Does this phenomenon have anything to do with self-image?

2. Harley-Davidson Company reports that motorcycle customers no longer fit the shabby, tattooed, long-haired, black-leather-jacket-wearing stereotype. Rather, many Harley buyers are professionals (e.g., physicians, lawyers, and top-level executives). What factors may account for this change in the makeup and profile of Harley-Davidson's customer base? What might motivate professionals to buy Harleys?

3. A few years ago, Anheuser-Busch, Inc. conducted a psychographic study of the beer-drinking market.[71] The study revealed that this market was composed of four different subgroups, each of which would drink for different reasons and on different occasions. The company labeled these subgroups as social, reparative, oceanic, and indulgent drinkers. *Social drinkers* are usually young persons who are driven by a need to get ahead. This group drinks in social settings and views drinking as a means of gaining social acceptance. *Reparative drinkers* are usually middle-aged people who are sensitive and responsive to the needs of others. They drink at the end of the workday and view drinking as a reward for sacrifices made for others. *Oceanic drinkers* are insensitive to the needs of others. Many members of this group are failures who blame their lack of achievement on themselves. They drink heavily, especially when under pressure to achieve. For them, drinking is a form of escape. *Indulgent drinkers* are insensitive to others and blame their own personal failures on other people's lack of sensitivity toward them. Like oceanic drinkers, indulgent drinkers drink as a form of escape. What insights can studies such as this one offer to marketers?

In reference to the chapter opening vignette, assume that you are the human resource director of a major airline. In the process of filling a few vacant positions for flight attendants, you receive a number of applications. Upon interviewing these candidates, you discover that several otherwise qualified applicants are obese. Because flight attendants are front people for the airlines, you deny employment to these individuals. Is your action defendable from a legal perspective? Is it defendable from a human resource point of view? Is it defendable from an ethical standpoint? Are there potential public ramifications of your selection process? How might portly flight attendants impact the corporate image?

CASE

A Psychographic Profile of the Porsche Buyer

In May 2006, Luxury Institute of New York awarded Porsche the title of the most prestigious automobile brand. The award was based on a survey of 500 households with a gross annual income of at least $200,000 and a net worth of at least $720,000. In addition, Porsche was awarded the 2006 J. D. Power and Associates Award for the highest Nameplate Initial Quality Study (IQS) of automobile brands.

Today, Porsche's profit margin is the greatest of any major auto manufacturer in the industry. Pre-tax profit as a proportion of sales was, in most recent fiscal years, 18.8 percent compared with a 9 percent margin for Toyota. On the average, Porsche reportedly makes $28,000 profit on each car it sells. With an annual sales in the United States of around 57,000 vehicles, the total profit figure is staggering.

However, this rosy picture was not always the case for this company. Porsche has had its share of downs over the years. In fact, it was not until 1993, when Mr. Wendelin Wiedeking, the present chairman of the Stuttgart-based Porsche, took over the company's operations that matters started to change for the better.

He was the fourth chairman hired by Porsche to replace his three predecessors—Peter Schutz, Heinz Branitzki, and Arno Bohn—all of whom had been fired by the company in the last six years as sales dropped from 53,000 units in 1986 to around 12,000 units in 1993. In these six dismal years, the company had lost over $200 million.

At that time, Mr. Wiedeking knew the challenges that faced him. His first concern was cost. Porsche automobiles had always been expensive. The rising mark and high German labor costs were threatening to price the car right out of the market. In the 1990s, for example, Porsche's prices ranged from $40,000 to almost $100,000. Another challenge was knowing the type of person who buys a Porsche or who would like to be a Porsche owner.

Holding a doctorate degree in mechanical engineering, and armed with previous experience as Porsche's chief of production, Mr. Wiedeking set out to reduce cost. Knowing that the Japanese are best at production matters, he decided to hire a Japanese consulting firm that had among its principals Toyota's longtime top production engineer. The Japanese helped Porsche reengineer the whole factory. Just-in-time methods were initiated to replace the old systems; suppliers were reduced from 900 to 300; and time required to build a car dropped from 120 hours to only 74.

As to the second issue of the profile of the car buyer, Mr. Wiedeking asked Mr. Richard Ford, Porsche's vice president of sales and marketing for the United States, to commission a study that would reveal that profile. Mr. Ford, based on Wiedeking's recommendation, hired a consulting team of anthropologists to find out who Porsche owners are.

A few months thereafter, Mr. Ford received a report from the consulting team that detailed the psychographic profile of the Porsche owner. The report indicated that the typical owner is a 40-something male college gradate earning over $200,000 per year. The report further categorized owners into five personality types as follows:

- *Top Guns* represent 27 percent of owners. These individuals are driven and ambitious. Of primary importance to them are the matters of power and control as well as a strong desire to be noticed.
- *Elitists* represent 24 percent of owners. These individuals are old-money blue bloods. To them, a car is just a car, no matter how expensive it happens to be. They do not feel that the car is an extension of the owner's personality.
- *Proud Patrons* represent 23 percent of owners. To this group, ownership is an end in itself. Their car is a trophy earned for hard work.
- *Bon Vivants* represent 17 percent of owners. These individuals are worldly jet-setters and thrill seekers. To them, the car is a means of heightening the excitement in their busy lives.
- *Fantasists* represent 9 percent of owners. To these individuals, their car is an escape. Feeling a little guilty about having a Porsche, they avoid impressing others with the fact that they own one.

As Mr. Ford glanced over the report, he thought of its possible implications to the two areas of car design and promotions. Concerning the first area, he wondered if it would be desirable to produce a different car model to fit the psychographic profile of each segment. Concerning promotions, he realized that ad appeals have to take into consideration both what motivates buyers and what turns them off. He regretfully recalled previous Porsche ads he once had approved that told buyers how good they look in the car and how fast they could go. He realized that those appeals were perhaps the wrong things to say when addressing a personality category such as the Elitists.

Based on these studies, as well as other marketplace facts and trends, today Porsche offers four lines of automobiles: two Boxter roadsters; two Cayman coupes; the 911 (a whopping 14 varieties including Coupes, Convertibles, Targas, Turbos, 2WD, and 4WD); and the mid-size Cayenne SUV (3 kinds, including a Turbo). Joining them in 2009 will be the four-door Panamera Sports Coupe. With this impressive lineup of luxury sports cars, the award-winning company's motto, "the epitome of sports driving," seems to have been truly fulfilled.

Questions

1. Postulate advertising appeals and themes that would effectively promote the Porsche to each of the five psychographic categories listed in the report.
2. Do you think the expansion of Porsche into the line of SUVs is consistent with the firm's reputation for high-speed, luxury automobiles? Why or Why not?
3. In addition to the two specific areas Mr. Ford was concerned about when he glanced over the report (advertising appeals and car models), what are the ramifications of this psychographic report to Porsche with regard to other areas of the marketing mix such as pricing, distribution, and media selection?

Notes

1. Marsha L. Richins, "Social Comparison and the Idealized Images of Advertising," *Journal of Consumer Research* 18 (June 1991), pp. 71–82; Lois W. Banner, *American Beauty* (Chicago: University of Chicago Press, 1980).

2. Calvin S. Hall and Gardner Lindzey, *Theories of Personality* 2nd ed. (New York: John Wiley, 1970), pp. 7–9.

3. Ibid.

4. Barbara Dominguez, "Enlightening New Science of Birth Order," *The Daily Sundial, in Northern Star* (May 1, 1997); Cheryl Russell, "What Your Birth Order Says About You," *USA Weekend* (May 9–11, 1997), p. 16.

5. "Can Birth Order Predict Your Personality?" *EEO Bi-Monthly, Equal Employment Opportunity Career Journal* (February 28, 1997), p. PG.

6. Paul Gray, "The Assault on Freud," *Time* (November 29, 1993), pp. 47–51; "Sigmund Freud," www.wynja.com/giganto/psych/freud.html (accessed July 9, 1997); Dr. W. Boyd Spencer, "Sigmund Freud" Outline, www.oldsci.eiu.edu/psychology/Spencer/Freud.html (accessed July 9, 1997); Austrian National Tourist Office, "Sigmund Freud's Biography," www.austria-info.at/personen/freud/freud1_e.html (accessed July 9, 1997); Austrian National Tourist Office, "The Epochal Significance of Sigmund Freud's Work, www.austria-info.at/personen/freud/freud2_e.html (accessed July 9, 1997); Austrian National Tourist Office, "Freud's Followers and the Impact of His Theories," www.austria-info.at/personen/freud/freud3_e.html (accessed July 9, 1997); "Freud: The Master . . . or a Has-Been?" www1.rider.edu/suler.freud.html (accessed July 9, 1997).

7. Paul Gray, "The Assault on Freud," *Time* (November 29, 1993), pp. 47–51.

8. Spenser Rathus, *Psychology* (New York: Holt, Rinehart and Winston, 1981).

9. Hall and Lindzey, *Theories of Personality*; Duane Schultz, *Theories of Personality* (Monterey, CA: Brooks/Cole, 1976).

10. Bob Murray and Alice Fortinberry, "Depression Facts and Statistics," *Uplift Program* (January 15, 2005), www.upliftprogram.com/depression_stats.html.

11. "Depression Guide—Medication Options," WebMed, www.webmed.com/depression/guide/medication-options.

12. "Antidepressants: Medications for Depression," *HealthyPlace.com* (February 23, 2002), www.healthplace.com/communities/depression/treatment/antidepressants/index.asp.

13. "Depression Hurts," http://depressionhurts.com/index.jsp.

14. Louise Knapp, "Help for Overly Frisky Felines," *Petnews* (April 2002), www.pets.ca/forum/showthread.php?s=&threadid=508.

15. Hall and Lindzey, *Theories of Personality*; Schultz, *Theories of Personality*, pp. 48–66; "Alfred Adler," www.wynja.com/giganto/psych/adler.html (accessed July 9, 1997); Dr. W. Boyd Spencer, "Alfred Adler" Outline, www.oldsci.eiu.edu/psychology/Spencer/Adler.html (accessed July 9, 1997); "Adler on Social Feeling," www.wynja.com/giganto/psych/sfeelingf.html (accessed July 9, 1997).

16. Hall and Lindzey, *Theories of Personality*, pp. 134–37; Schultz, *Theories of Personality*, pp. 68–83.

17. Hall and Lindzey, *Theories of Personality*, pp. 130–34; Schultz, *Theories of Personality*, pp. 86–101.

18. Hall and Lindzey, *Theories of Personality*, pp. 137–57; Schultz, *Theories of Personality*, pp. 104–16; Harry Stack Sullivan, *The Interpersonal Theory of Psychiatry* (New York: Norton, 1953), p. 111.

19. Joel B. Cohen, "An Interpersonal Orientation to the Study of Consumer Behavior," *Journal of Marketing Research* 4 (August 1967), pp. 270–78; Joel B. Cohen, "Toward an Interpersonal Theory of Consumer Behavior," *California Management Review* 10 (Spring 1968), pp. 73–80; Jon P. Noerager, "An Assessment of CAD—A Personality Instrument Developed Specifically for Marketing Research," *Journal of Marketing Research* 16, (February 1979), pp. 53–59.

20. Jerome Kernan, "Choice Criteria, Decision Behavior, and Personality," *Journal of Marketing Research* 5 (May 1968), pp. 155–64; Joel B. Cohen and Ellen Golden, "Informational Social Influence and Product Evaluation," *Journal of Applied Psychology* 50 (February 1972), pp. 54–59; Noerager, "An Assessment of CAD—A Personality Instrument Developed Specifically for Marketing Research"; Arch Woodside and Ruth Andress, "CAD Eight Years Later," *Journal of the Academy of Marketing Science* 3 (Summer–Fall 1975), pp. 309–13; Michael Ryan and Richard Becherer, "A Multivariate Test of CAD Instrument Construct Validity," *Advances in Consumer Research* 3 (1976), pp. 149–54; Pradeep K. Tyagi, "Validation of the CAD Instrument: A Replication," *Advances in Consumer Research* 10 (1983), pp. 112–18; Mark E. Slama, Terrel G. Williams, and Armen Tashchian, "Compliant, Aggressive, and Detached Types Differ in Generalized Purchasing Involvement," *Advances in Consumer Research* 15 (1988), pp. 158–62.

21. Gordon R. Foxall, "Cognitive Styles of Consumer Initiators," *Technovation* 15, no. 5 (June 1995), pp. 269–88.

22. Marsha L. Richins and Scott Dawson, "A Consumer Values Orientation for Materialism and Its

Measurement: Scale Development and Validation," *Journal of Consumer Research* 19 (December 1992), pp. 306–16; Marsha L. Richins, "Special Possessions and the Expression of Material Values," *Journal of Consumer Research* 21 (December 1994), p. 531; Richard G. Netemeyer, Scot Burton, and Donald R. Lichtenstein, "Trait Aspects of Vanity: Measurement and Relevance to Consumer Behavior," *Journal of Consumer Research* 21, (March 1995), pp. 612–26; Susan Schultz Kleine, Robert E. Kleine III, and Chris T. Allen, "How Is a Possession 'Me' or 'Not Me'? Characterizing Types and an Antecedent of Material Possession Attachment," *Journal of Consumer Research* 22, (December 1995), pp. 327–43.

23. Ronald E. Goldsmith and Charles F. Hofacker, "Measuring Consumer Innovativeness," *Journal of the Academy of Marketing Science* 19, no. 3 (1991), pp. 209–21; Curtis P. Haugtvedt, Richard E. Petty, and John T. Cacioppo, "Need for Cognition and Advertising: Understanding the Role of Personality Variables in Consumer Behavior," *Journal of Consumer Psychology* 1, no. 3 (1992), pp. 239–60; Richard Petty et al., "Personality and Ad Effectiveness: Exploring the Utility of Need for Cognition," in Michael Houston (ed.), *Advances in Consumer Research* 15 (Ann Arbor: Association for Consumer Research, 1988), pp. 209–12; John T. Cacioppo, Richard Petty, and Katherine Morris, "Effects of Need for Cognition on Message Evaluation, Recall, and Persuasion," *Journal of Personality and Social Psychology* (October 1993), pp. 805–18; James W. Peltier and John A. Schibrowsky, "Need for Cognition, Advertisement Viewing Time, and Memory for Advertising Stimuli," in Chris T. Allen and Deborah Roedder John (eds.), *Advances in Consumer Research* 21, (Provo, UT: Association for Consumer Research, 1994), pp. 244–50.

24. Anastasia Toufexis, "365 Shopping Days Till Christmas," *Time* (December 26, 1988), p. 82; Ronald J. Faber and Thomas C. O'Guinn, "Compulsive Consumption and Credit Abuse," *Journal of Consumer Policy* 11 (1988), pp. 109–21; Mary S. Butler, "Compulsive Buying—It's No Joke," *Consumer's Digest* (September 1986), p. 55; George Witkin, "The Shopping Fix," *Health* (May 1988), p. 73; Rajan Nataraajan and Brent G. Goff, "Manifestations of Compulsiveness in the Consumer-Marketplace Domain," *Psychology & Marketing* 9 (January 1992), pp. 31–44; Thomas C. O'Guinn and Ronald J. Faber, "Compulsive Buying: A Phenomenological Explanation," *Journal of Consumer Research* 16 (September 1989), p. 154; Elizabeth C. Hirschman, "The Consciousness of Addiction: Toward a General Theory of Compulsive Consumption," *Journal of Consumer Research* 19 (December 1992), pp. 155–79; Dan L. Sherrell, Alvin C. Burns, and Melodie R. Phillips, "Fixated Consumption Behavior: The Case of Enduring Acquisition in a Product Category," in Robert L. King (ed.), *Develop-*

ments in Marketing Science (Richmond, VA: Academy of Marketing Science, 1991), pp. 36–40; Ronald J. Faber and Thomas C. O'Guinn, "A Clinical Screener for Compulsive Buying," *Journal of Consumer Research* 19 (December 1992), pp. 459–69; Allison Magee, "Compulsive Buying Tendency as a Predictor of Attitudes and Perceptions," in Chris T. Allen and Deborah Roedder John (eds.), *Advances in Consumer Research* 21, (Provo, UT: Association for Consumer Research, 1994), pp. 590–94; see also Ronald J. Faber and Thomas C. O'Guinn, "A Clinical Screener for Compulsive Buying," *Journal of Consumer Research* 19 (December 1992), pp. 459–69; Elizabeth C. Hirschman, "The Consciousness of Addiction: Toward a General Theory of Compulsive Consumption," *Journal of Consumer Research* 19 (December 1992), pp. 155–79; Thomas C. O'Guinn and Ronald J. Faber, "Compulsive Buying: A Phenomenological Exploration," *Journal of Consumer Research* 16, (September 1989), pp. 147–57; Ronald J. Faber, Gary A. Christenson, Martina De Zwaan, and James Mitchell, "Two Forms of Compulsive Consumption: Comorbidity of Compulsive Buying and Binge Eating," *Journal of Consumer Research* 22, no. 3 (December 1995), pp. 296–304.

25. Satya Menon and Barbara E. Kahn, "The Impact of Context on Variety Seeking in Product Choices," *Journal of Consumer Research* 22 (December 1995), pp. 285–95; Morton I. Jaffe, "Brand-Loyalty/Variety-Seeking and the Consumer's Personality: Comparing Children and Young Adults," in Scott B. MacKenzie and Douglas M. Stayman (eds.), *Proceedings of the Society for Consumer Psychology* (LaJolla, CA: American Psychological Association, 1995), pp. 144–51.

26. William Bearden and Randall Rose, "Attention to Social Comparison Information: An Individual Difference Factor Affecting Conformity," *Journal of Consumer Research* 16 (March 1990), pp. 461–71.

27. "MBTI Basics," The Myers-Briggs Foundation, www.myersbriggs.org/my-mbti-personality-type/mbti-basics/.

28. Zorika Petic Henderson, "Neurobiology's Role in Personality and Emotion," *Human Ecology Forum* 23 (March 1, 1995), pp. 8–11.

29. Ibid.

30. Richard P. Ebstein et al., "Dopamine D4 Receptor (D4DR) Exon III Polymorphism Associated with the Human Personality Trait of Novelty Seeking," *Nature Genetics* 12, no. 1 (January 1996).

31. Ibid.

32. Joseph D. Brown and Russell G. Wahlers, "The Environmentally Concerned Consumer: An Exploratory Study," *Journal of Marketing Theory & Practice* 6, no. 2 (Spring 1998), pp. 39–47.

33. Tim Triplett, "Brand Personality Must Be Managed or It Will Assume a Life of Its Own," *Marketing News* 28 (May 9, 1994), p. 9.

34. Hans Baumgartner, "Toward a Personology of the Consumer," *Journal of Consumer Research* 29, no. 2 (September 2002), pp. 286–293.

35. Raymond L. Horton, "The Edwards Personal Preference Schedule and Consumer Personality Research," *Journal of Marketing Research* 11 (August 1974), pp. 335–37; Harold H. Kassarjian and Mary Jane Sheffet, "Personality and Consumer Behavior: An Update," in Harold H. Kassarjian and Thomas S. Robertson (eds.), *Perspectives in Consumer Behavior*, 4th ed. (Glenview, IL: Scott, Foresman, 1991), pp. 291–353; Jennifer L. Aaker, "Measuring Brand Personality," unpublished manuscript, Stanford University (September 1994).

36. William D. Wells and Arthur D. Beard, "Personality and Consumer Behavior," in Scott Ward and Thomas S. Robertson (eds.), *Consumer Behavior: Theoretical Sources* (Upper Saddle River, NJ: Prentice Hall, 1973), pp. 141–99.

37. Kathryn E. A. Villani and Yoram Wind, "On the Usage of 'Modified' Personality Trait Measures in Consumer Research," *Journal of Consumer Research* 2 (December 1975), pp. 223–26.

38. Todd A. Mooradian and James M. Olver, "I Can't Get No Satisfaction: The Impact of Personality and Emotion on Postpurchase Processes," *Psychology & Marketing* 14, no. 4 (July 1997), pp. 379–93.

39. N. Hanna and J. S. Wagle, "Who Is Your Satisfied Customer?" *The Journal of Services Marketing* 2, no. 3 (Summer 1988), pp. 5–13; Wann-Yih Wu, "The Role of Risk Attitude on Online Shopping," *Social Behavior and Personality*, vol. 35, no. 4 (May, 2007), pp. 453–468.

40. James F. Engel, Roger D. Blackwell, and Paul W. Miniard, *Consumer Behavior*, 7th ed. (Fort Worth: Dryden Press–Harcourt Brace Jovanovich College Publishers, 1993), pp. 358–59.

41. SRI Consulting Business Intelligence, http://www.sric-bi.com/ VALS/

42. Ibid

43. "What is VALS," http://www.mediamark.com/memri/quicksheets/VALS_Quick_Sheet.pdf

44. SRI Consulting Business Intelligence, "VALS Applications," http://www.sric-bi/VALS/applications.shml

45. Lewis C. Winters, "International Psychographics," *Marketing Research: A Magazine of Management and Applications* (September 1992), pp. 48–49.

46. Judith Wardrop, "Markets with Attitude," *American Demographics* (July 1994), pp. 20–52).

47. SRI Consulting Business Intelligence, http://future.sri.com/vals/jVALS.index.html, http://future.sri.com/vals/JVALS.bkgrd.html

48. Marsha L. Richins, "Social Comparison and the Idealized Images of Advertising," *Journal of Consumer Research* 18 (June 1991), pp. 71–83.

49. Harrison G. Gough, Mario Fioravanti, and Renato Lazzari, "Some Implications of Self Versus Ideal-Self Congruence on the Revised Adjective Check List," *Journal of Personality and Social Psychology* 44, no. 6 (1983), pp. 1214–20; Steven Jay Lynn and Judith W. Rhue, "Daydream Believers," *Psychology Today* (September 1985), p. 14.

50. A. Ben Oumil and Orhan Erdem, "Self-Concept by Gender: A Focus on Male–Female Consumers," *Journal of Marketing Theory & Practice* 5, no. 1 (Winter 1997), pp. 7–14; Ibrahim Hafedh, "A Multi-Dimensional Approach to Analyzing the Effect of Self-Congruity on Shoppers' Retail Store Behavior," *Innovative Marketing*, vol. 3, no. 3 (2007).

51. Russell W. Belk, "Possessions and the Extended Self," *Journal of Consumer Research* 15 (September 1988), pp. 139–68; Russell Belk, "My Possessions Myself," *Psychology Today* (July–August, 1988), pp. 50–52; Amy J. Morgan, "The Evolving Self in Consumer Behavior: Exploring Possible Selves," in Leigh McAlister and Michael L. Rothschild (eds.), *Advances in Consumer Research* 20 (Provo, UT: Association for Consumer Research, 1993), pp. 429–32; Raj Mehta and Russell W. Belk, "Artifacts, Identity, and Transition: Favorite Possessions of Indians and Indian Immigrants to the United States," *Journal of Consumer Research* 17 (March 1991), pp. 398–411; Marsha L. Richins, "Special Possessions and the Expression of Material Values," *Journal of Consumer Research* 21 (December 1994), pp. 522–33; Kleine, Kleine, and Allen, "How Is a Possession 'Me' or 'Not Me'? Characterizing Types and an Antecedent of Material Possession Attachment."

52. Morgan, "The Evolving Self in Consumer Behavior: Exploring Possible Selves."

53. Erving Goffman, *The Presentation of Self in Everyday Life* (Garden City, NY: Doubleday, 1959).

54. Morris B. Holbrook, Michael R. Solomon, and Stephen Bell, "A Re-Examination of Self-Monitoring and Judgments of Furniture Designs," *Home Economics Research Journal* 19 (September 1990), pp. 6–16; Mark Snyder, "Self-Monitoring Processes," in Leonard Berkowitz (ed.), *Advances in Experimental Social Psychology* (New York: Academic Press, 1979), pp. 851–928.

55. Arnold W. Buss, *Self-Consciousness and Social Anxiety* (San Francisco: Freeman, 1980); Lynn Carol Miller and Cathryn Leigh Cox, "Public Self-Consciousness and Makeup Use," *Personality and Social Psychology Bulletin* 8, no. 4 (1982), pp. 748–51; Michael R. Solomon and John Schopler, "SelfConciousness and Clothing," *Personality and Social Psychology Bulletin* 8, no. 3 (1982), pp. 508–14.

56. Mark Snyder and Steve Gangestad, "On the Nature of Self-Monitoring: Matters of Assessment, Matters of Validity," *Journal of Personality and Social Psychology* 51 (1986), pp. 125–39.

57. Michael R. Solomon, "The Role of Products as Social Stimuli: A Symbolic Interactionism Perspective," *Journal of Consumer Research* 10 (December 1983), pp. 319-29; Robert E. Kleine, Susan Schultz-Kleine, and Jerome B. Kernan, "Mundane Consumption and the Self: A Social Identity Perspective," *Journal of Consumer Psychology* 2, no. 3 (1993), pp. 209-35; Newell D. Wright, C. B. Claiborne, and M. Joseph Sirgy, "The Effects of Product Symbolism on Consumer Self-Concept," in John F. Sherry Jr. and Brian Sternthal (eds.) *Advances in Consumer Research* 19 (Provo, UT: Association for Consumer Research (1992), pp. 311-18; Susan Fournier, "A Person-Based Relationship Framework for Strategic Brand Management," Ph.D. dissertation, University of Florida (1994).

58. Jack L. Nasar, "Symbolic Meanings of House Styles," *Environment and Behavior* 21 (May 1989), pp. 235-57; E. K. Sadalla, B. Verschure, and J. Burroughs, "Identity Symbolism," *Housing, Environment, and Behavior* 19 (1987).

59. E. L. Grubb and L. Grathwohl, "Consumer Self-Concept, Symbolism, and Market Behavior: A Theoretical Approach," *Journal of Marketing* 31 (October 1967), pp. 22-27.

60. Sak Onkvisit and John Shaw, "Self-Concept and Image Congruence: Some Research and Managerial Implications," *Journal of Consumer Marketing* 4 (Winter 1987), pp. 13-24; George M. Zinkhan and Jae W. Hong, "Self-Concept and Advertising Effectiveness: A Conceptual Model of Congruency, Conspicuousness, and Response Mode," in Rebecca H. Holman and Michael R. Solomon (eds.), *Advances in Consumer Research* 18 (Provo, UT: Association for Consumer Research, 1991), pp. 348-54; C. B. Claiborne and M. Joseph Sirgy, "Self-Image Congruence as a Model of Consumer Attitude Formation and Behavior: A Conceptual Review and Guide for Further Research," (a paper presented at the Academy of Marketing Science Conference, New Orleans (1990); Marsha L. Richins, "Special Possessions and the Expression of Material Values," *Journal of Consumer Research* 21 (December 1994), pp. 522-33; Kleine, Kleine, and Allen, "How Is a Possession 'Me' or 'Not Me'? Characterizing Types

and an Antecedent of Material Possession Attachment"; Mary K. Ericksen, "Using Self-Congruity and Ideal Congruity to Predict Purchase Intention: A European Perspective," *Journal of Euromarketing* 6, no. 1 (1996), pp. 41-56; Michael Lynn and Judy Harris, "The Desire for Unique Consumer Products: A New Individual Differences Scale," *Psychology & Marketing* 14, no. 6 (September 1997), pp. 601-16; Susan Fournier, "Consumers and Their Brands: Developing Relationship Theory in Consumer Research," *Journal of Consumer Research* 24, no. 4 (March 1998), pp. 343-73; Mark P. Leach and Annie H. Liu, "The Use of Culturally Relevant Stimuli in International Advertising," *Psychology & Marketing* 15, no. 6 (September 1998), pp. 523-46.

61. Rajagopal, "Impact of Advertising Variability on Building Customer Based Brand Personality under Competitive Environment," *Latin American Business Review*, vol. 6, no. 3 (2005), pp. 63-84.

62. Frank Kressmann, et. al., "Direct and Indirect Effects of Self-Image Congruence on Brand Loyalty," *Journal of Business Research*, vol. 59, no. 9 (September 2006), pp. 955-964.

63. Mary K. Ericksen and Joseph Sirgy, "Employed Females' Clothing Preference, Self-Image Congruence, and Career Anchorage," *Journal of Applied Social Psychology*, vol. 22, no. 5, (March 1992), pp. 408-422.

64. Joseph Z. Wisenblit, "Person Positioning: Empirical Evidence and a Paradigm," *Journal of Professional Services Marketing* 4 (1989), pp. 53-84; Betsy Wiesendancer, "Do You Need an Image Consultant?" *Sales & Marketing Management* (May 1992), pp. 30-36.

65. R. A. Wicklund and P. M. Gollwitzer, *Symbolic Self-Completion* (Hillsdale, NJ: Lawrence Erlbaum, 1982).

66. A. Dwayne Ball and Lori H. Tasaki, "The Role and Measurement of Attachment in Consumer Behavior," *Journal of Consumer Psychology* 1, no. 2 (1992), pp. 155-72; Raj Mehta and Russell W. Belk, "Artifacts, Identity, and Transition: Favorite Possessions of Indians and Indian Immigrants to the United States," *Journal of Consumer Research* 17 (March 1991), pp. 398-411.

Consumer
Decision Making

LEARNING OBJECTIVES

- To understand the factors at play in the process of consumer decision making.
- To conceptualize the difference between programmed versus nonprogrammed buying decisions.
- To gain insight into Dewey's five-stage problem-solving process as applied to consumer purchasing decisions.
- To recognize the importance of post-purchase feelings and their effect on the behavior of consumers.
- To ascertain the causes of consumer satisfaction/dissatisfaction.
- To identify the reasons for and causes of consumer behavior as well as recognize methods to maximize consumer satisfaction.

KEY TERMS

constructive processing
involvement
low involvement
high involvement
nonprogrammed decision
extended problem solving
limited problem solving
impulse purchases
programmed decisions
brand loyalty
internal search
sharpening
leveling
external search

evoked set
heuristics
evaluative criteria
salient attributes
determinant attributes
prospect theory
framing
decision rules
compensatory decision rule
noncompensatory decision rule
instrumental performance
expressive performance
consumer satisfaction

Ominous words such as massive layoffs, double-digit inflation, housing market collapse, the demise of Wall Street, and the government rescue package have become familiar terms in everyday conversations between people as well as among reporters in the media. The downturn started in the year 2007 with the subprime mortgage crisis, a condition caused by contracted liquidity in credit markets resulting from failures of banks, mortgage companies, investment firms, and government-sponsored enterprises.

Subprime lending is the practice of making loans to borrowers who do not qualify for receiving them due to various risk factors such as low income levels, size of down payment, credit history, and employment status. Subprime borrowing was a major contributor to the increase in the home-ownership rates and the unusual rise in housing demand. The overall rate of U.S. home-ownership increased from 64 percent in the 1990s to a peak of over 69 percent in 2004.

This rosy picture of a society where every person can fulfill the American dream of owning a home soon faded away. As the financial conditions worsened, the market faced one of its major economic challenges.

Finger-pointing and blame-setting became rampant. Views varied with regard to who was responsible for the mounting calamities. Some observes attributed the collapse to unethical practices of banks that offered high-risk loan options and incentives to entice unqualified borrowers. The high-risk loans included forms such as "no income, no job, and no assets" loans (a practice referred to as ninja loans). In 2005, for example, the median down payment for first-time home buyers was only 2 percent, while almost half of those buyers made no down payment whatsoever. Other deceptive loan practices included "interest-only adjustable-rate" mortgages (ARM) which allow home owners to pay just the interest during the initial period. Still other forms of loans extended to borrowers are known as "option loans," in which homeowners repay variable amounts, while any unpaid interest is added to the principal.

Most observers, however, place a great deal of blame on consumers' faulty decision making processes. They blame those consumers who received these questionable loans just as much if not even more than the banks that offered them. These home borrowers basically made poor financial decisions and should not have received those loans. In most cases, these individuals should not have aspired to own homes in the first place, especially knowing that they would be unable to repay their loans if interest rates were to rise.

Blame for the collapse of Wall Street, in these observers view, may partially rest on AIG, Freddie Mac, and Fannie Mae; but to a major extent, the fault rests on the shoulders of every single person who made the decision to apply for and get one or more of these subprime loans.[1]

The decision making process of both the executives of the failing financial institutions as well as those of the subprime mortgage loan borrowers were cited as major causes of the financial crisis that plagues our economy in the year 2008 and beyond. The first group was blamed for deceptive lending practices, while the sec-

ond group was criticized for knowingly taking advantage of loans they were unqualified to receive. Learn more about these issues by visiting Womens' Voices for Change at www.womensvoices-forchange.org/2008/10/financial-collapse-why-all-americans-are-responsible.html. *Which group are you inclined to blame more for the collapse? Are there other parties that you suspect were involved, failed to take action, or should have foreseen the problem before it arose? Explain.*

© 2009, Catalin Plesa, Shutterstock, Inc.

Investment decisions are among the most consequential decisions consumers make.

Whether or not consumers choose to invest their hard-earned money and how they elect to do so are among the most consequential decisions that individuals ever make. Sometimes, these investments yield a hefty return. Unfortunately, some individuals end up paying dearly for their financial ignorance and bad investment choices, as was the case in the recent housing and financial market collapse.

This chapter addresses consumer decision-making processes. We begin by differentiating between nonprogrammed and programmed decision processes. Next, we analyze the stages that comprise the decision-making process, from the problem-recognition phase through postpurchase evaluation. Finally, we examine determinants of consumer satisfaction or dissatisfaction with a purchase.

The Decision Process

The U.S. consumer today is simply one of the most cared for and pampered in the world. There is significantly more product selection, more product information, and more places at which to shop than in any other country in the world. A multitude of suppliers offers a complex mix of products and services. They utilize highly sophisticated pricing, distribution, and promotional strategies in a continuous race to please finicky consumers.

We have only to consider the variety of alternatives available to a new car buyer to realize the complexities of choice. A bewildering array of automobile makes, both domestic and foreign, with dozens of models available within each make and diverse features, power ranges, and options, present buyers a true challenge.

Although a wide range of choices represents a positive sign of progress and reflects a society's high standard of living, it nevertheless complicates the choice process. When confronted with an excessive number of alternatives from which to select, consumers may become perplexed and bewildered. They may simply patronize their usual brands and stores, or information overload may lead them to arrive at a product selection based on gut feeling.

The many and varied options available to new car buyers illustrate the complexity of choice.

One of the assumptions made in consumer behavior research is that most purchases are preceded by a decision process. A decision is an act that prevails only if the consumer is faced with two or more alternative courses of action, all of which have good probabilities of bringing about a desired end result. Decision making is the process of considering, evaluating, and choosing between these alternatives. Consumers who face a no-choice buying situation are simply not exercising decision making.

Consumers make many types of decisions. One type relates to whether or not they should buy a product under consideration. A recent college graduate commencing a new job in a large city mulls over a decision about the practicality of commuting to and from work via public transportation versus purchasing a new automobile. Assuming the consumer elects to purchase a new car, a further issue relates to the make of car. Once that decision has been made, the specific model, color, and options package remains to be decided. The graduate must still decide on the dealership from which the auto will be purchased, how the new car purchase should be financed, and whether or not extended warranty coverage is desirable.

When faced with two or more options in relation to any given problem or need, we tend to subjectively evaluate the alternatives, pondering the available information in light of our present and future expectations. We establish an order of preference among the alternatives that may shape the outcome of the final purchase selection.

ARE CONSUMERS RATIONAL?

Classical economic theory painted a picture of consumers as rational decision makers. Consumers are assumed to attempt to maximize their utility or satisfaction (supposing they can measure it) continuously within the constraints of limited resources. It further presumes that this rational consumer is able to select from among all possible alternatives a combination of products and services that will provide the greatest total utility given limited resources.[2]

This view suggests that the consumer is knowledgeable about all the possibilities or alternatives available in the marketplace, their features, their qualities, their prices, and the utilities that can be extracted from acquiring and using them. It ignores the sociopsychological factors that influence human behavior, however, and the effect of information such as advertising and promotion on consumer preferences.

Thus the traditional portrait of the rational, objective, utility-maximizing, information-processing, decision-making consumer is greatly simplified. Consumers are unlikely to be computing, calculating entities that mathematically gauge the outcome of each alternative considered.

A recent study by ComScore Network analyzed pre-purchase search activity across the four categories of apparel, computer hardware, fitness/sports, and travel. The study found that approximately one out of every two online purchases was preceded by an inquiry on a search engine. It also revealed that most searchers completed their purchase-related search activity two or more weeks in advance of the purchase transaction. For example, on average, buyers on fitness/sports Web sites conducted 2.5 relevant searches in the 12 weeks preceding a purchase; apparel buyers made 4.7 relevant searches; computer hardware purchasers made 4.9 searches; and buyers of travel services made 6 relevant searches in the 12 weeks prior to purchasing.[3] Another study by Compete, Inc., surveyed two million Internet users regarding their search during the automobile purchase process. The investigation showed that among consumers who purchased a vehicle, Web search was considered the most credible source in helping them with their auto purchase. Approximately 70 percent of them stated that they searched the Web throughout the entire research and purchase process. Over half of the buyers indicated that Web search helped them narrow down the list of vehicles they were originally considering, a procedure known as *winnowing*, as well as helped them evaluate the few surviving options side-by-side, a process known as *comparison*.[4] Today, shopping search engines provide valuable information to consumers during the search stage. Consumer reviews, merchant ratings, popular product lists, and total price that includes tax and shipping are but some of the facts needed by consumers in order to locate the best deal.[5]

Other studies provided evidence concerning the way brand purchases occur without prior consideration of alternatives. Feldman and Spencer reported that 75 percent of newcomers to a community selected physicians solely on the basis of a recommendation.[6] Further, Ferber stated that 20 to 25 percent of durable goods and clothing purchases appear to be impulsive.[7] It has also been reported that up to 50 percent of supermarket purchases and 33 percent of transactions in variety and drugstores are impulsive in nature.[8]

Researchers have come to realize that decision makers may engage in a variety of shortcuts in making choices. This is particularly true when they feel that the effort of systematic search and information processing is not justified, given the outcomes. A consumer may use what is known as **constructive processing** by evaluating the effort required to make a particular choice, then choosing an effort level best suited to the task. In this sense, consumers are tailoring their degree of cognitive effort to the task at hand.[9]

constructive processing
a tendency of consumers to tailor their cognitive effort to suit the task at hand

EFFORT VARIATIONS IN CONSUMER DECISION MAKING

The decisions consumers make vary widely in importance and so require different amounts of effort.[10] The amount of effort consumers expend when buying products or services is often a function of their degree of interest in and involvement with a particular purchase. **Involvement** depends on the degree of personal relevance that a product or service holds for the consumer and on the extent to which it serves as a vehicle of personal identification. In the case

involvement
the degree of personal relevance that a purchase holds for the consumer

low involvement
a case in which consumers attach minimal personal relevance to a purchase

high involvement
a case in which consumers attach elevated relevance to a purchase

nonprogrammed decision
a case in which a novel or infrequently encountered situation requires a customized solution

For most families, the purchase of a new home is a nonprogrammed decision entailing significant financial, social, and psychological consequences.

of **low involvement**, a consumer views a purchase as unimportant and regards the outcome of his or her decision as inconsequential. Because the purchase carries a minimal degree of personal relevance or identification, the individual feels there is little or nothing to be gained from attending to the details of a purchase. For example, a purchase of a candy bar requires minimal or no premeditation and planning.

High involvement purchases are those that are important to the consumer either from a financial, social, or psychological point of view. The purchase is characterized by personal relevance and an identification with the outcome. An individual anticipates a potentially significant gain from expending time and effort in comparison shopping before buying. A wine connoisseur purchasing an expensive bottle of wine to give as a house gift perceives the brand choice as having a high degree of personal identification. A high level of felt involvement can increase an individual's willingness to search for, process, and transmit information about a purchase.[11]

One way of looking at a classification of the decision-making process is to think of it in terms of a continuum, anchored at one end by programmed decisions and at the other extreme by nonprogrammed decisions. Many decisions fall somewhere between these two extremities.

Nonprogrammed Decisions

When a purchase decision involves products or services that are financially, socially, or psychologically important, consumers are likely to diligently seek out information from many sources, take time to analyze the information, and methodically sift through all the details before arriving at a final purchase decision. Such would be the case when consumers buy a new home or make a major investment in the stock market. **Nonprogrammed decisions** are either novel to consumers or are infrequently encountered, and experience appears to be of little value in reaching a decision. No standardized solution for handling the problem exists. A customized, tailored approach seems to be required in order to handle the situation.

Such cases are likely to activate a variety of cognitive processes. The consumer is willing to expend major cognitive effort, is more receptive to information sources, and is more inclined to process the acquired information. Evaluation of the acquired information is conducted in view of consumers' lifestyles and self-images, as well as against present and future needs and anticipated resource availability.

Marketers recognize consumers' need for detailed information when non-programmed decisions are being made. Marketers who provide such information are likely to receive favorable

© 2009, Christy Thompson, Shutterstock, Inc.

responses from consumers who would otherwise, in the absence of such information, feel skeptical and ambivalent about specific product and brand offerings and drop them from active consideration.

Nonprogrammed decisions include a range of decision process possibilities. As in the case of purchasing a new home, **extended problem solving** is a decision situation characterized by a high degree of perceived risk. Decisions, in this case, may require significant financial commitments, involve social or psychological implications, and entail symbols that communicate an image of the owner to others. In such cases, internal and multiple external information sources are sought. Information is likely to be processed actively and carefully. Alternatives are meticulously evaluated, and their attributes are painstakingly matched and compared.

In the case of **limited problem solving**, consumers have some experience in dealing with the purchase situation. They have already established criteria for evaluating products, services, or brands within the choice category. It is unlikely, for example, that a consumer whose wristwatch needs replacement would systematically search for information and rigorously evaluate each available alternative. A simpler approach, such as buying the same watch brand used previously or purchasing a well-known brand, may work well.

Impulse purchase situations are quite common. **Impulse purchases** involve little deliberation and limited or no external search. Cues such as price deals, special offers and targeted messages on the Internet, point-of-purchase displays, advertising messages, or a salesperson's comments, strategically situated by marketers, frequently trigger such purchasing responses. The purchase takes place within a short time span, and limited or no cognitive effort is allocated to the decision process. Emotional appeals usually play a major role in such purchases.[12]

extended problem solving
an elevated level of expended effort used in making risky and significant decisions

limited problem solving
a reduced level of expended effort used in making less-risky decisions

impulse purchases
spontaneous and unplanned purchases made in response to environmental cues

Programmed Decisions

At the other end of the continuum are decisions made with little or no conscious cognitive effort. Purchases of many products, such as soft drinks, toothpaste, coffee, or the daily newspaper, are repetitive and routine. Such **programmed decisions** require no special thought on the part of the consumer and are performed with minimal effort and conscious control.

Much consumer behavior can be classified as programmed decisions. The habitual or routine nature of many purchases allows consumers to minimize the time and effort spent on purchasing familiar, frequently bought, and often-used goods. **Brand loyalty** represents a special case of habitual purchasing behavior. Repetitive purchasing of brands that have proven satisfactory in the past is an effort-minimization strategy that speeds the shopping experience and eliminates the risk of selecting an unsatisfactory alternative.

From the perspective of brand managers, routine purchasing of a given brand by loyal consumers is a coveted accomplishment. However, such good fortune is not necessarily permanent. Programmed decisions are not irrevocable and

programmed decisions
cases where consumers follow habitual routines to deal with frequently encountered situations

brand loyalty
an attachment to brands that have proven satisfactory in the past

can be reprogrammed at some point in the future. Customer loyalties are fickle. They can change at any time if the product fails to provide the desired benefits or a competitor succeeds with price or promotional tactics to uproot the previous purchasing routine.

The Nature of the Consumer Decision Process

Consumer decision processes can be characterized as a form of problem solving. When consumers perceive a discrepancy between an actual state of affairs and a desired or ideal state of affairs, problem recognition arises. Individuals then become involved in a problem-solving process. This process entails a sequence of activities designed to arrive at a decision leading to a satisfactory solution to the perceived problem.

John Dewey identified five stages in problem solving.[13] In a slightly modified and adapted form, they are as follows.

1. Problem recognition
2. Search activity
3. Identifying and evaluating alternative solutions
4. Purchase or commitment
5. Postpurchase considerations

Although these steps are suggestive, shoppers may proceed directly from problem recognition to purchase. In some instances, a problem may not even exist before the purchase occurs, such as in the case of impulse purchases. The mental or physical activity associated with each stage may vary significantly based on the cost of the product or service. The following sections of this chapter explain each of Dewey's stages as they relate to consumer decision processes. Exhibit 9.1 is a depiction of these stages.

EXHIBIT 9.1   **Stages of the Consumer Decision Process**

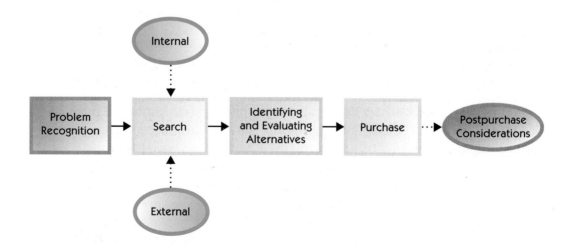

PROBLEM RECOGNITION

A problem exists when an individual is enticed by a goal but lacks certainty about the best solution for the specific dilemma that he or she faces. A young man experiencing hair loss perceives this predicament as a major problem. Desiring to appear attractive, he feels threatened that hair loss will reduce his attractiveness and limit his ability to socialize. The consumer, in this case, perceives a variance between an actual and a desired state of affairs. The result is a form of incongruity or dissonance that triggers behavior.

From a consumer behavior point of view, the chance of buying a product or service is enhanced when marketers successfully create a tension state for the consumer. If the disturbance in an individual's psychological field is strong enough, a problem surfaces at the conscious level. The tension may be sufficiently intense to arouse motives or reasons that impel the consumer to think about the problem and trigger a need for him or her to take corrective measures. One form of treatment is purchase of a product or service as a solution to the problem. For example, today many individuals worried about facial age lines resort to treatments such as Botox injections to alleviate their concerns over looking older. However, unfortunately, not every problem is solvable through product purchase and use. In some instances, individuals process information or engage in physical or mental activity that leads only to frustration or further anxiety. Consumers may discover that there is no viable, simple, or instant solution to their problem. They may even discover that a course of action they hoped would bring their problem to a satisfactory resolution has failed to provide the anticipated end result. For instance, a consumer may come to realize that the promised loss of weight from a certain diet pill may never materialize.

Problem recognition is not merely an outcome of marketing efforts aiming at making consumers aware of product groups or brands. It is, in many instances, the outgrowth of consumers' striving to fulfill the demands of everyday life.

Consumer problems can be the result of *assortment depletion*, wherein individuals experience inadequacies in their stock of goods. A family can run out of milk, breakfast cereal, aspirin, soft drinks, or some other commodity. At other times, *changes in consumers' life circumstances* may cause them to need something they never had occasion to need or use before. Career changes may require that individuals purchase a PC in order to maintain a home office. Retirement causes some to search for hobbies to occupy their newly found free time. *Product acquisitions* frequently require the purchase of further products such as supplies, accessories, and energy sources. Consumers who buy a PC may soon purchase a printer, various software packages, disks, and other related accessories to use in conjunction with their computer. *Product obsolescence* may cause individuals to replace goods. Some products break or wear out; others go out of fashion. *Expanded means*, financial or otherwise, may lead to expanded desires and higher levels of aspiration. A promotion and corresponding pay raise may translate into a desire for more possessions, expanded roles, or changes in lifestyle—causes for generating new consumer problems. Similarly, *contracted means* (such as a job layoff) may cause some-one to cancel a planned vacation. Finally, *expanded awareness* can also be a source of problem recognition. Consumers constantly receive new information about their surroundings, largely through marketing stimuli such as advertising and other promotional activities, as well as from the Internet. Discoveries of *new* and *improved* products create cognitions that may alter consumers' satisfaction with their present state of affairs. Discoveries of *new* and *improved* products create cognitions that may alter consumers' satisfaction with their present state of affairs.

SEARCH ACTIVITY

Problem recognition is followed by search activity. The objective of search activity is to identify and familiarize oneself with the courses of action available to solve the perceived problem. A patient who was advised by a physician to exercise daily may look at alternative fitness-equipment choices, such as a treadmill, Step Master, rowing machine, or NordicTrack. Later in the decision process, a consumer will examine the relative merits of the various options and contemplate the consequences of selecting one of them.

The amount of search activity undertaken varies greatly from casual to systematic, based on a number of factors such as the importance of the problem, the urgency of the purchase, the degree of involvement with the product or service, and the availability of such alternatives.[14] For example, a consumer who discovered a dandruff problem may do nothing more to find a solution than consider the experience of friends or family members who had a similar problem. On the other hand, a novice investor in the stock market may spend a great deal of time and effort to learn about the various companies listed on the NASDAQ.

Types of Search

Information search can be internal, external, or a combination. An internal search entails scanning one's memory for product-related information, and an external search involves physical (and perhaps mental) efforts to solicit and gather information from outside sources.

Internal Search

internal search
search the process of retrieving relevant information from memory

Internal search is the mental activity of retrieving information that has been stored in long-term memory and deals with products or services that can help an individual solve a problem. Past experiences, positive or negative, with products, services, stores, salespeople, or other aspects of the purchase situation as well as ads or conversations with friends may be recalled. Consumers may recollect previous experiences such as how nicely they were treated by a waitress at a particular restaurant, how wonderful the entrées were, and how delicious the desserts tasted.

Consumers' memory structure has profound implications to marketers. Because of the extensive amount of sensory stimulation that strikes the consumer almost daily, sharpening and leveling, both simplification strategies, take place.

Sharpening is a process of changing stimuli from ambiguous forms to more conventional ones as people attempt to make a complex situation consistent with preexisting simple schemas. Sharpening deals with encoding redundant or confusing information. The result is categorizing the information into chunks that are meaningful to a person. For example, we often hear people say that they take Centrum vitamins daily to enhance their health and vigor. Similarly, because of the numerous attributes of a product such as a headache remedy (pain relieving, gentle, fast acting, easy to swallow, long lasting, etc.), people use sharpening as a shortcut to abbreviate the product selection process. Evidence points to the fact that as consumers become familiar with a product category, they tend to evaluate the alternatives in it by *brand* rather than by *attributes*, and they tend to make more global evaluations of brands.[15] In the headache remedy example, a consumer may simply select a well-known brand such as Excedrin for headaches and another like Bayer for colds.

Leveling, on the other hand, is a process of generalization, wherein details are omitted in order to simplify the memory structure. Leveling also occurs when information about one object can be transferred or generalized to another object. For example, the generic term "hybrid cars" has been used to indicate energy-saving vehicles regardless of their make or model.

Sharpening and leveling often promote brand loyalty and hinder the marketing efforts of a newcomer into a product category. From the perspective of the consumer, making global evaluations based on *brand* is a preferred strategy, because it offers a shortcut compared with the effort-laden process of considering and evaluating products in terms of their attributes.

Stimulating consumers' memory is a necessity for marketers who stand to benefit from a simplified consumer evaluation process. Brand advertising, point-of-purchase materials, hang tags, store shelf talkers, gondolas, slogans, and other materials are designed to jog consumers' memories and prompt global and effortless evaluations.

External Search

External search seeks out new information through a variety of avenues that may include *market-oriented sources* such as advertising, promotional materials, packaging, and Internet shopping search engines; as well as *interpersonal sources*, such as taking with salespeople and peers, or e-mail and participation in online communities like MySpace and FaceBook.

The Internet facilitates consumers' access to consumption-related information. It permits obtaining such data more quickly and saves the effort and cost that would have been needed to collect this information from traditional comparison shopping and interpersonal sources. Moreover, the Internet improves consumer search effectiveness by providing a mixture of sound, image, text, and visual tools (e.g., animation and avatars) to enhance consumer learning.[17]

Today, the Internet as a search tool is a significant factor in the search process. It plays a key role in the decision-making and purchase process for the majority of higher-involvement consumer products and services. Recent surveys by DoubleClick indicate that 74 percent of respondents used Internet

sharpening
a process of changing stimuli from ambiguous forms to more conventional ones

leveling
a process in which details are omitted in order to simplify the memory structure

external search
the process of seeking information from exogenous sources

Today, the shopping experience has been greatly simplified and enhanced as the Web has provided both the convenience and wealth of information needed for consumers to make wise choices.

search before making any online purchase; and 57 percent did so before making any offline purchase. The survey also revealed that the majority of pre-purchase search activity (searches and clicks) involved generic product categories rather than merchants' specific brands. However, brand names peaked in the search activity as the moment of purchase approached.[18]

It has been observed that consumers use Internet search in a variety of ways. They may search for information through the Internet and end up buying the product online. Alternatively, they may search the information on the Internet, but then buy the product through traditional channels. In a third case, they may search the information through traditional channels, then buy the product online.[19]

Recognizing that consumers use search throughout the multi-channel shopping process, retailers now incorporate *search marketing* into their overall multi-channel strategy. Retailers came to realize the key role that search plays in the overall shopping cycle, including offline purchases. Through search marketing, companies now have a better chance of building awareness for their brands and influencing purchase decisions. Retailers can expand search marketing campaigns to promote offline events and sales, in-store pickup and return, multi-channel gift and redemption, as well as other multi-channel benefits.[20]

Researchers suggest that consumers tend to adapt and modify their external search effort to match the significance of the specific decision-making problem at hand. In this view, the research strategy for a specific decision-making problem is contingent upon a number of personal factors that characterize an individual decision maker. The four factors that appear to be significant in determining the amount of external search undertaken are:

- *Individual learning style:* Not all consumers have the same ability to explore, search, and process information. For example, novelty- and fashion-conscious consumers are likely to be passive learners, willingly accepting new things with little concern for outcomes and implications of their actions.[21]
- *Product involvement:* The higher the degree of involvement, the more likely a consumer will seek and systematically process information. For example, for most people, the decision to purchase a new automobile involves deliberate and exhaustive search for and processing of external information.
- *Experience:* Consumers facing new or unfamiliar purchase situations are likely to expend more search time and exert greater effort than experienced buyers. A novice investor in the stock market is more apt to seek advice from investment counselors than veteran investors.
- *Risk perception:* The amount of external search positively correlates with the degree of perceived risk. In general, the higher the perceived risk,

the greater the time and effort expended on external search. For example, when purchasing toys or garments for children, many parents attempt to learn about their safety before purchasing. The topic of risk perception is discussed in detail at the end of Chapter 4 on Consumer Perception.

IDENTIFYING AND EVALUATING ALTERNATIVE SOLUTIONS

The third step in the consumer decision process is the evaluation of alternative resolutions to the perceived market-related problem. This process may be executed simultaneously with the search process or it may emerge only after the consumer identifies and acquires sufficient information on the available alternatives. The goal of this step is to determine a choice set and compare the attributes of alternatives that fall within it. Two activities are involved in this evaluation process. The first is to narrow down product alternatives to a manageable number. The second is to evaluate the attributes of each alternative in order to choose the best option.

Identifying Alternatives

At this point in the decision process, the consumer has a pool of alternatives that he or she has become aware of through advertising, peer influences, previous experiences, or visits to stores and Web sites. However, the consumer is unlikely to consider all these. More often, consumers consider a modest subset of alternatives and tend to obtain information about that restricted set of options. The small set of brands that come to mind when one contemplates buying a product is known as the **evoked set**. Contrary to the traditional notion that consumers engage in an effortful, systematic search for information on a large number of alternative products, recent research suggests that such incidents are rare, even when decisions involve major purchases. In most cases, consumers tend to reduce alternatives in the evoked set to a manageable number in order to save time and effort. The *consideration set* is composed of those brands the consumer would actually contemplate purchasing (such as those brands that an individual is favorably impressed with and may indeed buy).

> **evoked set**
> those few brands that come to mind when one thinks of a product category

Consumers use simple rules of thumb or **heuristics** to reduce the effort involved in the decision-making process. Chaiken suggests that over time, consumers attempt to automate their decisions by seeking shortcuts to the extent that their decisions become programmed.[23] For example, research has revealed that consumers under conditions of time constraint were more likely to choose (1) higher-quality, higher-priced brands; (2) higher-quality brands over low-quality brands; and (3) top-of-the-line products. One possible explanation for these time-constraint effects is that consumers used a "brand-name" heuristic. Heuristic processing entails following simple practices, such as *always buy the brand on sale, buy a well-known brand, buy the store brand, buy what the family uses, buy what a neighbor recommends, buy the most expensive model*, or other similar routines.

> **heuristics**
> simple rules of thumb consumers use as shortcuts to reduce shopping effort

Consumer Behavior in Practice

Step Aside Men . . . Women Are in Charge

Marketing automobiles to women is very different than marketing them to men. Men and women tend to look at cars in totally different ways. Whereas men tend to think of their vehicles as extensions of their personalities, women are more apt to consider the practical aspects of a car.

When searching for an automobile, women tend to set different priorities then men. A recent survey showed that women placed a higher value on the attribute of dependability of the vehicle than men did. The chance that a car may fail to start on a dark and deserted road at night presents a more threatening situation for women than for men. In the case of luxury cars, the top five attributes for women, in order, were safety, styling, comfort, reliability, and quality.

With safety and dependability being of primary importance, other attributes that appeal to women include keyless entry, front and side airbags, traction control, antilock brakes, and interior design that accommodates the small body structure of women, such as front seats that easily adjust forward to reach the pedals.

Other important features for women include maneuverability of the vehicle, step-in height, texture of the seat fabric, and other details such as door convenience for seating kids and loading groceries, ease of getting into the backseat, and even whether a driver can operate small control buttons with long fingernails.

Car-buying trends have significantly shifted in recent years. Trends point to the fact that women have become the major decision makers for new car purchasing. According to *Road and Travel* magazine, women now purchase 65 percent of all new cars and 53 percent of used cars. They also influence 95 percent of all auto purchases.

Women, in general, tend to find the shopping experience for a new car intimidating and unpleasant. According to a recent survey by Capital One in 2005, women did not feel as empowered as they should in the car-buying process. The majority (75 percent) did not feel comfortable unless they brought along a male compan-

ion to the dealership. 74 percent of women surveyed reported that the most difficult aspects of the car-buying process relate to the financial elements of the transaction. Women's inability to get a good deal on price, pressure from the salesperson to buy more than the woman can afford, the inability to understand the purchase fees and costs, as well as the likelihood of obtaining a good deal on a loan, were among the negative aspects cited by women in the survey.

Today, dealers are anxious to capitalize on this growing market segment. They are initiating Web sites offering information about automobiles targeted specifically to women. These sites include the online magazine *Roadandtravel.com, Edmunds.com/women*, and *Motherproof.com*. Another site, *AskPatty.com*, runs a program to certify dealerships as female-friendly places to shop. Although car dealerships have traditionally been populated with primarily male employees, progressive dealerships are recruiting female employees to help create a safe and comfortable shopping environment for women. Moreover, they are recruiting better educated and more sophisticated salesmen and training them to better assist women.[22]

Changes in the roles of women have caused marketers to adjust traditional marketing strategies, many of which automatically presumed that males played the dominant role in decision making. Visit the Web sites of Roadandtravel.com *and* Edmunds.com/women. *These sites are designed to help women select the car that is right for them. Consider the marketing mix for a product like an automobile. Identify the ways in which the four Ps—product, price, place (distribution), and promotion—would differ when marketers specifically target women.*

Marketers must ensure that their brands are included in the evoked sets of target consumers. This becomes particularly crucial at those points in time when these consumers are actually considering the purchase of brands within a particular product category. It is essential that marketers' brands be well publicized both off- and online, be made readily available both in stores that carry the product category and on their Web sites, and be supported with promotion, service, financing options, and warranty coverage. Such tactics are effective and necessary means to achieve brand inclusion in the consumer's evoked set.

Evaluating Alternatives

Once alternatives representing possible solutions to the perceived problem have been assembled, evaluation of these options commences in order to arrive at a choice among them. Recall that decision rules that guide this selection process can range from systematic information search (which considers many alternatives and the various attributes of each option) to simple and quick choice strategies. The choice can be effort laden in the case of systematic processing or effortless in the case of heuristic processing.

In contemplating the various alternatives, consumers may focus on particular product features and ignore others. The product characteristics or features that consumers use to judge the merits of the competing options are known as the **evaluative criteria.** How individuals evaluate alternatives is influenced by both individual and environmental factors. In this sense, evaluative criteria become a product-specific manifestation of an individual's needs, values, lifestyle, and roles. Consumers employ these evaluative criteria to decide both what to buy and where to buy it.

evaluative criteria
product characteristics consumers use to judge the merits of competing options

Consumers' evaluative criteria are not static. These criteria vary from one individual to another; and in different situations, certain criteria become more important than others. For example, when eating at a fast-food restaurant, how important are criteria such as food preparation, freshness of ingredients, and speed of service to patrons? Beyond the client's goal of consuming a filling meal at a reasonable price, how do diners trade-off taste versus fat content or speed versus ambiance? This understanding of how important certain criteria are to the patrons of an establishment can help the firm develop effective internal and external marketing strategies.

Some attributes upon which alternatives are evaluated are **salient** in nature, while others are **determinant**. Both types, however, affect the marketing and advertising strategies of firms. In a purchasing situation, consumers would normally consider salient attributes first. In the case of buying a new automobile, salient attributes include the vehicle's make, price, model, gas mileage, and quality ratings. However, it is the determinant attributes, such as the vehicle's color, display panel, seating capacity, comfort, roominess, and wheel design that usually determine which brand or dealership buyers frequent, especially when the alternatives are equivalent on salient attributes.[24]

salient attributes
important aspects of a product that affect the choices consumers make

determinant attributes
those features on which alternatives are believed to differ

Assessing the Positiveness or Negativeness of Alternatives

Three factors appear to impact individuals' judgement concerning the positiveness or negativeness of potential consequences of their decision. The first is how a person values the alternatives; the second is how the outcomes of these alternatives relate to that person's memories; and the third is how a decision is framed.

prospect theory
a view of how decision makers, under risk conditions, value different options and assess their outcomes

Prospect theory attempts to explain how decision makers under risk conditions value different options (prospects) and assess the positiveness or negativeness of their outcomes.[25] According to prospect theory, an individual's perceptual apparatus is attuned to the evaluation of changes or differences rather than the evaluation of absolute magnitudes. For example, an object at a given temperature may be judged as hot or cold to the touch, depending on the temperature to which one has adapted. The same principle applies to nonsensory attributes such as health, wealth, and prestige. Thus, the method that a decision maker uses to evaluate the positiveness or negativeness of options (prospects) does not necessarily coincide with their objective or *actual* value, but rather with their *psychological* valuation.

Prospect theory explains the difference between actual and psychological valuation through the use of a *hypothetical value function*, a depiction of the relationship between the *psychological* valuation of gains and losses resulting from a course of action and the *actual* value of those gains and losses.

In Exhibit 9.2, the horizontal axis represents the actual value of an alternative, whereas the vertical axis represents the psychological value of that alternative. It has been observed that in decisions involving risk taking, losses loom larger than gains. In a betting situation, for example, the anguish an individual experiences in losing a sum of money appears to be greater than the pleasure associated with winning the same amount. Thus, the value function (*VL*) for losses in the graph (the lower-left quadrant of the diagram) is steeper than the value function (*VG*) for gains (the upper-right quadrant of the diagram). The graph reflects this tendency by showing that the value function for gains (*VG*) is concave above the reference point A and convex below it.

This analysis points to the conclusion that in decision-making situations that involve assumption of risk, increasing gains have decreasing psychological value. This tendency is consistent with the economic concept of diminishing marginal utility, which proposes that each additional unit of an item obtained by a consumer results in proportionately lower utility or satisfaction for each subsequently added unit. Conversely, in the domain of losses, additional losses are weighted more heavily than gains. For example, gamblers in the loss domain who have already squandered large sums of money are prone to take further risks to recoup losses and break even. On the other hand, a gambler in the gain domain is likely to act more conservatively, because each additional gain is perceived as having less and less psychological value.

Linkages to Memories

When consumers evaluate the possible consequences of a decision, they may recollect the outcomes of similar incidents. Linkages that a person makes between prior events and the alternatives currently under scrutiny can precipitate positive or negative evaluations of these options. For example, an athlete shopping to replace tattered sports gear may reminisce about winning or losing previous tournaments as that athlete tries on or tests out new goods. One's feelings about a brand worn or used during a winning season are likely to be positive. Conversely, brands that kindle memories of a losing season may be viewed negatively.

Source: Daniel Kahneman and Amos Tversky, "Prospect Theory: An Analysis of Decision Under Risk," *Econometrica* 47, no. 2 (March 1979), p. 229. Reprinted with permission.

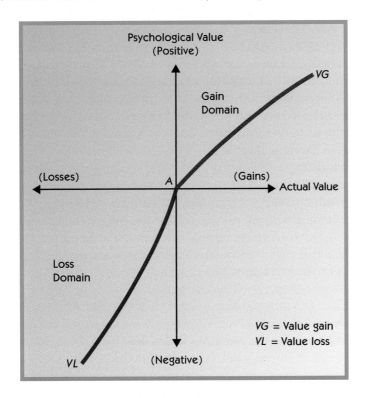

Framing of Decisions

Prospect theory also incorporates the concept of **framing,** which posits that the same decision can be viewed from either a gain or a loss perspective, depending on the reference point an individual applies.[26] It is analogous to describing a drinking glass as half full or half empty. In one experiment, for example, subjects were asked to give their impressions of ground beef.[27] Identical product information was provided, but the descriptions were framed positively (75 percent lean) or negatively (25 percent fat). Ratings were taken on four scales: good–bad tasting, greasy–greaseless, high–low quality, and fat–lean. When the evaluation was framed positively, subjects rated the ground beef as significantly better tasting, less greasy, higher quality, and more lean.

Another type of framing effect can be observed in regard to price cuts and sales promotions that accomplish a similar purpose. A price reduction framed as an adjustment from a product's base price seems smaller than if it were framed from a zero point. Assume that a $100 product is reduced to $90. Outright price cuts and coupon offers usually amount to a small change in the overall appraisal of price. On the other hand, a rebate for the same amount—if perceived independently of the product's base price—would make a larger psychological impact on the consumer and represent a gain. For example, automobile pricing is often done using rebates rather than

framing
a view that a given decision can be structured from either a gain or a loss perspective

outright discounts from the original price because selling prices of $22,000 and $21,250 are not that different. By contrast, when we get a $750 rebate check in the mail, it seems as if we have gained a large sum of money compared to receiving nothing at all.

Similarly, when customers receive a free gift or an opportunity to win a prize, they would likely frame the outcome as a gain rather than a price reduction. For instance, assume a customer buys a DVD-CD player for $150. The retailer tosses in a couple of CDs free of charge. In such a case, the CDs would be valued independently of the price paid for the player. In other words, the consumer would perceive the $20 value of the CDs as a gain rather than as a reduction in the player's selling price. As a consequence, the gift or prize would have greater psychological value.[28]

The time interval between a decision and the onset of gains or losses also affects perceived valuation. For instance, credit customers take immediate possession of a product and defer payment. Those who incur interest charges prefer having an item now (gain) and discount the psychological value of future payment (loss). The further into the future a cost will be experienced, the less psychological impact it tends to have.[29] Consequently, some people lose self-control when buying on credit.[30]

PURCHASE OR COMMITMENT

The purchase decision is the outcome of the search and evaluation process. As we discussed earlier, the degree of ease or difficulty associated with making a purchase commitment or actually purchasing a product or service is a function of the financial, social, and psychological importance placed on the outcome.

Choosing Among Alternatives

decision rules
alternative analytical procedures consumers use to process information and arrive at a selection

Consumers use a number of **decision rules** to reach a choice among alternative courses of action. These decision rules specify how consumers combine and process information in order to compare product alternatives. Decision rules can be divided into two broad categories—compensatory and noncompensatory rules. **Compensatory decision** rules involve simultaneously evaluating available alternatives on a number of product attributes. Such an evaluation procedure enables a high standing on one of a brand's attributes to make up for other perceived shortcomings. A car buyer may still contemplate a hybrid vehicle by Honda even though it does not offer the attractive sporty design of other alternatives, provided that the Honda hybrid does offer other features that the car shopper considers desirable, such as economy and environmental friendliness.[31]

compensatory decision rule
a selection procedure where a high score on one attribute of a brand can make up for a low score on another

noncompensatory decision rule
a selection procedure where a high score on one attribute of a brand cannot offset a low score on another

Noncompensatory decision rules, on the other hand, evaluate alternatives one at a time, eliminating all the alternatives that fail to meet specific attribute requirements. In this evaluation procedure, a brand's high standing on some attribute cannot offset a poor standing on another attribute. A homemaker who purchases breakfast cereal for family members may eliminate any sugar-coated cereals from the evoked set even though these sweetened cereals may be superior in other ways. Descriptions of the decision rules appear in Exhibit 9.3.

Compensatory: a high score on one attribute of a brand can make up for a low score on another

- To preserve the environment, a consumer acquires solar panels for her home, even though her investment in this technology far exceeds the cost of relying on traditional energy sources.
- A consumer patronizes a pricy department store due to the fact that the retailer supports a charitable cause that the consumer strongly endorses.
- In the search for financial security, a consumer chooses a bank's CDs offering relatively low interest rates rather than opting for the significantly higher returns offered by other more-aggressive types of investments.

Noncompensatory: a high score on one attribute of a brand cannot offset a low score on another

- In her effort to protect her children from lead poisoning, a mother refrains from purchasing reasonably priced toys made in China due to fear that the toys' paint may be tainted with lead.
- A consumer stops dining at his favorite restaurant due to perceived indifference on the part of the establishment's waiters.
- A supporter of animal rights ceases to purchase her favorite makeup from a well-known cosmetics firm upon learning that the company runs cosmetics tests on animals.

Selecting a Decision Rule

Consumers employ a number of decision rules to make product or brand selections. These include the simple-additive, weighted-additive, affect-referral, elimination-by-aspects, conjunctive, disjunctive, and lexicographic rules. In the process of decision making, consumers may use these rules singly or in combination. Descriptions of the various decision rules appear in Exhibit 9.4.

POSTPURCHASE CONSIDERATIONS

The act of purchasing does not conclude the decision-making process. For progressive marketers today, it is considered the first step toward building a coveted long-term relationship with the prospect-turned-customer. The outcome of postpurchase evaluation is a critical factor in this process. Feelings of satisfaction or dissatisfaction are instrumental in determining whether consumers will repeat the act of purchasing the brand, recommend it to others, and form positive attitudes toward the brand and the company that sponsors it.

Today, in order to establish firms as service leaders—those that offer improved customer experiences and relationships—companies are adopting the concept of Customer Touchpoints Management (CTM). These touchpoints are the various stages constituting the totality of a customer's experiences with the firm during all interactions, human or mechanical, that occur during a customer's relationship lifecycle with the firm. This relationship spans the gambit from prospect, to buyer, to user, to repeat buyer, to a switcher or disposer,

EXHIBIT 9.4 **Decision Rules Used by Consumers**

- *Simple-Additive Rule:* In the simplest case, consumers merely count the number of positive brand characteristics and select the brand that offers the greatest number of positive attributes. For example, to evaluate a product like a soft drink, consumers may rate each brand attribute (such as flavor, sweetness, carbonation, and color) on a scale from one (poor) to five (excellent). Consumers sum the attribute ratings for each brand and select the brand with the highest composite score.

- *Weighted-Additive Rule:* To evaluate a product like a soft drink, consumers take into account both a product's attribute ratings as well as the importance of its attributes. The importance of a drink's flavor and sweetness, for example, could be rated on a scale ranging from one (very unimportant) to four (very important). In effect, consumers multiply attribute ratings by their corresponding importance and sum these for each brand. Consumers then select the brand with the highest composite score.

- *Affect-Referral Rule:* Decisions are made without considering product attributes. Consumers merely use global or holistic evaluation to determine their choice. For example, a consumer in a restaurant may order a bottle of Perrier because of brand familiarity or due to lack of interest in scrutinizing a vast beverage menu.

- *Elimination-by-Aspects Rule:* Alternative brands are compared one attribute at a time after these attributes have been ordered according to their importance. Only the alternatives that meet the most important attribute requirement remain in the consideration set. The process of elimination continues until only a single brand remains.

- *Conjunctive Rule:* The consumer establishes a minimal acceptable quality or standard of performance for each product attribute. Alternatives are compared against each attribute requirement. Any brand that fails to meet the minimum acceptable level is eliminated from further consideration, regardless of whether or not it rates highly on other attributes.

- *Disjunctive Rule:* In this rule, the consumer establishes more demanding quality standards for each attribute. A brand alternative has to surpass the minimum cutoff for only one of the attributes to be acceptable. For example, a consumer buying a dress shirt sets a 50 percent minimum for cotton content *or* a price limit of $40. A shirt remains a viable alternative as long as its fabric contains more that 50 percent cotton *or* its price is less that $40.

- *Lexicographic Rule:* The consumer first ranks the attributes according to the order of their perceived importance or relevance. He or she then compares the various alternatives against the single most important attribute and selects the brand or brands that perform(s) best on that attribute. If two or more brands tie on the first attribute, then they are evaluated on the second most important attribute. The process of breaking ties continues until only one brand remains. The lexicographic rule seems to be the most common decision strategy that consumers use.[32]

and even to a returning customer. At each one of these lifecycle touchpoint stages, the goal is to design and implement procedures and protocols whose primary objective is to attain the highest possible level of customer satisfaction. By improving customer relationships, organizations can improve market share, sales, and both customer and employee loyalty.

Swan and Combs propose that consumers evaluate products based on a limited set of attributes.[33] Some of these determinant attributes are relatively important to consumer satisfaction. Other factors, although not critical to determining satisfaction, can still relate to dissatisfaction when their performance is deemed unsatisfactory. In this regard, two facets of product performance can be identified. **Instrumental performance** refers to product performance as a means to a set of ends. In other words, instrumental performance involves the utilitarian performance of the physical product per se. **Expressive performance,** on the other hand, entails performance that a consumer considers as an end in itself. Expressive performance pertains to social or psychological attributes; that is, stylistic and self-expressive aspects of a product, rather than its functional characteristics.

Sometimes the determinant attributes for a specific purchase are the product's expressive performance rather than its instrumental performance. Nevertheless, inferior instrumental product performance may lead to consumer dissatisfaction with the purchase, even though its expressive performance happens to be superior.[34] For instance, an individual may buy a jacket because of its fashionable styling (an expressive attribute). This person may later become dissatisfied with the jacket if it fails to keep him or her warm, the seams tear, or the zipper breaks (instrumental attributes).

Determinants of Consumer Satisfaction

Consumer satisfaction is an attitude formed toward a purchase. Research suggests that customer satisfaction is influenced by both the level of effort expended by consumers and their level of expectations. The level of effort expended mediates product evaluation and the resulting degree of satisfaction. Effort is a flexible, highly unstable, and individual yardstick. Equal amounts of effort extended by different individuals may be perceived by each as an investment or sacrifice of different magnitude and, as such, may yield different amounts of reward or satisfaction.[36]

Effort is often equated with sacrifice. Wasson asserts that every exchange in the marketplace can be viewed as a combination of some sacrifices.[37] Almost always, some relinquishing of financial resources, some loss of time in searching for the product and in consummating the purchase, and some commitment to spend time and effort necessary to learn the product's use system are required. In this sense, effort can be measured in financial, physical, or mental units.

Satisfaction, on the other hand, has been described by Howard and Sheth as a mental state of feeling adequately or inadequately rewarded in a buying situation for the sacrifice a buyer has undergone.[38] Reward is meant to include not only those benefits resulting from consumption of a brand but also any other satisfactions received in the purchasing and consuming process.

© 2009, Yuri Arcurs, Shutterstock, Inc.

instrumental performance
consumers' view of the utilitarian performance of the physical product as a means to an end

expressive performance
social or psychological aspects of product performance that consumers regard as ends in themselves

consumer satisfaction
the mental state of feeling adequately rewarded in a buying situation

The pleasant and respectful treatment customers receive from sales personnel in a store is often a major reason for consumer satisfaction with that store.

Global Opportunity

America on Sale for the Global Investor

In this era of the catalytic financial storm that has threatened to bring down the American economy, it is difficult to curtail the prevailing sense of hopelessness, despair, and depression caused by the late devastating events of the housing crisis, rising prices, the collapse of Wall Street, and massive layoffs. If this news is not bad enough, many observers feel that the ills of our economy are by no means over. The dire repercussions of the financial breakdown are expected to haunt us for many years to come.

One such gloomy view relates to the billions of dollars that Americans spent on purchases from the oil barons. These dollars are now being used to buy distressed and foreclosed properties from the very country that created these windfall profits for them. This form of colonization seems to have escalated in recent months, as cash-loaded oil-rich countries' wealth continues to grow. Many managers of sovereign wealth funds amounting to trillions of dollars now feel that this is a defining moment for them to invest in U.S. real estate. They are searching for and grabbing single- and multi-family homes, major U.S. corporations, financial institutions, and even farmland.

What makes these deals true bargains for the picking is their present dirt-cheap prices, caused by the urgency of sellers to dispose of such assets in search for desperately-needed cash. It is true that the United States needs the help of foreign investors to keep the economy running. This is particularly true now, when many companies face a choice between the two evils of either closing down operations and letting workers go, or the other alternative of allowing foreign investors to own part of the business.

Recently, the *Financial Times* reported that the CEO of an Abu Dhabi sovereign wealth fund worth over $875 billion has already launched its strategy to buy up America. The *New York Post* reported that another Arab sovereign wealth fund valued at an estimated $29 billion has hired consultants and brokers to locate and purchase single- and multi-family homes as well as those under foreclosure.

As this scenario continues to materialize, a major concern for us is when progressive American companies and our biggest financial institutions grant huge ownership positions to foreign entities, there is a chance that such groups may use their financial muscle to impose their cultural or religious views over U.S. owned businesses and properties.[35]

The declining value of the U.S. dollar against foreign currencies, cheap American real estate, and businesses offered for sale at foreclosure prices all have invited oil-rich and other trading partners to spot great investment opportunities in the U.S. by owning part of America. Learn more about this trend by visiting the Web site of Doc's Talk at http://docstalk.blogspot.com/2008/08/financial-demise-of-america.html *In view of this trend of foreign investors' ownership of America's properties and businesses, what would you recommend as policies to allay concerns over the imposition of other countries' views and practices upon U.S.-owned businesses and financial institutions? Are the policies you suggest enforceable? Explain.*

LITERATURE REVIEW OF CUSTOMER SATISFACTION

A number of studies affirm that the level of satisfaction is positively associated with the amount of expended effort. Cardozo introduced *shopping effort* into the evaluation process and observed that customer product evaluation or satisfaction is lower when the product does not measure up to expectations, but that satisfaction rises as effort expended to obtain the product increases.[39] Woodside asserted that effort may affect product evaluations whether individuals obtain more, less, or the same as what they expected.[40] According to Woodside, customers who expend greater effort and receive a product they consider appropriate for that amount of effort tend to perceive less disparity between effort and reward, compared to those who extend little effort to acquire the same product. Anderson reported similar findings.[41] His conclusions supported Cardozo's contention that the mere possession of information about a product may lead to a more favorable evaluation of that product, not only because customers have greater knowledge on which to base evaluation but also because the processing of information constitutes a form of commitment to the product. Golden and Peterson confirmed this tendency and found that the type of product is the most important factor in determining customer satisfaction expectations; that is, customers expect to expend more time and effort in purchasing a consumer durable than a nondurable.[42] As a result, the incremental time and effort involved in the purchase of the durable causes expectations to be higher. Thus, effort has been stressed by many scholars as an important variable in the determination of customer satisfaction with and evaluation of a product.

Customer satisfaction is also an evaluative judgment related to the level of consumer *expectations* rather than to actual product performance. Satisfaction is a function of the discrepancy or contrast between obtained and expected outcomes. If expectations are high and performance falls below one's expectations, dissatisfaction arises. If, on the other hand, actual performance meets or exceeds expectations, the consumer is delightfully pleased. Consequently, a major concern of many marketers today is the ability to create realistic consumer impressions in order to avert disappointment due to elevated expectations. For example, auto manufactures in the United States continue to express concern over how long it will take public perceptions to catch up with objective improvements in the industry. Similarly, airlines engaged in reducing service levels to control costs long for a quick match between passengers' expectations and the reduced service level necessitated by these cost-reduction measures.

The promotional strategy used by a firm and the claims it makes can influence the level of formed expectations. Overstated product claims raise very high expectations. A recent Federal Express ad promised users of the firm's services second business day delivery to Europe. Such promises produce expectations of very high service quality. If actual experience with the service is disconfirmed, the resulting consumer dissatisfaction would most likely be higher than it would have been had the claims not been made. On the other hand, slightly understating product claims may in fact lead to higher satisfaction. Understated product claims generate moderate expectations that can then be surpassed by actual product performance and lead to a higher level of satisfaction. Dick's Last Resort is a popular Chicago restaurant deliberately understates its atmosphere and offerings as a means of affecting customers' satisfaction when they actually experience dining there.

Consumer Complaint Intentions and Behavior

Even a single dissatisfied consumer means a loss to an organization. Customer dissatisfaction is of great concern to marketers because it is more cost effective to keep existing customers than try to win new ones. Dissatisfaction is a potential source of negative word-of-mouth communication. Morgan cites the findings of various recent surveys on the topic of customer dissatisfaction.[43]

- When consumers stop purchasing from a business, only 14 percent do so because of poor product quality. Sixty-eight percent indicate that someone was rude, indifferent, or discourteous to them.
- One in every five supermarket customers switches stores in any given year, mostly because of treatment received at the checkout counter.
- The cost of retaining customers versus that of gaining new ones varies from 2:1 to 20:1.
- A typical dissatisfied customer informs 11 others about quality or service failures. In turn, each of these individuals tells 5 more people. Thus, 67 persons get a bad impression of a business as a result of a single dissatisfied customer.
- Ninety-six percent of most firms' customers do not complain when they encounter a product or service problem. They simply stop purchasing the brand or patronizing the firm.
- 50 percent of consumers who experience dissatisfaction complain to a front-line employee.
- Front-line employees seldom report customers' complaints to a senior manager.
- Customer complaints have become a major concern in electronic commerce.
- Major online customer complaints are generated from conflicts with Web customer service centers.
- Complaint rates vary by type of problem. Problems that result in out-of-pocket monetary loss have high complaint rates (50 to 70 percent), while mistreatment, quality, and incompetence evoke only 5 to 30 percent complaint rates.

Many firms today have started to look at complaints as an opportunity rather than as a liability.[44] The value of complaints lies in their ability to reveal to the firm what consumers do and do not want. An effective complaint handling system is vital today in view of the emphasis on customer service quality. Such systems should allow for both prompt handling of individual complaints and for aggregate complaint analysis.[45]

Most studies of consumer complaints have been done in the context of the physical marketplace. Today, handling customer complaints and managing customer service in electronic commerce have become new areas of concern to marketers. Maximizing customer satisfaction and/or minimizing dissatisfaction often relate to the issue of resolving consumer complaints that revolve around service failures. While Internet advances have allowed customers varied conveniences such as Web-based service centers, where customers can ask questions, get product information, and handle payment issues, delivery, and product returns, faulty e-commerce transactions can occur. These service failures can be seen on sites such as www.epinions.com, www.thirdvoice.com, or www.complaints.com. In such cases, these customer feedback systems not only provide a medium for delivering customer complaints, they likewise disseminate the reputation of the business.

Whether a company is a traditional manufacturer, brick-and-mortar dealership, or online marketer, firms need to recognize that in response to faulty

Automated Decision Making in Consumer Lending: A Blessing or a Curse?

In the past few years, a number of progressive consumer home equity loan companies have moved to a higher level of financial efficiency in granting loans by adopting innovative technological systems capable of significantly facilitating and automating the consumer decision-making process of obtaining home equity loans.

In the past, a loan application used to take between 60 to 90 days to close, and cost an average of $2,000 to process. However, the automated financial decision-making systems adopted by these companies were able to cut the processing time and cost to a fraction of its previous levels. For example, in the case of one well-known online home equity lender, once a customer completes an online application (usually in less than five minutes), an automated process starts by pulling the customer credit report, invoking a scoring process, initiating an online valuation of the property, and checking fraud and flood insurance status. Within two minutes, the customer receives a financial decision regarding his or her loan application. For consumers, this ease of applying for and acquiring loans encouraged many to purchase homes or to refinance existing ones. This borrowing trend was further encouraged by the historically low interest rates and the various competitive lenders' offers that the Internet has brought about. This situation made "rate shopping" almost too easy and raised consumers' expectations and belief that they should be able to borrow money as quickly and easily as they would like to.

However, in the competitive efforts of such firms to grant loans, many lenders did not hesitate to offer subprime mortgages to homeowners with spotty credit who did not qualify under a securitized conforming product. These loans carry higher interest rates, and are basically short-term and high-risk types. Added to this chaotic mix are some nontraditional products such as Alt-A loans, where less documentation is required to qualify than with a conforming loan, option ARMS, which give borrowers the option to pay less than the monthly interest owed, no-money-down loans, and interest-only loan offerings. In many cases, all these factors combined tempted borrowers to seek loans sometimes well beyond their financial capability.

In 2007, the problem started with excesses and defaults in the subprime lending and housing markets when many consumers could not pay their mortgages. As the bubble burst, foreclosures mounted, and the housing activity came to a grinding halt. In time, the harm spread slowly from subprime borrowers and home builders to middle-class homeowners, causing lenders and banks to suffer huge losses. The result was what some have labeled as the mild recession that took place in 2008.[46]

Many home equity lenders developed innovative systems that would connect the consumer with hundreds of financial institutions. Consumers who complete a loan request receive multiple loan offers from up to four lenders, usually within one business day, and many offers come within just five minutes. Learn more about these practices by visiting the Web site of LendingTree at LendingTree.com. Do you believe that such automated systems are helpful to borrowers? Why or why not? Do you think that the government should interfere by imposing strict financial regulations to prevent lenders' psychological pressure and other abuses that prevail in the industry? Defend your answer.

complaint handling for a product or service, consumers may hold a grudge against the offender. Dissatisfaction results in grudgeholding, which in turn leads to an emotionally charged negative attitude toward the product or company in question. Consumer avoidance of the brand or store can also occur. Avoidance is a form of exit behavior that persists over time. Grudgeholding, on the other hand, is an exit behavior that is laden with strong negative emotion that persists for possibly many years.

Research has shown that negative emotion decays extremely slowly. However, by providing factual, objective, and counter-attitudinal information from credible sources (such as positive word of mouth, blogs on the Internet, and testimony from expert sources like *Consumer Reports* magazine), attitudes may change in the direction of the new information and lessen the likelihood of negative behavior.

TO WHOM DO CONSUMERS COMPLAIN?

Consumers direct their complaints to a variety of places. These include firms' customer service departments, state agencies (such as the State Attorney's Office), the Federal Trade Commission, the mass-media, credit card companies, and the Better Business Bureau (BBB).[47]

Firms need to assemble all dissatisfied customers' complaints, wherever the customers may have directed them. The company's customer service department or the Web-based service center are the logical starting points. In the case of third-party complaints made against the firm to other entities, such as state agencies, The Better Business Bureau, the FTC, the media, or credit card companies, extra effort is required to locate and diligently address them. Such complaints are especially important because they are potentially more damaging to the firm's reputation than those addressed directly to the firm. Negative publicity in the media, legal actions against the firm, or charge-backs from credit card companies as a result of third-party complaints place the firm in a compromising position.[48]

WHAT CAN BE DONE?

Many consumer-oriented firms today take matters of customer contentment and complaints seriously and make systematic efforts to learn the degree of consumer satisfaction or dissatisfaction with their products and services. Since most online firms establish Web-based customer service centers to deal with customer comments and complaints, experience has shown that the major causes of online customer complaints are the unsatisfactory responses provided by these centers.

To improve these centers' operations, progressive online firms today establish technologically advanced customer service centers referred to as *Web-enabled customer contact centers* (for example, www.iirny.com), which provide online chat services to the firm's customers and include efficient customer self-help centers, or a combination of several customer communication channels (for instance, www.rightnow.com). Further, to overcome delayed responses to customers, these firms now offer real-time customer service such as that provided by Neiman Marcus (www.neimanmarcus.com), which operates a real-time service that enables customers to solve their problems or answer their questions without delay.

Another inexpensive method used to facilitate complaint handling is a toll-free consumer hotline that offers consumers a way to air their gripes. They encourage dissatisfied consumers to conveniently voice their concerns rather than become angry and cease to purchase the brand altogether. Customers whose problems are promptly brought to satisfactory resolutions are likely to be pleased and continue to be loyal customers.[49]

A third way to handle customer complaints is to establish consumer affairs offices. These offices, headed by a top-level executive of the firm, are assigned responsibility for collecting complaints, analyzing their nature, contacting complainants, suggesting corrective actions, and following up with the suggested solutions. In some firms, consumer affairs offices are given responsibility for *aggregate complaint analysis*, which tracks complaints based on numbers, trends, and major sources of dissatisfaction. This type of analysis allows firms to establish complaint benchmarks against which they monitor the effectiveness of service quality over time. Western Union's consumer affairs department conducts a complaint analysis program that computerizes consumer complaints in one central file, analyzes them, and disseminates them to appropriate areas within the company.[50] In some instances, this department also conducts periodic surveys to ascertain customer attitudes.

Consumer education programs constitute a fourth method employed by some firms to reduce the occurrence of consumer complaints. The philosophy behind this method is the proposition that knowledge is a vital ingredient in forming expectations. Because consumer expectations are the basis for their satisfaction or dissatisfaction, knowledge enhances awareness and thus influences expectations. Some pharmaceutical companies, for example, go beyond the requirements of the law and make an extra effort to publicize the negative side effects of their medications in order to influence consumer expectations. Such knowledge can be disseminated through advertising (pamphlets and package inserts), speakers, ads, and videos.

In the last six chapters, we have examined in detail the way consumers perceive, learn and remember, form attitudes, and come to need and want. We have also investigated how consumers' personalities, lifestyles, and self-concepts influence what they choose to buy. In addition, we have studied how consumers process information and seek solutions to their problems. However, consumer behavior does not occur in a vacuum. We exist in the context of a larger population, where our actions are influenced by others around us. From the very moment of our birth, we are subject to social factors that play a major role in shaping our values, aspirations, and purchasing patterns. In the remaining chapters, we cover such topics as group, family, and personal influences, social class, and culture. We also investigate the role of marketing communication in enhancing the spread of innovations across a society. Herein lies its important role in the diffusion process. Diffusion is the process by which a new idea—be it a product or service, a practice, or a belief—spreads throughout the marketplace. The topic of diffusion is treated in the next chapter.

A Cross-Functional Point of View

The topics of problem solving and decision making have a number of implications for business disciplines other than marketing. Relevant issues might include

- **Energy/Public Policy:** In our society, the goal of reducing dependency on foreign oil cannot be attained without aggregate consumer decisions to alter their energy consumption habits in favor of conservation and alternative energy sources. In this regard, the U.S. government attempts to encourage consumers to take such action by offering tax incentives and rebates to energy-conscious consumers. In February 2008, the House passed $18.1 billion in renewable energy tax incentives, including an extension of the tax credit for energy-efficient home improvements, as well as a tax credit for up to $3,400 for consumers who purchase hybrid vehicles.

- **Ethical/Cost:** Management of a large fast-food corporation faces a critical decision concerning possible changes in the cooking procedures for the entire chain. Executives have reviewed a number of reports on the issue of severe allergic reactions that some people have to peanuts. Some schools and airlines have stopped serving peanuts to their students and passengers.

  The chain in question traditionally used peanut oil to fry foods ranging from fish filets to french fries. If the chain were to change the type of oil, a significant investment in additional equipment such as friers would be required for each different type of food. Because the public is unable to detect taste differences in fried foods, management can easily stick with the original oil choice and avoid incurring the added expense for new equipment. However, customers may suffer allergic reactions that could negatively affect the company's reputation.

- **Accounting/Finance:** In one state lottery program, the awards-granting committee is debating whether its recent move to allow winning parties to claim their awards either in a lump sum shortly after the drawing or in yearly installments received over 20 years was a smart move. Almost all winners have chosen lump sum awards at the time of winning. This has placed financial burdens on the state coffers, because the original idea behind the lottery was to finance the yearly award installments from future ticket sales. This has left the state with an immediate large cash outflow. The committee wonders whether it would be wise to rescind the instant-payment option.

These issues, and a host of others like them, show that the topic of decision making transcends marketing to other business disciplines.

Summary

This chapter deals with the decision-making process. It starts with a discussion of the degrees of cognitive effort that are employed by consumers in the decision-making process. These efforts can range from significant to minimal, depending on whether a decision is nonprogrammed or programmed. Some nonprogrammed decisions—such as those that are financially, socially, or psychologically important—occur after intense deliberation and cognitive effort. Some nonprogrammed decisions entail limited problem solving on the part of consumers, because buyers have some prior experience with the product. Still other nonprogrammed purchases are impulsive. Programmed decisions are usually made with little or no cognitive effort, such as when consumers have become loyal to a particular brand.

Dewey identified five stages of the consumer decision process. Specifically applied to the study of consumer behavior, these stages are (1) problem recognition, (2) search activity, (3) identifying and evaluating alternatives, (4) purchase or commitment, and (5) postpurchase considerations.

In the problem-recognition stage, marketers attempt to establish conscious awareness of a problem. If consumers become cognizant of a problem that can be lessened or eliminated through purchase behavior, the second stage—search activity—begins. Search can be either internal (consumers draw from information stored in memory) or external (consumers visit stores, speak to salespersons, read promotional materials and package information). Several factors influence the extent of search activity, such as consumers' learning style, product involvement, experience, and risk perception.

Once consumers acquire needed information, the evaluation stage emerges. Consumers narrow down the number of product alternatives they actually consider to a manageable number, a process known as winnowing. Various heuristics or simple rules of thumb may be used to reduce the effort one expends. Consumers may evaluate both the salient and determinant attributes of each alternative under serious consideration. They may also contemplate the potential outcome (positiveness or negativeness) of selecting a particular option. In this regard, prospect theory is discussed, including concepts such as the hypothetical value function, linkages to past memories, and framing.

In the process of choosing a particular alternative, consumers may apply various compensatory and noncompensatory decision rules (e.g., simple-additive, weighted-additive, affect-referral, elimination-by-aspects, conjunctive, disjunctive, lexicographic rules) by which they compare alternatives and arrive at a selection.

The act of committing to a particular alternative—purchasing—does not terminate the decision-making process, because postpurchase considerations arise. The satisfaction or dissatisfaction consumers experience from their product choice largely relates to the product's instrumental or expressive performance, the amount of effort or resources consumers expend to obtain the product, and consumers' level of product expectations.

It is more cost effective for marketers to satisfy and retain existing customers than to try to win new ones. Dissatisfied consumers are a potential source of negative word of mouth. Many firms now view complaints as valuable feedback about what consumers do and do not want. Well-handled complaints may alter consumers' final disposition toward the complaint encounter in a positive direction. Because consumers may complain to firms' customer service departments, Web-based service centers, state agencies, the FTC, the mass media, credit card companies, and the BBB, firms must assemble complaints, wherever customers may have directed them, to avert negative publicity or the possibility of a boycott.

Review Questions

1. It has been suggested that decision-making processes fall along a continuum that ranges from programmed decisions at one end to nonprogrammed decisions on the other. Explain the difference between these two types of decision-making formats. What are the implications of this knowledge to marketers?

2. According to Dewey's five stages of problem solving, two types of search—internal and external—take place after a consumer recognizes a problem. Discuss both types and elaborate on the factors that are likely to affect the amount of external search consumers tend to undertake.

3. Prospect theory has been advocated as a tool to assess the positiveness or negativeness of alternatives in consumers' decision-making processes. What are the main tenets of prospect theory? Explain this theory in terms of gains or losses experienced in a gambling situation.

4. Research suggests that customer satisfaction is influenced both by the level of effort expended by consumers as well as by their level of expectation. Explain this view, and show through an example how marketers can enhance customer satisfaction for a product or service.

5. Many companies today have started to view complaints as an opportunity rather than as a liability. What are the major causes of consumer complaints? What efforts can businesses undertake to deal with these complaints?

Discussion Questions

1. Many companies, such as those selling antiperspirants, mouthwashes, and dandruff shampoos, use ads that depict potentially embarrassing situations that consumers may face at some time. The ad then recommends the company's product as the solution to the problem. Cite some specific examples of this tactic that you are familiar with and explain the techniques used to evoke anxiety feelings.

2. Recently, an increasing share of automotive advertising appears to be directed to women. Some people attribute the switch to the increasing number of careered, financially independent women. Others claim that the shift reflects an increased awareness of the growing role of women in household decision-making processes. Still others claim that increased diversity in the workplace is largely responsible for this phenomenon. What do you think? In your opinion, is there any reason for advertisers to believe that men and women look for different things when buying a car?

3. A few years ago, Sears introduced a brand of blue jeans called Tough Skins, targeted to young people ages 6 to 16. The company promoted the jeans by advertising to parents that they were indestructible, would not fade, and would not shrink. The product failed miserably. What factors, in your opinion, contributed to the failure of these jeans? What insight does the consumer decision-making process suggest concerning the reasons for the product's demise?

In reference to the chapter opening vignette, many Americans have taken for granted the effectiveness of our government in overseeing our financial markets. Many consumers know very little about the roles of the Securities and Exchange Commission (SEC), the Treasury Department, and the Federal Reserve in the protection of the country's financial health. This lack of knowledge was one of the reasons the government felt free to grant financial institutions unusual powers and privileges which they abused. For example, the SEC allowed banks in 2004 to use billions of dollars to invest in risky financial instruments like mortgage-backed securities—the main reason for the financial collapse—all in the spirit of deregulation. While critics accuse financial institutions' deceptive practices, others point the finger at the government that failed to uphold the trust placed in it by consumers. Still others place the blame on consumers' unwise decisions to seek risky and questionable loans. On which side of this argument do you place the greatest blame—the financial institutions, the government, or consumers? Why?

CASE

Choosing a College

Mr. Walker, the admissions director at a well-known Ivy League university, is meeting with his staff to discuss the changes that characterize today's students' college selection processes and the significant implications of that change on admissions and financial aid policies of schools nationwide.

One of the driving forces behind the change has been the low birth rate in most of the 1980s, except for the last couple years of the decade, as well as the significant drop in the birth rate that started in 1991. This scarcity of prospective students created a competitive environment in which each school raced to lure students in order to fill the vacant seats in its classrooms. In addition to this situation, there seemed to be an emerging market composed of non-traditional students who were seeking full- or part-time educational programs, mostly for purposes of retraining in order to meet their career objectives.

Mr. Walker claimed that from his experience and from the reports he has been reading, *value* seems to have been the most important factor in college choice among many high school seniors as well as transfer students. The college choice decision has become much more money driven, and availability of student aid has become a significant component of that decision. It is not uncommon today to see college recruits lavish high school seniors with gifts, merit awards, and hard-to-refuse financial aid packages to get them to apply to a specific school. Such practices are common today among many public as well as private college recruiters.

Student decisions regarding college choice have also been influenced by the special annual issues published by *Money* magazine and *U.S. News & World Report*, which rank colleges according to criteria such as "the best value" per dollar. Such guides seem to have grown in popularity among many students in guiding their college choice.

Students also *shop* for colleges online. Most high school upperclassmen have Internet access at home or at school. They surf the Internet to determine which school can give them the best value for their money. In this sense, many students have come to regard the college experience as a *product* rather than a *process*. These consumerist students shopping for a college tend to study the product's long-term yield—that is, the potential job that will materialize or the quality of the graduate program for which the degree will qualify them.

This change has forced college recruiters to defend tuition rates by citing job placement and graduate school acceptance figures that prove there *is* a payoff to the large investment required to obtain a college education.

Questions

1. The concept of *value* treats selecting a college like purchasing a car. It ignores the important issue of *fit* (is a particular school the right choice for a specific student?). How do you feel about this issue?
2. In your opinion, what factors truly affect most students' choice of a college? Did these same factors apply in your own choice of a school?
3. What additional information, activities, or incentives could schools provide to help students, perhaps in conjunction with their parents, arrive at a better-informed choice of which college to attend?

Notes

1. Chris Pummer, "We're All to Blame for this Financial Mess," *FOX TRANSLATOR*, (October 20, 2008), www.foxbusiness.com/story/markets/industries/media/blame-financial-mess/.
2. Paul J. H. Schoemaker, "The Expected Utility Model: Its Variants, Purposes, Evidence and Limitations," *Journal of Economic Literature* 20 (June 1982), pp. 529-63.
3. "Search Activity Before Online Purchase Holds Opportunity for Marketers," *Internet Retailer* (February 16, 2005); DoubleClick "Search Before the Purchase" Report, www.doubleclick.com/about/press.aspx?id=586.
4. "Yahoo and Compete, Inc. Find Internet Search Plays Key Role in Automotive Research and Purchase Decisions," *Yahoo Media Relations*, http://docs.yahoo.com/docs/pr/release1264.html.
5. "Shopping Search Engines," *ClickZ* (December 10, 2003), www.clickz.com/showPage.html?page=3287081.
6. Sidney P. Feldman and Merlin C. Spencer, "The Effect of Personal Influence in the Selection of Consumer Services," in Peter Bennett (ed.), *Marketing and Economic Development* (Chicago: The American Marketing Association, 1965), pp. 440-52.
7. Robert Ferber, "Family Decision Making and Economic Behavior: A Review," in E. B. Sheldon (ed.), *Family Economic Behavior: Problems and Prospects* (Philadelphia: Lippincott, 1973), pp. 29-61.
8. James F. Engel et al., *Consumer Behavior* (Hinsdale IL: Dryden Press (1978), p. 483.
9. John W. Payne, James R. Bettman, and E. J. Johnson, "Behavioral Decision Research: A Constructive Processing Perspective," *Annual Review of Psychology* 4 (1992), pp. 87-131.
10. Judith Lynne Zaichkowsky, "The Personal Involvement Inventory: Reduction, Revision, and Application to Advertising," *Journal of Advertising* 23, no. 4 (December 1994), pp. 59-70; Edward F. McQuarrie and J. Michael Munson, "A Revised Product Involvement Inventory: Improved Usability and Validity," in John F. Sherry Jr. and Brian Sternthal (eds.), *Advances in Consumer Research* 19 (Provo, UT: Association for Consumer Research, 1992), pp. 108-15; William C. Rodgers and Kenneth C. Schneider, "An Empirical Evaluation of the Kapferer-Laurent Involvement Profile Scale," *Psychology & Marketing* 10, no. 4, (July-August, 1993), pp. 333-45; Deborah J. MacInnis, Christine Moorman, and Bernard J. Jaworski, "Enhancing and Measuring Consumer's Motivation, Opportunity, and Ability to Process Brand Information from Ads," *Journal of Marketing* (October 1991), pp. 332-53; J. Craig Andrews, Srinivas Durvasula, and Syed H. Akhter, "A Framework for Conceptualizing and Measuring the Involvement Construct in Advertising Research," *Journal of Advertising* (December 1990), pp. 27-40; Sharon Shavitt, Suzanne Swan, Tina M. Lowrey, and Michaela Wanke, "The Interaction of Endorser Attractiveness and Involvement in Persuasion Depends on the Goal that Guides Message Processing," *Journal of Consumer Psychology* 2 (1994), pp. 137-62.
11. Richard L. Celsi and Jerry C. Olsen, "The Role of Involvement in Attention and Comprehension Processes," *Journal of Consumer Research* 15 (September 1988), pp. 210-24; Marsha L. Richins, Peter H. Bloch, and Edward F. McQuarrie, "How Enduring and Situational Involvement Combine to Create Involvement Responses," *Journal of Consumer Psychology* 1 (September 1992), pp. 143-54.

12. Dennis W. Rook and Robert J. Fisher, "Normative Influences on Impulsive Buying Behavior," *Journal of Consumer Research* 22 (December 1995), pp. 305–313, and Francis Piron, "Defining Impulse Purchasing," in Rebecca H. Holman and Michael R. Solomon (eds.), *Advances in Consumer Research* 18 (Provo, UT: Association For Consumer Research, 1991), pp. 509–514.

13. John Dewey, *How We Think* (Boston: D. C. Heath, 1910), Ch. 8.

14. Gordon C. Bruner, II., "The Effect of Problem-Recognition Style on Information Seeking," *Journal of the Academy of Marketing Science* 15 (Winter 1987), pp. 33–41.

15. James R. Bettman and C. Whan Park, "Effects of Prior Knowledge and Experience and Phase of Choice Process on Consumer Decision Processes: A Protocol Analysis," *Journal of Consumer Research* 7 (December 1980), pp. 234–48; Phillip A. Dover and Jerry C. Olsen, "Dynamic Changes in an Expectancy-Value Attitude Model as a Function of Multiple Exposures to Product Information," in Barnett A. Greenberg and Danny N. Bellenger (eds.), *Contemporary Marketing Thought* (Chicago: American Marketing Association, 1977), pp. 455–60; and Jacob Jacoby, Robert W. Chestnut, and William A. Fisher, "A Behavioral Process Approach to Information Acquisition in Nondurable Purchasing," *Journal of Marketing Research* 15 (November 1978), pp. 532–44.

16. Peter R. Dickson and Alan G. Sawyer, "The Price Knowledge and Search of Supermarket Shoppers," *Journal of Marketing* 54 (July 1990), pp. 42–53.

17. R. E. McGaughey and K. H. Mason, "The Internet as a Marketing Tool," *Journal of Marketing Theory and Practice*, vol. 6, no. 3 (1998), pp. 1–11.

18. "Search Before the Purchase," *DoubleClick* (February, 2005), www.doubleclick.com/emea.

19. Byeong-Joon Moon, "Consumer Adoption of the Internet as an Information Search and Product Purchase Channel: Some Research Hypotheses," *International Journal of Internet Marketing and Advertising*, vol. 1, no. 1 (2004).

20. "DoubleClick Performics Unveils Holiday E-Commerce Trend Data," *DoubleClick Performics* (November 14, 2007), www.performics.com/news-room/press-release/doubleclick-performics-unveils-holiday-ecommerce-trend-data.

21. Elizabeth K. Sproles and George B. Sproles, "Consumer Decision-Making Styles as a Function of Individual Learning Styles," *The Journal of Consumer Affairs* 24, no. 1 (1990), p. 145.

22. Tim Triplett, "Automakers Recognize Value of Women's Market," *Marketing News* (April 11, 1994), pp. 1, 2; and Tim Triplett, "The Rich Are Even Different from the Rich," *Marketing News* 28, no. 16 (August 1, 1994), pp. 2, 3; "Women's News &

Views Concerning Car Buying Blues," *Colorado Women News*, (November 2001); and "Men, Women Approach Car Buying with Different Ideas," The Iowa Channel.com, posted December 30, 2002.

23. Shelley Chaiken, "The Heuristic Model of Persuasion," in M. P. Zanna, J. M. Olson, and C. P. Herman (eds.), *Social Science: The Ontario Symposium* 5 (Hillside NJ: Lawrence Erlbaum, 1986).

24. Stephen M. Nowlis and Itamar Simonson, "Attribute-Task Compatibility as a Determinant of Consumer Preference Reversals, *Journal of Marketing Research*, vol. 34, no. 2 (1997), pp. 205–218.

25. Daniel Kahneman and Amos Tversky, "Prospect Theory: An Analysis of Decision Under Risk." *Econometrica* 47, no. 2 (March 1979), pp. 263–91.

26. Alice A. Wright and Richard J. Lutz, "Effects of Advertising and Experience on Brand Judgments: A Rose by Any Other Name," in Leigh McAlister and Michael L. Rothschild (eds.), *Advances in Consumer Research* 20 (Provo, UT: Association for Consumer Research, 1992), pp. 165–69; Donald J. Hempel and Harold Z. Daniel, "Framing Dynamics: Measurement Issues and Perspectives," in Leigh McAlister and Michael L. Rothschild (eds.), *Advances in Consumer Research* 20 (Provo, UT: Association for Consumer Research, 1992), pp. 273–79.

27. Irwin Levin, "Associative Effects of Information Framing," *Bulletin of the Psychonomic Society* 25 (1987), pp. 85–86.

28. William D. Diamond and Abhijit Sanyal, "The Effects of Framing on the Choice of Supermarket Coupons," in Marvin E. Goldberg and Gerald Gorn (eds.), *Advances in Consumer Research* 17 (Provo, UT: Association for Consumer Research, 1990), pp. 488–93; John Mowen, Alan Gordon, and Clifford Young, "The Impact of Sales Taxes on Store Choice: Public Policy and Theoretical Implications," *Proceedings of Summer Educators' Conference* (Chicago: American Marketing Association, 1988).

29. John C. Mowen and Maryanne M. Mowen, "Time and Outcome Valuation: Implications for Marketing Decision Making," *Journal of Marketing* (October 1991), pp. 54–62; Joan Meyers-Levy and Durairaj Maheswaran, "When Timing Matters: The Influence of Temporal Distance of Consumers' Affective and Persuasive Responses," *Journal of Consumer Research* 19 (December 1992), pp. 424–33.

30. Stephen J. Hock and George F. Lowenstein, "Time-Inconsistent Preferences and Consumer Self-Control," *Journal of Consumer Research* 17 (March 1991), pp. 492–507.

31. C. Whan Park, "The Effect of Individual and Situation-Related Factors on Consumer Selection of Judgmental Models," *Journal of Marketing Research* 13 (May 1976), pp. 144–151.

32. Wayne D. Hoyer and Stephen P. Brown, "Effects of Brand Awareness on Choice for a Common, Repeat-Purchase Product," *Journal of Consumer Research* 17 (September 1990), pp. 141–48.

33. J. E. Swan and L. J. Combs, "Product Performance and Consumer Satisfaction: A New Concept," *Journal of Marketing* 40 (April 1976), pp. 25–33.

34. Ibid., p. 32.

35. Michael Webster, "Financial Demise of America," Doc's Talk, (August 21, 2008), http://docstalk.blogspot.com/2008/08/financial-demise-of-america.html.

36. Nessim Hanna, "Can Effort/Satisfaction Theory Explain Price/Quality Relationships?" *Journal of the Academy of Marketing Science* 6, no. 1, (Winter 1978), pp. 91–100.

37. C. R. Wasson, *Consumer Behavior: A Managerial Viewpoint* (Austin, TX: Austin Press, 1975), p. 256.

38. J. A. Howard and J. Sheth, *The Theory of Buyer Behavior* (New York: John Wiley, 1967).

39. R. N. Cardozo, "An Experimental Study of Customer Effort, Expectation, and Satisfaction," *Journal of Marketing Research* 2 (August 1965), pp. 244–49; R. N. Cardozo, "Customer Satisfaction: Laboratory Study and Marketing Action," *Reflections on Progress in Marketing*, AMA (December 1964), pp. 283–89; R. N. Cardozo and D. Bramel, "The Effect of Effort and Expectation on Perceptual Contrast and Dissonance Reduction," *Journal of Social Psychology* 79 (October 1969), pp. 52–62.

40. A. G. Woodside, "Positive Disconfirmation of Expectation and the Effect of Effort on Evaluation," *Proceedings*, 80th American Psychological Association Conference (1971), pp. 743–44.

41. R. E. Anderson, "Consumer Dissatisfaction: The Effect of Disconfirmed Expectancy on Perceived Product Performance," *Journal of Marketing Research*, 10 (February 1973), pp. 38–44.

42. L. L. Golden and R. A. Peterson, "Post-Purchase, Pre-Trial Satisfaction Expectations as a Function of Message Content and Source," in K. L. Bernhardt (ed.), *Marketing 1976–1976 and Beyond*, (Proceedings AMA (1976), pp. 143–46.

43. TARP, Technical Assistance Research Programs, Consumer Complaint Handling in America: Summary of Findings and Recommendations (Washington, DC: U.S. Office of Consumer Affairs, 1979); and TARP, Consumer Complaint Handling in America: An Update Study (Washington, DC: U.S. Office of Consumer Affairs, 1986); Yoon Cheong Cho, "The Impact of E-service Failures and Customer Complaints on Electronic Commerce," *Journal of Consumer Satisfaction, Dissatisfaction, and Complaining Behavior* (January, 2003)

44. Sweta Chaturvedi Thota, "Do Consumers Hold Grudges and Practice Avoidance Forever?" *Journal of Consumer Satisfaction, Dissatisfaction, and Complaining Behavior* (January 2006), http://findarticles.com/p/articles/mi_qa5516/is_200601/ai_n21406176/print.

45. John A. Schibrowsky and Richard S. Lapidus, "Gaining Competitive Advantage by Analyzing Aggregate Complaints," *Journal of Consumer Marketing* 11, no. 1 (1994), pp. 15–26.

46. "DeepGreen Bank Home Equity Information," DeepGreen Bank, www.home-equity-info.us/lenders_banks_deepgreen-bank.php; "Ellie Mae Partners with DeepGreen Bank to Offer Paperless Loans," *Business Wire* (June 17, 2002), www.allbusiness.com/banking-finance/banking-lending-credit-services-mortgages/5895277-1.html.

47. "Complaint Procedure Assists in Resolutions," *Chicago Sun-Times* (Special Advertising Supplement) (October 27, 1996), p. E7.

48. Ron Kurtis, "Dealing with Customer Complaints," *School for Champions*, www.school-for-champions.com/tqm/complaints.htm.

49. A. F. Wysocki, et. al., "Consumer Complaints and Types of Consumers," *University of Florida* (May 2001), http://edis.ifas.ufl.edu/HR005.

50. Mary Gardiner Jones, "The Consumer Affairs Office," *California Management Review* 20 (Summer 1978), pp. 63–73.

3

SOCIAL AND CULTURAL INFLUENCES ON BEHAVIOR

Diffusion of Innovation

LEARNING OBJECTIVES

- To understand the diffusion process and identify its four basic components.
- To become familiar with the process, forms, and categories of innovation.
- To conceptualize what constitutes a "new" product.
- To examine aspects of new products that enhance their chances of acceptance in the marketplace.
- To recognize and distinguish between five categories of adopters.
- To examine the adoption process as well as its stages.
- To recognize the functional and psychological sources of consumer resistance to adopting innovations.

KEY TERMS

diffusion
adoption
discontinuous innovations
dynamically continuous innovations
continuous innovations
symbolic innovations
relative advantage
compatibility
simplicity
observability
trialability
divisibility
rate of adoption
frequency of purchase
innovators

early adopters
early majority
late majority
laggards
S-shaped diffusion curve
knowledge
persuasion
decision
implementation
confirmation
value barrier
usage barrier
tradition barrier
risk barrier
image barrier

When the motorcycle was introduced in the United States around the late 1800s, it was merely a motorized bicycle. A feeble internal combustion engine strapped to the frame powered the rear wheel by means of a belt. Almost all of the 4,000 cycles registered in the United States in 1900 were used solely for transportation rather than recreation.[1] From the very outset, Harley-Davidson envisioned an opportunity in this market. The first Harley-Davidson motorcycle was built in 1903 in Milwaukee, Wisconsin. William Harley, together with the Davidson brothers, designed and built high-quality motorcycles from scratch. At that point of operations, the entrepreneurs' goal was simply to develop technically superior motorcycles that would sell themselves. To bikers of the era, reliability was a most salient feature. Cyclists depended on a bike's ability to withstand the poor road conditions that prevailed at that time.

Following the Industrial Revolution, the United States was evolving quickly. Harley-Davidson at the time foresaw the potential for growth and profits ahead. The firm, at that point, was one of more than 100 U.S. motorcycle manufacturers. When Ford Motor Company first introduced its Model-T car in 1908, the motorcycle market was devastated. Most motorcycle companies folded as a result. Harley-Davidson, however, thrived due to its popularity with the public and contracts to equip the government (military) and police with specially designed motorcycles. This trend continued during World War I and helped the firm to survive the Great Depression.

In the 1950s, many factors helped enhance the motorcycle's popularity. New roads across the United States were being constructed, and existing roadways were being improved. In addition, family income rose after World War II. Discretionary income had made it possible for people to buy products they could not purchase during the war years. Because purchasing an automobile was still beyond most people's means, many bought a motorcycle instead. Today, Harley-Davidson holds over 60 percent of the heavyweight motorcycle market in the United States and claims over 50 percent of that market in Canada and Australia.[2]

In 2006, Harley-Davidson's customer research profiled the average buyer as male, 47 years old, with a median income of about $80,000 per year. However today, women in increasing numbers are becoming equally proud Harley-Davidson owners. Because a major segment of the heavyweight motorcycle market, aging baby boomers, is expected to grow in size in the next few years, Harley-Davidson's promotional strategy will continue to stress appeals such as status, freedom, and a carefree approach to living in order to lure this segment of the *young-at-heart* boomers.

Certain makes of bikes, such as Harley-Davidson, have taken on a distinguished personality of their own and have created an image that far transcends the bike's functional or utilitarian value. Learn about Harley-Davidson by visiting www.harley-davidson.com. *How does this site promote the "Harley lifestyle"? Is this lifestyle an integral part of the brand? What motivates the brand's "cult" of followers?*

This brief account of Harley-Davidson reveals how a company introduces new products and how consumers react to new-product introductions. Whereas the former perception of the motorcycle was that of a machine designed mainly for inexpensive transportation over rugged roadways, Harley-Davidson has transformed that conception into something that delivers a lifestyle experience without equal.

This chapter focuses on two closely related processes. The first of these is the subject of how innovations spread within a social system. Afterward, the chapter takes up the topic of the way consumers decide to accept or reject an innovation. Comprehension of both processes is critical for marketers striving to introduce new products into the marketplace successfully.

Where Did It All Begin?

The origins of research in diffusion can be traced back to the nineteenth century in the fields of anthropology, sociology, and religion. Initially, German and British anthropologists and sociologists investigated the spread of ethnic traditions and religious doctrines, transfer of technology, expanse of political beliefs, and spread of commerce among nations. By the early twentieth century, marketers in the United States began to apply this type of research to the issue of new-product acceptance. During the 1920s, the study of diffusion accompanied the introduction of hybrid seeds, which held the potential for significantly increasing agricultural yields. The U.S. Department of Agriculture conducted extensive research concerning those farmers who adopted hybrid seeds, those who were reluctant to do so, and the reasons behind both decisions. Other diffusion-related studies soon followed and addressed such varied topics as insurance purchases, voting tendencies, and new-product acceptance.

The study of diffusion addresses two main issues. First, these studies explore how acceptance of a *new product* or *new idea* spreads within the marketplace. This is termed **diffusion**. Second, these studies probe into the decision-making process that leads toward a consumer's acceptance or rejection of a new product or idea. This is termed **adoption**. The *diffusion process* is a macroprocess concerned with the spread of a new product or idea from its original source to and throughout the general public. In contrast, the *adoption process* is a microprocess dealing with the stages that an individual goes through before accepting a product. In the following sections of the chapter, we examine the process of diffusion and explain its four components. We then shift our attention to a discussion of adoption.

diffusion
the spread of a new product or idea within the marketplace

adoption
the decision-making stages an individual goes through before accepting a product

The Diffusion Process

The word *diffusion* is derived from a Latin word meaning "to spread out." Thus, scientists may speak of gaseous vapors that diffuse or gradually unfurl through the expanse of available space. In a marketing sense, diffusion deals with how an innovation spreads within the marketplace by means of communication (which may include the mass media, sales representatives, opinion leaders, and members of a social system) over a period of time. Diffusion is simply the sum total of many individual adoption decisions. There are four basic components in the diffusion process:[3]

- The innovation,
- The channel of communication,
- The social system, and
- Time.

Let us clarify the role played by each of these four components in the diffusion process.

THE INNOVATION

New-product development is big business. Although consumer products firms tend to derive a slightly greater percentage of sales from new products than do business products firms, the introduction of new products has been and continues to be a critical activity for all companies.[4] In the food industry alone, around 34 new food products are launched every day.[5] More than ever, existing products can be expected over the course of time either to be preempted by new and improved products or to degenerate to a position where profits are nonexistent.[6] Think of the fate of products such as Burma Shave, Brylcream, Hai Karate, and Black Jack Gum, which were once widely recognized and frequently purchased.[7] Today, however, many of them have either disappeared from the marketplace or at least reached the end of their life cycle.

Without a doubt, the long-term health of most organizations is tied to their ability to provide existing and new customers with an ongoing stream of new products.[8] Over 10,000 new products are marketed in the United States every year, and hundreds of thousands of people make their living producing and marketing new products.[9] Almost 3 percent of this country's gross national product (GNP) is spent on the technical phase of new-product development; this percentage represents research and development (R&D) only, not manufacturing and marketing costs.[10] The ad in Figure 10.1 highlights one of the many new product innovations that are launched by a host of progressive companies and that continue to infiltrate the marketplace daily.

Classifying Innovations

Innovations take a variety of forms. Some innovations represent genuine technological advances that become embodied into new-to-the-world products (e.g., iPhone, WiFi, Blackberry, GPS navigation systems). More commonly, innovations involve modifications or improvements to existing products, such as adding a new feature, ingredient, color, or scent to a product. Still others involve symbolic representations that alter the social and psychological meaning of products (new car designs or hairstyles).

life before nüvi®

Think back to the last time you were lost. Completely adrift, with panic rising and confidence sinking. Now imagine finding anything your heart desires with nüvi 750, the portable GPS navigator from Garmin. Just tap the screen to look up addresses, intersections, businesses and more and nüvi takes you there with clear, voice-prompted directions. nüvi's great for navigating on foot or in the car, and the 750 can even find the most efficient route when you have several stops.

Once you nüvi®, you'll never go back.

www.garmin.com

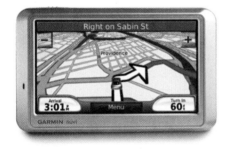

 NASDAQ **GRMN**

Figure 10.1
Today, more so than any other time in history, innovative products, such as the Nüvi GPS from Garmin are being increasingly introduced into the marketplace.

Consumer Behavior in Practice

Stealing, Robbing, and Bootlegging Are OK at 3M

3M Company, based in St. Paul, Minnesota, takes great pride in designing and maintaining a corporate environment that nurtures product innovation. Within 3M, it is expected that every one of the firm's 6,000 scientists worldwide *steals* 15 percent of the time, money, equipment, and personnel allotted to specific projects in order to work on creating and developing new products. What is the impact of *robbing* resources from one assignment to work on innovative ventures? The practice, known among 3M scientists as *bootlegging*, has enabled 3M, with over 40 divisions, to develop hundreds of new products every year. Ninety percent of these are developed in direct response to customer needs. One such 3M product is Post-it notes, the yellow strips of paper with a sticky backing.

The inspiration for Post-it notes came about in church. Arthur L. Fry, a 3M division scientist, was singing in the choir at St. Paul's Cathedral. Because performing the service music required singers to skip around in their hymnals, Fry prepared his songbook in advance by place marking the appropriate selections. He wished that some sort of bookmark were available that would stick to the pages but not damage the book when the markers were removed. Fry recalled that a lab scientist had recently experimented with an adhesive that failed to meet normal testing standards. He suspected this substandard adhesive—when applied to strips of paper— would serve the page-marking purpose perfectly.

Fry made samples in various sizes. Almost immediately, he found them to be quite handy for writing and affixing brief memos. To his amazement, he found that the nearly disregarded glue attached to most surfaces and could easily be removed after a few minutes or several years later without damaging the surface to which it had been affixed.

Samples of Post-it notes were circulated throughout the 3M organization. They were also sent to secretaries of Fortune 500 CEOs along with an explanation of how to use them. Soon personnel in these organizations were asking their corporate purchasing agents to order them. It was not long before the public had found many uses for Post-it notes and began asking for them too. Today, 3M has sales of $16.7 billion from many top branded consumer products, among the major ones is Post-it Notes, which has become an integral part of everyday life.[11]

Companies like 3M are known for the frequency with which they launch innovative products into the market. To familiarize yourself with the 3M Innovation Network, visit www.3m.com and http://www.3m.com/about3m/century/index.jhtml. In your opinion, what constitutes a truly new product? Despite the high costs and risks of failure, why is it more imperative than ever that firms today pursue growth via new-product introductions?

Robertson identified three classes of new products: discontinuous, dynamically continuous, and continuous innovations. His distinction between these three classes of products is founded on two elements: the extent to which they represent changes in technology and the extent to which the innovation requires changes in established consumption or usage patterns of adopters.[12] From a consumer behavior perspective, the greater the required change in established consumption habits resulting from the innovation, the less the chance that the innovation will gain quick acceptance. Conversely, the less disruptive the innovation is to these patterns, the greater the likelihood that it will gain widespread adoption. This section explains Robertson's threefold classification of innovations.

Discontinuous Innovations

Discontinuous innovations are unique, pioneering products that significantly disrupt and alter established purchasing and consumption routines. Discontinuous innovations involve major technical advances on the part of their creators. As a result of this striking newness, learning of new consumption or usage patterns is required.

Because discontinuous innovations require learning of new behavior patterns on the part of consumers, marketers must first sell prospective customers on the concept behind the innovation before they can sell the product. In other words, they need to educate consumers to respond to the new idea and then supply the product. Once the concept has gained acceptance, selling the product is relatively easy. This fact may explain the reason why it is often difficult for truly new products to gain quick acceptance in the marketplace. For example, it took many years for products such as the facsimile machine or contact lenses to become accepted by the masses.[13]

Discontinuous innovations are rare. Early examples include automobiles, airplanes, and telephones as well as more recent ones such as multi-media phones, MP3 players, portable video gadgets, GPS navigation devices, and supergizmos. Innovations of this type have changed and will continue to change the way we live and conduct business.

discontinuous innovations
unique products that significantly alter established consumption routines

Dynamically Continuous Innovations

Dynamically continuous innovations are new-product creations or alterations in existing products that entail minor technical advances and do not strikingly alter established consumer buying and usage patterns. Dynamically continuous innovations include adaptations of, replacements for, or improvements to existing products. Such innovations are new in some respects; in other ways, however, they are just slightly different or are simply minor modifications of existing products. Dynamically continuous innovations have some disrupting influence on customary consumption practices and require some new learning on the part of consumers Examples include digital cameras, hand-held computer organizers, laptop computers, voice-activated electronics, new computer operating systems, and conventional cell phones.

dynamically continuous innovations
new products that do not strikingly alter consumers' established usage patterns

Continuous Innovations

Continuous innovations are extensions or modifications of existing products with little or no change in technology. Continuous innovations are low-learning cases and require minimal, if any, adjustments in conventional consumption routines. Continuous innovations frequently take the form of imitative products. That is, they are new to the sponsoring company but perhaps not new to the marketplace, such as organic foods, high-pixel resolution digital comeras, or a diet or low-fat product extension to an existing food line. Other continuous innovations incorporate very slight changes, such as those related to appearance, packaging, size, color, new flavors, or style and fashion. Examples include new automobile models, new styles of clothing, whitening-formula toothpastes, flavored dental floss, liquid handsoaps, and moisturizing hand sanitizers. Continuous innovations may also incorporate

continuous innovations
new products that require minimal, if any, adjustments in consumption routines

new uses or applications of a familiar product. The present popularity of iced teas and coffees stands as a case in point. The ad for Fresh Step in Figure 10.2 informs pet owners of the odor-free feature of this new cat litter.

Extending Robertson's work, subsequent researchers have expanded the list of innovation classes to include what they have labeled symbolic innovations.[14] **Symbolic innovations** are those that convey new social or psychological meanings. In marketing, a classic example of symbolic innovation involves designer mineral water, which takes an existing product and gives it a new social meaning. Water, in this case, is repositioned as a purifying body cleanser (as in Evian ads) or as a fashionable alternative to alcohol (as in Perrier's ads).

Although innovations can be either symbolic or technological or even both, their effect on established consumer behavior patterns varies widely. Multi-media phones, iPods, and video game technologies, for example, have considerably altered social patterns of communication and recreation. However, most symbolic innovations, such as those related to style and fashion, are continuous in nature and involve minimal change of consumption habits.[15]

symbolic innovations

cases where a product conveys new social or psychological meanings

Figure 10.2

This eye-catching Fresh Step ad from the Clorox Pet Product Company reflects the concept of continuous innovation. The ad highlights the odor-eliminating feature of this new product.

What Is a "New" Product?

Whereas, in the eyes of the Federal Trade Commission, use of the word *new* in advertising is restricted to products distributed and made available in the marketplace within a time span of less than six months, the very notion of innovativeness, novelty, or newness is subjective and relative. In fact, time may or may not have anything to do with newness. For example, products qualify as new if consumers within a particular market lack awareness of or experience with them. In other words, that which is old to some may be brand new to others and vice versa. While cellular phones, PCs, VCRs, and CDs are standard household items within developed nations, they remain unavailable to millions of people in Third World countries.

New, therefore, may be thought of as anything that consumers perceive as new. Perception of newness, in many cases, can result from changes to packaging, price, distribution, and promotional strategies. In the same sense, newness of a product to the firm that manufactures or distributes it does not necessarily constitute novelty to the marketplace and consumers. From the perspective of newness, products enhanced by high-technological breakthroughs may excite product engineers, but it still remains to be seen whether they will do so for consumers.

Multiplicity of New-Product Strategies

Firms do not restrict themselves to any single type of new product. Rather, organizational efforts tend to emphasize a variety of endeavors. In both consumer firms and business firms, line extensions, which add related products to the current line, are the most common way of generating new products. Examples include Kellogg's introduction of Smart Start Antioxidents breakfast cereal, Jello Gelatin's creation of Jello Pudding Pops, or Danon's launch of Activia yogurt.[16] After line extensions, in decreasing order of importance, consumer products firms tend to focus on totally new products; efforts to improve existing product quality; adding features to current products; adding value to current products through distribution, price, and promotion; and finding new uses or markets for existing products. Business products firms, on the other hand, exhibit a somewhat different order of emphasis. After line extensions, they tend to focus on adding features to current products, developing totally new products, improving the tangible quality of current products, finding new uses or markets for current products, and adding value to current products through distribution, promotion, and price.[17] The Kawasaki Corporation ad in Figure 10.3 depicts an assortment of motorcycles that the diversified firm offers in just one of its many product lines.

These facts reveal that a good number of organizations are deemphasizing truly innovative products and are relying instead on defensive approaches such as flooding markets with line extensions. This trend has been confirmed by a study of the U.S. consumer products field that revealed that only about 5.7 percent of all new products introduced during a half-year period could be considered innovative.[18] This result does not compare

under the influence of drugs or alcohol. Adhere to the maintenance schedule in your owner's manual. Kawasaki's KFX50 is recommended for use under 16 riding ATVs should *always* have direct adult supervision. Kawasaki ATVs with engines of 90cc and above are recommended for use only more information, see your dealer, or call the ATV Safety Institute at 1-800-887-2887. **Warning:** ATVs can be hazardous to operate. For your safety, influence of drugs or alcohol. Never ride on public roads or pavement. Avoid excessive speeds and stunt driving. Be extra careful on difficult terrain. 1-800-661-RIDE

Kawasaki
Let the good times roll.

Figure 10.3

This ad from Kawasaki Corporation depicts several different motorcycle models the company offers in one of its product lines.

favorably to findings of a study of British and Japanese firms, which revealed that approximately 80 percent of these foreign competitors were developing radically new products as part of their development efforts.[19] In one investigation, a disappointingly low share of U.S. business products firms—just over one-third—engaged in the development of totally new-to-the-world products.[20]

Factors That Influence Consumer Acceptance of New Products

Some new products meet with instant success, such as the iPhone, MP3 and iPod, whereas others such as solar-energy powered heating and cooling systems are taking many years to gain acceptance. Certain features of product innovations appear to contribute to their success, whereas others seem to have no effect whatsoever on that success.[21] At the Marketing Science Institute, a research group backed by giants such as Procter & Gamble and Apple Computer, the first priority of business is improving new-product development procedures. Companies as diverse as Apple, Yahoo, Google, Hewlett-Packard, Motorola, Colgate-Palmolive, Honda, and Toyota are all tackling new-product issues in order to learn what contributes to the success of new products and how to keep flops to a minimum. When executives at Hewlett-Packard's Medical Product Group studied 10 of their new-product failures along with 10 of their successful products, they were able to identify a number of factors that determined which products flourished and which did not—information that led to future successes.

Based on studies of the adoption of new products and practices, Rogers identified five product characteristics that seem to influence consumer acceptance of new products. These characteristics are:

1. relative advantage,
2. compatibility,
3. simplicity–complexity,
4. observability, and
5. trialability and divisibility.[22]

Relative Advantage

Consumers are more inclined to purchase a new product when it offers a relative advantage over alternative merchandise. **Relative advantage** is the degree to which consumers perceive a new product as different from and better than its dated substitutes. For example, Dean Food Company has introduced a new package concept to enhance milk consumption. Instead of the square cartons that were used before, single servings are now packaged in attractive plastic bottles with screw-on caps called Chugs.[23] The greater the advantage, the greater the new product's chance of selection and the sooner the innovation will be adopted. Many consumers have made the switch from cassette tapes and vinyl records to CDs, and music downloads from typewriters to word processors, and from glasses to contact lenses. ATMs achieved quick acceptance because they made banking transactions available around-the-clock, a high perceived advantage to consumers. On the other hand, although debit cards and POS (point-of-sale) cards offered advantages to banks and retailers, consumers perceived little relative advantage over credit cards or personal checks, and they thus had significantly lower usage rates.

A good example of relative advantage is found in the competitive floral industry. FTD offers floral arrangements and specialty gift items, including boxed flowers, plants, dried flowers, gourmet food selections, holiday gifts, bath and beauty products, jewelry, wine and gift baskets, and stuffed animals.[24] FTD was

relative advantage
the perceived property of a new product as better than its dated substitutes

established in 1910 by a few florists who agreed to exchange orders for out-of-town deliveries via telegraph. Today, FTD encompasses 20,000 independent florists in the United States and is linked by state-of-the-art technology to 28,000 florists in 150 countries around the world. FTD was both the first floral wire service made available to the public and the first among such services to publish a selection guide containing photos of hundred of floral arrangements to help consumers make appropriate choices. A few years ago, FTD added a toll-free number—800-SEND-FTD—making it still easier for consumers to send flowers. In addition, FTD has its Web site—www.ftd.com—which offers1,000 floral arrangements and specialty gifts for holiday and special occasions. Convenience and speed of sending flowers to anyone, anywhere, anytime offers customers a genuine relative advantage. Similarly, in the case of paint, manufactures originally packaged paint in metallic cans, which caused the paint to spill while pouring. New and improved plastic containers that are designed to prevent spills were introduced to the market in the past few years. The ad from Whirlpool in Figure 10.4 recommends the Duet Steam Washer and dryer, that gives consumers the choice of a wash cycle or a Steam Refresh Cycle.

Compatibility

compatibility
the perceived property of a new product as being consistent with consumers' beliefs, values, experiences, and habits

A new product should be consistent with consumers' existing needs, beliefs, values, attitudes, experiences, and habits. The better the **compatibility** of a new product with consumers' lifestyles and established practices, the more quickly the innovation will be adopted. The success of Oscar Mayer's Lunchables is a case in point. It is a meal-in-a-box that parents of school-age children love. It solves the parents' problem of what to make for lunch every day, and at the same time, provides an expanded choice of lunch items kids enjoy.[25]

Recently, after six years of costly development, Microsoft introduced the Windows Vista operating system. PC professionals and enthusiasts gave a sigh of relief after a decade of eagerly waiting for this system to be introduced. This enthusiasm, however, promptly turned into disappointment when users discovered Vista's incompatibility with some existing hardware, its requirement for human interaction to close security dialogue box warnings, and its use of hated DRM. Lack of compatibility was a barrier that delayed acceptance of the new operating system.

Simplicity–Complexity

simplicity
the perceived property that an innovation is easy to understand, assemble, and operate

Simplicity is the extent to which consumers perceive a new product as easy to understand, assemble, and operate. The simpler an innovation is to comprehend and use, the greater its chance of being selected and accepted by consumers. Conversely, the more complex an innovation is, the less likely it is to find favor among the public. In 1998, Apple Computer introduced the Apple Puck Mouse, a puck-shaped mouse, along with its introduction of iMac G3. This ill-fated excuse for a human interface device was one of Apples most dubious creations. The device had a single button that was difficult to find without looking for it, and made the experience of "mousing" totally impractical due to the fact that users could not figure out which direction the mouse was pointing.

Sometimes clothes don't need a wash. They need a refresh.

Before

STEAM

After Steam Refresh Cycle

Introducing the Whirlpool® Duet® Steam washer and dryer. The one-touch Steam Refresh Cycle in the dryer naturally steams out wrinkles and odors. So skip needless washing, ironing and dry cleaning because now clothes can go from lying there to ready to wear in just 15 minutes. Visit **whirlpool.com** to learn more about the Duet® Steam pair with Laundry 1-2-3™ pedestals, towers and worksurfaces.

Whirlpool
Home Appliances

The power to get more done.

Photographs used with permission of Whirlpool Corporation

Figure 10.4

The relative advantage of the Whirlpool Duet Steam washer and dryer is a Steam Refresh Cycle that removes wrinkles and odors from clothes, as well as eliminates the need to iron or dry clean them.

With the sweeping technological advances of the day, some products have become so complex that consumers continue to shy away from them. Observing this trend, camera manufacturers—both still and video—were among the first to realize the importance of simplicity. Modern still cameras, for example, feature drop-in film loading, automatic film advance, automatic focus, and built-in flash so that amateur photographers can obtain professional results with minimal confusion and effort. Many popular software packages for Macintosh and Windows machines have been specifically designed to be user-friendly in order to overcome apprehensiveness on the part of nontechnically oriented prospects. Similarly, VCR manufacturers have sought to simplify programming activities with such features as VCR Plus and on-screen programming. Similarly, many computers—like Dell—come preloaded with software.

Observability

observability
the perceived property that an innovation is visible and communicable to potential adopters

Observability is the extent to which an innovation is visible and communicable to potential adopters. Highly visible products, such as automobiles and fashions, are more quickly adopted and diffused than, say, headache remedies or soaps, which are used in private. Studies of adoption of solar power panels by consumers in the United States show that acceptance often occurred within concentrated areas, such as California, Arizona, and Oregon, rather than throughout the entire country, and within certain concentrated neighborhoods within each one of these states.[27] Neighbors, once exposed to the comfort of air conditioning, wanted a unit for themselves. Manufacturers of sporting goods such as Wilson and athletic footwear such as Nike or Reebok frequently induce professional athletes to use their equipment or wear their shoes in order to enhance brand visibility. Use of a new product by talented heros at sporting events and celebrities in movies or on TV can enhance the speed of adoption.

trialability
the perceived property that a new product can be experienced before purchase

The case of AriZona iced tea offers a good example of the importance of observability. The tea comes in a bottle that is so well designed many consumers buy it just for the container. Each new variety of AriZona iced tea is anxiously awaited by collectors. As a result, AriZona iced tea stands out in a busy product category of soft drinks, replete with hundreds of other competing brands.

The attractive packaging of AriZona iced tea makes this brand stand out among the many other soft drink brands in the marketplace.

Trialability and Divisibility

When consumers can experiment with a new product on a limited basis and evaluate its merits before making a purchase commitment, adoption occurs more quickly. This property of a product is known as its **trialability**. When consumers can be given a free sample of a new product to test, achieving trial is simple. Toward this end, Procter & Gamble spends millions of dollars annually to distribute free *trial-size* new-product samples to households throughout the United States. Such minispecimens are sent directly to consumers' homes or handed out inside retail stores to allow consumers to try new products that few would have ventured to try otherwise. Although this practice is relatively easy in the case of sampling consumer goods, such as foods, soaps, or toothpaste, the case of durable goods presents a challenge. Limited trial of these types of goods, however, may be possible via tactics such as demonstrations in retail showrooms or consumers' homes, trial in-home placements, lease-with-option-to-buy plans, and 100 percent satisfaction guarantees. For this reason, most automobile companies, such as Ford and General Motors, woo car rental companies to get them to carry their recent models. The objective is obvious—when drivers try a new-car model, they are often impressed with its performance and frequently become potential buyers.

© 2009, Miodrag Gajic, Shutterstock, Inc.

Word of mouth is considered more effective than advertising because of the credibility and trustworthiness of the source.

In recent years, trialability has also been enhanced electronically through virtual reality. Recent developments in this technology have enabled consumers to experience a product before making a purchase choice. The use of Web-based virtual reality (VR) technology has been an effective way to facilitate shopping for many products, including furniture and clothing. VR offers consumers realistic product trials in cyberspace without the temporal and physical constraints of brick-and-mortar stores. In the case of furniture, VR technologies offer dynamic interaction with pieces of furniture by allowing users to zoom-in, zoom-out, move, or rotate an object. Among the biggest problems that furniture buyers face has been their inability to view the product in their home setting and to match choice alternatives with their currently owned pieces of home decor. However, realistic trialability—including close inspection of individual items and combinations of items—can be attained when the furniture and the environment for which it is intended are all generated in three-dimensional real-time interactive computer graphics. Similarly, in the marketplace for clothing, VR has made and will continue to make the shopping experience practical and convenient. A consumer looking for a dress will soon be able to step into a fitting room online, try it on, view herself from all angles, adjust the lighting and dress color, and send a snapshot to a family members or friends for their opinion. Through virtual shopping, she will also be able to use an avatar, a virtual representation of herself, to shop with friends in a three-dimensional online environment in real time, and try on virtual merchandise, as well as make purchases.

Divisibility is also an important factor in encouraging adoption. If consumers can try new products in small quantities, achieving trial is relatively easy. In a study of five packaged goods by Shoemaker and Shoaf, nearly two-thirds of consumers were found to make trial purchases of new brands in

divisibility
the perceived property that a new product can be sampled in small quantities

quantities smaller than those they usually purchased.[28] Realization of this tendency, in part, prompted Campbell's to introduce individual servings and smaller-sized packages of its soups and other ready-to-eat meals.

THE CHANNEL OF COMMUNICATION

Communication is essential for widespread acceptance of innovation. Communication enables marketers to promote their brands and thus sell their products or services. Without communication channels, consumers would remain largely unaware of new goods and services available in the marketplace. Diffusion researchers focus their attention on the process of transmitting product-related information through various channels of communication. Their objective is to understand the relative impact of messages and channels employed on new-product acceptance or rejection.

Marketing communication can be divided into two major types: mass communication and personal communication. **Mass communication** relies on the mass media to disseminate information to a target audience. Mass-media vehicles include magazines, newspapers, television, radio, and the Web, as well as many of today's electronic technologies such as multi-media phones. **Personal communication**, on the other hand, involves two or more persons interacting directly with each other either face-to-face, person-to-audience, or over conventional phone lines.

Over the years, diffusion researchers have argued that personal communication is the major key to persuasion. They further supported the contention that mass-media channels are merely effective in creating awareness and knowledge concerning innovations, while interpersonal channels are the force in forming and changing consumer attitudes regarding a new product or idea. According to this view, it is the influence of personal communication that brings about the decision to adopt or reject an innovation.

Today, however, with the recent overwhelming advances in technology, the Internet—which is considered a mass medium—has the ability to reach an unlimited number of audience members without many of the limitations that characterize other forms of mass media, such as absence or delay of feedback as well as restrictions in the amount of information communicated. Through interactivity, consumers can receive information on any topic upon demand and respond to messages they receive instantaneously. In fact, no mass medium can match the Internet's ability to convey as much specific, up-to-date, and detailed information.

With the present accessibility of the Internet for most consumers, information on virtually any topic, product, service, or company imaginable lies just a few keystrokes away. The Web has taken on the role of an interpersonal medium. Internet blogs, online communities, social networks, virtual worlds, photo galleries, and e-mail, are but a few of the vehicles that have helped to fuel the diffusion and adoption of present-day products and ideas.

New avenues of communication opened by the information superhighway make possible the transfer of information with simple strokes on a keyboard or flips of a switch. Through interactive TV, as we have discussed in chapter 1, consumers can receive any type of information on demand, ranging from educational programming and news broadcasts to product lists and grocery services. Via interactivity, direct-mail campaigns that used to cost thousands of dollars in the not-so-distant past can now be accomplished electronically for pennies per contact and at a much faster speed than ever before.

Beyond methods of reaching likely consumers through traditional media types such as newspapers, magazines, television, and radio, the rapid growth of interactive technology has prompted many companies to rethink the way they can reach prospects. By ascertaining where customers congregate on the Internet, some companies have opted to affiliate with certain content-driven Web sites. Through sponsorship of one of these content-driven sites, a tactic known as *co-branding*, a company can maintain direct equity in the Web site's show content, which is then designed to complement the company's mission, products, or services. For example, a strategic alliance was formed between MSN and Verizon Online, which have joined forces to deliver innovative high-speed digital subscriber line (DSL) Internet access and services that can be offered across the country over Verizon's DSL-capable lines.[30]

Marketers must understand the specific norms, values, traditions, standards, attitudes, and expectations of varied social systems in order to influence the acceptance of a new product or idea.

No matter how large a company's promotional budget may be, marketers of new products stand to benefit greatly when positive word-of-mouth communication among consumers supplements the firm's paid advertising and personal selling efforts. Positive word-of-mouth communication occurs when satisfied adopters of an innovation recommend the new product to their friends or relatives. Although the marketer of an innovation *can* control new-product advertising, word-of-mouth *cannot* be controlled by the firm. Consequently, it may be positive and helpful, or negative and harmful.[29] Both exposure to advertising in the media and hands-on product experience can have the effect of precipitating word of mouth among consumers. Word of mouth is considered more effective than advertising due to the credibility and trustworthiness of the source. Diffusion largely depends on a chain of positive interpersonal communications, whereby successive layers of consumers adopt a new product upon the advice of slightly more venturesome acquaintances.

THE SOCIAL SYSTEM

Humans do not exist in a social vacuum. Rather they are members of social systems. A social system is a physical, social, or cultural environment to which individuals belong and within which they function. Social systems unite groups of persons who interact, at least occasionally, because they share certain common needs, problems, activities, interests, places of residence or employment, and the like. Members of a social system have at least one characteristic in common (same sex, similar age, same occupation), which makes them potential buyers of or influencers for a marketer's product. In the case of men's cordless electric shavers, the social system consists of males who are old enough to grow unwanted facial hair. For a suntan lotion, the social system includes all individuals, male or female and young or old, who like to sunbathe.

Within a social system, each member possesses a particular status and plays a specific role. Positive and negative sanctions are in place to ensure that behavior complies with group expectations. The social system serves as a reference group as individuals carry over its norms and values into their purchase decisions. Keep in mind, however, that individuals exist at the intersection of multiple social systems (personal, familial, social, and professional) and frequently face interrole conflicts that must somehow be resolved.

The specific norms, values, traditions, standards, attitudes, and expectations of the social system are instrumental in influencing the acceptance of innovative products and ideas. These can make or break a new product. Traditional versus modern, religious versus secular, or adventurous versus cautious cultural orientations can influence an innovation's acceptance or rejection. New, revealing styles of swimsuits may be quickly endorsed in liberal, secular societies but may be swiftly shunned by more conservatively aligned social systems.

Not only do norms, values, attitudes, and expectations vary between social systems, but the expanse of specific orientations can vary between societies. The varied degree of diffusion of innovation across cultures is a fact of life. The World Bank report entitled "Global Economic Prospects 2008: Technology Diffusion in the Developing World" finds that the rate of diffusion of innovation in various cultures is a function of a number of factors, including socioeconomic differences, the availability of a critical mass of technological competencies in a country, as well as the affordability of the particular technology.[32]

Some of the documented cases of cross-cultural diffusion stand to clarify the varied degrees of speed at which innovation spreads within different cultures, and to pinpoint the factors that underlie the associated diffusion rate. Such cases include, for example, the way in which AIDS awareness and AIDS treatments differ from one country to another, due to factors such as socioeconomic conditions in each nation and differential access to patient care.[33] Another example includes the case of the rapid pace of diffusion for cell phones in many areas of the world, including sub-Sahara Africa as well as other places that have no landlines.[34] Still other cases include the 100-dollar laptop project, initiated by the One Laptop Per Child Association (OLPC), and the degree to which coverage was achieved in various countries. This level of success was influenced by the extent of each country's governmental interest and willingness to cooperate with OLPC. Further, the recent cases of the quick diffusion of automobiles in both China and India stand to confirm the positive association between the rate of diffusion and cross-cultural socioeconomic conditions, especially the gains in the income level of the middle class in these two countries.

Three aspects of the social system have been found to influence the speed of diffusion:

- The greater the degree of compatibility between the innovation and values held by a social system's members, the more brisk the pace of diffusion.
- The more homogeneous (nonsegmented) the social system, the quicker the diffusion process. Homogeneity maximizes interpersonal contact.[35]
- The diffusion of innovations across cultures depends largely upon the distance between the countries and the social similarity of their cultures.[36]

The acceptance of new products is both shaped and emulated by interaction among the people who belong to a particular social system. Huge multinational corporations have been known to falter occasionally in global markets when attempting to introduce domestically successful products. Why? They simply fail to adjust the product or its supporting marketing strategy to accommodate the dissimilar social systems in host countries. For example, Crest toothpaste initially failed in Mexico. When Procter & Gamble tried to use its U.S. campaign, Mexicans neither appreciated its promised decay-prevention benefit nor its scientifically oriented copy.[37] On the other hand, 3M's successful introduction of Post-it notes into Japan is due, at least in part, to recognizing the need to use long, narrow paper shapes suited to the vertical character of Japanese writing.[38]

Since norms and values vary cross-culturally, the same product may take on different meanings in different cultures.

TIME

The inclusion of time as a variable in diffusion research serves a number of important functions. Knowing the *rate of adoption* or relative speed with which consumers adopt an innovation is vital in planning production schedules and inventory requirements. Initial overproduction of an innovation as a result of high sales expectations can be financially devastating for a business. If the rate of adoption turns out to be slow, the excessive production ties up capital in unsold goods, causes overstocks in distribution outlets, and forces lower prices in order to move excess goods. Similarly, knowledge of the *frequency* with which consumers purchase a new product is an important factor in streamlining distribution practices. Scheduling new-product deliveries to dealers is founded on knowledge of the frequency with which consumers repurchase that product. The two time-related factors in the diffusion process can thus be identified as the rate of adoption and the frequency of purchase.

© 2009, JupiterImages, Inc.

rate of adoption
the relative speed with which consumers adopt an innovation

The **rate of adoption** refers to the length of time it takes a new product to become accepted by potential adopters within a given social system.[39] This rate is measured by the time span it takes consumers to adopt an innovation. In the field of photography, for example, consumer reaction to two types of recently introduced cameras—the digital camera and the high-definition digital camera with AMOLED display—stands to demonstrate the relevance of the rate of adoption to production and inventory management.[40] In the case of the digital camera, the number of units sold has increased more than fifty-fold since its introduction in 1994 by Apple (i.e., Apple Quick Take) and in 1995 by Kodak (i.e., Kodak DC).[41] Annual increases in sales also continued to surpass 10 percent. In the second case, however, the diffusion of the HD digital camera, which offers the advantages of superior-quality photos and AMOLED display, appears to be significantly slower due to its lofty price tag, the need for high-definition sets, and unfamiliarity of consumers with its advanced features. Considering this situation, Samsung's new HD digital camera, introduced in 2008, would be expected to face a slow pace of diffusion, at least in the short run.

frequency of purchase
the rate at which consumers purchase a product after the initial purchase

Frequency of purchase refers to the rate with which a consumer purchases the product after the initial purchase—sometimes referred to as the repurchase rate. This measurement differentiates between heavy users (who buy more of the product and do so frequently), moderate users (who display an average usage and purchase rate), and light users (who buy less of the product and do so infrequently). For manufacturers of new products, frequency of purchase represents valuable information in directing distribution schedules. Failure to identify this rate can result in stock outs for dealers if mammoth demand for the new product materializes or overstocks if demand is slow to come about.

Time and the Adopter Categories

Consumers exhibit individual differences in their readiness and willingness to try and accept new products. In other words, whereas some people test and accept an innovation soon after its introduction, others wait for additional information or rely on learning about the experiences of persons who are more venturesome than themselves when deciding whether to try or adopt. Some people delay longer than others before adopting a new product, and still others may never adopt altogether. As a result, marketers are interested in learning how long after product introduction various consumer groups adopt, how long adoption takes, reasons for time differences among consumer groups, and which individual and environmental variables distinguish earlier adopters from later adopters.

Marketers of new products recognize the important role of more innovative individuals in gaining new-product acceptance. As opinion leaders, they pass along information about the new product to others—a concept referred to as word of mouth. Marketers often research the demographic and psychographic characteristics as well as the media habits of these more venturesome consumers so that promotion and distribution can be first targeted to them. This is no small task, because researchers have yet to prove the existence of a general personality trait among consumers known as *innovativeness*. Rather, individuals tend to be venturesome in some product categories and more traditional in others. A sales professional, for example, may dress conservatively yet might drive the latest new model of automobile, loaded with all the options. Similarly, one who relishes sampling new and exotic cuisines may be politically quite conservative. Marketers of new products face the challenge of identifying the characteristics of those consumers who are likely to be venturesome in a specific product category.[42]

Rogers conceived a classification consisting of five adopter categories based on innovativeness as manifested by the length of time it takes consumers to adopt an innovation.[43] His model, depicted in Exhibit 10.1, follows the normal (bell-shaped) distribution. In other words, after a slow start, increasing numbers of people adopt the new product as it becomes more apparent. The number of adopters eventually reaches a peak and then gradually drops off as fewer potential adopters remain. Rogers assumes that eventually there will be 100 percent adoption and thus excludes nonadopters from his groupings and percentages. This is a bold assumption because, regardless of their merit, few innovations ever achieve universal acceptance. The following paragraphs provide a brief profile of the types of individuals who make up each of the five categories proposed by Rogers.

Innovators

Representing 2.5 percent of the market, **innovators** are venturesome individuals and the first to adopt a new product, even at some risk.[44] Innovators tend to have higher social status and enjoy higher incomes. They tend to be younger, better educated, more cosmopolitan and mobile, more self-confident, and more reliant on their own values and judgment than on group norms. Innovators are more likely to obtain information from nonpersonal sources, scientific sources, and experts. Promotional appeals targeted to innovators frequently use factual appeals that emphasize product attributes and corresponding customer benefits. Innovators tend to be less brand loyal and more attracted to products or situations that provide diverse challenges.

innovators
the first 2.5 percent of the market to adopt a new product

Adopter Categories Based on Innovativeness

EXHIBIT 10.1

Source: Everett M. Rogers, *Diffusion of Innovation*, 4th ed. (New York: Free Press, 1955). Copyright ©1955 by Everett M. Rogers.

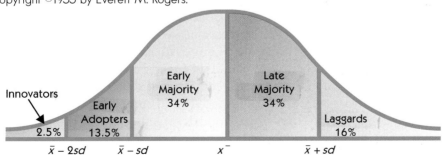

Early Adopters

Early adopters represent the next 13.5 percent of the market to adopt a product. Although early adopters are not the first to adopt, they adopt early—but carefully—during the product's life cycle. Unlike innovators who are characterized by broad involvement outside the local community, early adopters tend to be socially integrated and involved within their local community. They are more reliant on group norms and values and are most likely to be *opinion leaders* in their community. Because they are likely to transmit word-of-mouth influence to their acquaintances and colleagues, and because other people are interested in and influenced by their opinions, early adopters are probably the most important group in determining whether a new product will succeed. Early adopters play critical roles as trendsetters and tastemakers. Consequently, they are largely responsible for determining which new products will be deemed acceptable by future adopters.

© 2009, JupiterImages, Inc.

In the diffusion process, *agents of change* (parties who seek to accelerate the spread of a given innovation) usually focus their initial persuasive efforts on early adopters. When marketers succeed in attracting early adopters to an innovation, the broader market eventually follows, due to the respect other consumers have for early adopters' opinions. For example, in the wine industry, marketers attempt to attract early adopters by holding wine-tasting events where guests taste new wines and learn about each variety from hosting reps. Promotional messages targeted to these early adopters frequently employ factual appeals. In addition to their dependence on mass media to acquire knowledge about new products, early adopters rely on sales personnel as an important information source. They tend to display high usage rates in the product category in which the innovation falls. Marketers of new products are keenly interested in identifying and reaching these early adopters. They are an important target for ads and other promotions aimed at creating a market where none previously existed.[45]

Innovators tend to be younger, better educated, more cosmopolitan and mobile, more self-confident, and more reliant on their own values and judgment than on group norms.

The Early Majority

The **early majority** represents the next 34 percent of the market to adopt. Although the early majority adopts just before the average consumer in a social system, they deliberate their decision carefully. Members of the early majority are likely to gather more information and evaluate more brands than early adopters and are likely to be opinion leaders' friends and neighbors. This group is slightly above average in social and economic standing. The early majority tends to rely considerably on ads, salespeople, and contact with early adopters as information sources. Promotional appeals targeting the early majority frequently employ expert appeals and celebrity endorsements.

The Late Majority

The **late majority** represents still the next 34 percent of the market to adopt. The late majority is skeptical. They may lack the financing to purchase the innovation, or they at least feel that the new item is not worth its cost. Members adopt an innovation to save time or effort or in response to social pressure to conform, but only after most acquaintances have already done so. The late majority tends to be below average in income and education level. Trusting group norms, the late majority relies primarily on word-of-mouth communication from peers—the late or early majority—rather than on the mass media as a source of information. Advertising and personal selling are less effective with this group. Promotional appeals targeting the late majority frequently employ conformity appeals ("Everyone else does, why not you?").

Laggards

The **laggards** are the last 16 percent of the market to adopt. Laggards tend to fall at the low end of the socioeconomic scale and, like innovators, do not rely on group norms. Laggards are independent and tradition bound. Feeling estranged in a progressive marketplace, laggards are suspicious of change and resist adopting an innovation until it has become something of a tradition itself. By the time laggards adopt an innovation, it has probably been superseded and abandoned by the innovators in favor of more recent models. Promotional efforts targeted to laggards may suggest that a new product does what familiar products do, only better.

Given the preceding classification, the obvious question concerns how marketers can identify innovators and early adopters among personal and business consumers in order to focus early marketing attention and efforts toward them. A review of the literature suggests five traits that often differentiate innovators and early adopters from the masses:[46]

1. *Venturesome:* an obvious need to be daring and different
2. *Socially integrated:* extensive and frequent contact and interaction with others in one's community or profession
3. *Cosmopolitan:* interest in world affairs and perspectives that extend beyond the immediate locale
4. *Upwardly mobile:* capable of moving upward along the social scale, and
5. *Privileged:* wealthy (or at least possessing adequate resources) and financially independent.

The S-Shaped Diffusion Curve

Studies suggest that as diffusion progresses, a fairly predictable path of dissemination is followed. For marketing managers, this pattern, called the **S-shaped diffusion curve**, holds forecasting implications. Strategists can anticipate that cumulative adoption effect of an innovation, if successful, will likely proceed as follows.

- Initially, market acceptance for an innovation increases rather slowly.
- Then, after a rather lethargic beginning, market acceptance for an innovation accelerates more rapidly.
- Finally, market acceptance continues to grow but at an increasingly sluggish pace, because nearly all candidates for adopting the innovation have already done so.

In other words, the *S-shaped diffusion curve* concept holds that the probability of purchase at any point in time is directly related to the number of previous buyers. The rationale is that among consumers, two groups can be identified: early buyers who provide initial sales growth for an innovation, and followers who require broader distribution, more industry advertising, and word-of-mouth exposure before they become sufficiently confident to make the decision to purchase a new product.[47] Eventually, the pool of potential adopters becomes increasingly exhausted, and the growth rate decelerates as a sort of *glass ceiling* is approached. For example, in the case of the diffusion of Beanie Babies, which were introduced in 1993, the rate of adoption started at the zero point in that year, climbed slowly in the following three years, then shot up dramatically to reach approximately 25 million adopters by 1999. In 2000, however, sales started to decline, and the popularity of the product began to fade. By 2003, roughly 11 million adopters remained interested in Beanie Babies. This declining trend appears to continue throughout the present day, amounting to only 1.5 million adopters. The graph in Exhibit 10.2, which is a modified S-shaped diffusion curve, illustrates this effect. In this depiction, the course of time (by year—1993 through 2008) is plotted across the horizontal axis, and the number of Beanie Baby adopters is plotted along the vertical axis. Notice how the resultant curve approximates the shape of

EXHIBIT 10.2   **A Modified S-Shaped Diffusion Curve for Beanie Babies Allowing for Discontinuance**

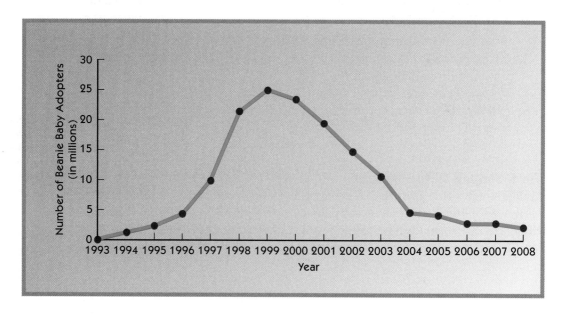

an elongated letter *s*. This curve depicts a slow start in the first four years to the diffusion of Beanie Babies, followed by a period of rapid growth during 1998 and 1999, then by a decline since the year 2000.

It should be noted here that diffusion patterns can vary from a curve that extends for many years to a rapidly declining curve of short duration. For example, today's popularity of many successful products and services such as movies, computer software, game software, and music CDs shows a quick diffusion at first, followed by a rapid decline occurring within a brief time span.

The Adoption Process

In order to improve the probability of success for a new product, marketers must understand the adoption process. The more innovative the new product, the more important at first this knowledge becomes. Simply stated, adoption entails a sequence of stages that an individual passes through along a road leading toward the acceptance of new products, services, or ideas. Marketers who develop insights into how and why products or ideas spread, how and why they are accepted or rejected, and the types of consumers who are most likely to purchase or embrace them soon after their introduction are in a better position to design effective introductory marketing strategies.

STAGES OF THE ADOPTION PROCESS

Adoption requires a series of successive judgments in an individual's decision process regarding acceptance of a new-product offering. The adoption process begins when a consumer or other adopter unit (a family, community, organization) first learns of a new product and ends when that unit finally decides to adopt or reject it. Rogers proposed a decision-making model for adoption of innovations. His original model depicted six stages of the adoption process: awareness, interest, evaluation, trial, adoption, and confirmation. However, his revised model defines the innovation-decision process as consisting of five stages: knowledge, persuasion, decision, implementation, and confirmation.[48] We discuss each in turn.

Knowledge
In the **knowledge** stage, a consumer is exposed to an innovation's existence and obtains some understanding of how it functions. At this point, consumers are aware of the innovation but have made no judgment concerning its relevance to a recognized problem or need. A family, for example, may learn from ads about a new home security system. Knowledge is largely the result of selective perception and is more likely to occur via the mass media than later stages, when it is more influenced by opinion leaders. Prior conditions (such as felt needs or problems) and characteristics of the decision-making unit (such as socioeconomic status) can influence the reception of information about the new product. Figure 10.5 presents an ad from LaBrada Nutrition, Inc., designed to enhance consumers' knowledge regarding a new product, Lean Body high-protein shakes.

knowledge
a state of being exposed to and aware of an innovation's existence

We asked Billy what he would improve in his biceps. His response, "Nothin', they're pretty much perfect!"

Some were just born with it!

For those who weren't, Lean Body® Shakes will help you build muscle and burn fat.

*L*ean Body® *shakes taste delicious*--- just like soft serve ice cream! But don't let their taste fool you---they're packed with 40g of muscle-building protein, yet contain no sugar or lactose. And, at 50% less fat than competing RTDs, you'll build muscle, not your waistline. Lean Body® shakes are a bodybuilder's best friend--- powerful, muscle building, fat-burning nutrition on the go.

Try one today and you'll be hooked, we guarantee it!

**Zero Sugar • Half the Fat
#1 in Taste!**

LABRADA
N U T R I T I O N ®
"The Most Trusted Name in Sports Nutrition!"™
©Copyright 2008, LBN, Inc.

Figure 10.5

The Lead Body ad from LaBrada Nutrition, Inc. communicates to consumers the benefits of these high-protein, low-fat shakes in building muscle and burning fat.

A Sparkle of Youth . . . In a Bottle

Herbal supplements such as ginkgo bilova, echinacea, St. John's Wort, burdock root, and ginseng are the fastest growing herbal remedies that the market has witnessed in recent years. Consumer adoption of herbs and supplements has gained vast momentum since Congress ruled that manufacturers could make health claims for nutritional supplements and that the Food and Drug Administration couldn't treat them like drugs. Sales of these natural remedies as a result have grown over 25 percent annually. Annual sales in the United States now exceed $21.4 billion according to the Council for Responsive Nutrition in Washington, D.C.

Presently, more than 1500 companies compete in this promising field. Companies such as Warner-Lambert, Pharamanex, Celestial, and Bayer offer a variety of products ranging from cholesterol-lowering herbal remedies to vitamins and minerals designed to enhance health, treat tension, and permit mood control.

Observing consumers' enhanced interest in these new herbs, many beverage companies have jumped on the bandwagon and have introduced new drinks laced with a variety of these herbs. Some of these drinks contain beta carotene, ginseng, aloe vera, and high doses of chromium. However, unlike sports drinks such as Gatorade that are formulated to replenish body nutrients, the makers of the new beverages claim that these drinks can bring back youth, improve health, and result in a longer, happier life.

Similarly, operations that market Chinese herbal supplements in the United States often claim that the products they sell treat or cure diseases. For example, a vendor of a pill called Dia-Cope claimed that the pill prevents, treats, and cures diabetes. Another supplier claimed that "Sagee," a Chinese herbal supplement, could improve memory and concentration, repair damaged brain cells, slow the aging of the brain, and increase the learning ability of people with mental handicaps including Alzheimer's disease. These sellers often advertise their products on Web sites available in multiple languages, including English, Chinese, Japanese, Korean, Indonesian, Spanish, and Russian.

Such claims are questionable at best because no scientific proof exists to support them. This may explain the 21st-century terminology and jargon used by marketers of these products to appeal to the same basic human dreams that have existed since the dawn of history.[49]

In the past few years, many consumers have come to believe in the benefits of herbal remedies. Visit the Web site of GNC at http://www.gnc.com/Default.aspx?lang=en *and the site of the Mayo Clinic at* www.mayoclinic.com/health/herbal-supplements-SA00044. *What do you think about the health claims made by makers of these herbal remedies and beverages? Who are the most likely prospects for consuming these products? Should legislation be passed to regulate and monitor such health claims?*

Persuasion

At the **persuasion** stage, the prospect formulates a favorable or unfavorable attitude toward the new product. A consumer may mentally imagine how helpful or satisfying the product might be in some anticipated future-use situation. The perceived risk associated with buying and using the new home security system, for example, may cause the family to weigh the potential value of state-of-the-art home protection against the potential costs involved. Communications (such as Web sites, advertising, catalogs, in-store materials, talking to other people) and the perceived characteristics of the innovation (such as its relative advantage and cost) influence this process of attitude formation. In the realm of persuasion, companies attempt to reduce consumers' perceived risk associated with new-product acquisitions. This goal is usually accomplished by

persuasion
a stage where a prospect formulates a favorable or unfavorable attitude toward an innovation

allowing consumers to sample or try a product before purchase. Computer and automobile companies, as mentioned earlier, offer lease contracts with the option for purchase to reduce risk perceptions.

Decision

Decision occurs when the prospect engages in activities that lead to a choice to adopt or reject the new product. Adoption is a decision to make full use of an innovation as the best course of action. According to Antil, adoption involves both a psychological and a behavioral commitment to a product over time.[50] In other words, we decide to continually use the product unless situational variables (such as lack of resources or product unavailability) prevent usage. In the example of the home security system, the family may conclude that due to an escalating crime rate in the neighborhood, the protection is well worth its cost. As a result, the decision is made to adopt. Rejection, on the other hand, is a decision not to adopt. Rejection can be either active or passive. In the case of active rejection, a prospect considers product adoption (perhaps including even its trial) but then decides not to adopt. Passive rejection, on the other side, consists of never really considering use of the innovation. By presenting facts about its features and benefits, marketing communications help consumers to evaluate an innovation and decide whether to accept or reject it.

Implementation

Implementation occurs when a prospect puts the adoption idea into action. At this point, the innovation-decision process shifts from a mere mental exercise to one that entails actual behavioral change. Active information seeking addresses such questions as where to obtain the new product, how to use it, what operational problems the user is likely to encounter, and how to solve them. Agents of change dispense technical assistance to clients as these clients begin the process of implementation to help them with various aspects of product use, maintenance, or service. A marketer's introductory strategies relating to financing, delivery, installation, and service are usually designed to make consumer purchasing easy.

Confirmation

Even after a consumer makes the decision to accept a new product, the newly converted customer may perceive some degree of postpurchase doubt. That is, an individual may seek reassurance that the decision to purchase and use the product was appropriate or correct. In the **confirmation** stage, the consumer assesses his or her satisfaction with the product and decides whether or not to continue to purchase and use it. As a result of confirmation or disconfirmation, adopters may strengthen their commitment to a new product or cease to utilize it altogether. For example, in some cases, consumers may reverse their adoption decision after being exposed to conflicting messages about the new product or when using the innovation conflicts with established habits. In the case of the home security system, family members may find that too many false alarms are being accidentally triggered by children in the house to the point

decision
a stage where a prospect makes a choice to either adopt or reject an innovation

implementation
a stage where a person acts on his or her decision to adopt

confirmation
a stage where an adopter experiences postpurchase doubt and seeks reassurance for the decision made

378   PART 3   Social and Cultural Influences on Behavior

of aggravating the parents, the neighbors, and the police—a situation that may lead them to discontinue the service altogether.

HOW TYPICAL ARE THE STAGES OF ADOPTION?

From the preceding, we should not suppose that all consumers pass through all stages of the adoption process each and every time they purchase goods and services. The adoption process specifically addresses the individual's deliberation about whether or not to accept new, previously unfamiliar products and services. The more novel, complex, expensive, or potentially risky the innovation is perceived to be, the more likely an individual is to systematically progress through the entire process or spend more time at any given stage. The duration of the time interval spent at any given stage or between stages varies among different individuals. For example, innovators and early adopters are less likely to go through a lengthy deliberation process compared with other adopter categories. Also, the stages leading up to adoption may not always occur in the specific order proposed, some stages may be omitted, and multiple stages may occur simultaneously. It is conceivable, for example, that upon becoming aware of a new product such as Ginko health supplement, a prospect may instantaneously become interested in it, mentally evaluate it, and arrive at an intention to adopt it. In another instance, a prospect may reject an innovation at one stage of the adoption process but resume the process at a later date. Thus, an individual could eventually adopt a product or service that he or she had previously rejected.

RESISTANCE TO ADOPTION

Some obstacles create serious barriers to new-product adoption and may cause consumers to reject an innovation altogether. A model proposed by Ram and Sheth identified three functional obstacles (value, usage, and risk barriers) and two psychological obstacles (tradition and image barriers) that serve as sources of consumer resistance to adopting innovations.[51]

Value Barriers

A **value barrier** is any potential lack of product performance relative to its price compared to that of substitute goods. A new technologically advanced brand of digital camera may carry a price tag of $500, whereas traditional cameras may be available for less than $50. A number of avenues are open to marketers in this case in order to overcome a perceived value barrier. First, marketers may explore technological advances that lower production costs and, in turn, the innovation's selling price (as has been the case for PCs and cellular phones). Second, marketers may significantly improve product performance and, ultimately, utility to prospective adopters. Third, marketers may improve the new product's positioning and sponsor informative advertising to convince prospects of the innovation's merit. For example, the new camera's advanced digital technology and its unique features, such as ease of editing and archiving photos, may be presented to the public as major improvements over traditional cameras and well worth the investment.

value barrier
a perceived lack of product performance relative to its price compared to that of substitute brands

Usage Barriers

A usage barrier exists when an innovation is not a part of prospects' routines. Marketers in this case may attempt to boost usage by identifying and cultivating markets that are unfamiliar with the product. The global expansion of American fast-food establishments, for instance, gave many of these companies unlimited opportunities in new markets all over the world. Second, marketers may follow a systems perspective. That is, they may coordinate the new product with a network of other interlocking products and activities. Horizontal cooperative advertising between complementary products (cameras and brands of film) or services (airlines, car rental companies, and hotels) are prime examples in point. Figure 10.6 illustrates how this strategy was used in the case of M&M's and the film *Indiana Jones and The Kingdom of the Crystal Skull.*

Third, marketers may utilize change agents, such as opinion leaders, to actively endeavor to switch peoples' mind-sets and habits. In the fashion industry, for example, designers sponsor well-publicized fashion shows attended by the elite as a means of creating opinion leaders who, when they adopt, spread the fashion to others.

Figure 10.6

This horizontal cooperative advertising effort between the Mars Company and the filmmakers of the movie *Indiana Jones and the Kingdom of the Crystal Skull* has the effect of benefitting both entities.

Global Opportunity

Cheers to the Wines from California

The U.S. wine industry has gone though a radical transformation, from being a largely domestic industry to a globally respected wine exporter. Until the 1980s, the wine market was largely a domestic one, with imports mostly arriving from France, Italy, and Spain. Today, the situation has changed dramatically, and California has risen as one of the most productive regions of superior wines.

Historically, it wasn't until the repeal of Prohibition in 1933 that Napa Valley's wine industry began its renaissance. During the years of World War II, a group of vintners came together to share the ideas of growing grapes and making wine. They laid the foundation for the Napa Valley Vintners, a dynamic trade organization dedicated to advancing the valley's wines. As time went by, the ingenuity, inventiveness, and freethinking of these pioneers came to bear fruit. First, they embarked on the issue of obtaining grape vines from Europe. This was followed by adopting creative methods of making these vines put out huge amounts of fruit. And instead of using the tradition-driven, old-world ways of winemaking, they created modern approaches that were developed in California. These approaches were based on tinkering, cloning, cataloging, and earth-science experimentation in order to give California wines their desired properties. By so doing, the vintners were able to produce high-quality wines that are full of character and distinctiveness—equal to those from Europe.

During the 1950s and 1960s, Napa Valley continued to gain notoriety in wine circles. It attracted a whole new generation of winemakers. A unique group of human resources came to age in the 1970s due to a success story generated by a public victory for the small California wine region at an international wine tasting competition in Paris. Napa Valley wines went head to head with the legendary French Bordeaux in a blind taste test and won critical acclaim.

Today, there are over 400 California wineries, and many of them export to over 165 markets worldwide. The United States now ranks as the fourth leading wine producer in the world. The United Kingdom is the premier customer of the California wines internationally.

In the year 2007, California wines set a record for overseas sales revenue, which surpassed $951 million. The U.S. wine exports, with about 95 percent coming from California, amounted to 453 million liters (120 million gallons), which represented an increase of around 9 percent in value and 12 percent in volume compared to the year 2006. This impressive trend is expected to persist as California wines continue to invade markets traditionally held by older winemaking countries, such as France and Italy.[55]

From the dawn of history, wine has been produced by various regions in the world. Some of the countries that traditionally dominated the making and exportation of wine include France, Italy, Spain, Portugal, Greece, and even Australia. The United States is actually a newcomer to this industry, but the quality of its wines has equaled or even surpassed that of those other regions. To what factors do you attribute this success story, particularly in the international market? Would you expect this successful trend to continue in the future if you knew that other low-cost producers of wine in some foreign countries, such as China, are already becoming formidable producers and aggressive marketers of their low-price wines globally? To learn more about California wines, visit the California Wine Institute at www.wineinstitute.org/resources/statistics/article 122. Do you think that the growth of demand for domestic wine will eventually help reduce American wine imports—positively influencing the balance of trade for the United States? Explain.

Risk Barriers

A **risk barrier** occurs when uncertainty lingers concerning the economic-value, functional-performance, safety, social, or psychological aspects of adoption. Marketers can surmount such reservations among consumers via strategies such as reducing price, increasing consumers' product education, and expediting experiences with and trials of a product. Marketers can also elicit product endorsements and testimonials from product authorities, celebrities, and ordinary satisfied customers. Advertisers frequently use seals of approval from respected associations to support their claims. This has been proven to be a successful strategy used by many firms in order to reduce risk barriers. For this reason, Crest toothpaste ads often contain an endorsement by the American Dental Association, and many other household products bear the Good Housekeeping Seal of Approval.

Tradition Barriers

A **tradition barrier** exists when cultural norms and values hamper product adoption. For example, life insurance is frowned upon in some fundamentalist Islamic countries on the basis that it is unthinkable to insure against the will of *Allah* (God). To surmount such obstacles, marketers must be sensitive to social mores and customs. Under such conditions, marketers should promote the service in a way that ties in with widely held cultural values rather than in a manner that abruptly alters established traditions. By utilizing appropriate agents of change over time, marketers may successfully reshape consumer ideas, opinions, and practices.

Image Barriers

An **image barrier** exists when a product or brand is unknown by the public or suffers from a relatively unfavorable image. In this case, marketers may be able to use well-known spokespersons to draw positive attention to the brand and boost its image, license a brand name with a solid image, or initiate an image-building ad campaign to enhance the firm's reputation. Hyundai automobile company, for example, suffered from a low-quality image compared to Japanese cars such as Toyota, Honda, and Mazda. As a result, Hyundai initiated a comprehensive and costly ad campaign that appeared in most U.S. media. The message highlighted the quality, design, safety, and economy of the firm's vehicles, and significantly enhanced the image of the brand.

As a new idea or product becomes available, information about it spreads from its source to receivers in the marketplace. This process may involve the mass media, word of mouth, observation of the new product in use, or any of a variety of other vehicles that help bring about widespread adoption of the product or idea in a social system. Diffusion of an innovation is therefore a part of the collective behavior of a group. Information about a product or an idea flows within and between the tiers of a social system. Group influence within the society functions as a powerful force leading toward final acceptance or rejection of an innovation. Group influence and its ramifications for marketers and researchers of consumer behavior is the topic of the next chapter.

---

tradition barrier
a condition where cultural norms and values hamper product adoption

risk barrier
a condition where uncertainty lingers about adopting an innovation

image barrier
a condition where a product or brand is unknown by the public or suffers from an unfavorable image

A Cross-Functional Point of View

The topics of diffusion and adoption have a number of implications for business disciplines other than marketing. Relevant issues might include

- **Ethics:** Supermarket shelves are rapidly becoming the world's most expensive real estate. Across the country, supermarkets are demanding thousands of dollars from manufacturers of new products just to place the products on their store shelves. Known as "slotting allowances," these fees have become the rule rather than the exception, driving away from the market many new food items whose creators cannot pay these hefty fees. For example, to stock Old Capital microwave popcorn, Shoprite Stores in New York City asked for $86,000 from its producer. Similarly, R. W. Frookie Cookies was asked by Ralph's, a major West Coast chain, to pay $100,000 to introduce the company's cookies in the chain's 100 stores. Aside from the fact that this practice raises the price of a new product to consumers to cover these fees, it is particularly open to abuse. Because these fees are negotiated privately and paid in cash or in merchandise, retailers feel that they command the power to charge manufacturers of new products what the traffic will bear.

- **Pop Culture/Marketing:** Fads come and go. Some are serious, while others are transient. Whatever the variety, fads are a means of expressing trends in our society. They result in the creation of pop culture and enhance the popularity and sales of certain products and services. Among the fads that prevailed in our culture in past years are the Hula Hoops of 1950s,

the pet rocks and tie-dyed t-shirts of the 1960s, the video arcades of the 1980s, the tattoos of the 1990s, and body piercing in the 2000s. Some experts suggest that in our present-day society, it is the teenage group that constitutes the primary force in fad creation, since its members are on the cutting edge of current trends and media awareness.

- **Strategy/Cost:** Whereas many companies such as 3M and Procter & Gamble pride themselves on being at the forefront of innovation and new-product development, other companies are slowing down the rate at which they are putting out innovative products into the marketplace. The reason is simply the high cost of launching new products. Although new-product research and development costs can vary between companies, launching a new-to-the-world product such as a high-tech item usually runs into hundreds of millions of dollars. This cost does not even include the necessary investment in promotion and distribution. These companies, instead, use a line-extension strategy to launch their version of new products into the market. By taking their current products and modifying them in some way—such as by adding a color, a scent, or a new package—these companies are able to spend only thousands of dollars on these modifications compared with the hundreds of millions of dollars they would have had to spend to come up with a new creation.

These issues, and a host of others like them, serve to show that the topics of diffusion and adoption transcend the field of marketing to other business disciplines.

Summary

Diffusion is a macroprocess concerned with the spread of a new product or idea from its original source to and throughout the general public. There are four basic components in the diffusion process: the innovation, the channel of communication, the social system, and time.

Innovations or *new* products are any products, services, or ideas that consumers perceive as new. New products can result from changes in technology and production processes, from changes in a firm's marketing strategy, or from a combination of these. One classification of new products distinguishes between discontinuous, dynamically continuous, and continuous innovations. Five product characteristics influence consumer acceptance of new products: relative advantage, compatibility, simplicity–complexity, observability, and trialability–divisibility. Communication of product-related information is essential for the widespread acceptance of an innovation across the marketplace. Without communication, consumers would remain largely unaware of new products. Channels of communication include the mass media, interpersonal communication, and interactive technologies. Diffusion depends on a chain of interpersonal communications, whereby successive layers of consumers adopt a new product upon the recommendation of slightly more venturesome acquaintances.

Diffusion occurs within the context of a social system in which individuals play specific roles, adhere to group norms and values, interact with others, and influence others as well as receive influence from them.

The time dimension includes such aspects as the *rate of adoption* and *frequency of purchase*. Consumers exhibit individual differences in their readiness and willingness to try and accept a particular new product, service, or idea. Thus five adopter categories can be identified: innovators, early adopters, early majority, late majority, and laggards. The S-shaped diffusion curve depicts the fairly predictable pattern of market acceptance for new products over time—slow at first, then more rapid, then at an increasingly sluggish pace.

Adoption is a microprocess dealing with the stages that an individual goes through before accepting a new product. Stages of the adoption process, which Rogers termed the innovation-decision process, are knowledge, persuasion, decision, implementation, and confirmation. In some cases, an innovation fails to become integrated into an adopter's life routine.

Five types of barriers—value, usage, risk, tradition, and image—serve as sources of consumer resistance to adopting innovations.

Review Questions

1. Explain the difference between discontinuous, dynamically continuous, and continuous innovations. In what way do these categories of innovations help marketers understand the consumer process of adopting new products?
2. Select and explain two of the factors that influence consumers' acceptance of new products and give an example for each.
3. The social system plays a major role in the diffusion process. Explain how.
4. Based on the amount of time it takes to adopt an innovation, consumers are typically classified into a number of categories that reflect how soon they acquire a specific innovation after its introduction. Cite and explain each of these adopter categories.
5. Rogers proposed a five-stage decision-making model for the adoption of innovations. Briefly discuss each stage and indicate how typical this model is in reflecting the adoption of an innovation phenomenon.

Discussion Questions

1. Considering the adoption rate for VCRs around the world, the United States lagged behind most Far Eastern, Middle Eastern, and European nations by as much as five to seven years. What factors do you imagine accelerated pace of adoption and diffusion abroad compared to the United States?
2. A number of companies, such as 3M and Rubbermaid, pride themselves on introducing large numbers of new, innovative products into the marketplace annually. Recognizing the high cost of developing and promoting new products, and further considering the low success rate for new products, why do companies continue to aggressively pursue new-product development activities? Would it be more advantageous (more economical, less risky) for firms to focus on improving their existing products rather than venturing into the new-products sphere?
3. IBM and Apple Computer have outdone each other in donating computers to grade schools so that children can learn how to use them. Although this act is admirable in itself, managers of such companies may have their own, perhaps less altruistic, agenda. Discuss *other* motives of the management of these firms for donating computers to schools.

In reference to the chapter opening vignette, assume the production manager at Harley-Davidson must deal with a dire situation. Highly frustrated customers find themselves waiting up to two years to finally obtain the motorcycle they ordered. In response to this volatile situation, the production manager contemplates expanding the production of Harleys into three foreign countries—namely, China, Korea, and Mexico. In presenting the proposal to the board, the executive claimed the company could attain reductions in manufacturing costs, due to cheaper labor, as well as increase the supply of bikes to promptly satisfy overwhelming consumer demand more. From human resource, production, finance, marketing, legal, logistical, and cross-cultural perspectives, what specific concerns would you expect board members to raise in reaction to this proposal? If you were on the board, how would you likely vote on this proposal. Why?

CASE

America's Love for the Emerald Bottle

It was the birthday of Mr. James Ward, the laboratory director of the Mecklenburg County Environmental Protection Department in Charlotte, North Carolina, whose agency in 1990 reported Perrier bottled water's chemical contamination. His colleagues at that lab had planned to celebrate the occasion of Mr. Ward's birthday by getting together for dinner at Sullivan's Steak House, a popular spot in the city of Charlotte.

As the group sat at an extended table in the midst of the restaurant enjoying a few drinks and munching on various hors d'oeuvres, Mr. Ward could not help but notice the large percentage of patrons who had ordered mineral water bottles such as Perrier, San Pellegrino, and Evian in lieu of cocktails. His observation confirmed a report from Beverage Marketing Corporation (BMC) that he had read a week earlier, which revealed the overwhelming increase in the demand for bottled water of all types in the United States. The report stated that Americans consumed 9.4 billion gallons of bottled water in 2008 at a cost of $12.6 billion. This figure translates into over 30 gallons of water per person, and places the United States as the world's top consumer of bottled water.

The sight of these familiar-shaped emerald bottles of Perrier brought to Mr. Ward's mind the memory of Perrier's success story in the United States, and its demise in 1990, when the company mishandled the issue of benzene contamination that year. Back in its 1970s hey day, when Perrier was first released in the United States, the brand was perceived as cool and chic. Health- and image-conscious consumers were seen ordering it instead of wine, beer, or mixed drinks, and were happy to sport the bottles at their table.

While a few consumers today remain unfamiliar with the cool and refreshing taste of Perrier, only a small minority could recount the company's humble beginnings. It was in early 1946 when Mr. Gustav Leven's father, head of a family brokerage firm, asked him to find a buyer for a small spring known since Roman times located in the town of Vergeze in southern France. Instead of finding a buyer, Mr. Levin (the son) bought the spring along with its bottling plant, even though the whole operation—spring and factory—were in shambles.

Hard work paid off, and by the 1970s, Gustav Levin not only controlled more than half of the maturing French market for sparkling mineral water, but had succeeded in invading the U.S. market. Sales of Perrier in the United States continued to climb over the years. Demand soared from 3 million bottles a year in 1976 to 200 million in 1979. By 1989, just before the benzene incident, Perrier accounted for 80 percent of the bottled water imports into the United States.

In 1990, Perrier's reputation for purity suffered a blow when the lab workers at the Mecklenburg County Environmental Protection Department reported finding traces of benzene in Perrier water bottles. Some of the tested bottles contained minute quantities of benzene, an industrial solvent and a carcinogen—a discovery that proved extremely costly to Source-Perrier, the parent company behind the French mineral water. Within weeks, the company had withdrawn every bottle from worldwide circulation. Over 160 million bottles in total were recalled, costing the company over $200 million. Since then, demand for Perrier in the United States never regained its previous level—a hefty price to pay for a problem that was eventually traced to a mere 13 bottles.

Today, Perrier is part of the Nestle family of companies, owned by Nestle-Waters. Interestingly, Nestle-Waters also owns San Pellegrino, and Vittel, as well as other brands. Nestle-Waters estimates that annual consumption of bottled water in the United States will increase by 10 percent annually and will surpass 32 gallons per capita by the year 2010. While this level of consumption lags far behind demand in continental Europe, sales in the United States over the past eight years have grown at an average rate of 9.5 percent.

As Mr. Ward thought about this emerging trend, he wondered about its ramifications for various industries such as soft-drink bottlers, liquor suppliers, wineries, and breweries. He also dreaded the thought of the resulting impact on the environment by the billions of bottles that would be thrown into landfills annually.

Questions

1. How do you account for the widespread popularity of carbonated mineral water back in the 1970s as well as today? Are the reasons you propose also typical for the consumption of regular bottled water?

2. Since the United States has become one of the world's largest consumers of bottled water, what industries here would be affected by this trend? What ramifications would this trend have on these affected industries?

3. There are approximately 430 facilities for bottling water in the United States that produce more than 700 different brand labels, as well as 75 brands of imported mineral waters. In view of these figures, the problem of bottle disposal (approximately 38 billion bottles per week) becomes an major issue. What would you suggest to lessen the effects of this threat to our environment?

Notes

1. T. Bolfert et al. (eds.), *Harley-Davidson, Inc: Historical Overview, 1903–1993* (Milwaukee, WI: Harley-Davidson, Inc., 1994).

2. Thomas Gelb, "Overhauling Corporate Engines Drive Winning Strategies," *Journal of Business Strategy* 19, no. 6 (November–December 1993), pp. 6–12; Milia Boyd, "Harley-Davidson Motor Company," *Incentive* (September 1993), pp. 26–31.

3. Vijay Mahajan, Eitan Muller, and Frank M. Bass, "New Product Diffusion Models in Marketing: A Review and Directions for Research," *Journal of Marketing*, 54 (January 1990), pp. 1–26; for a model of diffusion processes in developing countries, see Eric J. Arnould, "Toward a Broadened Theory of Preference Formation and the Diffusion of Innovations: Cases from Zinder Province, Niger Republic," *Journal of Consumer Research* 16 (September 1989), pp. 239–267.

4. Nessim Hanna, Douglas Ayers, Rick Ridnour, and Geoffrey Gordon, "New Product Development Practices in Consumer Versus Business Products Organizations," *The Journal of Product & Brand Management* 4, no. 2 (1995).

5. Marcia Mogelonsky, "Product Overload," *American Demographics* (August 1998), pp. 65–69.

6. T. D. Kuczmarski, *Managing New Products: The Power of Innovations* (Upper Saddle River, NJ: Prentice Hall, 1992).

7. Brian Wansink, "Making Old Brands New," *American Demographics* (December 1997), pp. 53–58.

8. E. Yoon and G. L. Lilien, "New Industrial Product Performance: The Effects of Marketing Characteristics and Strategy," *Journal of Product Innovation Management* 2, no. 3 (1985), pp. 134–44.

9. C. M. Crawford, *New Products Management* (Boston: Irwin, 1994).

10. Hanna, Ayers, Ridnour, Gordon, "New Product Development Practices in Consumer Versus Business Products Organizations."

11. "Post-it Notes Click Thanks to Entrepreneurial Spirit," *Marketing News* (August 31, 1984), p. 21; Melissa Hughes, et al., "3M Post-it Notes, www.mathcs.bethel.edu/~jankri/xml-3_6/PNotes.html.

12. Thomas S. Robertson, "The Process of Innovation and the Diffusion of Innovation," *Journal of Marketing* 31 (January 1967), pp. 14–19.

13. Page C. Moreau, Donald R. Lehmann, and Arthur B. Markman, "Entrenched Knowledge structures and Consumer Response to New Products," *Journal of Marketing Research* 38, no. 1 (February 2001), pp. 14–16.

14. Elizabeth C. Hirschman, "Symbolism and Technology as Sources for the Generation of Innovations," in Andrew Mitchell (ed.), *Advances in Consumer Research* 9 (Ann Arbor, MI: Association for Consumer Research, 1982), pp. 537–41.

15. Rosella Capetta, et. al., "Convergent Designs in Fine Fashions: An Evolutionary Model for Stylistic Innovation," *Research Policy*, vol. 35, no. 9 (November 2006), pp. 1273–1290.

16. "Good Food, All Day Long," Kelloggs, www2.kelloggs.com/Product/Product.aspx.

17. Hanna, Ayers, Ridnour, Gordon, "New Product Development Practices in Consumer Versus Business Products Organizations."

18. C. Miller, "Little Relief Seen for New Product Failure Rate," *Marketing News* 27, no. 13 (1993), pp. 1, 18.

19. S. Edgett, D. Shipley, and G. Forbes "Japanese and British Companies Compared: Contributing Factors to Success and Failure in NPD," *Journal of Product Innovation Management* 9, no. 1 (1992), pp. 3–10.

20. Hanna, Ayers, Ridnour, Gordon, "New Product Development Practices in Consumer Versus Business Products Organizations."

21. Lee Eun-Ju, Lee Jinkook, and David Eastwood, "A Two-step Estimation of Consumer Adoption of Tech-nology-Based Service Innovations," *Journal of Consumer Affairs* 37, no. 2 (2003), pp. 256–282.

22. Everett M. Rogers, *Diffusion of Innovations*, 4th ed. (New York: Free Press, 1995).

23. Mogelonsky, "Product Overload," p. 69.

24. "FTD Group Inc." Yahoo Finance Site, http://finance.yahoo.com/9/pr?s=ftd.

25. Mogelonsky, "Product Overload," p. 68.

26. "Flops: Too Many New Products Fail. Here's Why—And How to Do Better," *Business Week* (August 16, 1993), pp. 76–80, 82.

27. "To Cut Price, SolarCity Leases Solar Panels," C/netNews.com (April 1, 2008), www.news.com/8301-11128_3-9907982-54.html.

28. Robert W. Shoemaker and F. Robert Shoaf, "Behavioral Changes in the Trial of New Products," *Journal of Consumer Research* 2 (September 1975), pp. 104–9.

29. Michael J. Etzel, Bruce J. Walker, and William J. Stanton, *Marketing*, 11th ed. (New York: McGraw-Hill, 1997), p. 211.

30. "The Future of Interactive Marketing," *Harvard Business Review* (November 1996); "Verizon Online and MSN Join Forces To Offer Consumers DSL Internet Access and Unique Online Services," Microsoft, www.microsoft.com/presspass/press/2002/jun02/06-20msniaverizonpr.mspx.

31. Hubert Gatignon and Thomas S. Robertson, "A Propositional Inventory for New Diffusion Research," *Journal of Consumer Research* 11, no. 4 (March 1985), p. 859–67.

32. Yoram Wind, Thomas S. Robertson, and Cynthia Fraser, "Industrial Product Diffusion by Market Segment," *Industrial Marketing Management* 11 (1982), pp. 1–8; World Bank, *Global Economic Prospects 2008: Technology Diffusion in the Developing World,* http://econ.worldbank.org.

33. Stephen Crystal, "The Diffusion of Innovation in AIDS Treatment: Zidovudine Use in Two New Jersey Cohorts," *BNET.com* (October, 1995), http://findarticles.com/p/articles/mi_m4149/is_n4_v30/ai_17635052/print.

34. Joel Garreau, "The Fastest Global Diffusion of Any Technology in Human History," *12 Degrees of Freedom* (March 1, 2008), http://12degreesoffreedom.blogspot.com/2008/03/fastest-global-diffusion-of-any.html.

35. Gatignon and Robertson, "A Propositional Inventory for New Diffusion Research." Frank M. Bass, "A New Product Growth Model for Consumer Durables," *Management Science* 15 (January 1969), pp. 215–27.

36. Gatignon and Robertson, "A Propositional Inventory for New Diffusion Research"; Kristiaan Helsen, Kamel Jedidi, and Wayne S. DeSarbo, "A New Approach to Country Segmentation Utilizing Multina-

tional Diffusion Patterns," *Journal of Marketing* 57 (October 1993), pp. 60-71; Robert Fisher and Linda Price, "An Investigation into the Social Context of Early Adopter Behavior," *Journal of Consumer Research* 19 (December 1992), pp. 477-86.

37. Philip Kotler, *Marketing Management*, 8th ed. (Upper Saddle River, NJ: Prentice Hall 1994), p. 412.

38. William G. Zikmund and Michael d'Amico, *Marketing*, 4th ed. (Minneapolis: West, 1993), p. 301.

39. Scott Roberts and Rajiv Dant, "Socioeconomic, Cultural, and Technical Determinants of Contemporary American Consumption Patterns," in Stanley Shapiro and A. H. Walle (eds.), *1988 AMA Winter Educators' Conference* (Chicago: American Marketing Association, 1988), p. 321.

40. "Imerge Consulting Group Worldwide Digital Camera Forecast and Market Overview, 2002-2007," www.imergeconsulting.com/reports/abs-dsc -worldwide%202002-2007.htm.

41. "HD Digital Camera with AMOLED Display Launched by Samsung," *Crunch Gear* (March 27, 2008), www.crunchgear.com/2008/03/27/hd-digital -camera-with-amoled-display-launched-by-Samsung.

42. Kotler, *Marketing Management*, pp. 348-49.

43. Rogers, *Diffusion of Innovations*.

44. Gatignon and Robertson, "A Propositional Inventory for New Diffusion Research"; David Midgley and Grahame Dowling, "A Longitudinal Study of Product Form Innovation: The Interaction Between Predispositions and Social Messages," *Journal of Consumer Research* 19 (march 1993), pp. 611-25; Ronald E. Goldsmith and Charles F. Hofacker, "Measuring Consumer Innovativeness," *Journal of the Academy of Marketing Science* 19 (Summer 1991), pp. 209-21.

45. William G. Zikmund and Michael d'Amico, *Basic Marketing* (Minneapolis–St. Paul, MN: West, 1996), p. 170.

46. C. Merle Crawford, New Products Management (Burr Ridge, IL: Irwin, 1994), p. 292.

47. Edwin E. Bobrow and Dennis W. Shafer, *Pioneering New Products: A Market Survival Guide* (Homewood, IL: Dow Jones–Irwin, 1987), p. 139; Vijay Mahajan, Eitan Muller, and Frank M. Bass, "New Product Diffusion Models in Marketing: A Review and Directions for Research," *Journal of Marketing* 54 (January 1990), pp. 1-26.

48. Rogers, *Diffusion of Innovations*.

49. D. Kirk Davidson, "Products new, but Puffery Same as Always," *Marketing News* 28, no. 23 (November 7, 1994), p. 14; and David Vaczek, "Herbal Effervescence," *Promo* (November 1998), pp. 37-41; John Greenwald, "Herbal Healing," *Time* (November 23, 1998), pp. 59-69.

50. John M. Antil, "New Product or Service Adoption: When Does it Happen?" *Journal of Consumer Marketing* 5 (Spring 1988), pp. 5-15.

51. S. Ram and Jagdish N. Sheth, "Consumer Resistance to Innovations: The Marketing Problem and Its Solutions," *Journal of Consumer Marketing* 6 (Spring 1989), pp. 5-14.

52. "Chinese Commit Faux Pas, Too, in Export Marketing," *Marketing News* (October 14, 1983), p. 13.

53. Zikmund and d'Amico, *Basic Marketing*, p. 301.

54. Kotler, *Marketing Management*, p. 412.

55. "California Vintners Step Up Marketing Efforts," Beach California.com, www.beachcalifornia.com/wine2.html; "California Wineries," Beach California.com, www.beachcalifornia.com/wine.html; "2007 California Wine Sales," Wine Institute, wineinstitute.org/resources/statistics/article122.

Group Influence

LEARNING OBJECTIVES

- To grasp the meaning and nature of social groups.
- To identify various types of social groups.
- To distinguish between roles and status within the context of a group.
- To explore five types of social power as well as the way marketers employ them.
- To comprehend the nature, types, and influence of reference groups.
- To identify the levels of conformity to group mandates.
- To conceptualize the impact of reference groups on consumer behavior.

KEY TERMS

group
socialization
consumer socialization
primary groups
secondary groups
formal groups
informal groups
virtual community
Roles
role-related
   product cluster
status
conspicuous consumption
fraudulent symbols
stealth wealth
parody display
role-relaxed consumers
reward power
coercive power

legitimate power
referent power
expert power
Conformity
norms
social comparison
reference groups
memership reference groups
aspirational reference groups
anticipatory aspirational reference
   groups
symbolic aspirational reference groups
negative reference groups
disclaimant reference groups
compliance
reactance
classical identification
reciprocal identification
internalization

Marketing of illegal drugs in the United States, as well as globally, is a huge business consisting of various groups that compete to capture a slice of this multi-billion dollar market. It is interesting to observe the social interaction patterns among the members of one segment of this illicit and notorious distribution mechanism, namely, gangs.

Not long ago, police sources made public the house rules of Chicago's Mickey Cobras street gang. Many of the 46 regulations, as well as the gang's bylaws and constitution, provide rules for drug dealing, give instructions for drive-by shootings, and chart gang hierarchy. The rules specify that gang members should be 16 years old to work on the line, should report to work on time, limit bathroom breaks to 15 minutes, and sign in and out each day. The rules also forbid sitting down or horsing around while on duty and warn against getting high or drinking on the line.

The house rules include a detailed explanation of how to act as security for drug sales and how to sell packs of crack cocaine in buildings controlled by the gang. The operation is set up so that shifts of security patrol the lobby areas of the buildings, looking out for police or rival gangs who might interfere with drug sales. One gang member on security duty patrols the front door of each building while the other secures the back door. All customers entering the building are searched. The rules make it clear that any gang member who violates the code will be tried before the gang's board and punished. Loyalty is rewarded. Street-level security and sellers are rewarded with money, occasional parties, and prospects of moving up the gang ladder.

Similar rules and bylaws were found by gang investigators over the years. Among the edicts confiscated from one imprisoned gang leader was a memorandum from the chairman and board of directors of the gang. The memo noted that interrogations by police are inevitable because "not all business can be taken care of in a smooth way" and addressed a fundamental mandate: Don't talk to law enforcement investigators. It reiterates that, by law, police must inform suspects of their rights to remain silent and to have an attorney present during the grilling. The memo goes on to cite the moral of the duck story. "If the duck had kept his mouth shut, instead of quacking, he wouldn't have given his position away and, naturally, wouldn't have been our dinner."

Just like a corporate charter, gangs' bylaws, rules, and constitutions provide guidelines for their operations. They specify what is expected from members and outline authorities, responsibilities, rewards, and punishments.[1]

Government, corporations, schools, and churches, as well as gangs all have one thing in common—an organizational structure that guarantees the flow of authority from policy makers to followers. Check the flowchart of a justice-upholding government entity by visiting www.usdoj.gov/dojorg.htm. *Design a similar flowchart for your school, sorority, fraternity, dorm, or place of work. On what basis do you determine the tiers of your chart? What systems are in place to guarantee the continuous functioning of the structure?*

When individuals join together in groups—whether as corporations, unions, associations, clubs, gangs, or any other type—a complex set of interrelationships emerges. Within these structures, various levels of authority, power, and status evolve. Peculiar sets of roles, with their attached rights and responsibilities, also appear. Members act out roles formally prescribed by the group or play roles based on an informal structure that develops within a formal one.

This chapter explores how groups attain conformity to their expectations, why individuals comply with group standards, and what forms of power are at play in group interaction. The powerful impact of groups on consumers, particularly the effect of those social networks with whom individuals interact frequently, mandates that marketers examine their characteristic relational processes. Such knowledge can then be applied to guide the formation of effective marketing strategies.

When individuals join groups, a complex set of interrelationships emerge, including set roles.

The Meaning of Groups

The term **group** refers to two or more individuals who share a set of norms, values, or beliefs; have certain role relationships; and experience interdependent behavior.[2] Based on this definition, a group is not merely a collection of individuals who happen to be at the same place at the same time. People attending a show, patronizing a shopping mall, or riding a bus do not constitute a group. A group is a social system with its own hierarchy of interlocking roles. Ideally, within this structure, group members display regular contact; cooperatively interact with one another; and share a common goal, common norms, and a sense of belonging.

Rarely, if ever, does a single group provide for all human needs and wants. Thus, there are many groups to which people may belong. Family and friendship groups, Internet community groups, work groups, religious groups, civic groups, athletic groups, charitable groups, educational groups, and work groups are among the most familiar. As evidenced by their diverse names and labels, different groups exist for different purposes. The common purpose that binds group members together may, however, hold higher priority for some members than for others. Similarly, the purpose for joining the group can vary, depending on an individual's priorities. For example, although universities are established as institutions of higher learning, some students' motivations for going away to college may be to get away from their parents, to party, or to meet a spouse. Similarly, some people may join a church not to participate in its worship services and reflect on the true meaning of life, but rather to acquire community standing for themselves or private education and day-care facilities for their children. Thus, a single group sometimes satisfies different needs for different people.

group
people who share beliefs, have role relationships, and experience interdependent behavior

The diffusion of new style throughout the marketplace depends largely on its acceptance first among the fashion leaders.

socialization
the process by which individuals develop patterns of socially relevant behavior

consumer socialization
the process by which consumers acquire knowledge, skills, and attitudes relevant to the marketplace

THE IMPORTANCE OF GROUPS

The real significance of groups rests with their role in **socialization**. Socialization is the process by which an individual develops, through interaction with other group members, specific patterns of socially relevant behavior and experience. Socialization is not restricted to learning that occurs during childhood or within the family. Rather, it applies to behavior over the entire life span of any individual as he or she progresses through successive stages of the family life cycle. Consumers continually, regardless of their age, learn to adjust to new or altered roles and to relinquish antiquated ones. Socialization within the group allows group standards and requirements to be imposed through the processes of modeling, reinforcement, and social interaction.

Modeling involves imitation. Either the member makes a conscious attempt to emulate others in the group, or the prescribed behavior is the only option available. For example, it has been observed that successful diffusion of new fashions to female purchasers of clothing is a function of acceptance of these fashions by the opinion leaders. Once fashion leaders accept a new fashion, this group serves as role models and information sources for subsequent purchasers.[3]

Reinforcement is based on mechanisms of reward or punishment. Group members repeat behaviors that have been rewarded and avoid behaviors for which they have been punished. In sports, for example, the pride of winning and fear of losing empower players to excel in their sport.

Social interaction is the mechanism that defines a group's expectations from each of its members. These expectations are founded on the role a member occupies in the specific group. For example, the history of cults in the United States reveals that members were often expected to surrender all their material means of personal independence such as money and belongings to the group. Only the leader was allowed to have funds and property.

Socialization is instrumental in shaping consumer behavior. **Consumer socialization** is the process by which we acquire the knowledge, skills, and attitudes relevant to our effective functioning as consumers in the marketplace.[4] An individual learns to think and behave according to society's expectations as modeled by various groups the individual interacts with. Groups are responsible for shaping a person's consumption roles, product types acquired, purchasing behavior, consuming characteristics, as well as roles in family decision making.

Types of Social Groups

Groups can be classified based on a number of variables, such as regularity of contact, size, availability of membership, and degree of intimacy within the group. For our purposes, however, it suffices to classify groups on the basis of *intimacy* (primary versus secondary) and *formality* (formal versus informal).

PRIMARY VERSUS SECONDARY

Primary groups are usually small and intimate groups whose members come together on a regular basis, exhibit spontaneous interpersonal behavior, communicate face-to-face, and maintain commitment of self and concern for others in the group. The family represents an important primary group. Other examples of groups with close ties include athletic teams, local chapters of fraternities or sororities, monasteries, and convents.

primary groups
small, intimate groups that meet regularly and communicate face-to-face

Secondary groups, on the other hand, intimacy and personal interaction are less evident than in primary groups. Secondary groups lack the regularity of contact and personal commitment or concern for other members that characterize primary groups. Although communication may still involve face-to-face interaction, other communication efforts are impersonal in nature and occur via the mass media, such as in the case of virtual or online communities. Examples of other secondary groups may include professional organizations, religious denominations, alumni associations, labor unions, and similar groups.

secondary groups
groups in which regular, face-to-face contact is lacking

The distinction between primary and secondary groups lies in their degree of influence on a person's beliefs, values, attitudes, and behavior. While a family's influence can mold a member's lifelong behavior patterns, a secondary group's influence is typically moderate at best.

FORMAL VERSUS INFORMAL

Formal groups are highly organized hierarchical groups in which the structure is explicitly defined, objectives are clearly specified, roles and statuses are clearly delineated, and procedures and responsibilities are strictly observed. In the business world, major corporations within practically every industry have formal organizational structures that ensure the continuity of their mission, objectives, operational strategies, and policies, regardless of the specific individuals that occupy various positions in these groups.

formal groups
highly organized groups with an explicit structure and specified goals and procedures

Informal groups, on the other hand, frequently emerge within the formal group. Informal group relationships, for example, emerge between people working together as they socialize. This socialization provides a setting for exchange of ideas, viewpoints, and behavior patterns that may add to the efficiency of the organization structure or, as is the case in many present-day corporate structures, may impede its functioning. For example, workers on an assembly line in a factory may have an unspoken informal rule restricting their output to a slower pace than would otherwise be possible. A system of informal rewards and punishments guarantees persistence of these rules. An informal group may also emerge outside the confines of a formal group, such as

informal groups
groups in which structure, goals, and procedures are less explicit

Informal groups, which have their own centers of power and systems of rewards and punishments, often emerge within formal organizational structures.

groups that emerge between neighbors, acquaintances, and friends. A special case of informal groups is an online or **virtual community**, which has become an important supplemental form of communication between people in cyberspace. Virtual communities are social networks involving individuals with common interests, ideas, tasks, or goals who interact in a virtual society across time and geographic boundaries, with the objective of forming interpersonal relationships. Virtual communities take different forms depending on the level of interaction and participation among members. They can take the form of traditional structured online communities, such as message boards and chat rooms, or they may simply be individual-centric types, such as blogs and instant messaging buddy lists.

From the point of view of group influence, an online community allows members to interact with like-minded individuals instantaneously from anywhere around the globe, creating a powerful social network that is capable of influencing participants' views and behavior patterns.

virtual community
a social network with common interests, ideas, tasks, or goals that interacts in cyberspace

Effect of Technology on Group Behavior

Virtual communities are social networks that people join to fulfill their need for affiliation. Online communities encourage the important group dynamics of socialization and working together with others. The dynamic of working with others encompasses a variety of online connections, ranging from business teams cooperating on projects (e.g., www.bigbangworkshops.com), to linkages between members of local communities who share common goals (e.g., www.freenets.com), to links between people who share interests in various issues and causes (e.g., www.safer-world.org). The dynamic of socializing, on the other hand, occurs between persons who simply enjoy conversing online with like-minded others (e.g., www.salon.com).

A number of investigations have been conducted concerning the effect of online activities on particpants' offline lives, virtual identities, body in cyberspace, as well as community members' roles and types. One recurring theme in most of these studies is that the Internet encourages anonymity in both the technical and social senses. While it is true that with the right technological knowledge, all but the most expert users can be identified, postings to electronic bulletin boards, newsgroups, chatrooms, and MUDs (multiple-user domains or dungeons) are usually done under a fictitious screen name. As such, the sources of these postings are unknown and are thus subject to the control of the participants. This anonymity allows participants to safely and freely experiment with their multiplicity of selves. In fact, this anonymity is part of the allure of these sites for social interaction. It induces participants to engage in more risky behavior than they would dare to undertake in real-life situations.

Individuals and groups in cyberspace are more readily and completely inclined to express their most intimate views and release feelings ranging from rage to erotic obsessions. They often successfully develop online personas with bigger-than-life characteristics, or simply adopt imaginative identities in order to explore hidden or unexplored components of their personalities or social life. In so doing, a forum is created for self-disclosure and discovery.

On the issue of "disembodiment" engendered by the Internet, cyberspace is considered a liberating medium for those uncomfortable with their physical appearance, abilities, or social stature. The Internet gives such persons the power to become what their fantasies allow them to be. It is interesting to observe that the textual expression of self online often seems more real and gratifying to them than their physical self offline. This observation led many psychologists to propose that the Internet serves as a therapeutic medium via its ability to offer individuals an escape from some of the most distressing aspects of life, and allows them to work through their personal issues in a productive manner.[5]

Roles

Roles are major determinants of groups' expectation from their members. Role patterns as well as role—related expectations have major effects on consumer behavior. Shakespeare adeptly summarized role theory when he wrote:

> All the world's a stage,
> And all the men and women merely players.
> They have their exits and their entrances;
> And one man in his time plays many parts.

Just as a playwright's script calls for actors to wear indicated costumes, speak assigned lines, handle certain props, and perform designated actions, specific functions are assigned to or voluntarily assumed by persons who occupy particular positions within groups. **Roles** are patterns of behavior performed by individuals within a given social context. Such behavioral patterns may derive from formal role definitions prescribed by the group, from informal rules of the group, or from a history of prior experiences. For example, in virtual communities, individuals' patterns of participation in an online interaction vary significantly. Research has revealed at least 15 role types played by participants. A sample of these roles includes *core participants* who provide a large proportion of an online group's activity, *readers* who are not comfortable in posting but mainly read, *dominators* who post frequently and influence the space of an online interaction, *flamers* who send hostile and unprovoked messages, *actors* who develop different online personas, and *spammers* who post the same thing over and over again.[6]

Roles entail clusters of rights and responsibilities that are based on positions within a group, not on the specific individuals who occupy them. Some roles allow greater freedom than others. *Role parameters* delineate the range of behavior deemed appropriate for a specific role. The role parameters for university students are wide compared to, say, members of the clergy, who

Roles
patterns of behavior performed by individuals within a given social context

must follow a fairly straight and narrow path. A person's *role style* refers to individual variations in the performance of a given role. This means that the way in which role expectations are met may differ considerably from person to person. For example, two professors may teach the same course but require different textbooks and use dissimilar teaching methods.

Rarely, if ever, do individuals' lives entail a single role. Rather, their role repertoire includes multiple ones, each of which is valid only within a specific social context. Behavior deemed permissible in one role may be unacceptable in another. Similarly, roles may evolve over time. For instance, in contemporary society, the increased involvement of women in business has brought about marketing opportunities for the clothing, transportation, and food preparation industries. Increased involvement of men in homemaking chores, on the other hand, has caused changes in grocery shopping and child rearing.[7]

New roles can also be acquired. For example, when a husband or wife dies, the surviving spouse is left with total responsibility for managing the home. In other cases, individuals may face the stress of overextending themselves. *Role overload* occurs when the sheer volume of behavior demanded by the roles in a person's life set exceeds available energy, time, or money.[8] For example, due to the expanding number of dual-career couples, family and household groups frequently require that one or both spouses or partners bear multiple household roles.

Sometimes individuals hold incompatible roles. This situation, known as *role conflict*, occurs when individuals simultaneously occupy multiple roles and when pressures associated with membership in one group become incompatible with those stemming from participation in others. An individual's career ambitions, for example, may conflict with meeting his or her family responsibilities and vice versa.[9] The ad from Phoenix in Figure 11.1 addresses the case of high-net-worth individuals who earn—and spend—large sums of money. In the ad, the company highlights its long-term wealth strategies available to financial advisors designed to enhance and preserve the resources of prosperous clients.

In still other instances, expectations or demands placed on a person occupying a role are vague. *Role ambiguity* is a situation in which there is uncertainty about one's duties and responsibilities. Newcomers to a role and people experiencing role transitions often experience role ambiguity. A number of life events such as graduation, new employment, purchase of a home, marriage, birth of a child, retirement, divorce, and death of a spouse clearly delineate turning points in people's lives and the necessary assumption of new roles.[10]

ROLES AND CONSUMPTION BEHAVIOR

Roles in which people serve greatly influence their consumption behavior. In a study by Rassuli and Harrell, a predominantly male sample composed of professionals and skilled workers was asked to create sets of living room furniture.[11] It was found that the members of each occupational group had similar notions regarding what constituted an appropriate cluster of furniture. In other words, physicians in the sample tended to select similar items, as did a subsample of firefighters and a subsample of professors.

Figure 11.1

This ad from The Phoenix Companies, Inc., a financial services company, depicts a role conflict situation faced by an individual who earns a great deal of money yet spends lavishly. In view of such conflict, the company offers long-term wealth strategies for affluent and high-net worth clients.

role-related
product cluster
the set of goods
necessary for a person
to play a given role
competently

Certain products are essential to meeting the requirements associated with specific roles. A consumer's **role-related product cluster** is the set of goods necessary to play a given role competently.[12] Products can be functionally or symbolically imperative to meeting role-related expectations. Today, corporate sales reps cannot function without a laptop computer, a cellular phone, and a pager to satisfy the requirements of their job. Role-related product clusters define both appropriate and inappropriate products for a given role. The tuxedo required of instrumentalists performing with an orchestra would be unsuitable when flipping hamburgers at McDonald's.

As the environment changes over time, definitions of the behavior befitting to a role and pertinent product clusters also change. In many business offices, paper files have been replaced by PCs running word-processing, spreadsheet and database software. Changes in the roles of women and the expanding female presence in the workplace also have serious implications for marketers. Product lines, distribution strategies, and promotion tactics as well as retail store locations and hours must reflect evolving roles and consequent changes in shopping patterns.

The criteria that consumers use to evaluate products and services when occupying one of their roles may be quite different from the criteria they would use when serving in another capacity. Consider the case of a consumer who is both parent and purchasing agent for a corporation. Such a person would seek different features in a PC bought for the home than in a unit purchased for use in the corporation.

Within a group or a society as a whole, the role an individual plays or the position he or she occupies carries with it a certain degree of importance, influence, and prestige. Think of the stature associated with a position such as the CEO of a major corporation or the power held by a governor of a state. Such status is an inseparable component of group functioning and merits mention in the following section.

Status

status
the relative position a
person occupies along a
group's social continuum

Status represents the relative position a person occupies along a specific group's social continuum. Stated differently, status is one's rank within a group's power or prestige hierarchy. Status materializes in different ways; it can be either achieved or ascribed. *Achieved status* within a group reflects an individual's efforts, accomplishments, or contributions to the group. For example, individuals who earn an MBA degree and have several years of business experience possess credentials that qualify them for a highly paid managerial position in a major corporation. In such cases, individuals are said to possess achieved status. *Ascribed status*, on the other hand, can be a result of factors such as social class, wealth, age, gender, and ethnicity. For example, a person who is born into an affluent, aristocratic family may have ascribed status as part of the elite upper class.

Generally, higher status implies greater power and influence within the group. Furthermore, the range of acceptable behavior to which individuals must conform varies according to their status in the group. Higher-status members are permitted a wider range of acceptable behavior than are other group members. A company's president, for example, can arrive late to a meeting with subordinates; subordinates, however, would risk penalties if they were to arrive tardy for that same meeting.

STATUS AND CONSUMPTION BEHAVIOR

Consumers frequently purchase products, services, and brands suggestive of their elevated status in a group. They do so because prestigious products, services, and brands communicate a desirable image of them to others. Massive, elegantly furnished homes built on several acres of wooded land and luxurious automobiles, as well as hired household help (butlers, maids, cooks, gardeners, chauffeurs), exemplify status symbols. The term **conspicuous consumption** has been applied to the acquisition and prominent exhibition of these extravagant luxuries in order to provide evidence of the ability to afford them. Although such items in reality possess little in common, many consumers tend to group them together as a symbolic unit.[13]

Using material items to exhibit status has become essential within large, anonymous societies where reputation alone fails to convey to others who we are.[14] Frequently, individuals rely on visual cues such as material possessions to ascertain the status of people they do not know. If symbols are to convey status, they must be exclusive. Some goods, however, become so widely diffused among people of diverse statuses that they lose their exclusive meaning. In this case, they become **fraudulent symbols**. At that point, new symbols are needed to set the elite apart from the masses and satisfy consumers' need for uniqueness.[15]

Within some groups, however, symbolism operates contrary to consumers' social standing and wealth. Whereas big, flashy cars and flamboyant clothing may be status symbols in impoverished urban neighborhoods, smaller cars and jeans may be the norm among more affluent suburbanites who do not feel the need to flaunt their wealth. Flaunting one's wealth appears to be a tendency among the *nouveaux riche* (new rich); among the really rich, on the other hand, conspicuous consumption is *déclassé*. The term **stealth wealth** is sometimes applied to people who neither want to nor need to show off. These individuals are more likely to purchase quality items that do not scream money, glamour, and glitz.[16]

Some people engage in a peculiar type of conspicuous consumption. They deliberately avoid widely used, fashionable status symbols. In fact, they pursue status by snubbing it. Such paradoxical behavior has been called **parody display**, a phenomenon that may explain why some wealthy individuals shun designer brands and instead elect to drive utility vehicles or wear ragged jeans and shabby sneakers.[17]

conspicuous consumption
the acquisition and exhibition of extravagant luxuries to portray one's ability to afford them

fraudulent symbols
formerly unique goods that become common and lose their exclusive meaning

stealth wealth
a case where a person avoids showing off one's product acquisitions

parody display
a case in which a person pursues status by snubbing it

Conspicuous consumption refers to the acquisition and exhibition of extravagant luxuries to prove one's ability to afford them.

© 2009, Happy Alex, Shutterstock, Inc.

Due to current adverse economic conditions, it appears that many consumers have moved from conspicuous to rational consumption. The role-relaxed consumer of the past has reemerged. **Role-relaxed consumers** are frugal and crave good value.[18] A number of companies such as Subaru, the Japanese auto manufacturer, have identified role-relaxed consumers as their target consumer profile. Others like Filene's Basement, Target, and Wal-Mart, as well as many known merchandisers' "outlet stores," are examples of companies that have elected to employ a role-relaxed positioning.

Social Power

The ability of a group to influence the beliefs, attitudes, and behavior of individuals stems from the power it possesses over them. Marketers, as influencing agents, have at their disposal a number of power bases to influence consumer behavior. Although the extent to which marketers possess these power bases varies, a combination of them can often bring about desired changes in consumer behavior and consumption patterns.

TYPES OF SOCIAL POWER

French and Raven identified five types of social power.[19] These include reward, coercive, legitimate, referent, and expert power. This section explains each.

Reward Power

Reward power is based on the ability of the group to dispense rewards. Rewards offer reinforcements that are instrumental in influencing or altering behavior. The greater the reward a group can administer, the stronger its power to attain compliance with group norms.

Rewards occur in many forms. They can be tangible (gifts, monetary compensation, awards for achievement) or intangible, such as those that are psychological in nature like praise and recognition. Marketers employ a variety of methods to reward consumers. Perhaps the most important of these is satisfaction of consumer needs offered by marketers' products or services. Other forms of reward include price deals, coupons, premiums, rebates, sweepstakes and contests, as well as corporate sponsorship of popular entertainment programming in the media or cause-related marketing efforts. Such rewards provide an incentive for prospects to select a particular brand or patronize a particular retailer.

Coercive Power

Coercive power involves the power of a group to punish members to obtain compliance to norms and expectations. A new army recruit quickly learns to obey officers' orders to avoid harsh sanctions. The impact of coercive power on compliance is a function of the magnitude of the sanction. The more severe the threatened punishment, the greater the degree of conformity.[20]

role-relaxed consumers
consumers who buy rationally and crave good value

reward power
an influence based on a group's ability to dispense rewards

coercive power
an influence based on a group's ability to administer punishments

Global Opportunity

"Buy American" . . . Buy Toyota?

Waves of economic nationalism triggered by various causes such as recessions, calls for national pride, or periods of military conflict with another nation have occurred throughout U.S. history. The "Buy American" slogan is a form of legitmate power used by marketers to capitalize on such episodes. It emphasizes the need for national self-reliance and raises fears that foreigners increasingly control the country's economic destiny. For example, commercial spots from Worwick/Baker & Foire, an apparel firm in New York, depict plant closings and the personal impact of unemployment in an industry that has lost a half million jobs in the past decade.

Although "Buy American" fervor has a therapeutic dimension, leading consumers to believe that the ritual of buying goods made in the United States can treat economic problems at their root, the campaign, in reality, is nothing more than wishful thinking. It ignores the complexity of international markets and the dynamics of the trade, where quality and low-priced products are produced in other nations and marketed with little regard to international boundaries.

Specifying precisely what constitutes U.S.-made products poses a stumbling block. The confusion becomes evident when so-called U.S.-made products are merely assembled in the United States from parts and components made abroad. In the case of electronics, for example, the closest thing to a U.S.-made television set is one assembled by a French company in Indianapolis, using parts from Asia. Similarly, buyers of U.S. automobiles are buying U.S. *names*. While the 2008 models of Ford Mustang, Ford Focus, and Ford Escape contain 35 percent foreign parts, the same-year models of Toyota Camry and Honda Civic contain 80 and 70 percent, respectively, American parts.[22]

U.S. consumers are torn between their patriotic loyalties and market reality. To industry observers, it became evident that foreign carmakers had discovered a successful formula for getting American consumers to favor their foreign cars over domestic ones simply by placing a higher percentage of U.S.-made parts in their models. By so doing, foreign carmakers have been able to defeat the cries of those who advocate the "Buy American" slogan.

In one shopping mall, a couple was intercepted and asked what they had bought at the mall that evening. "Nike shoes and a Japanese stereo system" was the reply. When asked whether they had purchased anything that was made in the United States, the husband raised his soda cup and said, "Pepsi."[23]

Many patriotic U.S. consumers prefer to purchase products that carry the "Made in the U.S.A." label. To learn about actions being taken to reduce reliance on imports in the United States, visit the Made in the USA Foundation, a nonprofit organization concerned about American competitiveness and economic leadership, at www.madeusa.org. In your opinion, how effective is a legitimate power strategy in enhancing the sale of U.S.-made products? Does this strategy work equally well for the majority of consumers? If equivalent-quality foreign-made substitute products were available to U.S. consumers at a lower price, would this patriotic appeal still work? Why or why not?

Tupperware and lingerie parties are sometimes thought to employ coercive power as a selling strategy, particularly when a number of people attend these events less out of interest in the products than out of social obligation.[21] Guests at such in-home sales events tend to feel that because their peers are buying, failure to place at least a token order would be embarrassing and disappoint the hostess. Group pressure creates a social obligation for attenders to purchase something to save face.

In general, marketers do not possess coercive power. They cannot reprimand or discipline consumers for failure to follow a recommended course of action. However, marketers frequently employ a modified type of coercive power in the form of fear or guilt appeals used in ads. Crusades against drug abuse warn against the destruction of the human mind and body. Antismoking campaigns frequently focus on cancer and heart or lung disease. Mothers Against Drunk Driving (MADD) emphasize death or disablement due to accidents caused by intoxicated drivers.

In other instances, advertising emphasizes the negative consequences that can result if consumers fail to use the product. Condom advertisers, for example, build on the public's anxiety over catching AIDS as a consequence of engaging in unprotected sexual activity. Ads sponsored by the American Dairy Association may warn women that lack of calcium, a prime nutrient found in milk, can lead to osteoporosis. Sales reps for firms selling home security systems may describe dire consequences faced by the victims of home intruders. Unfortunately, elements of this power base have occasionally become the tools of intimidation employed by unscrupulous salespersons, particularly when dealing with the elderly and other unsuspecting, vulnerable consumers. The ad in Figure 11.2 from EpiPen, a treatment for sudden allergic reactions, employs a fear appeal directed at parents of young children in order to raise product awareness.

Legitimate Power

In any group there are norms, values, roles, and expectations, as well as pressures to uphold the principles that the group endorses. It is anticipated that each member's attitudes and behavior will coincide with these standards. Eventually, group members internalize feelings that they *should, ought to*, or *must not* undertake certain actions or think in certain ways. These feelings of propriety may originate from mandates of one's parents, religion, patriotism, or other groups. Individuals, over time, adopt these standards of conduct as their very own.

legitimate power an influence that occurs as a result of individuals' feelings of obligation	The feeling of legitimacy created through internalized norms and values has the same property as power. It engenders the same response as that created through reinforcing or punitive actions. Such influence is know as **legitimate power**. Individuals in a group sense a personal obligation to think or act in accordance with group expectations. Doctors and lawyers adopt a code of professional ethics that includes a responsibility to protect the confidentiality of their patients or clients. Members of MADD would not drink and drive because of internalized beliefs regarding such irresponsible behavior.

Marketers sometimes employ legitimate power to promote products or concepts. Campaigns founded on themes of patriotism or environmentalism as well as those that make references to propriety and tradition employ legitimate power. Ads stressing the *buy American* principle, for instance, exemplify the assumption that patriotic citizens should possess a desire to protect and help American industry and labor. Such consumers would prefer products manufactured in the United States over imported goods. The ad from the Marines in Figure 11.3, employs power by virtue of promising a leadership role in service to one's country.

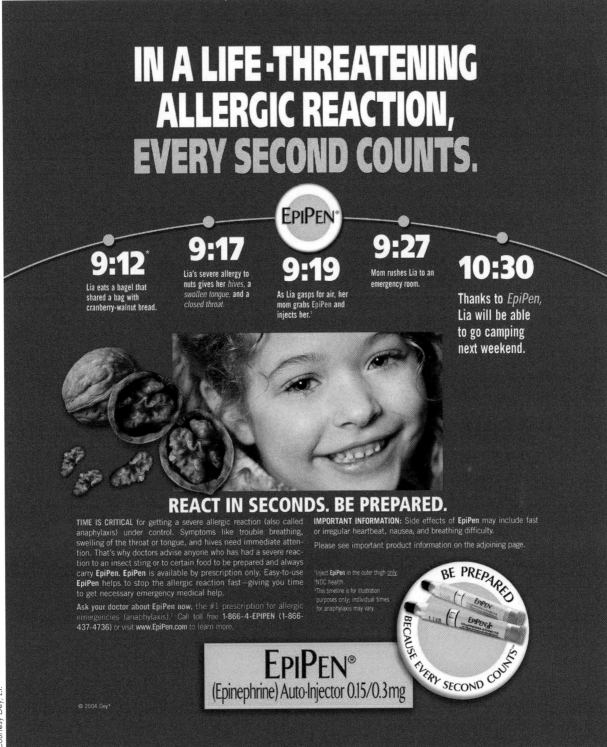

Figure 11.2

Hinting to a connection between sudden allergic reactions and loss of life, this ad for EpiPen employs a fear appeal to encourage parents to have the treatment on hand.

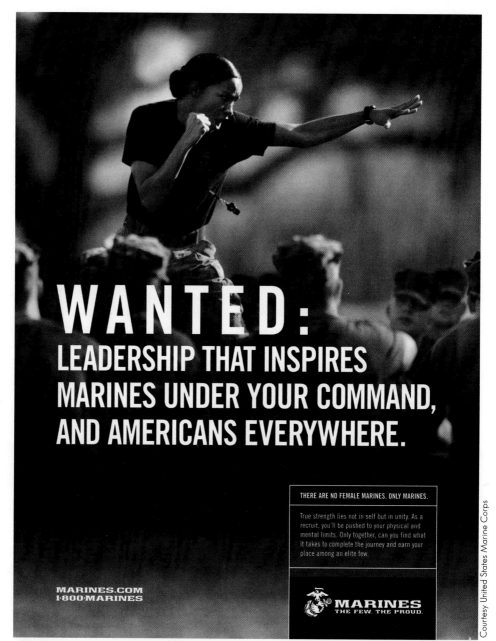

Figure 11.3

This ad from the Marines employs legitimate power to entice prospects to enlist by stressing the pride of playing a leadership role in the service of one's country.

Referent Power

A group's **referent power** is manifested through an individual's desire to identify with a group and to share a sense of oneness with it. For example, a study dealing with parental influence on their children's selection of a college major revealed that parental encouragement had a significant positive influence on their children's choice of major.[24]

referent power
an influence based on a person's desire to identify with an admired group

We can think of reference groups as sources of referent power. No one can deny the influence of professional athletic teams on sports fans, music groups on music lovers, or the Boy Scouts or Girl Scouts on participating youth. The greater the attraction of the referent, the greater the identification, and consequently the more powerful the referent influence. Marketers find referent power valuable in product and service promotions.

Consumers crave a sense of belonging to and identification with a group or structure that can offer them feelings of security and belonging. Consequently, advertisers spend handsomely to secure well-known and liked characters, such as movie superstars, sports heroes, public figures, and TV personalities to help promote their brands, boost awareness of their companies and brands, strengthen their image, or increase attention to their messages. Many sponsors feel that the payback in terms of product recognition and image enhancement justifies the cost incurred.[25]

A study by Agrawal and Kamakura suggests that using celebrities in ads may increase a firm's value.[26] Celebrity endorsers can affect attitude formation and change because they may attract more attention or possess more credibility than noncelebrities. Furthermore, consumers may identify with or want to emulate celebrities. Consumers may also relate traits of celebrities with product attributes in a way that coincides with their own personal wants. A number of recent studies have shown that celebrity endorsers are most influential when their image matches the personality of the product and the actual or ideal self-concept of the target market.[27]

Expert Power

Expert power is derived from an influencing agent's possession of specific knowledge or skills in which an individual is lacking. The wisdom or ability the expert exhibits in a specific area is sufficient to induce compliance. Legal counsel provided by an attorney or medical advice given by a physician exemplify cases of expert power. The scope of expert power is restricted to the specific area in which the expert possesses extraordinary knowledge or ability. In the pet food field, for example, companies that sell "designer" chow are borrowing a strategy from pharmaceutical companies, which routinely persuade doctors to prescribe their drugs. Marketers of pet foods reportedly spend hundreds of thousands of dollars to get veterinarians to recommend their premium-priced products to pet owners.[28]

expert power
an influence based on a person's regard for an agent's knowledge or skill

Advertisers frequently use experts such as engineers, doctors, scientists, or researchers to present an objective evaluation of a product or service. The audience's acceptance of claims made by such experts is a function of how credible they are perceived to be. The ad from Kyocera Document Solutions, shown in Figure 11.4, uses this strategy to promote the company's products.

SOCIAL POWER USED BY MARKETERS

Although marketing strategies may use one or more of the various types of social power, those employed most frequently are reward, referent, and expert power. Psychological sanctions (coercive power), when used, tend to decrease

Figure 11.4

In this ad, an expert purchasing director at Northeast Company attests to the quality and low cost of Kyocera copiers. Such expert testimony tends to boost the credibility of product claims advanced by the firm.

the attractiveness of the source and may elicit the opposite reaction of the response desired. In addition, their effect is often short-lived, because sanctions fail to produce permanent attitudinal or behavioral change. Likewise, marketers' use of legitimate power is limited. Its effect is confined to those cases where consumption of a product or a stand on an issue can be cleverly linked to some socially prescribed behavior, where a person ought to do or should refrain from performing some act.

Conformity to Group Mandates

Conformity is the change that occurs in beliefs, attitudes, or actions of group members as a result of real or imagined group pressure. Most groups have rules or norms to govern the conduct of their members. **Norms** are legitimate, shared guidelines to accepted and expected behavior.[29] They specify proper and improper actions under particular circumstances and serve as standards against which members evaluate the appropriateness of their own behavior and that of others. Norms stipulate what is required, acceptable, and

Conformity
the change in individuals' beliefs, attitudes, or actions as a result of group pressure

norms
shared guidelines to accepted and expected behavior

prohibited. They may cover such issues as styles of dress, table etiquette, roles assumed, manner of speech, personal hygiene, and other recommended modes of behavior. Some group norms apply equally to all members. Other sets of norms apply only to those persons who occupy specific roles (doctors, lawyers, judges, professors, clergy).

For a group or society as a whole to function effectively and smoothly, members must conform to norms. Chaos would result if each group member were to maintain his or her own set of behavioral patterns. Although some degree of deviation from group norms is to be expected, the range of permitted departure is restricted. When an individual crosses these limits, it is interpreted as *deviant behavior*, and sanctions are employed.[30] Imagine, for instance, the case of a driver who decides to violate the U.S. norm (encoded into law) and drives a car on the left-hand side of the road—a practice that is the norm in Britain and Japan.

When individuals join a group, they tend to note the conduct of others in the group in order to ascertain what constitutes proper behavior. This tendency, which is known as **social comparison**, implies that observing the behavior of others provides a yardstick for suitable actions of our own.[31] Peer pressure among teens offers a vivid example of this behavioral tendency. As newcomers to a group, we search for characteristic norms of the group. If our norms do not match those of others in the group, we may modify our norms, keep them intact and tolerate the consequences, challenge the group, or withdraw from it. Social comparisons occur in instances where certain behavioral patterns are expected but not necessarily clear to everyone in the group, or where behavioral choices are available but there is no objective clue as to which choice is deemed most appropriate.

> **social comparison**
> individuals' tendency to self-evaluate by noting the conduct of others in a group

Now, let us turn our attention to another aspect of group influence that deals with the consequences of group interaction. As social beings, humans tend to model their beliefs, attitudes, and behaviors after those of other members of the groups they affiliate with. Most individuals relate to particular groups and exhibit a great deal of concern over how they are perceived by other people whose opinions they value and whose acceptance they seek. The specific groups individuals identify with and emulate, or whose approval is of concern to them, are called reference groups.

In the following section, we investigate some aspects of reference groups such as their composition and types, as well as their influence on us and on our behavior.

Reference Groups

Reference groups are any sets of people that provide individuals with a standpoint or perspective for evaluating or patterning their own beliefs, values, attitudes, goals, or behavior. Thus, any group that influences consumer purchase decisions can be considered a reference group. Our desire to identify with and emulate admired groups underlies the purchase of many products as well as the specific brands that we select. Advertisers, as a result,

> **reference groups**
> groups that provide a perspective for evaluating or patterning one's own behavior

Popularity among reference groups is one major reason why a sport like golf has an army of faithful followers.

often show products used and enjoyed within group settings. Such groups can exert an influence on information processing, attitude formation, and purchase behavior.[32]

In most cases, reference groups do not dictate what individuals must do. Rather, individuals are influenced by actions of these groups, by respect for the group's opinion, or by concern for the group's feelings. Reference groups take various forms. Private online communities represent one such form. As an example, in one online community devoted to weight loss and sponsored by Glaxo-SmithKline, women dieters meet other like-minded women who support their dieting struggles through instant messaging and chat discussions. Realizing the power of online communities to influence target groups, a growing number of companies such as Glaxo, Kraft, Hewlett-Packard, and Coty are learning how to use the Web to harness such power by teaming up with Communispace Corp., a startup that hosts private online communities.[33]

Reference groups play a pivotal role in shaping consumer decisions by pressuring individuals to conform to group norms, providing believable information, and offering a set of values to identify with and express.[34] One's family and peers are prime examples of groups that serve as models in this way. Recently hired employees of a firm, for example, use their new colleagues as a reference group when making decisions about styles of clothing to wear at work, appropriate topics for conversation, and acceptable viewpoints to express.[35] In this situation, normative influence occurs as these recently hired employees apply group norms and values to define the new situations they encounter.

Similarly, reference groups frequently serve as credible sources of potentially useful information for uncertain or uninformed consumers.[36] A person who observes others using a given brand or acting in a particular way in an ambiguous situation may emulate that behavior simply because it seems to be the right thing to do. Teens, for example, often look to their peers to determine which brands of jeans or shoes to purchase. Consumers may select a brand because its widespread use in the group suggests that it is indeed good. Studies have revealed that insurance and medical services were susceptible to reference group influence due to the fact that individuals lack confidence when purchasing such services and, as a result, are open to group influence in the form of peer recommendations.[37]

Individuals also tend to make self-appraisals, compare their behavior, and gauge the outcomes of their actions against those of like-minded others of equivalent standing. We frequently appraise our own status, measure our accomplishments, and verify our ideas against those of our peers.[38] Then we pattern our beliefs, feelings, or actions accordingly. This process of social comparison is especially strong when no tangible, objective yardsticks are available.[39] For example, stylistic preferences for music are largely a matter of personal taste. However, when selecting the right mix of music for a party, hosts often assume that the types liked by their guests are more appropriate choices to play.[40] As such, reference groups set standards for self-evaluation or serve to validate one's personal beliefs, attitudes, and behavior.[41]

Reference groups vary in size, structure, and composition. Consequently, individuals can be influenced in dissimilar directions by different reference groups. The following section addresses the different types of reference groups.

TYPES OF REFERENCE GROUPS

Individuals may belong to a group they feel offers them a model or guide, or they may merely aspire to membership in a group, or they may even shun membership in a certain group they feel offers them a negative frame of reference. In general, reference groups can be classified as membership, aspirational, and dissociative reference groups.

Membership

Membership reference groups are those to which an individual currently belongs or qualifies for membership. Family, friends, fraternities, churches, and work groups are examples of membership reference groups. Similarly, individuals who reach 55 years of age can join the American Association of Retired Persons (AARP), and those who contribute to a public TV channel are members of its supporting group.

Within membership reference groups, a person has been accepted and is perceived by others as belonging to the group. Whereas membership in some groups is automatic, such as being an alum when a person graduates from a university, membership in some others—such as a political party—is voluntary. Individuals are free to join, refrain from joining, or withdraw from the group after joining.

Aspirational

Individuals need not be members of groups that offer them a frame of reference. Individuals may seek membership in a group for which they lack the needed qualifications or abilities. Such groups are called **aspirational reference groups**. For example, an individual may seek entry into a prestigious country club. However, the club's hefty annual membership dues and the person's social standing may prevent him or her from joining. Individuals generally try to emulate the beliefs, values, attitudes, and behavior of members of those groups that they aspire to join.

Aspirational reference groups can be anticipatory or symbolic. **Anticipatory aspirational reference groups** are those with which an individual has at least some direct contact and somewhat reasonable expectations of joining at a future time. A middle manager may aspire to move up an organizational hierarchy to a top management position.

Symbolic aspirational reference groups, on the other hand, are groups in which individuals' chances of achieving membership are remote at best, regardless of their sincere desire to join and their willingness to adopt and

memership reference groups
groups to which a person currently belongs or qualifies for membership

aspirational reference groups
groups in which a person seeks membership but lacks the qualifications to join

anticipatory aspirational reference groups
groups a person has reasonable expectations of joining in the future

symbolic aspirational reference groups
groups in which one's chances of gaining membership are remote at best

The intensity of group influence on beliefs, attitudes, and behavior is a function of individuals' willingness to accept the mandates of the group.

emulate group beliefs, norms, values, attitudes, or behavior. Few aspiring, talented individuals ever become professional athletes, famous recording artists, or movie superstars even though, as fans, they pattern their lives after highly successful role models. The influence of well-known symbolic groups, such as sports teams or rock groups, have a great influence on consumer behavior as can be observed in fans' imitation of group members' appearance, mannerisms, or behavior.

Dissociative

Not all groups provide consumers with a positive frame of reference. Some offer individuals a negative reference point.[42] Consumers may wish to differentiate themselves from or establish distance between themselves and certain undersirable groups. In some cases, individuals simply reject the objectives, agenda, or methods of the negative group. In other cases, however, a disassociation with a particular group is based largely on the biases of those outside the negative group (rather than on the group itself).

There are two types of dissociative reference groups: negative and disclaimant. **Negative reference groups** are groups with which individuals wish to avoid association or identification. Individuals may go out of their way to avoid contact with members of certain groups such as the KKK, street gangs, cults, skinheads, and drug abusers. **Disclaimant reference groups**, on the other hand, are those that individuals may have previously joined or otherwise belonged to, but whose values they later rejected. A person who registers as a member of a political party may later switch to another party because of disagreement with the party's stand on particular issues.

Negative reference groups can affect consumption behavior. Some consumers, for example, regard censorship advocates as negative reference groups. Attempts by certain organizations to purge the sexually explicit and violent lyrics of particular rap artists' music or ban their CDs altogether only cause some fans to crave them more. Similarly, some moviegoers who consistently disagree with particular critics' movie reviews are attracted to those films that such commentators abhor. However, marketers rarely appeal to the desire to avoid or disclaim a group. Rather, advertisers attempt to ensure that targeted consumers do not link their products to dissociative groups. In this vein, Honda motorcycle ads have depicted "you meet the nicest people" (rather than hair-raising Hell's Angels) riding Honda cycles. In many cases, marketers' appeals to nonconformity tend to take on a positive rather than a negative tone. Some campaigns, for example, encourage consumers to flaunt their individuality and dare them to be a bit different compared to other group members. The Hennessy Cognac ad in Figure 11.5 exemplifies such a strategy.

negative reference groups

groups with which individuals wish to avoid association or identification

disclaimant reference groups

groups to which a person previously belonged, but whose values one later rejects

DEGREES OF REFERENCE GROUP INFLUENCE

The intensity of group influence on beliefs, attitudes, and behavior is a function of individuals' willingness to accept the mandates of the group. Three degrees of group influence have been identified.[44] In the first case, an individual merely goes along with group mandates. In the second case, which reflects a more intimate relationship, the individual identifies with the group. In the third case, which is more of a union between the individual and the group, the person professes group norms and values as his or her own. These degrees of influence, which have been labeled compliance, identification, and internalization, are briefly explained in the following paragraphs.

Compliance

Compliance, the weakest degree of reference group influence, occurs when a person goes along with a group to obtain approval or avoid disapproval. The person adopts group dictates not out of genuine belief in their content or worth, but rather because they are instrumental in producing a satisfying social effect. An individual learns to do or say the expected things in public, regardless of what his or her private convictions may be. Behaviors adopted via compliance are expressed only when a person's behavior is visible to the influencer.

A number of studies have confirmed this tendency.[45] For example, a study by Lascu, Bearden, and Rose investigated the effect of group size and expertise on subjects' susceptibility to social influence.[46] In their experiment, a number of students were asked to evaluate a liquid diet drink, and confederates were

compliance
the act of going along with a group to obtain approval

ETHICAL DILEMMA

Electronic Town Halls for Political Campaigns

The Internet has become an integral element of political campaigns in the United States. It has forever changed American presidential campaigns and has brought back the roots of American politics, where communities got together and discussed public issues in town halls and parlors. Being a form of electronic town hall, the Internet allows people to communicate directly with elected officials via their online presence. From Web sites and Twitter accounts to YouTube videos, voters can discuss issues in real time with the candidates as well as with each other. For example, in the fall of 2007, YouTube teamed up with CNN to sponsor Democratic and Republican presidential debates, in which citizens submitted questions to the candidates through videos they produced themselves and uploaded to the site.

Today, candidates, political parties, fund raisers, lobbyists, and legislators all have online strategies for advocating their goals. Politicians on the Left and Right alike use the Internet to spread their message by means of videos, disseminated primarily on YouTube, as well as by maintaining active campaign blogs.

A recent PEW Research Center investigation revealed that 24 percent of Americans received at least some of their information about the 2008 political campaign from the Internet. The study also showed that 42 percent of younger voters aged 18 through 29 regularly turned to the Internet for political news. On the question of where Web searchers went for news, 26 percent cited msnb.com, 23 percent cited cnn.com, and 22 percent cited Yahoo News. As far as social networking sites like FaceBook and MySpace, 37 percent of searchers aged 18 through 24 got at least some political news from such sites.

In this sense, the Internet has become a valuable yet inexpensive medium that promotes grassroots democracy, and allows true communication among people who exchange views on matters of common concern in a rational process of debate. Likely voters can thus form opinions that would shape the important political decisions.

The growing importance of the Internet in the political arena, however, does not necessarily mean that the medium fosters greater democracy. On one side, many households lack Internet access. Furthermore, the vast nature of the Internet makes finding authoritative, factual, trustworthy, and objective information difficult. The big media channels that currently dominate the Internet, as well as any anti-democratic force, can circulate materials and views that may sway public opinion in a direction that is harmful to the free election process. The campaign of Sen. Hillary Clinton in 2007, for example, registered the names of two Web sites with the expressed goal of attacking her chief rival Sen. Barack Obama, and labeling him as cowardly for having occasionally voted "present" as an Illinois legislator when it came to contentious issues.[43]

The digital age has forever changed the way presidential campaigns are run globally and in United States. Learn more about the major role of the Internet in world politics by visiting the Web site of the Office of International Outreach of Texas A&M University at http://intlcenter.tamu.edu/NewsJun12.asp. What social forces are at play in political campaigns conducted over the Web? Do you think that the Internet as a medium for political campaigns promotes or hinders the democratic process? Explain your answer. What are the drawbacks, if any, of this medium in the political arena?

used to influence student ratings of the drink. The results revealed that not only did conformity to group pressure exist in the case of less-knowledgeable students, but conformity equally prevailed even when the group members were highly knowledgeable about dietary products.

Occasionally, group pressures to conform become too intense and seem to violate people's freedom. Evidence exists that pressure to conform works only up to a point and that excessive pressure may lessen the degree of compliance. In such cases, consumers may reject the group or its norms altogether and demonstrate independent behavior. This tendency is known as **reactance**. For example, in our society, deliberate and intense pressures placed by the public and the government on getting smokers to kick the habit has prompted some to become more adamant about smoking than otherwise would have been the case. Similarly, teenagers who face parental disapproval regarding tattooing or body piercing often engage in such practices as a form of reactance to such pressure.

Reactance becomes increasingly likely as individuals encounter restrictions on their rights to choose and the attraction of the proscribed behavior option increases.[47] A study by Lessne and Notarantonio concluded that soft drink ads that restricted the quantities customers could purchase had the effect of increasing the brand's attractiveness to shoppers.[48]

Identification

Identification denotes a somewhat closer and more dependent relationship with the group than suggested by compliance. *Identification* occurs when a person accepts influence because doing so is associated with a satisfying self-defining relationship with the influencer.[49] It serves to validate our connection to a group in which our self-identity is anchored. We model our behavior along particular lines to meet the expectations of fellow group members. Children, for example, take on parental beliefs, attitudes, and behaviors. Similarly, physicians who join the AMA or attorneys who join the bar association take on many of the group's conventions as part of their socialization into it. Identification differs from compliance in that the identifier actually believes in the attitudes or behaviors adopted. They are accepted both publicly and privately.

At least two forms of identification can be distinguished: classical and reciprocal. In the case of **classical identification**, accepting influence is a means of establishing or maintaining one's self-image or relationship to the group. The identifier desires to be like (or even to be) the influencing agent and takes on some part or all of the influencer's role. An actor in a supporting role in a movie often yearns to play the role of the leading star. Those who occupy a role desired by the identifier or who possess attributes he or she lacks tend to be attractive influencers. In the case of **reciprocal identification**, a person may be involved in a complementary relationship with another individual (friend or spouse) or enact a social role defined with reference to the influencing agent, such as in the cases of interactions between doctors and patients or lawyers and their clients. The identifier and influencer share expectations of each other's behavior. The identifier empathically reacts in terms of the influencer's expectations, views, or recommendations. Many environmentally conscious consumers can identify with this mother shown in Figure 11.6, who chooses to purchase products that sustain and protect our planet.

Internalization

Internalization occurs when an individual accepts group influence because the induced behavior is intrinsically rewarding, congruent in some way—rationally or otherwise—with the person's own value system. Behavior adopted via internalization tends to become integrated with the individual's existing values. Consumers may adopt the recommendation of a credible group

MEET THE NEW ENVIRONMENTALIST.

Millions of people have found a way to shop for the wood and paper products they need while still being good to our forests. They simply look for products with the ⊕ SFI® label at all their favorite stores. From cereal boxes to paper towels to wood flooring:

⊕ SFI labeled products come from forests managed to rigorous environmental standards.

⊕ SFI standards conserve biodiversity and protect soil and water quality, as well as wildlife habitats.

⊕ SFI forests are audited by independent experts to ensure proper adherence to the SFI Standard.

⊕ SFI participants also plant more than 650 million trees each year to keep these forests thriving.

SUSTAINABLE FORESTRY INITIATIVE
Good for you. Good for our forests.

To learn more about the SFI Standard, visit *www.sfiprogram.org*

Courtesy of the Sustainable Forestry Initiative, Inc.

Figure 11.6

As people increasingly came to realize the damage that our modern lifestyle has caused our planet, they chose to avidly support and join members of the movement to protect the environment.

Consumer Behavior in Practice

Plastic Symbols of Affiliation

If you are a student, you are likely to own a sweatshirt, jacket, duffel bag, or coffee mug with your school's logo on it. You may even carry plastic money or have a license plate bearing your university's name. Affinity marketing, which identifies a person with a particular group, offers an excellent example of how marketers creatively synthesize both reference groups and referent power in order to influence consumer behavior. Affinity marketing enables consumers to flaunt their identification with some membership group (school, church, corporation), symbolic group (NFL team, rock group), or cause (animal rights, environment protection, safe sex, AIDS research).[50] Affinity marketing capitalizes on the allegiance that many people feel to the organizations they belong to or the causes they believe in. It attaches symbols of consumers' group affiliations to the tools of their daily life.

The premise behind affinity marketing is that when offerings within a product or service category are all basically similar, consumers would prefer to support the specific groups or causes they are personally associated with. In what has become an extremely pervasive variety of affinity marketing, many financial institutions now offer distinctive affinity credit cards. Here's how the arrangement works. A bank and an organization, such as a college alumni association, form an alliance whereby the bank promotes its credit cards to the school's faculty, staff, and current as well as former students.[51] The charge card identifies the school rather than the bank as the card's sponsor (State College Visa card rather than Citibank Visa card). The arrangement benefits both partners. The school receives a percentage of all ensuing credit card charges. The bank, in return, acquires access to a special-interest market niche.[52]

A distinction, however, should be made between an affinity card and a co-branded card. An *affinity* card carries the name of an organization, school, sports team, or a hobby that generally benefits from each purchase a consumer makes using the card. The objective in this case is to tap into consumers' desire to support an organization or a cause. *Co-branded* cards, on the other hand, carry the name of a for-profit partner, such as an airline or store. They promote brand loyalty by offering rewards of free miles, gifts, or discounts.[53]

Presently, it is estimated that there are over 30,000 affinity and co-branded credit card programs worldwide, offered mostly by large financial institutions such as MBNA and Bank One corporations. Among the 1.2 billion bank-issued credit cards in 2006, there were 320 million affinity and co-branded cards, an impressive percentage to say the least.[54]

The success of affinity credit cards has led banks, nationally and internationally, to offer them to various groups. Learn more about affinity and co-branded credit cards by visiting http://www.mba.com/creditcards/index.html *and* http://www.creditcards.com/articles/affinity-card.html. *What are the underlying forces behind individuals' attraction to affinity credit cards? Other than financial advantages, what social or psychological benefits do groups or individuals obtain through these cards?*

such as Greenpeace because they find its views regarding environmental issues to be relevant to their perceptions and congruent with their values.

Here, the individual accepts the values and norms of the group as his or her personal values and norms. For example, consumers who prefer to purchase environmentally friendly products do so because of their inherent belief that such actions are necessary to protect the fragile environment. Similarly, vegetarians abstain from consuming meat due personal convictions concerning the rights of animals. The call to recycle magazines suggested by this ad in Figure 11.7 from Magazine Publishers of America relies on consumers' internalization of environmentally sound values.

GO THE EXTRA MILE,
RECYCLE YOUR PILE

We all love our magazines,
but when it's time to let go, it just takes
a little extra effort to recycle.
After all, helping the environment
is everyone's responsibility.

For more information on how
to recycle your magazines, go to
www.Earth911.com.

MAKE IT A HABIT. RECYCLE.

Brought to you by the Magazine Publishers of America.

Figure 11.7

Commitment to a pristine environment is the motivation behind this ad from Magazine Publishers of America. It prompts environmentally conscious consumers to recycle their magazines.

REFERENCE GROUP INFLUENCE ON CONSUMER BEHAVIOR

A survey of the literature reveals that a number of factors such as consumers' demographic characteristics and personality traits, as well as group characteristics, situational factors, and product types, affect the likelihood that group influence will occur.[55] Among these influences, it appears that the main determinant of whether or not consumer purchases are influenced by reference groups is a product's social value. Products that are conspicuous, such as homes, automobiles, clothing, jewelry, and luggage, possess a high level of social value. As such, their purchase is much more likely to be influenced by reference groups. On the other hand, products like salt, waxed paper, lightbulbs, and antifreeze have little or no social value. Consequently, their purchase is less susceptible to group influence.

A study by Bearden and Etzel confirmed the presence of reference group influence on publicly consumed (conspicuous) versus privately consumed (inconspicuous) products.[56] Publicly consumed items are those that an individual owns and that other people can see. As such, their purchase is likely to be influenced by what other people may think. Privately consumed products, on the other hand, are those that the individual uses at home or in private and that other people are not aware one has. The purchase of these types of products is less likely to be susceptible to group influence.

In addition to considering group influence on the consumption of public versus private products, Bearden and Etzel investigated the degree of that influence by adding a luxury versus necessity product dimension. Thus, the interaction between the two dimensions of public–private and luxury–necessity resulted in four different product-brand combinations: public luxuries, public necessities, private luxuries, and private necessities. Strong reference group influence was found in the case of public-luxury products. Negligible influence occurred in the private-necessity product case. Differential influence materialized in the cases of public-necessity and private-luxury items. These conclusions are shown in Exhibit 11.1.

Conspicuousness, however, is not a fixed characteristic of products, but rather one that depends largely on the circumstances and ways in which they are used. One study found that group influence on brand choice was important when beer was served to friends but not when it was consumed privately.[57]

Other studies have addressed the issue of changes in reference group influence as products proceed through the phases of their life cycle.[58] In the introduction stage, others around us strongly influence our initial decision to buy the product; brand choice, however, is less influenced by others. In the growth stage, group influence on both product and brand choice becomes strong. In the maturity stage, influence on product choice weakens, but the brand is strongly influenced by others. In the decline stage, group influence on both product and brand choices practically ceases to exist. Exhibit 11.2 depicts the occurrence of reference group influence over the stages of the product life cycle.

Reference Group Influence on Public–Private, Luxury–Necessity Purchase Decisions

EXHIBIT 11.1

Source: Adaped from W. O. Bearden And M. J. Etzel, "Reference Group Influence On Product And Brand Purchase Decisions," *Journal Of Consumer Research* (September 1982), p. 185.

Public

Public Necessities	Public Luxuries
Example: clothing	Examples: jewelry and furs
Reference group influence:	Reference group influence:
Product −	Product +
Brand +	Brand +

Necessity ——————————————————— Luxury

Private Necessities	Private Luxuries
Example: electric blanket	Example: interactive home entertainment center
Reference group influence:	Reference group influence:
Product −	Product +
Brand −	Brand −

Private

(+) = Strong reference group influence
(−) = Weak reference group influence

EXHIBIT 11.2   **Reference Group Influence During Product Life Cycle**

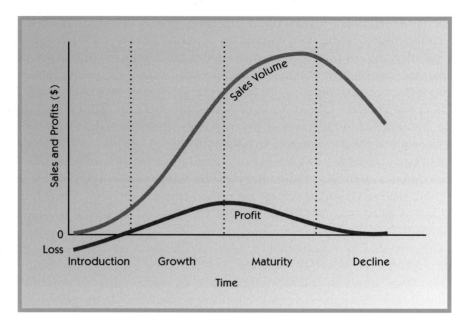

- **Introduction stage:** Group influence is mostly on the product. For instance, the launch of the very first generation of cell phones represents this situation.

- **Growth stage:** Group influence is on both the product and the brand choice. This situation is exemplified by the market condition that existed when growth of competition in the cell phone industry occurred after a successful launch.

- **Maturity stage:** Group influence is mostly on brand choice. This situation is represented by the current condition of the cell phone market, as technology constantly brings about new features in order to revitalize industry sales.

- **Decline stage:** Group influence ceases for both product and brand. As far as the future demand for cell phones as we now know them, this situation remains to be seen.

REFERENCE GROUP INFLUENCE AND MARKETING STRATEGY

Marketers who intend to employ reference group influence as part of their strategy must realize that consumers have multiple reference groups. Different groups are known to influence different types of people and different purchase decisions. Individuals may look to reference groups in their community, on the Internet, at work, at school, and at the gym. They may look to a neighbor for recommendations regarding lawn-care products, to a business colleague for advice concerning their car, and to a virtual community on the Web for ideas about sporting apparel or equipment.

It follows that marketers who employ group influence as part of their strategy face multiple tasks. First, they must determine the types of groups that various kinds of people are likely to refer to when making decisions about the specific product class. Having identified the groups that are truly germane to the purchasing situation, marketers are in a position to choose pertinent emissaries to deliver their messages and plan their campaign strategy.[59]

The topic of group influence has a number of implications for business disciplines other than marketing. Relevant issues might include

- **Strategy/Investment:** One form of group influence is seen vividly in the practice of collecting as a hobby. The collected objects can be pieces of art, antique furniture or cars, jewelry, stones, butterflies, dolls, sports paraphernalia, clocks, or myriad other items. Stamp collecting, one form of this passion, is known as philately. Philately is a popular and widespread hobby among millions of people throughout the world. It is estimated that in the United States today, 30 million people hunt for their coveted stamps and feel elated whenever they find a rare stamp for their collection.

  A stamp can cost from a penny to thousands of dollars. Philately is an immense business, involving sales of millions of dollars annually. Philately, as such, is a large revenue producer for postal services as well as for many governments. The U.S. Postal Service, for example, sells hundreds of millions of dollars' worth of stamps every year to collectors. Realizing this business opportunity, the U.S. Postal Service set out to increase its revenues in October 1996 by launching an innovative program known as Stampers. The program is designed to introduce a new generation to the hobby of collecting stamps. Stampers offers youngsters an opportunity to enter the USPS program without charge by calling (888) STAMPFUN. As members, they receive free mailings that include magazines, posters, and educational items designed to help kids start their stamp collection.

- **Rituals/Fraternal Organizations:** Freemasonry is a fraternal organization that arose from the stone masons' guilds during the Middle Ages. The language

and symbols used in the fraternity's rituals date back to this era. Freemasonry is an organization of individuals based on the "fatherhood of God and the brotherhood of man," using builders' tools as symbols to teach basic moral truth. Membership in the fraternity is about 5 million worldwide, with an estimated 3.5 million members located in the United States. Past members include historic figures such as George Washington, Benjamin Franklin, Paul Revere, and Joseph Warren. Only recently has membership been opened to women. Masons are known for their social and charitable activities, which range from operating children's hospitals and funding medical research to engaging in local community service projects.

- **Politics:** Group political views and biases are influential in shaping the public's political opinions and party evaluations. For example, in our political party system, the stand of a party on issues considered important by an individual can have a significant effect on that person's evaluation of the party and on his or her inclination to support or oppose it.

  Not only does perception of a party influence an individual's political inclination, but it is also instrumental in shaping how that person evaluates other people affiliated with the opposite political party. Clearly, these evaluations have a bearing on the extent of support or opposition the individual is likely to display toward candidates running for public office during election campaigns.

These issues, and a host of others like them, serve to show that the topic of group influence transcends the field of marketing to other business disciplines.

Groups influence many aspects of our lives. We use groups as reference points against which we measure our own behavior or accomplishments. Groups also influence our consumption behavior as we tend to emulate the consumption behavior of others. Similarly, views and opinions of groups around us significantly affect how we feel about the issues and occurrences in our environment.

Group membership and participation often yield tangible as well as psychological benefits. Such is the case with the family group. The family is an extremely influential social group that dramatically shapes our beliefs, views, behavior, and consumption patterns due to the close contact and the length of time we spend with this social group. The family as well as significant age groups are the topics covered in the next chapter.

Summary

Groups are defined as two or more individuals who share a set of norms, values, or beliefs; have certain role relationships; and experience interdependent behavior. True groups display regular contact; cooperatively interact with one another; and share a common goal, common norms, and a sense of belonging. The real significance of groups rests with their role in socialization. Through the processes of modeling, reinforcement, and social interaction, individuals are indoctrinated with group norms and values.

Groups can be classified as primary or secondary, and formal or informal. Members occupy specific roles, which are valid only within the context of the group. Role-related product clusters are sets of goods necessary to play a given role competently. Some group members may experience role overload, role conflict, and role ambiguity. Members hold a specific status within the group. Conspicuous consumption entails the use of goods as status symbols.

There are five types of social power: reward, coercive, legitimate, referent, and expert power. Conformity expresses the change in individuals' beliefs, attitudes, and behavior as a result of real or imagined group pressure. Social comparisons provide a yardstick by which individuals can ascertain what constitutes proper behavior.

Reference groups are sets of people that provide individuals with a perspective for evaluating or patterning their own beliefs, values, attitudes, or actions. Reference groups exert normative, informational, or comparative influence on individuals. Reference groups can be classified as membership, aspirational, and dissociative types. The degree of reference group influence can be classified as compliance, identification, and internalization.

Reference groups can influence consumers' product or brand choices. A fourfold product classification (publicly versus privately consumed, luxury versus necessity) explains whether or not reference groups impact product or brand choices.

Marketers who employ group influence as part of their strategy must identify the groups that are looked to by their target consumers, determine the nature and degree of influence these groups exert, and select effectual representatives of influential groups to deliver their messages.

Review Questions

1. Modeling, reinforcement, and social interaction are cited as components of the group socialization process. Explain the process of socialization in terms of its three components.

2. The roles that individuals occupy in groups determine group expectations of them as well as their rights and responsibilities. How do roles influence consumption behavior? Give specific examples.

3. Choose two types of social power covered in this chapter and show through specific examples how marketers use these types of power to influence consumer behavior.

4. Reference groups are classified into three major categories as membership, aspirational, and dissociative types. Explain each briefly, emphasizing in each case the type of effect it has on an individual.

5. Degrees of reference group influence vary from weak to strong. They range from compliance to identification and even to internalization. Explain each case and speculate about the circumstances under which each type of influence would occur.

Discussion Questions

1. In an effort to get people to contribute money to charity, many charitable organizations send mailers to potential donors that contain a free gift. Items such as a set of greeting cards, address labels, or a holiday ornament are mailed to prospects along with an urgent plea to contribute. The objective of these campaigns is to make recipients feel guilty if they were to keep the gifts without making a donation to the charity. In your opinion, do such tactics work? What type of social power is being used when such methods are employed?

2. Buy American campaigns, utilized by many retailers (e.g., Wal-Mart) are intended to enhance public perceptions of the store, promote patronage, and increase the sales support for American-made products. Recognizing that the majority of so-called American-made products are assembled in the United States from parts and components manufactured abroad, how effective and how ethical are such claims and appeals? To be ethical, should the American-made label be restricted to products made totally in the United States?

3. Excessive violence on television has been the subject of ongoing criticism by many concerned parties. It is believed that observing violent scenes on TV encourages imitation and sets a bad example for youth to follow. In defense of such scenes, some network officials contend that savage depictions repel viewers and implant a desire to stop violence and abuse. Which view do you support and why?

Cross-Functional Debate

In reference to the chapter opening vignette, compare the organizational structures of three different types of groups: the military, a large corporation, and a street gang. In making your comparison, consider the following criteria:

1. Is the organizational structure flat or multitiered with many intermediate levels?
2. Are the patterns of authority and responsibility formally defined?
3. Does the flow of information within the organization necessarily follow the specified routes?
4. How do systems of rewards and punishments operate?
5. Does planning originate from the top or from the bottom of the organization?
6. What roles do formal and informal leaders play in each type of group?
7. How are conflicts resolved in each type of organization?
8. In your opinion, which—if any—of these organizational structures most effectively and efficiently realizes the group's objectives?

Teen Peer Pressure

The last history class of the day for Spencer, a junior at an urban high school in Dallas, Texas, was about to end. He looked at his watch as he prepared to leave the class to meet with Mr. Rambush, the school's principal, and Ms. Kurzan, the student counselor. Two other students—Shaunte, a sophomore, and Maria, a senior—were also attending the same meeting. The three students had agreed to talk to school officials, who were increasingly getting concerned about the problems of violence, drug abuse, and increased sexual activity that were taking place on campus. These problems had become major concerns for many parents. As a result, school officials thought that perhaps talking to students about the possible causes of these problems might provide clues regarding how to deal with them.

As the three students, along with Mr. Rambush and Ms. Kurzan, sat down around a small table in the principal's office, Mr. Rambush started the meeting by thanking the students for their willingness to talk about these important issues and assured them of the confidentiality of their conversation. After this brief introduction, he proceeded by saying, "We feel that the school campus is no longer a safe haven for many of our students. Parents tell us that they are concerned about the safety of their children here. The increased violence, sexual activity, and drug abuse that we have all witnessed here scares everyone," he added. "Parents don't know what to do about it. We too feel responsible to some extent." Then, in a desperate tone, Mr. Rambush added, "If we only knew where the problem lies, perhaps we could do something about it. But until then, our hands are tied..." He then paused to allow the students to speak.

"Well, I think peer pressure has a lot to do with many of these problems," said Spencer. "You've got to be aware of your surroundings and have your head clear. That's why I'm playing baseball...to stay off the streets," he added.

Nodding her head in approval, Maria supported Spencer's comments saying, "To me, this is a whole different generation. I think that's why we have a harder time than our parents when they were in high school," she added. "Generations change and people change...sex and drugs...that's pressure for us. Your boyfriend is pressuring you to have sex...your friends want you to share drugs...and you see everyone else is doing it. If you are part of a group...what're you going to say?" she asked. "Saying 'no' isn't that easy. Besides, no one would want to be with you if you always said 'no,'" she claimed.

Shaunte, who had been listening quietly to the conversation up to this point, joined in, "You know...it's like in this whole world, everyone thinks violence now," she commented. "It's dangerous out there...you may not be able to go to the next street without fear for your life. That's why I feel the need to do everything *now*...I may not be here tomorrow. My philosophy?...Enjoy life with your friends...even if it's dangerous."

Listening carefully to the students' comments and taking notes, Ms. Kurzan joined the discussion at this point. "I have a child eleven years old. I try to tell him that if someone asks him to do something that's wrong, he should just say 'no' or get up and leave...but I see you don't think this is an easy way to avoid trouble," she said.

In a somewhat sarcastic tone, Shaunte responded to her comment and said, "You parents don't recognize how serious peer pressure is. You think of your kids as little darlings who will always do the right thing. I can assure you...this isn't the way it is in real life. You have to see your kid in a group situation...then you'll understand," she said.

As the meeting went on for another couple of hours, it became evident to the school administrators that peer pressure plays a significant role in bringing about a major part of these problems to the school environment.

When the students had left his office, Mr. Rambush and Ms. Kurzan commenced to consider alternatives that could help tackle these issues. Ms. Kurzan suggested looking into a corrective program based on peer pressure she had read about in the newspaper the previous week. Developed by a school in Kilgore, Texas, the program was designed to maintain a drug-free school environment. The Kilgore group is a student-run program that relies mostly on peer pressure to keep its members off drugs. Perks include recognition from the school and community, discounts at local business, and other privileges. Students who join the Kilgore group pledge to remain drug free. They are subjected to initial drug testing and then random future testing. The results of these tests are handled in such a way that the identities of the test subjects are known only to other students, but not to the students' parents.

As Mr. Rambush contemplated this possibility, he recognized that initiating this program at his school would require a lot more than the school's commitment to adopt it. Community support, he thought, would be vitally needed for such a program to bear fruit.

Questions

1. What factors underlie the strength of peer pressure as a type of influence? Why is it difficult for most people to go against group mandates?
2. Do you agree with the claim that today it is peer pressure that underlies most of teens' devious behavior? Support your answer.
3. Do you feel that corrective programs such as the one developed by the school in Kilgore Texas, would be effective in alleviating the drug problem in schools? Why or why not?

Notes

1. Andrew Martin, "Street Gang Membership Often Comes with Instructions," *Chicago Tribune* (May 13, 1995), pp. 1, 6; *Rolling Stone* (December 1, 1994), pp. 108-14.
2. D. Cartwright and A. Zander, *Group Dynamics* (New York: Harper & Row, 1968).
3. R. E. Goldsmith, J. R. Hietmeyer, and J. B. Freiden, "Social Values and Fashion Leadership," *Clothing and Textile Research Journal* 10, no. 1 (Fall 1991), pp. 37-45.
4. George Moschis, *Consumer Socialization: A Life-Cycle Perspective* (Lexington MA: Lexington Books, 1987); and Scott Ward, "Consumer Socialization," *Journal of Consumer Research* 1 (September 1974), pp. 1-14.
5. "What Is the Value of Participating in an Online Community?" *Full Circle Associates* (December 2000), www.fullcirc.com/community/whyparticipate online.htm; Robin B. Hamman, "Cybersex Amongst Multiple Selves and Cyborgs in the Narrow-Bandwidths Space of America Online Chatrooms," www. greenlloyd.com/bodyincyberspace.htm; Julian Dibbell, "Where Do We Actually Go When We Go Somewhere in Cyberspace?" www.greenlloyd.com/ bodyincyberspace.htm; Sue Boetcher, et. al., "What Is a Virtual Community and Why Would You Ever Need One?" *Full Circle Associates* (January 2002), www. fullcirc.com/community/communitywhatwhy.htm
6. Nancy White, "Community Member Roles and Types," *Full Circle Associates*, (January 12, 2001), www.fullcirc.com/community/memberroles.htm.
7. K. R. Evans, T. Christiansen, and J. D. Gill, "The Impact of Social Influence and Role Expectations on Shopping Center Patronage Intentions," *Journal of the Academy of Marketing Science* (Summer 1996), pp. 208-18.
8. Michael Reilly, "Working Wives and Convenience Consumption," *Journal of Consumer Research* 8 (March 1982), pp. 407-18; and A. C. Burns and E. R. Foxman, "Some Determinants of the Use of Advertising by Married Working Women," *Journal of Advertising Research* (November 1989), pp. 57-63.
9. R. G. Netemeyer, M. W. Johnston, and S. Burton, "Analysis of Role Conflict and Role Ambiguity in a Structural Equations Framework," *Journal of Applied Psychology* 75 (1990), pp. 148-57; C. J. Thompson, "Caring Consumers," Journal of Consumer Research (March 1996), pp. 398-99.

10. M. Solomon and O. Anand, "Ritual Costumes and Status Transition," in E. Hirschman and M. Holbrook (eds.), *Advances in Consumer Research 12* (Provo, UT: Association for Consumer Research, 1985), pp. 315–18; A. Andreasen, "Life Status Changes and Changes in Consumer Preferences and Satisfaction," *Journal of Consumer Research* (December 1984), pp. 784–94; and J. McAlexander, "Divorce, the Disposition of the Relationship and Everything", J. Schouten, "Personal Rites of Passage and the Reconstruction of Self; M. Young, "Disposition of Possessions During Role Transitions"; and S. Roberts, "Consumption Responses to Involuntary Job Loss"; all in R. H. Holman and M. Solomon (eds.), *Advances in Consumer Research 18* (Provo UT: Association for Consumer Research, 1991), pp. 33–51.

11. Kathleen M. Rassuli and Gilbert D. Harrell, "Group Differences in the Construction of Consumption Sets," in Kim P. Corfman and John G. Lynch (eds.), *Advances in Consumer Research 23* (Provo, UT: Association for Consumer Research, 1996), pp. 446–53

12. M. R. Solomon and B. Buchanan, "A Role-Theoretic Approach to Product Symbolism," *Journal of Business Research* (March 1991), pp. 95–109; Rassuli and Harrell, "Group Differences in the Construction of Consumption Sets."

13. James H. Leigh and Terrance G. Gabel, "Symbolic Interactionism: Its Effects on Consumer Behavior and Implications for Marketing Strategy," *The Journal of Consumer Marketing 9*, no. 1 (Winter 1992), pp. 27–38; Dong H. Lee, "Symbolic Interactionism: Some Implications for Consumer Self-Concept and Product Symbolism Research," in M. E. Goldberg et al. (eds.), *Advances in Consumer Research 17* (Provo, UT: Association for Consumer Research, 1990), pp. 386–93; Marsha L. Richins, "Social Comparison and the Idealized Images of Advertising," *Journal of Consumer Research 18*, no. 1 (June 1991), pp. 71–93; Irfan Ahmed, "The Role of Status in Service Interactions," *AMA Winter Educators' Proceedings 3* (1992), pp. 142–43; Elizabeth C. Hirschman, "Cocaine as Innovation: A Social-Symbolic Account," in John F. Sherry and Brian Sternthal (eds.), *Advances in Consumer Research 19* (Provo UT: Association for Consumer Research, 1992), pp. 129–39; and Eva M. Hyatt, "Consumer Stereotyping: The Cognitive Bases of the Social Symbolism of Products," *Advances in Consumer Research 19* (1992), pp. 299–303.

14. C. R. Snyder and H. L. Fromkin, Uniqueness: *The Human Pursuit of Difference* (New York: Plenum Press, 1980).

15. Scott Dawson and Jill Cavell, "Status Recognition in the 1980s: Invidious Distinction Revisited," in Melanie Wallendorf and Paul Anderson (eds.), *Advances in Consumer Research 14* (Provo UT: Association for Consumer Research, 1986), pp. 487–91; William H. Form and Gregory P. Stone, "Urbanism, Anonymity, and Status Symbolism," *American Journal of Sociology 62* (1957), pp. 504–14.

16. Michelle Osborn, "Conspicuous Consumption is Déclassé," *USA Today* (November 29, 1991), pp. 1A–2A.

17. John Brooks, *Showing Off in America* (Boston: Little, Brown, 1981), p. 13.

18. Howard Schlossberg, "Conspicuous Consumption Is a Thing of the Past for 'Relaxed' Consumers, "*Marketing News* (January 4, 1993), pp. 7, 16.

19. J. R. P. French Jr. and B. Raven, "The Bases of Social Power," in D. Cartwright (ed.), *Studies in Social Power* (Ann Arbor MI: Institute for Social Research, 1959), pp. 150–67.

20. A. Gaviria and S. Raphael. "School-Based Peer Effect and Juvenile Behavior," *The Review of Economics and Statistics 83*, no. 2 (2001), pp. 257–268.

21. Ellen Graham, "Tupperware Parties Create a New Breed of Super-Saleswoman," *Wall Street Journal* (May 21, 1971), pp. 1, 18; Flavia Krone and Denise Smart, "An Exploratory Study Profiling the Party-Plan Shopper," in Robert H. Ross, Frederick B. Kraft, and Charles H. Davis (eds.), 1981 *Proceedings, Southwestern Marketing Association*, Wichita State University (1981), pp. 200–203; Manli Ho, "Peddling Naughty Lingerie . . . in Suburban Livingrooms," *Boston Globe* (March 2, 1976); and J. K. Frenzen and H. L. Davis, "Purchasing Behavior in Embedded Markets," *Journal of Consumer Research* (June 1990), pp. 1–12.

22. Jim Mateja and Rick Topely, "Made in America? Hard to Tell," *Chicago Tribune* (September 24, 2006).

23. Kelsey Mays, "The Cars.com American-made Index," *cars.com* (December 28, 2007), www.cars.com/go/advice/Story.jsp?section=top&subject=ami&story=amMade1207.

24. Cathy Pearson and Mary Dellmann-Jenkins, "Parental Influence on a Student's Selection of a College Major," *College Student Journal* (September 1997), pp. 301–13.

25. Kevin Goldman, "Year's Top Commercials Propelled by Star Power," *Wall Street Journal* (March 16, 1994), p. B1.

26. J. Agrawal and W. A. Kamakura, "The Economic Worth of Celebrity Endorsers," *Journal of Marketing* (July 1995), pp. 56–62.

27. M. A. Kamins, "An Investigation into the 'Match-up' Hypothesis in Celebrity Advertising," *Journal of Advertising* no. 1, (1990), pp. 4–13; S. Misra and S. E. Beatty, "Celebrity Spokesperson and Brand Congruence," *Journal of Business Research* (September 1990), pp. 159–73; J. Lynch and D. Schuler, "The Matchup Effect of Spokesperson and Product Congruency," Psychology & Marketing (September 1993), pp. 417–45; and M. A. Kamins and K. Gupta,

"Congruence Between Spokesperson and Product Type," *Psychology & Marketing* (November 1994), pp. 569-86; C. Tripp, T. D. Jensen, and L. Carlson, "The Effects of Multiple Product Endorsements by Celebrities on Consumers' Attitudes and Intentions," *Journal of Consumer Research* (March 1994), pp. 535-47; M. F. Callcott and W. N. Lee, "Establishing the Spokes-Character in Academic Inquiry," in F. R. Kardes and M. Sujan (eds.), *Advances in Consumer Research, 22* (Provo, UT: Association for Consumer Research, 1995), pp. 144-51.

28. Tara Parker-Pope, "Why the Veterinarian Really Recommends That 'Designer' Chow: Colgate Gives Doctors Treats for Plugging Its Brands, and Sees Sales Surge," *Wall Street Journal Eastern Edition* (November 3, 1997), p. A11.

29. Arnold Birenbaum and Edward Sagarin, *Norms and Human Behavior* (New York: Praeger, 1976).

30. Danielle E. Warren, "Constructive and Distructive Deviance in Organizations," *Academy of Management Review* 28, no. 4 (October 2003), pp. 622-633.

31. William O. Bearden and Randall L. Rose, "Attention to Social Comparison Information: An Individual Difference Factor Affecting Consumer Conformity," *Journal of Consumer Research* 16 (March 1990), pp. 461-71; Marsha L. Richins, "Social Comparison and the Idealized Images of Advertising," *Journal of Consumer Research* 18 (June 1991), pp. 71-83; Terry Bristol and Edward F. Fern, "Using Qualitative Techniques to Explore Consumer Attitudes: Insights from Group Process Theories," in Leigh McAlister and Michael L. Rothschild (eds.), *Advances in Consumer Research* 20 (Provo, UT: Association for Consumer Research, 1993), pp. 444-48.

32. William O. Bearden, Richard G. Netemeyer, and Jesse E. Teel, "Measurement of Consumer Susceptibility to Interpersonal Influence," *Journal of Consumer Research* 15 (March 1989), pp. 473-81.

33. Heather Green, "It Takes a Web Village," *Business Week* (September 4, 2006), p. 66.

34. Terry L. Childers and Akshay R. Rao, "The Influence of Familial and Peer-Based Reference Groups on Consumer Decisions," *Journal of Consumer Research* 19 (September 1992), pp. 198-211; William O. Bearden and Michael J. Etzel, "Reference Group Influences on Product and Brand Purchase Decisions," *Journal of Consumer Research* 9 (September 1982), pp. 183-94; C. Webster and J. B. Faircloth III, "The Role of Hispanic Ethnic Identification on Reference Group Influence," in C. T. Allen and D. R. John (eds.), *Advances in Consumer Research* 21 (Provo, UT: Association for Consumer Research, 1994), pp. 458-63.

35. Bearden, Netemeyer, and Teel, "Measurement of Consumer Susceptibility to Interpersonal Influence"; W. O. Bearden, R. G. Netemeyer, and J. E. Teel, "Further Validations of the Consumer Susceptibility to Influence Scale," in M. E. Goldberg et al. (eds.), *Advances in Consumer Research* 17 (Provo, UT: Association for Consumer Research, 1990), pp. 770-76; O. A. J. Mascarenhas and M. A. Higby, "Peer, Parent, and Media Influences in Teen Apparel Shopping," *Journal of the Academy of Marketing Science* (Winter 1993), pp. 53-58.

36. Childers and Rao, "The Influence of Familial and Peer-Based Reference Groups on Consumer Decisions."

37. R. C. Becherer, W. F. Morgan, and L. M. Richard, "Informal Group Influence among Situationally/Dispositionally Oriented Customers," *Journal of the Academy of Marketing Science* (Summer 1982), pp. 269-81; W. O. Bearden and R. L. Rose, "Attention to Social Comparison Information: An Individual Difference Factor Affecting Consumer Conformity"; D. N. Lascu, W. O. Bearden, and R. L. Rose, "Norm Extreme and Interpersonal Influences on Consumer Conformity," *Journal of Business Research* (March 1995), pp. 201-13; L. R. Kahle, "Role-Relaxed Consumers," *Journal of Advertising Research* (May 1995), pp. 59-62; B. G. Englis and M. R. Solomon, "To Be and Not to Be," *Journal of Advertising* (Spring 1995), pp. 13-28; see also P. Choong and K. R. Lord, "Experts and Novices and Their Use of Reference Groups," *Enhancing Knowledge Development in Marketing* (Chicago, IL: American Marketing Association, 1996), pp. 203-8.

38. Jay C. Wode and Charles J. Gelso, "Reference Group Identity Dependence Scales: A Measure of Male Identity, Male Reference Group Identity Dependence," *The Counseling Psychologist* 26, no. 3 (1998), pp. 384-411.

39. Leon Festinger, "A Theory of Social Comparison Processes," *Human Relations* 7 (May 1954), pp. 117-40; George P. Moschis, Social Comparison and Informal Group Influence," *Journal of Marketing Research* 13 (August 1976), pp. 237-44; Robert E. Burnkrant and Alain Cousineau, "Informational and Normative Social Influence in Buyer Behavior," *Journal of Consumer Research* 2 (December 1975), pp. 206-15; M. Venkatesan, "Experimental Study of Consumer Behavior Conformity and Independence," *Journal of Marketing Research* 3 (November 1966), pp. 384-87; Childers and Rao, "The Influence of Familial and Peer-Based Reference Groups on Consumer Decisions"; M. Deutsch and Harold B. Gerard, "A Study of Normative and Informational Social Influences upon Individual Judgment," *Journal of Abnormal and Social Psychology* 51 (1955), pp. 624-36.

40. Chester A. Insko, Sarah Drenan, Michael R. Solomon, Richard Smith, and Terry J. Wade, "Conformity as a Function of the Consistency of Positive

Self-Evaluation with Being Liked and Being Right," *Journal of Experimental Social Psychology* 19 (1983), pp. 341–58.

41. Childers and Rao, "The Influence of Familial and Peer-Based Reference Groups on Consumer Decisions"; Bearden and Etzel "Reference Group Influence on Product and Brand Purchase Decisions."

42. Englis and Solomon, "To Be *and* Not to Be."

43. Vanessa Fox, "Super Tuesday, Internet Style: How We're Using the Web in the 2008 Elections," *Search Engine Land* (February 5, 2008), http://searchengineland.com/080205-190713.php; Merlyna Lim and Mark E. Kann, "Politics: Democratic Deliberation and Mobilization on the Internet," *Networked Publics*, http://networkedpublics.org/book/politics; Jake Tapper, "Clinton Launches Obama Attack Websites," *abcnews* (December 20, 2007), http://abcnews.go.com/print?id=4032659.

44. Herbert C. Kelman, "Processes of Opinion Change," *The Public Opinion Quarterly* 25, no. 1 (Spring 1961), pp. 57–78; Herbert C. Kelman, "Compliance, Identification, and Internalization: Three Processes of Attitude Change," *Journal of Conflict Resolution* 2, no. 1 (1958), pp. 51–60.

45. Jennifer D. Campbell and Patricia J. Fairey, "Informational and Normative Routes to Conformity: The Effect of Faction Size as a Function of Norm Extremity and Attention to the Stimulus," *Journal of Personality and Social Psychology* 57 (March 1989), pp. 457–68; Barbara C. Perdue and John O. Summers, "Checking the Success of Manipulations in Marketing Experiments," *Journal of Marketing Research* 23, (April 1986), pp. 317–26.

46. Lascu, Bearden, and Rose, "Norm Extreme and Interpersonal Influences on Consumer Confomity"; P. F. Bone, "Word-of-Mouth Effects on Short-Term Product Judgments," *Journal of Business Research* (March 1995), pp. 213–23.

47. R. D. Ashmore, V. Ramchandra, and R. Jones, "Censorship as an Attitude Change Induction," a paper presented at meetings of the Eastern Psychological Association, New York (1971); R. A. Wicklund and J. Brehm, *Perspectives on Cognitive Dissonance* (Hillsdale, NJ: Lawrence Erlbaum, 1976); see also Michael B. Mazis, Robert B. Settle, and D. C. Leslie, "Elimination of Phosphate Detergents and Psychological Reactance," *Journal of Marketing Research* 10 (1973), pp. 390–95; Snyder and Fromkin, Uniqueness: *The Human Pursuit of Difference.*

48. Greg J. Lessne and Elaine M. Notarantonio, "The Effect of Limits in Retail Advertisements: A Reactance Theory Perspective," *Psychology and Marketing* 5, no. 1 (1988), pp. 33–44.

49. Aida Hurtado, Patricia Gurin, and Timothy Peng, "Social Identities—a Framework for studying the Adaptations of Immigrants and Ethnics: The Adaptation of Mexicans in the United States," *Social Problems* 41(1994), p. 129.

50. Judith Waldrop, "Plastic Wars," *American Demographics* (November 1988), p. 6.

51. P. Rajan Varadarajan and Anil Menon, "Cause Related Marketing: A Coalignment of Marketing Strategy and Corporate Philanthropy," *Journal of Marketing* 52 (July 1988), pp. 58–74; Scott M. Smith and David S. Alcorn, "Cause Marketing: A New Direction in the Marketing of Corporate Responsibility," *Journal of Services Marketing* 5, no. 4 (Fall 1991), pp. 21–37.

52. Terry Lefton, "Discovery Channel's Credit Card Includes Animal Protection Hook," *Brandweek* 39, no. 26 (June 29, 1998), p. 12.

53. "Popular, Personalized Credit Cards Losing Punch in Saturated Markets," *The Clarion Ledger Business* (December 23, 2002).

54. "Co-banded and Affinity Credit Cards in the US," *the-infoshop.com* (May 2007), www.the-infoshop.com/study/pf51662-co-branded.html.

55. Donald W. Hendon, "A New Empirical Look at the Influence of Reference Groups on Generic Product Category and Brand Choice: Evidence from Two Nations," in *Proceedings of the Academy of International Business: Asia-Pacific Dimension of International Business* (Honolulu, Hawaii: College of Business Administration, University of Hawaii, December 18–20, 1979), p. 757; Robert T. Green, Joel G. Saegert, and Robert J. Hoover, "Conformity in Consumer Behavior: A Cross-National Replication," in Neil Beckwith et al. (eds.), *1979 Educator's Conference Proceedings* (Chicago, IL: American Marketing Association, 1979), pp. 192–94; Lyman O. Ostlund, "Role Theory and Group Dynamics," in Scott Ward and Thomas S. Robertson (eds.), *Consumer Behavior: Theoretical Sources* (Upper Saddle River, NJ: Prentice Hall, 1973), p. 245; Harold H. Kassarjian, "Riesman Revisited," *Journal of Marketing* 29 (April 1965), pp. 54–56, and Richard W. Mizerski and Robert B. Settle, "The Influence of Social Character on Preference for Social Versus Objective Information in Advertising," *Journal of Marketing Research* 16 (November 1979), pp. 552–58.

56. Bearden and Etzel, "Reference Group Influence on Product and Brand Purchase Decisions", see also Childers and Rao, "The Influence of Familial and Peer-Based Reference Groups on Consumer Decisions."

57. Paul W. Miniard and Joel E. Cohen, "Modeling Personal and Normative Influences on Behavior," *Journal of Consumer Research* 10 (September 1983), pp. 169–80.

58. Philip Kotler, *Marketing Management*, 8th ed. (Upper Saddle River, NJ: Prentice Hall, 1994), p. 178.

The Family and Generational Cohorts

LEARNING OBJECTIVES

- To ascertain the role of the family in the process of consumer socialization.
- To become cognizant of family consumption roles.
- To explore the dynamics of the family decision-making process.
- To learn how children influence the process of family decision making.
- To examine the issue of advertising to children.
- To understand the concept of the family life cycle.
- To review nontraditional living arrangement patterns prevalent in contemporary society.
- To comprehend the concept of generational cohorts and its implications for market segmentation.

KEY TERMS

family	cohort
enacted role	Postwar cohort
perceived role	Boomers I cohort
prescribed role	Boomers II cohort
family life cycle	Generation X cohort
latchkey kids	Generation Y cohort
boomerang children	Generation Z cohort
sandwich generation	Techno-savvies
generational marketing	

The roles of men and women in the family and in society have changed drastically over the last few decades. Traditional households headed by male wage earners have waned, giving way to a variety of living arrangements that combine single-person households to cohabitating couples to families of mixed races.

One of the most notable trends in this social evolution has been the rise of what has been termed the "unmarriage revolution," which is the decoupling of formal man/woman legal ties. Statistics indicate that more than 100 million unmarried people now reside in the United States, many of whom are professional women who have chosen not to marry or who have decided to spend a longer portion of their lives as unmarried individuals. They are mostly upwardly mobile women who have accomplished status in boardrooms and who have been buying their own homes and funding their own retirement. They reject the notion that what is "normal" and standard is a household composed of a married man and woman and their kids. Marriage to them is an option. It may happen only if the right partner comes along. They are free to choose relationships that best complement their personal values and needs.

A notable social trend is the "unmarriage revolution," which includes many women who see marriage as one of many options.

© 2009, Galina Barskaya, Shutterstock, Inc.

However, even though many of these women question the necessity for marriage, their desire for having children is nevertheless uncompromised. Just like married women who set out to become pregnant, they too long for kids. Motherhood, they feel, would give them the sense of empowerment and self worth they yearn for.

Fortunately today, technology in the form of sperm banks provided the answer for these single women to fulfill their dreams of having a dad-free family. The California Cryobank, the country's largest sperm bank, estimates that about 40 percent of its customers are single women. The sophisticated marketing of these sperm banks appeals to such women who pay handsomely to procure the bank's services, particularly since technology has made pregnancies safer and fertilizations more likely to succeed. For example, clinics such as Genetics & IVF Institute in Virginia now boast a 70 to 90 percent pregnancy success rate.

As married couples become a minority of all American households, both government and business employers will be forced to reshape their workplace policies, including ways of distributing benefits to various forms of contemporary "family" groups.[1]

Sperm banks around the United States report that demand from single women has been increasing steadily in the past few years. Visit the Web site of Single Mom.com. at www.Singlemom.com/Resources/Children_Resources/Adoption_infertility.HTM *to learn more about the services available to women who desire to create families outside of the traditional means. Does this trend reflect a modern era of re-lationships or does it pinpoint the lack of one? How do you feel about commercializing and tampering with natural reproductive functions? Explain.*

The success story of sperm banks is based on their ability to fulfil a vital human need—the desire of women to have children and raise a family in the absence of a traditional father figure.

This chapter deals with the family and significant age groups. The first half addresses consumer socialization, family consumption roles and decision processes, the family life cycle, and recent household trends. The second half covers generational marketing, or market segmentation by life experiences.

The Family

The mere mention of the word *family* conjures up a host of images ranging from warmth, love, sharing, and caring to instances where neglect and physical abuse may prevail. Whichever is the case, the family context of interpersonal communication is believed to have the greatest influence on consumer socialization.

The Census Bureau defines **family** as "two or more persons, related either through birth, marriage, or adoption, living under one roof." This definition gives rise to the conventional image of family consisting of a mother, father, and two children. However, the reality may be quite different. Contemporary families come in different forms and sizes. These include traditional families, stepfamilies, blended families, single-parent households, childless couples, and extended families, as well as other possibilities. Thus, the definition of family has become almost personal, taking in those to whom we are connected in a fundamental way.

> **family**
> two or more persons, related either through birth, marriage or adoption, living under one roof

Communication among family members plays a significant part in shaping a family's consumption behavior. Family influence emerges as a result of the frequency and impact of contact within the household. In this section, let us consider the forces that underlie this influence and observe how the roles played by various family members determine the extent of that influence.

CONSUMER SOCIALIZATION

As we have seen in chapter 11 on group influence, socialization is the process by which individuals develop, through interaction with others, specific patterns of socially relevant behavior and experience. Today's adolescents learn about the world in completely different ways than young adults of previous generations. Their socialization occurs within the confines of the technological revolution that has swept their lives and influenced their learning, recognition, and consumption behavior. Through online communities, virtual realities, text messaging, and the various electronic gadgets they possess, they are perpetually in touch with and affected by other people with whom they communicate.

Most children today have Internet and video game access; many also have a cell phone and iPod. The number of children joining social networking Web sites such as Facebook and MySpace is growing daily. Technological advance has enabled 'tweens to access the same content from different media, often from mobile ones, as well as surf the Internet through their cell phones.

The Entertainment Software Association revealed that nearly a third of Americans who are online are under 18 years of age. Similarly, the Pew Internet & American Life Project reports that 93 percent of teenagers are avid users of the Internet. These chip-driven gizmos that fill the modern life of adolescents have exposed the 'tweens to marketplace realities unknown to previous generations and have made them savvy consumers.

Parental influence is another important factor in the development of various dimensions of children's consumption patterns. A study by Moore and Moschis found that the family affects the development of adolescents' materialistic orientation.[2] A separate longitudinal study by the same researchers investigated the effects of the family on adolescents' consumption learning, in both the short and the long run. This study found that parent–child interaction has some long-run influence on development of brand preferences as well as on ability to distinguish facts from exaggerations in ads as the child reaches adolescence.[3]

In addition, many studies confirm the family's influence on the development of children's decision-making patterns. For example, a cross-sectional study of the development of an adolescent's decision-making process confirmed that parents are more likely to be influential at the information-seeking stage than at the product-evaluation stage.[4] However, the development of the child's consumer decision-making patterns appears to be based on certain parent and child characteristics such as age, social class, sex, and family characteristics.

As far as *age* is concerned, children generally attain greater family independence in decision making as they grow older, although the degree of independence varies with the product type. Further, once the children begin to earn money outside the family, they are less subject to parental control through manipulation of resources.

Independence in decision making can also be a function of *social class*. For example, middle-class children appear to attain less independence in purchasing as they grow older than do children in lower and upper social classes. This tendency is due to middle-class families' greater consciousness of the normative standards of their class and their subsequent greater desire to supervise their children's activities closely in an effort to socialize them into the class norms.[5]

As children grow older, they begin to acquire greater independence in purchase decisions, partially because of their age and partly due to earning their own money outside the family.

© 2009, Elena Elisseeva, Shutterstock, Inc.

Alternatively, this phenomenon may be attributed to the possibility that children from working classes need to work and earn money to support the family, thus attaining greater independence from their parents. Middle-class children, on the other hand, whose parents have long-range plans for them (such as attending college), are likely to display less independence because their parents are able to continue to exercise influence through control of resources.[6]

Sex of the child also affects parental influence on the child's consumption behavior. Studies show, for example, that female adolescents display a greater need for conformity to peer group norms. As a result, they have purchasing patterns that reflect greater family independence, particularly in purchasing products relevant to physical appearance such as health care products and clothing.[7]

Finally, *family characteristics* are also likely to affect parental influence on children. Aldous, for example, concluded that children of working mothers are likely to be socialized better or faster because they are often expected to take on more consumer responsibilities than children of nonworking mothers.[8]

Studies indicate that although the family plays an important role in consumer socialization of the young, parental influence is often casual and can hardly be characterized as premeditated or deliberate consumer training. Research reveals that parents often expect their children to learn through observation.[9] Parent–child discussions about consumption are most likely to take place when the child requests a product seen via advertising.

FAMILY CONSUMPTION ROLES

Each member of a family plays a role. This role specialization affects the decision-making process as well as what is or what is not purchased. In most purchase situations, it is individuals (rather than entire families) who buy products. A consumer analyst must be able to identify such role specialization because of its impact on how marketers should target their efforts and to whom, as well as on where products should be offered for sale. For example, wives and girlfriends purchase 70 percent of the fragrances and colognes used by men, 90 percent of all greeting cards are purchased by women, and it is usually parents who purchase school supplies for young children, not the children themselves.[10] This realization, even though logical, eluded Crayola, the maker of children's drawing and coloring instruments. At first, the company targeted only children with advertising shown on Saturday morning TV programs. Later, however, realizing that it is usually mothers who actually purchase the product, the company shifted a portion of its advertising to mothers by placing ads in women's magazines. Figure 12.1 is an example of an ad from Crayola directed toward parents of young children.

Family consumption involves at least eight definable, sometimes overlapping roles. These roles, described in Exhibit 12.1 on page 435, can be assumed by a husband, wife, or child, or they can be performed by more than one person.

The term *role* has at least three meanings. There is an **enacted role**, which is the actual overt behavior displayed by an individual in a particular situation. There is also a **perceived role**, what an individual interprets his or her obligations or behavioral patterns to be. There is also a **prescribed role**, which is the set of expectations held by others as to what modes of behavior should be displayed by an individual in a situation.[11] The concept of prescribed role is usually the most evident in family role structure, because culture prescribes what is appropriately masculine and feminine and who is responsible for what. However, recent trends show a blurred image of family role structure as a result of the social changes that are taking place in contemporary society. For example, the present generation of fathers is more involved in child care than ever before.

enacted role
the overt behavior displayed by an individual in a particular situation

perceived role
an individual's perceived obligations

prescribed role
the set of expectations held by others as to what modes of behavior should be displayed by an individual in a situation

Figure 12.1

Recognizing that adults are equally part of the decision process when buying art supplies for children, Crayola directs this ad to parents of young children.

A recent study by Nielsen Media Research reveals that women now represent 45 percent of the 9.2 million book buyers, 38 percent of the 7.2 million CD/video buyers, 24 percent of the 5.4 million buyers of computer hardware, and 53 percent of the 4.5 million online buyers of clothing. Women also purchase more than half of all new vehicles, and influence more than 80 percent of all new vehicle purchases.[13]

Family buying roles, in this sense, can affect every aspect of the marketing strategy for a product. Marketers need to be mindful of buying roles when they design products and packages, set prices, select distribution channels, choose media, and create advertising appeals.

1. *Influencers* are members of the family whose beliefs or opinions affect product purchase or selection. A child can influence the selection of a family pet.

2. *Gatekeepers* are members of the family who oversee and regulate the flow of information into the household. Parents may allow or disallow viewing of particular TV programs by their children.

3. *Deciders* are members of the family with the power or authority to make decisions concerning consumption behavior. One spouse may request the other to pick up a particular wine when he or she goes shopping.

4. *Buyers* are family members who act as purchasing agents, visiting the store or placing a phone or online order.

5. *Preparers* are family members who adapt, transform, assemble, modify, or otherwise ready a product so as to make it suitable for consumption by members of the household.

6. *Users* are family members who consume or use the product or service purchased or prepared. Users may or may not be the same parties who purchase and prepare the product.

7. *Maintainers* are family members who attend to the maintenance, service, repair, cleaning, and upkeep of products including, for example, appliances, automobiles, yard equipment, home furnishings, and electronic devices.

8. *Disposers* are family members who have the authority to determine when to discontinue the use of a product and how and when to do so. Awareness of recycling and other environmental issues has added an important dimension to this family role, especially with regard to packaging materials.

THE FAMILY DECISION PROCESS

The relative influence of husband, wife, and children in decision making has been a topic of great interest in the study of consumer behavior. Although information about it is clearly very important from a marketing perspective, research in this area remains most challenging. Families differ significantly from each other in terms of wealth, social status, lifestyle, age, number of children, and other variables. They also vary regarding the personalities of family members. Furthermore, specific types of products or services under consideration for purchase must be taken into account.

Decisions in the family range from individual choices made by each member separately to joint decisions involving two or more members. Decision patterns can be classified into four categories:

(1) *autonomic,* in which each spouse independently makes about half the decisions
(2) *husband dominant*
(3) *wife dominant* and
(4) *syncretic,* in which decisions are made jointly by the husband and wife.[15]

During the past two decades, the study of marital roles in the decision-making process has evolved from a focus on stereotypical depictions of these

Consumer Behavior in Practice

The Multiple Roles of Working Mothers

Over the past few decades, the role of women in contemporary society has changed dramatically. Millions of women with children have entered the labor force and have become major breadwinners. This shift in roles has resulted in fewer mothers (less than one-third) who remain at home and provide full-time care for their children. It has been reported that half of all preschoolers spend at least part of the day in the care of adults other than their parents. This change in the lifestyle of many women has resulted in rapid growth in the number of day-care centers and other forms of nonparental care for children.

Child-care arrangements take different forms. According to the National Center for Educational Statistics, the most common form of child care in the year 2006 was center-based programs, accounting for 56.4 percent of children, with 22.8 percent left in the care of relatives, and 14 percent in the care of nonrelatives. The remaining 26.1 percent of the children were under parental care.

A number of factors affect the choice of child-care arrangements used by mothers. Among the more important influences are age of the child, family income, marital status, and cost. Regarding *age* of the child, child-care centers are used more frequently for two- to four-year-old children than for infants. This may be attributable to parental preference as well as to the fact that many child-care centers do not accept infants.

Income also affects the type of child care that mothers use. Families in the higher-income category are more likely to use child-care centers than are families in lower-income groups. However, as family income increases, the use of public child-care centers declines while use of private centers increases. This is due to the fact that upper-income families can more easily afford the private centers. In addition, dual professional couples may use a nanny or *au pair* to provide full-time in-home child care and support.

Marital status is another factor affecting the choice of child-care arrangements. Younger single women usually turn to their relatives and child-care centers more often than do married women, who receive some child-care help from the child's father. Older single women do not use child-care centers as often as do married women. They find it more economical to rely on relatives or have the children care for themselves.

Cost is a factor in the choice of child-care arrangement. In 2007, child-care costs for a single infant ranged anywhere from $4,388 to $14,647 annually. Younger mothers utilize child-care services an average of 40 hours per week, compared with around 25 hours for older women. The reason may be that older mothers tend to have more children, and older children can care for younger ones.

One of the most frequently cited problems relative to the child-care issue is that the lack of affordable quality child care hinders the careers of many women. Even if the mother is employed, tardy arrivals to or absences from a job due to child-care problems could delay advancement. A catch-22 situation exists: without child care women could not seek work, and without work they could not afford the costs of child care.[14]

One of the major problems facing women with children today is the ability to maintain a balance between their family role on one hand and their professional role on the other. Learn more about the services of Child Care Experts National Network by visiting its Web site at www.childcare-experts.org. Although the human resource policies of many companies and organizations accommodate family obligations, others still lag behind. In your opinion, what types of policies or actions should firms undertake to help women with children maintain this balance? In your opinion, is the cost of such programs justifiable? Why?

roles in a family setting to investigations of changing roles in our contemporary society. More recent research has focused on investigating how roles vary across product categories and across decision phases. These studies typically rely on respondents' perceptions, impressions, or recollections of their involvement in decisions that occur within the confines of the family and whether they acted autonomously or jointly. The Allstate ad in Figure 12.2 depicts the added role of fathers as providers of care and protection for their family and young children.

An early study by Davis and Rigaux pointed out that the dominant marital roles in family decision making varied according to the phase of the decision process (information-search stage versus purchase-decision stage).[16] Subsequent studies by others confirmed this tendency. For example, Putnam and Davidson found that the tendency toward autonomic decisions was predominant in the information-search stage; however, there appeared to be an obvious shift toward joint decisions in the final stage of purchase.[17] They also found less sex-role dominance and more autonomic decision making for less-risky purchases. The tendency toward joint final decisions makes intuitive sense when we view the final decision as a culmination of the purchase process— a most important stage for accenting the individual roles of each spouse. This tendency is particularly prevalent when the decision concerns a high-involvement item and when the couple is concerned about living with the consequences of a poor autonomous decision.

Several factors have been suggested by researchers as significant in influencing the relative roles of husband and wife in family decisions. These factors can be summarized as follows.

Egalitarianism

Egalitarianism can be defined as a general value system stressing equality in marital relations.[18] The degree of influence attributed to either the husband or the wife in a family decision is thought to be a function of the level of "traditional marital values" present in the family. For example, in households where *traditional* marital-role values exist, the husband would be expected to make the majority of the decisions whereas the wife's role would be limited to domestically oriented tasks.[19] One study compared two samples from the United States and China.[20] The less-egalitarian, more patriarchal Chinese culture was found to foster less joint decision making and more husband dominance. Some observers attribute this pattern in part to China's one-child policy, which seems to have reinforced China's male-dominant attitude. Reports reveal that this rule has caused a disdain for female infants. Abortion, neglect, and abandonment, as well as infanticide, have been known to occur in the case of female babies.

Several factors influence the level of egalitarianism manifested within the family. As the level of education, income, and occupational prestige experienced by the wife increases, so also does her input into the family decision-making process.

Involvement

Involvement is the degree of relevance an individual assigns to an object or issue. A spouse's level of involvement depends on the degree of personal

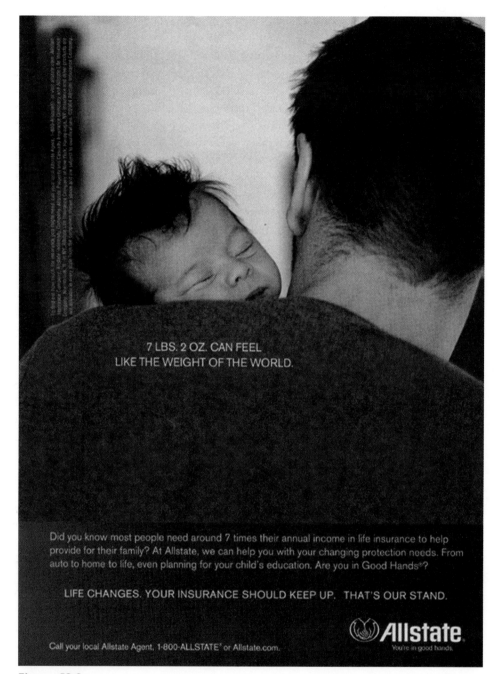

Figure 12.2

This ad from Allstate reflects the added roles played by fathers within the contemporary American family. The ad emphasizes the need to provide sufficient insurance coverage to protect the future of both family and children.

significance that the product or service holds for that individual. For example, when investigating spousal purchase patterns for consumer products and professional services, studies reveal some differences in the types of decisions undertaken by either the husband or the wife. A study by Cosenza showed that purchase of women's clothing tended to be wife dominant, whereas purchase of life insurance and homeowners' insurance tended to be husband dominated.[21] A second study by Kasulis and Hughes found that the selection of insurance agents and lawyers tended to be husband dominant, whereas the selection of pharmacists was a wife-dominated decision.[22] Involvement is basically a function of interest and the perceived utility of the expected outcome of the decision. For example, in household financial-management decisions, either the husband or the wife can be the dominant decision maker. The propensity toward autonomic versus joint decision making in this case is a function of which of the two is more interested and involved in this activity.

Empathy

The degree to which spouses exhibit *empathy* toward each other's preferences is an important influence on family decision making. The empathic response is a reaction in which one spouse feels as if he or she were a participant in the sensations and feelings of the other spouse. In households where empathy projection exists between the spouses, joint decision making is more likely to occur. In this case, joint decisions are not simply made to avoid the risk of a negative long-term reaction from the other spouse where a poor autonomic decision was made. Rather, they reflect a spouse's willingness to participate in the feelings of the other and a desire to go along through sharing his or her view regarding the issue.

Recognized Authority

Recognized authority is a mutually agreed-upon or culturally recommended and socially acceptable right to decide, assigned to one spouse. In family decision making, this recognized authority may result from a deliberate division of functions or roles between the husband and the wife. Each spouse is perceived to possess different talents, interests, and functions, many of which are complementary to those of the other spouse. Such recognized authority is not usually perceived as threatening. Instead, it promotes and enriches the common family well-being.

Recognized authority varies among different households and between cultures. What constitutes a husband's or wife's domain within one household or culture may not be the same in another. However, research indicates that general patterns do exist with regard to the types of recognized authority. Wives, for example, have more recognized authority in caring for young children, whereas the husbands' sphere may include taking care of the mechanical aspects of the family's automobile. Conflict arises when a couple fails to agree on recognized authority, where one spouse is less empathic to the preferences of the other, or where an egalitarian atmosphere is lacking within the family.

Now that we have briefly reviewed consumption roles and the factors at play in the family decision process, let us examine the increasingly important role that children play in household decision processes.

CHILDREN'S INFLUENCE ON FAMILY DECISION MAKING

In 2008, there were 48.9 million children between the ages of 6 and 17 in the United States who reportedly spent over $160 billion of their own money on goods and services. In addition, these same children exerted direct influence on $130 to $670 billion of family purchases, which involve products and services bought for them by parents or others, purchases made with them in mind, as well as major family purchases, such as automobiles, home electronics, and vacations.[23] This group's influence on the marketplace should only accelerate as its members get older and earn their own wages. The amount of money they spend has been growing at a rate of 15 to 20 percent annually during the past decade. MarketResearch.com reported that in 2008, 'tweens ages 8 to 14 spent an average of $2,000 each annually, for an aggregate total of approximately $58 billion. Add to this the more than $150 billion that their parents spent on them by the end of the same year.[24]

Children make their biggest impact in the food and beverage category. Products such as candy, soft drinks, and sweetened cereals account for a good share. It is here that they spend one-third of their income—more than $40 billion of their own money. Furthermore, kids influence an additional $110 billion of family food and beverage purchases.

The second category of expenditure for kids is electronic items, such as gizmos, games, music and movie downloads, as well as toys. Approximately $38 billion are spent on this class of goods every year. Kids also influence an additional $76.62 billion of their family's expenditures on electronics and various forms of entertainment.

The third category on which children spend their money is apparel. Expenditure in this category is estimated to exceed $20 billion. Kids in the 10-to-13 age bracket make more than two-thirds of their apparel decisions.

Children's influence on their parents' purchasing behavior has been the subject of many studies.

© 2009, Losevsky Pavel, Shutterstock, Inc.

The fourth category of expenditure for kids, children's personal care products (which could be purchased by family members or by the children themselves), reached a figure of over $15 billion in 2008. This category includes items such as oral hygiene, facial creams and medications, soap and bath products, shampoos and conditioners, as well as suncare products.

For children, the primary source of income is their parents. Much of this money comes in the form of allowances. In addition, kids receive money as gifts for birthdays, holidays, and other occasions. They also earn money for performing some household chores and for doing occasional jobs outside the home, like baby-sitting and delivering newspapers.

Regarding their shopping behavior, children prefer stores that play popular music and incorporate an element of theater into their environment.[25] Kids aged 8 to 12 like mass merchandisers because of these stores' breadth of product offerings, including such items as electronic gadgets, games, toys, clothes, school supplies, and snacks. These children also like specialty stores due to their depth of merchandise assortment.[26]

Kids prefer shopping in groups and tend to spend many hours in shopping locations, such as malls or strip centers. Unlike their parents, this group is unconcerned with price. Kids tend to spend between $14 and $19 on an average purchase. Cash is the usual method of paying for their purchases. However, a whopping one-third of them have use of a credit card.

Children today are shrewd. In addition to being Internet savvy, they get some of their information from TV. Their shopping behavior is characterized by having disposable cash, buying on impulse, and visiting multiple stores.

Children's influence on their parents' purchasing behavior has been the subject of many studies. Children attempt to manipulate parents to get them to yield to their requests. A number of factors seem to have a bearing on the degree of children's impact on their parent's purchase decisions. The age of the child and personality of the parents, as well as the specific product being purchased, are important factors that determine the extent of that influence. In general, the younger the child, the less the influence. Strict versus permissive parental personalities also affect the child's role in a family's decision-making style. Recently, many parents started ceding unprecedented decision-making power to their kids—perhaps due to changes in family lifestyles, as well as to the rising number of dual-income parents. For example, in the area of family car, children as young as eight have been reported to influence the car-buying selection process.[27] This trend of children's influence is largely due to the tendency of parents to include the children in a family's leisure and recreation travel episodes. In so doing, the kids play the consumption role of *influencers*.

Children affect parental spending through either direct or indirect types of influence. *Direct influence* occurs in the form of children's requests, demands, and hints directed toward their parents in a purchase situation. A child, for example, may specifically ask for a bag of M&M candy. *Indirect influence*, on the other hand, occurs when the parents know the brands their children prefer and buy them without being asked to do so. In 2008, it was estimated that indirect influence accounted for as much as $300 billion of the nearly $600 billion in household spending.[28]

It is anticipated that the market potential for kids will continue to grow at the same double-digit annual rate that characterized its growth during the past decade. The importance of children's purchasing power and their influence on parents can be observed in the variety of products offered to them. Kids' versions of many adult products find their way to the marketplace every day. Virtually every adult consumer product, from books to foods, to shoes, to clothes, to medications, to music, to video games, has been scaled down and dolled up to suit children. The increasing attractiveness of the youth market is due to a number of factors, such as the extra money that kids have today, their unlimited access to media, and the fact that they are more savvy and informed than their predecessors. Today's youth seek any number of adult products, such as cell phones and iPods.[29]

Marketers have coined a name for their strategy of getting kids to buy adult merchandise. This tactic is known as "age compression," which involves pushing adult products and attitudes on young children. In many cases, the strategy merely involves extending an already existing adult product to this market by scaling it down and adding youth appeal to its package and/or brand name. In this sense, the "new" product targeted to children is merely a slight variation of the adult version, with a modified brand name or package—for example Nike Kids Lil Nike Shox Turbo Infant/Toddler shoes, which are merely miniatures of the adult item.[30]

One major advantage of the age compression strategy is the fact that through this early targeting, a brand can increase its chance for a greater share of each customer's business in later life. Brand preference is more lasting when formed in childhood years, resulting in greater lifetime revenue for a firm. It has been suggested, for instance, that lifetime revenue from one customer of hamburger chain might be $12,000. Since it is relatively possible for a hamburger chain to develop a relationship with children, this target of $12,000 should be manageable.[31]

ADVERTISING TO CHILDREN

In recent years, marketers' efforts to reach children through electronic media have gone through dramatic changes. The world of media, particularly TV, which for many years dominated the children's field, has given way to a new arena crowded with cell phones, iPods, video games, instant messaging, virtual reality Web sites, online social networks, and e-mail.

For many years, television had been an important vehicle for reaching children. According to a report from the American Medical Association, children between the ages of 2 and 17 watch an annual average of 15,000 to 18,000 hours of TV, compared with 12,000 hours spent per year in school. Today however, the new forms of electronic media have cut into hours spent in front of the television and have become a main avenue for reaching the young. Since interactive media incorporate and build on the child's actions, they are considered more influential than traditional media such as TV. Interactivity can take into account each individual learner knowledge base and adapt the message to match each kid's developmental level. Advertisers, thus, can develop a campaign that can almost target each child individually.[32]

Over the years, the government has attempted to regulate advertising directed at children. A number of laws have been enacted to protect the vulnerability of children from various abusive tactics. Exhibit 12.2 summarizes some of the main pieces of federal legislation that pertain to media directed to children.

In addition, the Children's Advertising Review Unit (CARU) of the Council of Better Business Bureau provides guidelines and evaluates consumer

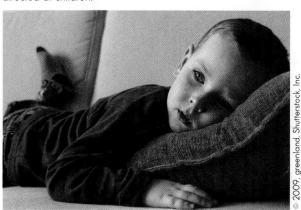

Over the years, the government has attempted to regulate advertising directed at children.

© 2009, greenland, Shutterstock, Inc.

Policy Title	Mandates
Children's Television Act of 1990	Requires educational TV for children; establishes commercial time restrictions; and bans host selling.
Three-Hour Rule (1997)	Specifies three hours per week of educational programming to qualify for expedited license renewal for TV stations.
Telecommunications Act of 1996	Requires TV sets to include a V-chip to block programs with content parents find objectionable.
Communications Decency Act of 1996	Imposes criminal sanctions on those who knowingly transmit obscene materials to children under the age of 18.
Children's Online Privacy Protection Act of 1998	Requires operators of Web sites and online services directed to children (or heavily used by children under the age of 13) to obtain verifiable parental consent and to keep confidential any information disclosed from others, including parents.

complaints regarding advertising that targets kids. For example, CARU guidelines state "advertisements should not convey to children that possession of a product will result in greater acceptance by peers or that lack of the product will result in less acceptance by peers." Advertisers are also admonished not to advertise to children products that "pose safety risks to them, i.e., drugs and dietary supplements, alcohol, and products labeled 'keep out of the reach of children.'"

Food Advertising Directed at Children

Traditionally, the food and beverage industry in the United States viewed children as a major market for its products due to their high collective spending power and their potential as lifelong customers for the business. Marketers have used multiple techniques and channels to reach kids, including television advertising, in-school marketing, product placements in movies and programming, kids' clubs, the Internet, toys with brand logos, and tie-ins. One form of promotion to children that has recently received much attention is the food

Ethical Dilemma

Wombs for Rent

The primal drive to have children has prompted many couples in our society who are unable to conceive on their own to seek the services of artificial insemination clinics, invitro fertilization, and gestational surrogacy operations. There are two reasons for the overwhelming rise in demand for such reproductive assistance services: first, infertility affects more than 6 million women and their partners in the United States; and second, major advances in medical technology have significantly enhanced the success rate of invitro fertilization.

In the case of commercial surrogacy, the practice of having "wombs for rent" has been growing steadily over the past few years. The idea of a woman bearing a baby for another is as old as civilization itself and has even been regulated in the Code of Hammorabi back in the year 1800 B.C.E. Surrogates are impregnated in vitro with the egg and sperm of couples unable to conceive on their own. The surrogates carry the baby for 24 hours a day, 7 days a week, until birth—when they undergo the hardship, pain, and risks of labor. Industry experts estimate that there were about 1,000 surrogate births within the United States in 2007, and the number globally is reported to surpass that figure fivefold.

The motivations of gestational carriers vary widely. Some perform this service because they believe that one of the greatest rewards surrogate mothers experience is the sense of self-worth and empowerment gained by helping others fulfill their dream of having children. Other surrogates also feel that performing this service is equivalent to offering an organ transplant to someone who truly needs it. However, many surrogates perform this service to earn fees, where the compensation usually amounts to over $20,000. Surrogate mothers and the parents sign a contract that specifies, among other things, the couple's responsibility for all the medical expenses and the surrogate's fee, as well as arrangements for receiving the baby at birth.

Surrogacy is not just an American phenomenon. It has spread globally to a large number of foreign countries. In India, for example, baby making comes at the intersection of high productive technology and a plentiful cheap labor market. At a clinic in Kaival Hospital in the town of Anand, a number of women carrying children for infertile couples from many countries, including the United States and the European Union, are kept in the clinic throughout the months of pregnancy, are provided with medical care, and are paid more than many of them would have earned in 15 years. This form of womb outsourcing has flourished in India and has become a viable growth industry.

Surrogacy is viewed by some as a creative method of assisting reproduction that benefits individuals who cannot conceive or carry a pregnancy to term. Ethically, such programs raise a host of questions that touch on the values of society, tampering with the miracle of life, the morals of modern science, exploitation, and globalization. One concern, for instance, is the fear that wealthy, self-obsessed, and shallow women may decide to have their babies via surrogates merely to avoid stretch marks.

In the United States, at the time of this writing, 13 states permit surrogacy agreements, and 6 other states forbid such practices. Learn more about state laws regarding surrogacy by visiting the Human Rights Campaign Web site at www.hrc. org/issues/parenting/surrogacy/surrogacy_laws. asp. Do you think that surrogacy is a sound solution to family building? Do you think that surrogacy is an ethical solution for family building? Cite the pros and cons of this practice by visiting a new blog called "Conception Connections" at www. conceptionconnections.wordpress.com, which is designed to generate conversations regarding the surrogacy issue.

and beverage advertising that targets them. In view of the sharp increase in the childhood obesity rate in our society, "junk food marketing to children" has been singled out by advocacy groups as the culprit in today's overweight epidemic. As such, it has received increased scrutiny from lawmakers.

Obesity has been linked by many observers to heavy advertising of unhealthful foods. This condition led in 2007 to the creation of a joint task force on marketing and childhood obesity by both Congress and the Federal Trade Commission. The function of this task force is to recommend actions or policies dealing with the obesity issue. With new regulatory action looming on the horizon, more than a dozen of the largest food companies and establishments pledged to limit junk food advertising directed at children and to promote healthier alternatives. Examples include McDonald's pledge in 2008 to limit ads that target children under the age of 12 to meals with less than 600 calories; and Coca Cola's decision also in 2008 to halt ads to children under 12 and to limit beverages offered in school to water, 100 percent juice, and milk for elementary and middle-school students.[33]

The Family Life Cycle

For years, sociologists and marketers have recognized the fact that most families tend to pass through a fairly steady and predictable series of stages as household members grow older. These stages constitute what has become known as the **family life cycle** (FLC). The stages of the FLC model are primarily based on four characteristics:

family life cycle
the sequence of stages that families tend to pass through

- age,
- marital status,
- employment status of the head of household, and
- the absence or presence of children as well as their ages.

Marketers usually infer the ages of the parents and the relative amount of disposable income from the household's stage in the FLC. At each stage, there are unique needs, differences in earning power, and specific demands placed on household resources.

Traditionally, starting with *bachelorhood*, most individuals move on to form a family unit by marriage. *The honeymooner* stage ends when the first child is born. The *parenthood* stage continues as long as at least one child resides in the married couple's home. Eventually, in the *postparenthood* stage, the mature children depart from their parent's home, leaving behind an "empty nest." Finally, the *dissolution* stage occurs when one of the spouses dies. Figures 12.3 and 12.4 depict two ads. The first from State Farm targets honeymooners. The second from Go RVing targets parents with children.

As people move from one FLC stage to the next or as they assume different life roles, various types of products and services increase or decrease in importance. Young bachelors and newlyweds, for instance, are the most likely to exercise, to consume alcohol, and to frequent bars, concerts, and movies. Families with young children are major purchasers of health foods and fruit

Figures 12.3 and 12.4

These two ads from State Farm Insurance and Go RVing reflect changing family needs for products and services as the family progresses from honeymooner's need for combined insurance coverage to parenthood, when children's desire to experience outdoor recreation becomes paramount.

juices, whereas single-parent households and those with older children tend to buy more junk food. Home-maintenance services are most likely to be used by older couples ("empty nesters") and bachelors. An understanding of such consumption patterns coupled with knowledge of demographic trends in the marketplace can help marketers forecast demand for specific product and service categories over time. Monitoring changes over time in needs, preferences, and priorities of consumers is essential for segmenting markets, targeting prospects, and positioning products. For example, Procter & Gamble introduced Folger's Singles for people who live alone and who don't need to brew a full pot of coffee at a time.[34]

A MODERNIZED FAMILY LIFE CYCLE

Not long ago, this traditional FLC model typified the overwhelming majority of U.S. households. In recent years, however, a number of cultural, sociodemographic, and lifestyle trends in the United States, as well as technological advances, have reconfigured the structure and profile of the U.S. family. For instance, significant increases have occurred in the number of singles, unmarried cohabitants, same-sex unions, dual-career couples, childless couples, single-parent households, adoptions by single persons, late-in-life marriages, blended families, and divorces and separations. There has also been a notable decrease in the number of extended families.[35] This diversity coupled with other developments such as changing roles of men and women, spousal abuse, family planning, artificial insemination, and legalized abortion strongly suggest that the contemporary notion of the family must be expanded to include eclectic situations.

The U.S. Census Bureau reports that in 2007, the number of grandchildren living with their grandparents reached 5.8 million, compared with only 2.2 million in 1970.[36] A litany of contemporary sociocultural maladies have precipitated this phenomenon—teen pregnancy, abandonment, drug and alcohol abuse, homicide, neglect, poverty, AIDS, imprisonment, unemployment—all ills that ignore race and income.

Moreover, some aging but successful males are acquiring young, glamorous wives and even young children through second marriages. In the past, marketers would have pigeonholed a 55-year-old male into a vague 50-plus age category and, consequently, assumed his lifestyle and consumption behavior mirrored that of others in the class. In reality, however, this person's consumption would be drastically different than marketers would have presumed. Similarly, a young woman in her teens, while never having been married, may have one or more children who may have different fathers. For marketers, lumping such a person—now a single parent—into the teenage or bachelor category would seriously misrepresent her consumption behavior.

Although many people still maintain the traditional view of marriage for themselves and others, some individuals contend that social changes such as these necessitate updating standard terminology. In particular, the definitions of single and married persons require revision. Perhaps *Singles* should include anyone who is presently unmarried, regardless of past marital status. Perhaps *Married* should embrace any couple that resides together and intends to share an extended relationship. In this view, a man and woman living together with or without formally exchanging vows would fall into the married category, and homosexual couples would qualify as married if they contemplate a long-term partnership. These are but a few of the departures from the traditional family life cycle concept that realistically reflect metamorphoses occurring in modern society.

With the advent of such diverse types of households and living arrangements, it becomes obvious that the traditional FLC no longer adequately represents the typical path through which contemporary households and living arrangements progress. To compensate for the limitations of the traditional model, researchers of consumer behavior have sought out expanded FLC models that better reflect today's heterogeneity of households and living arrangements.[37] Nontraditional households include both family and nonfamily types. *Nontraditional family households* include childless couples, same-sex unions, career-oriented couples who delay having children until later in life, couples who enter into marriage with a child, single parents (widows or widowers, persons with custody of a child after divorce, persons who have children out of wedlock, singles who adopt a child), and extended families. Today, the range of extended families includes single adults who return home to their parents to lessen the expenses of living alone while establishing a career, divorced sons and daughters who return to their parents' home (perhaps with grandchildren), infirm elderly parents who move in with their children, and newlyweds who live with their in-laws. *Nonfamily households*, on the other hand, include single persons (most of whom are young), unmarried couples (including gays and lesbians), divorced persons without children, and widowed persons.

In view of these social changes, researchers such as Gilly and Enis as well as Murphy and Staples, among others, have proposed redefined family life cycles. Gilly and Enis proposed a FLC that depicted three age groups (under 35, 35 to 64, 65 years and over) and divided these age groups into 14 categories.[38] Murphy and Staples, on the other hand, developed a model that depicted 14 FLC categories and divided heads of households into separate categories of young, middle-age, and older life phases.[39]

Let us now consider some of the forms of nontraditional living arrangements that have recently emerged in our society and that reflect a marked deviation from the traditional FLC.

Nontraditional Living-Arrangement Patterns

Nontraditional households are supplanting conventional family units as the norm. In fact, according to the U.S. Census Bureau, only 15 percent of all U.S. households in 2006 fit the traditional family mold, leaving the rest as a challenge to be tackled by astute marketers.[40] During the last half of the twentieth century, marketers have become increasingly aware of and responsive to various nontraditional living-arrangement patterns, such as latchkey kids, boomerang children, single-parent families, single-person households, as well as gay and lesbian households. Ramifications of these trends extend to many areas of consumer behavior. For example, the rise in the number of latchkey kids and single-parent families impacts various facets of consumer behavior such as the number of meals eaten out; consumption of convenience foods; eating meals on the run; use of beepers or cellular phones to keep track of kids; and demand for errand services, dry cleaning pickups, and the like.

LATCHKEY KIDS

latchkey kids
children who return home from school to a locked and empty home

Today, about one-third of all school-age children, an estimated five to seven million children between the ages of 5 and 13, are the so-called **latchkey kids**—children who return from school to a locked and empty home while their parents are away at work.[41] The term *latchkey* originated from the early nineteenth century, when children who were responsible for their own care would wear the key to their house on a string that hung around their neck.[42] What has contributed to the growing ranks of latchkey kids is changing demographics. An increase in the number of working mothers, as well as single-parent families, combined with a decrease in the number of extended families that once helped with child care together account for this phenomenon. According to the Council on Contemporary Families, Stanford University, 65 percent of mothers with preschoolers and 79 percent of those with school-age children were employed in 2007, up from 30 percent and 56 percent respectively in 1970.[43]

Companies such as Whirlpool, General Electric, Lipton, American Home Products, and Hasbro have recognized that latchkey kids together with their parents comprise a fairly significant market niche for products ranging from convenience foods to household appliances and home security systems. They also realize that brand loyalties formed early have the potential to persist for a long time. Lipton, for example, distributes *Kidsmarts* magazine to 150,000 households so that after-school hours might be spent more securely and beneficially until parents come home from work. *Kidsmarts* includes ads and coupons for Lipton products that latchkey kids consume.

BOOMERANG CHILDREN

Recent reports reveal that 39 percent of single women and almost 46 percent of single men ages 20 through 29 lived with parents in 2005, up from 36 percent of women and almost 42 percent of men in the year 2000.[44] These so-called **boomerang children** include increasing numbers of college graduates who have headed home after facing a disappointing job market and expensive housing. Such young people seem to abound, particularly if they happen to be in low-paying creative careers such as acting, publishing, and music. They try to maintain the amenities of their well-heeled upbringings. Studies show that return-home rates tend to rise during periods of high unemployment, but student debt and high housing costs are also factors. Whereas some return out of economic necessity, others reappear because they have been spoiled by their parents' affluence and feel disinclined to accept a lower standard of living if they were to reside on their own.[45] Evidence suggests that men are more likely than women to reappear on parents' doorsteps, due in part to the fact that the median age at which men marry is 27—more than two years later than the average for women. Although boomerangers are largely single, statistics reveal that many married couples with children also return to their parents' home. The length of stay, in most cases, ranges between six months and two years.[46] Boomerang children tend to spend more on discretionary purchases such as entertainment, clothing, and personal-care items.[47]

It is interesting to note that many families with a boomerang child at home are simultaneously providing some form of financial assistance to an elderly parent, which places a heavy burden on the family's resources. Demographers refer to such families as a segment of the "**sandwich generation**," which includes any household with children and parents who concurrently provide assistance to their *own* aging parents. According to the Pew Research Center, slightly more than one out of every eight Americans ages 40 to 60 falls into the sandwich generation category.

boomerang children
grown children—now adults—who continue to live in or return to their parents' home

sandwich generation
parents who simultaneously support both their kids and their elderly parents

SINGLE PARENTHOOD

Over the last few decades, the proportion of traditional two-parent families has been declining while that of single-parent households has been on the rise. According to the Custodial Mothers and Fathers Report released by the United States Census Bureau in 2007, there were approximately 13.6 million single parents in the United States, who were raising 21.2 million children, a figure that represents about 26 percent of all children in our society under the age of 21. The report revealed that 84 percent of these single-parent households are headed by mothers, and only 16 percent by fathers. Many single-parent families are low-income households. Around 27.7 percent of households headed by a custodial single mother with children live in poverty, compared to only 11.1 percent of households headed by a single father with children.[48] Three major subgroups of one-parent families can be identified:

- displaced homemakers,
- adolescent mothers, and
- single fathers.

In the *displaced homemakers* group, marital dissolution drastically reduces the new single-parent family's available income. Displaced homemakers are at a disadvantage because they often lack an employment history, training, and marketable skills. Concerning the *adolescent mothers* group, one-third of girls in the United States become pregnant before reaching the age of 20. Pregnancy statistics from DataBank show that in 2006, birth rates among girls between the ages of 15 and 19 reached a high of 41.9 per thousand. This vast subgroup of single parents faces many obstacles to self-sufficiency, such as lack of education, job readiness, and emotional maturity. The third group consisting of *single fathers* tends to have a more healthy economic status compared with its female single-parent counterpart. However, single fathers often find their sole child-rearing role conflicting with work expectations and often feel that they are filling social roles for which they are unprepared.[49]

More than one in four children in the U.S. is being raised in a single parent household.

© 2009, Andresr, Shutterstock, Inc.

Changes in the structure of the U.S. family, such as the work and living arrangements of single parents, have many ramifications for marketers. These arrangements affect buying responsibilities and decision centers within the family. For example, it has been found that teens and even children often act as pseudoadults in divorce situations and acquire responsibility for shopping for groceries and other major purchases.[50] Restaurant patronage and purchase of convenience foods are also influenced. One study revealed that single-parent families differ with respect to their weekly dollar expenditures at full-service restaurants and their frequency of eating at such restaurants, compared with two-parent family structures.[51]

Another study investigated the demand for services such as child care, housekeeping, and food prepared away from home as a result of the employment status in families headed by a single mother.[52] The study revealed that single mothers' demand for these services significantly increased as their work hours–wages increased. The study also revealed that single mothers tended to compensate for reduced time inputs in the family by substituting a different mix of products (such as purchasing frozen dinners rather than ingredients to make dinner from scratch) or by getting an older child to prepare the meal instead of the mother.[53]

THE LIVE ALONES

Marketers are just beginning to realize the buying power of the live-alone market.[54] Men and women who live alone can and do spend heavily—any way they please. In the year 2005, estimates reveal that there were over 17.4 million single-female households and 13 million single-male households, resulting in a total of more than 30.4 million single-person households.[55] Those who live alone constitute an attractive market in certain product and service sectors. Recent reports from market analyst Datamonitor indicate that single-person households spend around 150 percent more per person on rent than those who live in households of two people or more. They also account for 41 percent of the personal-care market and tend to spend more on alcohol. In addition, they lay out more per person for reading materials, tobacco products, and smoking supplies.[56]

A number of traits characterize the live-alone market. Singles tend to be self-reliant and gravitate toward products that are low maintenance, affordable, quiet, and safe.[57] Because they prefer living close to where they work, they are willing to move into the dense, attached homes as well as lofts and condos that most families with children tend to avoid. Singles also tend to be among the best customers for restaurants. They tend to spend more on travel, convenience foods, and sporty automobiles than married adults. This segment constitutes a lucrative market for many items ranging from dating services to fashionable clothing.

A variety of companies target the live-alone market. One such group of firms is online dating services, which help singles meet the right mate via videos and computerized databanks. Other firms include, among others, Web sites that address the needs of singles (such as americansingles.com), food processors, home builders, as well as travel and recreation agencies. Club Med designs vacations filled with opportunities to meet others. Royal Cruise Line offers a program that furnishes men as social hosts and dance partners for single women over 50.[58]

Singles tend to be among the best customers for restaurants.

© 2009, konstantynov, Shutterstock, Inc.

Many singles feel ignored by marketers, who seem to be enamored of families. Strategies that cater to average households may subtly discriminate against singles, who often complain that it is difficult to find offerings designed and sized for those who live alone. Their criticism covers a wide variety of products and services. Few packaged food items are available in single-serving packages. Likewise, individuals who travel solo must pay the same rates for hotel rooms that couples pay for double occupancy.

Generational Marketing

generational marketing

the cataloging of generations in terms of external events that occurred during their members' formative years

cohort

an aggregate of people who have undergone similar experiences and share common memories

Generationally defined lifestyles and social values exercise as much influence on buying as more commonly known demographic factors such as income, education, and gender.[59] Marketers are discovering how to exploit the life experiences that define each generation of consumers. This practice is known as **generational marketing.** Unlike a mass-marketing strategy, where consumers—regardless of their demographics—are viewed as a whole, generational marketing identifies and addresses smaller segments of the market based on the significant experiences they share.[60] Whereas a generation is usually defined by dates of birth, a cohort catalogs each generation in terms of external events that occurred during its members' formative years.

A **cohort** is an aggregate of people who have undergone similar experiences, passed through cultural milestones and historical events, and shared common memories of events that transpired during a particular time frame. Because members of a cohort share common recollections, it is possible to appeal to them through symbolism meaningful to each cohort. Feelings of nostalgia could be created by using familiar appeals based on prior experiences. The success of the new Volkswagen Beetle is largely due to nostalgia for the old Bug. Clothing fashions and music keep coming back in cycles, fueled by generations that are emotional about things they experienced when they were children. Similarly, commercials for many products today, such as cars, soft drinks, and financial services, borrow hits from the 1960s and classic rock era in an effort to stimulate sales among the Boomers.[61]

© 2009, Radoman Durkovic, Shutterstock, Inc.

Because members of a cohort share common recollections, it is possible to appeal to them through symbolism. Feelings of nostalgia can be created through familiar appeals based on past experiences.

CLASSIFICATION OF CONSUMERS BY LIFE EXPERIENCES

A contemporary glance at the lifestyles of the present-day generations in our society reveals a need to update the classification of cohorts that prevailed in the 1990s and that were suggested by authors such as Meredith and Schewe.[62] Today's generations have expanded, and may be classified into six major cohort types. These are labeled the Postwar Cohort, the Boomers I Cohort, the

Boomers II Cohort, the Generation X cohort, the Generation Y Cohort, and the Generation Z Cohort. It is worth noting that demographers disagree about each of these groups' exact parameters, and certainly these classifications overlap to some extent.

The Postwar Cohort

Also called the silent generation, the **Postwar cohort** is comprised of individuals born between 1928 and 1945 and represents 21 percent of the population. While in their teens, its members lived through the period of economic growth and social tranquility that followed the war years. Thoughts of war and fears of nuclear attacks, however, were still fresh in their minds, creating a need to alleviate uncertainty in their lives through material possessions. Their financial philosophy is to save some and spend some. They have fond memories of singers such as Frank Sinatra and Andy Williams. They also enjoy folk rock.[63]

Postwar cohort
individuals born 1928 to 1945

The Boomers I Cohort

Also called the Woodstock generation, the **Boomers I cohort** consists of individuals born between 1946 and 1954 and represents 17 percent of the population. Brought up with the experience of the Vietnam War, the assassinations of John F. Kennedy and Martin Luther King Jr., and the first moon walk, this group embraces the values of youthfulness, invincibility, and freedom. The hippie movement was a natural outcome of this orientation. They created a new meaning of the youth culture, popularizing blue jeans, rock music, and sexual permissiveness. They vowed to stay forever young, but at the same time exhibit concerns about health, old age, and retirement. Boomer I members are dissimilar to their parents in that they like to spend, borrow, and, in many cases, live beyond their means. They enjoy owning conspicuous products. The Beatles and Elvis Presley are among their favorites.

Boomers I cohort
individuals born 1946 to 1954

The Boomers II Cohort

Also called zoomers, the **Boomers II cohort** embraces individuals born between 1955 and 1965 and represents 25 percent of the population. The Watergate era took its toll on this group, resulting in a loss of faith in the existence of an idealistic political system. Their ingrained sense of entitlement has been overtaken by unmet expectations. They tend to be somewhat self-absorbed, pursuing personal goals and instant gratification.[64] In order to have a lifestyle as good as that of their predecessors and to flaunt their success, they like to spend and will go into debt to acquire material possessions. Concerned about the environment, they tend to prefer environmentally friendly products. They like rock and roll and have a permissive view of sex.

Boomers II cohort
individuals born between 1955 and 1965

The Generation X Cohort

Also called baby busters, individuals born between 1965 and 1976 (other demographers use the dates 1963 and 1977) represent 21 percent of the population.[65] The **Generation X cohort** grew up in the era of X-rated movies, legalized abortion, and the information superhighway. They are the first to have

Generation X cohort
individuals born between 1965 and 1976

grown up with computers and, perhaps more importantly, the first to play video games. Unhappy about the environmental and economic problems they inherited, they are cynical and display seemingly contradictory behavior. They tend to be antihype and reject the concept of conspicuous consumption. Products that hype their own success with copy points such as upscale or best-selling are unlikely to persuade Generation Xers, whose money motto was once "Spend, spend, and spend," are now worried about the debt being loaded into their future. For example, although they represent only 25 percent of all credit card holders, Generation Xers account for about 38 percent of the industry's outstanding debt. Their political views are colored by the principle of "What's in it for me?" It is interesting to note that improving public education is one of the highest public policy priorities for Xers.[66]

This group has been unfairly described as flannel-wearing and underachieving slackers. Despite this somewhat unflattering depiction of Generation X, other observers of this group note that not all Xers fit the stereotype. In fact, many Xers are shedding the psychographic and behavioral certainties that once defined them. Many are the dotcom world-changers who blossomed only a few years later, as well as the engaged leaders of causes like MoveOn.org. Many members of this cohort are also altruistic and genuinely interested in societal causes, such as helping the poor and conserving the environment. Some Xers, for example, are actively involved in such organizations as Habitat for Humanity and Greenpeace.

Generation Y Cohort

Generation Y cohort
individuals born between 1977 and 1994

Born between 1977 and 1994 (other demographers use the dates 1980 and 1995), the approximately 70 million consumers dubbed **Generation Y cohort** or echo boomers—represents the result of 78 million baby boomers reaching childbearing age. This cohort can be divided into three subgroups based on the formative experiences shaping their lives.[67]

- The first is *generation Y adults*, born between 1977 and 1983 (as of this writing, age 25-31) who witnessed such events as the Iranian revolution, Vietnam draft dodgers, CNN, and MTV, and artificial heart implants.
- The second is *generation Y teens*, born between 1984 and 1989 (age 19-24) who witnessed the fall of the Berlin Wall, 1987 stock market crash, Prozac debut, CDs, Apple Mac, and the break up of the Bell phone system.
- The third is *generation Y kids*, born between 1990 and 1994 (age 14-18) who witnessed events such as the attack on the World Trade Center, Los Angeles earthquake, the cloning of human cells, Woodstock '94 concert, and the debut of *Friends*.

Generation Y has been described as idealistic, socially conscious, and individualistic. Members of this group tend to be anticorporate, speak their minds, and dress as they please. Many use extreme fashions, such as body piercing, dyed hair, and tattoos. Generation Y tends to be more of an activist group than Generation X.[68] According to a survey sponsored by the Horatio Alger Association of Distinguished Americans, Generationer Yers spend far more time with personal computing, iPods, and television than with homework or reading for pleasure. When it comes to loyalty, the companies they work for are last on their list of priorities, behind their families and friends. They see crime as the most important issue facing the nation and worry about government dishonesty, corruption, and gang violence.[69] Their favorite music is grunge, retro, and rap, and their choice of clothing includes such brands as FUBU, Tommy Hilfiger, and other hip-hop styles.

Members of Generation Z are children of older, wealthier parents. They tend to have unlimited access to information through the Internet as well as other forms of mobile technology.

Generation Y is more radically diverse than boomers. One in three is not Caucasian. One in four lives in a single-parent household. Three in four have working mothers.[70] Having grown up in an even more media-saturated, brand-conscious world than their parents, Yers respond to ads differently. The type of advertising that pushed slogans and images and worked well with boomers has proven to be ineffective with Generation Y. Yers respond more to humor, irony, and the unvarnished truth. In addition, celebrity endorsements play an important role in luring them to purchase cosmetics and toiletry products. Lancaster's licensing agreement with Jennifer Lopez for a line of products under the J.Lo brand name is one example.

Yers are a less-homogenous market than their parents due, on one hand, to their racial and ethnic diversity and to the multiplicity of media types they are exposed to on the other. The proliferation of newer types of media such as the electronic and mobile media, particularly the Internet, and—to a lesser extent—the broad spectrum of cable and satellite TV channels as well as niche magazines such as *Sports Illustrated* and *Seventeen*, has sped up the fashion cycle and allowed Yers to find out about the most obscure trends the very moment they emerge.

Generation Z Cohort

Generation Z cohort chronologically follows Generation Y, beginning roughly in the year 1995 and lasting through approximately the year 2008. Members of Generation Z are mostly in their childhood years; but at the oldest edge, they are in their early teens. They are the children of older and wealthier parents who have fewer siblings. From a materialistic point of view, they constitute the most supplied generation of children ever. Technologically, no other generation before them could claim its exposure to or experience with the digital world. They have unlimited access to information through the Internet as well as from other forms of mobile technology. As such, information has become an integral part of their existence. Recent reports reveal that before they can even read, almost one in four children in nursery school is learning the skill of using the Internet. According to the Department of Education, about 23 percent of children in such schools ages 3, 4, and 5 have gone online. By kindergarten, 32 percent of them were reported to have used the Internet, typically under adult supervision.[71]

Generation Z cohort individuals born between 1995 and 2008

Global Opportunity

You Can Enjoy Your Music and Wear It Too!

It is music that sets the tempo in clothing for Generation Y. Yers tend to emulate the style of dress worn by the recording artists they admire. One style of music that has greatly influenced fashion is hip-hop, popularized by African Americans a number of years ago. Described as loose-fitting urban streetwear, hip-hop is perfect to relax and sweat in. The style includes baggy jeans, sweatshirts, hiking boots, and baseball caps—usually worn backwards. However, creative hip-hop teens frequently add their own personal touches with such accessories as flannel shirts, Lycra jackets with sport logos, and Nike or Adidas athletic shoes. In this world of fashion, boys and girls dress alike.

Hip-hop, as a class of music and clothing, represents a fusion of U.S. and European styles. In the 1980s, African-American kids in Detroit and Chicago started to wear baggy street clothes in dance clubs. A few years later, urban dance music invaded Europe. Hip-hop stormed Manchester, England, which is the European capital of rock music. When Manchester's bands such as the Stone Roses and Charlatans UK toured the United States in 1989 and 1990, the marriage between white British bands and black American performers was consummated, and a style of music and an international fashion sensation were born.

Over the past few years, this baggy-preppy scene has been dominated by giants like Ralph Lauren and Tommy Hilfiger. This dominance, however, did not stop other boutique labels such as FUBU, Naughty Gear, Phat Farm, Pure Playaz, UB Tuff, Wu-Wear, Rocawear, Sean John, Mecca USA, and Ecko Unlimited from claiming a large share of the market. In 2003, sales of these brands amounted to over $15 billion and is growing at the rate of 50 percent annually. This male urban-clothing niche is growing faster than any other apparel category except, perhaps, lingerie.

Obsession with hip-hop is a worldwide phenomenon. In Japan, for example, junior high students, the best barometer of mainstream America, are buying FUBU's and Hilfiger's look almost exclusively and dragging their wide-bottom jeans through the streets of Kyoto and Tokyo. Similarly, Phat Farm, the cartoonishly rural-themed stores selling the hip-hop label started by Russell Simons, the founder of Def Jam Records, report that over one-third of their styles are sold in Asia.[74]

The secret to success in marketing hip-hop fashions to Yers seems to lie neither in offering slick styles nor in spending huge sums of money on advertising, but rather in getting a rapper—preferably one in heavy rotation on MTV—to wear the brand. Visit U.S. and British hip-hop shopping malls at http://www.ballersmall.com/ and www.darkncoldhiphop.com. Compare hip-hop fashions in the two countries. What similarities or differences do you detect between the two? What factors might explain these similarities or differences? In your opinion, are there specific traits that distinguish those Yers who are attracted to this fashion sensation?

AN ADDITIONAL GENERATIONAL COHORT

In recent years, marketers have identified an additional generational cohort to supplement the six original segments discussed so far. This cohort is known as the Techno-savvies.

Techno-Savvies

Techno-savvies
electronically
sophisticated consumers

According to a Pew Internet & American Life Project in 2007, 85 percent of Americans own computers and use the Internet. However, only 8 percent of those, or around 20.4 million, are electronically sophisticated and constitute a group that has been labeled the **techno-savvies**. About 77 percent of this group are married, and techno-savvy households are likely to include children. Techno-savvies typically live in a single-family dwelling within 20 minutes of a big city, such as Los Angeles, New York, San Jose, or Chicago. Their average income is over $100,00, and about 54 percent earn in excess of $150,000 annually.

Techno-savvies can be subdivided into three subgroups. The first group, called the *perpetual motion consumer*, consists of business executives whose activities revolve around the computer and travel. This consumer is typically male, married, and around 42 years old and always travels with a computer notebook and mobile phone. The second group, known as the *networked consumer*, frequently works in technical fields such as computer programming. Also mostly men, these consumers are generally in their early thirties and are the so-called early adopters of new gadgets. They spend much of their leisure time online. Finally, there is the *home-bound consumer* working from a home office as a self-employed entrepreneur or satellite employee of a corporation. Members of this group are as likely to be women as men, are usually married, and average about 42 years in age.

Recent research indicates that techno-savvies are independent learners, preoccupied with free expression as a result of being exposed to extensive information on the Internet. They have strong visual-spatial skills and readily integrate the visual with the physical world. They learn by discovering and are comfortable multitaskers capable of using a range of technologies. Global connectivity allows them to communicate with a broad range of users and exposes them to a wide spectrum of ideas and cultural differences, leading to a more socially inclusive outlook.[72]

Techno-savvies are image conscious and upscale from a consumer marketer's point of view. They are likely to be either *innovators or early adopters* of new high-tech products. This group has the highest ownership and usage rates of technology-based products and services and tends to display high response rates to electronic sales pitches. Among time-pressed techno-savvies' usual array of products and services are travel, computers, and software, as well as entertainment.[73]

MARKETING APPLICATIONS OF GENERATIONAL COHORTS

Generational marketing systems hold high promise for marketers of many products and services. The power of this system lies in its ability to categorize consumers into groups of individuals with homogeneous life experiences. Common experiences of a generation create a specific sensibility that touches all its members in some way. Through these experiences, individuals' views are formed regarding what is funny, what is stylish, and what is taboo. It directs them to what is appropriate and what is not. Consequently, those who have similar life experiences are most likely to be similar with respect to other behavioral characteristics, such as product purchase, motivations, and media behavior. This implied psychological coherence of these segments allows marketers to use language and symbols and to make offers that are meaningful to them and likely to produce a desired response.

Cohort segmentation, for example, allowed Weber Company, the maker of grills, to profile the buyers of its products.[75] The company's executives determined that generational cohort differences are useful to identify who is buying their grills and to ascertain the type of grills they are most likely to purchase. The company produced a 20-minute video that dramatized the lifestyles of cohorts and made it available to its distributors and sales staff. Each cohort vignette pictured its home environment, complete with appropriate lifestyle items. The vignette portrayed the typical cohort family, their guests, their food preferences, and the type of grill its members are most likely to purchase.[76]

The cohort approach to understanding consumer tastes has helped many marketers select appeals—whether through music, images, jokes, or values—that evoke the shared experiences of people belonging to the same generation. Companies such as Jaguar Cars Ltd., Volkswagen, VH1, and Levi Strauss & Co. have similarly reported they have successfully used this approach to design products or services that suit particular cohorts or create appeals that win their favor.[77]

As we have seen while investigating the process of decision making within a family setting, decisions can range from individual choices made by a single family member to joint decisions that entail input from multiple parties, including husband, wife, and/or children. In these cases, each member of the family influences others as well as receives influence from others. The family, in this sense, is but one example of social groups in which personal influence plays an important role. Personal influence describes the process by which others influence us either verbally (friends, neighbors, or colleagues) or virally (through communication on the Internet). The significance of personal influence lies in its credibility as a source of product-related information due to perceived objectivity of the source. The topic of personal influence is covered in detail in the next chapter.

A Cross-Functional Point of View

The topics of the family and generational cohorts have a number of implications for business disciplines other than marketing. Relevant issues might include

- **Human Resources:** Many companies today view work–family initiatives as a business imperative. At IBM, for example, a survey of employees revealed that the primary reason for employee resignations was problems in achieving work versus family-life balance. The company found that 62 percent of its employees were part of a dual-income couple, 32 percent had child-care needs, 32 percent had some elder-care responsibilities, and 4 percent were single parents. As a result, the company's work-life programs were designed to include child-care and elder-care resource and referral, adoption assistance, personal leaves of absence for up to three years, flexible work schedules and workplace arrangements, personal financial planning, and a consulting and referral program to help employees and their families manage a personal problem.

- **Legal/Ethics:** The Children's Advertising Review Unit (CARU) as a self-regulatory group has its own suggested guidelines for ads directed to kids but wields no legal authority to change or pull misleading and deceptive ads off the air. As a result, children's commercials that run on network television, where the standards for children's advertising are very strict, remain firmly within CARU's guidelines. However, commercials that are produced for nonnetwork TV can run the gamut from being fictional to being outright deceptive. A Barbie doll, for example, which is no more than a plastic figure incapable of movement, can be made to come alive in a commercial designed for nonnetwork TV. In one such commercial from Mattel, Barbie and her friends appeared to move by themselves, holding guitars and dancing amid flashing pink and blue lights. Because children, especially youngsters, cannot distinguish between fantasy and reality, CARU views commercials of this type as crossing the ethical boundary but realizes its hands are somewhat tied because it lacks the authority to curtail such practices.

- **Investment Planning:** In most states, single parents, homosexuals, and those who choose to live together outside marriage face formidable retirement-planning challenges. Although the law in such states provides plenty of protection for married couples, it fails to do the same for everyone else. Taxes, insurance benefits, retirement pay, and inheritance rules—factors that have traditionally been incentives for and benefits of marriage—are but some aspects of the law that discriminate between conventional families and other forms of households. Similarly, corporate benefits routinely extend to spouses of employees but do not always protect unmarried partners. This situation necessitates that people with nontraditional living arrangements set up their own safety nets, prepare special legal documents, and plan independently for retirement.

These issues, and a host of others like them, serve to show that the topics of the family and generational cohorts transcend the field of marketing to other business disciplines.

Summary

The U.S. Census Bureau defines *family* as "two or more persons, related either through birth, marriage, or adoption, living under one roof." Nevertheless, contemporary families or households come in myriad forms, sizes, and compositions. The family plays an integral role in the process of consumer socialization—the process by which individuals acquire the knowledge, skills, and attitudes relevant to their effective functioning as consumers in the marketplace.

At least eight family consumption roles can be identified. These include influencers, gatekeepers, deciders, buyers, preparers, users, maintainers, and disposers. The family decision process can be classified into four categories: autonomic, husband dominant, wife dominant, and syncretic. The relative roles of the husband and wife in family decisions are impacted by such factors as egalitarianism, involvement, empathy, and recognized authority.

The family life cycle refers to the series of stages through which households pass as their members grow older. The stages of the FLC model are primarily based on age, marital status, employment status of the head of household, and the presence or absence of children as well as their ages. At each stage, there are unique needs, differences in earning power, and specific demands placed on household resources. Five distinguishable stages of the traditional FLC are bachelorhood, honeymooner, parenthood, postparenthood, and dissolution. Modernized family life cycle models recognize the diversity of contemporary households and societal trends, such as increases in the number of singles, unmarried cohabitants, dual-career couples, childless couples, single-parent households, adoptions by single persons, late-in-life marriages, blended families, and divorces and separations. Accompanying such increases is a notable decrease in the number of extended families. Still other nontraditional households include latchkey kids and boomerang children.

Generational marketing targets segments of the population based on external events that occurred during the formative years of a generation. Whereas a generation is defined by dates of birth, a cohort catalogs each generation in terms of external events that occurred during its members' formative years. Generational cohorts include the Postwar, Boomers I, Boomers II, and Generation X, Generation Y, and Generation Z cohorts as well as Techno-savvies.

Generational marketing systems can help marketers of many products and services identify groups of consumers with homogeneous life experiences. Those who have similar life experiences are likely to be similar with respect to other behavioral characteristics, such as product purchase, motivations, and media behavior. The implied psychological coherence of such segments allows marketers to use language and symbols, select appeals, and make offers that are meaningful to them.

Review Questions

1. In general, why is the U.S. Census Bureau's current definition of the term *family* considered inadequate? In light of the ever-increasing number and diversity of nontraditional households, what revised definition of *family* would you propose?

2. China's one-child policy was established by then Chinese leader Deng Xiaoping in 1979 to limit Communist China's population growth. Even though it was designated as a temporary measure, it remains in full force even today. The policy limits

couples to one child. Punishments for violators include fines, pressures to abort pregnancies, or even forced sterilization. The government claims that such a policy is vital to China's survival, considering the limited natural resources available to support the country's massive population. Do you think the one-child policy is justified in view of this claim? What arguments can you present for and against this policy?

3. As households progress through the successive stages of the family life cycle, the categories of products and services acquired at each stage tend to change. Cite examples of products and services that are likely to be needed and purchased during the two stages of honeymooners (young married couples without children) and those that are typical during the parenthood stage.

4. Assume you are a marketer of family vacation cruises and would like to broaden your customer base to include singles. What strategies or actions would you consider taking in order to accomplish this objective?

5. One of the benefits of generational marketing is its ability to help segment the market based on the similarity of life experiences within specific customer groups. Consider the generation known as the Boomers I cohort. What specific language and symbols would you suggest advertisers use to evoke an emotional response from members of this group?

Discussion Questions

1. The change of spousal roles due to the expanded participation of women in the labor force has affected family decision-making processes. Not only did this change affect who makes certain types of decisions, but it also influenced who does the actual shopping, when the shopping is done, and where. Cite a number of changes that you have observed in this regard. Comment on how these changes may require marketers to adapt their traditional strategies.

2. Television advertising directed to children has been the subject of a great deal of controversy. It has even attracted the attention of various government bodies, which either closely scrutinize ads for children or seek to regulate their content and manner of presentation. Why is this topic of importance to marketers? How much influence do children have on parental purchasing behavior? When and for which types of product purchases are children most likely to be influential? When are children least likely to be influential?

3. Singles often complain that despite their large numbers in society and their vast purchasing power, it is often difficult for them to find product offerings designed and sized for those who live alone. Critics claim that marketers seem to be enamored of families and choose to ignore singles. They cite examples that range from food packages that are unsuitable for single servings to hotels that charge identical rates for single versus double occupancy. Do you feel that such complaints from singles are justified? Should marketers adjust their strategies to cater to the needs of singles? How?

In reference to the chapter-opening vignette about singles and the rise of what has become known as the "unmarriage revolution," some observers feel that there are at least three reasons for the tendency of individuals in our society to remain single today. The first relates to a person's desire for autonomy brought about by specific career goals that force his or her relationships to the back burner. An obsessive sense that one's independent lifestyle must not be curtailed in any way becomes that person's driving force. Relationships, in this sense, may impair one's self-oriented, carefree lifestyle and cause one to make undesirable compromises.

The second reason lies in the unlimited social relationship choices individuals have available today. Driven by the Internet and electronic media, these types of opportunities have multiplied and created countless options—making it difficult to commit to one person. The third reason pertains to the fact that many individuals in our society, more so than in any previous generation, realize that they are products of divorced parents. This revelation leaves many of them suspicious about marriage and sensing a great statistical risk of having to face divorce themselves. Do you agree with this assessment of the "unmarriage revolution" phenomenon? In your view, what other significant influences underlie this singles trend?

CASE

Club Med Woos Families

On a sunny, warm day, around the middle of April 2008, the airport at the Pacific resort of Ixtapa, Mexico, seemed exceptionally busy. A number of newspaper reporters and photographers, and French as well as Mexican TV crews, were gathering in the main airport lobby. The reason for the assembly was the expected arrival of Mr. Henri Giscard D'Estaing, the CEO and Chairman of the Board of Club Mediterranee, and members of his board, as well as dignitaries and guests from around the world. The purpose was the celebration of the Grand Opening of the new Club Med Premium Resort in Ixtapa, which was one of the first resorts to receive part of the $530 million renovation project spent by Club Med. Other upgraded properties included Sandpiper, Punta Cana, Cancun, Yucatan, Columbus Isle, Turkoise, and Bora Bora

Upon arrival, Mr. D'Estaing spoke to reporters about the new strategy that Club Med has adopted. The present focus of the firm, Mr. D'Estaing explained, has shifted from the old strategy of appealing to single adults—the main market segment the company catered to in the past—to families and their children.

Originally, the company's vacations had been designed to relieve singles from everyday cares and preoccupations and to give them a memorable vacation full of fun, as well as a chance to meet other singles. Club Med vacations included airfares, ground transfers, accommodations in straw huts or in hotel or bungalow-style rooms, exotic meals served in romantic atmospheres, sports and activities that included swimming, scuba diving, horseback riding, skiing, tennis, and golf, as well as nightly entertainment.

The company had done very well for many years. In the 1960s and 1970s, for example, when Club Med was at its height, thousands of singles flocked to camps on Greek islands, in the Pacific Ocean, and on the Mexican shores to have fun and to meet other singles. However, as the years went by, Club Med's followers began to trail off into more responsible lives. The majority settled down, got married, formed families, and became parents. In 2007, for example, the company found out that the average age of clients had climbed to over 48 years. Many had already deserted Club Med and had started to frequent "family-friendly" competitive resorts run by companies such as Apple Vacations, a top tour wholesaler in the Caribbean and Mexico that converted 51 of its resorts into family-style accommodations. Similarly, cruise ships such as Disney Magic as well as Carnival Cruises started to steer a great many families their way. Moreover, hotels such as the Westin, Marriott, and Hyatt had started to appeal to families through programs such as kids' clubs, menus, activities, day care, game rooms, and free accommodations and meals.

These changes took their toll on Club Med's business. In 1997, the company ran up losses in excess of $235 million. As a result, the company's board of directors fired Serge Trigano, the firm's founder, and replaced him with Philippe Bourguignon, the French industrialist who put Disneyland Park in France on the road to profitability.

One of the first strategic moves Bourguignon made was the recognition of the need to change the emphasis of Club Med vacations from singles to families. Out of the company's 114 villages, he designated only 11 for grown-ups. The rest were targeted to families. Providing vacations to the middle-aged, he believed, would turn around the negative financial picture of the company.

Leaning toward adopting the strategy of his predecessor, Mr. D'Estaing decided to continue this emphasis on families, but with increased quality in hotel services and upgraded accommodations. Special emphasis was placed on family vacations. Activities would be offered for children 4 months to 17 years of age, ranging from hip-hop dance to mini-chef cooking classes. Children, based on their age, can also enjoy one of four facilities in each resort such as Baby Club Med, Petit Club Med, Mini Club Med, and Junior Club Med.

When Mr. D'Estaing undertook the transformation of Club Mediterranee, he had a number of goals in mind that included improving the entire village portfolio and upgrading 98 percent of its properties to three Tridents or higher. He worked on shifting the vacation trend toward more frequent but briefer vacations, and organ-

ized them around four themes—exploration, well-being, golf, and first snowfall. He also continued to focus the company's emphasis on families, as well as expand the market the company wishes to target. The identified target market was set at 60 million individuals, with particular attention directed to families in the United States, Asia, and Europe. To reach members of this target market, Club Med used innovative techniques that included, among other media, the Internet.

In January 2008, the company launched a multicultural, worldwide advertising campaign called "Where Happiness Means the World." The campaign, the company hoped, would emphasize the moments when families, couples, and friends create their own meaningful experiences, free from difficulties of worldly pressures.

The main emphasis of the new campaign is markedly different than that of previous years. The new campaign is designed to downplay the exotic and erotic fun vacations, once the trademark of Club Med, that were peddled to swinging singles. The updated emphasis, instead, is the family—vacations for couples or singles who like to take their children along everywhere.

The concern, however, with this campaign is that after years of trying to lure singles to Club Med resorts, the switch to families may have the negative effect of confusing customers and blurring one of the premier brand names in the singles vacation world. The fact that Club Med was once the unchallenged leader in the all-inclusive vacations for young singles might make the new family emphasis backfire. The campaign may alienate singles, who would then avoid kid-crowded resorts and, at the same time, may disinterest families who still believe that Club Med is a place for swinging singles only.

Questions

1. Considering the firm reputation that Club Med had established over the years in serving singles, do you think the new strategy of targeting families will meet with the desired success? Explain.

2. Some observers feel that the new emphasis on families by Club Med may cause confusion among young single guests. In your opinion, what possible negative effects might this repositioning campaign precipitate? During the transitional period, what is the expected reaction of both singles as well as families when they find out that they share the same resort? What can Club Med do to minimize such reactions?

3. Knowing that Club Med has targeted the market segment consisting of families at full force, what policies or attractions might the company employ to raise families' interest and enhance the demand for the firm's vacations?

Notes

1. Sam Roberts, "51% of Women Are Now Living Without Spouse," *New York Times,* (January 16, 2007), www.nytimes.com/2007/01/16/US/16census.html; Ellen Connolly, "Career Women Empty Nation's Sperm Banks," News.com.au (January 20, 2008), www.news.com.au/story/0,23599,23077288-2,00.html.

2. R. Moore and G. P. Moschis, "Role of Mass Media and Family in Development of Consumption Norms," *Journalism Quarterly* 80, no. 1 (Spring 1983), pp. 67–73.

3. R. Moore and G. P. Moschis, "The Effects of Family Communication and Mass Media Use on Adolescent Consumer Learning," *Journal of Communication* 31, no. 4 (Fall 1981), pp. 42–51.

4. G. P. Moschis and R. Moore, "A Longitudinal Study of the Development of Purchasing Patterns," in P. Murphy (ed.), *Proceedings of the Educators' Conference,* (Chicago: American Marketing Association, 1983), pp. 114–17.

5. G. P. Moschis et al., "Mass Media and Interpersonal Influences on Adolescent Consumer Learning," in B. Greenberg (ed.), *Proceedings of the Educators' Conference* (Chicago: American Marketing Association, 1977), pp. 68–71.

6. J. A. Clausen, "Perspectives on Childhood Socialization," in J. A. Clausen (ed.), *Socialization and Society* (Boston: Little Brown, 1968).

7. Moschis et al., "Mass Media and Interpersonal Influences on Adolescent Consumer Learning."

8. J. Aldous, "Commentaries on Ward, Consumer Socialization," *Journal of Consumer Research* 1 (September 1974), pp. 15–16.

9. S. Ward, D. B. Wackman, and E. Wartella, *How Children Learn to Buy: The Development of Consumer Information Processing Skills* (Beverly Hills, CA: Sage, 1977).

10. P. Sloan, "Matchabelli Name Readied for Men's Fragrance Line," *Advertising Age* (September 18, 1978), p. 3; B. Voss, "Selling with Sentiment," *Sales & Marketing Management* (March 1993), pp. 60–65.

11. J. W. McDavid and H. Harari, *Social Psychology* (New York: Harper and Row, 1968), pp. 268–69.

12. Bernice Kanner, "Toplines: Are You Normal?" *American Demographics* (March 1999), p. 19.

13. "Women Driving the Internet," *Mom's Refuge* (2006), www.momsrefuge.com/carrer/9906/biznotes/index.html; "The Changing Roles of Men and Women," *Ketchum Inc.* (2007), www.ketchumcomms.co.uk/node/564.

14. "Child Care Resource Group Releases 'Book of Families' to Congress, President," *US Newswire* (February 26, 1998); J. R. Veum and P. M. Gleason, "Child Care: Arrangements and Costs," *Monthly Labor Review* (October 1991), pp. 10–17; and P. Cattan, "Child-Care Problems: An Obstacle to Work," *Monthly Labor Review* (October 1991), pp. 3–9; and "Family Finance, The Cost of Raising a Child: 2003," http://www.gov.mb.ca/agriculture/homuc/cba28502.html; "Parents and the High Price of Child Care: 2007 Update," National Association of Child Care Resources & Referral Agencies, www.naccrra.org/docs/press/price_report.pdf.

15. H. L. Davis and B. P. Rigaux, "Perception of Marital Roles in Decision Processes," *Journal of Consumer Research* 1 (June 1974), pp. 51–62; M. A. Straus, "Conjugal Power Structure and Adolescent Personality," *Marriage and Family Living* 24, no. 1 (February 1962), pp. 17–25.

16. Davis and Rigaux, "Perception of Marital Roles in Decision Processes."

17. M. Putnam and W. R. Davidson, *Family Purchasing Behavior II: Family Roles by Product Category* (Columbus, OH: Management Horizons, 1987).

18. L. H. Rogler and M. E. Procidano, "Egalitarian Spouse Relations and Wives' Marital Satisfaction in Intergenerationally Linked Puerto Rican Families," *Journal of Marriage and the Family* 51 (February 1989), pp. 37–39.

19. W. J. Qualls, "Household Decision Behavior: The Impact of Husbands' and Wives' Sex Role Orientation," *Journal of Consumer Research* 14 (September 1987), pp. 264–79.

20. J. Ford, M. S. LaTour, and T. L. Henthrone, "Perception of Marital Roles in Purchase Decision Processes: A Cross-Cultural Study," *Journal of the Academy of Marketing Science* 23, no. 2 (Spring 1995), pp. 120–31.

21. Robert M. Cosenza, "Family Decision Making Decision Dominance Structure Analysis—An Extension," *Journal of the Academy of Marketing Science* 13, nos. 1, 2 (Winter–Spring 1985), pp. 91–103.

22. Jack J. Kasulis and Marie Adele Hughes, "Husband–Wife Influence in Selecting a Family Professional," *Journal of the Academy of Marketing Science* 12, nos. 1, 2 (Winter–Spring 1984), pp. 115–27.

23. "Children as Consumers," *Global Issues"* (January 8, 2008), www.globalissues.org/TrendRelated/Consumption/Children.asp.

24. "American Children: Key National Indicators of Well-Being 2007," *Child Stats.gov*, www.childstats.gov/americaschildren/tables.asp.

25. Liebeck, "The Consumer Connection: Children under 13."

26. Datamonitor, "Best Practices in Teen and Tween Personal Care 2002," http://www.marketresearch.com/map/prod/829427.html; and David G. Kennedy, "Coming of Age in Consumerdom," *Am. Demographics* (April 2004), p. 14.

27. "Kids Now Have a Bigger Say in the Car Buying Decision," *Easier Motoring* (August 11, 2006), www.easier.com/view/News/Motoring/articles-64579.htm/.

28. "Children as Consumers," *Global Issues"* (January 8, 2008), www.globalissues.org/TrendRelated/Consumption/Children.asp.

29. "Selling to Kids: Kid-Sizing Adult Products by the Book," *BNET.com's FindArticles* (March 7, 2001), http://findarticles.com/p/articles/mi_m0FVE/is_4_6/ai_71352186/print.

30. James U. McNeal, *The Kids Market: Myths and Realities* (Paramount Market Publishing, Inc., Ithaca, NY).

31. "The ABCs of Adult Marketing to Children," *PR Watch* (July 7, 2006), www.prwatch.org/node/4957.

32. Anup Shah, "Behind Consumption and Consumerism/Children as Consumers," *Global Issues* (January 8, 2008), www.globalissues.org/TradeRelated/Consumption/Children.asp; CARU Guidelines at www.caru.org/guidelines/index.asp.

33. Children's Advertising Review Unit, Council of Better Business Bureau, www.caru.org.

34. Christy Fisher, "Census Data May Make Ads More Single-Minded," *Ad Age* (July 20, 1992), p. 2.

35. U.S. Census Bureau, "Households and Families 2000," http://www.census.gov/prod/2001pubs/c2kbr01-8.pdf

36. Molly Ginty, "Grandmothers Strain Resources to Raise Grandkids," *Women's e News*, (June 17, 2008), www.womensenews.org/article.cfm/dyn/aid/3282/context/archive.

37. Charles M. Schaninger and William D. Danko, "A Conceptual and Empirical Comparison of Alternative Household Life Cycle Models," *Journal of Consumer Research* 19 (March 1993), pp. 580–94.

38. Schaninger and Danko, "A Conceptual and Empirical Comparison of Alternative Household Life Cycle Models"; Mary C. Gilly and Ben M. Enis, "Recycling the Family Life Cycle: A Proposal for Redefinition," in Andrew A. Mitchell (ed.), *Advances in Consumer Research* 9 (Ann Arbor, MI: Association for Consumer Research, 1982), pp. 271–76.

39. Schaninger and Danko, "A Conceptual and Empirical Comparison of Alternative Household Life Cycle Models"; Patrick E. Murphy and William A. Staples, "A Modernized Family Life Cycle," *Journal of Consumer Research* 6 (June 1979), pp. 12–22.

40. Jan Hare and Elizabeth Gray, "All Kids of Families: A Guide for Parents" (2006), CYFERnet, www.cyfernet.org/parent/nontradfam.html/21K.

41. "About Our Kids," New York University's Child Study Center, www.aboutourkids.org.

42. "Latchkey Kids," http://www.scpd.org/crime/latchkey-kids.html

43. "Highly Educated Mothers Likely to Stay in Workforce, Sociologists Find," News Service, Stanford University (May 11, 2007), www.lisatrei@stanford.edu.

44. Sharon Jayson, "Analysis: Boomerang Generation Mostly Hype," *USA Today* (March 14, 2007), www.usatoday.com/news/nation/2007-03-13-analysis-boomerang_N.htm.

45. Jay MacDonald, "How to 'Gently' Toss Your Boomerang Kid," *Bankrate* (September 9, 2005), www.bankrate.com/brm/news/pf/20050909a1.asp.

46. Gary Picariello, "They're Back: Boomerang Kids," *Associated Content* (June 1, 2007), www.associatedcontent.com/article/259628/theyre_back_boomerang_kids.html?cat=12.

47. Pamela Paul, "ecoboomerang," *American Demographics* (June 2001), pp. 44-49.

48. Jennifer Wolf, "Who Is the 'Average' Single Parent?" *About.com* (2007), http://singleparents.about.com/od/legalissues/p/portrait.htm?p=1.

49. "Single-Parent Family: Career Help," www.baycongroup.com/word2007/SamplePrint.docx.

50. Rickard, "Friendship and Choice Now Thicker than Blood."

51. R. D. Ahuja and Mary Walker, "Female-headed Single Parent Families: Comparisons with Dual Parent

Households on Restaurant and Convenience Food Usage," *Journal of Consumer Marketing* 11, no. 4 (1994), pp. 41-54.

52. Cathleen D. Zick, Jane McCullough, and Ken R. Smith, "Trade-offs Between Purchased Services and Time in Single-Parent and Two-Parent Families," *Journal of Consumer Affairs* (June 1, 1996), pp. 1-23.

53. Ibid.

54. "Single Parents (Household Projections)," *American Demographics* 15 (December 1993), pp. 36-37.

55. United States Census Bureau, *Current Population Survey, 2008 Annual Social and Economic Supplement.*

56. "People Living Alone Account for 41 Percent of the Personal Care Market," *Goliath* (2008), http://goliath.ecnext.com/coms2/gi_0199-3010729/People-living-alone-account-for.html.

57. Sara Hammes and June Fletcher, "Selling to Singles and Couples," *Builder* 17, (February 1994), p. 52.

58. Ted J. Rakstis, "Wanted: The Single Consumer," *Kiwanis Magazine* (August, 1992), pp. 34-37.

59. Jock Bickert, "Waging War on the 98%," *Direct Marketing* (February 1996), pp. 40-43; and Jock Bickert "Cohorts II: A New Approach to Market Segmentation," *Journal of Consumer Marketing* 14, no. 5 (1997), pp. 362-79.

60. Geoffrey Meredith and Charles Schewe, "The Power of Cohorts," *American Demographics* 16, no. 12 (December 1994), pp. 22-27, 31; Faye Rice, "Making Generational Marketing Come of Age," *Fortune* (June 26, 1995), pp. 110-14.

61. Tony Laidig, "Using the Power of Nostalgia as a Marketing Strategy," *Scribd* (2007), www.scribd.com/doc/3192077/Using-the-power-of-nostalgia-as-a-marketing-strategyLAIDIG; Nedra Weinrich, "Harnessing Nostalgia," *MarketingProf Daily Fix* (June 1, 2007), www.mpdailyfix.com/2007/06/harnessing_nostalgia.html

62. Meredith and Schewe, "The Power of Cohorts," summarized in Rice, "Making Generational Marketing Come of Age," pp. 110-14.

63. Geoffrey E. Meredith, "Defining Markets Defining Moments," *Life Stage Marketing,*" www.lifestagemarketing.com.

64. J. Walker Smith and Ann Clurman, "Generational Marketing," *Inc.* (April 1997), pp. 87-88, 91.

65. "Toplines: Conflicting Signals," *American Demographics* (November 1998), p. 19.

66. Laura Barcella, "Generation X's Debt Headache," *Alter Ne,* (May 31, 2006), www.alternet.org/workplace/36658/.

67. "Generation Y: Today's Teens—the Biggest Bulge since the Moomers—May Force Marketers to Toss Their Old Tricks," *Business Week* (February 15, 1999), www.businessweek.com/1999/99_07/b36/6001.htm.

68. Lisa Reilly Cullen, "Ride the Echo Boom to Stock Profits," *Money* 26, no. 7 (July 1997), pp. 98-104; Len Lewis, "Generation 'Y,'" *Progressive Grocer* 76, no. 3 (March 1997), p. 18; Suzanne Kapner, "Understanding," *Restaurant Business* 96, no. 14 (July 15, 1997), pp. 48-52, and Pamela Paul, "Getting Inside Generation Y," *Am. Demographics* (Sept. 2001), pp. 43-49; and Nadira Hira, "You Raised Them, Now Manage Them," *Fortune*, (May 28, 2007), pp. 38-46.

69. "A Vague View of '90s Teenagers," *Chicago Sun-Times* (August 18, 1996), p. 6.

70. Ellen Neuborne and Kathleen Kerwin, "Generation Y," *Business Week* (February 15, 1999), pp. 81-88.

71. Susan Walsh, "Kids as Young as 2 Using Internet," *Chicago Sun-Times* (June 5, 2005).

72. Barbara Comes, "Techno-Savvy or Techno-Oriented: Who Are the Net Generation?" Proceedings of the Asia-Pacific Conference on Library Information Education and Practice" (2006), http://elist.sir.arizona.edu/1410/01/57.Barbara_Comes_pp401-408_pdf.

73. Laura Bird, "Techno-Savvies Are New Target of Advertisers," *Wall Street Journal* (January 11, 1994), pp. B1, B2.

74. Shawn Tully, "Teens: The Most Global Market of All," *Fortune* (May 16, 1994), pp. 90-97; Joel Stein, "Getting Giggy with a Hoodie," *Time* (January 19, 1998); Google Answers, "Apparel Sales Market Research," http://answers.google.com/answers/threadview?id=74610.

75. Bickert, "Cohorts II: A New Approach to Market Segmentation."

76. Ibid.

77. Michael M. Phillips, "Demographics: Selling by Evoking What Defines a Generation," *Wall Street Journal* (August 13, 1996).

Personal Influence and Word of Mouth

LEARNING OBJECTIVES

- To examine the nature of personal influence and opinion leadership.
- To comprehend the power and vividness of word-of-mouth communication.
- To develop a basic understanding of four models of the personal influence process.
- To gain insight into the methods of identifying and/or creating opinion leaders and e-fluentials.
- To examine the three personal influence strategies that marketers use to benefit their firms.
- To review how marketers harness word of mouth and combat negative buzz.

KEY TERMS

personal influence
word of mouth (WOM)
opinion leaders
e-fluentials
opinion leadership
agents of change
availability-valence hypothesis
hypodermic needle model
trickle-down model
trickle-up model
trickle-across model
two-step model
multistep model

sociometric method
sociogram
self-designation method
key informant method
objective method
shopping pals
market maven
surrogate consumer
brand reps
teaser campaigns
product placement
testimonials

In January 2007, at the MacWorld Expo in San Francisco, Steve Jobs announced to the world his plans to introduce the new iPhone, the first most important product to be launched by Apple. Almost immediately, his announcement created overwhelming press attention, resulting in thousands of articles appearing in over 50 major publications discussing and speculating about the features of the new iPhone. In addition, consumers' excitement and anticipation for the iPhone caused bloggers to blog furiously and techno-savvies to debate the phone's expected features, price, and partnership with AT&T.

All components of Apple's strategy, including the timing of the press announcements, the sequence in which the ads were released, and even the caption and illustrations used in these ads, combined to produce an aura of suspense and anticipation that got everyone talking about the new device. At this point, the full power of word of mouth was obviously in play at full force. On one side, the product offered a superior substitute for consumers' current cell phones; and on the other side, the exclusive image that was created by the iPhone's initial lofty price appealed to the vanity of many consumers.

The full force of the power of word of mouth, however, was realized after the iPhone was released. On June 29, 2007, the day after the phone was officially introduced, an incredible amount of chatter, speculation, and discussion took place among consumers in all known forms of media. Consumers, experts, and techno-gurus exchanged views about all aspects of the iPhone, including its technical and nontechnical features, components, applications, and looks. Consumers evaluated, speculated, and praised or criticized some of the phone's new features, price, and exclusivity.

As soon as some fortunate consumers were able to get their hands on the new iPhone, they could not wait to show it off to their friends and colleagues. Everyone was fascinated by this technological marvel. The iPhone features and its capability of finger-motion screen image change dazzled consumers. Groups clustered around the lucky possessors, looking, touching, and testing the new device.

This extraordinary interest created high awareness for the innovative product. Consumers were very receptive to news about it and even sought sources of further details. Experts and opinion leaders trusted by consumers praised the new phone and gave it glowing reviews. Demand for the new phone exceeded supply, and the shortages even helped in creating a sense of suspense and urgency to acquire one.

In a similar fashion, Apple employed this strategy to introduce the iPhone 3G, which was released on July 11, 2008. The iPhone 3G was introduced along with the opening of the iTunes App Store, featuring over 500 third-party applications for the new phone. Three factors significantly contributed to the immediate success of the iPhone 3G. These factors include the unique combination of an extremely capable device, millions of customers looking for ways to expand the usefulness of their current phone, and an enthusiastic community of developers—all sustaining an avalanche of positive word of mouth for the new device.

By harnessing the power of word of mouth, Apple succeeded in masterfully manipulating public eagerness for an innovative device, as well as enhancing the anticipation and excitement that surrounded the product's release—actions that resulted in unparalleled levels of sales. This word-of-mouth success story of the iPhone is, and will continue to be, a unique case about which marketers will marvel for many years to come.[1]

> *Online social networks have greatly enhanced the power of word of mouth. Thousands of comments, stories, compliments, and/or complaints in blog postings change the narrow meaning of "word of mouth" from verbal face-to-face communication between two individuals to a massive phenomenon that shares information among millions of consumers. Learn more about word of mouth by visiting two Web sites, the first from the Word of Mouth Marketing Association at www.womma.org/about/ and the second known as Twitter at twitter.com To what extent should marketers encourage such online chatter? What are the ramifications of ignoring the things that consumers say? What action would you suggest for firms to address both positive and negative types of word of mouth? Explain.*

Word of mouth derives its power simply from the high level of consumers' interest and involvement due to its ability to create an environment in which people can freely share their thoughts and views with others either personally or via e-mail, blogs, and postings in social networks. We begin this chapter by exploring the dynamics of personal influence and word-of-mouth communications, as well as by ascertaining the role played by opinion leaders in disseminating product and service information to others. We then examine the characteristics of opinion leaders and cite strategic marketing implications of these concepts to the field of consumer behavior.

Personal Influence

Our purchasing behavior is frequently affected by the folk with whom we intermingle. Just as reference groups and family members shape our beliefs, attitudes, and behavior, so also do other individuals with whom we interact. These interactions between two or more persons frequently influence the ideas, feelings, or conduct of one or more participants in the dialogue. This phenomenon is known as personal influence.

Personal influence refers to any change, whether deliberate or inadvertent, in an individual's beliefs, attitudes, or behavior that occurs as the consequence of interpersonal communication. Word of mouth is one of the means through which personal influence can occur. **Word of mouth (WOM)** is communication between a source and a receiver, where the receiver perceives the source as independent regarding a product, service, or brand. Such communication may be personal or may alternatively occur online through the use of preexisting social networks. WOM is originated by a third party, transmitted spontaneously in a way that is somehow autonomous of the party being talked about. In this sense, in WOM, both the message and the medium are independent.[2] People generally think of WOM in terms of advice given and received

personal influence
any change in beliefs, attitudes, or behavior due to interpersonal communication

word of mouth (WOM)
sharing of an opinion about a product, service or company between an independent source and a receiver

© 2009, Michael Shake, Shutterstock, Inc.

The increasing popularity of hybrid cars at the present time is largely due to both word of mouth concerning energy costs, as well as visual influence as this type of car debuts on the nation's highways.

within the context of face-to-face communication. In reality, WOM recommendations of products, services, brands, and stores can be transmitted either in person, over the phone, through the mail, or online through social networks, review sites, blogs, and forums. In this sense, WOM is the actual sharing of an opinion about a product or service between consumers. As such, it should be distinguished from viral marketing, which is typically reserved for programs where the advertising is talked about as opposed to the product itself. For example, viral videos, where the humor overshadows the brand, represents a case in point. The ad in Figure 13.1 from Allianz, a global financial network, stresses the value of verbal word of mouth spoken by a father to his son regarding selection of the right network to accelerate financial growth.

The effects, as well as the form, of WOM vary with the blend of industries, products, and services to which the WOM pertains. In research specific to health-care marketing, for example, studies conclude that personal influence has a more decisive effect on the purchase decision than do commercial sources of information.[3] For example, in the selection of obstetric–gynecologist health professionals, friends, family, and other doctors and nonphysician health-care practitioners were found to be important word-of-mouth sources. Similarly, family and other doctors were found to be important word-of-mouth sources in the selection of an internist.[4] Personal influence, in these cases, was the main determinant of the choice of physician.

Personal influence can be verbal, visual, or both.[5] Consumers may track product, service, and store comments from blog postings, forums, and message boards, or simply overhear other peoples' opinions about them. In other cases, consumers observe what other people are doing, wearing, or using and may even ask them what an item is, how much it costs, and where it was purchased. The consequence of these information-sharing exchanges is influence that can be either one way or mutual. In the area of clothing, for example, visual influence can be so dramatic that a new style becomes fashionable across the entire nation in a matter of just a few weeks.

WHO ARE THE OPINION LEADERS?

When confronting unusual circumstances, unfamiliar issues, or challenging decisions, individuals in search of pertinent information frequently turn to others within their social sphere who are better informed on the subject. Those more knowledgeable persons who casually provide advice are known as **opinion leaders**. Opinion leaders play a key communications role by conveying credible information via WOM and influencing the viewpoints or actions of others.

opinion leaders
knowledgeable, influential persons who casually provide advice

Figure 13.1

The tagline and illustration in this ad for Allianz Financial Network reflects the notion that word of mouth is an effective medium for communicating financial advice.

Many products and services that are an integral part of our lives today get their initial boost from opinion leaders. These individuals are the experts, gurus, and mavens. Their sphere of influence may be global, national, or local in nature. The attribute that gives them their influence is the trust that consumers place in their recommendations. They are perceived as objective evaluators of the overwhelming amount of information that consumers are faced with. They process marketers' communications as well as translate the messages for the rest of us. They spread marketers' information to us by conspicuously displaying their recent purchases, vocalizing their thoughts, or urging us to try something unfamiliar and new.

These tiers of experts and influencers are the ones who start the chain reaction of WOM and give the products, services, or ideas they support their initial jump start. Examples of opinion leaders abound. Simply think of recommendations provided by movie critics or food gurus on Web sites such as Zagat's Guide to Restaurants and Hotels, or tech buffs for the latest models of home electronics.

Progressive companies have come to realize that in order to run a successful word-of-mouth marketing campaign, they have to reach and maintain relationships with a highly effective group of influencers. And, because those influencers use both online and offline media channels, they are able to provide a communications shortcut—thereby helping companies effectively and inexpensively reach their intended market.

A 2007 survey by Burson-Marsteller Public Relations and Public Affairs Firm has revealed a profile of a group of opinion makers called the **e-fluentials**. These individuals defy the limits of traditional viral marketing and spread the word to millions of people. They are defined according to their intensive use of e-mail, chatrooms, and message boards, as well as company and opinion Web sites. They constitute 10 percent of the U.S. online adult population, or approximately 11 million individuals, but are capable of reaching a total of 155 million American adults online and offline as they relay their experiences.[6]

E-fluentials love to chat. They spend over 21 hours per week conversing both with colleagues at work (9.2 hours) and with friends and family outside of work (11.7 hours). Moreover, they additionally spend approximately 21 hours each week online. The survey also showed that 96 percent of the e-fluentials talk about both good and bad product experiences face-to-face, and 79 percent of them share product news over the phone. These points demonstrate the fact that e-fluentials still spend a significant amount of time using old-fashioned personal and telephone conversations to get their messages across.

Some of the characteristics of e-fluentials include the tendency to crave knowledge, to acquire more information than general Internet users, and to obtain it from a wider variety of sources. The Burson-Marsteller survey revealed that e-fluentials are socially and politically engaged and are vocal citizens in cyber- and traditional spheres. They are in constant touch with companies, the media, and government agencies through e-mail and other forms of communication, thereby connecting the dots between companies, the media, policymakers, and consumers.[7]

e-fluentials
Internet users who influence other consumers online

E-fluentials are Internet experts. Three out of four e-fluentials classify themselves as advanced expert Internet users, versus less than half of general users who classify themselves in the same manner. More than three-quarters of e-fluentials go online at least once a day, and half of them spend at least two hours online daily.[8]

From the perspective of social scientists, **opinion leadership** is the extent to which an agent is informally able to incline the beliefs, attitudes, or behaviors of other people in some desired way. In a marketing sense, however, opinion leadership refers to the influence that individuals conversant with a product/service, or company exert on the minds and actions of other consumers. A distinction, however, must be drawn between unpretentious opinion leaders and those individuals or organizations that actively seek to change other people's minds. Parties, whether political, religious, or commercial, whose personal or collective agendas entail active attempts to modify other people's beliefs, attitudes, or behaviors are more correctly termed **agents of change**.

Opinion leadership is an inherent and indispensable element in the give-and-take of interpersonal relationships. It is not a personality trait that some people possess and others don't. In fact, most people would qualify as opinion leaders in some subject or product category. The 110 million online adults *not* designed by the 2007 Burson-Marsteller survey as e-fluentials give advice too.

opinion leadership
an agent's ability to informally incline the beliefs, attitudes, or behaviors of others

agents of change
parties who actively seek to modify other people's beliefs, attitudes, or behavior

THE POWER OF PERSONAL INFLUENCE AND WORD OF MOUTH

There are many ways to cause, deliver, or steer WOM in various industries and in the cases of specific products and services. WOM works differently in diverse situations. Let us consider the following cases.

- Nike created an onslaught of WOM when, in 2006, the company erected a large interactive billboard in Times Square (New York). Passersby could use their cell phones to text in their own custom design for a pair of Nike shoes, and in return receive a free pair of Nike IDs. Although Nike gave away 3,000 pairs of shoes in this promotion, consumers were just as excited about seeing their own shoe designs posted live on the jumbotron as they were by getting the free footwear.[9]
- When promoting the Focus automobile, Ford tapped influential young consumers in five key markets: New York, Miami, Los Angeles, Chicago, and San Francisco. Each of the 120 young people selected was given a Focus to drive for six moths, and was asked to simply be seen with the car and to hand out Focus-themed trinkets to anyone who expressed interest in it.[10]
- Hasbro Games deputized hundreds of youth and fifth graders as "secret agents" to tantalize their peers with Hasbro's then-new POX line of electronic games.[11]

Just how powerful is verbal or viral WOM? Ernest Dichter summarized 6,000 case studies and concluded that nearly 80 percent of all purchases can be traced to WOM influence.[12] Dichter's findings were echoed by an advertising executive who stated, "Today, 80 percent of all buying decisions are influenced by someone's direct recommendations."[13] The effectiveness of word of mouth applies across the board in terms of the kinds of responses marketers traditionally seek. Word of mouth increases awareness and knowledge as well as persuades and leads to action. Day found that word of mouth was important in gaining awareness of an innovation and the decision to try a new product.[14] He believed that word of mouth is more important than advertising because the source is seen as more reliable and capable of providing the potential buyer the impetus to take action.

Social pressure to conform often backs up advice given via WOM.[15] In one study, Myers and Robertson found that consumers' estimates of how much their friends might like furniture items appeared to be a better predictor of purchase than buyers' own evaluations.[16] Such findings suggest that the opinions of others carry considerable influence and sometimes may be more convincing than one's own perceptions and judgments.

In another study, Herr, Kardes, and Kim found that WOM had a much stronger impact on brand evaluations of personal computers than objective brand information received in detail from *Consumer Reports*.[17] The same study, however, found that WOM was not the dominant factor in *all* purchases. WOM tended to be less consequential in the evaluation of an automobile when consumers already had a strong impression of the product or when negative product information was available. In other words, it was unlikely that WOM would change the attitudes of consumers who already had strong loyalties or valid apprehensions about a brand. When our knowledge and memory prove sufficient to make a decision, the impact of WOM is lessened.

Many providers of professional services, such as doctors, dentists, and lawyers, build up thriving practices without advertising in the media or using other formal types of promotion. One possible explanation for the success of such businesses is the informal WOM networks that develop among the consumers of these services.[18] Any business, whether large with a huge promotional budget, or small with no funds available for promotion, stands to benefit from referrals, positive WOM, and the impact of e-fluentials.

VIVIDNESS AND IMPACT OF WORD-OF-MOUTH COMMUNICATION

Compared to pallid messages carried by the conventional mass media, verbal or viral WOM information tends to be more vivid and salient, largely because it emanates directly from another individual who personally recounts his or her own experiences. WOM has been described as "live," not canned like most other company communication.[20] It is live because it is custom tailored to the people who are participating in it. Consumers are not receiving a sales pitch but rather are getting answers to their important questions. As such, consumers pay more attention to word of mouth because it is more relevant and complete compared to any other form of communication.

Word of mouth is limitless in the sense that it would take only a few influencers to ignite a chain reaction, where successive tiers of receivers influence the next tier. In a successful campaign, recipients of a message become

Global Opportunity

The World Gets the Word on Word of Mouth

Word of mouth as a marketing strategy is still uncommon in many foreign countries, possibly because it is difficult to define as a promotional tool. However, the last few years have witnessed an increasing number of foreign companies starting to reap the benefits of this important tool. Recently, for example, word of mouth put the Tamagotchi, an egg-shaped virtual pet from the Japanese toy maker Bandai, on the global map. When the company test-marketed the toy among schoolgirls in Tokyo, word about it spread like wildfire as the youngsters told their friends, and the toy sold out as soon as it reached stores. Success of the toy in Japan and the consequent media coverage forced the company to launch the product in other countries ahead of schedule—a case similar to Rubik's cube, which blanketed the globe in the 1980s.

To promote its flat-rate program for mobile phone users, T-Mobile in 2007 had a literal "talk till you drop" contest in the firm's home country, Germany. The contest involved getting teams of two people between the ages of 18 and 25 to talk continuously to each other day and night. Any team that remained silent for more than 10 seconds was eliminated. The team that persisted until the end won a prize of 10,000 euros.

In Korea, one available technology is known as QR codes, which turn a phone into a bar code scanner. Adidas in Korea used these codes on retail merchandise tags and clothing imprints. Potential customers could take a photo of the color code on a sleeve; the handset would then upload the manufacturer's WAP site. Over the course of the test run, 60,000 consumers participated in the Korean Adidas program, and Adidas received over 2 million page views.

Encouraged by these success stories, a number of European companies decided to employ the word-of-mouth strategy to enhance their sales performance. Ericsson, the Swedish mobile phone company, throws parties to spread its brand message among trendy customers. Similarly, Siemens, a German-based firm, in cooperation with its advertising agency FCA, designed a campaign for its mobile phones in the United Kingdom in which cab drivers were paid to chat about the phones to customers riding in their cabs. Even though the scheme failed to get off the ground due to U.K. advertising regulations, ensuing media coverage of the event became the topic of many conversations and comments over the Internet, giving the company a great deal of free publicity.[19]

Realizing that consumers like to talk about products and brands, many companies now opt to stimulate word of mouth by establishing Web sites on which they provide newsworthy stories, ideas, and facts to the public. See how Ericsson stimulates word of mouth by providing news such as its press room, publications, environmental and health issues, Internet awards, and career opportunities on the firm's Web site by visiting www.ericsson.com. Globally, are consumers similar in their tendency to spread, accept, and use word of mouth? In your opinion, is gregariousness (or lack of it) as a cultural trait a determining factor in the spread of word of mouth throughout a society? Explain.

powerful carriers spreading the word to still more carriers, much like a virus rampages through a given population. Since the receiver of advice determines what to ask, whom to approach, in what forum, and whether to continue the dialogue or drop it altogether, the custom-tailored nature of WOM is paramount.

As a consequence of its vivid character, WOM information is more accessible in memory and exerts a relatively greater impact on consumers.[21] A number of reasons explain why WOM appears more vivid than messages received via the conventional mass media. First, WOM has personal relevance, which increases receivers' involvement levels and, consequently, its impact. Second, WOM is concrete, containing detailed facts about specific people, situations, actions, and outcomes. Third, WOM testimony occurs in close temporal, spatial, and sensory proximity to receivers. The story is fresh and new, its setting and context are local and recognizable, and the account describes the narrator's firsthand experience, to which listeners can likely relate.

Messages that are vivid and concrete tend to wield greater influence on receivers than does more abstract information.[22] Vivid information tends to attract and hold receivers' attention, to stimulate their imagination, to make its way into their long-term memory, and to be recalled longer and more easily. Highly vivid messages can conjure up positive or negative impressions among receivers because of what has become known as the availability-valence hypothesis. The **availability-valence hypothesis** states that vivid information tends to be stored in semantic memory with more links to other concepts. This more elaborate mode of storage can make vivid information more accessible for retrieval. Our product judgments depend on the favorableness of the information available in memory.[23] If this information is positively valenced, judgments tend to be positive. If, on the other hand, the information is negatively valenced, judgments tend to be negative.

availability-valence hypothesis
a view that vivid information tends to be stored in memory with more links to other concepts

FORMS OF VIRAL WOM

As was discussed earlier, due to today's highly advanced technology-based communication, WOM is no longer restricted to the small circle of family and friends that opinion leaders were formerly assumed to have. The exponential growth of the Internet rendered this process one of the most powerful communication means in our society today—capable of reaching an unlimited number of Internet users.

The explosiveness of Internet WOM can be observed in online newsgroups and blogs that articulate product/service praises and complaints, seek information, report experiences, and ask for or offer assistance.[24] In a newsgroup, for example, one may see a letter praising a company for its quality products. One may also find a complaint with a description of a negative incident. Some of these are written as open letters addressed not only to the company but to the mass media, opinion leaders, and Internet users in general. To accomplish an effective distribution of their messages, some individuals make their message part of their own home page and join a link-exchange program.

Another form of Internet WOM is online chatrooms, which may be text-based or graphic. The text-based variety is the oldest form of true chatrooms. Some chatrooms, such as Yahoo, use both text and voice simultaneously. However, the graphical chatrooms, such as Active Worlds,

WOM, both viral and verbal, is described as "live" since it is custom tailored to specific needs and quests of receivers.

© 2009, Monkey Business Images, Shutterstock, Inc.

Habbo Hotel, There, Home, and Second Life, add visualization to the chat experience in either 2D or 3D through the use of avatars. These chatrooms have become well-established venues for personal influence. On the promotional side, for example, companies use chatrooms to host online sessions in which celebrities or experts of special interest to their clients make presentations and respond to questions. However, whether the communication format is through chatrooms, e-mail, newsgroups, bulletin boards, or blogs, one influential online individual has an impact on the beliefs, attitudes, and behavior of thousands of people.[25] In this new e-society, the challenges that marketers must confront are to understand e-fluentials and somehow harness their impact to achieve desired marketing objectives.

Social networks have become a powerful global phenomenon. It is estimated by Forrester Research that Facebook in 2008 had the highest growth rate, with more than 60 million active users, and an average 250,000 new registrations per day since 2007. In addition, it maintains 85 percent market share of the four-year United States universities. MySpace, which is the largest social network in North America, maintains the dominant position as a media site primarily aimed at youth. Monthly, the site reaches more than 110 million active users around the globe, with an average of 300,000 new registrations daily.[26]

The forms that virtual communities take vary. One form is multi-user dungeons (MUDs), a computer-generated environment where participants interact socially in formats of role and game playing. A second form is weblogs or blogs, which are online personal journals where users post their random thoughts on the Web site and read similar musings placed by others. Still other forms include instant messengers, forums, and RSS, among others.[27]

Virtual communities can be highly effective at fostering viral WOM. Among the benefits to a company from stimulating virtual communities is the help it gets in the form of suggestions regarding product design. WOM can also serve as a public relations tool with a firm's customers. Cobra Golf, Inc., for example, created a space on its Internet site for people to post unedited messages on blogs. Although such companies obviously take a risk when allowing virtual community members to discuss a firm's own and competitors' products freely on a site, such firms significantly benefit from the public relations this promotional effort nets.

The Occurrence of Personal Influence

When individuals who are involved in purchasing decisions lack product knowledge, they often turn to the Internet or to more knowledgeable friends, neighbors, relatives, and colleagues as credible sources of information or counsel. WOM, whether viral or verbal, expedites their buying tasks by lessening the time and effort required for comparison shopping. When purchasing products or services that are new, infrequently bought, costly, important, complex, or difficult to evaluate personally, consumers frequently reduce risk by learning about other people's firsthand experiences. When differences between brands are ambiguous and objective criteria to assess products are lacking,

Influence Is More Likely When Consumers:	Influence Is More Likely When Products:
• Lack product knowledge	• Are expensive
• Lack objective criteria to assess alternative brands	• Are new
	• Are infrequently bought
• Are highly involved with the product	• Are important
• Have strong ties to information givers	• Are complex
• Join new groups	• Are difficult to evaluate
• Face new life experiences	• Are highly visible
• Have Internet access	• Have expressive value
	• Reflect personal taste

consumers often draw from the experience of others as a form of vicarious trial. This is particularly true in the case of services—such as medical, legal, investment, and repair—which are hard to evaluate.

Whereas consumers are more likely to turn to informative sources or knowledgeable others for advice in the case of high-involvement products, they are less likely to seek advice for low-involvement purchases. Nevertheless, in the latter case, an individual's more involved peers may still volunteer unsolicited guidance. For instance, whereas most people would consider the purchase of snack foods to be relatively unimportant, a person who is deeply concerned with nutrition might offer unsolicited views on the health repercussions of eating foods high in fat, salt, or sugar content.

Personal influence is likely to occur when strong social ties exist between information receivers and transmitters.[28] Many consumers prefer products that carry their peers' stamp of approval, especially when goods possess a public character, such as cars, clothing, and furniture. Buyers of products that are highly visible, have expressive value, or reflect personal taste frequently contemplate what their acquaintances might think about their selections. This is especially likely when an individual joins a new group or faces a new life experience (going away to college, getting married, having a child, contemplating retirement). Those who buy products that have been recommended by knowledgeable others feel confident of peer acceptance and approval. Exhibit 13.1 summarizes the consumer and product characteristics that enhance the probability that personal influence would occur.

Models of the Influence Process

Over the years, a number of models were coined to explain the manner in which people are influenced by marketers' communication efforts. Whereas one model advocated that it was the media that exerted direct influence on their audiences, alternative models presented opinion leaders as the most important influentials in the communication process. Let us now consider these varied perspectives and examine the role of opinion leaders in human interactions.

THE HYPODERMIC NEEDLE MODEL

One communication approach is the so-called **hypodermic needle model**. The term conjures up an image of a huge syringe with which a communicator injects the public with a message. Through the needle flows a one-way stream of ads directed to target consumers. The hypodermic needle model speculates that the media have an immediate, direct, and forceful impact on new-product acceptance by a mass audience. Following this approach, huge advertising budgets and effective, cost-efficient (in terms of cost-per-thousand impressions) mass-media strategies are assumed to expedite new-product introductions as well to create demand for established products. Advertisers, in this case, attempt to reach their target market through advertisements in a variety of media types using precision targeting methods. More precise targeting is made possible by today's network, magazine, and newspaper regionalization efforts to localize ad reach.[29]

The basic assumption of the hypodermic needle model is that messages will reach and influence captive audiences. The drawback of this model, however, lies in the selective perception processes of consumers, where many of them tend to tune out promotional messages or disregard them due to lack of interest, disagreement with the messages, or based on a belief that they are biased and untrustworthy.[30] The Hypodermic Needle Model is illustrated in Exhibit 13.2.

> **hypodermic needle model**
> a view that the media have an immediate, direct, forceful impact on a mass audience

THE TRICKLE-DOWN MODEL

While the traditional version of the trickle-down model presumed that personal influence passes from higher social classes to classes below them, the new view of the trickle-down process greatly extends the circle of those

The Hypodermic Needle Model: Influence Flow | **EXHIBIT 13.2**

| EXHIBIT 13.3 | **The Trickle-Down Model: Influence Flow** |

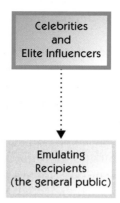

high-status influencers to include others who are prominent in a society. This updated concept recognizes the power and influence of those who are in the media spotlight and for whom the public holds affection, admiration, or fascination. This group may include public figures, celebrities, professional athletes, movie stars, and TV personalities. For example, no one can deny the influence of public figures and celebrities like Senator Bob Dole who endorsed Viagra, Reese Witherspoon and Patrick Dempsey who promote Avon, Sally Fields' appearances in ads for Boniva, Ellen DeGeneres for American Express, William Shatner for priceline.com, Sam Waterson for Ameritrade, and Tiger Woods for the myriad of consumer products he promotes. The **trickle-down model** is illustrated in Exhibit 13.3.

trickle-down model
a view that influence flows from celebrities and elite influentials to emulating recipients (the general public)

The growth of the mass and electronic media and their use by many people, particularly the young, has opened the floodgate to a highly exclusive circle of figures of influence. A study by Boon and Lomoroe into admirer-celebrity relationships among young people reported that 75 percent of young adults at some time in their life had a strong attraction to a celebrity, and 59 percent of them stated that their idols had influenced many aspects of their attitudes and behavior.[31] In the updated trickle-down model, influence flows downward from both the elite and celebrities to the emulators. Celebrities can play a key role in influencing others, since they offer a variety of possible selves that individuals may wish to test. They provide living examples of how to dress and to behave.[32] In a recent *Newsweek* poll, for example, 77 percent of respondents stated that young female celebrities like Britney Spears, Paris Hilton, and Lindsay Lohan have too much influence on young girls in our society today.[33] In this special case, the influence may be more negative than positive, as these celebrities' haircuts, tattoos, smoking habits, dating, and manner of dress are imitated by adoring young women.[34]

British academicians studied how celebrities influence young people and their social networks. They reported that in the past, it was parents, teachers, and friends who were the key influencers. However, the overwhelming growth of the mass and electronic media today coupled with their constant campaigns to make celebrities bigger than life have helped compound people's attachment to media figures, including pop stars, actors, and sports heros. This sense of attachment underlies and helps explain much of the attitudes and behavior of their fans.[35]

On occasion, influence has been known to follow a vertical upward path. The **trickle-up model**, an exception to the general rule, refers to cases where a product or style originating among those who are typically emulators or influence-recipients eventually gains acceptance and popularity among the elite and celebrity influencers. In cases of trickle-up, grassroots pioneers less inclined to closely conform to the dominant culture's norms constitute the innovators. Eventually, the novel product or style disseminates upwards to the elite and celebrities who find the novelty appealing. Products and services that have benefitted from trickle-up processes include jeans, sneakers, many ethnic foods, baggy pants, tattoos, body piercings, and various styles of music, including jazz, blues, country, rock and roll, and rap.

Another path of influence may follow a horizontal pattern, where consumers emulate the beliefs, attitudes, and behaviors of people just like themselves within their own peer groups. In this view, new technologies have given everyday people the ability to converse with anyone. As a result, consumer power shifts from the "expert" to everyone, giving everyday individuals the ability to shape, make, and share news and information, as well as give and receive advice. This type of influence is known as the **trickle-across model**.

trickle-up model
a view that influence flows upward from usual recipient emulators to the general public as well as to celebrities and elite influentials

trickle-across model
a view that influence flows horizontally among peers

two-step model
a view that it is opinion leaders who receive messages first from the mass media and then pass them on to others

THE TWO-STEP MODEL

The **two-step model** advocates that it is the opinion leaders and e-fluentials who have greater topic-bound exposure to the mass and electronic media than those they influence, and that it is these individuals who mediate the flow of message content to a large number of passive information recipients. These opinion recipients constitute the majority of consumers. This model is depicted in Exhibit 13.4.

According to the two-step model, many consumers in their purchasing behavior do not rely on firsthand exposure to ads run in the media nor do they require personal experience with products before buying them. Rather, they learn a great deal from the experiences and opinions of other people around them—the influentials. In this view, the role of mass media is to transfer information to those influentials who, in turn, transfer product

The Two-Step Model   **EXHIBIT 13.4**

| Message | Via mass and electronic media → | Opinion Leaders and E-Fluentials | Via word of mouth → | Opinion Followers |

information or advice to others via WOM. As a consequence, those influentials or opinion leaders informally shape other people's consumption-related beliefs, attitudes, and behaviors. For example, wine-tasting events are sponsored by wineries, distributors, and liquor stores. These occasions are advertised to wine opinion leaders through wine-related magazines and direct mail or at wine related Web sites. Wine opinion leaders, as a result of knowledge gained from these events, pass this information along to others. Likewise, the travel and hospitality industries have raised this technique to a fine art. Las Vegas hotels such as Luxor, Caesar's Palace, and Bally's, for instance, successfully attract millions of visitors every year based on WOM received from influentials.[36]

In its time, the two-step theory was a significant contribution because it countered a then-accepted view that the mass media were consumers' primary information sources. In contrast, it proposed that interpersonal communication, not advertising, carried the greater influence. Today, however, many marketers discern shortcomings in the two-step model. First, seldom do opinion leaders simply propagate mass-media dispatches to a set of inert followers. Second, opinion leaders often base their opinions on product trial rather than views injected by marketers through the mass media.

Today, marketers are cognizant of the fact that advice seekers frequently initiate WOM exchanges. Ads carried by the media sometimes prompt fact seekers to approach opinion leaders for advice. Thus, influence from the mass media extends beyond opinion leaders to information seekers as well.[37]

THE MULTISTEP MODEL

multistep model
a view that mass-media messages reach both opinion leaders and followers who then share that information with others

The **multistep model** is largely an elaboration and extension of the two-step model. It postulates that information transmitted through the mass media reaches opinion leaders as well as opinion followers. A distinguishing characteristic of this model is the assumption that opinion followers are not passive. Rather, they are active seekers of information from both opinion leaders and media sources.

In the multistep model, nearly everyone is potentially reachable through mass communication. Although both opinion leaders and opinion followers may receive product news from the mass and electronic media, this information is more apt to reach opinion leaders and e-fluentials first. They, in turn, pass along this information to others. It should be noted here, however, that in some instances, gatekeepers—individuals who have the power to forward or restrict messages—may choose to block messages' availability to others. Examples include parents who restrict their children's exposure to certain Internet sites and TV programs or government censors who prevent certain news or facts from reaching the general public.

Opinion followers, according to this model, actively seek information regarding products, services, and stores from online, media, and interpersonal sources. They also may receive unsolicited advice from various sources. In this sense, bidirectional influence can flow between opinion providers and opinion receivers. In other words, roles of opinion leader and opinion follower may reverse, depending on the specific situation or product of interest.[38]

Exhibit 13.5 illustrates the multistep model. In this depiction, movement downward (following the solid arrows) involves advice giving, which can be initiated as a result of a situation causing one to seek advice or a conversation that triggers giving the advice. The model shows that information from the media or the Internet can reach both opinion leaders or e-fluentials and opinion followers at the same time. However, due to e-fluentials' and opinion leaders' greater interest in the product or service, they frequently externalize this information and share it with other opinion leaders or opinion followers, who in turn may share the information with others like themselves.

In this depiction, movement upward (following the dashed arrows) entails information acquisition, which can similarly be initiated by advice-seeking situations or conversations. Opinion followers may actively seek advice from persons like themselves, from opinion leaders, or from the media. Opinion leaders may also seek information from other opinion leaders or from the media.

For example, motion picture studios regard critics as important sources of information for moviegoers. Consequently, studios invite critics to sneak previews and expend considerable effort to befriend and cajole them. At preview events, movie studios wine and dine the critics. Critics in attendance also discuss the film among themselves. Sometimes, studios bring out the stars so

The Multistep Model: Influence Flow　　　　　　　　　　　　　　　**EXHIBIT 13.5**

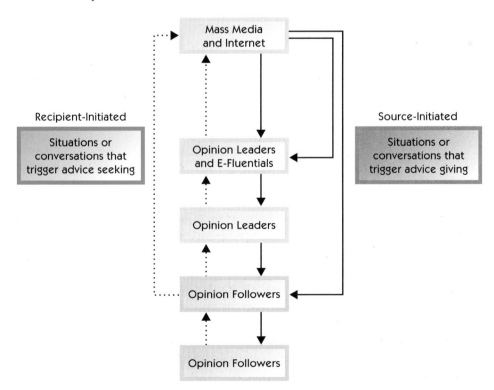

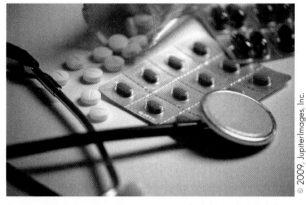

critics can meet and interview them, all in an effort to promote positive reviews that can then be quoted in movie ads. Critics' influence is likely to be greatest when a film first opens and little other information about it is available. Later on, critics exert a lesser influence on box office revenues; as more people view the film and as WOM from other moviegoers becomes increasingly available, the influence of critics is likely to wane.[39]

Because pharmaceutical firms identify physicians as opinion leaders, their sales staff visit physicians and distribute drug samples and supporting literature.

Identifying Opinion Leaders

In order for marketers to use opinion leaders as part of their strategy, they need to identify those individuals who fit that profile. In some instances, it is relatively easy to identify opinion leaders for a company's products or services. For example, publishers of college textbooks recognize that professors who teach a certain course usually have authority to adopt and require the text they prefer. Experienced professors may even recommend a text to recently hired instructors who are teaching a course for the first time. Thus, professors are opinion leaders for textbooks. Similarly, pharmaceutical firms identify physicians as opinion leaders, because doctors prescribe or recommend medication for their patients. Drug companies' sales staffs visit physicians and drop off samples and supporting literature. In other instances, however, it is difficult to know who the opinion leaders are, and the task of identifying opinion leaders may prove to be a challenging undertaking. For example, who are the opinion leaders for speedboats, garden tools, and luggage?

Once opinion leaders have been identified, marketers can proceed to use personal influence as a supplement to or even a substitute for advertising. There are four basic methods of identifying opinion leaders. These include:

1. sociometric,
2. self-designation,
3. key informant, and
4. objective techniques.[40]

THE SOCIOMETRIC METHOD

sociometric method
a technique to identify opinion leaders in small groups

The **sociometric method** involves close scrutiny of interpersonal communication patterns within small, intact communities. First, researchers ask that all group members indicate to whom or to which Web sites they turn when seeking information or advice about a particular topic or product category. After procuring the Internet sites or the names of specific people who influenced specific decisions, they validate the data by locating and checking with the named Web sites and with the influencers mentioned. In the case of named individuals, those who receive numerous mentions are the likely opinion leaders or influentials within the group. For example, if a pharmaceutical company developed a new cancer drug and was trying to identify opinion leaders among oncologists (cancer specialists), investigators could ask various doctors to indicate with which clinics and with whom they had consulted when a patient posed a particularly difficult cancer case to diagnose and treat. Knowledgeable doctors reported to have given advice can then be contacted to verify the consultation.

Having identified the likely opinion leaders in a group, researchers are in a position to trace the flow of both verbal and viral WOM linkages and construct a sociogram. A sociogram is a diagram that systematically maps out verbal and viral interactions that occur among individuals within a group and tracks the informal communication network or web that exists among its members.

sociogram
a diagram that maps out the communication network in a group

The sociometric method is precise and highly valid. It is, however, very costly to implement, difficult to manage and analyze, and not as useful if only a sample of the social system is interviewed. As a result, the sociometric method is primarily used to identify opinion leaders in relatively small, self-contained communities (a university, retirement community, organization, neighborhood, hospital, prison, army base). However, because most product and brand studies extend beyond a small social system, marketers must usually turn to other techniques.

THE SELF-DESIGNATION METHOD

The self-designation method is the most common procedure for studying opinion leadership patterns. It is based on inviting respondents to recount their own opinion leadership activities in order to determine the extent of their influence. This method is suited for use on a broad scale with large, diverse, geographically dispersed groups. For example, in a Roper Starch Study of e-fluentials, over 2,000 Internet users were interviewed online and were asked to assess their opinion-leadership activities on the Internet. The objective of the self-designating technique is to ascertain whether certain types of people serve as influencers but usually *not* to designate specific individuals by name. As such, the self-designation method does not enable researchers to construct a sociogram.

self-designation method
a technique to profile opinion leaders in large, dispersed groups

In the self-designating approach, questionnaires are administered to a large group of individuals who display interest in a certain product or service. It is not always necessary to survey the entire populace of interest. For example, an investigation of motorcyclists may be restricted only to people who own Harley-Davidson motorcycles. *Self-designation questionnaires* contain a litany of items specifically designed to measure the characteristics of the respondents and pertain to the specific product category, such as buying, riding, and maintaining a motorcycle. Subjects are asked to self-report such qualities as the following:

- The extent to which they visit motorcycle-related Web sites.
- The extent to which they have been sought out by other people for advice about motorcycles online or offline.

- The extent to which they have provided others with information about motorcycles online or offline.
- Whether or not they are regarded by others as a good source of advice for motorcycles.
- The degree to which they believe they have influenced others in purchase decisions for motorcycles.

Based on respondents' replies, researchers develop a single score that permits them to categorize subjects as *opinion leaders* (frequently influence others), *opinion followers* (never or rarely influence others), or something in between (occasionally influence others). Self-designation appears to be acceptably valid, but validity relies on subjects' objectivity. Bias could occur should respondents perceive opinion leadership as a desirable trait and consequently exaggerate their estimates of their own influence on others.

THE KEY INFORMANT METHOD

key informant method
using knowledgeable persons to identify opinion leaders in a group

In the **key informant method**, which is more applicable to verbal WOM, researchers seek out individuals who are knowledgeable about a specific group and who can objectively identify persons most likely to be influential within it. Those selected as key informants need not be members of the group under investigation but must be keenly cognizant of communication patterns among its members. A teacher, for example, might act as a key informant about colleagues. A business executive may be a source of information about coworkers and a physician about other physicians. Key informants are normally people who engage in frequent WOM with the group of interest.

The key informant method is relatively quick and inexpensive, because a single informant or just a few informants can be interviewed and asked to rate the stature of members of a specific group. For example, heads of the PTA or school board, prominent local businesspersons, and clergy may serve as key informants for studies of the communities in which they serve. Drawbacks of this technique, however, are that application is restricted to a singular group, and that the method cannot be used for studies requiring samples from large, diverse populations.

THE OBJECTIVE METHOD

objective method
a technique that involves creating opinion leaders

The **objective method** artificially *creates* opinion leaders. E-fluentials, for example, may be stimulated by bits of news or facts placed online by a company or other entity such as seeding agency (e.g., BzzAgent). Influence from such nuclear implants usually multiplies geometrically, creating as it spreads many opinion leaders. Alternatively, marketers send free product samples, offer special deals, or direct new-product information to selected individuals to boost their enthusiasm about the product and get them to communicate the information to others. Companies also create events that foster word of mouth, such as holding seminars, parties, conferences, and swap meets to bring people together. Other firms, such as automobile companies, loan cars to consumers to drive for a period in order to stimulate WOM. In an effort to win the college market, for example, many carmakers lend a new car model for a semester or year to graduate assistants and presidents of the student government or campus business organization. As these individuals drive the new automobile on campus, much interest and many inquiries emerge. In this manner, the graduate assistants or organizations' presidents, in effect, serve as opinion leaders.

In addition, marketers attempt to direct newsworthy materials to socially involved, influential persons who are likely to become opinion leaders. Recipients, in this case, are encouraged but are not required to chat with others on the Internet about the information the company provided.

Now let us turn our investigation to other matters of interest to marketers. These include sources of personal influence other than traditional opinion leaders and e-fluentials, and what motivates these individuals to communicate the information received to others.

ARE THERE OTHER SOURCES OF PERSONAL INFLUENCE?

In addition to opinion leaders, three other types of influencers can be identified. These sources include shopping pals, market mavens, surrogate consumers, and brand reps.

shopping pals
other persons who accompany a consumer on a shopping trip

Shopping Pals

Sometimes another person physically accompanies a consumer on his or her shopping trip and acts as a source of information, advice, influence, and support. Such individuals are called **shopping pals**. In a study by Harman and Kiecker, shopping pals were used 25 percent of the time by purchasers of electronic goods.[41] In that study, male and female shopping pals tended to serve different roles for the shoppers they accompanied. Male shopping pals tended to be used as sources of product-category expertise, product facts, and retail store and price information. Female shopping pals, on the other hand, were more used to provide moral support and boost buyers' confidence in their decisions.

Shopping pals often accompany consumers to help them with their merchandise choices.

© 2009, Simone van den Berg, Shutterstock, Inc.

Interestingly, an electronic shopping pal called the UScanShopper, mounted to the handle of shopping carts, was introduced to the marketplace in 2005. It is a battery-powered device that uses wireless communication and infrared triggers around the store. It is designed to get information into consumers' hands as they shop. It reveals prices on items, alerts consumers about discounts, reminds them of items on their shopping list, points out the store's specials, directs shoppers to the aisle where products can be found, and speeds them through the checkout process. If and when this type of technology diffuses throughout most stores, it would likely lessen the advice function of human shopping pals, but boost their moral support function.

Ethical Dilemma

Ford's Desperate Search for Buzz

In September 2007, Ford Motor Company staged an elaborate stunt in which dozens of people who had recently bought new cars from competitors, such as Saturn and Toyota, were encouraged to trade them temporarily for Ford vehicles. On September 4th, Ford introduced its new campaign "Swap My Ride," a play on the similarly named MTV show. The campaign encouraged drivers to swap their new non-Ford automobile with a Ford vehicle for a period of one week, so that consumers could experience the quality improvements made by Ford Motor Company over the years.

The main purpose of the campaign was to solicit and tape raw, unedited, and unbiased testimonials from real consumers who swapped their cars for Fords. Company executives felt that these impartial opinions would be more effective in raising the sagging image of the Ford automobiles than pitches coming from the firm's officials.

To execute the campaign, Ford's ad agency, JWT, had workers in New York, Miami, Los Angeles, and Dallas pretend to represent a fictitious market-research firm. The workers were instructed to track down the owners of cars made by Toyota, Honda, and Saturn, as well as other competitors, and ask them to drive new Ford models for a supposedly impartial week-long test. Camera crews then interviewed those drivers after the test in order to solicit their comments about the driving experience.

In its efforts to obtain unbiased opinions from participants, the ad agency had to trick them into believing that the research study was done for a nonexistent market-research firm, "In-Home Test Drive Experience." Not only were the testimonials obtained or solicited under the guise of market research, but the identity of the auto firm, Ford, behind the project was never revealed. Respondents, after the facts were disclosed, indicated that they were surprised to learn that "In-Home Test Drive Experience" was not a real research company and that the entire project was linked to Ford.

As a result of this campaign, hundreds of media articles and thousands of Web posts discussed, debated, and reprimanded Ford for delaying information disclosures to participants, misleading the unsuspecting public, and unethically collecting data under the guise of market research. Ford executives, however, defended their action by arguing that this aggressive marketing tactic was necessary due to the low-quality perception of American cars among buyers of foreign automobiles.[43]

In Ford's "Swap My Ride" campaign, two points of view are apparent. The first is the public's negative reaction to this campaign. The second is Ford executives' defense that the aggressive campaign was necessary to overcome the unfavorable perception of American automobiles. Learn more about this controversy by visiting the Web site of Sentientservices at www.sentientservices.com/blog/2007/09/ford-and-jwt-blur-line-between.html. Which of the two points of view do you support? Explain your choice. Some observers argue that this campaign is an example of stealth marketing, which, in the view of the Word of Mouth Marketing Association, may be unethical. Do you agree with this assessment? Visit this organization's Web site at www.womma.org/wom101/06/ to learn about the definition of stealth marketing and other unethical marketing tactics.

Market Mavens

In your daily interaction with other people, you may have encountered friends, colleagues, or neighbors who appear to be sensitive to their shopping experiences and tend to be highly motivated to talk about products, services, stores, events, and prices. This type of individual belongs to a consumer category known as **market mavens**. Market mavens are not necessarily authorities in any particular product category. Rather, they are a sort of generalized opinion leader in the sense that they display interest in diverse types of marketplace information. Market mavens tend to be sociable and enjoy talking to others about

market maven
person who actively transmits marketplace information

their knowledge and experiences. They feel confident about their overall understanding of how and where to procure products and in their ability to help others find the best prices and places to shop.

Studies show that market mavens enjoy introducing new products and talking about events or stores with others. Market mavens' knowledge is a factor in getting *others* to approach them as a good source for advice. Even though market mavens would appear to fit the profile of opinion leaders in the sense that they have wide knowledge of products, stores, prices, and events, studies show that market mavens tend to help diffuse information on low-involvement and less-significant purchase decisions, such as in the case of advice on food items, clothing, jewelry, shoes, cosmetics, and items for children.

Surrogate Consumers

Sometimes consumers lack the know-how, time, or ambition to personally search for information, evaluate alternatives, and arrive at a decision. They may detest particular shopping chores and prefer to employ an intermediary who will gather and evaluate information, narrow down their options, or make a purchase selection. Such go-betweens are called surrogate consumers. A surrogate consumer is "an agent retained by a consumer to guide, direct, or transact marketplace activities."[42] Surrogate consumers can play a wide variety of roles, including tax consultants, lawyers, wine stewards, interior decorators, financial managers, stockbrokers, professional shoppers, wedding planners, and reunion planners.

surrogate consumer
agents a consumer retains to guide, direct, or execute transactions

Surrogates tend to be utilized for high-involvement purchases (expensive furniture, complex investment securities) by persons willing to delegate a task to a more competent external agent—frequently a paid professional. Essentially, surrogate consumers become an extra tier in the distribution channel between manufacturer and final consumer, charged with performing all or part of a decision process. Although the extent of surrogates' influence varies, marketers cannot ignore it. Rather, marketers should assess the extent to which surrogates influence purchases of their firm's products or services by final consumers. Marketers should then target promotional materials to surrogate consumers as well as direct ads to end users.

Brand Reps

Brand reps, also known as brand ambassadors, are everyday consumers who promote brands or companies, both publicly and among their friends. For performing this service, they often receive cash and free goods from the companies they represent. Among the firms that use this type of influential representative are JP Morgan Chase Bank, Ford Motor Company, Macy's Inc., and Pepsico Inc. For example, at Northwestern University, in the greater Chicago area, brand reps from Macy's Inc. wore free clothes from the retailer's American Rag line and promoted a one-day sale and a casting call for an online documentary. Similarly at Northwestern, brand ambassadors for Pepsico Inc. placed banners and videos for Mountain Dew on their Facebook and MySpace

brand reps
consumers who promote brands or companies publicly and among friends

pages. They also staged faux rallies on campus, complete with buttons and signs, as well as offered students samples of three prospective flavors of the soda. According to a study by PQ Media, companies paid an estimated $1.4 billion for this type of word-of-mouth influentials in the year 2007.

WHAT FORCES MOTIVATE INFLUENTIALS TO GIVE ADVICE?

Opinion providers engage in product-related conversations or Internet activities for a number of reasons. These reasons can be explained by a number of factors such as an individual's high extent of product-involvement, or self-involvement, other-involvement, or message-involvement.

Regarding *product involvement*, the tendency to initiate viral or verbal WOM is directly proportional to that individual's degree of involvement with a specific product or service.[44] Persons who have an inherent interest in a subject or product category tend to enjoy communicating about it. Individuals who like attending movies and watching TV often talk about their favorite films and shows. When consumers buy or use a new, unique product, they are often so fascinated, pleased, or disappointed that they feel compelled to inform others. Product-related talk simply provides a way to release this energy.[45]

Self-involvement is also a reason for giving advice. Years ago, Dichter suggested that initiating WOM fulfills emotional needs or goals of influencers.[46] These personal satisfactions include gaining the attention of others, showing connoisseurship, implying elevated social status, suggesting access to inside information, demonstrating awareness and expertise, asserting superiority, promulgating a view and bringing others to accept it, personally identifying with the newness or uniqueness of an innovation, or anticipating a reciprocal benefit when advice recipients return the favor. At other times, consumers attempt to confirm their own good judgment and eradicate their own post-purchase doubts by extending advice to others. An individual who feels unsure about an acquisition frequently tries to relieve anxieties by talking up its advantages to his or her acquaintances. If they too buy the product, the original decision to buy is bolstered.

Other-involvement constitutes still another motive for the spread of word of mouth. Those who are motivated by concern for others feel the need to share their product-related experiences. Such influencers use product-related advice as expressions of friendship, neighborliness, caring, and love. This is particularly likely to occur when the influencer has experienced high satisfaction from the consumption of a product or service that is of interest to another person.[47] For example, the mother of a newborn baby may advise her soon-to-be-mother best friend about a crib or a brand of formula that she found to be acceptable.

Finally, *message-involvement* may explain some instances where advice is given due to fascination with promotional messages. Product-related WOM may be precipitated by intrigue with an advertising campaign. Some consumers like to comment on or critique unusually interesting, original, or entertaining promotional appeals. Such was the case for AFLAC'S talking duck and the Geico Insurance Company's gecko lizard.

Strategic Applications of Personal Influence and Word of Mouth

Personal influence can often be used as an element of a company's marketing strategy. As mentioned earlier, favorable WOM is a valuable supplement to any size promotional budget. Strong positive WOM enables many companies such as Apple, Wal-Mart, and Harley-Davidson to decrease their advertising budgets.[48] In a few rare instances, firms have been known to omit advertising and sales efforts completely and to rely solely on personal influence and word of mouth. Such was the case of the movie *Cloverfields* in 2008, where elements of the viral marketing campaign included MySpace pages created for fictional characters and Web sites created for fictional companies alluded to in the film, as well as numerous postings on YouTube.[49]

When deciding whether and how to utilize personal influence, marketers must ascertain the extent to which personal influence is likely to affect prospective purchasers of their products or services. Products in some categories stand to benefit more from operative personal influence than others. Within some merchandise categories, consumers derive personal satisfaction or opportunities for self-expression from product ownership and use. Opinion leaders are more apt to actively disseminate, via WOM, product information related to conspicuous products like automobiles and fashion merchandise. However, in our technologically-sophisticated environment, we also tend to seek advice for just about everything we buy. WOM is an important means of acquiring this information.

In general, three approaches are available to marketers who wish to capitalize on personal influence as a promotional strategy. They are:

1. creating and enlisting opinion leaders,
2. stimulating opinion leadership, and
3. simulating opinion leadership.

CREATING AND ENLISTING OPINION LEADERS

Marketers can employ a number of strategies to create and enlist opinion leaders. These strategies may vary based on the type of industry or business the firm is in. Companies that market products may find certain strategies more effective than others employed in the service domain. For example, whereas Ford Focus loaned cars to customers to initiate buzz, the company Shortcuts, an online grocery coupon service, used a flurry of blog posts following the service launch. The following strategies are among those that have proven effective in enhancing WOM:

- Using seeding agencies to help plant viral WOM. Companies such as Bzz Agent and SheSpeaks work with consumers who like to try new products and services. If those consumers like the product, they are encouraged (but not required) to spread the word about it.
- Offering incentives to a group of everyday consumers (known as brand reps or brand ambassadors) in a "tell a friend" program is an increasingly

popular strategy. The company, in this case, grants financial and/or other type of credit (such as free merchandise) to customers who are willing to participate in a program that entails recommending the firm and its products to people they know.

- Reaching community experts through their Web sites (which most of them have). Newsworthy information about the company as well as product samples can then regularly be directed to them in order to enhance their awareness of a firm's products, policies, and events. The purpose, of course, is to help them spread the news to others.

- Working with promotion agencies that target local grassroots organizations, such as Parent Teachers Associations (PTAs). Such social networks provide excellent grounds for viral buzz.

- Creating and implementing events that foster WOM, such as holding seminars, conferences, and swap meets where customers and prospects can be brought together.

- Gaining media coverage of a company's newsworthy activities or creating stories pertaining to the company's line and how it relates to consumers' lifestyle and emotions. Hallmark generated a great deal of WOM when the company asked customers to relay personal experiences relating to the firm's line of greeting cards. The company made and aired brief videos of some of these experiences. One particularly successful video that brought tears to the eyes of viewers and created a significant amount of buzz centered around the mother of a young girl whose husband had passed away. Her little girl wanted to send her daddy a message of love and farewell. The segment showed the young girl and her mother tying a Hallmark greeting card bearing the emotional message to a helium-filled balloon and releasing it into the heavens.

- Using canned WOM methods—including audio, video, and the Web, as well as brochures—to deliver customer recommendations and positive WOM about the firm's products and services.

- Establishing affiliation programs by formally joining customers and the company together in a mutually beneficial manner. Both Saturn Corporation and Harley-Davidson created successful nationwide affiliation "family" programs that bring satisfied customers together with each other, as well as with the top executives of the firm.

Creating opinion leaders in the print media has also been a popular strategy to initiate the flow of personal influence. Popular personalities and celebrities are frequently pictured along with the promoted product to enhance the item's appeal. Figure 13.2, the appearance of a star, such as John Lithgow, along with Campbell's Select soups demonstrates the use of a personal influence strategy in promotion.

STIMULATING OPINION LEADERSHIP

teaser campaigns
promotions that drop bits of information while withholding the particulars

In addition to identifying and creating and enlisting opinion leaders and e-fluentials, marketers can *stimulate* or encourage consumers to discuss a product.[51] One such approach entails running teaser campaigns. **Teaser campaigns**

Figure 13.2
Brands that are recommended by admired celebrities, such as John Lithgow for Campbell's Select soups, are more likely to be noticed and recalled by consumers.

are promotions that drop bits of information and withhold the particulars. Motion picture and TV show producers have effectively used this technique by releasing advance teaser ads about a movie or upcoming program that arouse audience interest and heighten its anticipation. Teaser campaigns expose just enough details about the movie or show to arouse audience curiosity and get people talking.

Similarly, clever and imaginative campaigns may entice a desire on the part of the audience to comment on them. The ad in Figure 13.3 from PickensPlan.com, along with its caption, "It's time to stop America's addiction to foreign oil," has directed the public's attention to the perils of our dependency on foreign oil. It has also generated a great deal of interest and comments about the need to switch to other alternative sources of energy. In a different promotional format, some local automobile, electronics, and appliance dealers concoct bizarre and sometimes obnoxious ads just to get people to talk about their retail outlet.[52]

Inaugurating activities around a product can help marketers increase brand awareness and stimulate WOM. Some firms sponsor events such as parades, open houses, sweepstakes, contests, or athletic tournaments in order

Figure 13.3

This ad from T. Boone Pickens raised awareness and caused a great deal of word of mouth about America's problems with regard to scarcity of energy resources and dependency on foreign oil. Such an ad caused many public and private entities to commit to taking corrective action.

Consumer Behavior in Practice

How Wild Is the Party When the Main Attraction Is a Facial Cream?

Mary Kay Cosmetics, Inc., a direct selling company, was established in 1963 by Mary Katherine Ash. The company is the largest direct seller of beauty products in the United States, ranking first ahead of Avon. Mary Kay Cosmetics sells its range of over 200 beauty products through approximately 1.8 million independent salespeople, who operate in more than 35 markets worldwide. The company's sales figure in 2007 reached a staggering $2.7 billion. The firm's astounding success was due in large part to Ash's idea of creating opinion leaders out of ordinary folks in order to sell cosmetics. The sales technique she employed is known as the party plan. Parties are usually held in the afternoon or evening and no more than five guests are invited. The parties last about two hours, during which a hostess, who is known as a *beauty consultant*, gives a free facial to each guest and explains or demonstrates beauty tips. At the end, refreshments are served, and guests place their orders for a number of products from the 200-product line of Mary Kay. Guests are gently, but firmly, pushed into buying several of the products in the line, not just one.

Under the party plan, the hostess-beauty consultant assumes the role of an opinion leader in her specialty area. She is perceived as a knowledgeable individual in skin-care products and an expert in giving facials. She raises the interest of her guests in her product line by suggesting the benefits that the products will yield in terms of softer and more beautiful skin. Because the hostess-consultant is known on a firsthand basis to her guests and because the brand has a national reputation, she is more successful in influencing the opinions and purchasing intentions of her customers.

Party-plan selling is based on the power of personal influence. The consultants basically sell to their extended family, friends, and neighbors. This type of selling is most effective in ordinary neighborhoods, small towns, and urban working-class or ethnic areas where people tend to know each other. However, in large cities where personal ties are weak and where working women have little time to spare for attending parties, such techniques are difficult to implement.[50]

> Whereas many cosmetic companies follow the traditional strategy of selling their products through department stores, Mary Kay uses personal influence as an alternative selling tactic. Learn more about Mary Kay products and operations by visiting www.marykay.com. In your opinion, why does Mary Kay regard this approach of selling cosmetics to be more effective than the conventional method? From market-exposure and sales-volume points of view, would Mary Kay be more successful if the firm sold its products through mass merchandisers? Why or why not?

to gain public exposure and generate talk. Others arrange for product demonstrations or sample giveaways at strategic visible locations like shopping malls and airports. Still other companies employ a tactic known as a **product placement**, where branded merchandise appears in movie scenes, TV programs, or video games. Firms frequently approach movie studios to publicize their brand within motion pictures and television shows. In the Warner Bros. Movie *The Dark Night*, Bruce Wayne shows his allegiance to Belstaff and Lamborghini's Murcielago line of sports cars, and Nokia has gadget fans buzzing with a cameo of its touchscreen phone. In the Paramount movie *Indiana Jones and Kingdom of the Crystal Skull*, the chase scenes that carry the stars from the desert of Nevada to the jungles of South America promoted the Fedor

product placement
display of branded merchandise in movie scenes or TV shows

and Harley-Davidson brands. Product placement is not currently as widespread in TV shows as in the movies. However, its use on television is a rapidly growing trend, where the phenomenon is more commonly referred to as *product integration*. A good example of this tactic can be observed in the popular talent show *American Idol*. In 2008, Nielsen counted over 4,348 product placements in the previous season's *American Idol* shows.[53]

SIMULATING OPINION LEADERSHIP

In addition to stimulating opinion leadership, advertisers use a variety of formats that *simulate* impartial persons informally giving and receiving information via WOM. Slice-of-life, hidden camera, and testimonial ad formats employ simulated influence. *Slice-of-life* commercials allow the audience to eavesdrop on an exchange. These miniskits depict a troubled individual encountering another person who spontaneously proposes a solution. A physician, for example, can be shown to recommend an over-the-counter stomach antacid to a patient. In other ads, the simulated opinion leader reiterates what a real opinion leader had previously advised, as in the "My doctor said Mylanta" commercials. *Hidden-camera* commercials portray individuals going about the task of buying a product without suspecting that they are being recorded. A commercial may depict a shopper who observes which brand other customers (the simulated opinion leaders) are buying and who then purchases the same brand.

testimonials
ads that depict a
celebrity or expert who
endorses a brand

Ads frequently employ testimonials in which relevant celebrities or experts endorse a brand. Celebrities are effective givers of testimony, particularly when they have some believable connection with the advertised product. Testimony from experts enhances the credibility of advertising claims and is effectual when a purchase involves financial, functional, or physical risk.

Occasionally, advertisers use their own current or former corporate executives as spokespersons, such as Steve Jobs for Apple. Present or past company owners, CEOs, or presidents speaking on behalf of their firms appear to be highly credible and can be good sources for buzz.[54]

Harnessing Word of Mouth

It has been reported that word of mouth is far and away the most powerful force in the marketplace. It has been described as the proximal cause of purchase—the most recent encounter that happens just before buying and a powerful purchase trigger.[55]

Three situational factors seem to increase the likelihood that word-of-mouth communication will take place: (1) when consumers who enjoy talking about purchase alternatives become familiar enough with a company's products or services that they can discuss them, (2) when consumers of a product or service experience an emotional reaction—favorable or unfavorable—to it, and (3) when dissatisfied consumers of a product or service find it difficult to complain to the party that caused the dissatisfaction.

Recognizing these factors has led many firms to significantly enhance information availability about their products or services through media sources such as the Internet as well as to build consumer excitement and emotional ties with their products. They also attempt to keep all avenues of communication open with consumers of their products.

The following are a few examples of companies' attempts to accomplish the objective of harnessing word of mouth:

- In 2007, the American skiing company called Affinitive initiated a campaign known as "My A41.com pass-holder community" and hosted an online site for its "All for One" season pass-holders. Nearly 4,000 users signed up and posted photos, stories, ski tips, and videos on the "My A41" site and spread the word about the "All for One" pass.[56]
- Quicken Loans was able to leverage Yahoo! Answers to field questions that users were asking about home loans, in its campaign "How Quicken Loans Became a Yahoo! Answers Knowledge Partner." The only rule Quicken Loans imposed to guide answers was: "Answer the question. Don't tell them how great Quicken Loans is. Don't tell them how they will benefit from our products. Don't tell them anything except what they ask." This campaign provided potential customers with basic information instead of a sales pitch, and generated a great deal of buzz for the company.[57]
- The launch of the Pontiac G6 was a major publicity stunt. To kick off the launch, two hundred and seventy six G6 cars were given away to audience members of the *Oprah Winfrey Show* in the fall 2004 season premier. This promotion generated international attention, a reported $110 million in publicity, and put the G6, a previously unknown name, solidly on the lips of many car shoppers.[58]
- In conjunction with the movie *Snakes on a Plane*, a mobile promotion allowed users to generate a customized phone call from Samuel L. Jackson. To set the call up, participants went online to select their personal attributes via pull-down menus and provided the necessary phone numbers. As a recipient, it looked like the phone call was coming in from a friend; but when recipients picked up the phone, they heard the voice of Mr. Jackson. This program was phenomenally successful in rasing movie buzz, with over 4 million phone calls placed during the core promotional period.[59]

Tactics such as these precipitate a strong tie between the company and its customers, enhance customer loyalty, and encourage an avalanche of positive word of mouth. The benefits of such actions almost always far exceed their cost.

Combatting Negative Word of Mouth

As tools that simplify WOM exchanges dominate our society, they have forever changed the old belief that 1 out of every 10 dissatisfied customers takes the time to formally complain to a firm's customer service department. Today, popular social networks, review sites on the Internet, blogs, and forums have become powerful tools in the hands of consumers to communicate their dissatisfaction with businesses. According to a 2008 study by the Society for

New Communications Research, 59 percent of consumers use social media to vent their frustrations about customer service. In addition, 74 percent choose companies or brands based on online shared experiences from others, and 72 percent search companies' online customer service records prior to purchasing products and services from them.[60]

Three dimensions of consumer complaint behavior can be identified. Formal complaints that involve complaining directly to the seller; private complaints that entail complaining to friends, family members, and online; and third-party complaints that consist of formal complaints directed to the media, to consumer groups, to the Better Business Bureau, or to government agencies. Researchers have suggested that complaint behavior may be sequential in nature; that is, certain complaint actions are taken only after other avenues have been exhausted.[61] For example, third-party complaints usually occur after formal complaints have proven unsuccessful. A recent case in point occurred between Dell and a blogger. The blogger noted on his own personal blog, BuzzMachine, about his lengthy quest to get Dell to fix his $1,600 computer that malfunctioned. He wrote about the ordeal that entailed countless unanswered e-mails and calls to Dell's customer service line. He was finally told to send the computer in to get it repaired. When it came back, it still did not work. Frustrated by Dell's indifference, he launched a series of attacks on the company and its CEO, Michael Dell. The offensive resulted in receiving a refund. More important it caused a great deal of negative WOM for the company, as the episode attracted more than 10,000 daily visits to the blog.

Thus, it is both the nature of the firm's response (product replacement, repair, or refund) *and* the speed of that response (days versus weeks) compared to consumers' redress expectations that appear to be the key factors in determining how consumers will react toward the company. To avoid incidents of consumer dissatisfaction and probable negative WOM, progressive marketers have adopted measures to *exceed* consumers' redress expectations. Such companies attempt to learn about consumer dissatisfaction at the individual level *before* it surfaces. Their reasoning is that to restore satisfaction and its favorable effect on repurchase intention, the company should find out about product failures ahead of time.

Companies can take several steps to prepare for and protect themselves against negative WOM. First, the company can establish a crisis-watch program to monitor, assess, and regularly check what is being communicated about it online. Monitoring feeds allows the company to immediately respond to negative WOM posts. This objective can be attained by using Google Alerts or by subscribing to feeds on Google Blogsearch.

Second, the company can be proactive in building relationships with the WOM community in which it operates. For example, the company can respond to a negative posting directly in the blog comments, since most blogs have a comment feature enabled. The company can also establish its own blog, so that consumers can easily send and receive communication relating to their concerns. In so doing, the company can come to understand its customers' needs and be able to spot market opportunities.

Third, the company should provide truthful facts whenever any event touching the company threatens to turn into a public controversy. Honest

The topics of personal influence, viral marketing, and word of mouth have a number of implications for business disciplines other than marketing. Relevant issues might include

- **Trading in the Viral World:** Buying and selling in the viral marketplace has become big business. Some of the massively popular multiplayer online games (MMOS), such as Dark Age or Camelot, are confined to trading of items that possess in-world value. On the other hand, the virtual economies of life-simulation games, such as Second Life's economy, are structured in the Linden Dollar, which is closely monitored by the Linden Lab. The Linden Dollar can be traded and sold for U.S. dollars on the Linden Lab's Lindex Service. In such games, avatar-to-avatar dealings are currently (2008) running at U.S. $15 million per month.

- **Global Cosmetics Marketing/Public Relations:** Employing movie stars is a costly undertaking for companies that employ them as spokespersons and endorsers. Avon, due to declining sales in 2007, has increasingly turned to Hollywood in order to polish and glamorize the firm's image domestically and globally, as well as to dissociate the company's old perceived image as targeting suburban homemakers. Avon retained the services of Oscar-winner Reese Witherspoon, who, along with appearing in the company's ads, travels worldwide as the Avon Foundation's first-ever global ambassador and honorary chairwoman.

- **Ethics:** Like doting stage parents, many companies today vie for starring roles for their products in movies. Coca-Cola, Pepsi, Budweiser, and Miller are among the most aggressive in attempting to get into films. Companies even hire specialized product-placement agencies in California and New York, which scan more than 100 movie scripts each year looking for potential hits. They then negotiate placements of their products with studios. Every major studio has opened a product-placement department replacing informal systems that in the past included under-the-table gifts to prop masters. These companies often pay studios fees that typically range from $5,000 to $50,000, but many companies including McDonald's and AT&T prefer instead to provide their products or services free to movie producers. Critics argue that product placement is a deceptive and often distracting form of advertising. Companies and movie studios, however, say that as long as it is not overdone, product placement can make scenes look more natural and save studios money.

These issues, and a host of others like them, serve to show that the topics of personal influence, viral marketing, and word of mouth transcend the field of marketing to other business disciplines.

---

information disclosure has the power to neutralize the potential negative effect of WOM that can harm the firm.[62]

In this chapter, we have seen how influence travels between and within the various layers of a society. Influence flow depends on who occupies the roles of influencers and receivers. The roles of influence provider and influence receiver, in turn, are largely determined by demographic characteristics and behavioral patterns that distinguish between individuals. Such characteristics, in the final analysis, constitute the grounds for assigning a particular social standing to each individual within a particular society.

Thus, the cumulative social standings of individuals in a culture constitute the basis for identifying tiers that sociologists have labeled social classes. Social class studies are deemed valuable to marketers because the different consumption and behavior patterns of these societal tiers hold significant implications to practitioners and researchers in the field of consumer behavior. The following chapter deals with the topic of social class and its many implications for segmenting, targeting, and positioning strategies in the disciplines of marketing and consumer behavior.

Summary

This chapter covers the topic of personal influence, which refers to any change in a person's beliefs, attitudes, or behavior that results from interpersonal communication. Personal influence is transmitted both verbally and virally. WOM is personal communication between a receiver and a source whom the receiver perceives as noncommercial regarding a product. In a marketing sense, opinion leadership refers to the influence that individuals conversant with a product or service category exert over the minds and actions of other consumers. Verbal or viral WOM is powerful. Compared to messages carried by the media, WOM information tends to be more vivid, more salient, and more accessible for retrieval from memory.

When consumers lack product knowledge, they often turn to more knowledgeable acquaintances as credible sources of counsel. The passage of product-related information to others tends to be incited by situational or conversational circumstances and normally occurs within the context of casual interaction or through planned or unplanned surfing of the Internet. A number of models have been proposed to explain the flow of messages from message sources and target audiences. These models include the hypodermic needle model; trickle-down, trickle-across, and trickle-up models; the two-step model; and the multistep model.

Opinion leaders can be identified through sociometric, self-designation, key informant, and objective methods. E-fluentials are a special group of influentials that constitute 10 percent of the adult U.S. population. They crave knowledge and are socially and politically engaged individuals.

When deciding whether and how to use influence as part of their strategy, marketers may elect to identify and enlist opinion leaders directly, stimulate opinion leadership, or simulate opinion leadership. Many firms enhance the availability of information about their products via the mass media and/or the Internet and try to build consumers' excitement and emotional ties with their products to harness WOM. Occasionally marketers find themselves in situations where they must combat negative WOM. Negative WOM may result from consumer dissatisfaction and resulting unredressed complaints. Among the strategies that marketers employ to reduce dissatisfaction and combat negative WOM are establishing a crisis-watch program, being proactive in building relationships with the WOM community in which the company operates, and providing truthful facts when a crisis threatens the firm's operations.

Review Questions

1. Enumerate some of the conditions under which consumers are more likely to seek advice from others regarding a particular purchase or other behavior. Alternatively, when are individuals less apt to seek such advice from others?

2. Sports heroes, movie stars, and other popular celebrities are often used by advertisers as opinion leaders and influencers. How do you explain people's tendency to heed such advice, particularly in cases where no relationship exists between a celebrity's expertise and the promoted product or service?

3. The exponential growth of the Internet has significantly altered the way WOM operates in our society. As a result, a group known as the e-fluentials has emerged. What characteristics tend to distinguish individuals who fall into this category?

4. Assume that a popular motorcycle company hired you as a consultant to identify influentials the firm can contact to help promote its line of bikes. What method or methods of identifying opinion leaders would you employ to accomplish this objective?

5. Executives of a California winery were wrestling with the question of how best to spend the company's promotional dollars. One alternative was to allow tours to the winery during which wine tasting would occur as guests sample hors d'oeuvres. The second alternative would be simply to spend money on an advertising campaign in the mass media. The third alternative does not require major dollar expenditures for advertising, but rather relies on viral WOM by circulating newsworthy information about the winery on the Internet. In your opinion, which strategy would likely be more effective in promoting the winery's products? Why?

Discussion Questions

1. Many households have had the experience of being targeted for visits by members of various religious groups (e.g., Jehovah's Witnesses and other fundamentalist denominations). At the doorstep, assertive members of these groups attempt to preach their doctrines and distribute literature. How effective are such efforts to proselytize? Would you listen to their presentations? Are such presentations likely to impact your personal beliefs?

2. Superstar athletes, such as Tiger Woods, are often sought after and employed by advertisers as spokespersons, endorsers, and givers of testimony on behalf of their brands. Considering that the royalties for employing celebrity athletes run into the millions of dollars, is it worth the cost for companies to use this strategy? In your opinion, how effective is this type of appeal?

3. In order to drum up votes during political election campaigns, candidates visit many communities, speak at rallies, and personally shake hands with as many potential voters as possible. What effect do these activities have on voters? Compare the impact of these efforts with the influence created through the candidates' Web sites and political ads appearing in the mass media.

In reference to the chapter-opening vignette, assume that a few months prior to the introduction of the iPhone, an executive meeting was held to determine an appropriate strategy that Apple should adopt to promote its new product. Assume further that Apple's Promotional Manager had prepared a proposal that included four possible strategies for consideration. The first strategy entailed initiating an intensive advertising campaign to be rolled out one month before the actual introduction of the iPhone. The campaign would demonstrate the phone and its advanced features through ads on television, in the print media, as well as the Web—all designed to reach every consumer in the United States and Canada. The second strategy involved employing a group of celebrities and public figures to be included in ads and promotional materials for the iPhone. Even though this step may require a large initial financial outlay for celebrity royalties, the enhanced sales resulting

from their testimonials would more than surpass the incurred costs. The third strategy entailed creating an army of opinion leaders by identifying influentials (including e-fluentials) and giving each a free iPhone three months prior to the actual launch. The buzz generated would constitute the major force in promoting the innovation. The fourth strategy involved doing nothing, and having Steve Jobs announce to the world news about this innovation from a public platform, an action that would occur a few months before the iPhone introduction. This would be accomplished via announcements made by him at expositions, where the hungry media and electronic buffs are looking for news and gadgets to talk about. Hindsight aside, assume you had been asked at that time to give your opinion on the viability of each proposal. What would your evaluation of each alternative strategy be? What arguments would you present to support and defend your chosen strategy over the other options?

CASE

A Questionable Celebrity Spokesperson to Promote Lipitor

On a Monday morning in early January 2008, the secretary to Mr. Ian Read, Pfizer's President of Worldwide Pharmaceutical Operations, entered his office and handed him an urgent sealed envelope addressed to the company from the Chair of the Committee on Energy and Commerce, Representative John Dingell (D-Michigan). The enclosed letter from the leaders of the Congressional Committee addressed and raised House concerns regarding a number of ads featuring Dr. Robert Jarvik as a spokesperson for Pfizer's cholesterol-lowering drug known as Lipitor. The letter requested the submission of all contacts, e-mails, correspondence, and scripts of television and print advertisements that Pfizer exchanged with all parties connected with the ad, including Dr. Jarvik, the ad agency Kaplan Thaler Group, and the FDA's Advertising Review Department.

The 2006–2007 ad campaign for Lipitor from Kaplan Thaler Group was a highly successful promotion, leading to sales in excess of $12.7 billion in the year 2007. The campaign was rolled out in early 2006, the same year that Zocor, Lipi-

tor's chief generic competitor, was introduced. Since Zocor was being sold at a fraction of Lipitor's price, Pfizer initiated the Jarvik campaign to protect its Lipitor's franchise, and reportedly spent over $258 million on advertising from January 2006 to September 2007. Much of this advertising outlay went for the Jarvik campaign.

Celebrity advertising endorsements are nothing new to promotional campaigns. Celebrities are employed by many companies and their ad agencies due to their popularity and mass appeal. But the Lipitor campaign was a rare instance of a well-known doctor and his questionable qualifications to endorse a drug used by millions of heart patients. Dr. Robert Jarvik is best known for the artificial heart he developed more than a quarter century ago. However, some of the House Committee concerns involve his credentials. Even though Jarvik holds a medical degree, he is not a cardiologist and, as such, is not licensed to practice medicine or prescribe medications to heart patients. The question, therefore, is what qualifies him to recommend Lipitor to patients on television.

In the commercials, Dr. Jarvik was depicted in various outdoor pursuits. One ad depicted him rowing a one-person racing shell swiftly across a mountain lake with a pitch line, "When diet and exercise aren't enough, adding Lipitor significantly lowers cholesterol." In another ad, where he was presented jogging with his stepson, Jarvik was featured saying, "Lipitor is one of the most researched medications. I'm glad I take Lipitor, as a doctor and a dad."

When the Congressional Committee looked into when Dr. Jarvik began taking Lipitor, its members found out that he did not start taking Lipitor until after he was hired by Pfizer to do the commercials. In addition, the committee discovered that in producing the commercials where Dr. Jarvik was shown rowing a racing shell, the crew that filmed the commercial used a stunt double, who was picked partially for his size and partially because, like Dr. Jarvik, he had a receding hairline. The frames that actually included Dr. Jarvik were shot in a rowing apparatus on a fixed platform in a film studio.

During the investigation, the Committee also uncovered that Dr. Jarvik was guaranteed $1.35 million for appearing in the advertisements. All these facts caused the Committee to suspect wrongdoing and perhaps realize the need to change existing laws in order to give consumers a better level of protection against such forms of questionable direct-to-consumer pharmaceutical advertising. Based on the findings of the probe, Pfizer, in February 2008, pulled its controversial Lipitor ads featuring Dr. Jarvik. The pharmaceutical company also promised to do a better job of clarifying its use of spokespersons in future advertising messages.

While the line between acceptable puffery and outright deception is not always clear, the Jarvik ads transfer this doctor's fame as an inventor to a vaguely authoritative giver of testimony for a drug treatment. When consumers see and hear a doctor endorsing a medication, they automatically perceive the expert to be credible with requisite knowledge of the drug he or she recommends. Testimonials are not unethical per se; however, what makes the stakes in this case high is the fact that the endorsement deals with a drug that affects the lives of millions of people. Dr. Jarvik, in these commercials, offers himself up as living proof of how well the drug works. Not only is the faked footage demonstrating his athletic prowess misleading, the deceptive claim of his medical expertise as well as his financial motives may have promoted him to offer this drug-endorsement testimony.

Questions

1. In your opinion, why are ads depicting public figures and celebrities usually more effective in promoting products than non-celebrity ads? Is the degree of influence on recipients uniform for all categories of products and services? Is the degree of influence the same for various celebrities? What characteristics are needed to qualify public figures and celebrities as effective givers of advertising testimony?

2. In clarifying his involvement with the Lipitor ads, Dr. Jarvik stated, "I accepted the role of spokesman for Lipitor because I am dedicated to the battle against heart disease, which killed my father at age 62 and motivated me to become a medical doctor. I believe the process of educating the public is beneficial to my patients, and I am pleased to be part of an effort to reach them." Do you believe that such a statement should have been a good enough reason for the House Committee to allow Pfizer to continue with the Jarvik campaign? Why or why not? Explain.

3. Would you recommend passage of legislation that governs celebrity involvement in promotion, such as rules on the types of products and services they can or cannot endorse? Would you support laws that require celebrity endorsers to possess appropriate credentials and expertise in the product or service category they promote? What time span of bonafide prior use should be required before spokespersons who claim to use a brand can legally be allowed to promote a product to the public?

Notes

1. Dave Balter, *The Word of Mouth Manual, Volume II* (Print Matters, Inc., 2008); and Stephen H. Waldstrom, "A Stroll Through the iPhone App Store," *Business Week*, (July 28, 2008), p. 74.

2. Paula Fitzgerald Bone, "Determinants of Word-of-Mouth Communication During Product Consumption," in John F. Sherry and Brian Sternthal (eds.), *Advances in Consumer Research* 19 (Provo, UT: Association for Consumer Research, 1992), pp. 579–83; W. R. Wilson and R. A. Peterson, "Some Limits on the Potency of Word-of-Mouth Information," in T. K. Srull (ed.), *Advances in Consumer Research* (Provo: UT: Association for Consumer Research, 1989), pp. 23–29; J. E. Swan and R. L. Oliver, "Postpurchase Communication by Consumers," *Journal of Retailing* (Winter 1989), pp. 516–33; and P. M. Herr, F. R. Kardes, and J. Kim, "Effects of Word-of-Mouth and Product-Attribute Information on Persuasion," *Journal of Consumer Research* (March 1991), pp. 454–62; C. Walker, "Word-of-Mouth," *American Demographics* (July 1995), p. 38.

3. Betsy Gelb and Madeline Johnson, "Word of Mouth Communication: Cases and Consequences," *Journal of Health Care Marketing* 15, no. 3 (Fall 1995), pp. 54–58.

4. Ibid.

5. Thomas S. Robertson, *Innovative Behavior and Communication* (New York: Holt, 1971), p. 170; and Deborah Sue Yeager, "Markdown Mecca," *Wall Street Journal* (July 6, 1976), p. 1

6. "New Survey Reveals E-fluentials' Cynical About Commercial Activity on Consumer Websites," *Businesswire* (October 24, 2007), http://findarticles.com/p/articles/mi_mOEIN/is_2007_Oct_24/ai_n27418558/print?tag=art.

7. Idil Cakim, "E-fluentials Expand Viral Marketing," *iMedia Connection* (October 28, 2002), www.imediaconnection.com/printpage/printpage.aspx?id=1146.

8. David Schemelia, "e-fluentials: News/Press Kit," http://www.efluentials.com/news/2001/news061500.html

9. "Top 10 Mobile Marketing Campaigns," *Christine* (November, 2006), www.christine.net/2006/11/top_mobile_mark.html.

10. "Buzz Marketing: Suddenly This Stealth Strategy Is Hot—But it's Still Fraught with Risk," *Business Week* (July 30, 2001), www.businessweek.com/print/magazine/content/01_31/b3743001.htm?chan=mz.

11. Ibid.

12. *Ad Forum* (July 1983), p. 55.

13. Quoted in Barbara B. Stern and Stephen J. Gould, "The Consumer as Financial Opinion Leader," *Journal of Retail Banking* 10 (Summer 1988), pp. 43–52; Elihu Katz and Paul F. Lazarsfeld, *Personal Influence* (Glencoe, IL: Free Press, 1955); Stephen P. Morin, "Influentials Advising Their Friends to Sell Lots of High-Tech Gadgetry," *Wall Street Journal* (February 28, 1983), p. 30.

14. George S. Day, "Attitude Change, Media, and Word-of-Mouth," *Journal of Advertising Research* 11, no. 6 (1971), pp. 31–40.

15. Johan Arndt, "Role of Product-Related Conversations in the Diffusion of a New Product," *Journal of Marketing Research* 4 (August 1967), pp. 291–95.

16. James H. Myers and Thomas S. Robertson, "Dimensions of Opinion Leadership," *Journal of Marketing Research* 9 (February 1972), pp. 41–46.

17. Paul M. Herr, Frank R. Kardes, and John Kim, "Effects of Word-of-Mouth and Product-Attribute Information on Persuasion: An Accessibility-Diagnosticity Perspective," *Journal of Consumer Research* 17 (March 1991), pp. 454–62.

18. Karen Maru File, Diane S. P. Cermak, and Russ Alan Prince, "Word-of-Mouth Effects in Professional Services Buyer Behavior," *Service Industries Journal* 14 (July 1994), pp. 301–14.

19. Amanda Lutchford, "Why the Word on the Street Works," *Marketing* (September 18, 1997), p. 18; "Top 10 Mobile Marketing Campaigns," *Christine* (November, 2006), www.christine.net/2006/11/top_mobile_mark.html; "Interactive Marketing and Other Great Advertising Ideas since 2003," *Adverblog* (July 22, 2007), www.adverblog.com/archives/003139.htm.

20. Silverman, "How to Harness the Awesome Power of Word-of-Mouth."

21. Herr, Kardes, and Kim, "Effects of Word-of-Mouth and Product-Attribute Information on Persuasion: An Accessibility-Diagnosticity Perspective."

22. Richard Nisbett and Lee Ross, *Human Inference: Strategies and Shortcomings of Social Judgment* (Upper Saddle River, NJ: Prentice Hall, 1980).

23. Jolita Kisielius and Brian Sternthal, "Examining the Vividness Controversy: An Availability-Valence Interpretation," *Journal of Consumer Research* 12 (March 1986), pp. 418–31.

24. Bernd Stauss, "Global Word-of-Mouth: Service Bashing on the Internet Is a Thorny Issue," *Marketing Management* 6, no. 3 (Fall 1997), pp. 28–30.

25. "A Hitchhiker's Guide to the Virtual World," *Four Corners* (March 19, 2007), www.abc.net.au/4corners/content/2007/s1876121.htm.

26. "Social Network Stats: Facebook, MySpace, Reunion," Forrester Research (January, 2008), www.web-strategist.com/blog/2008/01/09/social-network-stat-facebook-myspace-reunion.html.

27. Mike Reid, "Online Social Networks, Virtual Communities, Enterprises, and Information Professionals—Part 1," *Information Today, Inc.* (July 29, 2008), www.infotoday.com/searcher/jul07/reid_grey.shtml.

28. Jacqueline Johnson Brown and Peter H. Reingen, "Social Ties and Word-of-Mouth Referral Behavior," *Journal of Consumer Research* 14 (December 1987), pp. 350–62.

29. Elihu Katz and Paul F. Lazarsfeld, *Personal Influence: the Part Played by People in the Flow of Mass Communication* (Transaction Publishers, 2005).

30. "Mass Media: Types and Influences," *Word Press* (October 23, 2007), http://maxibona.wordpress.com/2007/10/23/mass-media-types-and-influences/.

31. S. D. Boon and C. D. Lomore, "Admirer-Celebrity Relationship Among Young Adults: Explaining Perceptions of Celebrity Influence on Identity," *Human Communication Research*, vol. 27 (2001).

32. D. C. Giles and J. Maltby, "The Role of Media Figures in Adolescent Development: Relations Between Autonomy, Attachment, and Interest in Celebrities," *Personality and Individual Differences*, vol. 36 (2004).

33. "Britney Spears Shaven 'Hair Cut': Is It Worth the Media Buzz?" *Huliq News* (February 18, 2007), www.huliq.com/11471/brittney-spears-shaven-hair-cut-is-it-worth-the-media-buzz.

34. "Long-Term Harmful Effects of Britney, Paris, and Lindsay's Bad Behavior on Young Women," *Huliq News* (February 17, 2007), www.huliq.com/11469/long-term-harmful-effects-of-brittney-paris-and-lindsays-bad-behavior-on-young-women.

35. Sarah Cassidy, "Celebrities Now More Influential on Young People Than Parents," BNET.com (March 1, 2004).

36. Thomas W. Valente and Rebecca L. Davis, "Accelerating the Diffusion of Innovations Using Opinion Leaders," *Annals of the American Academy of Political and Social Science* 566 (November 1999), pp. 55–67.

37. P. H. Reingen and J. B. Kernan, "Analysis of Referral Networks in Marketing," *Journal of Marketing Research* (November 1986), pp. 370–78.

38. L. F. Feick, L. L. Price, and R. A. Higie, "People Who Use People," in R. J. Lutz (ed.), *Advances in Consumer Research* 13 (Provo, UT: Association for Consumer Research, 1986), pp. 301–5; P. H. Reingen, "A Word-of-Mouth Network," in M. Wallendorf and P. Anderson (eds.), *Advances in Consumer Research* 14 (Provo, UT: Association for Consumer Research, 1987), pp. 213–17; and L. J. Yale and M. C. Gilly, "Dyadic Perceptions in Personal Source Information Search," *Journal of Business Research* (March 1995), pp. 225–37.

39. "Film Critics: Influencers or Predictors?" *Marketing News* (April 28, 1997), p. 18.

40. Everett M. Rogers, *Diffusion of Innovations*, 4th ed. (New York: Free Press, 1995).

41. Ibid., Leisa Reinecke Flynn, Ronald E. Goldsmith, and Jacqueline K. Eastman, "Opinion Leaders and Opinion Seekers: Two New Measurements," *Journal of Academy of Marketing Science*, vol. 24 (Spring 1996), pp. 137–47.

42. Michael R. Solomon, "The Missing Link: Surrogate Consumers in the Marketing Chain," *Journal of Marketing* 50 (October 1986), pp. 208–18.

43. "Ford and JWT Blur the Line Between Marketing and Research," *Sentientservices* (September 14, 2007), www.sentientservices.com/blog/2007/09/ford-and-jwt-blur-line-between.html.

44. Meera P. Venkatraman, "Opinion Leadership, Enduring Involvement and Characteristics of Opinion Leaders: A Moderating or Mediating Relationship?" in Marvin E. Goldberg, Gerald Gorn, and Richard W. Pollay (eds.), *Advances in Consumer Research* 17 (Provo, UT: Association for Consumer Research, 1990), pp. 60–67.

45. Katz and Lazarsfeld, *Personal Influence*, Ch. 10.

46. Ernest Dichter, "How Word-of-Mouth Advertising Works," *Harvard Business Review* 44 (November–December 1966), pp. 147–66.

47. Bone, "Determinants of Word-of-Mouth Communications During Product Consumption"; Dichter, "How Word-of-Mouth Advertising Works."

48. Christy Fisher, "Wal-Mart's Way," *Advertising Age* (February 18, 1991), p. 3.

49. "Viral Advertising Spreads Through Marketing Plans," *US Today* (June 23, 2005); Manohla Dargis, "We're All Gonna Die! Grab Your Video Camera," *New York Times* (August 1, 2008), movie review of *Cloverfield*.

50. Sandra Mardenfeld, "Mary Kay Ash," *Incentive* 70, no. 1 (January 1996), pp. 54–55; Jennifer Robertson, "Mary Kay Cosmetics: A Review of the Mary Kay Cosmetics Line," *Ezine Articles* (September 2, 2007), http://ezinearticles.com/?Mary-Kay-Cosmetics---A-Review-of-the-Mary-Cosmetic-Line&id=713721.

51. R. L. Bayus "Word-of-Mouth: The Indirect Effects of Marketing Efforts," *Journal of Advertising Research* (June–July 1985), pp. 31–35.

52. Gordon M. Henry, "And Now a Gag from Our Sponsor," *Time* (May 19, 1986), pp. 71, 74.

53. Katherine Neer, "How Product Placement Works," *Howstuffworks* (2008), http://money.howstuffworks.com/product-placement.htm/; "Product Placement Growth Fueled by Increase in Channels," *Howstuffworks*, (June 9, 2008), http://howstuffworks.com/framed.htm?parent=product-placement.htm&url=http://www.productplacement.biz1.

54. Judith Dobrzynski and J. E. Davis, "Business Celebrities," *Business Week* (June 23, 1986), pp. 100–107; Leslie Schultz, "Not Quite Ready for Prime Time President," *Inc.* (April 1985), pp. 156–60.

55. Silverman "How to Harness the Awesome Power of Word-of-Mouth."

56. Igor Holas, "Ford's Car Swap," *Autosavant* (September 7, 2007), autosavant.net/2007-09-fords-car-swap.html.

57. Duncan Carver, "Here's How to Tap into Yahoo! Answers' 60+ Million Targeted Visitors," *Anwersniper* (March 27, 2008), www.answersniper.com/.

58. "Pontiac G6 GT (2005) with Pictures and Wallpapers," NetCarShow (2005), www.netcarshow.com/pontiac/2005-g6_gt/.

59. "Top 10 Mobile Marketing Campaigns," *Christine* (November, 2006), www.christine.net/2006/11/top_mobile_mark.html.

60. Linda Bustos, "Negative Word of Mouth: Crisis or Opportunity?" *Get Elastic* (May 7, 2008), www.getelastic.com/reputation-management-damage-control/.

61. Diane Halstead, "Negative Word of Mouth: Substitute for or Supplement to Complaints?" *Journal of Consumer Satisfaction, Dissatisfaction, and Complaining Behavior* (January, 2002).

62. Paul Rand, "Understanding and Managing Negative Word of Mouth," *Ketchum* (September 28, 2005), www.ketchum.com/paul_rand_managing_negative_word_of_mouth_article; Glen Allsopp, "How to Deal with Negative Blog Posts," *Viper Chill* (February 19, 2008), www.viperchill.com/how-to-deal-with-negative-blog-posts/

Social Class

LEARNING OBJECTIVES

- To examine the concept of social class and the way our society regards the class issue.
- To gain insight into the multi-tiered class structure of the United States.
- To ascertain patterns, causes, and ramifications of the evolving social class structure in contemporary society.
- To probe the criteria and methods used in measuring social classes.
- To identify and examine five relevant issues associated with the concept of social class in contemporary society.
- To review the impact of social class membership on various aspects of consumer behavior.

KEY TERMS

social class
stratification
egalitarianism
mobility
nonproductive reach
subjective measures
reputational measures

objective measures
single-variable indexes
composite-variable indexes
status crystallization
overprivileged
underprivileged

Even though Americans are not all equal in status, most of us perceive ourselves as members of a huge middle class. This belief stems largely from an ingrained self-perception of being average, normal, and about equal in stature to everyone else. Within this theme of equality that runs through American social relationships, being on par with everybody else seems to be the "right thing to say and do" socially.

However, in many other societies, class is a more prominent issue, and social rankings bestow different degrees of importance, influence, and prestige to specific members of a society. In few other places is this social demarcation more evident than in Great Britain. To U.S. citizens, the English aristocracy is mysterious and confusing. Who are the aristocrats and how did they inherit their titles? Although some may wonder why the British are still fascinated with this group that seems to be a relic of the past, the fact remains that this part of society is the very backbone of England.

Only about one-third of British aristocracy are honored with noble titles such as Sir, Lord, or Knight. Traditionally, aristocrats did not work for a living. They inherited their money, which was usually spent on elegant homes, horses for hunting or racing, gaming, fine wines, and exquisite possessions.

Foremost among characteristics that distinguish British aristocrats is a deeply ingrained sense of duty, coupled with impeccably good manners. This sense of duty is manifested in deep involvement with charity events and needy causes. Because aristocrats have a supreme sense of self-confidence, they do not care what other people think of them. They tend, as a result, to be unimpressed by the achievement of others. They are preoccupied with the countryside and country sports, such as cricket, rugby football, polo, and croquet. During winter evenings, favorite pastimes include billiards, bridge, and backgammon. Most of them dislike living in cities and prefer out-of-the-way country homes, which they never name, believing that the people who matter would know where they live.

In Ireland and Scotland, many aristocrats live in old castles, adorned with furniture that is inherited, never bought, and rarely matches. Walls are decorated with an abundance of portraits of ancestors. The more portraits a castle has, the greater the prestige and honor accredited to its occupants.

British aristocrats tend to send their children to be educated at Eton, the top British public school established in 1440 by Henry VI. Annual tuition there exceeds £23,000. This was the school chosen by the Royal Family to complete Prince William's education. Old Etonians hold a great deal of power and prestigious posts in Britain. Exclusively male at one time, the school today accepts a limited number of females.

British aristocrats have their own mode of speech. They sit not in the lounge but in the drawing room. They do not go to the toilet, but to the lavatory. To avoid attention in public eating places, British aristocrats seldom eat in restaurants. They prefer the privacy of their own homes or a friend's dinner table, where good plain English food and fine wines from personal cellars are served. Along with this love of home is a significant attachment to the club—an aristocrat's inviolable refuge from reality. Most prestigious London clubs have changed very little over the years. In these for-men-only clubs, the staff upholds old traditions with great pride, only whispering as they talk, and making sure that members are elegantly served. Business discussions in the club are rarely heard. They are simply not allowed.[1]

> *Values and traditions in any culture dramatically influence how the society is stratified, as well as how people in each stratum live, what they like, and what interests them. Find out more about the British culture by visiting www.geocities.com/TheTropics/2865/index.htm. Compared to our seemingly classless society in the United States, what factors account for the permanent, formal caste system that characterizes British society? In your opinion, are the modern social-economic realities likely to change the way the British feel regarding their present rigid class structure?*

Many of the older societies around the globe have distinct social class structures in roughly the same way that the British monarchy thinks of class. However, whereas people in the United States readily admit to racial, ethnic, cultural, and gender distinctions or inequities, they tend to be less class conscious and largely choose to overlook social class divisions. Lacking obligations to class and social position, Americans can, at least, move from one group to another based on their accomplishments.

In this chapter, we examine the impact of social class on consumer behavior and the implications of class differences for marketers when designing strategies. Specifically, we cover the concept of social class, the U.S. class structure, class measurement, and the influence of class on purchasing and consumption patterns.

Introduction to Social Class

Marketers are keenly interested in the distribution of wealth across the marketplace, because this phenomenon largely demarcates which groups of people exhibit the greatest purchasing power. The marketing literature clearly establishes that income—the amount of resources an individual or household earns—exerts a major impact on consumer purchases. Some companies, such as Rolex and Bentley Motors, vie for the upper, more affluent levels of society. Others firms, such as Wal-Mart, successfully target less opulent, working-class consumers.

Although income and social class are related, they are not synonymous. **Social class** refers to the overall rank assigned to large groups of people, according to the values held by a particular society. From a marketing perspective, social class identifies large groups of people who share common ideas about how life should be lived. Whereas income influences purchasing behavior through availability of resources, social class affects how consumers spend that income. This may include where a person lives, what recreational activities he or she pursues, how to decorate his or her home, and the types of products and services he or she acquires.

Socioeconomic status and lifestyle are, to a great extent, inseparable.[2] Social class membership and relative standing within a class impact people's

social class
a societal rank assigned to large groups of people

The less opulent consumers constitute the main target of box stores like Wal-Mart and KMart.

© 2009, emin kuliyev, Shutterstock, Inc.

stratification
a system of classifying members of a population based on economic and social characteristics

beliefs, values, and behaviors.[3] People's lifestyles and tastes, as well as their consumption patterns, can be viewed largely as expressions of their socialization into a particular class. People learn the values and behaviors appropriate to their class formally via schooling as well as vicariously by observing their peers.

The Concept of Social Class

Many species of animals, such as wolves and chickens, arrange themselves into multitiered or stratified societies in which the most aggressive creatures command the first pick of food, mating partners, and living space. A study by Schjelderup-Ebbe described a barnyard community where each hen held its own definite position in the pecking order of the group.[4] Within the brood, each hen was found to dominate those of lesser standing and acquiesce to those of higher stature. Broadening the notion of a dominance–submission hierarchy to apply to humans, Ries and Trout noted that "Consumers are like chickens. They are much more comfortable with a pecking order that everybody knows and accepts."[5]

All but the smallest and most primitive societies have demonstrated **stratification**, or formal systems of economic and social inequality.[6] Social identity comes about when a culture establishes limits on interactions between people of unequal status. The existence of deference (social honor paid to members of higher classes by those of lesser social stature) is well accepted among social scientists. According to Weber, social class demarcates individuals' future opportunities and possibilities.[7] Furthermore, both social class and relative standing within a class are considered important sources of consumer beliefs, values, and behaviors.[8]

HOW U.S. CONSUMERS VIEW SOCIAL CLASS

It is a common belief that, compared to the class system in Europe, the United States does not have a rigid and clearly defined class system. Class distinctions in the United States are so subtle that foreign observers—especially those accustomed to a rigid caste system like that of India—often miss class nuances.

Many people associate the word *class* with unpleasant connotations. For many, particularly those who harbor deep feelings of egalitarianism, the idea of typing people is disturbing. Such persons feel that the United States was founded on a principle of equality, and people should be measured by their own accomplishments, not by whom their families happen to be. As a consequence, most U.S. citizens feel they belong to a massive middle class that seems, at the first glance, to engulf everyone around. However, no one can deny that in the eyes of others, all of us are defined, at least in part, according to an elaborate system that includes our occupation, education, income, family standing, type of residence, possessions, appearance, and manner of speech.

These distinctions between people who otherwise are assumed to be equal not only occur on an interpersonal basis, but also abound in every aspect of the business world. Examples include major airlines' three-tiered categorization of fliers, theaters with graded sections, and manufacturers' *good, better*, and *best* product gradations. Similarly, corporate, government, and ecclesiastical organizational structures are based on rigid *clan* hierarchies and various employment cadres.

FACTORS OBSCURING THE RECOGNITION OF SOCIAL CLASS IN THE UNITED STATES

A number of factors obscure the recognition of divergent social classes in the United States. These include the doctrine of egalitarianism, the size of the middle class, the possibilities for mobility in an open-class system, and confusion between social class and income.

Egalitarianism

Whereas very few Europeans, especially among the British, would offer apologies for their country's social hierarchy, the United States was founded on the principle of **egalitarianism**, which advocates equality among people. Egalitarian beliefs run counter to any idea implying that some members of society are more privileged and, in some way, superior to others.

> **egalitarianism**
> a principle that advocates that all people are equal

Size of the Middle Class

The size of the middle class in the United States to some extent hides the existence of a social class structure. Unlike many societies in which there are the very rich, the very poor, and only a few in-between, the United States has a comparatively large middle class, accounting for roughly between 45–47 percent of the population, depending on how the middle class is defined.

Mobility

Mobility, both social and economic, is a third factor that plays a significant role in the failure to recognize class distinctions. The Horatio Alger story, a partly real and partly mythical tale about a penniless young orphan who became successful in business and in life, has made a strong and lasting impression on the U.S. consciousness. Similarly, anecdotes about Commodore Vanderbilt (the skipper of a Staten Island garbage scow), Swift (a pushcart meat peddler on Cape Cod), and Kennedy (a rum-runner), as well as a host of other rags-to-riches narratives, have served to inspire many people in the United States with dreams of climbing the social ladder.

> **mobility**
> the movement upward and downward in the socioeconomic hierarchy

Social Class versus Income

Finally, many people confuse social class with income. Income is a gauge of the amount of money that individuals or families have available to spend, but income figures can obscure the many factors that truly differentiate between classes such as occupation, education, lifestyles, values, and attitudes. Although jobs that rank relatively low in social prestige may earn as much or even more than jobs that rank relatively high, the reverse also frequently occurs. With the downturn in our country's economic activities that started in 2007, some highly qualified individuals have been marginalized and are underemployed or working for lower pay and fewer benefits.[9]

WHY LEARN ABOUT SOCIAL CLASS?

The benefit of social stratification lies in its ability to provide a basis for market segmentation. Although social classes are tremendously large social aggregates containing vast differences in individual behavior and great diversity of life circumstances, the presence of certain shared values, attitudes, behavioral patterns, and lifestyles among members of each social class can facilitate the targeting process.

Marketers can now pinpoint the class status and buying patterns of just about everyone in the market. As we mentioned in the segmentation chapter, PRIZM from Nielsen Claritas Inc. broke down the entire United States into geo-demographic clusters, some as small as 300 households, in order to allow for more precise targeting. For example, according to Nielsen Claritas, a person at the highest level of the suburban elite class would most likely live in Upper Crust or Blue Blood Estate territories like Scarsdale (outside New York), Winnetka (outside Chicago), or Atherton (south of San Francisco). That person would probably own a new convertible, read one or more business magazines, and patronize a full-service brokerage firm. If that person were an Urban Gold Coaster, he or she would be likely to live on the Upper East Side in Manhattan, along Lake Michigan in Chicago, or in the Pacific Heights section of San Francisco. This person's inclinations would most likely include sailing, preference for informational TV, and investing in the stock market.

Ownership of expensive "toys" such as this yacht is among the characteristics of PRIZM's *Upper Crust* cluster.

© 2009, Volodymyr Kyrylyuk, Shutterstock, Inc.

Beneficiaries of such targeting efforts include direct marketers and advertisers who use precision targeting through the localization strategies of media. Dividing consumers into groups with common demographic, lifestyle, or behavioral characteristics allows the firms to zero in on minute niches of the population whose characteristics are known. Members of these niches thus are most likely to respond to particular offerings crafted specifically to suit their particular needs and interests.

nonproductive reach
the effort wasted on contracting consumers who are unlikely prospects

The intention is to eliminate **nonproductive reach**, otherwise known as the junk mail or spam phenomenon. Conventional promotion aimed at broad audiences usually translates into waste. Disinterested consumers who receive Web communications, ads, or unsolicited items in the mail usually ignore them or discard them without even a second glance. To overcome this problem, database marketing came to the rescue. Marketers are now able to identify and reach clusters of consumers who share common characteristics, interests, incomes, professions, lifestyles, and preferences. By knowing the characteristics of a group, marketers can design messages precisely calibrated to get members to act. For example, using its database, Hilton Hotels Corporation designed award-winning programs for business executives, such as its Hilton Meetings product for business travelers, Hilton HHonors, and its frequent guest programs.[10] Among the many users of database marketing are credit card companies, banks, food and non-food companies, pharmaceutical firms, as well as liquor, travel, and recreation establishments.

Advertising agencies are also avid users of this type of focused data. Advertisers today are forced to cater precisely to specific groups as a result of the present highly fragmented class structure in the United States. Whether the appeals are subtle or blatant, they are designed with class characteristics and aspirations in mind. Ads for domestic beer versus French wines, and for Hyundai versus Bentley, are designed to touch off a personal response and signal to a specific class that the product is appropriate for its tastes and social status. As depicted in Figure 14.1, this ad from Gucci is designed to appeal to members of the upper-middle class.

Class Structure in the United States

Most highly industrialized nations exhibit neither strict and tightly defined class systems nor pure social strata. Rather, in countries like the United States, a series of *status continua* can be identified.[11] These status continua reflect various factors that the society as a whole values. In achievement-oriented cultures like our own, income, occupation, education, residence, and possessions would be more likely to endow us with status than factors unrelated to accomplishment like family heritage, race, or gender. By contrast, more traditional societies such as China, India, and to some extent Great Britain might ascribe greater importance to such factors as ancestry or the social status of one's parents.

It is estimated that there are about 744,000 homeless persons in the United States, living in substandard conditions.

Researchers of the social class phenomenon differ with regard to the number of classes that exist in the United States. Estimates vary from as few as two classes to as many as nine. Those who propose a two-tiered society believe that the distinction between classes lies in the domain of ownership of the means of production. The *haves* own the means of production and employ the *have-nots*. The have-nots, on the other hand, sell their labor power to the haves in order to survive. This situation, inevitably, leads to antagonism between the two classes, which, in turn, is the main driving force in the system.[12]

Other authors such as Paul Fussell, for example, identified nine distinct classes that range from an elite class, virtually invisible behind the tall walls of their mansions, all the way to an underclass, equally invisible in their hovels. Still others, such as William Thompson, Joseph Hickey, and Dennis Gilbert,

© 2009, wrangler, Shutterstock, Inc.

Figure 14.1

A chic and attractive model along with the quality-laden image of Gucci are symbols that appeal to consumers in the upper-middle class.

proposed a six-class structure that ranges from high-level executives, celebrities, and heirs at the top all the way down to others who occupy poorly paid positions, who lack job skills and have little or no participation in the labor force, or who rely on government transfers for survival.[13]

MULTI-TIERED SOCIAL CLASS STRUCTURE OF THE UNITED STATES

Based on classifications by contemporary sociologists such as William Thompson, Joseph Hickey, Leonard Beeghley, Dennis Gilbert, and others, the social class structure in the United States can be summarized as follows:[14]

The Upper Class

The *upper class*, which accounts for about 1 percent of the population, includes top executives, celebrities of superstar stature, high-rung politicians, multimillionaires, and heirs. In addition to those blue bloods who inherited their wealth, some members of the upper class are the corporate elite who control or own America's corporations as well as those who earn exceptionally high income through boardroom memberships. For this group, income and wealth statistics serve as the standard for placing them in this category. There is, however, disagreement over the inclusion of those "*nouveau riche*" as members of the upper class—an issue that perhaps caused sociologist W. Lloyd Warner in 1941 to divide the upper class into the two distinct subgroups known as the "upper-upper" and "lower-upper" classes. Nevertheless, many observers feel that members of this group are the achievers who, rather than inheriting their wealth, have ambitiously worked hard to earn it.[15]

The Middle Class

The *middle class* constitutes a large share, between 45 and 47 percent of the population. Most contemporary sociologists divide this group into two distinct subgroups, the upper middle (about 15 percent of the population) and the lower middle (about 30 to 32 percent of the population).

The upper middle class consists of highly educated, salaried professionals and managers with above-average income, mostly in the six-figure range. Many of these individuals hold graduate degrees, enjoy greater work autonomy, and are often members or officers of professional organizations. Examples include professionals, executives, scientists, esteemed authors, and journalists.

The lower middle class, on the other hand, consists of semi-professionals and craftspeople who have some degree of work autonomy. Most of the members of this group have at least some college education and mostly occupy white-collar positions. Their income is average, ranging between $35,000 and $95,000. However, it should be noted that the distinction between the two segments of the middle class based on income levels alone could be misleading. Household income distribution can neither reflect the standard of living for a household nor its class status with complete accuracy.

The Working Class

Sociologists estimate the size of the *working class* to be between 40 and 43 percent of the population. This group also consists of the two categories known as the working class (about 30 to 32 percent of the population) and the working poor (about 13 percent).

The first group includes individuals who occupy clerical and blue- and pink-collar jobs that normally carry minimum job security. These positions entail routinized work schedules and processes, and require no decision-making capabilities. Members of this group usually hold a high school degree. Once again, it should be noted here that the standard of living of households within this category varies widely based on the number of wage earners within the household. For instance, husband–wife households with no children where both spouses work have been observed to enjoy a higher standard of living than other households with a single wage earner and a number of children to support.

The working poor segment, on the other hand, is made up of individuals holding retail, service, and low-rung clerical jobs. Those who occupy such positions are characterized by low levels of education often gained in substandard school systems. The types of jobs they hold offer little security, low chances for advancement, and minimal protection from poverty—conditions that create feelings of vulnerability and susceptibility to changing economic circumstances.

The Under Class

Located at the very bottom of the social hierarchy, the *under class* accounts for about 12 percent of the population and consists of individuals who either occupy poorly paid positions, are infrequent participants in the labor force, or those who rely on government support or charity for survival. In August 2008, the U.S. Census Bureau reported that there were 37.3 million individuals living in poverty in our society. With a low educational level of some high school or less, their chances of acquiring or maintaining well-paying jobs are severely restricted. Many members of this group live below the poverty level, with food insecurity present among one-third of them. In 2006, the Center on Hunger and Poverty reported that approximately 25 million Americans participated in the food stamps program.[16]

The Evolving Social Class Structure of the United States

Today, new social trends continue to alter the profile of social classes in the United States. The growing gap between those who are well off and everyone else is among the more troubling phenomena in our time. For example, in the past few years, the concentration of wealth among a handful of people at the top has set new records. According to a 2008 report, the super richest 1 percent of Americans currently hold wealth worth $16.8 trillion, nearly $2 trillion more than the bottom 90 percent of the population.[17] The broad category of the rich, however, includes over 12 million persons. This group has been labeled by the *Wall Street Journal*'s wealth reporter as the "richistan"—almost a separate society from the rest of the U.S. population.[18] The richistans are not necessarily about old wealth. While some of these individuals accumulated their assets through hard work, others made their fortunes from short-term speculation, such as hedge funds and other largely manipulative financing schemes. Growth of the segment known as the richistans has been accelerating over recent decades. The number of billionaires rose from 13 in the year 1980 to over 500 in 2008. The count for millionaires inflated from half a million to 10 million over the same time frame.

Against this glamorous picture of the rich lies another gloomy image of the poor. The U.S. Census Bureau reports that the poverty rate in our society in 2006 was 12.3 percent, placing about 37 million individuals below the official poverty thresholds. Moreover, due to the current economic downturn, this rate is rising even higher. Many working-class individuals are now facing even less access to income and wealth due to recent corporate layoffs. For example, in January 2009, reports indicated that the job losses during 2008 amounted to 2.6 million jobs, and that the unemployment rate rose to a 7.2 level. There were 11 million individuals looking for work at that point of time. In the meantime, the rising standard of living among the more financially privileged members of our society has further pushed down the already low standard of living for our poor. Add to this the long-term rise in prices for the necessities of life, such as energy, health care, and food, that has taken an even larger bite out of their already-low income.

This dire situation has resulted in many calls for a national effort to cut the poverty rate in our society. Suggested remedies include government initiated public projects, raising the minimum wage rate, granting an income tax credit for the poor, investing more in rural communities, supporting education and training for the less fortunate, expanding family literacy programs, providing for access to health care, and strengthening labor laws to protect the rights of workers.

SOCIAL CLASSES AND THE NET

During the last 25 years, technology has become an integral component of society's everyday information environment. For a large segment of our population, technology is transparent and has become a part of its social, economic, and educational landscape. A Pew Internet & American Life Project in 2008 reported that 73 percent of Americans now use the Internet, compared with only 47 percent in the year 2000.[19] This technology has affected the way we live and has influenced nearly every aspect of our daily lives. However, the skills required to access information continue to be more diverse and reflect the complexity of both the technology being used to store, retrieve, and disseminate information as well as its multiple delivery formats.[20] This fact requires that the user is someone who has proficiency in a wide-ranging skill set that is constantly evolving. And that is where one differentiating element between social classes—namely education—explains the issue of the digital divide among members of our society.[21]

Concerns about racial disparity and Internet access/use were discussed and debated in the press as well as among scholars throughout the 1990s. The issue quickly changed direction when subsequent reports presented concrete demographic evidence that the digital divide should not be viewed along racial lines, but rather be regarded as a product of the standard of living of individuals within the society.[22] In the year 2000, Forrester Research presented a study revealing that the existing divide is actually based not on ethnicity, as had been advocated by many, but rather resulted from disparities of income, age, and educational levels existing within the social groups that make up our society.[23] In fact, the 2008 Pew Internet & American Life Project's report revealed that the rate of Internet use by English-speaking Hispanics was 80 percent, compared to only 75 percent for whites. It also showed that the black rate of use was close to 59 percent, and was accelerating every year.[24]

Some observers were quick to conclude that the digital divide issue is a myth, and that the "have-nots" are in fact "want-nots" who did not care for the technology in the first place. A study conducted by the U.S. Department of Commerce reported that when members of the Internet nonusers category were questioned regarding the reasons underlying their choice of rejecting the Internet, the reasons given included cost/value and availability issues. Other

Ethical Dilemma

Ego or Hard-Work Driven CEO Pay?

Everyone today realizes that the gap between the rich and the poor is widening. The concentration of financial resources at the top of the economic ladder has left average families with inadequate income to maintain a decent standard of living. With the recent mortgage meltdown, and with household debt at its highest level since 1933, many families now face difficulties in maintaining their former levels of consumption.

Against this bleak backdrop, recent reports in the media have revealed that the five biggest firms on Wall Street paid a record of $39 billion in bonuses to their executives for 2007, a year in which three of these five companies suffered the worst quarterly losses in their history. While the International Monetary Fund (IMF) estimated that the financial turmoil set off by the collapse of the mortgage market reached $1 trillion, the CEOs of the firms most responsible for causing the crisis collected hundreds of millions of dollars in pay and benefits.

At the center of this issue lies the question of the fairness of CEO pay levels and the alarming rate at which they have been growing over the past few years. According to an AFL-CIO Executive Watch report, the average CEO of a Standard & Poor's 500 company in 2006 received $14.78 million in total compensation. This report also revealed that in the same year, the ratio of average CEO's pay to that of the average worker's pay was 364 times. If that exponential rate of growth were to continue, the average CEO would make the salary equivalent of more than 150,000 American factory workers by the year 2050.

The exceptionally high income of CEOs consists of a number of components. In addition to their salaries and bonuses, CEOs receive stock-based pay. This means that the executives are also owners of the corporation for which they work. Stock-based pay takes the forms of either stock options or stock grants. The first type gives the executive the right to buy a share of stock at a fixed price for a specified period of time, such as 5 or 10 years. The executive can then trade a stock bought at a low price by selling it when prices rise. In the case of grants, the company endows the executive with shares of the company's stock and, in effect, makes him or her a part owner of the business.

A number of factors help preserve this unusual practice. A large portion of the benefits that top executives receive are hidden. The law does not require that they be disclosed. A second factor is the lack of a system that gives shareholders the right to approve executive compensation packages. A third factor entails compensation consultants' drive to encourage CEOs to reach for the sky in their salary negotiations in order to surpass the pay of their peers.

Critics argue that this exorbitant level of CEO compensation has taken earnings away from company shareholders and working families. It has also resulted in lowering the standard of living of those who constitute the actual workforce behind the production and marketing of products and services in our society. Many observers wonder whether the government should intervene by placing limitations on these skyrocketing CEO salaries. However, they realize that if history serves as a guide, the action taken by Congress back in 1933 to prohibit pay of more than $1 million to CEOs was ineffectual. Unless Wall Street moguls and boardroom professionals step up to their social responsibilities, this wealthy group of executives will continue to get even richer over the years.[28]

Reactions concerning the inequity of the income issue in our society have risen dramatically in recent times due to the mortgage meltdown of 2007-2008 and the perceived complicity of Wall Street in this situation. Learn more about this topic by visiting the AFL-CIO Executive PayWatch Web site at www.paywatch.org. Examine a few case studies the site provides, such as CitiGroup, Merrill Lynch, and Morgan Stanley. Are the CEOs of such financial firms responsible for the meltdown of the market? Was it wise for the government to intervene and bail out such corporations? Explain. What actions would you suggest to curtail the excessive compensation packages offered to CEOs in the United States?

rationalizations offered included lack of need, disinterest, limited financial capability, absence of technical knowledge, and unavailability of service in some rural areas where nonusers resided.[25]

On the topic of class and Internet use, sociologist Nalini Kotamraju has argued that class divisions in the United States have more to do with lifestyles and social stratification than with income.[26] Lifestyles, she believes, can better explain people's online activities than do their social backgrounds, which instead better explain household adoption practices, such as computer ownership.

In one application of this proposition, Danah Boyd investigated preferences for Facebook and MySpace among high-school and college students. She noted that until recently, America's young were flocking to MySpace. This picture, she argued, is now being blurred, where many of these young people are flocking to Facebook. MySpace was launched in 2003, and was used by young adults between 20 to 30 years old. Facebook was established in 2004 as a Harvard-only site, but gradually expanded over time to welcome many other young people. For all of the year 2005 and most of 2006, during which MySpace was the preferred site for high-school teens, Facebook was the favored site among college students. In her effort to frame the labels that demarcate the class to which these students belonged, Boyd coined names for two groups of young people—the "hegemonic teens" and the "subaltern teens." The first group, which mostly uses Facebook, consists of kids who tend to come from families that emphasize education and higher learning. They are primarily white, enrolled in honors classes, and live in a world dominated by after-school activities. The subaltern teens, on the other hand, tend to be users of MySpace. They usually come from parents who did not attend college. Their families expect them to get a job or enlist in the military after graduating from high school. They are somewhat socially ostracized at school because they seem to be different from their peers. Whether or not Boyd's framing of Internet users will confirm what Kotamraju advocated remains open to interpretation.[27]

IMPLICATIONS OF EVOLVING SOCIAL CLASS TRENDS

Recent changes in the profile of the social class structure in our society are affecting where and how consumers shop. For example, since the year 2000, the percentage of households that visited and purchased products from dollar stores, discount supercenters, warehouse stores, and thrift shops has soared and surpassed 67 percent in 2007, up from 55 percent in 2000. Meanwhile, traditional merchandisers have been losing customers.[29]

Some of the biggest marketers in the United States are adopting a two-tiered strategy, tailoring their products and pitches to two different Americas. Companies from AT&T through Disney to General Motors now openly embrace this two-tier marketing strategy, which deliberately polarizes products and services as well as their sales pitches to the two market segments of the rich and the poor.[30]

In the same vein, Paine Webber, Inc. has advised investors to follow a Tiffany/Wal-Mart strategy and avoid companies that serve the middle of the consumer market. Some companies try to attract customers on both sides of the divide with an upstairs–downstairs approach. For example, at Gap's

Banana Republic stores, denim jeans sell for $78. Gap's Old Navy stores sell a similar version for $29. Both chains are thriving.[31]

A glance at the changes just described reveals an evolving marketplace. On one side, the shrinking income of many households translates into frugality that will characterize their buying patterns. On the other side, the *selectively affluent* offer excellent opportunities. They are the consumers whose incomes may not qualify them for entrance into exclusive country clubs or gated communities, but who have an affluent mind-set and sufficient discretionary income to satisfy their aspirations. This newly emerging class, which is well educated and generally highly paid, provides a market for many quality and prestigious products and services, such as expensive cars, jewelry, and vacations. The ads in Figures 14.2 and 14.3 are aimed at selectively affluent audiences.

Measuring Social Class

We informally apply a variety of criteria in order to judge the social status of other persons around us, to classify or grade other people in terms of the location of their residence and their possessions. Criteria may include such things as the other party's ancestry, occupation or income, education or intelligence, authority or influence, associations, behavior, speech, tactfulness, and grooming. In fact, the specific yardsticks we employ to rank other people along some sort of social scale reflect, to a large extent, the norms, values, and ideals of the society in which we live.

More formally, social scientists have applied three basic techniques to research the topic of social class. In one approach, individuals rate their own social standing. Second, individuals can be requested to evaluate the social position of others. In still another technique, impartial measurement criteria are applied as indicators of the particular social class that an individual belongs to. These procedures, known respectively as subjective, reputational, and objective measures, are discussed in paragraphs that follow.

SUBJECTIVE MEASURES

subjective measures
ways of determining social class membership based on individuals' classification of themselves

Subjective measures of social class probe individuals' class-consciousness or sense of belonging and identification with others. When employing these measures, researchers give participants an opportunity to classify themselves, based largely on their self-images, in order to determine the social class structure. Although this method of measuring class offers simplicity and convenience, it can lead to an erroneous profile of the social classes. Some respondents over- or understate their class standing, thereby causing over- or undercounts of various class memberships. For example, in a 2008 national survey by the Pew Research Center, 53 percent of Americans of all races and regions self-defined themselves as middle class. But by applying the standard measure that defines middle-income households as those earning between 75 and 150 percent of the median family income, now about $60,000, only 35 percent of the population met that criterion.[32]

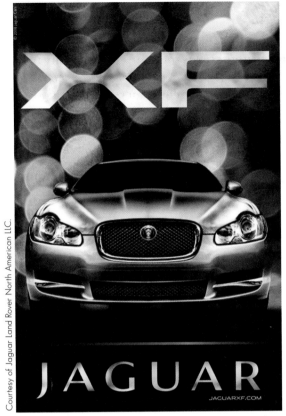

Performance Runs in the Family

INTRODUCING THE 2008 GRANTURISMO AND QUATTROPORTE SPORT GT S

With their style, performance and exclusivity, the new GranTurismo and Quattroporte Sport GT S express values that have made Maserati automobiles overachievers from the very beginning. Like the championship-winning MC 12 GT 1, each is a Pininfarina masterpiece; unequalled in style and impossible to ignore. At their heart is a powerful, 400 hp Ferrari-engineered V8 engine that delivers brilliant performance and an unforgettable driving experience. And each is truly rare; limited production combined with unmatched personalization options ensure the exclusivity for which Maserati is famous. Join the family of overachievers; visit maseratiamerica.com to build your own Maserati and locate your local authorized dealer.

MSRP for base Quattroporte Automatic starts at $119,000, Sport GT S (shown) starts at $132, 415. GranTurismo starts at $113,750, including gas guzzler tax, dealer prep and transportation. Dealer price may vary. ©2008 Maserati North America. All rights reserved. Maserati and the Trident logo are registered trademarks of Maserati SpA.

Figures 14.2 and 14.3

Prestigious names such as Jaguar and Maserati suggest distinction and exclusivity–images that are desirable to affluent members of our society.

REPUTATIONAL MEASURES

Rather than having subjects estimate their own social standing, **reputational measures** of social class ask individuals to rank the social position of other individuals in the community with whom they are familiar. When employing these measures, researchers request key informants within a group (a coworker, manager, neighbor, member of the clergy, colleague) to provide preliminary judgments of other members' social class. Trained researchers, however, are responsible for making the definitive assignments of community members into the various social class positions.[32]

Although many social scientists regard reputational measures as the most accurate and thoroughly validated approach to investigate social class structures, reputational approaches hold lesser value to marketers and researchers of consumer behavior, who are interested in identifying specific class attributes that have a bearing on consumption patterns.

reputational measures
ways of determining social class based on individuals' ranking of others in a society

OBJECTIVE MEASURES

Unlike subjective and reputational techniques of social class measurement, which rely on self- or peer-evaluations, respectively, studies that use **objective measures** apply relevant demographic and socioeconomic criteria in order to assess individuals' social class membership. Specific variables employed when using the objective method include amount or source of income, location or type of residence, occupation, education, and possessions. These variables, as well as other factors, can be used separately or in combination to evaluate an individual's social standing.

Some investigations of social class rely on just one socioeconomic gauge in order to estimate an individual's social class membership. Such studies are said to employ **single-variable indexes**. Among the single-variable indexes used to measure social class, occupation is probably the most widely accepted sole indicator of social standing. To a great extent, occupation reflects level of education, determines income, and influences the type of people that someone associates with, as well as the products and services bought to perform the occupational role. Other commonly accepted singular yardsticks of social class include an individual's level of formal education and amount or source of income. Education is likely to influence a person's beliefs, values, activities, and opinions. Income determines one's ability to purchase goods and services.[33]

Other sociologists have used possessions as an index of social class.[34] Chapin's Social Status Scale offered a rating scheme for evaluating a family's social class that hinged on the presence of certain furniture items and accessories in the living room (types of floor covering, drapes, fireplace, etc.) and the condition of the room.[35] In another study, Kron found that lower-class families tended to place their TV sets in the living room, whereas middle- and upper-class families usually placed their TVs in the bedroom or family room.[36] The quality of the neighborhood where a person lives and the dollar value of his or her residence, although seldom used as sole gauges of an individual's social standing, are useful to verify social class membership that has been assigned on the basis of a single variable such as occupation or income.

Because social class is a truly multidimensional phenomenon and synthesizes many different aspects of people's lifestyle, consumer researchers typically prefer to systematically combine and differentially weigh several socioeconomic measures into an overall index of social class. Such gauges, known as **composite-variable indexes**, better reflect the complexity of social class than do single-variable indexes. When composite-variable indexes are used, an individual's overall score is computed as a weighted average. Evaluation criteria such as income source, occupational status, educational level, housing type, and dwelling areas can be rated on a multipoint scale from most to least prestigious or from excellent to poor.[38] For example, when rating income source on a 7-point scale, inherited wealth would be assigned a rating of 1, whereas public relief would receive a rating of 7. Other criteria such as occupation and education level can also be evaluated on multipoint scales as shown in Exhibit 14.1.

Income Source	**Rating**
Inherited wealth	1
Earned wealth	2
Profits and fees	3
Salary	4
Wages	5
Private relief (from relatives or friends)	6
Public relief	7

Educational Level	**Rating**
Professional (earned doctorate or master's degree)	1
Four-year college diploma	2
Associate's degree or some college–business school (but without a four-year degree)	3
High school graduate	4
Some high school, no diploma	5
Elementary school diploma	6
Less than elementary school diploma	7

Occupation	**Rating**
Major professionals, owners and high-ranking executives of large businesses	1
Professionals, owners and managers of medium-size businesses	2
Minor professionals, administrative personnel, owners of small-to-medium-size businesses	3
Clerical sales workers, technicians, owners of small businesses	4
Skilled laborers	5
Semiskilled laborers	6
Unskilled laborers	7

Researchers would also assign each of the socioeconomic factors chosen to measure individuals' social class its own weight. For example, subjects' income source may be given a higher weight than their dwelling area. Multiplying each socioeconomic criterion rating by its respective weighting and then summing produces an individual's overall score. This composite score, in turn, is used to designate the individual's class standing.[39] Interestingly, Zaltman, LeMasters, and Heffring note that it is extremely difficult to define social class by cataloging its components. Although members of a social class and similarities in their attitudes may be influenced by their education levels, occupations, and financial wealth, "social class is not a combination of these factors but a fusion of effects resulting from these and other factors. This fusion becomes a unique entity with its own character that does not resemble any of its contributory factors."[40]

Global Opportunity

Would the Consumer in Rwanda Pay $1 for a Can of Coke?

The changing class structure in many developing countries due to rising incomes and escalating standards of living have attracted the attention of many U. S.-based businesses that aim to expand their operations abroad. The problem that faces most of them, however, is how to assess the purchasing power in a foreign country and how to determine which class represents a feasible group to pursue. Fortunately, two methods of measuring foreign consumers' income and purchasing power have been developed by economists to help marketers in their pursuits. These methods are the *Socioeconomic Strata* (SES) system and *Purchasing Power Parity* (PPP) analysis. The logic behind either method is simple: household income in developing countries does not always equate with the comparatively high household income in the United States, thus restricting the ability of consumers in these countries to pay the same prices for similar goods and services. The fact that standards of living vary significantly from one country to another creates a pricing dilemma for American companies selling globally.

In one application of the SES system, Strategy Research Corporation classified Latin American households based on measures such as the number of durables in the household, employment of domestic servants, and the householder's education level. Based on the SES, the company was able to divide Latin American households into five social classes ranging from the elite at the top, to those society members who are struggling for neces-

sities at the bottom. Similarly, the SES system was employed in a recent study to ascertain value perceived by consumers in Argentina, Brazil, Chile, Colombia, Costa Rica, and Mexico as these individuals considered baskets of retail offerings.

PPP analysis, on the other hand, differs from measures such as household income or GNP per capita. It is based on the cost of a standard *market basket* of products bought in each country expressed in U.S. dollars. This method allows marketers to compare the relative purchasing power of goods in a particular country to what it would cost in the United States. Thus, the price for the same product in each country can be set to coincide with the level of purchasing power in that nation. The World Bank now classifies all countries by the PPP system in its annual *World Bank Atlas*.[37]

Finding an easy measure for consumer demand and purchasing power in foreign countries is a familiar problem most U.S. marketers have to face. To learn more about Purchasing Power Parity (PPP), visit http://fx.sauder.ubc.ca/ppp.html and learn how PPP is calculated. In your opinion, is over-valuation or under-valuation of currencies with respect to their ability to acquire products a factor that affects the rank of individuals or households on the social class scale? Explain.

Issues Relevant to the Social Class Structure in the United States

Now that we have addressed some of the procedures used by researchers to measure social class, let us shift our attention to some of the issues relevant to the topic. These issues include the changing class stature of women, social class versus income, status crystallization, the over- and underprivileged, and finally the issue of social mobility. We discuss each of these topics in the sections that follow.

THE CHANGING CLASS STATURE OF WOMEN

The model of the nuclear family, with the breadwinner father out at work and the homemaker and child-minding mother at home, has run out of steam for a number of reasons. Single women, up until marriage or until the birth of their first child, either go to school or work. In addition, women with families are working in far greater numbers today than ever before. A record 68 million women were employed in the United States in 2007. Seventy-five percent of them were employed full time, and 25 percent were employed on a part-time basis. Employed women are also projected to constitute 49 percent of the total labor force in the next few years. Thirty-nine percent of employed women worked in managerial, professional, and related occupations; 34 percent in sales and office occupations; and 20 percent in service occupations.[41] With regard to education, women now surpass men in college enrollment. Further, among those with higher education, there is almost no difference between the percentages of men and women who are able to locate jobs. As women have furthered their education and acquired better jobs, their status and income have risen correspondingly.

Despite these changes in the social stature of women in our society, measurements of family social class standing traditionally classified women in accordance with the occupation of their fathers or husbands.[42] If social class measurements were to reflect a more accurate depiction of the class structure in our society, these measurements should use joint husband–wife assessments. Incorporating female education levels and occupations into social class measurement would significantly change many of the traditional generalizations regarding class differences in lifestyles and consumption.[43]

Today, women's educational and professional accomplishments have altered the traditional view of social class in our society.

SOCIAL CLASS VERSUS INCOME

Although it is not uncommon for people to casually equate money with social class, social scientists still ponder the precise nature of the relationship between income and other aspects of social class. The fact that some lower-class families earn lofty incomes while some higher-class families remain underprivileged has already been established. Coleman concluded that "class and income are not very well correlated."[46]

A number of authors have addressed the issue of whether social class or income better predicts consumption patterns. Both concepts appear to hold merit, and one is not a substitute for the other.[47] According to Stone, for example, buying decisions are less affected by income than by consumers' reference groups, social class, and cultural influences. Stone noted that the *ability* to buy needs to be distinguished from the *proneness* to buy.[48]

Consumer Behavior in Practice

For Richer, for Smarter . . . 'Til Death Do Us Part

America's matrimonial trends clearly indicate that the majority of marriages are between individuals who belong to the same social class. Clearly, individuals feel more comfortable when they are around people who are much like themselves. This phenomenon has been confirmed by looking at how closely a couple's "social ranks" match. Social ranking has been used by sociologists to reflect the extent of a couple's educational attainment—a measure that is less likely to change over time compared with the couple's income.

This trend toward educational homogeneity, or the tendency for men and women with similar educational achievement to marry each other, has had an obvious negative effect on the U.S. marriage rates, and has placed educated women in an adverse position in the matrimonial market. The increased educational attainment of women and their mass entry into the work force since the 1970s had given them an edge over many eligible males. Today, for example, the number of women who receive a bachelor's or master's degree each year far surpasses the number of men who do so.[44] Since this trend is expected to continue into the future, it simply would indicate that more educated women are and would likely continue to be available in the nuptial market. And herein lies the problem. Educated women are less likely to be attracted to males who lack comparable educational credentials. Less-educated men are less desirable to women because they do not fit the profile of what a woman looks for in a mate. An attractive companion has to be someone who shares similar interests, values, and views of the world as well as a party who can make a similar economic contribution to the family.

From a male's point of view, on the other hand, less-educated men tend to feel somewhat threatened by the higher educational accomplishment of their female companion. This would also mean that women with brains are less likely to be viewed by these men as the hottest commodities in the marriage market.[45]

Since many single Americans tend to look for marriage partners within their own social class, they often face the problem of infrequent opportunities to socially meet others. Marketers have seized this opportunity by providing dating/mating services to facilitate the task of meeting others online. Many dating Web sites have now proliferated the Interent, with some boasting membership of over 3 million. Visit the Web site of one such service at www.e-Harmony.com, a site that employs 29 personality dimensions of participants to effect successful matches. In your opinion, to what extent are such services successful in matching similar individuals? Will such services help to enhance or reduce the homogeneity trend in intra-class marriages prevalent in our society today?

Similarly, Schaninger suggested that social class appears to be a better predictor than income for consumer purchases that require low-to-moderate dollar expenditures, have symbolic value, reflect an underlying lifestyle, or mirror homemaker roles (various food items and beverages, domestic or imported wines, some cosmetic and makeup items).[49] Social class also appears to be more relevant than income for predicting the method and place of purchase for highly visible, symbolic, and more costly items such as living room furniture. Income, on the other hand, appears to be a better predictor than social class in the case of products or activities that require major expenditures and reflect ability to pay. Examples include home computers, as well as major kitchen and laundry appliances, which are not perceived to be class-linked status symbols. Combined social class and income data, however, appear necessary in order to predict purchases of moderate-to-expensive, highly visible products such as homes, automobiles, electronics, and clothing that serve as symbols of status within a class.

STATUS CRYSTALLIZATION VERSUS INCONGRUITY

When we attempt to gauge an individual's social class membership, that person's score on one class indicator may or may not concur with his or her standing on other class indicators. Whenever multiple objective criteria are applied to ascertain an individual's social class, researchers often find some degree of inconsistency among the indicators they employ.[50] Consider the case of a truck driver who never finished high school and who lives in a modest home in the older section of town but who earns a very high income. Such an individual would exemplify low-status crystallization, a case known as status incongruity.

Thus, **status crystallization** refers to the extent to which different indicators of an individual's social stature (income, occupation, education, residence, ethnicity) tend to coincide with one another. As consumer researchers, we are often interested in the exceptions to the phenomenon of status crystallization—incongruities between a consumer's social class standing and his or her consumption-related patterns.

status crystallization
the coincidence of the different indicators of an individual's social stature

The concepts of status crystallization and incongruity help consumer researchers appraise the impact of inconsistencies on consumption patterns. For instance, in the case of the truck driver mentioned earlier who earns a high income but lives in a modest home, the excess discretionary income may be spent on luxury items such as expensive high-tech electronics, a speedboat or a fancy automobile or motorcycle.

THE OVER- AND UNDERPRIVILEGED

Popular notions that all members of a given social class have approximately equal income or that individuals' or households' class standing is the consequence of their income are serious fallacies. In fact, significant earning differentials can be observed within every social class. For example, in the 2008 Pew Research Center's Report on the middle class, four in ten Americans with incomes below $20,000 self-defined themselves as middle-class, as did a third of those with incomes above $150,000.[51] Therefore, in addition to categorizing individuals and families by their class standing, we can further pigeonhole members of each class as:

(1) fairly average wage earners,
(2) those who make considerably more money than the average for their class, and
(3) those who make notably less than the average for their class.[52]

Marketers recognize that the purchasing, spending, and consumption patterns of these three subgroups differ according to their relative incomes.[53]

Average individuals and families are those who fall into the middle-income range for their assigned social class. Such households are likely able to afford the residence location, type of home, furniture, appliances, automobiles, clothing, and food, as well as other possessions and services that their class peers might expect. If we were to consider average individuals within present middle class, we would readily observe that their households have been increasingly squeezed by sagging incomes. The economic slowdown as well as rising energy costs have affected their expenditures on various products and services such as food, clothing, housing, medical care, and education. Even though most members of this category have working spouses, reports indicate that even with dual incomes, average middle-class families in the year 2007 spent 32 percent less on clothing, 18 percent less on food, and 52 percent less on appliances compared with their counterparts back in 1970.[53]

Those whose income level exceeds the median for their class are said to be the overprivileged. In these households, a good portion of earnings remains as discretionary income after basic necessities have been cared for. In other words, extra money is available to pursue some of the nicer things that life offers. For example, when the iPhone was introduced, it surprised folks at Apple to learn that adoption spread over all social classes, and not just the upper social class. The innovators were found to be the overprivileged—those with elevated incomes—in every social class. A similar pattern exists for other product categories, such as luxury automobiles, more expensive home electronics, appliances, and recreational equipment. The market for such items is not restricted to the upper social classes but rather extends to the overprivileged within each class. However, because these households continue to share the values and symbols of other members of their own class, ownership of such niceties does not mean that they are viewed as members of the next higher social class.

The underprivileged are those individuals and families whose incomes are under the median for their social class. Because the earnings of underprivileged households fall well below the average for their class, these less-affluent households must economize and skimp just to afford the products and services that other members of their class deem proper and appropriate. Similarly, if we were to consider an underprivileged family within the present middle class, we would readily observe that it is financially difficult for such a household to make ends meet. For example, The Warren Report mentioned earlier indicates that mortgage payments for such households rose by 76 percent, and employment-sponsored health insurance costs increased by 74 percent, compared with 1970. Due to such factors, families in this group are now spending over three-quarters of their income on basic needs compared to only 50 percent of wages in 1970.

SOCIAL MOBILITY

More than any other country in the world, the United States exhibits an *open class system*. In other words, individuals are not frozen into a fixed position along a social continuum by nature of their birth. Rather, it is possible to rise from rock bottom to top positions in industry and government. Because people are influenced by their socialization as children as well as by their present or aspired-to class standing, those who study the impact of social class on consumer behavior should take into account both individuals' past and present socioeconomic statuses.[54]

A study by Shimp and Yokum revealed a clear pattern of upward mobility (movement toward higher class membership) in U.S. society.[55] Nearly two-thirds of the households examined in this study included a spouse who had achieved higher social stature than his or her parents. In the meantime, social status remained the same for 25 percent of respondents and fell for a mere 8 percent. Most social mobility tends to be intergenerational (it occurs between generations) and is limited to the immediately adjacent social classes. In other words, children in a family may acquire slightly higher social standing than their parents. The parents, in turn, may have gained slightly higher standing than the grandparents.

Many people aspire to higher classes than they currently occupy. Higher strata serve as reference groups for those who have lesser standing but are on the move. Education, occupation, achievement, talent, and sometimes marriage are among the forces that propel upward mobility. Consider, for example, the cases of Steve Jobs and Bill Gates, who progressed from mere computer enthusiasts to heads of the two largest computer companies in the world; Ray Kroc, who leaped from being a modest salesman to the highest echelons of McDonald's; and Walt Disney, who advanced from an animation novice to the pinnacle of the world's largest entertainment empire.

The dynamic nature of an open class system is usually viewed in terms of upward social mobility—especially for the Yuppie set. Wanting it all is a hallmark of the middle class, and many members of this group buy products with the symbols and allure of elevated status. Occasional splurging and treating oneself to the best are ways that consumers set themselves apart from their peers and bolster their self-image. Consequently, ads for top-of-the line products are often designed to be sensual, provocative, and elegant.[56]

Unfortunately, open class systems also mean that families or individuals can tumble on the social ladder, and some downward mobility has been observed in recent years. Due to the recent economic downturn and high unemployment rate, many members of Generation Y have been finding it difficult to secure good-paying, entry-level employment that relates to their college degree or vocational training.[57] Many are having trouble exceeding or even matching their parents in terms of job opportunities, home ownership, income, and savings. Some of these young people in the United States are in danger of dropping out of the middle class.[58] Similarly, many displaced workers and farmers have been forced to go on welfare or join the ranks of the unemployed. One conservative estimate suggests that as many as 744,000 persons in the United States are homeless on a given night.[59]

The Impact of Social Class on Consumer Behavior

Characteristics that distinguish the various social classes also influence their behavior as consumers. Understanding the psychological differences between classes as well as the differences in their lifestyles can help marketers design

© 2009, prism_68, Shutterstock, Inc.

No retail store can equally appeal to all shoppers. Retailers like Nordstrom successfully target consumers in the upper and upper-middle classes.

effective strategies targeted to specific socioeconomic groups. This concluding section cites a number of generalizations regarding tendencies of the various classes and suggests likely influences on consumption. Although idiosyncracies can be observed in the situations faced by specific individuals and households within a class, these general inclinations have important implications for marketers when planning strategies.

While some product categories, such as purely functional staples like detergents and paper products, are classless, many of the more expensive and fashionable possessions that people own, like home furnishings and apparel, *are* expressions of class. Purchasing patterns are therefore likely to vary across social strata. One indicator of class membership is income, which largely determines the types, quantity, and quality of products and services that consumers in a particular class can afford. For example, relative to its size, the upper class consumes a disproportionate share of services. As another example, in regard to products, a recent study found that the relationship between income and willingness to buy store brands rather than national brand merchandise appeared to be curvilinear.[60] In other words, low- and high-income shoppers were less prone to buy store brands than those in between. Middle-class consumers tended to be the group most likely to experiment with store brands.

Other gauges of social class, such as education and occupation, also appear to affect shoppers in terms of what they contemplate when evaluating and selecting products as well as how they gauge the social acceptability of merchandise. Clothing, for example, has always been a peculiarly resonant class symbol.[61] Members of various classes differ in what they regard to be in good taste or fashionable. In her book, *The Language of Clothes*, Alison Lurie states, "The man who goes to buy a winter coat may simultaneously want it to shelter him from bad weather, look expensive and formidable, announce that he is sophisticated and rugged, attract a certain sort of sexual partner, and magically invest him with qualities of Robert Redford."[62] Lower-middle-class consumers seem to like apparel items that offer an external point of identification. In this sense, they constitute prime targets for licensed goods, such as T-shirts and caps that bear the names of famous celebrities and athletes, admired organizations, and valued company trademarks. Upper-class consumers, on the other hand, prefer clothing that has a more subtle look and is free of supporting associations.

Social class also influences shoppers' retail store choices. It is unlikely that any given store could simultaneously cater to all classes. For example, a study that dealt with shopping behavior and store avoidance of different social classes revealed that Kmart was seen as appealing to lower- and lower-middle-class customers, whereas Nordstrom was seen as appealing mainly to upper- and upper-middle-class consumers.[63] The study proposed the factor of *social distance* (the difference between the individual's social position and the store's perceived image) as an explanatory measure for the shopping preferences of different social classes. It is therefore customary in retailing to determine the class of the customer base a store is expected to draw from in order to design effective layouts, develop suitable in-store strategies, and communicate appropriate class messages via store advertising.[64]

Saving, investing, spending, and credit card usage patterns also seem to relate to social class. Higher-status consumers tend to be future oriented and confident in their financial discernment. They are willing to invest in insurance, stocks, and real estate. Lower-class consumers, on the other hand, tend to be interested in immediate gratification. Use of credit cards also differs according to social class. Whereas upper-status consumers use credit cards as an expedient substitute for cash, underclass consumers view credit as an indispensable means of fulfilling urgent needs that otherwise they could not afford to satisfy at the moment.

Social class also influences the recreational activities that people engage in during their leisure time. Upper-class consumers attend the theater, opera, and concerts, play polo and squash, and go to college football games. Playing bridge and playing tennis and racquetball are middle- to upper-class activities. Lower-class pastimes include watching TV, playing bingo, fishing, baseball, bowling, pool and billiards, and frequenting taverns, professional wrestling matches, and monster truck events.

Social class is also assumed to have a bearing on consumers' media habits. As the level of social class rises, so does consumers' access to media information. Middle- and upper-class consumers tend to engage in more information search, particularly from the Web, before and while shopping. Lower-class consumers, on the other hand, have limited information sources and rely less on the Internet, but more heavily on relatives, friends, salespeople, and in-store displays for information about purchases.

Recognizing lifestyle differences between social classes similarly can help advertisers allocate the advertising budget between various forms of traditional and electronic media, as well as select appropriate ad appeals. In ad messages, the appeal to class aspirations can be either subtle, as in ads from Ralph Lauren, or blatant, as in ads from Abercrombie & Fitch. Ralph Lauren ads often depict black-and-white close-up photos of average-status young people wearing Polo jeans and denim outfits. Abercrombie & Fitch ads, on the other hand, often show couples of elevated social stature in sexually provocative poses wearing stylish designs. The key is to touch off a personal response by signaling to a consumer that the product or service is appropriate for his or her taste and social status.[65] Concerning the selection of appropriate media types, higher-status consumers tend to have greater exposure to the print media than their lower-status counterparts. Similarly, access to and use of the Internet at home or outside the home is positively correlated to consumers' level of income or social class. According to the U.S. Census Bureau in 2007, 92 percent of those earning more than $100,000 per year were reported to have used the Internet compared with just 40 percent of those with family income under $25,00 a year.[66]

Further, because many people in working-class occupations get up early in the morning and engage in strenuous physical activity, they feel the need to go to bed earlier. Many middle-class workers, on the other hand, get up later in the morning, perform tasks that are mentally demanding, and stay up later at night to wind down before going to bed. Consequently, whereas prime-time TV reaches a large working-class audience, late-night TV reaches a sizable middle-class audience.

Martineau noted that psychological disparities between the classes regarding perceptions of the world may account for many of the dissimilarities in their consumption behaviors.[67] Lower-status individuals, for instance, tend to have a rural identification, focus on the immediate past, and exhibit limited horizons. Such persons view the world through their own experiences and describe it in personal, concrete terms. They also hold vaguely structured views of the universe; have a limited sense of choice making; are inclined to react intuitively or emotionally; and express concern for security, themselves, and their families. Members of the middle class, in contrast, tend to have an urban identification, focus on the future, have a broader view of the world, describe their experiences from diverse perspectives, see themselves tied to national happenings, and stress rationality. They also tend to think abstractly, display greater self-confidence, and exhibit more willingness to take risks.

So far, we have observed how the members of a society can be classified along a social continuum—a range of social positions into which a society's members fall. The outcome is a number of superimposed strata or social classes that consumer researchers find useful to delineate the behavioral patterns typical of each. In this sense, various social classes provide a natural basis for market segmentation, targeting, and positioning.

We have also observed that the social class structure in the United States is markedly different compared with that found in older societies. The unique values and beliefs held by members of our society regarding what determines an individual's standing in the class hierarchy largely explains our social class structure. These values and beliefs are integral parts of culture—aspects that determine how consumers in a society tend to think, feel, and act. The important influence of culture and its effect on consumer behavior are topics covered in the next chapter.

A Cross-Functional Point of View

The topic of social class has a number of implications for business disciplines other than marketing. Relevant issues might include

- **Public Policy/Taxation:** Although the president and Congress often debate over which taxes should be cut or raised, one argument that seems to win the working person's enthusiasm and support consistently is that of raising taxes on the upper classes. This sentiment may be due to the widening gap between the richest U.S. citizens and the rest of the populace. This feeling has motivated many politicians to call for the initiation of income equality through a policy of heavily taxing the rich while easing the burden of taxes on the working class. Many policy makers, however, feel that attempts to close the income gap by raising taxes on the rich could have dire effects on the nation by discouraging savings and investments needed for the economy to grow. Instead, they feel that the government should direct its efforts toward better educating, training, and retaining U.S. workers via programs such as Head Start, revamping inner-city schools, and extending more college loans and scholarships.

- **Home Economics:** Studies conducted in the United States, France, and the United Kingdom reveal a strong correlation between social class and dietary patterns and preferences of consumers. Eating habits are powerfully influenced by social class rather than by income alone. Class tastes and preferences considerably influence food-related choices such as the kinds of food purchased for home consumption, where people eat out, and their preferences among alcoholic beverages. The studies found that whereas money expenditure on food is a function of income, food preferences are definitely a matter of social class. For example, whereas members of the upper class tend to dine out at full-service restaurants with exquisite cuisine, seldom cook at home, select gourmet foods, and enjoy drinking wine, members of the working class tend to eat out at fast-food restaurants, cook regularly at home, and generally favor beer over wine.

- **History/Labor Relations:** An inquisitive glance at the roots of major world revolutions reveals that the main cause of most rebellions is resource inequity between the *haves* and the *have-nots* in a society. Whether it is the French Revolution, where the poor and working classes attempted to eliminate the elite, or where the masses in Russia rid the country of the czar, the culprit has always been interclass frustrations caused by social and income injustice.

   Although we in the United States have not experienced such revolutions per se, the clash between the haves and the have-nots may be observed in one form—labor strikes, which are often violent against owners and managers of big business. Laborers—the have-nots—often view themselves as the less-fortunate members of the society being taken advantage of by the haves. Many incidents such as Chicago's Pullman and meatpacking riots, in which hundreds of people lost their lives, stand as sad reminders of this form of class conflict. In this sense, the rise of labor unions can be viewed as a natural consequence of antagonistic feelings that often arise between social classes in a country.

These issues, and a host of others like them, serve to show that the topic of social class transcends the field of marketing to other business disciplines.

Summary

Social classes are permanent status categories within a social system. Each class is an aggregate of people with similar socioeconomic positions, values, and behavioral patterns. Between the various social classes, sharp economic, social, and psychological disparities can be observed. Marketers' interest in social class stems from the fact that it provides a basis for segmenting and targeting markets.

Certain factors such as egalitarianism, the large size of the middle class, opportunities for mobility, and confusion of income with class membership obscure the recognition of divergent U.S. social classes. Unlike more rigid societies, countries like the United States exhibit a series of status continua.

The class structure of the United States is evolving. A growing gap separates the affluent from everyone else. Both the higher and lower earnings groups are expanding. In terms of Internet access/use, an emerging view of the digital divide issue depicts access/use of the Internet as a function of the standard of living of a family and its income rather than its ethnicity.

Social class can be measured by employing subjective, reputational, or objective methods. Studies that follow an objective approach can use single-variable or composite-variable indexes to measure social class. Other relevant issues discussed include the changing class stature of women and status crystallization—the extent to which different indicators of an individual's social stature concur. In addition, every class has average, overprivileged, and underprivileged members. Significant differences in earnings and consumption patterns characterize these subgroups.

The United States exhibits an open class system, in which both upward and downward mobility are possible. Most mobility is intergenerational and limited to the immediately adjacent classes. Education, occupation, achievement, talent, and marriage can precipitate upward mobility.

Social class has a bearing on shopping and consumption patterns such as product and service choices; retail shopping and store selection; saving, investing, spending, and credit; as well as recreation and leisure activities.

Review Questions

1. In the United States, the middle class is currently going through some major changes and shifting patterns. Describe the nature and causes of these changes or shifts.
2. Consumer researchers use a number of methods to measure social class. Briefly explain each method and comment on its practicality and value from the perspective of studying consumer behavior.
3. The class stature of women in today's society has changed drastically. Comment on this statement citing the ramifications of this trend both to society as a whole and to the field of consumer behavior.
4. In contrast to some foreign countries, it has been said that the United States has an open class system. What are the main factors that permit such mobility in our society?
5. It has been suggested that social class influences various aspects of consumer behavior such as retail store choice as well as media habits. Explain, and support your answer with specific examples.

Discussion Questions

1. In the measurement of a family's social class standing in the United States, women traditionally have been classed in accordance with their fathers or spouses. As women increasingly earn advanced educational degrees and occupy prominent positions in the workplace, the true social class picture in the United States could be quite different from what it is reported to be. Comment on this statement.

2. Managers of retail institutions realize that stores cannot be everything to everyone. Consequently, retailers select certain social classes to target. For example, Macy's and Bloomingdale's appeal to what is sometimes called the *quality market* (i.e., upper-middle and upper classes), whereas Kmart and Wal-Mart primarily appeal to the *mass market* (i.e., lower-middle and upper-lower classes). Why can't a single retail institution simultaneously appeal to all social classes? How different are shopping habits between social classes? Give some examples.

3. Consider the readership of publications such as the *National Enquirer*, *The Star*, *The Globe*, and *True Confessions*. Contrast this audience with the readership of publications like *Fortune*, *Business Week*, *New Yorker*, *Esquire*, and *Smithsonian*. What distinguishes these types of readers? How would advertising appeals in the first set of publications differ from those in the second set?

Cross-Functional Debate

In reference to the chapter opening vignette, British people have always taken great pride in their heritage. Included in this tradition is the monarchy itself, and titled Britons such as princes, princesses, lords, dukes, duchesses, and knights. However, many young Brits today believe the royal monarchy system is an outdated mark of the past. They argue that the royal family serves no purpose and exists as a burden on an already-strained economy. Against this modern view lies the unwavering conviction of the traditional Brits that the mere thought of changing these traditions is a betrayal of the historically grand British identity.

Present arguments to support each view. Which of the two perspectives do you favor? Explain why.

Wal-Mart Chases the Affluent

The phone on Ms. Kaplan's desk was ringing. The caller was her boss, Mr. Donald Soderquist, chief operating officer of Wal-Mart. He asked her to bring in the file on the new Evergreen, Colorado, store. He requested the folder that morning to prepare for the executive planning session scheduled for later that afternoon.

The meeting was to be attended by other Wal-Mart top executives, including H. Lee Scott, the company's executive vice president of merchandising; Thomas Coughlin, chief operating officer of Wal-Mart's store division; and Robert Walker, manager of the newly planned Evergreen store. The purpose of the meeting was to address merchandising and other policies for a new store that Wal-Mart was planning to open the following year in Evergreen, Colorado. Additional topics to be covered in the meeting included planning the store layout, staffing, and promotions, as well as identifying the competition the new store was expected to encounter.

What was different about this meeting was Wal-Mart's new strategy of locating stores in upscale, ritzy suburbs. Evergreen, Colorado, was at that time a town of 20,000 upper-middle class residents, mostly composed of artists, engineers, scientists, and doctors, as well as other professionals whose median family income was $113,000, which is double the present national average. Until recently, the self-proclaimed "discount king" had catered mainly to rural and middle-income shoppers. Now, however, the company feels that beyond wooing middle-income shoppers, there is nowhere to go but upscale. The greatest potential for growth, the company executives felt, lies in catering to the high-income folks. With the company's over 2,400 stores nationwide, populating the majority of the rural and middle-income areas, little remained to pursue except the upper-middle class.

As Mr. Soderquist leafed through the folder on the Evergreen store, he recalled the modest beginnings of the Wal-Mart empire when its founder, Sam Walton, opened his first store in Rogers, Arkansas. Today, Wal-Mart is the no. 3 company in the Fortune 500, with annual sales of more than $100 billion. Basing his strategy on price discounting and driving costs out of the merchandising system, Sam Walton's chain rapidly began to take off. Mr. Soderquist has always marveled at how Sam Walton selected cities for his new stores. He would buzz towns in his low-flying airplane studying the lay of the land. When he had triangulated the proper intersection between a few small towns, he would touch down, buy a piece of farmland at that intersection, and build up another Wal-Mart store. Mr. Soderquist thought to himself how drastically different the site selection procedure today is in comparison to its predecessor. Today, sophisticated scientific and business analyses techniques are used to select the appropriate sites.

The challenge with opening stores in upscale neighborhoods is the folksy, down-home image customers have of Wal-Mart. The company's advertising and corporate culture have always stressed the working class and poked fun of the upper crust and the fashion conscious. The company's ads typically feature chunky, middle-aged employees in boxy clothes reiterating the low-price policy typical of Wal-Mart.

When the meeting commenced later that afternoon, two major issues dominated the discussion. The first dealt with the expected competition for the new store, and the second addressed the store's merchandising strategy and layout.

Regarding the first issue, the executives recognized that the competition in the Evergreen area was expected mainly from the Minneapolis-based Target chain. Long before Wal-Mart's efforts to invade urban areas, Target established its presence in cities and suburban markets with discount stores that appealed to both the upper-middle class as well as low-income shoppers. With its signature of wide aisles, shiny floors, upscale merchandise, and cheery "team members," a prevailing belief was that wealthier shoppers find Target stores appealing. The committee also examined a recent BearStearns report regarding the tendency of high-income Americans to shop at Wal-Mart versus other competing stores. In the category of "affluent Americans' favorite stores," Wal-Mart ranked first at a 35 percent preference rate versus Target at 22 percent, Home Depot at 17 percent, Best Buy at 15 percent, and Walgreen at 12 percent.

Concerning the layout, the committee felt that the store's design should be markedly different from the boxy style characteristic of other Wal-Mart stores. Members felt that it should feature a stone-pillar and oak exterior, vaulted roof, and a parking lot beautifully landscaped with evergreen trees. A layer of sod was also suggested to surround the store to create an atmosphere likely to attract a herd of elk that live in a nearby woods.

Regarding the merchandising strategy, the committee recommended stocking more high-end merchandise, including computers, sporting goods, jewelry, and apparel—particularly an expanded array of infant clothing. For example, the store was recommended to include a version of the Smartz Computer Store, which the company first launched inside its State College, Pennsylvania, store. The Smartz store carries six types of sophisticated Pentium-based machines and devotes more than twice as much space to computer-related goods as do regular stores.

As the committee deliberated for two hours over the plans for the new store, a disturbing issue arose—the Evergreen store's margin. At the crux of the problem are the operating costs of the Evergreen store, which were expected to be very high. In the meantime, Wal-Mart was anticipated to continue its low-price strategy. These facts meant that prices at the Evergreen store could never be high enough to reflect the exceptionally high operating cost. The result? Margins of stores run in such affluent suburbs are doomed to be substandard—a price Wal-Mart would have to pay if it were to continue its strategy of chasing after the upper class.

Questions

1. In your opinion, should Wal-Mart continue to pursue its strategy of opening stores in upscale suburbs in view of the low margins expected to materialize at these sites? Why or why not?
2. Some observers claim that the upscale appeal Wal-Mart is attempting to establish not only will confuse its present core customers in the working class but also will fail to gain sufficient volume from upscale shoppers. As such, this strategy appears doomed to fail. Do you agree?
3. Considering the strong competitive position that Target has already established in upscale suburbs, can Wal-Mart successfully compete? What strategies can Wal-Mart use to penetrate the competitive barrier?

Notes

1. Geraldine Trembath, "Uppercrust Brittania," *Hemispheres* (April 1996), pp. 66–71.
2. J. H. Myers and Jonathan Guttman, "Life Style: The Essence of Social Class," in William Wells (ed.), *Lifestyle and Psychographics* (Chicago: American Marketing Association, 1974), pp. 235–56.
3. James E. Fisher, "Social Class and Consumer Behavior: The Relevance of Class and Status," in Melanie Wallendorf and Paul Anderson (eds.), *Advances in Consumer Research* 14 (Provo, UT: Association for Consumer Research, 1987), pp. 492–96.
4. T. Schjelderup-Ebbe, "Social Behavior of Birds," in C. Murchison (ed.), *A Handbook of Social Psychology* (Worcester, MA: Clark University Press, 1935).
5. Al Ries and Jack Trout, *Positioning: The Battle for Your Mind* (New York: McGraw-Hill, 1981), p. 53.

6. Daniel W. Rossides, *Social Stratification* (Upper Saddle River, NJ: Prentice Hall, 1990).

7. Max Weber, in H. H. Gard and C. Wright Mills (eds.), *From Max Weber: Essays in Sociology* (New York: Oxford University Press, 1946).

8. Fisher, "Social Class and Consumer Behavior: The Relevance of Class and Status."

9. Rebecca Piirto Heath, "The New Working Class," *American Demographics* (January 1998), pp. 51–55.

10. "Hilton Hotels & Resorts Named Best Hotel Chain by Executive Travel Readers," *Reuters* (July 9, 2008), www.reuters.com/article/pressRelease/i/US91869+09-Jul-2008+BW20080709.

11. Fisher, "Social Class and Consumer Behavior: The Relevance of Class and Status."

12. Philip A. Klein, "Institutionalists, Radical Economists, and Class," *Journal of Economic Issues* 16, no. 2 (June 1992), pp. 535–45.

13. William Thompson and Joseph Hickey, *Society in Focus* (Boston, MA: Pearson, 2005); Dennis Gilbert, *The American Class Structure: In an Age of Growing Inequality* (Belmont, CA: Wadsworth, 2002).

14. Ibid.

15. Leonard Beeghley, *The Structure of Social Stratification in the United States* (Boston, MA: Pearson, 2004).

16. "Results: Center on Hunger and Poverty Statistics for the United States" (August 2006).

17. John Cavanagh and Chuck Collins, "The Rich and the Rest of Us," *The Nation* (June 11, 2008), www.thenation.com/doc/20080630/cavanagh_collins/print.

18. Ron Henderson, "The 'Lucky Rich' Emergence of a New Class," *Sociological Eye* (June 13, 2008), http://contexts.org/eye/2008/06/13/the-%E2%80%9Clucky-rich%E2%80%9D-emergence-of-a-new-social-class/.

19. Inside the Middle Class: Bad Times Hit the Good Life," *Pew Research Center* (April 9, 2008), http://pewsocialtrends.org/pubs/706/middle-class-poll; "Pew Internet & American Life Project: Demographics of Internet Users, *Pew Research Center*, (April 8–May 11, 2008), www.pewinternet.org/trends/User_Demo_7.22.08.htm.

20. D. Nicholas, et al., "Digital Information Consumers, Players and Purchasers: Information Seeking Behavior in the New Digital Interactive Environment," *ASLIB Proceedings* (2003), 55(1/2), pp. 23–32.

21. "Fact Sheet: Racial Divide Continues to Grow," (July 1999), NTIA, www.ntia.doc.gov/ntiahome/digitaldivide/factsheets/racial-divide.htm.

22. Tod Newcombe, "Debating the Racial Divide," *Government Technology* (March 29, 2001), www.govtech.com/gt/print_article.php?id=4210.

23. Ibid.

24. Inside the Middle Class: Bad Times Hit the Good Life," *Pew Research Center* (April 9, 2008), http://pewsocialtrends.org/pubs/706/middle-class-poll; "Pew Internet & American Life Project: Demographics of Internet Users," *Pew Research Center* (April 8–May 11, 2008), www.pewinternet.org/trends/User_Demo_7.22.08.htm.

25. Courtney Macavinta, "Study: Digital Divide Persists," CNET News (July 8, 1999), http://news.cnet.com/2100-1023-228150.html&hhTest=1?hhTest=1.

26. Nalini P. Kotamraju, "Living Like Me: Lifestyle, Social Stratification and Technology," *Berkeley University* (May 20, 2007), http://socrates.berkeley.edu/~nalinik/.

27. Danah Boyd, "Viewing American Class Divisions Through Facebook and MySpace," *ApopheniaBlog Essay* (June 24, 2007), www.danah.org/papers/essays/ClassDivisions.html.

28. "AFL-CIO's New Executive PayWatch Web site Shows How CEO Pay Packages Helped Create..." *Reuters* (April 14, 2008), www.reuters.com/article/pressRelease/idUS17899+14-apr-2008+PRN20080414; "Executive PayWatch Site Shows Continuing Excesses in CEO Salaries," *AFT* (2008), www.aft.org/news/2008/exec_paywatch.htm.

29. Booradly, "Thank Jeebus for Dollar Stores," *Gomestic* (December 18, 2007), www.gomestic.com/consumer-information/Thank-Jeebus-for-Dollar-Stores.67395; "On the Radar: Dollar Store Growth Forces Other Retail Formats to Take Notice," *Goliath* http://goliath.ecnext.com/coms2/gi_01994853376/On-the-radar-dollar-store.html.

30. Dan Schiller, "Marketing on the Net," *Le Monde Diplomatique* (November 1997), http://mondediplo.com/1997/11/interent.

31. Ibid.

32. "Inside the Middle Class: Bad Times Hit the Good Life," *Pew Research Center* (April 9, 2008), http://pewsocialtrends.org/pubs/706/middle-class-poll.

33. Rebecca Gardyn, "The Mating Game," *American Demographics* (July–August 2002), p. 34.

34. Janeen Arnold Costa and Russell W. Belk, "Nouveaux Riches as Quintessential Americans: Case Studies of Consumption in an Extended Family," *Advances in Nonprofit Marketing* 3 (Greenwich, CT: JAI Press, 1990), pp. 83–140.

35. F. Stuart Chapin, *Contemporary American Institutions* (New York: Harper, 1935), pp. 373–97.

36. Joan Kron, *Home-Psych* (New York: Potter, 1983), pp. 90–102.

37. B. A. Hamilton, "Creating Value in Retailing for Emerging Consumers: Breaking the Myths About Emerging Consumers," *The Coca-Cola Retailing Research Council Latin America* (May 1, 2003); Guillermo D'Andrea, et al., "Breaking the Myth on

Emerging Consumers in Retailing," *International Journal of Retail and Distribution Management* vol. 34, no. 9 (2006), pp. 674–687.

38. Warner, Meeker, and Eells, *Social Class in America: A Manual of Procedure for the Measurement of Social Status*; A. B. Hollingshead and F. C. Redlich, *Social Class and Mental Illness* (New York: John Wiley, 1958), p. 394; *Methodology and Scores of Socioeconomic Status*, Working Paper No. 15 (Washington, DC: U. S. Bureau of the Census, 1963); Coleman, "The Continuing Significance of Social Class to Marketing."

39. Ibid.

40. Sak Onkvisit and John J. Shaw, *International Marketing: Analysis and Strategy*, 2nd ed. (New York: Macmillan, 1993), p. 341.

41. "Status of Women: Quick Stats 2007," *U.S. Dept. of Labor: Women's Bureau* (August 21, 2008), www.dol.gov/wb/stats/main.htm.

42. Stephen Moore, *Sociology* (Lincolnwood, IL: NTC Publishing Group, 1995), p. 83.

43. Terence A. Shimp and J. Thomas Yokum, "Extensions of the Basic Social Class Model Employed in Consumer Research," in Kent B. Monroe (ed.), *Advances in Consumer Research* 8 (Ann Arbor, MI: Association for Consumer Research, 1981), pp. 702–7; Charles M. Schaninger and Chris T. Allen, "Wife's Occupational Status as a Consumer Behavior Construct," *Journal of Consumer Resarch* 8 (September 1981), pp. 189–96.

44. "Status of Women: Quick Stats 2007," *U.S. Dept. of Labor: Women's Bureau* (August 21, 2008), www.dol.gov/wb/stats/main.htm.

45. Rebecca Gardyn, "The Mating Game," *American Demographics* (July–August 2002), p. 34.

46. Coleman, "The Continuing Significance of Social Class to Marketing," p. 273.

47. Charles M. Schaninger, "Social Class Versus Income Revisited: An Empirical Investigation," *Journal of Marketing Research* 18 (May 1985), pp. 192–208; and Louis V. Dominquez and Albert L. Page, "Stratification in Consumer Behavior Research: A Re-examination," *Journal of the Academy of Marketing Science* 9 (Summer 1981), pp. 250–71.

48. Bob Stone, *Successful Direct Marketing Methods*, 2nd ed. (Chicago: Crain Books, 1979), p. 98.

49. Schaninger, "Social Class Versus Income Revisited: An Empirical Investigation."

50. Yoram Wind, "Incongruency of Socioeconomic Variables and Buying Behavior," in Philip R. McDonald (ed.), *Proceedings of the Educators' Conference Series No. 30* (Chicago: American Marketing Association, 1969), pp. 362–67.

51. "Inside the Middle Class: Bad Times Hit the Good Life," *Pew Research Center* (April 9, 2008), http://pewsocialfriends.org/pubs/706/middle-class-poll.

52. Coleman, "The Continuing Significance of Social Class to Marketing."

53. Elizabeth Warren, "The New Economics of Middle Class: Why Making Ends Meet Has Gotten Harder," *Harvard Law School* (May 10, 2007); Elizabeth Warren, "A 2007 Filmed Presentation," www.youtube.com/watch?v=akVL7QY0S8A.

54. George P. Moschis and Gilbert A. Churchill, "Consumer Socialization: A Theoretical and Empirical Analysis," *Journal of Marketing Research* 15 (November 1978), pp. 599–609; Shimp and Yokum, "Extensions of the Basic Social Class Model Employed in Consumer Research."

55. Shimp and Yokum, "Extensions of the Basic Social Class Model Employed in Consumer Research."

56. Jaclyn Fierman, "The High-Living Middle Class," *Fortune* 115 (April 13, 1987), p. 27.

57. Lawrence Mischel and Elise Gould, "Inhospitable Job Market to Greet College Graduates," *Economic Policy Institute* (May 14, 2008), www.epi.org/content.cfm/webfeatures_snapshots_20080514.

58. Katherine S. Newman, "No Room for the Young," *New York Times* (May 16, 1993), p. E17.

59. "Study: 744,000 Homeless People in US," *US News* (January 7, 2007), www.msnbc.msn.com/id/16564208/.

60. Alan Dick, Arun Jain, and Paul Richardson, "Correlates of Store Brand Proneness: Some Empirical Observations," *Journal of Product and Brand Management* 4, no. 4 (1995), pp. 15–22; Rajesh Kanwar and Notis Pagiavlas, "When Are Higher Social Class Consumers More and Less Brand Loyal than Lower Social Class Consumers?" in John F. Sherry Jr. and Brian Sternthal (eds.), *Diversity in Consumer Behavior* (Provo, UT: Association for Consumer Research, 1992), pp. 589–95.

61. Labich, "Class in America."

62. Alison Lurie, *The Language of Clothes* (New York: Henry Holt, 2000), p. 8.

63. John P. Dickson and Douglas L. MacLachlan, "Social Distance and Shopping Behavior," *Journal of the Academy of Marketing Science*, 18, no. 2 (Spring 1990), pp. 153–61.

64. Ibid.

65. Labich, "Class in America."

66. U.S. Census Bureau, "Households Using the Internet in and Outside the Home: By Selected Characteristics" (2008), www.ntia.doc.gov/reports/2008/table/_householdinterent200.pdf.

67. Pierre Martineau, "Social Classes and Shopping Behavior," *Journal of Marketing* 23 (October 1958), pp. 121–30

Culture and Microcultures

LEARNING OBJECTIVES

- To grasp the meaning of culture and the way it is learned by the members of a society.
- To become cognizant of the five dimensions of culture proposed by Hofstede.
- To examine ten socio-cultural dimensions proposed by Harris and Moran.
- To probe the concept of microcultures and recognize its importance in segmenting markets.
- To identify three major ethnic microcultures in the United States and examine their characteristics and purchasing patterns.
- To become cognizant of consumption microcultures.
- To explore marketing implications of culture and microcultures.

KEY TERMS

culture	power distance
socialization	uncertainty avoidance
enculturation	individualism
acculturation	masculinity
cultural lag	values
ethnocentrism	means-end chains
ethnography	norms
direct questioning	microcultures
content analysis	microcultures of consumption
key informants	rituals

For the past 50 years, the American way of life has been invading many European countries. Restaurants such as McDonald's and Pizza Hut, brands such as Nike and Disney, and American-made motion pictures, TV soaps, and news shows have found their way to major cities as well as many living rooms throughout Europe.

Although many Europeans were originally impressed and even fascinated by American novelties, stores, and shows, the appeal of these things seems to have waned, and sentiments in recent years seem to have taken the opposite direction. Many Europeans have started to fear that the American way of life is about to overtake their culture and rob them of their own rich heritage. Seeing that they are inundated with American expressions, products, and ideas, they are fearful that they may wake up one day and find themselves conforming to the American way of life.

Major differences exist between the mentalities of Europeans and Americans. The American mind-set is sometimes described as a *Swatch-watch* mentality, accustomed to produce a product that is functional, appears attractively styled, sells for an affordable price, and has a relatively short product life. For a veteran German craftsman, whose exactitude and expertise are the culmination of many years of formal training and apprenticeship, the American outlook is viewed as lamentable.

Many differences in lifestyle also exist. In most European countries, for example, workers continue to receive high wages and extensive employee benefit packages. They are entitled to at least six weeks of vacation every year. Long lunch breaks and midday shop closings remain customary in Italy, Spain, and parts of France. In Germany, shops throughout the country close at 8:00 P.M. on weekdays and 4:00 P.M. on Saturdays. Stores are never open on Sundays. Such hours and high wages are customary in Europe and are perceived as entitlements.

In the view of many Europeans, Americans are workaholics. Europeans do not understand why Americans are so obsessed with work and why they spend such long hours at the office. They wonder why it is that Americans seem unable to sit in a café and enjoy an extended conversation.

Countries are taking a number of steps in an effort to preserve their cultural integrity and protect it from the American cultural invasion. A few years ago, Canada called together 19 other governments to plot ways to ensure their cultural independence from the United States. Mexico is considering legislation requiring that a major percentage of its media programming remains in the hands of its citizens. In the arena of films, TV, and news, the governments in Britain, France, and Germany have designed programs to stabilize and promote home-grown films. There is also an obvious trend away from buying American TV services. In addition, many products—replicas of their American counterparts—have been developed in Europe as a defense against the flood of U.S. goods.[1]

An obvious trend in recent years is the growing negative sentiments on the part of consumers in many foreign countries toward U.S. products, stores, and programs. Learn about two cultures, the United Kingdom and Canada, by visiting http://www.odci.gov/cia/publications/factbook/docs/faqs.html. *Simply click your mouse on each of the two*

nations in the menu provided. What cultural forces underlie resent-
ment toward American products abroad? In your opinion, what
strategies should U.S. marketers adopt to ease these feelings?

Cultural contexts are at the root of differences in foreign versus American lifestyles and preferences. The traditions of many countries color the beliefs, values, likes–dislikes, and actions of their peoples. Because of the significant role that cultural heritage plays in consumer behavior, it is important that marketers understand the elements in various cultures that influence consumption choices. The objective, of course, is to design marketing mix elements that best suit a specific culture.

In this chapter, we deal with the issues of culture and microcultures. We broaden the scope of analysis and consider the marketing implications of cultural similarities and differences that prevail in world markets. We further investigate consumer behavior in a cultural setting and address issues such as values and modes of thinking and behaving. We also deal with similarities and dissimilarities in African, Hispanic, and Asian-American microcultures and investigate the impact of these characteristics on consumption behavior.

The Meaning of Culture

There are over two hundred definitions of *culture* proposed by writers in the field. Although they are beneficial in profiling a culture, most of these definitions are broadly based and lack the specificity needed by marketers. Unlike sociologists and anthropologists, marketers are mainly interested in discovering those elements of culture that influence the patterns of consumer behavior for a particular product or service within a specific society. For example, devout Muslims do not partake of alcoholic beverages. Pork is not consumed by adherents of the Jewish and Islamic faiths, and beef is not eaten in the Hindu tradition. Western cultures tend to emphasize youth, whereas traditional Eastern societies hold persons of advanced age in high esteem. Such knowledge can be translated into culturally sensitive marketing strategies. For example, canned-meat processors can sell nonpork products and breweries can sell nonalcoholic beer in the Middle East.

For the purposes of this book, **culture** may be defined as follows:

Culture is a society's distinctive and learned mode of living, interacting, and responding to environmental stimuli. This mode is shared and transmitted between members.

culture
a society's distinctive and learned mode of living, interacting, and responding to environmental stimuli

As people live with one another in a society, interaction between them requires them to adjust to the social environment. Modes of conduct, standards of performance, and systems of dealing with interpersonal and environmental relations are established to ensure harmony and growth. Within this process, certain values and behaviors emerge as helpful and desirable whereas others appear to be ineffective or even harmful. The first are shared and rewarded, and the latter are discouraged or even punished. Thus, it can be said that culture functions to establish, enforce, and transmit group norms and values.

Show Me the Box, I'll Tell You Your Worth

Among the cultural values that people learn are those that deal with appropriate behavioral patterns. The universal practice of gift giving presents an interesting case. A recent study compared how Americans and the Japanese give gifts. The study revealed that most gift purchases in Japan take place in department or specialty stores that have an upscale market image, carry well-known brand names, and are fashionable places from which to buy. For Americans, being practical and more value-oriented prompts many to include other outlets on the list, such as discount stores and food and drugstores.

Gift packaging and wrapping were also found to be of extreme importance by the Japanese compared with their American counterparts. Gift packaging and wrapping are so important in Japan that the package, in many cases, is more significant than the actual gift inside. Aware of this fact, Japanese product manufacturers often concentrate more effort on package design than on product contents.

Regarding the occasions on which gifts are given, over half of the gifts given by U.S. families are given during religious holidays such as Christmas and Easter. Other occasions for gift giving include family celebrations, such as birthdays and anniversaries. In Japan, only 17 percent of the gifts are given during religious holidays. However, 32 percent of the gifts given during *Ochugen* and *Osebo* seasons in early summer and at year end, are primarily for reciprocal giving between employers and employees. This is a direct result of the social- or work-group orientation of much Japanese gift giving.

Another issue in the study dealt with the value of the gift, which is an indication of the amount of respect or admiration one has for the receiver of the gift. Almost every Japanese person is brought up to be highly conscious of doing favors, which literally signifies one's honor to another. Conversely, in the United States, businesspeople fear that such a gift, particularly to superiors, may be misinterpreted and considered a form of a bribe or a means of flattery. Such concerns prevent many businesspeople from offering gifts or, at least, are factors in reducing their frequency or value.[2]

Cultural traditions influence what consumers consider appropriate as a gift, how much to pay for it, and where to buy it. Learn more about how Japanese traditions are being transmitted from one generation to the next by visiting http://www.japancorner.com/customs_traditions.asp. In your opinion, what factors influence the formation of cultural traditions? How should marketers address the fact that foreign traditions often differ from our own? Explain using specific examples.

HOW IS CULTURE LEARNED?

socialization
the process by which we acquire knowledge to function productively in society

Standards of acceptable behavior are shared and passed along from one generation to the next in a continuation of the cultural heritage. The process by which individuals learn the norms and values of a culture is referred to as socialization. More specifically, socialization refers to the process by which individuals acquire the knowledge, skills, morals, and ethics necessary to function as productive members of a society. Cultural learning occurs in a variety of ways, including living in the family environment, formal schooling, observing and imitating the behavior of others who serve as role models, and simply interacting with other people within the society. Within the United States, the sharing of cultural norms and values is facilitated by such factors as a common language, schools, and places of worship, as well as the mass media and advertising.

From early childhood, we begin to absorb the norms, values, and behaviors deemed appropriate by our culture. The process of indoctrinating youth with the norms and values of a society is often referred to as **enculturation**. On the other hand, some individuals, for one reason or another, leave the society in which they were born and raised and take up residence in another culture. Such persons need to assimilate the norms, values, and behaviors of an unfamiliar culture. The term **acculturation** is often applied to the process of learning the norms, values, and behaviors of a culture different from that in which individuals were brought up.

Culture includes both material and abstract elements. Tangible aspects of a culture include its tools, technologies, architecture, currency, and works of art. Intangible aspects include religion, knowledge, traditions, ideals, and language. Culture provides the language in which people communicate with others and in which they think their most private thoughts. Humans cannot think without language. Languages tend to vary across cultures, with many—but not all— being exclusive to a specific culture. Greek, for example, is spoken primarily in the Hellenic culture. English, on the other hand, is spoken in the U.S., Canadian, British, Irish, South African, New Zealand, and Australian cultures, among others.

Interestingly, the tangible and intangible components of a culture do not necessarily evolve at the same pace. Whereas mechanical and technical traits of a culture can mature quite rapidly, ideological traits of a culture tend to change more slowly. In recent years, breakthroughs in the fields of medicine and information systems, for example, have occurred so rapidly that we cannot possibly keep abreast of, take advantage of, or accept all the advances. In some cases, issues of morality and ethics have not had an opportunity to catch up and address what is right and wrong. A consequence of this unevenness in the pace of change can be friction among the components of a society, sometimes referred to as cultural lag. **Cultural lag** is the delay between the time that technological innovations are made available and the time the public accepts and makes use of them or rejects them and limits their use.

CULTURAL SENSITIVITY VERSUS ETHNOCENTRISM

In today's diverse culture, we must be able to understand, accept, and respect the views and actions of others, even though these views and actions may markedly differ from our own. **Ethnocentrism** refers to the tendency to make cross-cultural evaluations on the basis of prereflective beliefs and values that are rooted in one's own culture. Culture determines the way people think, feel, and act. As such, it becomes the lens through which individuals judge the world. Cultural programming can act as a sort of blinder to other people's ways of thinking, feeling, or acting. In other words, one's own views tend to become the *only* natural way to function in the world. The rest of the world is viewed through this cultural lens.[3] Ethnocentrism, per se, is not morally wrong. Its dangers become apparent, however, when individuals make cross-cultural judgments on the basis of such myopic beliefs. In doing so, one in effect declares the superiority of his or her own group above all others. Herein lie the perils

enculturation
the process of indoctrinating youth with society's norms and values

acculturation
the process of learning the norms, values, and behaviors of a different culture

cultural lag
the time delay between the introduction of innovations and their acceptance

ethnocentrism
the tendency to make cross-cultural evaluations based on one's own beliefs and values

of misunderstanding, ignoring, or suppressing those who hold different views or perspectives. Beliefs, attitudes, and behavior of people from other cultures can thus be perceived as wrong or somehow inappropriate.[4]

A recent case that reflects ethnocentrism is demonstrated by the feeling among the Japanese regarding the superiority of their domestically grown rice. The Japanese had always believed that their rice was unparalleled by that grown elsewhere. To the Japanese, domestic rice is sacred and represents the soul of the nation. A few years ago, when adverse weather conditions in Japan were predicted to cause a 10 percent shortage in the rice crop, panic ensued. In anticipation of the expected shortages, politicians suggested as a solution that domestic rice be blended with imported rice. As a consequence of this proposal, it was feared that there would be riots, hoarding of domestic rice, and even thefts. The emperor was enlisted to ease the predicted crisis; the Imperial Household Agency announced that he had consented "to eat foreign rice mixed with Japanese rice" and had survived. Fortunately for the Japanese, the "Great Rice Crisis" did not materialize. The rice crop was adequate to meet the demand.[5]

HOW TO ASSESS CULTURE

ethnography
the study of culture by unobtrusive observation

Culture can be studied in a number of different ways. Attempts to assess culture have employed such techniques as ethnography, direct questioning, content analysis, and consulting with key informants. **Ethnography** is the study of culture by observation. Anthropologists have been known to live in a foreign culture for lengths of time and unobtrusively scrutinize it from within.[6] Marketers sometimes observe shopping behavior or product-usage patterns abroad in order to determine the likelihood that their products will sell in these cultures. When attempting to sell cereal in Russia, Kellogg's observed what Russians customarily ate for breakfast. The firm discovered that cereal was seldom on the menu. Therefore, Kellogg's advertising had to help Russians form a new association and teach them a new dietary habit.

direct questioning
the study of culture through research questionnaires

Direct questioning, a second method of studying culture, entails constructing and administering questionnaires that relate to the likelihood of product purchase and use. For example, in the Middle East, Nivea circulated a questionnaire to determine whether or not people sunbathed, how often they did so, and what people used to protect their skin from the rays of the sun. The company found a negative correlation between desire for beauty and tanning. In other words, appearance-conscious consumers tended to spend less time in the sun.

content analysis
the study of culture by reviewing its media or literature

Content analysis, a third method of studying culture, entails attempting to assess cultural practices and values by reviewing the media or literature coming out of a society and searching for recurrent themes. Finally, marketers could consult with **key informants** who are familiar with the culture of interest. Key informants are knowledgeable persons, such as expatriates, who have lived in a foreign country for an extended period of time. Other examples of key informants include members of the diplomatic or commercial corps, as well as consulate and embassy personnel.

key informants
individuals who are knowledgeable about a culture of interest

Hofstede's Cultural Dimensions

From the perspective of consumer behavior, in order for us to analyze cultures in a meaningful manner, we must identify a number of sociocultural dimensions. Geert Hofstede, a Dutch researcher, has identified five cultural dimensions that help explain how and why people from various cultures behave as they do.[7] These dimensions are power distance, uncertainty avoidance, individualism, masculinity, and term orientation.

POWER DISTANCE

Power distance is the degree to which less-powerful members of a society accept the fact that power is not distributed equally. Societies in which people obey authority without question are labeled *high power distance* cultures. In *low power distance* cultures, on the other hand, people are seen as equals. Members of such societies place a great deal of value on independence and individuality. Hofstede found that many Latin American and Asian countries were typified by high power distance, whereas countries like the United States, Canada, and many European nations exhibited moderate to low power distance.

> **power distance**
> the degree to which society's members accept unequal power distribution

The effect of this dimension on consumer behavior can be observed in many areas, particularly in the areas of decision making and promotional strategies. In high power distance cultures, family decision making tends to be autocratic or paternalistic. Family members are inclined to obey the recommendations of the authority figure in the household. In promotions, the use of referents and authority figures in advertising can prove to be a highly successful strategy. Consumers in high power distance cultures value conformity and tend to behave as they are told. Conversely, in low power distance cultures, decisions are made after consulting with others. Conviction of merits rather than blind obedience is the main motivation underlying behavior.

UNCERTAINTY AVOIDANCE

Uncertainty avoidance is the extent to which people feel threatened by ambiguous situations and have created institutions and beliefs for minimizing or averting uncertainty. People in societies characterized by *high uncertainty avoidance* attempt to reduce risk and attain security by developing systems and methods for dealing with ambiguity. They place significant trust in experts and their knowledge. Examples include Germany, Japan, and Spain. In such countries, many beliefs are formulated and rules or regulations are passed to ensure that people know what they are to do. High anxiety, stress, and concern with security characterize people who live in these societies. Conversely, in *low uncertainty avoidance* societies, such as Denmark, people have less of a need for structuring their activities and are willing to assume greater risk. They accept the uncertainty associated with the unknown and the notion that life must continue despite ambiguity and risk.

> **uncertainty avoidance**
> the degree to which people feel threatened by ambiguity and uncertainty

Uncertainty avoidance has applicability to consumer behavior and marketing in the areas of diffusion and adoption as well as branding, labeling, and channel strategy. The extent to which a culture is willing to try or accept new products and novel ideas is a function of the degree of uncertainty avoidance prevalent in that particular culture. Consumers in high uncertainty avoidance cultures are reluctant to accept innovations. The tendency of these consumers to prefer established brands, shop at well-known outlets, and seek information-laden product labels reflects their lower tolerance for accepting risk. Consumers in low uncertainty avoidance cultures, on the other hand, tend to perceive little or no risk in the purchase of new products and are much more likely to make innovative purchases than consumers who perceive a great deal of risk. The ad in Figure 15.1 from Life Insurance Company emphasizes uncertainty avoidance by stressing the fact that this type of insurance is for the protection of the family members left behind after a loved one passes on.

INDIVIDUALISM

individualism
a tendency of people to look after themselves and their immediate family only

Individualism is the tendency of people to look after themselves and their immediate family only.[8] This dimension is the antithesis of *collectivism*, which is the tendency of people to belong to groups that look after each other in exchange for loyalty. People in countries characterized by high individualism, such as the United States, Canada, Denmark, and France, tend to be self-sufficient and place strong emphasis on individual initiative. In such cultures, autonomy is given a high value. Consumers in highly individualistic societies tend to be inner directed and make individual decisions without reliance on or need for group support or approval. In contrast, countries with low individualism, such as Japan and Korea, tend to be other directed and place great importance on group decision making, affiliation, and approval of others.

From a consumer behavior perspective, consumers living in countries characterized by high individualism tend to rely on their own inner values or standards in evaluating new-product or -service offerings and are likely to be innovative consumers. Consumers in societies with low individualism, on the other hand, tend to look to others for direction concerning what is acceptable. Consequently, they are less likely to be innovative consumers.

This cultural dimension may also have a bearing on the type of promotional messages that marketers employ in each culture type. Individualistic (inner-directed) consumers tend to prefer ads that emphasize product attributes and personal benefits. These consumers, in turn, apply their own values to evaluate the product. Collectivistic (other-directed) consumers tend to prefer ads that feature a social environment or stress social acceptance so as to appeal to their need for approval. The ad depicted in Figure 15.2 contains an other-directed appeal from Mutual of America. The ad stresses the company's continued effort to help individuals fulfill their American dream.

LIFE INSURANCE ISN'T FOR THE PEOPLE WHO DIE. IT'S FOR THE PEOPLE WHO LIVE.

Dorsey Hoskins' father Bryan felt a tingling in his arm. The diagnosis— an inoperable brain tumor. Six months later, he died at the age of 33, leaving his wife to raise Dorsey and her sister Hattie.

Fortunately, Bryan bought life insurance when he married, and again when his daughters were born. Thanks to Bryan's foresight, Dorsey, Hattie and their mom are taken care of.

Are you prepared should the very worst happen? Without adequate life insurance, your financial plans may be just a savings and investment program that dies when you do. Consult a qualified insurance professional to help you create a plan that will continue to provide for the ones you love.

LIFE®
A NONPROFIT ORGANIZATION
www.lifehappens.org

The Life and Health Insurance Foundation for Education is a nonprofit organization dedicated to helping consumers make smart insurance decisions to safeguard their families' financial futures. For more information about life insurance or tips on finding a qualified insurance professional, visit www.lifehappens.org or call 1 888-LIFE-777.

Dorsey Hoskins

Figure 15.1

This ad from Life Insurance Company emotionally depicts the foresight of a father who preserved the financial status of his family by purchasing life insurance before passing.

Helping Barbara Sullivan live her American Dream

Before she had a third grade class, she had her own little "homeroom" of two girls and a boy. And somehow she's managed to treat them all with the same love and care.

For over 50 years, we've put our retirement and pension products to work to help make sure the American Dream has been safe and secure for the men and women who work so hard to make all our lives better. And the families they come home to.

401(k)
403(b)
457
ANNUITIES
TDA
RETIREMENT PLANS
LIFE INSURANCE

But we're not about to stop now. We've done our homework, and come up with programs that offer a serious choice of products. All without front-end charges, withdrawal fees or transfer charges,* from a local salaried consultant you get to know by name and who has a personal and professional interest in the financial well being of those we serve. For more information call us at **1-800-468-3785** or visit our web site at **www.mutualofamerica.com**

People like Barbara teach us lessons about hard work every day. Which is why it's so important that our programs score high marks.

MUTUAL OF AMERICA
the spirit of America

320 Park Avenue, New York, NY 10022-6839 1 800 468 3785 www.mutualofamerica.com Mutual of America Life Insurance Company is a Registered Broker/Dealer
*For complete information on our variable accumulation annuity products, including all charges and expenses, please refer to the applicable prospectuses which can be obtained from Mutual of America by calling 1 800 468 3785 and should be read carefully before investing.

Figure 15.2

This ad from Mutual of America employs an other-directed approach. It informs the public that the firm's retirement and pension products have helped people like Barbara Sullivan, a devoted classroom teacher, to live her American dream by helping others.

MASCULINITY

Masculinity was described by Hofstede as the degree to which the dominant values in society are success, money, and things.[9] Hofstede measured this cultural dimension on a continuum ranging from masculinity to femininity. *Femininity*, in this view, is a situation in which the dominant values in society are caring for others and the quality of life. Countries such as the United States and other Western societies with a moderate-to-high masculinity index place great importance on earnings and recognition. People in such societies place high value on material possessions, achievement, and challenge. Achievement, in this view, is defined in terms of wealth and recognition. By contrast, in low-masculinity cultures (high-femininity cultures), such as Norway, achievement is defined in terms of human contacts and concern about the environment. People in such societies tend to place importance on cooperation, maintaining a friendly atmosphere, and employment security. The Pioneer and Peace Corps ads depicted in Figures 15.3 and 15.4 illustrate high-masculinity and low-masculinity themes, respectively. The first ad from Pioneer emphasizes power and control through innovations in sound and vision. The second ad from the Peace Corps emphasizes caring for others around the world.

From a consumer behavior perspective, the masculinity–femininity dimension represents a viable segmentation variable, because achievement in countries with high masculinity scores is expressed through material possessions. In such societies, possessions reflect a person's achievements. Possessions are social symbols and serve as a means of communication between people in a society. Prestigious products and brands find lucrative markets in such societies. In countries with low-masculinity scores, on the other hand, concern for the environment would tend to create demand for products and services that are ecologically friendly.

masculinity
the degree to which dominant values are success, money, and things

Courtesy of the Peace Corps.

Figures 15.3 and 15.4

The dominant values of masculinity and femininity that characterize different cultures are exemplified here by contrasting themes in two ads from Pioneer and the Peace Corps.

TERM ORIENTATION

A country's term orientation is another dimension added later by Hofstede to the original four dimensions cited earlier.[10] According to Hofstede, in contrast to short-term-oriented cultures, long-term-oriented cultures are characterized by patience, perseverance, respect for one's elders and ancestors, along with a sense of obedience and duty toward the larger good. Examples of long-term-oriented cultures are found in Asia, including China, Singapore, Taiwan, and Japan.

The effect of this dimension on consumer behavior may be observed in the strong influence that elderly members of the family or other significant groups possess over other individual members. In addition, a long-term orientation would direct people toward seeking more permanent solutions to their problems, rather than making temporary quick fixes. A long-term perspective is also demonstrated in the belief that one's culture is venerable and worth giving one's life for.

Consumer Behavior in a Cultural Setting

Like Hofstede, many researchers have examined cultural dimensions that reflect similarities and differences among cultures. In one such work, Harris and Moran identified a number of sociocultural dimensions that they selected on the basis of their relevance to products and services being marketed in various societies.[11] They suggested that culture can be divided into 10 distinctive categories. These categories consist of communication and language, beliefs and attitudes, values and norms, sense of self and space, relationships, time and time consciousness, mental process and learning, rewards and recognitions, dress and appearance, and food and eating habits. Exhibit 15.1 depicts the interrelationship between these variables and consumer behavior within a cultural context. This section surveys the effect of each of these 10 cultural dimensions on consumer behavior. In practice, however, each dimension cannot be treated as separate or mutually exclusive. Rather, these dimensions are highly interdependent and interrelated.

COMMUNICATION AND LANGUAGE

Language as part of culture is the primary means of communication and the medium used to convey meaning, thoughts, and feelings. It embodies the culture's philosophy and heritage. Language is not only restricted to spoken and written words but also includes symbolic communication through spatial proximity, gestures, facial expressions, and body movements.

From a marketing perspective, at least two aspects of language must be investigated in any culture to gain a better understanding of that society. The first deals with language as a *communication tool*. In this regard, marketers examine the relevance of explicit and implicit elements of language (the spoken word and silent components of communication). The second aspect deals with the *heterogeneity* of languages in a culture, or the number of languages and dialects spoken within the borders of a particular country.

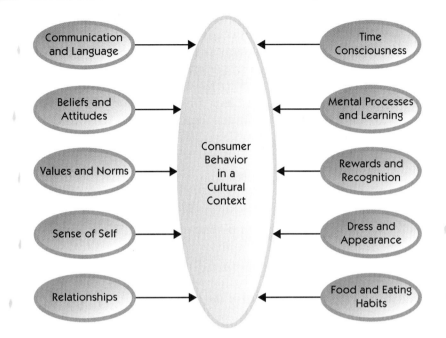

Concerning the first aspect, both spoken and silent languages are used to communicate thoughts and feelings. *Silent language* is the nonverbal component of language that involves gestures, grimaces, posture, color, and distance.[12] Silent language is typically conditioned by culture. The way people express themselves through hand gestures, facial expressions, and other forms of *body language* is culturally determined. In communicating with other people, for example, U.S. speakers stand approximately 18 inches apart. In Latin American countries, this distance is only 12 inches. In many Middle Eastern countries, it is about 7 inches.

The *spoken language*, on the other hand, involves vocal sounds and written symbols that make up the language. Even when people use the same language, misunderstandings can occur because the same words and symbols may have different meanings to individuals from different cultures. For example, U.S. expressions borrowed from the world of sports, religion, politics, and entertainment abound. These idiomatic expressions are meaningless to persons from other cultures, regardless of how fluent in English they may be. Expressions like *home run, piece of cake*, and *hot potato* would be confusing to individuals from abroad.

Acknowledging variations in language is important to marketers when communicating product information to various cultures. Translating a product–service benefit or campaign theme from one language to another can present a challenge. For example, When KFC entered the Chinese market, the company was shocked to discover that its slogan, "Finger Lickin' Good" came out as "Eat Your Fingers Off." Similarly, when the Dairy Association's "Got Milk" campaign was used in Mexico, it was read as "Are You Lactating?"[13] Such blunders can be avoided by a better awareness of each country's use of language and by *back translations*, where a translated message is retranslated into the original language by a different interpreter to catch possible errors. The Pepsi can design depicted in the ad in Figure 15.5 is an example of a product symbol that retains consistent meaning cross-culturally.

BELIEFS AND ATTITUDES

Culture has a significant influence on beliefs and attitudes. For example, in Western cultures, the prevailing outlook is youth oriented.[14] Youth is admired, and considerable efforts and funds are allotted to looking and feeling younger. Many people join health clubs, subscribe to physical fitness programs, and frequent beauty parlors. Some even undergo plastic surgery. In traditional societies, in contrast, old age carries great respect. Young people often seek advice and opinions from the elderly.

Beliefs, particularly religious beliefs, influence a culture's outlook on life and its meaning. Religions assert what is right and wrong, good and bad, and often are central to a culture because they influence the economic system,

Figure 15.5

"Fortunately, nothing's lost in the translation" is the tag line of this Pepsi ad. It communicates the thought that the brand is perceived uniformly throughout the world.

Consumer Behavior in Practice

An Aquarium with Six Black Fish Can Change Your Luck

Based on beliefs acquired from their homeland, many Asian Americans—especially those of Chinese ancestry—subscribe to *feng shui*, an ancient custom with roots deep in nature worship, Taoism, and yin and yang. *Feng shui* literally means "wind and water." Believers in this tradition profess that invisible power forces, called *ch'i* (chee) run through the world. A person's dwelling or place of business should attract a favorable *ch'i* and deflect an unfavorable one. If buildings, furniture, roads, and other human-made objects are placed in harmony with nature, it is believed that good fortune will prevail. If not, it is held that bad omens and great harm would befall the place and person(s) occupying it. It has been claimed, for example, that animals, such as dragons and tigers, reside beneath the surface of the earth. Consequently, humans must not cut into a dragon's flesh (exposing red earth), nor should they build under a tiger's mouth. Simply stated, buildings must fit the land's contours.

In order to ensure that buildings, offices, and furniture are arranged in harmony with nature, many Asian businesses operating in the United States retain the services of an expert *feng shui* practitioner, who examines the facilities and takes readings from a compasslike instrument covered with small Chinese characters. A geomancer may, for example, propose installing aquariums complete with black fish. Although these fish are fed, they are not pampered in fancy tanks. Rather, they are meant to die and be replaced. In doing so, the fish are presumed to absorb bad luck. Other likely recommendations include placing mirrors pointing out of offices to deflect bad luck, using wind chimes, plants, crystals, and weather vanes, among other things, in order to ease or block the flow of *ch'i*.

Many well-known American corporations operating in Asia, including Chase Manhattan bank and Citibank, use *feng shui* to help them achieve harmonious relationships with nature. These companies have found that this practice, which was originally used to ease the fears of local employees, really does work. After a Chase Manhattan bank manager, who had occupied a supposedly unlucky office in Hong Kong, was killed in an airplane crash, the bank moved its regional headquarters to a new building. Chase officials admit that the staff's concern about *feng shui* was one of the reasons for relocating, but these same officials also note that bank business seems to boom as a result of using this craft.[16]

Superstitions are part of the folklore of any culture, small or large. Businesses must be cognizant of and sensitive to these traditions when dealing with microcultures. To learn more about feng shui, visit www.planetbonsai.com and http://www.feng-shuiweb.co.uk/advice/business.htm. Think of some American superstitions. How might these superstitions affect the way a company designs its products, services, or brands? How might these same superstitions affect consumers' preferences for brands, institutions, and stores?

political structure, and social relationships between people. Religions place different emphases on material possessions and economic activities. Buddhism, for example, has been described as the striving for a state of *wantlessness* and contemplation. Its world-denying orientation is the core of its teachings. Emphasis on material wealth is considered ignoble.[15] Islam includes a belief system and detailed laws regulating many aspects of life. It can be described as fatalistic, seeing everything that occurs in life as predetermined, the result of divine will that humans can do nothing to change. Hinduism, while placing no sanctions on the acquisition of wealth, can also be described as fatalistic. Some groups within Christianity—Protestantism in particular—

emphasize the work ethic. To work hard is a religious duty and its rewards, therefore, are signs of God's approval. Many Eastern Orthodox Christians, by contrast, tend to value a leisurely, contemplative lifestyle.

Religion also influences male–female roles in a society. For example, in Western cultures, women play a major role in society today. In contrast, some traditional Islamic societies severely restrict the role of females outside the household. A Muslim male (outside the United States) may have up to four wives at a time (provided that he treats them equally and has a means to support them). Women, on the other hand, must practice monogamy.

Religion also establishes authority relationships, a person's duties and responsibilities, and the sanctity of various acts.[17] Many religions are replete with prohibitions and requirements. Gambling and consumption of alcohol are often prohibited. Practices such as wearing modest apparel, circumcision, and fasting may be required. For example, observant members of the Jewish faith (Orthodox and some Conservative Jews) circumcise their male children and follow strict dietary rules concerning what is *kashrut* or kosher.

Marketers who distribute their products globally need to understand the attitudes and sentiments of other cultures toward foreign products. The opportunities or difficulties that await U.S. marketers who attempt to do business abroad depend largely on whether these cultures view foreign products, ideas, and influence positively, negatively, or with suspicion. In some instances, being *foreign* can be a selling point, with exotic, luxurious, prestigious, or status-laden connotations. For example, in Japan, Borden sells Lady Borden ice cream and Borden cheese deliberately packaged and labeled in English exactly as they are marketed in the United States because the Japanese place a higher status value on imported products.

VALUES AND NORMS

values
ideals concerning what is right or wrong and goals worth pursuing

Values are enduring beliefs that involve ideals, such as what a person should or ought to do, goals that are worth pursuing, and ways to pursue these goals. Culture may be analyzed and categorized on the basis of its norms and value systems. For example, through analysis of a culture's values, it is possible to draw conclusions about how these elements affect behavior and modes of consumption. Values may influence whether consumers regard a product or service as desirable or undesirable. For example, unlike Western cultures, people in Eastern cultures avoid sunbathing because dark skin is associated with working social class. Therefore, to determine the acceptability or appeal of their products in various cultures, marketers often solicit the help of a technique known as **means–end chains**.[18] This analytical technique is simply a depiction of the postulated linkages between a product's *attributes, consequences* of that product's use, and consumer *values* as they exist in a particular culture. Means–end chains are based on the premise that consumers do not buy physical products—they buy *benefits* that these products yield. Yet, obviously the benefits that consumers seek are culturally determined. For example, if the tendency of consumers in Eastern cultures is to avoid sunbathing due to a culturally based belief of the undesirability of dark skin, any brand of skin-tanning

means–end chains
depictions of linkages between product attributes, use consequences, and consumer values

cream offered in such cultures is doomed to fail. In this case, the means–end chain may simply be as follows: "tanning creams enhance the acquisition of dark skin" (attribute); "dark skin is perceived by others in the society as a sign of the working class" (consequence); and "avoid any association with working class by maintaining fair skin" (value). The natural consequence of this value-based means–end chain is a strong tendency to avoid sun rays and tanning creams.

Values also exert an impact on the effectiveness of communication messages. Many U.S. multinational corporations that use standardized advertising campaigns in their global markets find that such advertising does not work in some cultures, because consumers in these markets do not identify with the situations, characters, or imagery depicted in these ads. Gieco's talking lizard ads, which played well in the United States, may mean very little to consumers in much of Africa.

From its value system, a culture sets norms of behavior for the society. **Norms** are shared guidelines to accepted and expected behavior and provide standards against which people evaluate the appropriateness of their behavior.[19] Norms address matters and issues that range from work ethic to manner of dress, and as such, influence consumption patterns. In the United States, for example, material possessions and manifestation of wealth are encouraged. An overt display of success is acceptable. In other cultures, such as Japan and Germany, thrift is emphasized. In the United Kingdom, a conspicuous display of wealth is considered to be in bad taste. Proverbs and idioms in a society often signify culture's norms. For example, "Time is money" or "The early bird catches the worm" are indicative of a culture that is busy and diligent.

norms
a society's shared guidelines regarding appropriate behavior

SENSE OF SELF

Self-identity and self-worth are influenced by culture. Being modest and humble or being aggressive or macho are reflections of what a culture values and rewards. In the United States, traits such as aggressiveness, sense of independence, and assertiveness are expected and encouraged. In many Western societies, people gauge their accomplishments in terms of the status symbols they acquire. In Eastern societies, the opposite is true. For example, in Japan, child rearing emphasizes modesty and self-effacement. If aggressiveness is one of the desirable traits for U.S. salespersons, the Japanese would tend to be judged as poor salespeople. Also, whereas U.S. consumers value independence, the Japanese are always under strong constraint to meet the expectations of others so as to maintain their face. They likewise avoid causing others to lose face. Hence, decision making in Japan is a collective or group-oriented act. Group cooperation, harmony, and conformity are signs of success and progress.

Humility is a key trait in the Japanese culture.

© 2009, JupiterImages, Inc.

Self-identity affects buying behavior in many ways. U.S. businesspeople, whose self-identities embrace feelings of competence and confidence, tend to project an idealized self through the consumption of conspicuous products and services. By means of owning an impressive home, furniture, automobile, and clothing, U.S. consumers attempt to match their self-identity with product imagery. A Japanese businessperson, on the other hand, may choose simplicity in the purchase of similar items as a result of a modest and humble evaluation of self-worth.

People in a culture may also be collectively labeled as formal or informal. In Japan, for example, formal authority, obedience, and conformance to hierarchical position are very important. Job-related promotions are mainly based on seniority rather than merit alone. The United States, on the other hand, is an informal culture in which people tend to be treated alike regardless of their hierarchical position. Job promotions and raises in pay are based for the most part on merit, regardless of age or seniority.

As we have seen in Chapter 14, cultures also may be classified based on the presence or absence of vivid differences between social classes. In some older societies, such as India, a caste system still remains in force, which demarcates a person's place in society from the moment of birth. On the other hand, in the United States, which has an open class system, social mobility is possible via education, achievement—especially economic success—and talent or ability.

RELATIONSHIPS

Personal and organizational relationships are subject to cultural influences. Culture, for example, determines the roles of managers and subordinates as well as how they relate to each other. In some traditional cultures, managers and subordinates are separated by various boundaries ranging from protocol to separate office facilities. In others, equality characterizes the operation. For example, Nissan USA has no privileged parking spaces for high-ranking officials and no private dining rooms. In addition, workers and managers wear the same type of white overalls, and the president sits in the same office with a hundred other workers.[20]

The family unit is another common expression of cultural relationships. The family unit in Western industrialized countries consists of parents and children. In traditional societies, on the other hand, the family unit is extended to include others such as grandparents, uncles, aunts, and cousins—all living under the same roof. In such societies, business is kept within the family and passed from one generation to the next. Family members demonstrate absolute loyalty to the family, often to the point of self-sacrifice. Centers of authority and responsibility within the family also vary dramatically. In the Middle East, for example, the authority figure in the family is the male. Children play an insignificant role in the decision-making process. Whereas female roles in Western societies are equivalent to those of males, in other societies women's roles are sometimes restricted to managing the household. In China, Japan, and Korea, the elderly are treated with great respect and honor and are considered wise. Their views are solicited and considered. In other Western cultures, the elderly may be considered burdensome, and little attention is given to their views or advice.

Relationships outside the family also vary based on culture. In the West, relations with friends, neighbors, and colleagues are casual and noncommittal, whereas in the Middle East, Latin America, and other cultures, relationships with others are closer, warmer, longer-lasting, and more candid. U.S. businesspeople, for example, shy away from doing business with friends and discussing family problems with colleagues. Conversely, the Japanese and Latin Americans prefer to conduct their business with friends. A Latin American person, in addition, would not hesitate to stay up all night in order to listen to the family problems of a colleague. Because working through friends often results in priority treatment, marketers conducting business in other cultures should learn to take the time to establish some friendships first before pursuing the necessary business matters.

TIME CONSCIOUSNESS

Sense of time differs by culture. In the United States, Germany, and the United Kingdom, people are punctual. Promptness is the norm, and tardiness leads to embarrassing or even costly consequences. In Latin America and much of Africa and the Middle East, however, the clock is not so rigidly adhered to. A person can arrive at a meeting half an hour late and be considered early. Tardiness is acceptable and expected. Concerning social functions, it is not considered polite to arrive at a party on time. In much of the Middle East, Africa, and Latin America, hosts are likely to be annoyed if a guest arrives precisely on time. In Japan, arrival at a meeting is governed by rank—junior people are expected to arrive early and wait. Those with seniority arrive last.

Another cultural time horizon is whether people in a culture focus on the past or the future. For example, in much of Europe, a sense of history, tradition, and heritage plays a more significant role in buying behavior than it does in the United States. This may be reflected in Europeans' resistance to change, to altering traditional ways of doing things, and to accepting recent innovations. In the United States, the focus on the future allows more willingness to change and seek new and different ways of satisfying needs.

The short-term versus the long-term time horizon philosophy is another element that distinguishes cultures. Some cultures focus most heavily on a short-term time horizon. For example, investors pressure corporate boards of directors to show profitability. Consequently, short-range profit goals characterize the outlook of many U.S. corporations. Other cultures, such as the Japanese, are more interested in long-range goals of profitability and are willing to accept losses for many years in order to build market share before profits start to materialize.

When U.S. firms conduct business abroad, their haste and impatience are often ridiculed. Others consider these traits to be weak points in the U.S. style of business negotiations. Often, U.S. haste is exploited when foreign negotiators simply adopt a strategy of waiting. This strategy usually nets better terms and concessions for foreign negotiators.

MENTAL PROCESSES AND LEARNING

The way people think and the ease or difficulty with which learning occurs is another aspect that differentiates people from various cultures. In some cultures, such as the British, myopic thinking modes are the pattern. Data, material objects, and other stimuli or activities are viewed in terms of a particular goal or result.[21] Therefore, attention is directed to details and procedures rather than general principles or abstract concepts. In this case, an activity's detail takes priority over what the activity as a whole is all about. In other societies, such as the United States, people place practical considerations ahead of details or procedures. Many Middle Easterners may act on emotions; in contrast, Americans are taught to act on logic. In still other societies, such as the French, general principles are placed ahead of practical considerations. These modes of mental activity precede behavior, and as such affect consumer behavior.

People in different cultures also vary in the degree to which they acquire information from various kinds of sources, as well as in the speed of such learning. This speed is a function of seemingly innate ability, which varies in different cultures. Psychologists have distinguished between at least five kinds of learning ability: verbal competence, spatial visualization, word fluency, general reasoning, and creativity. These capabilities, or lack of them, affect the way consumers react to new products or promotions appearing in various media. For example, in cultures in which visualization is high, the market is more easily reached through television. Conversely, in cultures in which verbal competence and word fluency is high, the market can be more effectively reached through print media. Where creativity is high, people tend to adopt new products more quickly.

Because some learning occurs via reinforcements and punishments, cultural interpretations of what constitutes rewards and penalties influence the learning process. For example, in some Middle Eastern or African countries, persons who are a bit overweight are deemed attractive (a reward). Products that increase body weight are thus considered desirable. In the Western world, on the other hand, being slim, trim, and fit is desirable. Obesity is viewed negatively. Thus, reduced-calorie, low-fat products that help consumers lose weight are perceived as desirable.

Marketers who deal with different cultures should consider the thinking modes of various societies to avoid misunderstandings in their communications with the marketplace. Within the context of business meetings, for example, the Japanese tend to listen, analyze what has been said, and seldom speak. The U.S. mode of behavior is almost the opposite.

REWARDS AND RECOGNITION

The methods of rewarding individuals for exceptional performance or accomplishments differ widely within cultural contexts. Monetary rewards, recognition, medals, honors, expense accounts, and impressive titles are used differently in various cultures. Although the process of motivation is universal, the methods used to attain goals are quite different. In the United States, for example, recognition, security, and monetary awards are important reinforcement systems. In China, however, group affiliation is an important need and reinforcer. A desirable reward in this case may involve having a picture of an employee hung on the wall as "employee of the month." In Canada, a study of what motivates workers revealed that relationships at work rank first, followed by security, then recognition, and pay in fourth place.[22]

An article entitled "Where Status Is Measured by Toilets and Showers" summarized some of the status symbols in the Washington, D.C., offices of government bureaucrats. A wooden desk and chair indicate that the office is occupied by a bureaucrat of grade GS-15 or higher. Less-important employees must make do with metal desks. An office with a private toilet and a sink points to an officially recognized government chief. An office with a private toilet, sink, shower, and vanity is occupied by a genuine big shot. In corporate America, the size of the office and its location are symbols of authority. In a towering headquarters building, the CEO and top executives usually occupy spacious, well-furnished top-floor office suites. In many Asian cultures, managers conduct business side-by-side with ordinary workers.

Although every country bestows honor and status on some occupations, those that are chosen vary from culture to culture. In the Middle East and Asia, religious leaders are revered and respected. In Latin America, poets and authors have considerable status. In Japan, honor is given to government and business leaders. In the United States, judges, physicians, lawyers, and well-known entertainers and athletes are held in high regard.

The manner of greeting may vary greatly in different cultures. Whereas a firm handshake is the norm in the United States, Europeans prefer a less-intense handshake. The Japanese bow as they greet each other. The depth of the bow reflects the stature of the other party. Middle Easterners embrace and kiss both cheeks. Indians greet with hands held in a prayerlike manner.

© 2009, Ronald Sumners, Shutterstock, Inc.

The sari is traditional garb for many Indian women. In addition to its attractiveness and colorfulness, the sari is styled to maintain a sense of modesty, because it covers most of a woman's body.

DRESS AND APPEARANCE

The clothes and body adornments people use in different cultures vary according to climate and tradition. The traditional Japanese still wear the kimono, Arabs the abaya, Polynesians the sarong, Indians the sari, and Middle Easterners the galabia. Although these articles of clothing may be designed first to protect against the elements, like white robes that reflect the Mideast sun's rays and allow for body ventilation, they may also be styled to maintain a sense of modesty and equality. Modesty is attained by covering most of the body, and equality through a look-alike appearance that eliminates distinctions between rich and poor.

Customs and traditions determine acceptable modes of dress, appearance, and hair length. Americans prefer loose-fitting suits, whereas Europeans prefer tight-fitting attire. Latin American men prefer to grow a beard and mustache and have long hair, styles that are acceptable in their business circles. Many

U.S. corporations, on the other hand, require their male employees to have a clean-shaven face and short haircuts.

Color of clothes and accessories also vary by culture. Black is a color of mourning in Western cultures, but white is used for this purpose in China and Japan. White flowers, for example, are associated with funerals and should be avoided as gifts for business or social occasions. Color preferences should be observed in packaging as well as in promotional materials. To Westerners, for example, white cotton inserts for pharmaceutical-product containers suggest that the product was packaged under sterile and sanitary conditions. In some societies, on the other hand, white-colored packaging as well as white medicine tablets may connote death.

In modern times, a new trend in men's dress and appearance seems to be sweeping many countries, particularly the USA. It is that of men's tendency to tread upon territories that once were the exclusive domain of women. Not long ago, a man who went to an aesthetician for a facial was ridiculed. Today, many men sign up for facials, manicures, pedicures, waxings, liposuction, and hair coloring. These men who have taken up the challenge of looking good have been labeled *metro-sexuals*—a description of straight men who like to look attractive and who refuse to surrender their youth. Jewelry, perfumes, ear rings, bandanas, and skin-care creams are but some of the products sought by metro-sexuals. Many companies are seizing the opportunity for substantial profits by catering to the needs of this group. Such companies include providers of fitness products, hair transplants, botox injections, cosmetics, and pharmaceuticals. Reports show that in the United States during the year 2007, the average annual household expenditure on such rejuvenation products and services was $7,940.

FOOD AND EATING HABITS

In many cultures, dining is a ceremony where family members gather for an hour or more to share food, drinks, and conversation.

Another way of observing culture is to note what people eat or refuse to eat, how food is prepared, when meals are served, and how quickly people eat. In Islamic countries, for example, pork is not eaten and liquor is not served. In most of Latin America, as well as in Africa and the Middle East, the main meal is served in the early afternoon, after which a nap is taken. Beer is the preferred drink in Germany, wine in France, and aquavit in Norway. Whereas most Americans are meat eaters, in some cultures, such as India, many people consume little or no meat. Foods that are common in one culture may sound repulsive to members of another. Among the Chinese, dog and cat are delicacies. Hummus, felafel, and tabouli are staples in most Middle-Eastern households, but are unknown taste sensations to many U.S. consumers who have been raised on hamburgers and hot dogs. In terms of how quickly people eat, individuals in the United States—especially those with active or stressful life-

© 2009, JupiterImages, Inc.

styles—tend to eat quickly or even on the run. On the other hand, Italians and some South Americans make a ceremony out of dining and may leisurely spend a couple hours or more at the dinner table.

So far we have seen that each culture tends to have its own customs and traditions. We have also recognized that cultural values determine how people in a particular society think, feel, and act. Today, sensitivity to these cultural dimensions is not a matter of choice for marketers—it is a practical necessity. Success in business hinges on the understanding that consumer behavior occurs within a cultural context and that the route to success lies within the confines of such sensitivity to cultural traditions.

Now let us move on to another culture-related issue—the view that culture is seldom homogeneous. Rather, a culture often consists of a number of **microcultures** or subgroups of individuals within the culture whose beliefs, experiences, traditions, and modes of behavior set them somewhat apart from those of the main culture. These unique patterns of various microcultures are a topic of interest to marketers in their pursuit of better ways to serve their customers.

microcultures
smaller, more homogeneous subsets of people within a larger culture

Microcultures

Within countries such as the United States and Canada, nations characterized by plurality and multiculturalism, researchers use a variety of criteria to delineate microcultures. Among these criteria, microcultures have been identified on such bases as demographic, geographic, and lifestyle variables. Although such classifications may be somewhat useful for purposes of sociological research and market segmentation, they are less actionable for purposes of designing culturally sensitive marketing strategies. For this very reason, we limit our coverage of microcultures to two forms: the first is an overview of those microcultures that can be identified on the basis of ethnicity; and the second is microcultures that are identifiable through observed consumption choices of products or services that consumers make. Examples of such microcultures include the Harley-Davidson Owners Group, Knights of Columbus, Masons, and Shriners, among others.[23]

Ethnicity, one of the most popular bases for delineating microcultures, embraces such factors as the race, nationality, and religion that individuals belong to. Ethnicity also takes into account how strongly or weakly individuals feel connected to their heritage.[24] The amount of influence that consumers' ancestry exerts on them depends largely on the strength of their association and affiliation with the microculture. Some consumers strive to preserve the language and traditions of their native homeland. Others opt for rapid assimilation into the mainstream of their new society. In addition, differences can be observed between first-, second-, and third-generation members of the various ethnic microcultures.

To the extent that the members of an ethnic group share common beliefs and perceptions that differ from those of other ethnic groups or society as a whole, these individuals constitute a distinct ethnic microculture or market segment.[25] It must be pointed out, however, that ethnic groups (African

Americans, Hispanics, Asians) that exist within the marketplace are, of course, very diverse in composition and may need to be segmented further.

Consumption, an alternative base, provides a different method for delineating microcultures. Microcultures of consumption are distinctive subgroups of a society that self-select on the basis of shared commitment to a particular product class, brand, or consumption activity. Researchers are able to reveal such microcultures through ethnography, an unobtrusive observation method that was discussed earlier in this chapter.

We will begin with an overview of ethnic microcultures, followed by brief coverage of what has become known as consumption microcultures.

ETHNIC MICROCULTURES

The following sections briefly profiles three major microcultures in U.S. society, namely African, Hispanic, and Asian American consumers.

African-American Consumers

According to the U.S. Census Bureau, the number of African Americans in the nation, including those of more than one race, will remain around 40 million, or about 13 percent of the population in the years to come. Projections reveal that their share of the population will drop to around 11.8 percent by the year 2050.[26] One myth concerning African Americans is that most are low income. However, while the median household income of blacks was $32,000 in 2007, the proportion of households now earning over $80,000 a year is around 36 percent. Financially, African Americans constitute a major force in the marketplace, with an estimated combined buying power of $964 billion in the year 2009.[27] With regard to education, 81 percent of African Americans ages 25 years and older hold at least a high school diploma, 18 percent have a bachelor's degree, and around 1.3 million have earned advanced degrees.[28] Concerning employment status, 26 percent of single-race blacks 16 years of age and older work in management, professional, and related occupations.[29] It is estimated that one-third of black buying power is concentrated in just four states: California, Texas, New York, and Illinois.[30]

African Americans are younger than the general population. Their median age is 30.1 years, which is more than 5 years younger than the median age for Whites (36.4 years).[31] Over half of all African Americans are between the ages of 18 and 34 years. As these young individuals form families, buy homes, and build careers, their spending power is virtually certain to grow.

The consumer adage of the 1980s, "Shop till you drop," is alive and well with many African Americans today, who tend to spend generously to enhance their personal image.[32] Although African-American households spend less than average on many things, from food away from home to charitable contributions, millions of middle-class and upper-class blacks have discretionary income to spend on other items. According to Focus USA, blacks tend to spend a greater percentage of their income on groceries and clothing than their white counterparts. African Americans are able to spend more on food and personal appearance because they tend to spend less on line items related to home-ownership. They spend 24 percent less than average on household furnishings and equipment, and less of their budgets than average on transportation, because many of them live in cities that have public transportation systems.[33]

Profile of African-American Consumers

In some ways, African-American shoppers are more discriminating than their white counterparts in their retail interaction. Although price is the number-one deciding factor for both African Americans and whites, for the former, the second most important factor is *respect*. African Americans often report being ignored or watched while shopping.[34] They tend to view shopping as a social experience. They often shop with friends and family and patronize discounters' upscale competitors, such as department and specialty stores. Almost two-thirds feel that they are willing to pay more to get the best brands. For many, it is quality—not quantity—that matters. This is largely due to the desire to enhance personal image. Among young African Americans, brand is synonymous with image. To members of this group, brand is a statement of a person's worth and status.[35]

© 2009, Stephen Coburn, Shutterstock, Inc.

African Americans are younger than the general population. As they form families, buy homes and build careers, their spending power will grow.

In a study dealing with how African Americans spend their time, blacks emerged as distinct in their greater use of free time for religious activities; Internet use; watching TV; stereo, radio, and iPod listening; electronic game playing; active sports; and talking (both on the phone and at home).[36] For example, African Americans spend almost twice as much time going to church as whites do and tend to consume four to five more hours a week watching TV. They also listen more to radio and recordings as a primary activity. These tendencies, however, are offset by their lower times spent on reading, hobbies, and going to social or cultural events such as fairs and museums.

How to Reach African-American Consumers

In reaching this market, an African-American advertising executive once commented, "Black people are not dark-skinned white people—there are cultural values which cause us to be subtly different from the majority population."[37] It is true that for products with broad appeal (such as paper products and detergents), the mass media—especially TV—may effectively reach all consumers. However, for other classes of merchandise (personal grooming supplies, home furnishings, clothing, and foods), additional media such as magazines, newspapers, and radio stations that are specifically targeted to African Americans may be more effective and should supplement firms' general advertising efforts. Simply running a company's usual ads in black media or substituting black actors into ads without adjusting the dialogue, appeals, or backdrop does not usually work.[38]

Astute marketers acknowledge the importance as well as the diversity of the African-American market. The belief that blacks are a demographic monolith or demonstrate a single mind-set is a myth.[39] Segmentation of the African-American market usually reflects socioeconomic standing (income, education, occupation).[40] Armed with this understanding, many companies target and position products to the African-American market. For example, recognizing that African-American women spend about $1.8 billion on cosmetics annually, Prescriptives (an Estée Lauder subsidiary), Maybelline, and Revlon introduced their All Skins, Shades of You, and Color Style makeup lines, respectively.[41] These lines are specifically formulated for African-American women. Hallmark added a Mahogany line of greeting cards. Similarly, dolls with African-American attributes are marketed by Mattel (a black Barbie and Shani) and Tyco. Procter & Gamble and Coca-Cola have been known to hand out samples in gift bags after Sunday services at African-American churches.[42] Similarly, there are approximately 50 magazines, such as *Ebony, O* (the Oprah magazine), *Essence, Upscale, Sister, About Time, American Legacy*, and *Hope Today*, that cover topics ranging from fashions to politics and social issues. An online magazine that addresses African-American fashions is *One Magazine.net*.[43] Mass marketers like Kmart, Wal-Mart, and Target have often courted the African-American clothing market.[44] Similarly, banks and brokerage firms have targeted African-American investors. For instance, Merrill-Lynch has formed partnerships with associations of African-American professionals. The firm also assigns teams of financial advisors to market to large population clusters of affluent African Americans.[45] Smith Barney, as well as Citigroup, have followed suit.[46]

Hispanic-American Consumers

About half of all immigrants to the United States today—legal and illegal—come from Spanish-speaking countries.[47] In fact, over 580,000 Hispanic immigrants come to the United States every year. Hispanics and their U.S.-born children accounted for 45 million individuals in 2007, representing over 15 percent of the population. These figures show that they have rapidly surpassed African Americans as the largest ethnic minority in the United States. In fact, the Hispanic population continues to grow at a rate faster than the black population, the Asian population, and the white population. This pace of growth is projected to continue well into the century, with projections indicating that Hispanics will constitute 29 percent of the U.S. population by the year 2050. Hispanics' growth rate is approximately 9.8 percent annually, compared with 2.5 percent for the overall population.[48] Interestingly, 53 percent of Hispanic population growth can be attributed to international migration, while the rest is the result of procreation. From a marketing point of view, Hispanics are estimated to represent as much as $1 trillion in annual buying power today, and this figure is projected to top $1.2 trillion by 2012.

The term *Hispanic* encompasses persons from many different cultural backgrounds. Hispanics in the United States come from a wide range of geographic areas: Mexico (61 percent), Central or South America (14 percent), Puerto Rico (12 percent), Cuba (5 percent), and other areas (8 percent).[50]

Ethical Dilemma

No School for You, Little José

Throughout our history, Americans have passed through cycles of anti-immigrant fervor. Many citizens have felt and continue to feel that the large numbers of immigrants, many of whom lack marketable skills, present a drain on the country's scarce resources and even pose a danger to its security.

The 1990s witnessed the height of such cycles when voters in California approved Proposition 187, which prohibited illegal immigrants from receiving virtually all public benefits, including public health coverage as well as primary and secondary education. Tens of thousands of children of illegal immigrants were prevented from attending public schools.

Critics of Proposition 187 were quick to point out the inhumanity of the initiative. They questioned the wisdom of denying education to an entire generation of children and the effect of such denial on society as a whole. As a result, Proposition 187 was overturned by a federal court, deeming it to be unconstitutional. Congress also backtracked on some of its extreme restrictions, such as denying food stamps even to legal immigrants.

This negative sentiment toward illegal immigrants has never subsided. It remains one of the hottest topics of debate both in the media and in political circles. Frustrated by the federal government's failure to curtail the inflow of illegal immigrants and to address the status of the 12 million illegal immigrants already in the United States, many states and local governments across the nation have been busily enacting immigration crackdowns. Oklahoma, for example, which shelters 100,000 illegal immigrants, recently passed immigration bill HB 1804 in November 2007. This bill cuts off undocumented immigrants from participating in most government programs, as well as mandates felony charges against anyone who transports or shelters illegals.

Such actions clearly pose positive as well as negative consequences. On the positive side, savings of $200 million a year, which represents the extra cost in health, education, and welfare spending for illegal immigrants, is a cause of rejoice to the law's supporters. On the negative side, however, the majority of the 100,000 illegal immigrants have fled the state, negatively affecting industries that rely heavily on undocumented laborers, such as construction companies, farms, groceries, and restaurants. In fact, illegal workers fulfill an important void in our society–since there are not enough U.S. citizens willing to staff the low-skill farming and construction jobs that keep our country's economy growing.[49]

Many U.S. citizens have mixed feelings on the issue of illegal immigrants and the costs associated with their education, health care, and welfare. Learn more about Oklahoma's state immigration bill HB 1804 by visiting the CNN Web site at www.cnn/2007/US/11/02/oklahoma.immigration/ as well as USA Today's Web site at www.usatoday.com/news/nation/2008-01-09-immigcover_N.htm. What are the social, political, economic, and ethical ramifications associated with this issue? Where do you stand on this matter? Defend your position.

Given this diversity, cultural differences may exist within the larger group that would be worth exploring for marketers. Such inquiries would be particularly important for marketers in the areas of product preferences and appropriate advertising appeals designed for each subgroup. For example, Anheuser-Busch, a beer brewer that aggressively pursues Hispanics, produces its radio jingles in four versions—with Puerto Rican, Cuban, Mexican (California), and Mexican (Texas) musical flavorings in order to suit the tastes of each subgroup. Similarly, its TV spots are geared to the nationality of each intended target audience. Spots directed to the heavily Mexican Los Angeles area have employed scenes that depict a small family fiesta and a restaurant gathering.

On the other hand, spots prepared for the heavily Cuban Miami area have featured a scene with a roasted pig and another person making cigars. The spots, instead of using known actors, employ "real people" from the local areas where the commercials are to be aired.

Whereas the median age of non-Hispanic Whites in 2007 was 36.4 years, the median age for Hispanics was only 27 years. Half of all American Hispanics are 25 years of age or younger, compared with half of the general U.S. population, which is 40 years of age and older. This youth orientation is due to the high birth rate that characterizes the Hispanic market. In fact, by the year 2020, the number of Hispanic teens will grow by 62 percent to 7 million individuals, compared with a 10 percent growth in the number of teens overall.[51] This youthful trend will have many ramifications both for the labor force and for marketers. It is estimated, for example, that presently Hispanics account for about 25 percent of the U.S. labor force growth.[52]

Profile of Hispanic-American Consumers

On average, the Hispanic population falls at the lower end of the socioeconomic scale, with only 15 percent of this population earning more than $75,000 per year compared to one-third of the total U.S. population. Approximately 22 percent live in poverty. Educationally, in the year 2006, 12.3 percent of U.S. Hispanics were college graduates, and 28.2 percent held a high-school diploma, while more than 40 percent never graduated from high school.[53]

A 2007 study by A C Nielsen investigated the spending patterns of Hispanic consumers on products and services ranging from grocery items to nonfoods. The study revealed that expenditures by Hispanic households exceeded those of white households in a large number of food and nonfood categories.[54] Other studies, however, show that Hispanic expenditures were much lower than the average for dwelling, entertainment, medical services, insurance, and education.

Expenditures on grocery items are high due to the fact that Hispanics tend to eat at home more often than non-Hispanic whites. Food expenditures amounted to a total of $51 billion, with $33 billion spent on meals consumed at home and $18 billion spent on meals away from home. Hispanics place high value on food and in-home meal preparation, as well as high priority on getting together to enjoy meals with the whole family. Hispanic entertainment is done mostly at home through sharing a meal with the extended family and friends. Expenditures on clothing are also sizeable, due to the greater need for infant clothing as a result of the high birth rate among Hispanics. With younger and larger families than the overall population, Hispanics in 2007 spent twice as much as the general population on infant clothing, which children quickly outgrow. Another area of elevated expenditure among Hispanics is phone services. U.S. Hispanics are heavy users of cellular phones, beepers, and pagers, as well as place many local, long-distance, and international calls. They spend considerably more than the general public on value-added phone services, such as call waiting and caller ID. According to Miami-based Strategy Research, a market research firm, this tendency is due to the large number of foreign-born Hispanics living in the United States and their need to call home.[55]

American Hispanics can be divided into three distinct acculturation segments. The first group is the *unacccultured* segment, which accounts for approximately 40 percent this market. Members of this subgroup retain close ties to the culture of their country of origin and prefer to communicate in the Spanish language. The second subgroup, which constitutes around 32 percent of the total, is the *bicultural* segment, and consists of bilinguals who desire to retain much of their original culture while adopting many elements of U.S. society as well. The third subgroup is the *accultured* segment, accounting for 28 percent of Hispanics, whose members have moved beyond their roots and have adopted U.S. cultural and family values. Members of this segment prefer to communicate in English, and many no longer speak the Spanish language. This segmentation pattern has major implications for marketers, particularly in the areas of employment, store preferences (e.g., unacculatured members often prefer large discount stores), and promotional media types as well as languages used to reach the Hispanic community.[56]

Hispanics tend to prefer established and prestigious brands, to avoid private brands and generics, and to be brand loyal—especially to brands from their country of origin. They buy brands advertised by their *bodegas* (neighborhood grocery stores) such as the Goya brand, like to buy what their parents bought, prefer fresh goods to prepared or frozen items, and willingly pay extra for quality products. Hispanics prefer shopping at smaller stores, enjoy socializing with friends and store owners while shopping, and dislike impersonal stores. They tend not to buy impulsively and are less-confident shoppers. Difficulty with English sometimes inhibits their adoption of new products. In-store promotions, sponsorship of community activities, and ad tie-ins to Hispanic life and culture can be more effective than coupons and price reductions to get Hispanics to try new products.[57]

How to Reach Hispanic-American Consumers

The AOL Latino 2006 Hispanic Cyberstudy, conducted by Synova, revealed that there were more than 25 million Hispanic Americans online, which accounted for 55 percent of the U.S. Hispanic population. Among those online, 77 percent had broadband access. The study reported that 68 percent of Hispanic Internet users consider the Internet to be the best source of information on brand choices. In addition, 77 percent of these Internet users rely on the Internet to learn about brands.[58] Beyond the Internet, a variety of media is available to reach Hispanic Americans. Spanish television networks, such as Univision and Telemundo, and hundreds of local Spanish-language TV and radio stations, as well as numerous Spanish-language magazines and newspapers, and even a Sunday newspaper supplement *(Vista)*, serve the Hispanic market. In February 2008, Canal Internet launched its Web site *canalinternet.com*, which offers without charge television shows and other video content in Spanish. Users of this service can watch their favorite programs in Spanish on their computer screens.

Hispanics are now the largest ethnic microculture in the United States.

Hispanics are passionate devotees to their Spanish language. Almost half of those who watch television during prime time are viewing Spanish-language programs. Hispanic audiences turn to English-language television mainly for what they cannot get in Spanish. Progressive advertisers realize that it is not sufficient to merely use the Spanish language correctly in advertisements; their ads must also depict models in appropriate roles and employ suitable appeals, symbols, and images.

Companies that vigorously pursue Hispanics include AT&T, Comcast, IDT, Coca-Cola, Miller Brewing, Mazda, McDonalds, Anheuser-Busch, Philip Morris, Colgate-Palmolive, Wal-Mart, Kmart, Ford Motor Company, and Quaker Oats.[59] IDT, for example, launched a holiday promotion aimed at Hispanics for the firm's Tuyo Mobile service. The promotion involved adding five dollars of free talk time to new customer account balances once each week for three months with the purchase and use of a new phone.[60] Some firms such as Estee Lauder, Faberge, and Frito-Lay have marketed makeup shades, hair products, and plantain chips, respectively, with Hispanic consumers in mind.

In addition, online marketing is fast becoming a major route to reach Hispanics. As mentioned, 55 percent of Hispanics are online. At this high level of penetration, the Web is reaching this market with sites such as Starmedia's www.us.starmedia.com and www.elsitio.com, sites that are dedicated to the Hispanic segment's language and needs.

Asian-American Consumers

In 2008, there were 15 million Asian-American consumers (Asian alone or in combination with one or more other races), constituting about 5 percent of the U.S. population.[61] This group is projected to reach nearly 41 million individuals by the year 2050, amounting to 9 percent of the total.[62] Like other microcultures, Asian Americans exhibit a strong ethnic identity and vast diversity. They are considerably more diverse than the African- or Hispanic-American markets.

The term *Asian* is used to refer to many ethnic groups. The Census Bureau's category "Asian and Pacific Islander" covers more than 17 countries. The Chinese comprise the single largest group (approximately 24 percent), followed by Filipinos (about 18 percent), Asian Indians (about 16.5 percent), Vietnamese (about 11 percent), Korean (about 11 percent), and Japanese (about 8 percent). Other subgroups include Laotions, Cambodians, Thais, Pakistanis, Hawaiians, Samoans, Guamanians, Fiji Islanders, as well as others. Within this group, however, generations—delineated by when they immigrated to the United States—distinguish between this large group's various members. The most affluent subgroup, Asian Indian, contains cohorts. Indians who came to the United States in the 1960s are well-educated professional men, homemaker wives, and grown children. Those who arrived in the 1970s tend to be well-educated, dual-career couples with teenagers. Recent arrivals, however, are younger, less educated, and likely to own small stores.[63]

Well over half of Asian Americans live in three states: California (especially the Los Angeles and San Francisco areas), New York, and Hawaii. It has been estimated that 4 out of 10 Asian Americans live in California. They also account for 25 percent of immigrants in Los Angeles and New York. Clusters of Asian Americans are also found in Philadelphia and Washington, D.C., as well as a number of other large urban centers, such as Oakland, San Jose, San Diego, Orange County, and Chicago.

Profile of Asian-American Consumers

The average age of Asian Americans is 35.4 years, compared with 36.4 years for the general population. Asian Americans are industrious and strongly driven to achieve a middle-class lifestyle. The most highly educated and affluent microculture, this group exhibits strong family ties and places a high value on education.[64] In 2008, about 49 percent of Asian Americans held a bachelors degree or higher, which is two points above the national average. Their median income was over $65,000, with certain segments such as Asian Indians earning over $78,000. In addition, 53 percent of Asian-American households had at least two wage earners, which is a higher proportion than other racial groups.[65] Asian Americans and Pacific Islanders tend to hold executive, professional, and technical positions, and many run their own businesses. Reports reveal that Asian Americans' purchasing power in 2008 amounted to $578.8 billion.[66] Asians value well-known, premium-quality brands and are both able and willing to pay for them. They consider quality more important than price when selecting retail outlets to shop; 54 percent shop as a leisure activity compared to 50 percent of the general population. Asian Americans are highly status conscious.[67] They are a good market for technically oriented products and services and are more likely to use automated teller machines and to own consumer electronics of all types.[68]

How to Reach Asian-American Consumers

Over 50 percent of Asian Americans do not speak English well. They tend to speak their native language at home, especially those of Korean and Chinese ancestry.[69] The most frequently spoken languages among Asian Americans are Mandarin Chinese, Korean, Japanese, and Vietnamese.[70] Filipinos are the only Asians who predominantly speak English among themselves.[71] This lack of familiarity with the English language makes it difficult to target all Asian Americans simultaneously. To date, there exists a small number of Asian cable TV networks, which include *AsiaVision*, *Imagin Asian*, and a new *Vision Asia*, with affiliate TV stations in many states. In addition, *STAR* (Satellite TV for Asian Region) is an Asian TV service based in Hong Kong, with programming directed to Asian viewers worldwide. At a regional or local level, heavy concentrations of specific Asian-nationality communities permit advertisers to run campaigns in other local and specialized media (the Internet, newspapers, and radio) and create opportunities for retailers to carry ethnic merchandise (foods, clothing, gift items). Due to this relative unease with English, most of them prefer media in their own language.[72] For example, 93 percent of the Vietnamese, 83 percent of the Chinese, and 81 percent of the Koreans prefer to communicate in their mother tongue. Therefore, advertising copy to them must be in-language and should be written specifically for each separate ethnic group, taking into account the mores and taboos of each. Moreover, representation of Asians in ads featuring appropriate nationality models is also critical.[73] Promotions featuring Asian celebrities and athletes are highly effective in reaching Asian Americans.[74] New media, such as Asian-American Web sites, attempt to address the needs of various Asian-American communities, while maintaining the cultural identities of each. Asian focused dot.coms of all types are now available through www.microviet.com a site which provides links to dozens of Asian Web sites covering various aspects of the Asian microculture.[75]

CONSUMPTION MICROCULTURES

microcultures of consumption
distinguishable subgroups of society that share a strong commitment to a product, brand, or activity

As mentioned earlier in this chapter, **microcultures of consumption** are distinctive subgroups of society that self-select on the basis of a shared commitment to a particular product class, brand, or consumption activity. Examples of such groups include Harley-Davidson Motorcycle Owner Group (HOG), Deadheads and the Grateful Dead Organization, bodybuilders and the Weider Brothers empire, and—to some extent—groups such as surfers and skateboarders. These are usually characterized by their identifiable, hierarchical social structures, unique ethos, shared beliefs and values, as well as distinguishing jargon, rituals, and modes of symbolic expression. The basis for the rise of these microcultures is their members' ritualistic consumption of certain products and brands or involvement in activities that distinguish them as cohesive groups. The unifying force, in this case, is the shared interest in the unique consumption pattern or the involvement in the singular activity.

Such microcultures are usually assessed through ethnography, which is the study of human behavior in its natural context. Ethnography involves observation of consumers' purchase behavior and/or activities in the physical settings in which they naturally occur. Depth interviews are also conducted to obtain participants' perspectives.

Due to the ritualistic devotion of members of these microcultures to certain products, brands, or activities, marketers can take active roles in inducting and socializing new members as well as cultivating the commitment of current members of such groups. Harley-Davidson, for example, has been highly successful in creating and maintaining a powerful and committed microculture of Harley owners by strategically supplying a steady stream of information geared to the needs of present and new members, as well as by providing a full range of clothing accessories and services that function to enhance members' pride and involvement. In return, Harley-Davidson receives the enviable benefits of steadfast customer loyalty, positive word of mouth, and a flow of highly beneficial feedback.

Marketing Implications of Culture and Microcultures

Marketers stand to profit from studying culture and microcultures. In reference to culture, this chapter has already demonstrated that the beliefs, values, norms, and traditions held by consumers within a culture influence the products/services they buy and use. When cultural values are deemed relevant to product consumption, marketers appeal to prevalent values and surround their brands with symbols of these values. For example, when advertising yogurt in Japan, Yoplait emphasized the product's pure, all-natural ingredients to capitalize on the Japanese love of nature.

Marketers also benefit from understanding microcultures. Delving into the psyche of members of a microculture to find out what is important to them and playing to their interest is simply good marketing practice. In this context, cultural *relevance* becomes a necessity. Cultural relevance requires understanding a group's values, customs, and aspirations and presenting products and promotions in light of these unique characteristics. For example, a depiction of a family reunion in an ad for a long-distance phone service directed to the Hispanic-American microculture would be considered highly apropos and effective. This appropriateness is due to the tendency of Hispanic Americans to care for their families and value familial relationships. Cultural relevance also means avoiding symbols, icons, holidays, and heroes that are often meaningless to members of the microculture. For example, using supermodels such as Niki Taylor and Molly Sims to advertise Cover Girl cosmetics is a plausible appeal when advertising to white America. For Hispanic and Asian Americans, the idea of a "cover girl" is unfamiliar. To members of these microcultures, a supermodel is simply just another pretty face.[76]

Interestingly, microcultures often exhibit different rituals than the macroculture. **Rituals** are sets of symbolic behaviors that occur in a fixed sequence and tend to be repeated periodically.[77] Rituals can be private or public and often reflect widely held cultural or religious values. For example, private rituals include bowing one's head for grace before meals or burning incense and making food offerings to the spirits or one's God. Public rituals, on the other hand, include such things as giving some Asian-American employees gifts during *Ochugen* and *Osebo* Japanese holiday seasons or fasting during the month of Ramadan for African-American Muslims. Ritual situations are important to marketers because specific products are bought and consumed within the context of these occasions.

rituals
sets of symbolic behaviors that occur in a fixed sequence and tend to be repeated periodically

In this chapter, we have seen that people's traditions, norms, and values comprise the cultural component of their external environment. Culture is simply people—how they live, what they think, and what they hold in esteem. Cultural norms and values affect consumer decision making, because they establish limits regarding what a society deems desirable or at least acceptable.

We have also observed that within diverse cultures, microcultures may exist that have their own distinguishing tastes and consumption patterns. Members of microcultures are frequently prime targets for products or promotions designed specifically with them in mind. In our society, the existence and rapid

A Cross-Functional Point of View

The topics of culture and microcultures have a number of implications for business disciplines other than marketing. Relevant issues might include

- **Communication/Linguistics:** In 2007, in a newsletter addressed to the staff, Rochester City School District Officials gave their approval for students and teachers to speak *ebonics* (the black English vernacular). The issue of using *ebonics* in schools dates back to 1997, when a firestorm of controversy arose in the media over a decision by the Oakland, California, school board to incorporate this dialect into the Oakland Public Schools' curriculum. As a consequence, African-American students in Oakland's classrooms were not penalized for violating the rules of standard English when they used double negatives ("Ain't nobody buyin' nothin',") or said such things as "She be at the store."

   Supporters of the resolution to incorporate ebonics into the curriculum include, among others, the Linguistics Society of America. This organization endorses the controversial decision, calling the plan "linguistically and pedagogically sound." Opponents of ebonics in the curriculum, on the other hand, fear that the movement would likely limit African-American students' ability to compete in school or the job market against those who master standard English.

- **Public Policy:** Our country's intensified efforts to force other countries to adopt our principles of free trade and our lifestyles and values can spell disaster for the future of our international relations. Many foreign countries are fed up with the U.S. efforts to invade their cultures through activities ranging from powerful rhetoric from the Treasury Department about the magic of the free marketplace, to cultural-shots from companies such as Walt Disney and Cable News Network. Protecting their national cultures could soon become a defensive rallying point for societies undergoing tumultuous change. Greater sensitivity to foreign values and ways of life would ease the prospect of backlash and would enhance our long-term ability to maintain amicable relationships with the rest of the world.

- **Politics/Research:** Unlike previous censuses, censuses since the year 2000 allow for multiple race categories. The increasing numbers of children born to people in mixed-race marriages fuel demands for means for people to identify themselves with more than one race category. For example, the 1990 census data for racial categories contained five cells: White; Black; American Indian, Eskimo, or Aleut; Asian or Pacific Islander; and Other. The corresponding table, for censuses since the year 2000 contains 64 race categories.

   Because census data are used for political redistricting plans to reapportion congressional seats, a major problem arises. Under section 2 of the Federal Voting Rights Act, to prove that a district is black or Hispanic, there must be enough minorities in that district to constitute a majority of voters. In attempting to establish a majority-black voting district, for example, it is unclear which count should be used: people who identify themselves as black; those who marked black and one other race; or those who marked black, regardless of how many other races they selected.

These issues, and a host of others like them, serve to show that the topics of culture and microcultures transcend the field of marketing to other business disciplines.

growth of such microcultures is anticipated to hold ramifications in many areas, including the composition of the labor force, social services and taxation, and the demand for culturally sensitive products and services.

As we have learned from this chapter and the previous ones, the study of consumer behavior integrates many fields of knowledge. It focuses on the behavioral, social, and cultural aspects involved in the process of satisfying human needs and wants. We also know that consumption-related activities extend across geographic boundaries, making the investigation of consumer behavior a necessary undertaking anywhere in the world. Equipped with this consumer knowledge, we as marketers hope to be able to use this information to serve our customers and society better.

Summary

Culture can be defined as a society's distinctive and learned mode of living, interacting, and responding to environmental stimuli. This response pattern is shared and transmitted between the members of a society. The process by which we learn the skills, norms, and values necessary to function as productive members of a society is referred to as socialization. Cultural learning occurs via living in a family environment, formal schooling, observing and imitating others, and simply by interacting with them. Within the U.S., the sharing of cultural norms and values is facilitated by a common language, schools, places of worship, and the mass media.

Culture includes both tangible and intangible elements. Whereas mechanical traits of a culture evolve rapidly, its ideological traits change more slowly. This unevenness in the pace of change can create cultural lag or friction among the components of society.

Ethnocentrism refers to the tendency to make cross-cultural evaluations on the basis of prereflective beliefs and values that are rooted in our own culture. To avoid this kind of bias, marketers and researchers of consumer behavior learn about different cultures via such techniques as ethnography, direct questioning, content analysis, and using key informants.

Five cultural dimensions help explain how and why people from various cultures behave as they do. These dimensions are power distance, uncertainty avoidance, individualism, masculinity, and term orientation. A set of 10 sociocultural dimensions offers a basis for comparing similarities and differences between cultures. These dimensions are communication and language, beliefs and attitudes, values and norms, sense of self and space, relationships, time and time consciousness, mental processes and learning, rewards and recognitions, dress and appearance, and food and eating habits.

Microcultures are smaller, more homogeneous subsets of people that exist within a larger, more diverse society. Within nations characterized by plurality and multiculturalism, researchers use a variety of criteria such as demographic, geographic, and lifestyle variables to delineate microcultures. Ethnicity, one popular basis for delineating microcultures, embraces such factors as the race, nationality, and religion that individuals belong to as well how strongly these individuals feel connected to their heritage. Three microcultures of particular importance to marketers today are African-, Hispanic-, and Asian-American consumers. Of course, these groups are very diverse in composition and may need to be segmented further.

In addition, microcultures can be delineated by distinguishing subgroups of society that share strong commitment to a particular product, brand, or activity.

Marketers stand to benefit from studying culture and microcultures because the beliefs, values, and attitudes held by people within a culture as well as the rituals they engage in can affect the products and services they buy and use. An understanding of both culture and microcultures is essential to develop sensitive and relevant marketing strategies.

Review Questions

1. Ethnocentrism is the tendency to make cross-cultural evaluations of others based on one's own views. What causes this tendency to arise, and what can be done to avoid or lessen it?

2. Researchers have developed a number of methods to assess culture. Explain these methods and comment on which would provide results quickly and economically.

3. Hofstede's five cultural dimensions help explain how and why people from various cultures behave as they do. Select two of these dimensions and discuss them from the point of view of their ramifications for consumption behavior.

4. One of the 10 sociocultural dimensions proposed by Harris and Moran on which culture can be analyzed is *values and norms*. How do values influence behavior? What is the relevance of *means–end chains* in learning about the relationship between values and behavior in a culture? Explain via an example.

5. Based on what you have learned from the discussion on microcultures in this chapter, compare and contrast the profiles of African- and Hispanic-American consumers. What cultural similarities or differences characterize these two microcultures?

Discussion Questions

1. U.S. executives who negotiate business with Japanese counterparts often remark that conducting business there can be frustrating. Decision making is slow and involves obtaining approval from almost everyone in an organization. Should Americans attempt to teach or impose on the Japanese executives our more efficient style of business negotiations? Why or why not?

2. Many American fast-food companies, such as McDonald's and Pizza Hut, are experiencing impressive success in foreign markets. This continues to be the case despite the fact that in some countries, such as Russia, a meal consisting of burgers, fries, and a Coke at a McDonald's restaurant may cost the consumer his or her wages for an entire day or two of work. What might prompt foreign consumers to buy these products? Do you believe this is a fad that will change over time?

3. Products come to mean different things to different people around the world. For example, Americans regard bicycles primarily as objects of leisure. To the Chinese, they are a key mode of transportation. Many Americans love to eat corn on the cob, whereas many Europeans believe that proper etiquette dictates serving corn that has already been removed from the cob. Beef and pork are staples of the American diet. In India, on the other hand, the cow is deemed sacred, and beef is never thought of as food. In much of the Middle East, the pig is considered an unclean animal, and pork is not served or consumed. Cite other examples of products that are perceived dissimilarly in different parts of the world.

In reference to the chapter opening vignette, assume that your company plans to expand operations into a number of countries across the European Union (EU), such as Germany, Spain, Greece, and the United Kingdom. Executives in your company realize that managerial styles must be adapted in each of these cultures according to the way employees respond to authority. Do you visualize any differences in managerial styles (authoritarian versus participatory) that your company should follow in each case? If so, form separate teams to compare and contrast appropriate managerial styles for each culture.

CASE

Diversity and Inclusion: Transcending Boundaries

During the months of May and June, 2008, Mr. Joe Carleo, Public Relations Society of America's (PRSA) chair of the Advanced Language and Media Services, along with PRSA's chief executive officer, Jeffrey Julin, held a number of meetings. These meetings included others in the organization, such as Manny Ruiz, PRSA's Diversity Committee co-chair and president of PR Newswire's Multi-Cultural Services, as well as other executives from Internet radio network WebmasterRadio.FM.

The purpose of these meetings was to place the final touches on the organization's diversity programs and to discuss the details of its planned launch on July 21, 2008. The program involved a new monthly podcast series, "PRSA's Diversity Today," which is designed to explore the many facets of diversity in America as they apply to business communicators. The program delves deeply into the ethical and economic value of diversity in today's dynamic business climate. The program features in-depth and frank discussions about diversity in the workplace and marketplace. These podcasts are designed to help professionals understand why a commitment to diversity is not just the right thing to do, but rather a wise action to take.

In planning the series, the committee envisioned a number of diversity-related topics that included:

- Men in public relations—an "endangered species"?
- Award-wining diversity programs from ERSA Chapters,
- Corporate best practices for your business or organization,
- An Alaskan lesson on what a "diverse-thinking society" is like, and
- Best practices for hiring and retaining a diverse workforce.

In order for the public to listen to the podcasts, the committee arranged for listeners to visit PRSA Diversity Today at www.prsa.org/diversity/communications.html. The programs were also planned to be posted on WebmasterRadio.FM on the PRSA Conference Channel. In addition, interested listeners can subscribe to the show via an RSS feed, or through iTunes, where they can download the product.

Applaudable efforts and programs such as these are often undertaken by progressive firms in today's marketplace. America's growing diversity has reached nearly every state, from South Carolina's budding immigrant population to the fast-rising number of Hispanics in Arkansas. Yet, in spite of these facts, problems still remain for minorities trying to assimilate into employment settings, as reflected in accounts of discomfort, alienation, and frustration experienced by some racial and ethnic minority employees.

Some of the issues covered by programs such as those from PRSA are aimed at revealing differences between *diversity* and *inclusion*. While *diversity* focuses on defining differences, *inclusion*, on the other hand, focuses on teaching people to value these differences. Many corporate executives confuse increases in the headcount among members of their workforce with evidence of a truly diverse culture. Diversity, however, is much more than merely a numbers game. True diversity requires an environment where differences are actually valued and appreciated by everybody in the organization. It is only through such a conviction that companies can claim success for their diversity program and attain the very concrete benefits of inclusion.

Questions

1. In view of the diversity that characterizes our society today, how do you explain the prejudicial treatment that some minorities still receive in the workplace?

2. What measures, programs, or actions do you recommend that companies take to reduce or eliminate incidents of discrimination based on ethnicity, race, and lifestyle?

3. Do you believe that programs such as those put forward by PRSA can be helpful in raising awareness of the diversity and inclusion issues in our society? Are they being directed to the right audiences? Why or why not?

Notes

1. Hedy Weiss, "The New Europe: What Europeans Think of Us—Fear and Fascination," *Chicago Sun-Times* (December 1, 1997), pp. 6–7; Hedy Weiss, "The New Europe: Nationalism—New Dangers, Old Dreams," *Chicago Sun-Times* (December 3, 1997), pp. 6–7; Hedy Weiss, "The New Europe: Prospects for a United Europe—Paying the Price of Unity," *Chicago Sun-Times* (December 4, 1997), pp. 6–7; and Jeffrey E. Garten "'Cultural Imperialism' Is No Joke," *Business Week* (November 30, 1998), p. 26.

2. Nessim Hanna and Tanuja Srivastava, "Cultural Aspects of Gift Giving: A Comparative Analysis of the Significance of Gift Giving in the U.S. and Japan," in Samsinar Sidin and Ajay K. Manrai (eds.), *Proceedings of the Eighth Biennial World Marketing Congress* VIII (Kuala Lampur, Malaysia: Academy of Marketing Science, 1997), pp. 269–73.

3. Barbara Applebaum, "Moral Paralysis and the Ethnocentric Fallacy," *Journal of Moral Education* 25, no. 2 (June 1996), pp. 185–200.

4. D. M. Gollnick and P. C. Chin, *Multicultural Education in a Pluralistic Society* (Columbus, OH: Merrill Publishing, 1986).

5. B. R. Schlender, "What Rice Means to the Japanese," *Fortune* (November 1, 1993), pp. 150–56; and "Going Against the Grain in Japan," *The Economist* (April 23, 1994), p. 34.

6. Alison S. Wellner, "The New Science of Focus Groups," *American Demographics* (March 2003), pp. 29–33.

7. Geert Hofstede, *Culture's Consequences: International Differences in World Related Values* (Beverly Hills, CA: Sage, 1980).

8. Ibid.

9. Ibid.

10. Geert Hofstede, *Cultures and Organizations* (London: McGraw-Hill, 1991).

11. Philip R. Harris and Robert T. Moran, *Managing Cultural Differences* (Houston, TX: Gulf, 1985), pp. 58–61.

12. E. J. Hall, *The Silent Language* (New York: Doubleday, 1959).

13. "Some Humorous Cross-Cultural Advertising Gaffes," *Taking On Tobacco*, www.takingontobacco.org/intro/funny.html.

14. David Aviel, "Cultural Barriers to International Transactions," *Journal of General Management* 15, no. 4 (Summer 1990), pp. 5–20.

15. Vern Terpstra, *The Cultural Environment of International Business* (Cincinnati, OH: South-Western, 1978), p. xii.

16. Olivia Wu, "Believers in Harmony with Old Chinese Practice," *Chicago Sun-Times* (February 14, 1996), p. 22; E. S. Browning, "When Fung Shui Speaks, Business Listens," *International Wildlife* 14

(September–October 1984), pp. 36–37; Patricia Corrigan, "Living in Harmony with Feng Shui," *Chicago Sun-Times* (November 10, 1996), p. 12CW.

17. G. Brooks, "Riddle of Riyadh: Islamic Law Thrives Amid Modernity," *Wall Street Journal* (November 9, 1989), p. 1.

18. T. Hofstede et al., "An Investigation into the Association Pattern Technique as a Quantitative Approach to Measuring Means–End Chains," *International Journal of Research in Marketing* 15, no. 1 (February 1998), pp. 37–50; and Jonathan Gutman, "Means–End Chains as Goal Hierarchies" *Psychology & Marketing* 14, no. 6 (September 1997), pp. 545–60.

19. A. Birenbaum and E. Sagarin, *Norms and Human Behavior* (New York: Praeger, 1976).

20. "The Difference That Japanese Management Makes," *Business Week* (July 14, 1986), pp. 47–50.

21. Endel-Jakob Kolde, *Environment of International Business*, 2nd ed. (Boston: Kent, 1985), p. 423.

22. G. E. Popp, H. J. Davis, and T. T. Herbert, "An International Study of Intrinsic Motivation Composition," *Management International Review* 26, no. 3 (1986), p. 31.

23. John W. Schouten and James H. McAlexander, "Subcultures of Consumption: An Ethnography of New Bikers," *Journal of Consumer Research* 22 (June 1995), pp. 43–61.

24. Rohit Deshpandi, Wayne D. Hoyer, and Naveen Donthu, "The Intensity of Ethnic Affliation: A Study of the sociology of Hispanic Consumptic," *Journal of Consumer Research* 13 (September 1986), pp. 214–19.

25. Elizabeth C. Hirschman, "An Examination of Ethnicity and Consumption Using Free Response Data," in *Proceedings of the Educators' Conference* (Chicago: American Marketing Association, 1982), pp. 84–88.

26. Damell Little, "Minorities Will Be in Majority," *Chicago Tribune* (August 14, 2008), www.chicagotribune.com/news/nationworld/chi-censusaug14,0,2584897.story.

27. "Projection of Total Black Buying Power by State, 2004," Selig Center (2005), http://nbbta.org/buyingpower.htm.

28. "Black History Month: February 2008, Facts for Features," U.S. Census Bureau, www.census.gov/Press-Release/www/releases/archives/population/010048.html; www.census.gov/Press-Release/www/releases/archives/income_wealth/010583.html; www.census.gov/Press-Release/www/releases/archives/income_wealth/012528.html; www.census.gov/Press-Release/www/releases/archives/facts_for_features_special_edition.

29. Ibid.

30. Brad Edmondson, "Minority Markets Take the Lead," *Forecast* (August 1997).

31. www.census.gov/Press-Release/www/releases/archives/facts_for_features_special_edition.

32. Christy Fisher, "Black, Hip, and Primed (to Shop)." *American Demographics* (September 1996), pp. 52–58.

33. MapInfo: American Demographics Analysis of 2000 Consumer Expenditure Survey, Bureau of Labor Statistics.

34. Fisher, "Black, Hip, and Primed (to Shop)."

35. Ibid.

36. John Robinson, Bart Landry, and Ronica Rooks, "Time and the Melting Pot," *American Demographics* (June 1998); "Inside the Middle Class: Bad Times Hit the Good Life," *Pew Research Center* (April 9, 2008), http://pewsocialtrends.org/pubs/706/middle-class-poll; "Pew Internet & American Life Project: Demographics of Internet Users," *Pew Research Center* (April 8–May 11, 2008), www.pewinternet.org/trends/User_Demo_7.22.08.htm.

37. H. Schlossberg, "Many Marketers Still Consider Blacks 'Dark-skinned' Whites," *Marketing News* (January 19, 1993), p. 1; Marie Spadoni, "Marketing to Blacks—How Media Segment the Target Audience," *Advertising Age* 19 (November 1984), p. 43.

38. "The Difference in Black and White," *American Demographics* (January 1993), p. 49.

39. Jon Berry, "6 Myths About Black Consumer," *Adweek's Marketing Week* 32 (May 6, 1991), pp. 16–19.

40. *The 1993 Minority Market Report* (Coral Gables, FL: Market Segment Research, Inc. 1993).

41. "Mining the Non-White Markets," *Brandweek* (April 12, 1993), p. 29.

42. "Buying Black," *Time* (August 31, 1992), p. 52.

43. "African American Magazines," Yahoo Directory, http://dir.yahoo.com/Regional/Countries/United_States/Society_and_Culture/Cultures_and_Groups/Cultures/American.

44. Dan Fost, "Reaching the Hip-Hop Generation," *American Demographics* (May 1993), pp. 15–16; Carrie Goerne, "Retailers Boost Efforts to Target African-American Consumers," *Marketing News* (June 22, 1992), p. 2.

45. Rachel Sams, "Banks, Brokerage Firms Target African-American Investors (November 18, 2005), *Baltimore Business Journal*, http://baltimore.bizjournals.com/baltimore/stories/2005/11/21/focus3.html.

46. Ibid.

47. Roberto Suro, "Recasting the Melting Pot," *American Demographics* (March 1999), pp. 30–32.

48. Bureau of the Census, U.S. Dept. of Commerce, "Population by Sex, Race, Residence, and Median Age 2002; "Hispanics Next Major Minority," *Chicago Sun-Times* (January 22, 2003), p. 6.

49. Emily Bazar, "Strict Immigration Law Rattles Okla Businesses," *USA Today* (January 10, 2008), www.

usatoday.com/news/nation/2008-01-09
-immigcover_N.htm; Ismael Estrada, "Oklahoma Targets Illegal Immigrants with Tough New Law," *CNN* (November 5, 2007), www.cnn/2007/US/11/02/oklahoma.immigration/.

50. Geoffrey Paulin, "A Growing Market: Expenditure by Hispanic Consumers," *Monthly Labor Review* 121 (March 1, 1998), p. 3.

51. Helene Stapinski, "Generation Latino," American Demographics (July 1999), pp. 62-68; and Bureau of the Census, "Population by Sex, Race, Residence, and Median Age 1970-2002."

52. Exito Latino, "First Career Guide Especially for Latinos," America Online, HAYMO (March 9, 1999), p. 1.

53. "U.S. Hispanic Market," Pan-American Life Insurance Company (2008), www.panamericanlife.com/ushispanic/facts.aspx.

54. Kylee Hall, "The Hispanic Consumer's Shopping List," *A.C. Nielsen Consumer Insight* (Summer 2006), http://us.nielsen.com/pubs/documents/ci_q2_06_000.pdf; "U.S. Hispanic Trends: The Basics and More," The Coca-Cola Company, www.heritageupdates.com/Hispanic/Hispanic/%20Basics%20v1.ppt#567,16,summary.

55. "U.S. Hispanic Use of Telecommunication Services 2006-2011," Insight Research Corporation, www.insight-corp.com/reports/ethnic06.asp.

56. "U.S. Hispanic Trends: The Basics and More," The Coca-Cola Company, www.heritageupdates.com/Hispanic/Hispanic/%20Basics%20v1.ppt#567,16,summary.

57. S. Livingston, "Marketing to the Hispanic-American Community," *Journal of Business Strategy* (March-April 1992), pp. 54-57.

58. "Hispanics Online: Demographics," eMarketer (2007), www.emarketer.com/Report.aspx?code=emarketer_2000514.

59. Ibid.

60. "Tuyo Mobile Launches New Holiday Promotion," *VoIP Monitor* (November 29, 2006), www.voipmonitor.net/2006/11/29/T%C3%BAyo+Mobile+Launches+New+Holiday+Promotion.

61. U.S. Census Bureau News, "Minority Population Tops 100 Million" (May 17, 2007), www.census.gov/Press-Release/www/releases/archives/population/

010048.html; "4 Important Statistics about Asian Americans," *Asian-Nation* (2008), www.asian-nation.org/14-statistics.shtml.

62. "Asian/Pacific American Heritage Month: May 2007 by the U.S. Census Bureau," *IM Diversity* (May 2007), www.imdiversity.com/villages/asian/reference/census_asian_pacific_american_heritage.

63. Brad Edmondson, "Asian Americans in 2001," *American Demographics* (February 1997), pp. 16-17.

64. Ibid., IM Diversity.

65. "Diversity in America," *Supplement to American Demographics* (November 2002), pp. S8-S10.

66. Miriam Muley, "Diversity and Direct Selling: How Much Money Are You Leaving on the Table?" *Direct Selling News* (September 4, 2008), www.directsellingnews.com/article_app.php?articleid=86.

67. Donald Dougherty, "The Orient Express," *The Marketer* (July-August 1990), p. 14.

68. Dan Fost, "California's Asian Market," *American Demographics* 12 (October 1990), p. 34-37.

69. "Taking the Pulse of Asian-Americans," *Adweek's Marketing Week* (August 12, 1991), p. 32.

70. Marty Westerman, "Fare East: Targeting the Asian-American Market," *Prepared Foods* (January 1989), pp. 48-51.

71. Dougherty, "The Orient Express."

72. Ibid.

73. Carol Kaufman-Scarborough, "Asian-American Consumers as a Unique Market Segment: Fact or Fallacy?" *Journal of Consumer Marketing* 17, nos. 2-3, (2000), pp. 249-260.

74. Hassan Fattah, "Asia Rising," *American Demographics* (July/August 2002), pp. 39-43.

75. Donald A. DePalma, "Multicultural Web Marketing," *Target Marketing* 23, no. 12 (December 2000), pp. 46-49.

76. Shelly Reese, "Cultural Shock: When It Comes to Marketing to Ethnic Populations, What You Don't Know Can Hurt You," *Marketing Tools* 5 (May 1, 1998), p. 44.

77. B. Gainer, "Ritual and Relationships," *Journal of Business Research* (March 1995), pp. 253-60; and C. Otnes and L. M. Scott, "Something Old, Something New," *Journal of Advertising* (Spring 1996), pp. 35-50.

Glossary

absolute (lower) threshold the lowest intensity level at which an individual can detect a stimulus

acculturation the process of learning the norms, values, and behaviors of a different culture

acquired needs drives that are conditioned by relationships with others in the environment

adaptation an indifference to a stimulus to which an individual has become overly accustomed

adoption the decision-making stages an individual goes through before accepting a product

affective component an individual's positive or negative reaction to an attitude object

agents of change parties who actively seek to modify other people's beliefs, attitudes, or behavior

AIO inventories questionnaires that reveal consumers' activities, interests, and opinions in order to create psychographic profiles

anticipatory aspirational reference groups groups a person has reasonable expectations of joining in the future

approach–approach conflict a situation in which a person faces a choice among two desirable alternatives

approach–avoidance conflict a situation in which a person must surrender resources to gain a desirable outcome

arousal a tension state resulting mainly from unfilled needs

aspirational reference groups groups in which a person seeks membership but lacks the qualifications to join

attention the allocation of an individual's mental capacity to a stimulus or task

attitude change a shift in the valence of an attitude from negative to positive or vice versa

attitude object anything about which consumers can form an attitude

attitude toward-the-object an individual's overall appraisal (like or dislike) of an attitude object

attitudes learned predispositions to respond in a consistent manner to a given object

attitude-toward-the-behavior one's overall appraisal of an act based on its consequences and one's evaluation of these outcomes

attribution efforts to ascertain the causes of events in our lives

availability-valence hypothesis a view that vivid information tends to be stored in memory with more links to other concepts

avoidance–avoidance conflict a situation in which a person faces a choice between two undesirable alternatives

basic needs essential needs that include physiological, safety, social, esteem, and self-actualization needs

behavior shaping the process of breaking down a complex behavior into a series of simple stages and reinforcing the learner at each step

behavioral (conative) component a person's action tendency or intentions with respect to an attitude object

behavioral segmentation a partitioning of the market based on attitudes toward or reaction to a product

bonding the connecting of a consumer and a product through an emotional tie

boomerang children grown children—now adults—who continue to live in or return to their parents' home

Boomers I cohort individuals born 1946 to 1954

Boomers II cohort individuals born between 1955 and 1965

brand equity the added value a brand name brings to a product beyond its functional worth

brand loyalty a consumer's consistent purchase of a specific brand within a product category

brand parity a situation where many consumers come to believe that no significant differences exist among brands

brand reps consumers who promote brands or companies publicly and among friends

brand-specific goals particular alternatives in a product category from which consumers can choose

cartoon a test where respondents provide missing dialogue in a situational drawing

central route to persuasion a view that under high involvement, consumers diligently process information provided in messages

centrality the extent of how closely an attitude reflects a person's core values and beliefs

chain word associations association tests in which subjects respond with a series of four or five words

chunk an organized grouping of data inputs

classical conditioning a view that learning involves linking a conditioned stimulus and an unconditioned stimulus

classical identification the case where one accepts influence in order to establish or maintain one's self-image within a group

closure the tendency to perceive complete structures even though some parts are missing

coercive power an influence based on a group's ability to administer punishments

cognitive component what a person thinks he or she knows about an attitude object

cognitive consistency a view that we strive to maintain congruity between beliefs, emotions, and behavior

cognitive dissonance theory a view that inconsistency between a person's beliefs and behavior causes psychological tension

cognitive learning a view that humans are goal-oriented, problem solvers and processors of information

cohort an aggregate of people who have undergone similar experiences and share common memories

compatibility the perceived property of a new product as being consistent with consumers' beliefs, values, experiences, and habits

compensatory decision rule a selection procedure where a high score on one attribute of a brand can make up for a low score on another

compliance the act of going along with a group to obtain approval

compliance-aggressiveness-detachment (CAD) scale a paradigm that classifies people based on how compliant, aggressive, and detached they are

composite-variable indexes objective measures of social class that combine several socioeconomic factors

concentration strategy a marketing effort that focuses on a single market segment

confirmation a stage where an adopter experiences postpurchase doubt and seeks reassurance for the decision made

conformity the change in individuals' beliefs, attitudes, or actions as a result of group pressure

congruity the relatedness of sequentially presented informational cues

conspicuous consumption the acquisition and exhibition of extravagant luxuries to portray one's ability to afford them

constructive processing a tendency of consumers to tailor their cognitive effort to suit the task at hand

consumer behavior the study of how consumers select, purchase, use, and dispose of goods and services to satisfy personal needs and wants

consumer panels groups of research participants who provide purchase and consumption data over time

consumer research systematic methods used by marketers to study consumer decisions and exchange processes

consumer satisfaction the mental state of feeling adequately rewarded in a buying situation

consumer socialization the process by which consumers acquire knowledge, skills, and attitudes relevant to the marketplace

content analysis the study of culture by reviewing its media or literature

context the setting in which a stimulus occurs affects how it is perceived

contiguity the spacial or temporal nearness of objects

contingency the notion that the conditioned stimulus should precede the unconditioned stimulus

continuous innovations new products that require minimal, if any, adjustments in consumption routines

continuous reinforcement a reinforcement schedule that rewards a desired behavior every time it occurs

controlled word associations word associations where respondents reply with a specified type of word

craft ethics ethical relativism whereby managers learn what their profession mandates in a situation and follow that mandate

cultural lag the time delay between the introduction of innovations and their acceptance

culture a society's distinctive and learned mode of living, interacting, and responding to environmental stimuli

customization strategy a personalized marketing effort to suit individual customer's needs

data mining the computer software that sifts through mounds of data to find meaningful relationships

database marketing the gathering, analyzing, and finding of specific information about propects

decision a stage where a prospect makes a choice to either adopt or reject an innovation

decision rules alternative analytical procedures consumers use to process information and arrive at a selection

defense mechanisms the tendency to protect our ego by denying and distorting anxiety-producing situations

demographic segmentation a partitioning of the market based on factors such as age, gender, income, occupation, education, and ethnicity

desires passions that involve longing, yearning, and fervently wishing for something

determinant attributes those features on which alternatives are believed to differ

differential threshold or just noticeable difference (JND) the smallest increment in the intensity of a stimulus that a person can detect

diffusion the spread of a new product or idea within the marketplace

direct questioning the study of culture through research questionnaires

direction an end toward which behavior is prompted

disclaimant reference groups groups to which a person previously belonged, but whose values one later rejects

discontinuous innovations unique products that significantly alter established consumption routines

divisibility the perceived property that a new product can be sampled in small quantities

dynamically continuous innovations new products that do not strikingly alter consumers' established usage patterns

early adopters the second tier of consumers (after the innovators) to adoptan innovation

early majority the third tier of consumers to adopt an innovation

ecological design the planning of physical space and other facets of the environment to modify human behavior

e-fluentials Internet users who influence other consumers online

egalitarianism a principle that advocates that all people are equal

ego a personality component that balances the id's hedonistic impulses and the superego's constraints

ego-defensive function the notion that some attitudes serve to protect an individual's ego or disguise a person's inadequacies

elaboration-likelihood model (ELM) a view that consumers' level of involvement determines the appropriate route to persuasion

emotion a feeling state such as joy or sorrow

emotional motives those aroused by stressing sentiments, fantasies, and feelings

enacted role the overt behavior displayed by an individual in a particular situation

encoding the process of employing symbols such as words or images to store a perceived idea

enculturation the process of indoctrinating youth with society's norms and values

ethical absolutism an ethical framework that assumes there is one true ethical or moral code

ethical relativism an ethical framework that recognizes the diversity of value systems and the moral consequences of an act

ethnocentrism the tendency to make cross-cultural evaluations based on one's own beliefs and values

ethnography the study of culture by unobtrusive observation

evaluative criteria product characteristics consumers use to judge the merits of competing options

evoked set those few brands that come to mind when one thinks of a product category

experiments investigations that manipulate one or more casual variables to measure the effect on one or more dependent variables

expert power an influence based on a person's regard for an agent's knowledge or skill

exposure the act of deliberately or accidentally coming into contact with environmental stimuli

expressive performance social or psychological aspects of product performance that consumers regard as ends in themselves

extended problem solving an elevated level of expended effort used in making risky and significant decisions

extended-self the self defined in terms of an individual's possessions

external search the process of seeking information from exogenous sources

extrinsic motivation behavior undertaken in order to acquire rewards

family two or more persons, related either through birth, marriage or adoption, living under one roof

family life cycle the sequence of stages that families tend to pass through

figure and ground objects are perceived in relation to their background

fixation a halt in personality progress at a particular developmental stage

focus groups sessions where 8 to 12 people—led by a moderator—freely discuss a topic

formal groups highly organized groups with an explicit structure and specified goals and procedures

framing a view that a given decision can be structured from either a gain or a loss perspective

fraudulent symbols formerly unique goods that become common and lose their exclusive meaning

free word associations a test where respondents reply to each given word with the first word that comes to mind

frequency of purchase the rate at which consumers purchase a product after the initial purchase

general sensation-seeking scale (GSSS) a scale designed to measure individual differences in sensation–seeking tendencies

Generation X cohort individuals born between 1965 and 1976

Generation Y cohort individuals born between 1977 and 1994

Generation Z cohort individuals born between 1995 and 2008

generational marketing the cataloging of generations in terms of external events that occurred during their members' formative years

generic goals nonspecific categories of products and services that can satisfy customer needs

geodemographic segmentation a partitioning of the market by considering data on neighborhoods, zip codes, or census tracts

geographic segmentation a partitioning of the market based on climate, location, surroundings, and terrain

gestalt a view that people perceive cohesive wholes and formulate total impressions

global village the increasingly interdependent global economic environment

goal the sought-after objective of motivated behavior

goals pursuits where an individual thinks impediments stand in they way of attaining a desired objective

green marketing advocating the environmental soundness of products and packaging

group people who share beliefs, have role relationships, and experience interdependent behavior

grouping the tendency to perceive data chunks rather than separate units

hemispheric specialization of the brain a view that the left and right hemispheres of the brain process, organize, and encode information differently

heuristics simple rules of thumb consumers use as shortcuts to reduce shopping effort

high involvement a case in which consumers attach elevated relevanceto a purchase

high sensation seekers (HSS) persons with stronger-than-average need to seek novel, surprising, and more intense activities

high-involvement learning a case where individuals are motivated to process information to be learned

homeostasis a self-regulating mechanism of the body that maintains harmony of all bodily systems

hypodermic needle model a view that the media have an immediate, direct, forceful impact on a mass audience

id a personality component that demands pleasure and immediate gratification

image a person's view of what a company, product, brand, or store is

image barrier a condition where a product or brand is unknown by the public or suffers from an unfavorable image

imagery the way consumers visualize sensory information in working memory

implementation a stage where a person acts on his or her decision to adopt

impulse purchases spontaneous and unplanned purchases made in response to environmental cues

individual factors the qualities of people that influence their interpretation of an impulse

individualism a tendency of people to look after themselves and their immediate family only

inertia a pattern of repeatedly buying a particular brand merely because it is familiar

informal groups groups in which structure, goals, and procedures are less explicit

information retrieval the process of sifting through memory to activate previously stored information

information-processing approach an effort to provide facts to help consumers reach a logical conclusion

innovators the first 2.5 percent of the market to adopt a new product

instincts genetically transmitted physical and behavioral characteristics of a species that enable it to survive in the environment

instrumental motives learned, social patterns of behavior that are solicited in the service of a basic need

instrumental performance consumers' view of the utilitarian performance of the physical product as a means to an end

intensity the extent of how strongly an individual feels one way or the other about an attitude object

intention one's subjective resolution to behave in a certain way toward an attitude object

intermittent reinforcement a reinforcement schedule that rewards a desired behavior only occasionally

internal search search the process of retrieving relevant information from memory

internalization an influence that occurs when individuals accept group norms and values as their own

intrinsic motivation behavior undertaken for the inherent pleasure of the activity itself

involvement the degree of personal relevance that a purchase holds for the consumer

key informant method using knowledgeable persons to identify opinion leaders in a group

key informants individuals who are knowledgeable about a culture of interest

knowledge a state of being exposed to and aware of an innovation's existence

knowledge function the notion that some attitudes provide people with a simple, predictable, and organized view of the environment

knowledge structures formations of related bits of information

laggards the fifth and last tier of consumers to adopt an innovation

latchkey kids children who return home from school to a locked and empty home

late majority the fourth tier of consumers to adopt an innovation

learning process by which changes occur in the content or organization of a person's long-term memory

learning curve (experience effect) the notion that tasks become easier as the number of repetitions increases

left hemisphere the area of the brain that specializes in analytical thinking, verbalization, and algebraic calculations

legitimate power an influence that occurs as a result of individuals' feelings of obligation

leveling a process in which details are omitted in order to simplify the memory structure

limited problem solving a reduced level of expended effort used in making less-risky decisions

long-term memory (LTM) the information warehouse in which data are organized and extendedly stored

low involvement a case in which consumers attach minimal personal relevance to a purchase

low sensation seekers (LSS) persons who prefer less-thrilling activities

low-involvement learning a case where individuals are less motivated to attend to and process material to be learned

market maven person who actively transmits marketplace information

market profile a portrait of the various market segments and competitors' positions in them relative to a specific product

market segmentation the act of dissecting the marketplace into submarkets that require different marketing mixes

market targeting the process of reviewing market segments and deciding which one(s) to pursue

marketing concept an operating philosophy in which the consumer is the focus of all company activities

masculinity the degree to which dominant values are success, money, and things

mass customization combining technology and customer information to tailor products and services to the specific needs of each customer.

massed (concentrated) practice lengthy learning sessions scheduled over a brief time period

mass-market strategy a philosophy that presumes consumers are uniform and that broad-appeal products and marketing programs suffice

means–end chains depictions of linkages between product attributes, use consequences, and consumer values

memership reference groups groups to which a person currently belongs or qualifies for membership

microcultures smaller, more homogeneous subsets of people within a larger culture

microcultures of consumption distinguishable subgroups of society that share a strong commitment to a product, brand, or activity

misinformation effect a case where false assertions taint a person's recall of what really occurred

mnemonic devices auditory or visual aids that promote retention of material by identifying it with easily remembered symbols

mobility the movement upward and downward in the socioeconomic hierarchy

mood an individual's current frame of mind

moral anxiety the fear of feeling shame and guilt

motivation a state in which our energy is mobilized and directed in a selective fashion toward desirable goals

motivation research the study of the why aspects of consumer behavior

motivational conflict situations in which multiple needs simultaneously act on an individual

motive a state of tension that pushes an individual to act

multi-attribute model a view that attitude objects have a number of desirable or undesirable features that differ in importance to the same individual

multisegment strategy a view that the market consists of multiple segments, and each requires its own marketing mix

multistep model a view that mass-media messages reach both opinion leaders and followers who then share that information with others

needs internal forces that prompt behavior toward goal-oriented solutions

negative reference groups groups with which individuals wish to avoid association or identification

negative reinforcement an inducement to repeat a behavior in order to remove an adverse situation

neo-Freudian theory a view that social variables rather than biological instincts and sexual drives underlie personality formation

neo-Pavlovian conditioning a view that reshapes traditional classical conditioning into a fully cognitive theory

neurotic anxiety the fear of the negative consequences of instinctual gratification

noncompensatory decision rule a selection procedure where a high score on one attribute of a brand cannot offset a low score on another

nonproductive reach the effort wasted on contracting consumers who are unlikely prospects

nonprogrammed decision a case in which a novel or infrequently encountered situation requires a customized solution

norms a society's shared guidelines regarding appropriate behavior

objective measures a method that applies relevant demographic and socioeconomic criteria to determine social class membership

objective method a technique that involves creating opinion leaders

observability the perceived property that an innovation is visible and communicable to potential adopters

operant (instrumental) conditioning a view that learning is driven by the positive or negative consequences of behavior

opinion leaders knowledgeable, influential persons who casually provide advice

opinion leadership an agent's ability to informally incline the beliefs, attitudes, or behaviors of others

optimal stimulation level (OSL) a measurement of people's tendency to seek or avoid thrilling, challenging activities

overprivileged households whose incomes exceed the median for their social class

parody display a case in which a person pursues status by snubbing it

perceived role an individual's perceived obligations

perception the process of selecting, organizing, and interpreting sensations into a meaningful whole

perceptual categorization the tendency to group somewhat similar objects together

perceptual defense a tendency to block threatening or contradictory stimuli from extensive conscious processing

perceptual inferences beliefs based on prior experience that a person assigns to products or stores

perceptual map n-dimensional depiction that provides a visual profile of a number of brands for comparison purposes

perceptual overloading the inability to perceive all the stimuli that compete for an individual's attention at a given moment

perceptual vigilance an individual's ability to disregard much of the stimulation one receives through the senses

peripheral route to persuasion a view that under low involvement, consumers are less likely to process information provided in messages

personal influence any change in beliefs, attitudes, or behavior due to interpersonal communication

personality the sum total of an individual's inner psychological attributes

personality tests paper-and-pencil questionnaires designed to measure personality traits

personalization making a product personal to the consumer. This concept is related to customization.

persuasion a stage where a prospect formulates a favorable or unfavorable attitude toward an innovation

physiological needs basic bodily requirements essential to maintain life

picture-sorting techniques tests where respondents sort a stack of pictures to reveal stereotypes

positioning establishing a differentiating image for a product or service in relation to that of the competition

positive reinforcement an inducement to repeat a behavior to receive a pleasant consequence

possible-self the self a person would like to or could become

postpurchase dissonance a state of doubting the wisdom of one's choice after making a purchase

Postwar cohort individuals born 1928 to 1945

power distance the degree to which society's members accept unequal power distribution

prescribed role the set of expectations held by others as to what modes of behavior should be displayed by an individual in a situation

primary data information or statistics originated by the researcher for the purpose of the investigation at hand

primary groups small, intimate groups that meet regularly and communicate face-to-face

proactive interference a case where prior learning interferes with recall of recently learned material

product placement display of branded merchandise in movie scenes or TV shows

programmed decisions cases where consumers follow habitual routines to deal with frequently encountered situations

projective techniques the psychological techniques that reveal the real reasons behind consumption behaviors

prospect theory a view of how decision makers, under risk conditions, value different options and assess their outcomes

proximity the tendency to assume relatedness due to spatial or temporal nearness

psychographic segmentation a partitioning of the market based on lifestyle and personality characteristics

psychographics a segmentation approach that classifies consumers based on their lifestyle

rate of adoption the relative speed with which consumers adopt an innovation

rational motives those aroused through appeals to reason and logic

reactance a situation in which one resists pressure to conform and behaves independently

reality (objective) anxiety jective) anxiety the fear of tangible danger in the real world

reciprocal identification the case where a person accepts influence due to playing a complementary role with another individual

reference groups groups that provide a perspective for evaluating or patterning one's own behavior

referent power an influence based on a person's desire to identify with an admired group

reinforcement schedule the pattern in which reinforcements are given

relative advantage the perceived property of a new product as better than its dated substitutes

repositioning modifying a brand, redirecting it, or stressing different features to boost sales

reputational measures ways of determining social class based on individuals' ranking of others in a society

retroactive interference a case where recent learning interferes with recall of previously learned material

reward power an influence based on a group's ability to dispense rewards

right hemisphere the area of the brain that specializes in interpreting and recognizing visual patterns

risk barrier a condition where uncertainty lingers about adopting an innovation

rituals sets of symbolic behaviors that occur in a fixed sequence and tend to be repeated periodically

role-related product cluster the set of goods necessary for a person to play a given role competently

role-relaxed consumers consumers who buy rationally and crave good value

roles patterns of behavior performed by individuals within a given social context

rototype matching the tendency to compare brands in a product category to the category's leading brand

salient attributes important aspects of a product that affect the choices consumers make

sandwich generation parents who simultaneously support both their kids and their elderly parents

schema a structure for understanding and interpreting new information

script the knowledge about procedures to follow in recurring situations

secondary data information or statistics not gathered for the immediate study at hand

secondary groups groups in which regular, face-to-face contact is lacking

selective attention a tendency of individuals to heed information that interests them and to avoid information that is irrelevant

selective exposure a tendency of people to ignore media and ads that address topics that are unimportant to them

selective interpretation the act of combining relevant knowledge structures with expectations and intentions to derive meaning from a stimulus

selective sensitization a tendency to perceive more readily information that is consistent with one's needs and beliefs

self-concept the overall image that a person holds of him or herself

self-designation method a technique to profile opinion leaders in large, dispersed groups

self-product congruence a tendency to select products that march some aspects of the self

sensation the responses of a person's sensory receptors to environmental stimuli and transmission of this information to the brain via the nervous system

sensory memory a storage system in which incoming data undergo preliminary processing

sentence completions association tests where respondents complete sentences with the first phrase that comes to mind

sharpening a process of changing stimuli from ambiguous forms to more conventional ones

shopping list technique a test where respondents surmise the type of person who buys items on a list

shopping pals other persons who accompany a consumer on a shopping trip

short-term memory (STM) a storage system in which an individual briefly holds a limited amount of information

simplicity the perceived property that an innovation is easy to understand, assemble, and operate

single-variable indexes objective measures of social class that employ one socioeconomic factor

situational self-image the physical and mental state a person is experiencing at a specific moment in time

situational variables environmental circumstances that constitute the context within which transactions occur

social class a societal rank assigned to large groups of people

social comparison individuals' tendency to self-evaluate by noting the conduct of others in a group

socialization the process by which individuals develop patterns of socially relevant behavior

sociogram a diagram that maps out the communication network in a group

sociometric method a technique to identify opinion leaders in small groups

spaced (distributed) practice brief learning sessions intermingled with rest periods scheduled over a lengthy time period

S-shaped diffusion curve a pattern of market acceptance for an innovation that begins with a slow start, followed by more rapid acceptance, and then a slowdown

status the relative position a person occupies along a group's social continuum

status crystallization the coincidence of the different indicators of an individual's social stature

stealth wealth a case where a person avoids showing off one's product acquisitions

stimulus discrimination the tendency to distinguish between, and respond differently to, similar—but nonidentical—stimuli

stimulus factors the physical characteristics of an object that produce physiological impulses in an individual

stimulus generalization the tendency to assign commonality to similar stimuli

stratification a system of classifying members of a population based on economic and social characteristics

subjective experience the notion that humans synthesize beliefs and experiences to gain insight into new situations

subjective measures ways of determining social class membership based on individuals' classification of themselves

subjective norms one's beliefs about what significant others think and inclinations to comply with their views

superego the social, moral, and ethical component of personality

surrogate consumer agents a consumer retains to guide, direct, or execute transactions

surrogate indicators the cues that consumers rely on to place products into categories

symbolic aspirational reference groups groups in which one's chances of gaining membership are remote at best

symbolic innovations cases where a product conveys new social or psychological meanings

symbolic self-completion a tendency to complement self by displaying symbols associated with one's identity

synethesia fusing together of the human senses

teaser campaigns promotions that drop bits of information while withholding the particulars

Techno-savvies electronically sophisticated consumers

telecommuting an arrangement whereby employees work at home using PCs, modems, faxes, and other communications equipment

terminal (upper) threshold the point beyond which further increases in the intensity of a stimulus produce no greater sensation

test markets evaluating a product or strategy in limited geographic areas

testimonials ads that depict a celebrity or expert who endorses a brand

Thematic Apperception Test (TAT) a test where respondents interpret an ambiguous situation

theory of reasoned action (TORA) a view that attitude toward the behavior, intentions, and subjective norms determine behavior

tradition barrier a condition where cultural norms and values hamper product adoption

traditional model of attitudes a view that attitudes consist of three components: cognitive, affective, and behavioral

trait theory a view that classifies people according to their predominant response patterns

traits relatively permanent and consistent response patterns that characterize individuals

trialability the perceived property that a new product can be experienced before purchase

trickle-across model a view that influence flows horizontally among peers

Trickle-Down Model a view that influence flows from celebrities and elite influentials to emulating recipients (the general public)

trickle-up model a view that influence flows upward from usual recipient emulators to the general public as well as to celebrities and elite influentials

two-step model a view that it is opinion leaders who receive messages first from the mass media and then pass them on to others

uncertainty avoidance the degree to which people feel threatened by ambiguity and uncertainty

underprivileged households whose incomes are below the median for their social class

undifferentiated strategy a view that the market is a single large domain and that one marketing mix suffices

usage barrier a condition where an innovation is not part of a prospect's routines

utilitarian function the notion that some attitudes serve as a means to an end—gaining rewards or avoiding punishments

valence an attraction or repulsion felt toward an attitude object

VALS™ a segmentation approach that classifies consumers according to primary motivations and resources/ innovation

value barrier a perceived lack of product performance relative to its price compared to that of substitute brands

value-expressive function the notion that some attitudes help consumers communicate the core values they revere to other people

values ideals concerning what is right or wrong and goals worth pursuing

verbal projective a test where respondents complete an incomplete story

vicarious learning behavior change due to observing others and the consequences of their actions

virtual community a social network with common interests, ideas, tasks, or goals that interacts in cyberspace

word of mouth (WOM) sharing of an opinion about a product, service or company between an independent source and a receiver

Zaltman Metaphor Elicitation Technique (ZMET) a test where respondents provide images that represent their feelings about a topic

INDEX

Enabled customer contact centers, 340

Enacted role, 433

Enculturation, 545

Endust, 176

Energizer, 260

Energy, decision making and, 342

Engel, James F., 5

Entertainment Software Association, 432

Environmental cues, defined, 234

Environmental Protection Department, 386, 387

EpiPen, 405

ESRI Business Information Solution, 86

Essence magazine, 566

Estée Lauder, 155, 566, 570

Ethical absolutism, defined, 26

Ethical issues, in consumer research, 60-64
    confidentiality and, 63-64
    deception and, 62-63
    informing participants, 63
    participant protection, 62

Ethical relativism, defined, 26

Ethics
    attitudes and, 222
    consumer research and, 60-64, 65
    craft ethics, defined, 26
    decision making and, 342
    diffusion and, 383
    emerging trends in, 13, 24-26
    family and generational cohorts and, 459
    focus on, 13
    motivation and emotion, 266
    perception and, 142
    personal influence and, 499
    personality and, 306
    segmentation and, 103

Ethnicity
    defined, 563
    demographic segmentation, 83

Ethnic microcultures
    African-American consumers, 563-66
    Asian-American consumers, 570-72
    Hispanic-American consumers, 566-70

Ethnocentrism
    cultural sensitivity *versus*, 545-46
    defined, 545

Ethnography, defined, 546

European Union (EU), 29, 31

Evaluation-based inferences, 135

Evaluative criteria, defined, 329

Eve Ultra Lights 120s, 82

Evoked set, defined, 327

Exchange processes, marketing concept and, 10-12

Expanded awareness, 324

Expanded means, 323

Expectations, consumer, 337

Expected price, 134

Experience, decision making and, 326

Experience effect, 173

Experiencers, VALS™, 296, 297

Experimentation, 175

Experiments, 48-49

Expert power, defined, 407

Exposure, 114

Expressive performance, defined, 335

Extended problem solving, 321

Extended self, 299

External search, for decision making, 325-27

Extinction, theories of, 178-80

Extrinsic *versus* intrinsic motivation, 238

F

Faberge, 570

Facebook, 325, 431, 477, 489, 519

Factory 121, 96

Family, 431-51
    Asian-American, 571
    characteristics, 43
    Club Med and, 462-63
    consumer socialization, 431-33
    consumption roles, 433-35
    decision process, 435-39
    defined, 431
    food advertising to children, 443-45
    nontraditional living-arrangement patterns, 448-52

Family and Medical Leave Act (FMLA), 18

Family life cycle (FLC), 445-48
    defined, 445-46
    demographic segmentation, 82
    modernized, 446-48

Fannie Mae, 24, 316

Fast-food caloric counts, 35

Federal Express, 337

Federal policies, for children's media, 443

Federal Trade Commission (FTC), 22, 340, 359

FedEx, 53, 54

Fellowes Shredders, 239

Femininity, 551

Feng shui, 555

Fidelity Investments, 166, 251

Fields, Sally, 480

Figure and ground, 131

Filene's Basement, 137

Finance/economics
    attitudes and, 222
    motivation and, 266

Financial risk, 141

Financial Times, 336

FirstSTREET, 196

Fishbein's multi-attribute model, 205-7
    limitations of, 206-7

Fisher-Price, 99

Fitness industry, emerging trends in, 16-17

Fixation, 281

Flamers, 397

Fleet Bank, 55

Florida Orange Growers Association, 242

Focus groups, 47-48

Food, culture and, 562-63

Food advertising, to children, 443-45

Food and Drug Administration (FDA), 35, 119, 376, 502

Ford, Henry, 75

Ford, Richard, 309

Ford Motor Company, 26, 75, 113, 114, 172, 221, 242, 250, 352, 403, 473, 488, 489, 491, 570

Forgetting
    rate of, 160
    theories of learning, 178-80

Formal groups, defined, 395

Forrester Research, Inc., 76, 477

Fortune magazine, 24

4MAT model, 170

Framing, decisions, 331-32

Franklin, Benjamin, 421

Fraternal organizations, 421

Fraudulent symbols, 401

Freddie Mac, 24, 316

Free word associations, defined, 58

Frequency of purchase, 369, 370

Fresh Step, 358

Freud, Sigmund, 246, 279

Freudian personality theory, 279-83
    marketing applications of, 282-83

Friends, 454

Frito Lay, 570

Fry, Arthur L., 356

FTD, 260, 361–62
FUBU, 455, 456
Fuji, 179
Functional risk, 141
Fussell, Paul, 513

G

G. Heileman Brewing, 123
Gallup poll, 24
Gambling, law and, 232–33, 268
Gap, 155, 519
Garmin, 355
Gatekeepers, family roles, 435, 482
Gates, Bill, 529
Geico Insurance Company, 211, 490
Gender
    decision making and, 328
    demographic segmentation and,
        82–83
    roles, 17–18
General Electric, 170, 171, 211, 242,
    449
General Mills, 155
General Motors, 18, 95, 113, 119, 145,
    192, 242, 519
General sensation-seeking scale
    (GSSS), 248
Generational marketing, 452–58
    applications, 457–58
    Boomers I cohort, 453
    Boomers II cohort, 453
    defined, 452
    Generation X cohort, 453–54
    Generation Y cohort, 454–55
    Generation Z cohort, 455
    life experiences classification,
        452–55
    Postwar cohort, 453
    techno-savvies, 456–57
Generation X cohort, 453–54
Generation Y cohort, 454–55, 456
Generation Z cohort, 455
Generic goals, 242
Genetics & IVF Institute, 430
Geodemographic segmentation,
    84–87
Geographic segmentation, 78
Gestalt psychology, 130–32
Gift giving practices, 544
Gilbert, Dennis, 513
Gillette, 192
Giorgio of Beverly Hills, 118, 254
G&J magazine, 82
Glass ceiling, 374
Glaxo Smith Kline, 140, 410

Global business, production and, 103
Global Economic Prospects 2008, 368
Global village
    defined, 29
    emerging trends of, 29–31
    rise of, 13
Goals, 209
    brand-specific, 242
    defined, 242
    generic, 242
GoDaddy.com, 242
Gone with the Wind, 260
Good Housekeeping magazine, 145
Good Housekeeping Seal of
    Approval, 382
Google, 361
Google Alerts, 498
Google Blogsearch, 498
Go RVing, 445
GPS navigation systems, 354, 357
Grateful Dead Organization, 572
Great Depression, 352
Great Rice Crisis (Japan), 546
Green Giant, 176
Green marketing, 28
Greenpeace, 454
Greeting Card Association, 200
Greeting card industry, 97, 200
Gross national product (GNP), 354,
    524
Group, defined, 393
Group influence, 391–425
    conformity to mandates, 408–9
    defined, 393
    effect of technology on, 396–97
    importance of, 394
    reference groups, 409–21
    roles, 397–400
    social groups, 395–96
    social power, 402–8
    status, 400–402
Grouping, 131
Gucci, 132, 194, 513, 514
Guess Jeans, 136, 137, 246
Guest Rewards program, 185
*Guidelines for the Use of
    Environmental Marketing
    Claims,* 29
Gulf Wars, 29
Gymboree Company, 240

H

Habbo Hotel, 477
Habit, learning curves and, 173–75
Habitat for Humanity, 454

Hai Karate, 354
Hallmark Corporation, 97, 200, 260,
    492
Halo effect, 135, 163
Harkin, Tom, 36
Harley-Davidson, Inc., 80, 140, 352,
    386, 485, 491, 492, 496
Harley-Davidson Owner Group
    (HOG), 80, 563, 572
Harrod's, 135
Hasbro Games, 449, 473
Haves *versus* have-nots, 513
HDTV, 133
Head Start, 533
Health Fanatics group, 28
Health industry, emerging trends in,
    16–17
Hearst, 145
Heinz, 199, 200
Hell's Angels, 412
Hemispheric specialization of the
    brain, 169
Hennessy Cognac, 412, 413
Henri VI (king), 508
Herbal supplements, 376
Hershey Chocolate Company, 93, 150
Heterogeneity, of languages, 552
Heuristics, defined, 327
Hewlett-Packard, 200, 201, 361, 410
Hickey, Joseph, 513
Hidden-camera commercials, 496
High involvement, defined, 9, 319
High-involvement learning, 152
High sensation seekers (HSS), 248
High *versus* low urgency motivation,
    235
Hilton, Paris, 480
Hilton Hotels Corporation, 82, 513
Hilton Meetings, 513
Hip-hop, 456
Hispanic-American consumers, as
    microculture, 566–70
History/labor relations, social class
    and, 533
Hofstede, Geert, 547
Hofstede's cultural dimensions,
    547–52
    individualism, 548
    masculinity, 551
    power distance, 547
    term orientation, 552
    uncertainty avoidance, 547–48
Home, 477
Home-bound consumer, 457
Home Depot, 537
Home economics, social class and, 533

Homeostasis, defined, 247
Honda, 91, 112, 132, 145, 283, 332, 361, 382, 403, 412
Honeymooner stage, 445
Hope Today magazine, 566
Horatio Alger Association of Distinguished Americans, 454
Howard, John A., 5
H&R Block, 169
Human actions, consumer behavior and, 9
Human resources, 103
    family and generational cohorts and, 459
    learning and memory, 182
    personality and, 306
Husband dominant decision pattern, 435
Hyatt Regency Hotels, 82, 463
Hypodermic needle model, 479
Hypothetical value function, 330, 331
Hyundai, 242, 243, 382, 513

I

IBM, 26
Id, 281
Identification
    classical, 415
    defined, 415
    reciprocal, 415
IDT, 570
iMac, 362
Image barriers, 382
Image management, 139
Imagery, perception and, 138-39
    promotion, 138-39
Images, perception and, 136-41
    brand equity, 140
    defined, 136
    image change, 139-40
    imagery and promotion, 138-39
    risk perception, 141
Imagin Asian, 571
Immediacy, in products and services, 20
Imperial Majesty, 135
Implementation, defined, 378
Impulse purchases, 321
Inclusion, diversity *versus,* 578
Income
    of CEOs, 518
    conceivable ratings for, 523
    social class *versus,* 511-12, 525-27

Incongruity, status crystallization *versus,* 527
Index of Investor Optimism, 24
India
    automobile industry and, 30
    caste system in, 510
Indiana Jones and the Kingdom of the Crystal Skull, 380, 495
Indirect influence, 441
Individual factors, of perception, 124-26
Individualism, defined, 548
Individual learning style, 326
Inertia, 174
Inference, perceptual, 134-35
Infertility, surrogacy and, 444
Infiniti, 101
Influence, by reference groups
    compliance, 413-15
    identification, 415
    internalization, 415-17
Influence, group. *See* Group influence
Influencers, family roles, 435, 441
Infomercials, 161, 166
INFOMINE, 52
Informal groups, defined, 395
Information, on consumer, 41-51
    buyers, 42-43
    customer loyalty, 43
    customer satisfaction, 43-44
    market segments, 43
    product use, 43
    purchase situation, 41-42
Information, sources of, 44-51
    primary data, 45-51
    secondary data, 44-45
Information-based strategy (IBS), 54
Information overload, 176
Information-processing approach, in attitude change, 215-18
Information retrieval, 177-78
Information superhighway, 13, 14-15, 453
Informing participants, ethics of consumer research, 63
Innovation, diffusion of, 351-87
    adoption process, 375-82
    diffusion process, 353-75
Innovation, in diffusion process, 354-66
    advantage of, 361-62
    classification of, 354-56
    compatibility, 362
    consumer acceptance of, 361

    continuous, 357-58
    discontinuous, 357
    divisibility, 364-66
    dynamically continuous, 357
    "new" product defined, 359
    observability, 364
    simplicity *versus* complexity, 362-64
    strategy multiplicity, 359-60
    symbolic, 358
    trialability, 364-66
Innovativeness, 287, 288, 371
Innovators
    adopter categories of, 371
    techno-savvies as, 457
    VALS™, 296, 297
Input variation, of perception, 121-22
Insight Research Group, 201
Instincts
    defined, 246
    theories of, 246
Instrumental motives, 254
Instrumental performance, defined, 335
Intel Centrino Pro Processor, 207, 208
Intelligent Transportation Systems (ITS), 297
Intensity, of consumer attitudes, 194-95
Intention, 207
Interest statements, 293
Intermittent reinforcement, 160
Internalization, defined, 415-17
Internal search, for decision making, 262, 324-25
Internet, 15, 44, 431
    as search tool, 325
    social class and, 517-18
    word of mouth, 476-77
Internet, consumer research and, 51-53
    data acquisition, 52-53
    online surveys, 52
    tracking visitors, 51
InterPage, 84
Interpersonal sources, 325
Intrinsic *versus* extrinsic motivation, 238
Investment planning, family and generational cohorts and, 459
Investments, group influence and, 421
Involvement
    defined, 319
    in family decision making, 437, 439

Value, personalized economy and, 20
Value barriers, 379
Value-expressive function, defined, 198
Value function, 330
Values, cultural, 556–57
Vanity sizing, 4
Variety seeking trait, 287, 288
Verbal projectives, 57
Verizon, 258
VH1, 120, 458
Viagra, 82, 197, 480
Vicarious learning, 171
Vicary, James, 127
Victoria Secret, 242
Video games, 245
Vietnam War, 453
Viral word of mouth, 476–77
Virginia Slims, 82
Virtual community, 396
Virtual offices, 19
Virtual reality (VR), 365
Vision, sensory system, 115–17
Vision Asia, 571
Volkswagen, 119, 226–27, 260, 458
Volvo, 18, 91, 101

W

Wall Street Journal, 131, 516
Wal-Mart, 28, 61, 137, 205, 491, 509, 510, 519, 570
  social class and, 536–37
Walton, Sam, 536

Ward, James, 386
Warner, W. Lloyd, 515
Warner Bros., 106–7, 495
Warren, Joseph, 421
Warren Report, 528
Washington, George, 421
Waterson, Ellen, 480
Weber, Ernst H., 126
Weber Company, 458
WebmasterRadio.FM, 577
Weider Brothers, 572
Weighted-additive rule, in decision making, 334
Weight Watchers, 90
Weight Watchers' Healthy Choice, 82
Wendy's, 49
Westin, 82, 463
Whirlpool Corporation, 291, 363, 449
Wiedeking, Wendelin, 309
Wife dominant decision pattern, 435
Wi-Fi, 133, 354
Williams, Andy, 453
Windows Vista, 362
Wine industry, 381
Winnowing, 319
Withdrawal, 282
Witherspoon, Reese, 480
The Wizard of Oz, 260
Women, changing class stature of, 525
Women's Voices for Change, 317
Woods, Eldrick (Tiger), 192
Woods, Tiger, 211, 226, 480

Word of mouth (WOM), 365, 467–503. *See also* Personal influence
  combatting negative, 497–99
  communications, 9
  defined, 469
  global, 475
  harnessing, 496–97
  impact of, 474–76
  opinion leaders and, 470–73
  power of, 473–74
  strategic applications of, 491–96
  viral, 476–77
  vividness of, 474–76
Workbench, 176
Working class, in United States, 515–16
Working mothers, roles of, 436
Workplace, diversity in, 22–24
Wu-Wear, 456

Y

Yahoo, 361
Yoplait, 573
YouTube, 414, 491
Yves Saint Laurent, 194

Z

Zagat's Guide to Restaurants and Hotels, 472
Zaltman Metaphor Elicitation Technique (ZMET), 60
ZMET, motivation research, 60
Zocor, 502